WITHDRAWN

Hitler's First Foreign Minister

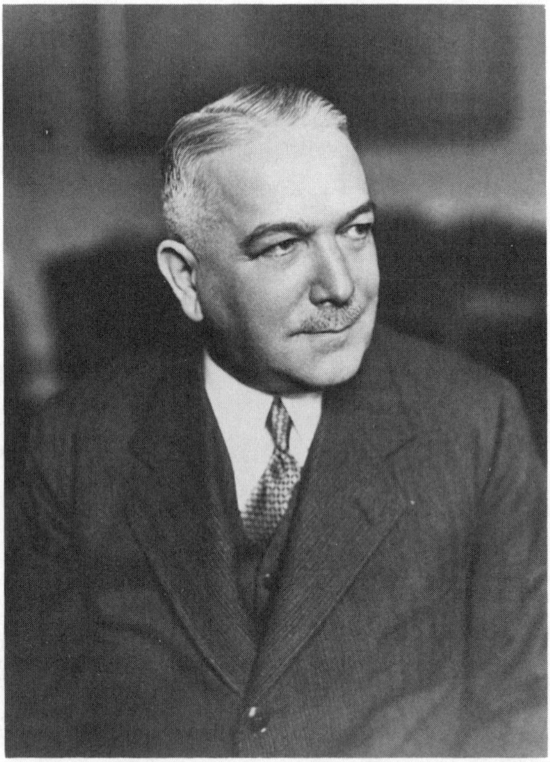

John L. Heineman

HITLER'S FIRST FOREIGN MINISTER

*Constantin Freiherr von Neurath,
Diplomat and Statesman*

University of
California Press
Berkeley
Los Angeles
London

University of California Press
Berkeley and Los Angeles, California
University of California Press, Ltd.
London, England
Copyright © 1979 by
The Regents of the University of California
ISBN 0-520-03442-2
Library of Congress Catalog Card Number: 77-71061
Printed in the United States of America

1 2 3 4 5 6 7 8 9

In the course of this book, I have acknowledged with appreciation the numerous archivists and personalities who have helped with the research, particularly the descendents of Freiherr von Neurath, his daughter, Frau Winifred von Mackensen, and his son, Constantin von Neurath.

In this place, I would like to express my deep gratitude to two people, without whose help and support this research would never have reached its final form. The first is my wife, Helen, who has lived with the Neurath problem for more than ten years, and whose constant interest and knowledge of the English sentence spurred me to expend my best efforts in telling this fascinating story. This book, as she knows, is as much hers as mine.

The second person to whom I owe so much was my dear friend and colleague, Dr. Allen M. Wakstein. His faith in this project, and his repeated readings of the material—in a number of versions—helped me sharpen its focus and saved it from infelicities and errors. I alone am responsible for whatever weaknesses are still present in the text, but its strengths are most often the result of his advice.

> Thus, in gratitude, this book is dedicated to
> my wife, Helen Kliegl Heineman
> and to the memory of
> Allen M. Wakstein
> (1931–1979)

Contents

Frequently Used Abbreviations	ix
CHAPTER I Introduction	1
CHAPTER II Early Life: 1873–1919	7
CHAPTER III Neurath as Ambassador: 1919–1932	18
CHAPTER IV Neurath Becomes Foreign Minister	33
CHAPTER V The Professional Diplomat as Minister	46
CHAPTER VI The Nonpolitical Minister	59
CHAPTER VII Neurath and Domestic Issues in the Hitler Cabinet	68
CHAPTER VIII Neurath's Influence on Foreign Policy: 1933–1936	86
CHAPTER IX Challenges to Neurath's Leadership: 1933–1937	117
CHAPTER X Neurath and the Personnel Crisis: 1936–1937	134
CHAPTER XI Neurath and German Foreign Policy: 1936–1938	148

CHAPTER XII
  The Year of Decision: 1938   167
CHAPTER XIII
  Neurath in Prague: 1939–1941   186
CHAPTER XIV
  Leinfelderhof, Nuremberg, Spandau   213

  Notes   247
  Bibliography   329
  Index   349

Frequently Used Abbreviations

AA	Auswärtiges Amt, Files of the German foreign office.
ADAP	*Akten zur deutschen auswärtigen Politik, 1918–1945*
BA	Bundesarchiv, the German federal archives in Coblenz
Cab. Mins.	Cabinet Minutes
DBFP	*Documents on British Foreign Policy, 1919–1939*
DDF	*Documents Diplomatiques Français, 1922–1939*
DDI	*Documenti Diplomatici Italiani,* 7th Series, 1922–1925
DGFP	*Documents on German Foreign Policy, 1918–1945*
DHCP	*Dokumenty z historie ceskoslovenske politiky, 1939–1943*
DZA	Central German Archives, Potsdam
FGN	Forschungsstelle für die Geschichte des Nationalsozialismus, Hamburg
FRUS	*Foreign Relations of the United States*
HSAS	Hauptstaatsarchiv, Stuttgart
IMT	International Military Tribunal, *Trial of the Major War Criminals before the International Military Tribunal,* Nuremberg
IZ	Archives of the Institut für Zeitgeschichte, Munich
NA	National Archives of the United States, Washington, D.C.
NCA	*Nazi Conspiracy and Aggression,* English

	translations of selected prosecution documents for IMT
RK	Reichskanzlei, Files of the Reichs Chancellery
RJ	Files of the German ministry of justice.
TWC	*Trials of War Criminals before the Nuremberg Military Tribunal,* Washington, D.C.
VJHZG	*Vierteljahrshefte für Zeitgeschichte*
ZS	Zeugenschrifttum

CHAPTER

1

INTRODUCTION

President Paul von Hindenburg installed a cabinet of conservative concentration to replace the coalition under which Heinrich Brüning had ruled Germany since the loss of his parliamentary majority in July 1930. Appointing a government under Franz von Papen in June 1932, the president deliberately bypassed the various rightist parties, conservative interest groups, and movements (including the neo-conservative revolutionaries) and turned instead to individual members from the conservative establishment: the officer corps, the civil service, and the aristocracy. Hindenburg hoped thereby to restore the authority and stability of the state—sorely tested by the depression—by reviving the civic virtues and political relationships of the Bismarck compromise: rule entrusted to neutral experts who would guarantee efficient government.[1]

This "presidential cabinet" reached back to the Empire's union of military, bureaucratic, and aristocratic values, to create not a reactionary government but a centralized force suitable to overcome the emergency. It was republican in form, but authoritarian in scope, a contradiction which by 1932 had become the basis of German conservatism, calling for a nonparliamentary government, resting upon presidential prerogatives. Such a nonpolitical cabinet, transcending all political interests and parties, would lead a country whose parliament had failed to combat unemployment, economic misery, the wounds of a lost war, and the growth of political radicalism on both the Left and Right.[2]

President von Hindenburg specifically reserved two cabinet positions for his own candidates: the foreign office and the ministry of defense. For the former, he selected the German ambassador to the Court of St. James's, Constantin Hermann Karl Freiherr von Neurath, a Swabian aristocrat, a gentleman-hunter, ex-soldier, career diplomat, and German patriot. From June 1932 Neurath served as foreign minister in the presidential cabinets of Papen and General Kurt von Schleicher, and continued in the coalition formed by Adolf Hitler in January 1933. Loyal to Hindenburg's mandate, Neurath stayed in the Hitler government until he asked to be removed in early 1938. Despite this resignation he continued to give the objective and neutral advice for which he had been selected minister in 1932, and subsequently was appointed Protector of Bohemia and Moravia, when that area was taken over by Hitler in 1939. He ended his life as a "war criminal," convicted of leading his country and his people into wars of aggression and crimes against humanity.

Neurath's story is one of a man trying to tame a whirlwind which he never quite understood. His fate reflects that of a generation of well-meaning Germans and speaks to one of the great questions of modern history: how could decent and honorable men serve the evil that was National Socialism? In Neurath's case, the answer lies in a totality of experiences which were common to many. Thus, while this study will necessarily touch on the important foreign policy developments over which Neurath presided, the changes in the foreign office during these years, and the creation of a Nazi dictatorship both in Germany and central Europe, the essential and pervasive focus will be on Neurath,[3] a conscientious German and dedicated civil servant, who will probably go down in history with the inglorious and incomplete epitaph: "Hitler's first foreign minister."

In his long life, Neurath appeared to many people a rather straightforward person, whose outstanding characteristics were a healthy common-sense approach to problems and an agreeable disposition. Standing nearly six feet tall, his heavy frame tending toward corpulence, he was a handsome man who made a sympathetic impression. With a good, though not profound, intelligence, and broadly human rather than specialized cultural interests, he appeared always calm and composed, exuding confidence and a sense of security. These considerable talents he combined with a sure touch in handling people, somewhat in the tradition of British colonial governors, whose similar traits were often described, for want of a more precise term, as eminent good sense.

Outwardly impressive, deliberate in speech and movements, and obviously well suited to a diplomatic career, Neurath was always courteous, friendly, and gentlemanly by breeding and taste. He struck observers as a man at home anywhere in the broad spectrum of middle and upper class European society. He could instruct the Sultan on the proper way to eat fresh asparagus, and take time to intercede for a train porter who was unhappy with his shift.* Yet beneath an easy joviality lay a native shrewdness and stubbornness, a combination popularly attributed to Swabians. His sense of humor and ability to put visitors at ease lulled many into regarding him merely as an easy-going country gentleman, interested mainly in hunting and tennis. His diplomatic colleagues, however, recognized him as a resourceful negotiator, able to extract himself and others effortlessly from even the most embarrassing situations. Neurath appeared to be born for the

---

*Stories from author's interview with Frau Winifred von Mackensen, May 2, 1968. Frau von Mackensen, the only daughter of Constantin von Neurath, graciously cooperated in all aspects of this biography. She permitted the author access to the surviving Neurath Nachlass and family papers in her possession, and on six occasions during the spring and summer of 1968 granted lengthy interviews on every phase of her father's life. Without her help, this book would have been impossible.

embassy; he told friends that in his profession, one should not appear to be working at all, but be able to move freely in the social and diplomatic worlds, meeting people and discussing a broad range of subjects, listening to everyone and antagonizing no one. This life style Neurath had understood since his childhood, and he perfected it during his years as ambassador and minister. Still, the image is superficial.[4]

In fact, Neurath was a well trained diplomat with insights into world problems, formidable linguistic skills, and determined political and economic views. Above all, he had mastered two difficult virtues: he could mask his feelings and private opinions from even the most astute observer, and he could remain calm in the most distressing circumstances. Like Bismarck before him, he described these qualities in hunter's language. Although he passionately loved hunting, Neurath refused to engage in the *Treibjagd,* in which animals are driven past a blind screening the hunters, but preferred stalking his prey on foot, a mode which called for patiently learning the animal's traits and individual quirks, waiting for the one false move which would betray the animal and bring it within range. He took joy in long waits in rain and storm, alternating between freezing and sweating, in pursuit of his game. He seldom killed any animals; in 1945 he could recall the exact number of deer, marmots, and chamois he had bagged since 1921. Often he never took a shot during his entire vacation, and his major enjoyment was watching and making an inventory of the foxes, owls, grouse, martins, and eagles which shared the preserve.[5]

These tendencies toward reserve and patient waiting he brought to his public life. Retiring and shy by nature, unwilling to thrust himself forward, Neurath's diplomatic training reinforced his innate cautiousness. He always worked best when circumstances permitted slow and natural evolution; he was reluctant to force issues, and preferred to await developments. He abhorred agitation of all kinds, and was personally and professionally incapable of fanaticism. He despised artificial solutions, which he claimed were concocted by intellectual scheming and marred by emotional involvement. Politicians and intellectuals, he frequently implied, could enjoy such pastimes; a civil servant, especially in the foreign service, had to live by another code: recognition that personal desires and fantasies must be submerged in serving the nation's broader realities. Firm in this conviction, Neurath rejected any single ideology or *Weltanschauung.* Jealously independent, he had no time for the endless discussions of tactics and programs by men he called "fantastists," who ignored historical truths in order to try to force reality into narrow limits. On principle, he preferred to deal with most problems by leaving them alone. If ignored, he was fond of saying, most difficulties would work themselves out. This characteristic attitude caused some contemporary observers and political enemies to charge him with laziness, ignorance, and indifference. The truth was quite different.

As his many years in the diplomatic service show, Neurath was an industrious worker. His reports and memoranda were always concise; he was, he once wrote, "no friend of lengthy letters" or reports. He expected others to condense their thoughts and speeches as he did his own. A trained observer and administrator, he would work long hours without complaint, devouring numerous dispatches and reports, thoroughly evaluating all relevant materials. In this work, he showed the pride and sense of service which characterized the German bureaucracy. Family tradition, his own experience, and a tough conscientiousness pervaded his career.

Yet, paradoxically, Neurath found it impossible to enjoy the public duties of his career. He frankly did not like society and he despised politics. On more than one occasion, he complained that the most difficult part of his life was the social whirl accompanying international diplomacy. Yet as ambassador and foreign minister, he was forced into an active social life in order to facilitate the more serious business of creating associations and obtaining information. Despite his unquestionable social grace, he preferred the retirement of his Württemberg estates, where among the forests and fields he sensed a singularity and a reality in sharp contrast to the quicksilver properties of political and diplomatic intrigue. This ambivalence for a man in the highest and most public area of society is an important key to understanding his personality and life. "Liberal democracy," one commentator has correctly noted, "requires a sense of public life, of the market of men and its rules, which is lacking in those who have fallen in love with private virtues." Neurath was such a man. Realizing his intensely private nature, he once remarked that no one would ever be able to write his biography. Skeptical of public virtues and abstract concepts of political or social equality and justice, the whole idea of society as a structured and rational organization to meet communal goals would have seemed incomprehensible to him. The morality or immorality of public actions escaped him.[6]

In his personal relationships with others, Neurath adhered to a strict moral code, believing that decency and honesty were necessary forms for daily life. His favorite poem, which he frequently quoted and which was read at his funeral, caught this sense of the private man struggling to endure the stresses of a public world:

> Think and be quiet
> Feel more than you show
> Bow down before God
> And you stay your own master.

Loyal to this precept, he found his greatest happiness in the heights and depths of friendship and family, in relationships that were honest and unaffected, in the "satisfaction of imprecise reveries." Participation in the social and political process was for him ever an "external" and he retained the choice and need to retreat on numerous occasions. Such was the real function of his frequent flights to his estates and hunting lodge.[7]

Critics have chosen to see Neurath's close and pervasive ties to the land as signs of his indifference and apathy toward foreign policy, especially when crucial events transpired while he was away from Berlin. But Neurath never neglected his public affairs and indeed his flying trips to his mountains and farms served a necessary and restorative purpose which made his public life possible. Much earlier, at eighteen, he had discovered the joys of an alpine vacation, and at the first opportunity he had rented a lodge in the Tyrolean Alps, intending to provide a refuge for himself and his family "away from people and society, the constant presence of which was unsympathetic to all of us, but unfortunately unavoidable because of my position." In 1928, he and his good friend Count Rainer Geldern rented a larger preserve, Baldurschwang in Allgäu, which remained Neurath's personal hideaway, with a house not big enough for family or friends. Most often, he spent his three weeks there with the game wardens. What he really sought were the mountains and the solitude. He worked at replenishing the herds, watched carefully over the winter forage and the proper plantings of alpine meadows and forests. He took pleasure in long treks in the summer sun and exhausting pursuits in knee-deep snow.[8]

Here, in a glorious surrounding, he could escape the stress and troubles of his public life. Recalling those days while in prison after the war, Neurath explained their importance:

> I needed a place in nature in which I could unharness, and move about, in order at least a few times in the year to get some necessary distance between myself and the destructive political work. This was particularly necessary after 1932, when I had to take over the office of minister. A few days in the lodge and out stalking regularly sufficed to bring refreshment, even when I arrived completely worked out.

The fields and woods of Leinfelderhof and the meadows and mountain peaks of Baldurschwang were, he recalled, a kind of therapy enabling him to derive strength and power from the land itself:

> The residence in open nature and the observation of the wild animals was my pleasure. What can be more beautiful than to experience a sunrise in the mountains, alone or with a dear like-minded friend beside you.
> That is now all over for me, and will never return, but the memory remains and can never be taken away.

Neurath is an example of an outmoded private individual whose deepest responsibilities were suddenly all public as he faced the challenges of a modern world. Albert Speer, who came to know the private lives of so many prominent figures of those days, recalls Neurath's flat refusals to interrupt this life, and his angry rejection of Hitler's offer of a grandiose palace. To Speer, the Neuraths showed "confident modesty and deliberately abstained from the craving for ostentation on the part of the new masters." This acute perception does not, however, go far enough. Neurath's innate dislike of society and politics set him sharply apart from the Nazis with whom he came into contact. Self-assuredly aloof, Neurath could never join this new establishment. "This man has nothing in common with us," Joseph Goebbels later complained of Neurath. "He belongs to an entirely different world." Not interested in honors, position, political intrigues, or power,

Neurath thought it was enough to take private refuge, even while he attempted to continue a responsible public career.[9]

His life became a shambles as he tried to satisfy these conflicting needs. To his career as civil servant he brought many strengths and a share of weaknesses, the greatest of which, ironically, was what he considered his finest private virtue: an obsessive preoccupation with "duty." Unwilling, or perhaps unable, to engage in the public world of social and political decision making, Neurath fell back upon his civil service training, and elected to do his duty, obediently carry out his responsibilities, prevent worse things from happening, trust that somehow the unpleasantness would go away, and when it did not, retreat to mountain walks with his frustrations. In another time and place, in which duty, private virtues, and a love of country would not have brought a horrible complicity in mass murder and wars of aggression, he would have lived an honorable life.

In personal decency and responsibility, Neurath was unexcelled, but in the time of trial, he was found grievously wanting. Born for another century, relying with too much trust upon an outmoded code of doing one's duty, Neurath never successfully defined the nature of the challenge that faced him. Ultimately, he saved neither his own integrity nor that of his country. Years afterwards he would write: "Destiny was stronger than I." That was the story of his life.[10]

CHAPTER

2

EARLY LIFE:
1873–1919

The Neurath family originated in Hesse, where the name appeared in the chronicles of Alsfeld as early as 1480. Numerous members of the family served the Counts of Leiningen, and in 1782 Johann Friedrich Albrecht Constantin Neurath (1739–1816) became a member of the Imperial Court at Wetzlar and was subsequently elevated to the nobility. His only son, Constantin Franz Fürchtegott von Neurath (1764–1817), had also been a member of the imperial court, and upon its dissolution entered the royal Württemberg service, presiding over the supreme court until his death. Henceforth the Neurath family remained devoted servants of the government of Württemberg. His son Constantin Franz Justus von Neurath (1807–1868) served that state for twenty years as minister of foreign affairs, justice minister, and finally president of the privy council. On March 30, 1851, he was elevated to the rank of Freiherr.[1]

The eldest son of Constantin Franz, Constantin Karl Sebastian Ludwig Peter Julius Freiherr von Neurath (1847–1912), was educated at Tübingen as companion to the future king, William II (1848–1927). Subsequently, he spent his life as the intimate friend, confidant, hunting partner, and chief courtier of his corps-brother monarch. After inheriting his father's 637-acre estate (Klein Glattbach and Leinfelderhof) northwest of Stuttgart near the small town of Enzweihingen, he married Mathilde Freiin von Gemmingen-Hornberg, daughter of a prominent Swabian family whose numerous members traced their descent from Götz von Berlichingen. Through this marriage, the family became related to many of Württemberg's court nobility, and the young couple adopted the life style of the landed aristocracy, rather than of the urban society to which previous Neuraths had been accustomed.[2]

Constantin Hermann Karl Freiherr von Neurath, the subject of this study, was the oldest of the family's three sons. Born February 2, 1873 in Klein Glattbach, his Swabian origins were reflected in much of what he later did and thought. Like his father, he pursued a simple and unaffected style of life. His style with servants, secretaries, officials of his staff, and the common people in general was easy and free. An attitude not learned or consciously adopted, it rose out of the childhood atmosphere of his Württemberg home.* Neither awed by the proximity of greatness, nor enamored of the outward manifestations of power, he had little inclination toward ceremonies. From his father too he developed an inability to make quick or impromptu conversation, both public and private. For him the important world was always his small estate on the Ems river, the fields and woods of his native land, and the hunting preserves of southern Germany and Austria. Despite his later positions of importance, Neurath never ceased to be primarily a Swabian gentleman farmer, with strong ties to the countryside of his birth.[3]

After a brief period of tutorial education, Constantin von Neurath attended the village *Volksschule* and then the Latin school in Vaihingen/Enz. Later, he and his brother Wilhelm enrolled in the humanistic Eberhard-Ludwig Gymnasium in Stuttgart, where the family moved temporarily. During his last year at the Gymnasium (1892), Neurath and his father helped to rescue from a minor fire Princess May of Teck, the future Queen Mary of Great Britain. Later appointed to posts in London, Neurath always felt welcome there because of this episode, and Queen Mary too recalled the bond between them, which was strengthened when he married one of the young women who had attended the princess on this visit. Throughout these early years, Neurath moved freely and naturally within court circles. In 1903, he was named *Kammerjunker,* and in 1910 *Kammerherr,* honors which entitled him to wear resplendent uniforms at all royal functions.[4]

Academically, Neurath was average; his education did not produce any deep commitment to intellectual pursuits. As an adult, outside of professional requirements, he seldom read anything more serious than hunting magazines. He could flavor his letters with a few quotations in Latin, and was fluent in French, English, and Italian, but in general he had not benefited greatly from a liberal education. His attitude toward learning was faintly patronizing; in later years he claimed that those who were first in class were seldom so in life. While believing himself a cultured and educated gentleman, he was in fact strongly anti-intellectual.[5]

He passed the *Abitur* examination in Stuttgart and, following the traditions of his family, enrolled at Tübingen to study jurisprudence. He joined the *Corps Suevia,* one of the oldest and most distinguished German student fraternities; he was active for the usual three semesters, and never ceased to be its energetic supporter. Many of its members were his lifelong friends. Characteristically, he remembered the corps as the heart of his educational experience. He avidly enjoyed dueling, and proudly bore the resultant scars.[6]

---

*In his autobiographical "Skizze," written in prison in 1945, Neurath stressed the simplicity of his family's way of life: "At home, I enjoyed with my two younger brothers full freedom accompanied by strict but benevolent parental discipline and supervision, with particular stress on one's own sense of responsibility. Our standard of living was as simple as could be imagined. In the morning, breakfast consisted of milk soup with a roll, and only on Sunday some coffee and butter. During the school hours we had only a simple piece of black bread."

In 1893, Neurath interrupted his college training to volunteer for the one-year military service and mandatory summers in the reserves, which was available to young men of family and education. In 1898, he was promoted to Lieutenant of the Reserves with the 119th Olga Grenadiers. Consistently in his seven summer maneuvers he received the highest commendations from the officers, who singled out his "excellent social forms and unexcelled spirit of camaraderie." All of his superiors agreed that "in case of mobilization, Freiherr von Neurath should be employed in the field and in higher command positions." Neurath treasured his military experience, and was never to deviate from the conviction that only armed strength permitted a nation to exercise its freedom.[7]

Moreover, he always considered himself bound by the military oath and its discipline, rather than by political or diplomatic codes. During his long career, he several times considered resignation, often because he believed higher officials had blundered into untenable situations. In almost every instance, he rationalized his decision to stay with the phraseology of military ethics—"desertion" and "leaving the field of battle." The military uniform was more congenial than the full diplomatic regalia which, he always insisted, gave him the look of a bohemian waiter. Not surprisingly, he would be one of the first German diplomats to reappear after World War I in full military dress.[8]

Neurath Enters the Diplomatic Service

In 1894, he returned to his studies at Tübingen and the University of Berlin. In 1897 he passed the *referendar,* and in 1901 the *assessor* examinations in Stuttgart. For some time now he had decided to enter the diplomatic service of the Reich. In those days, however, the foreign office separated the "diplomatic" and the "consular" careers. Financial requirements, designed to attract only suitable candidates, played a major role in determining entrance into either: for a career in the political and diplomatic aspect of foreign relations, the entrant was required to guarantee an annual income of 20,000 Marks; for the commercially oriented consular service, an annual income of 10,000 Marks. As the Neurath estate did not produce even the lower sum, any opportunity for the young man to enter such a career rested upon the dowry that a wife might bring.

For five years, Neurath had been engaged to Marie Auguste Moser von Filseck, daughter of a prominent Stuttgart banking family. Unimpressed by Neurath, the Mosers had tried to discourage the marriage, and insisted that Manny would receive no more than the predetermined dowry, a sum yielding income of about 10,000 Marks a year. On May 30, 1901, Manny Moser and Neurath were married, and contrary to predictions, it was an excellent union. Love grew with the years and the income from the dowry enabled Neurath to enter the consular service. Four months after his marriage, he began a probationary period as assessor in the economics division. In January 1903, he was posted to the consulate in London where he remained for five years. His son, Constantin Alexander, had been born in Berlin shortly before this transfer, and in 1904 a daughter, Winifred

Mathilde Christine Helene, was born in London. There he also made two friends who would remain close throughout his career: Gerhard Köpke, the witty Berliner who subsequently became minister-director of the West European desk in the foreign office, and Otto Göppert, who later was active in disarmament negotiations. Like Neurath, both men were vice-consuls in London, and formed (as they often joked) a mutual admiration society functioning primarily to praise one another in the presence of superiors.[9]

Neurath served his diplomatic apprenticeship at the center of one of the most powerful empires of modern times. When he left London, he not only had a sure command of English and valuable associations, but also the firm conviction that Britain's friendship—however valuable and desirable—could never be won with self-abasing policies. This attitude foreshadows much of his future policy and shows an already characteristic paranoia:

> We must really suppose that all of England has become an insane asylum. The only danger is that the inmates cannot be isolated and therefore represent a danger to their fellow humans. The sudden agitation, which under no observable condition is justifiable, is chiefly an election maneuver of the Unionists. But the extent to which this agitation has spread proves also upon what well-prepared ground the excitement falls and how widespread among the English, both high and low, is the idea: *Germania esse delendum.* For us there is absolutely no other countermeasure except a determined continuation of ship building. Any consideration of proposals for peace and disarmament is suicidal.

Throughout his long career, the usually genial Neurath combined this confidence in military strength with a distinct suspicion of all foreign intentions toward Germany. This confirmed distrust of the rest of the world and even stronger trust in the virtues of all that was German was to prove his undoing. This first post abroad confirmed both prejudices.[10]

His interest in the broad area of general foreign policy made Neurath impatient with the dullness of his assigned field of economic and commercial negotiations. In January 1908 he welcomed his reassignment to Berlin, even while he realized that transfers out of the consular career were extremely rare and that he still could not meet the financial requirements. He worked first as secretary for the International Copyright Conference of 1908, and in the following year was named Counselor of Legation in the commercial section of the West European division.[11]

In Berlin, Neurath soon grew bored with both his assigned work and the demands of the attendant social life. In July 1910, his situation suddenly improved when Alfred von Kiderlen-Wächter was named foreign secretary in the new cabinet of Bethmann-Hollweg. Kiderlen was a Swabian, whose sister had married a Gemmingen relative of Neurath's mother, and was a frequent guest of the Neuraths in Berlin. One of the main tasks awaiting the new secretary was a reorganization of the stagnating foreign service. Kiderlen believed that diplomats should have knowledge of economic and industrial developments and he introduced special courses on these topics, seeking recruits who would combine technical skills with the more traditional talents of linguistic ability, social grace, and political astuteness. Seeing Neurath as possessing these qualities, Kiderlen proposed that he transfer to the diplomatic service and offered to support his candidacy. Numerous others in the consular and translator divisions, however, had also requested such reassignment, and it seemed a blow to Neurath's chances when Kiderlen died suddenly in December 1912, before any decision had been made regarding the transfer.[12]

Since his own father had died in 1912, Neurath was now master of the Württemberg estate. Because his career until now had been somewhat disappointing, he was tempted to retire to the land; but this step was not to be necessary. In February 1913, he was transferred to the diplomatic service, where he was not, however, received with much cordiality. After nearly a year in the various national sections of the Berlin office, in May 1914 Neurath was named first secretary at the embassy in Constantinople. Telling his family: "Now everything is different," he made a settlement with his two brothers, dividing the estate. Ernst Josef received Klein Glattbach, the central portion of 345 acres, while Neurath kept for himself only Leinfelderhof, a 192-acre section lying along the Enz river. Having now resolved upon a diplomatic career, Neurath kept this property only to preserve a connection with Württemberg and the land. There was little chance that he could ever live off its income.[13]

Neurath was scheduled to report to Constantinople on August 1, 1914. First he completed army maneuvers and examinations for the rank of Captain of the Reserves, receiving his new commission in July. The threatening situation in Europe, however, prompted him to delay his departure for the East. "At such times," he told his family, "my place is in the army," and even before German mobilization was announced, he left Leinfelderhof to join his troops. His impetuosity thoroughly confused the military bureaucracy, and it was several months before the official order to report for duty caught up with him. He returned it with the characteristically laconic statement: "I am today marching with my troops at the front."[14]

Although conscious of his duty to the fatherland, Neurath told a friend that he believed Germany bore much responsibility for starting the war by forcing Austria to issue an ultimatum to Serbia. He suspected that the incompetence of William II, together with the almost proverbial blundering of his advisors, had significantly contributed to the catastrophe. But a soldier's duty was always clear: hesitation, weakness, or mental reservations meant treason. Perhaps because he recognized these interior doubts, he embraced more willingly the role of soldier-patriot, dropping his complex duties for service at the front. Thus, much to the displeasure of the foreign office, who considered his appearance in Constantinople a matter of utmost importance, Neurath ignored orders to report to his new post. "This is no time for diplomats," he told his family. "This is a time for soldiers."[15]

And he was a good soldier, entering the field on August 9 with the Olga Grenadiers at the battles at Breuschtal (August 17-19), and the Vosges (August 20-22), where he received shrapnel wounds. Remaining with the troops, he took part in the battle before Nancy (August 25–September 9), at the Somme (September 25–October 6), and at St. Quentin (October 7–10). Between October 1914 and March 1915, he was in the trenches near Artois, and participated in the December attack at Ovillers-La Boissele. On October 16, 1914, he was awarded the Iron Cross second class, and on January 1, 1915, the Iron Cross first class.[16]

In the battle before Nancy, his colonel's adjutant was killed, and Neurath was prompted to replace him. The foreign office, however, was still determined to regain his services for the understaffed embassy in Constantinople, where the ambassador was ailing and the German military mission was jeopardizing cooperation by indiscreet actions. In March 1915, the foreign office officially asked the Württemberg government to discharge Neurath. Furious when a representative of the office came to the front lines to escort him to Constantinople, he could do nothing. Orders were orders, and after a short rest at home—where he amused his children by sleeping on the floor because the beds now seemed too soft—he left the army and the war to take up his diplomatic service.[17]

In Constantinople

After a harrowing trip to Constantinople,* Neurath found a confused state of affairs and faltering cooperation between German military and diplomatic authorities. In the summer of 1914, General Otto Liman von Sanders, head of the German military mission in Turkey, had bluntly refused to consider himself subordinate to the embassy. The entrance of Turkey into the war on Germany's side in November did not ease the misunderstandings. Indeed, Neurath had been selected in the hope that he could strengthen the embassy in its struggle with an array of official and unofficial advisors from the military mission. Neurath arrived at the height of the chaos and disarray which accompanied the government's preparations to abandon Constantinople to the joint French-British units attempting to force the Dardanelles. The surprisingly strong Turkish resistance and the resultant withdrawal of the allied forces, however, terminated the threat, despite divided German counsels.[18]

Throughout the crisis, Neurath efficiently performed his duties and soon restored order, terminating the activities of irresponsible German officials who alienated the Turks and threatened official cooperation.† Through repeated protests to Berlin, he eventually made the embassy the real as well as the legal center of German activities in Turkey.[19] He was convinced that only well trained specialists,

*Recalling his trip, Neurath described it as "an adventure-filled expedition." When Romanian or Russian agents planted a bomb on his train and tried to capture him at the ferry over the Danube, Neurath eluded them by crossing the flooded river in a rented canoe. Neurath, "Skizze."

†In October 1915, Neurath warned the foreign office about one agent who had been "absolutely useless to us, and indeed only damaging. Our reputation, not only with the Turks but also with Germans who live here, will not improve if such parasites tramp around clothed in an official capacity." Neurath to Rosenberg, October 1915, AA, Deutschland 135, Nü. 1, Bd. 5.

fluent in Turkish, should be sent to help Germany's ally. His opposition to amateurs, here first demonstrated, remained one of Neurath's characteristic attitudes.

Originally sent to assist an ailing ambassador who soon died, for most of 1915 Neurath assumed full responsibility for the mission. Thanks to his efforts, the new ambassador, Count Wolff Metternich, formerly accredited to the Court of St. James's, found a well run embassy upon his arrival. He immediately supported Neurath's campaign for improved personnel and successfully terminated the practice of independent military reports to Berlin. The two seemed to enjoy a harmonious relationship, but it did not last long. Early in 1916, Neurath complained to Berlin that Metternich was uninterested in getting to know Turkish leaders, or in promoting close associations with Constantinople society. Neurath had to apply pressure to obtain even the slightest gesture of good will from the ambassador, and got little or no response on larger policy decisions. He asked Berlin for reassignment. Under Metternich's torpid leadership, anti-German sentiment was again on the rise and the semi-official German agents began to return. But the Kaiser supported his ambassador, and the matter was ordered resolved.[20]

Although Neurath enjoyed an excellent reputation in Constantinople, possessed the full confidence of the Turks, counted many friends among the diplomatic corps, and moved easily even in pro-Entente circles, his position had become impossible. Besieged by complaints against his own ambassador, Neurath carried the case to Berlin, even though within the acknowledged code of behavior junior officers should not report unfavorably upon their superiors. Neurath believed it was his duty to inform the government of the situation, and to tender his own resignation. On August 4, 1916, he outlined his specific charges:

> You will perhaps have noticed that for the past seven months you have not heard a word from me. During this period I have tried everything in order to cure the strife between M[etternich] and the Turks, which has been threatening since his arrival. After the situation became so hopeless that any improvement or even restoration of tolerable relations was out of the question, I considered it my duty to report to you, as the proper official. I am not by nature capable of participating in intrigues. In my last letter, I requested that you have me recalled from here. I now repeat that request. You can do me no bigger favor. You in the foreign office have no idea of the intrinsic difficulties I have had to contend with since the appearance of M. In peace time, I would not have stayed here a month. Now my patience and strength are exhausted. I have done my duty. You will not hear another word from me. I merely repeat once more: the conditions here are untenable and will not be improved.[21]

Somewhat condescendingly, the foreign office denied Neurath's request:

> Our good Neurath apparently does not know how to handle Metternich, for whose peculiarities one must stoically make allowances, and whose lack of consideration for others must be paid back in kind. Occasionally, one has to be colossally coarse with him.[22]

This incident illuminates several important facets of Neurath's character. He was an honest man, who would not engage in intrigues, but he was also unable to handle a superior with table pounding and scenes. One could have predicted his subsequent troubles with Adolf Hitler. In addition, Constantinople showed that Neurath would accept a personally repugnant position for a long time out of a sense of duty. This weakness he never outgrew and ultimately it cost him his reputation. Finally, Neurath's brave self-confidence must be stressed. Once determined that a course of action was correct, he would not waver. Aware of his external easy-going manner, officials in Berlin were perhaps justified in taking lightly his threat to resign. But when Neurath arrived in Berlin during his vacation in August 1916 he announced that under no condition would he return to Constantinople. Since he had already moved his family, the office was forced to accept his decision and assign him to a new job at the home office.[23]

Naturally, Neurath's action did not win him a warm reception. His recent transfer from the consular service and the unpleasantness surrounding the Metternich affair made him a marked man.* Neurath felt these slights and was also unhappy with foreign office bickering over better rooms and office space. Moreover, he was soon bored by his new job as deputy chief of the press division, which consisted primarily of attending daily conferences held by the military, and serving as liaison between an increasingly ineffective foreign office and members of the heavily censored press. After his front line experiences and important post at Constantinople, Neurath hated the dreary bureaucratic regime of wartime Berlin, and four months later he submitted his resignation from the foreign service.[24]

Behind this action also lay the fact that Neurath was "not at all in agreement with the current policy of the Wilhelmstrasse." In fact, he was increasingly skeptical of his government's conduct of the war. Suspicious of the grandiose schemes for expansion in Turkey which he had tried to oppose, he had concluded that Germany was getting involved in too many countries without tangible advantages. His brief experience in the press division confirmed his opinions of the political ineptitude and diplomatic naivete of the military dictatorship then ruling Germany. From his good friend Köpke, who was involved in a war aims study for the foreign office, Neurath also learned of the increasingly ambitious and unrealistic demands of many officials. Irritated by the superficial discussions preceding the decision to reintroduce unrestricted submarine warfare, Neurath predicted only one result: the entry of the United States into the war, and inevitable German

---

*Only a month after Neurath's resignation, Ambassador Metternich was removed. A perceptive report noted that the reasons were precisely those which Neurath had mentioned: "Because of his continuing conflict with the ambassador, the deserving German counselor of embassy, Baron von Neurath, has left on a so-called vacation. Neurath alone carried on the real work of the embassy and was greatly honored by all, even in those circles friendly to the Entente powers ... because of his tactful behavior.... The ambassador appears to have received a strong reprimand ordering him to pay more personal attention to the business of the embassy, and above all else, to show a more worthy demeanor. Constantinople is no place for an ambassador who by means of his bizarre conduct completely isolates himself, or for one who makes himself laughable through his unbelievable greed and miserly hospitality." Unsigned report from Pera, August 4, 1916, AA, Geheim, Der Weltkrieg, Bd. 33.

defeat. Depressed by the failure of diplomatic leadership to block these dangerous and foolhardy trends, and his own inability to assist the few good men left in the foreign office, Neurath decided he could no longer participate in the coming catastrophe. Thus, he was receptive to an offer to become *Kabinettschef*, or political advisor and private secretary, to his father's old friend, King William II of Württemberg.[25]

Apparently, Neurath had been asked on several occasions to accept this appointment, then held by his uncle, the 77-year-old Julius Freiherr von Soden. Now, in the late summer of 1916, he accepted the offer and officially assumed his new office on January 11, 1917, with a yearly salary of 10,000 Marks and pension credit of more than 22 years transferred from the Reich. Neurath seemed to have achieved a solid position, but from the beginning he expressed the hope that his assignment would not last long:

> Getting accustomed to Stuttgart, in spite of the kindness of my king, was not easy. But I had not expected anything else. My activities here are indeed quite different from my past ones, and therefore, in spite of my complete independence, I feel quite tied down. The work is not overwhelming, and most of it not very interesting, and therefore contrasts sharply with what I was doing in Constantinople. Naturally, on the other hand, many things are quite pleasant, and within the [Württemberg] borders, I have an enviable influence. In my daily contacts with the king, I can easily mention many subjects which otherwise no one would have an opportunity to raise. My royal master himself is charming and apparently very happy that I am with him which I, of course, learned only in a roundabout fashion. In spite of all this, the work is not satisfactory, and in the long run, I will probably not remain head of the *Kabinett*. But I have plenty of time, and rather can calmly await developments.

Later in the same letter, he commented: "I do not regret at least one thing: that I am not at present at the foreign office. The relationships there do not appear to be very satisfactory."[26]

For two years, Neurath served as the king's advisor, prepared daily briefings, and reported on legislation and other matters of importance. From the beginning, William placed confidence in him and old friends were amazed to hear the king refer to Neurath simply as "Constantin."[27] But this relationship did not relieve the boredom which Neurath described to his friend Köpke:

> For the past eight days I have been here [in Wiesbaden] with my royal master for the cure, that is, *he* needs it, and I guzzle along out of boredom and according to the motto: "Nil juvat, nil nocet." And I also discipline my old joints in hot salt baths.... Hilarious it is not. Except for me, only an adjutant is here. I see the royal master only at meal times, and if I have anything special for him. Otherwise, everyone goes his own way. I finish my work in the mornings, and this keeps me tied to my writing desk from 8 to 11:30. Then, other than some nonessential telegrams, I am finished for the rest of the day, and sleep, go walking, etc., and do those things one usually

does at a watering place. In the evening I retire to bed like a good boy between 10 and 10:30. This way of life should last another three weeks; then we are going hunting for a few days in Silesia, and then perhaps a trip to the front to visit the troops. From June onwards, I must be in Bebenhausen near Tübingen for the summer sojourn, so that my family has seen very little of me.

A few months later, he complained: "This constant round of obligations is no trivial thing, and has often reduced me to profanity." After fifteen months in office, he still longed for "some greater field of activity," and described his summer with the king with the phrase: "Delicta mea lustrare volens in solitudinem recepi" ("Solitude in order to atone for my offenses.")[28]

Revolution in Stuttgart

By the end of 1917, Neurath was close to despair; Germany's fate was being decided on the battlefield, where he could not be,* and the incompetence in Berlin was so widespread that he no longer expected any improvement. He feared that the much discussed introduction of full parliamentary control over the cabinet ministers would destroy the backbone of Germany's political system by bankrupting the civil service, "with damaging results for political morale and the quality of future recruits." By July 1918 he believed that domestic revolution was likely. For him, parliament was the guilty party: "In Berlin, apparently, such nervousness prevails that with each trivial event, one awaits an explosion dangerous to the whole state. Fortunately the source of the infection—called the Reichstag—is out of action at least for some time."[29]

Neurath's pessimism deepened, not only because of what he regarded as the dangerous trend toward parliamentary rule, as distinguished from authoritarian government under professional experts, but also because of the impending military defeat. He was bitterly critical of the high command: "Where are the repeatedly promised, infallible results of the [unrestricted] submarine warfare? One million Americans have landed in France, and in England rationing has been lifted as unnecessary."[30]

Closer to home, Neurath confronted a paralyzing dilemma. He clearly preferred the status quo and the monarchy his family had served for so long, for he believed that a parliamentary government with a democratic base was not well suited to the German temperament. On the other hand, he knew that a monarchical Württemberg could not survive within a republican Germany, the inevitable result of a lost war. When the revolution did come, therefore, Neurath advised the king to avoid useless bloodshed; he knew that nothing could be changed and his

---

*Two letters from Neurath illustrate his identification with the front soldiers: "I never pity the fallen soldiers. They have given their life for a great purpose and no better thing can be done. A soldier's death is always the most beautiful one." And a few days later: "It is unfortunate that vacations cannot really be enjoyed more during wartime. At least, I cannot enjoy mine; I always suffer under a bad conscience that I am at home, while others are at the front." Neurath to Köpke, June 19 and July 30, 1918, Köpke Nachlass.

principal interest became the safety rather than the position of the king. He was confident that the Swabians would respect the royal family, even if they overthrew the monarchy.[31]

The revolution in Württemberg proceeded like a carefully staged drama with a predetermined script. Well announced and orderly demonstrations featured singing in four-part harmony; an interim government of traditional politicians stepped forward to fill the void; then upon news of general strikes in Berlin and the abdication of the Kaiser and numerous kings, a republican coalition formed to defuse further revolution. Without violence, arrests, or executions, power somehow passed from king to ministers, and thence to socialists, labor unions, and workers' councils. Throughout, Neurath played a decisive moderating role. The 70-year-old monarch was obviously worn out and deeply shaken by the events. Neurath's perceptive handling prevented embarrassing scenes; at one crucial point with the help of a few servants, he diverted the mob from an unguarded passage leading to the king, persuading them to vacate the palace. The revolution was over, and a new political reality established itself rapidly. The king and his parliamentary ministers vanished, even as the new republican government was proclaimed.[32]

Immediately recognizing the republic, Neurath requested permission to take the king to Bebenhausen, but at the king's request, he stayed behind in Stuttgart to handle the negotiations. The king's farewell on the steps of his palace to this faithful friend was, in the words of one witness, "deeply moving." It is ironic that the king was furious at the Stuttgarters who had played an insignificant role, but was moved to tears by the loyalty of Neurath who had persuaded him to accept the revolution he detested.[33]

In the following weeks, Neurath negotiated the financial settlement and worked out the technical details of the abdication (November 30, 1918), but at 46, he refused the king's request to continue in his service. Neurath believed it was fairer that the monarch retain his older staff (in particular the master of ceremonies, Count von Stauffenberg, father of the future hero), since they might not be able to find suitable employment elsewhere. After the negotiations were completed, Neurath retired to his own estate.[34]

These events in Württemberg reveal the nature of Neurath's conservatism. Devoted to his king and reared in the traditions of the aristocracy, Neurath interrupted a diplomatic career to serve the dynasty his family had defended for generations. Yet he strengthened the resolve of the king to preserve the peace of Württemberg, even at the cost of the royal house. For Neurath, the state had a higher claim. In no sense could Neurath be considered a democrat, but in the unique Swabian experience, aristocracy and monarchy had never lost their original popular base. Neurath's conservatism included a realistic recognition that historical developments must be respected, even though they might run counter to personal preference. In the light of this principle, Neurath requested that his fellow Swabians stay in office to help the new republican government.[35] Eventually, similar arguments would persuade him to render continued service to a state whose principles he did not necessarily accept.

CHAPTER

3

NEURATH AS AMBASSADOR: 1919–1932

Neurath Reenters the Foreign Service

Although Neurath had no immediate plans when he left the Württemberg service in 1919, there were indications he would reenter his chosen profession. As early as summer 1918 he had been approached by the foreign secretary regarding a new appointment. Neurath wrote to his friend Köpke: "I finally explained that I would be available for service to the Reich, if they believed I was needed. I would reserve my decision, however, until I considered the particulars of each offer. Truthfully, I have no real reason to leave [Stuttgart], even though I often long for some more important activity." A few weeks later, more overtures came from Berlin, and again writing Köpke Neurath noted: "Someone in the office seems to have a longing for me, or to put it better, there is a shortage of men, but I have provisionally rejected the offer.* The proper moment has not yet come."[1]

After the revolution, Neurath was asked to assume a cabinet-rank position in the new Württemberg government. He refused "with polite excuses," but when the offer was renewed more strongly, he replied with "that greeting which my countryman and maternal ancestor Götz von Berlichingen, offered to those laying siege to his castle." Apparently resolved upon a diplomatic career, even under the new Republic, in his last audience with the ex-king, Neurath asked permission to return to the foreign service, although no firm offer had as yet arrived.[2]

In Berlin, the situation confronting the new foreign minister, Count Ulrich von

---

*Neurath's hesitation came from his distrust of the lack of reform within the foreign service—"a task worse than cleaning out the Augean stables," he wrote to Köpke who was on a commission charged with this responsibility. "If you do not have the full support of the highest authorities, you will not survive but remain stuck in camel droppings." Six months later he added: "I willingly believe that your progress with reform does not move forward. My fears remain that in the foreign office they will experiment with so many new ideas and for so long, until suddenly some outside force will step in and turn everything upside down. You and Edmund Schüler will work yourself sick, and in the end the same old measures will remain." Neurath to Köpke, November 27, 1917 and June 19, 1918, Köpke Nachlass.

Brockdorff-Rantzau, was incredibly chaotic. In the months ahead his office would have to make superhuman efforts to win an acceptable peace. He needed, but lacked, a well trained staff; by the end of the war only 138 higher officials (as compared to the prewar number of 335) were in active service. Ranks had been depleted when younger officials had joined the army, and during the revolution many of the remaining ones had resigned because they could not bring themselves to serve a republican government. Those approaching retirement used the opportunity to leave. Brockdorff-Rantzau's first need was to lure back the younger men and to recruit new blood. Neurath's name would have come up for consideration in any event, but he had already impressed the new minister with his talents well before the war, having frequently entertained Brockdorff-Rantzau in Berlin. In his first weeks in office, the minister offered to Neurath his own former position as consul in Copenhagen, an important post in one of the few capitals where German and allied diplomats still met, and where the court was relatively friendly to Germany.[3]

Brockdorff-Rantzau frankly described to Neurath the need for someone who would not, because of previous relationships, be condemned in advance. Still, the post required a trained diplomat who was dedicated to advancing the German cause and protecting German honor. Neurath's excellent reputation in Constantinople made him a logical choice; near the end of December 1918, he received the official invitation. Still committed to Stuttgart duties for several more weeks, Neurath replied: "Until then, unless extremely urgent circumstances occur, I cannot desert the king's affairs." Still, he indicated a willingness to reenter the service. That Brockdorff-Rantzau was now foreign minister was something "I truly wish had occurred earlier," Neurath wrote, adding:

> This fact provides a guarantee that [my] employment would be possible without too great a sacrifice of convictions. I do not need to assure you that the idea of working with you in order to preserve for the fatherland whatever can be saved appeals to me. But it must be in a post in which I will have sufficient independence to accomplish something. I will not return to the office as a *Geheimrat*.[4]

At the end of January, Brockdorff-Rantzau invited Neurath to Berlin, where he had a lengthy interview with Friedrich Ebert, then provisional chancellor and soon the first president of the republic. In describing the interview for his family, Neurath indicated that he had asked the president whether only socialists or fellow travelers would be eligible for service in the republic. Ebert denied the limitation, accepting Neurath's offer to serve the republic without adopting democratic principles. Specifically, Neurath said he preferred a moderate monarchism, not "red republican" ideas.[5]

This incident epitomizes Neurath's attitude toward the Weimar Republic. He was willing to serve even under the new form, for the state was higher than any mere political institution. Despite his monarchism, he conceded that a restoration of the princes was impossible. Principally, he objected to the prevalence of party rule, for as a devoted civil servant he believed that self-interest forced parties and politicians to serve the state poorly and inefficiently. He feared that the republic's parliament and cabinet would become the plaything of factions and coalitions, to the detriment of the nation. He himself refused to join any party. "They are all so limited in their views," he told his daughter, "and so limiting in their outlook." No supporter of the German Nationals, or any other conservative party, Neurath was one of a large number of conservatives who found no place within the Weimar political system, but gave passive and unenthusiastic loyalty to the new state. The republic would be well served by this aristocratic monarchist who was too honest, upright, and honorable to disguise his feelings, but also too patriotic ever to shirk his duties. After their conversation, Ebert claimed that he had received "a satisfactory guarantee of Neurath's loyalty," and offered him an appointment.[6] No republican official ever had cause to regret that decision. Over the next fourteen years, Neurath loyally served as consul and ambassador in Copenhagen, Rome, and London. Next to the factor of personality, his experiences in these posts shaped the man who was to become foreign minister in 1932.

In Copenhagen

In February 1919, Neurath arrived in Copenhagen to begin work under inauspicious circumstances. The Paris peace conference was just beginning, and because of Germany's absence, Berlin needed to learn the allied intentions through the Danish window to the West. Neurath provided both accurate information and advice. He urged that a stubborn diplomatic resistance (even perhaps to the extent of forcing armed occupation) might modify some of the unjust demands. He wanted Berlin to pursue a more active program and was especially annoyed at the failure to protest more strongly the harsh aspects of the continuing blockade. He wrote:

> If we ourselves do not resist the continuing acts of violence done to us by the Entente, then we cannot demand that neutral countries be disposed to help us. On the contrary, they will continue to gain the impression that one can carry out anything against Germany, without the slightest risk. This conviction on the part of the Danes is even now being expressed by their attitude in the question of North Schleswig.[7]

For Neurath, the Versailles Treaty was a vindictive humiliation. He saw no advantages in the new territorial changes, yet upon its ratification (July 19, 1919), rather than follow his friend and superior Brockdorff-Rantzau into retirement, he resolved "to assist more than ever in the resurrection of Germany and not to be humbled by all the shameful demands which would now be placed upon German representatives abroad." His dedication to the cause of removing the postwar treaty was to be the shaping force of Neurath's career, as he strove to demonstrate in his own person Germany's strength and independence, thus compensating for the shameful treaty. In 1921, for example, when William of Württemberg died,

Neurath attended the funeral in the full uniform of the royal *Kammerherr*, the only person to so honor the former monarch. Shortly thereafter, he was the first German diplomat to appear at receptions in full-dress military regalia.[8] The easygoing, friendly Swabian now held himself aloof from most personal ties, acutely conscious of his representative role. By nature gentle and polite, Neurath displayed an abrupt firmness in his unswerving insistence that German views be heard. His physical size, too, commanded respect, if not friendship, from diplomatic and government officials. Suppressing his own moderate political view, Neurath projected an unlimited and patriotic faith in the future greatness of his country. In short, Neurath aimed to create an image of a distinguished diplomat from a proud and vigorous land. Gradually, the image merged with the man.

For a German diplomat to maintain such a stance in 1919 was not only unusual, but in the view of most observers, unrealistic. Germany was prostrate, defeated in war, torn by internal revolutions, and now punished by a debilitating peace. Its representatives abroad were expected to adopt appropriate tactics, but Neurath never did. Traditional diplomatic usage, for example, demanded that newly appointed officials make courtesy calls on other diplomats. Although most officials in Denmark had been accredited later than the Neuraths, after the signing of the peace treaty they insisted that the German consul should reopen the customary relationship and Neurath refused. "If they are waiting for my visit," he said, "they will become as old as Methuselah." Not until late 1920 did this persistent equanimity end his family's isolation. Thereafter, he was happy to feel that he had emerged worthily because he had not abased himself before the triumphant allied diplomats.[9]

Neurath believed that power and property, not ideology or friendships, were the key to a successful foreign policy. Thus, after the signing of the treaty, he tried to impress upon the Danish government the danger of relying permanently upon German weakness or Entente strength. He aimed "to achieve direct negotiations between Germany and Denmark over all the outstanding questions" and thereby to recover for Berlin that independence of action in negotiations which the Paris talks and the treaty were seeking to limit. Throughout 1919 and 1920, Neurath made little progress although he worked patiently to change Danish attitudes, often resorting to unusual methods. Several times he firmly but politely terminated unproductive conversations with ministers. Germany could wait; there was always time for the proper moment; "ripeness is all." Convinced of the necessity of power, he tended to sweep aside disdainfully the rights and ambitions of smaller states:

> Individually and as a nation, the Danes are naturally cowardly. Only the strong make an impression upon them. At the present time, no one here [in Copenhagen] believes that they have reason to fear us. They feel secure within the protection of the Entente which, they presume, will always be ready to implement Danish wishes against us. We will be able to reckon with a more reasonable state of mind only when the Danes again begin to fear us.[10]

This attitude, revealed first in Neurath's prewar strictures against Great Britain and in his unfaltering opposition to disarmament programs, remained constant. In Denmark, Neurath first demonstrated his conviction that all meaningful international relations are cemented by fear, not by respect, trust, or confidence. In diplomatic negotiations, Neurath demonstrated stubborn determination and insensitive immovability. Slow to engage in talks, keenly aware of the realities of power, his attitude—especially toward small countries—was gruff and even arrogant.

In the North Schleswig question, however, this approach was spectacularly successful. While insisting that Germany gracefully recognize the cession of portions of North Schleswig determined in the February 1919 plebiscite, Neurath demanded that the occasion be used to bring Denmark into bilateral negotiations emphasizing Germany's real and permanent power. After months of such pressure, in October 1920 Neurath wired Berlin that the Danish government had agreed that "all future negotiations would be conducted directly with us, to the exclusion of allied commissions and the like." Under his constant manipulation, Copenhagen and Berlin began these talks on May 23, 1921. Neurath was triumphant; for the first time since the war, Berlin ignored Entente circles and resumed direct relations with a foreign nation on a matter related to the Versailles Treaty. Only in this way, Neurath believed, could German recovery be achieved.[11]

In the course of the talks, Neurath distinguished himself from many contemporary German diplomats. His principal motive remained the accomplishment of an agreement, which no excessive German demands must endanger. Thus he was constantly on the alert lest the delegation depart from his own sober insistence that "for the negotiations, we must take our stand upon the realities of the situation." He continually reproved those who introduced domestic politics into the discussion. Thus, despite his anger and dismay that the final boundary line was at odds with the plebiscite of the preceding year, he sharply resisted the temptation to make a fuss. "No practical value for the future is to be expected from the delivery of such a protest," he informed the office. He would not permit a symbolic gesture to damage the talks necessary for German recovery. Neurath's counsel prevailed, and the negotiations concluded successfully in November 1922.[12]

Thus within two-and-a-half years, Neurath had achieved his goals: the border treaty and transfer were complete and friendly relations were restored, according to the principle of Danish acknowledgment of German power. In the process, his own relationship with the diplomatic corps had become friendly; he had every reason to be satisfied with his first diplomatic post. And it must have given him special pleasure when Denmark requested Neurath's signature on the draft treaty, besides that of the head of the delegation. But this accomplishment was only the beginning. The solution of the North Schleswig dispute helped restore Germany's reputation throughout Scandinavia, but the real issue was the Treaty of Versailles, and in Copenhagen Neurath could do little to change that treaty. By the winter of 1921, he was becoming restless and bored, hoping to be employed soon in some more important position.[13]

During his Copenhagen stay, Neurath had been sporadically engaged in the important matter of foreign office reform, cooperating with the thorough reorganization initiated in July 1919 by Personnel Director Edmund Schüler. Soon, however, Schüler changed his mind. In attempting rapidly to assimilate new forces, the director had recruited men from business and financial circles, and bowed to pressures from political parties in making important appointments abroad. With a few exceptions, these "outsiders" (as they were called by the traditional diplomats) were mediocre and woefully inexperienced. When consulted, Neurath was openly critical. Although he had little patience with the incompetents who before the war had dominated the service through fraternal associations, family, or social connections, he saw that Schüler's changes constituted no improvement.[14]

In December 1920, under attack because of his "dictatorial manner," Schüler retired. On the same day, the foreign minister asked Neurath to participate in a review and thorough discussion of all candidates for foreign posts. In addition, the minister expressed his intention to slow down the reforms threatening to undermine the entire training program for future diplomats. For extended periods in early 1921, Neurath was called to Berlin to handle "organizational and personnel questions." His assignment primarily was "to restore the diplomatic training program to some professionally justifiable and acceptable form." To many in the foreign service, Neurath's real job was to rid the service of untrained amateurs and to see that in the future such political appointments did not recur.[15]

Subsequently, Neurath prepared a training program which represented a compromise between Schüler's ideas and the older system. Introduced by the foreign office in late 1921 with only minor revisions, Neurath's approach preserved the diplomatic service from a rash of encroachments. Language tests and oral examinations which demanded a mastery of history, economics, and international law made it logical that the republic would recruit its diplomats from the same classes which had provided officials under the empire. These procedures, effective throughout the republic, later protected the service from Nazi intruders, even as late as 1937. As foreign minister Neurath always kept an attentive eye on the recruitment and training of future diplomats.[16]

Although Neurath also assisted in the general reorganization of various divisions of the foreign office (subsequently known as the Schüler Reform), his major interest was in personnel. He was an influential advisor to the minister, and frequently served as liaison with other members of the service. Inevitably, there were speculations that Neurath might himself soon become personnel director, until he expressed strong preferences for a foreign post. He had not changed his earlier expressed abhorrence of serving as a *Geheimrat* in the Berlin bureau.[17]

In Rome

After the formation of a new cabinet in October 1921, Neurath was called to Berlin to advise the chancellor (who had assumed the foreign ministry as well) on personnel changes. There he was surprised by an offer of the ambassadorship to Rome, where he would replace one of the bumbling incompetents who had been appointed as a favor to one of the political parties. Thus Neurath began an eight-year assignment which was to prove decisive for the direction of his future career and political views.

Upon his arrival in Rome in February 1922, he found a totally disorganized embassy, a staff of well paid but incompetent agents, and an Augean stable of legal cases concerning confiscated German property including even the old embassy building. In his first official act (while presenting his credentials), he proposed withdrawing from the city "until worthy quarters were made available." To make the issue clear, he added: "It was not only a question of comfort . . . but, to an extraordinary degree, a matter of political and personal prestige." Having expressed his desire for suitable quarters, he set off for Genoa, returning only after negotiations had begun for the purchase of the Villa Volkonsky, which he furnished as an embassy with living quarters for himself and his family.[18]

During the interim, Neurath worked closely with the German chancellor and foreign minister at the Genoa reparations conference, where he genially served as official German host. Although dubious about the ultimate value of Soviet assistance as worked out in the Rapallo Treaty, and aware of the torrent of attacks which would deluge the delegation, Neurath supported the chancellor's determination. "We have done it," Neurath reportedly said to his superiors at the conclusion of one particularly stormy meeting, "and now we must carry it through."[19] Neurath here revealed his characteristic ability to resist external opposition.*

After his return to Rome another aspect of this trait appeared during Neurath's courtesy call upon Mussolini, newly named Minister-President in October 1922. Before the visit, the Austrian consul told the Neuraths of his own visit. He had been ushered into a large room at the end of which Mussolini stood with his back to the visitor. While the consul discreetly coughed, Mussolini continued to stare into the fire. After an embarrassed silence of about fifteen minutes, the Austrian diplomat bowed and quietly left. Neurath was much amused by the incident which seemed to him typical of the pompous new ruler.

Thus forewarned, the next day he too was ushered into the room to find Mussolini, hands tightly fisted on his hips, staring pensively into the fire. Walking heavily across the floor, Neurath also gave a diplomatic cough, but when this produced no reaction in the silent thinker, the Swabian Baron walked up, clapped him heavily on the back and said: "Buona serra, Mussolini. I am here!" Turning and glaring up at the tall Neurath, Mussolini grinned. Pleased that Neurath could

---

*Despite success, Neurath was pessimistic: "The Conference of Genoa was very interesting, but did not, I am sorry to say, give the world the desired peace. People and the men by whom they are [led] are still far away from understanding that the world is going to pieces, if they do not change the ideas they had until now. In Germany, matters are still going to the worse, . . . and I fear our way downwards is not yet at its end." Neurath to Cardinal O'Connell, July 2, 1922, Archives of the Archdiocese of Boston.

not be intimidated, he immediately took a liking to the German ambassador which was to last for years to come.[20]

While Neurath welcomed the good relations with Mussolini, he approached the fascist movement with less than friendly expectations. Suspicious of its boisterous brutality, he condemned its use of terror to achieve political goals and its disregard for the established channels of authority. Primarily, he was disturbed by the possibility that the fascist movement would replace the state, substituting armed militia, party bosses, and local party cliques for civil and military authority. Neurath's subsequent reaction to the National Socialist movement was largely determined by his early impressions of fascism. Thus his experiences here were among the most important of his career. First, Neurath saw the fascist party as containing both idealists who wanted to restore the authority of the state and a mass of disinherited and disgruntled lower-class opportunists. Sooner or later these two forces would clash. On the day after Mussolini was commissioned to form the government, Neurath wrote that should the new leader not quickly succeed in uniting the party, violence would follow, for his dynamic movement was on the verge of internal anarchy.[21]

Deeply troubled by this problem, Neurath was more disturbed by the method of its resolution. The fascists handled dissent with terror and tyranny—"billy clubs, revolvers, and castor oil."* After they had consolidated their power in Italy, Neurath observed, they had still failed "to develop the intellectual ability to deal with their enemies except with weapons in hand." Rather than erecting a national government with broad consensus and support from the king, army, and civil service, Mussolini had capitulated to the fascist militia, bosses, and "the scum for whom the [fascist movement] was only the most convenient way to satisfy personal, and not least of all financial ambitions." In fact, Neurath concluded, the party had taken both nation and Mussolini captive. His reports describe "nearly medieval events," brutality, and public hatred against the Freemasons and other enemies of the state.[22]

Then, to Neurath's surprise, Mussolini regained control, becoming undisputed master of both country and party. At first, Neurath was not enthusiastic over Mussolini's leadership, and criticized the lack of clear programs in both domestic and foreign affairs. Moreover, unlike a professional statesman, Mussolini entered too personally into these areas, was oversensitive to criticism and, when aroused, was difficult to placate. In short, he predicted that unless Mussolini learned self-control and acquired firm mastery over the party, his regime would be short-lived.† Neurath was pleased when in October 1926 Mussolini revised the party statutes, introducing strong centralization and bringing party appointments under

---

*As early as December 18, 1922, Neurath wired Berlin that "merging the fascists with the state is in practice coming to mean more and more the suppression of all dissent under the fascist strongmen." AA Abtl. II, Italien, PO 29, Bd. 1.

†Only a month after Mussolini took power, Neurath wrote: "As Minister-President, he will naturally have to restrain his impulsive manner and the principal danger to his government is that it might be hard for him to reconcile his actions as head of the administration with his previous words and deeds as party leader." Neurath to AA, November 3, 1922, AA K428/K123484.

his personal control. By year's end, Neurath admitted that while "terror remains an integral part of the system," Mussolini was rapidly substituting another form of authority: "Mussolini's greatest talent lies in his skill at playing off individuals and factions against each other. Until now, he has always known how to prevent unauthorized actions by his followers, or at least how to reduce the complications which arise from such actions."[23] Neurath's conviction of the importance of strong leadership—a lesson he learned in Rome—was carried into his own experience as foreign minister.

Gradually, Neurath came to believe that the so-called program of the fascist party was secondary to Mussolini's strong personality, specifically his ability to follow programs likely to bring success and to abandon quickly an unprofitable undertaking. Neurath realized that such opportunism provided a practical base from which to restore order in Italy. His criticism yielded to admiration, especially after negotiations of the Lateran Treaty with the Vatican in 1929 finally created a national front. In dispatches filled with praise for "cleverly selected," "exemplary," and "masterful" techniques, Neurath concluded Mussolini had made the transition from party leader to national figure. The attendant strengthening of the concept of the state, he believed, would be a healthy counterbalance to any residual revolutionary fascist ideas.[24]

By 1929, Neurath thought that the fascist party was thoroughly incorporated into and controlled by the state. The new party statutes of October represented "a further progress on the road to a gradual subordination of the party, the union of party and nation, and the merging of fascism into the totality of the nation." He hailed "attempts of the government gradually to roll back the influence of the fascist party in the life of the nation and to make it subordinate to the concept of the state," and he reasoned that tendencies to eliminate the party as a state within a state have "now become a reality":

> Even though fascism might continue to have a material existence by means of the preservation of the party structure, as an idea it has dissolved itself into the concept of the state. Henceforth, the party will only be a means to an end: to permeate the national will throughout the whole of the people, and to create a greater Italy with all its classes united. Mussolini himself is quite aware that this ideal destination is still in the distant future, and that if it is ever to be reached, the party must accept considerably greater concessions, and finally disappear entirely as an unnecessary 'state within a state.' He therefore plans to continue slowly with his gradual elimination of the shock troops, which however he still temporarily has need of.[25]

Neurath believed that Mussolini had curbed the excesses of the fascist movement by enlisting the aid of the professional civil servants, who stayed in office despite party pressures and thus prevented irresponsible policy. By the time he left Italy, he believed the state forces were in command; those of the party and ideological fanatics were in retreat. As he was later to testify, his own evaluation of German National Socialism was based on this experience. It too, he thought, was "a revolutionary phenomenon which would be gradually worn away in the manner

I had observed during the German revolution in 1917 and later during the fascist revolution in Italy." A friend recalled that Neurath "thought that [the excesses in National Socialism] would die down and that developments would be similar to those in fascist Italy, where things had been very wild in the beginning, but had settled down afterwards."[26] Neurath attributed this evolution to the civilizing of the party at the hands of a patient and efficient civil service. Here was the third lesson he brought away from his Rome years.

Neurath was particularly glad that in the Italian foreign office, experienced diplomats realistically appraised Italy's strengths and set limits to Mussolini's more flamboyant ambitions. Once, in mid-1925, when some signs indicated that this older guard was losing control, Neurath wrote a dispatch which accurately forecast his own position under Hitler ten years later, for like Contarini (the general secretary of the Italian foreign office), Neurath always warned against self-deception in evaluating strength:

> Therefore for months now the fascists have waged a vigorous campaign against [Contarini] with the goal of removing this all-powerful man from the Palazzo Chigi. Up to now, Mussolini has always withstood the pressure of his followers, because he could not dispense with the collaboration of this experienced official, who in turn has taken pains that a substitute would not be easy to find. Recently, the crisis, which has been latent for quite some time, has sharpened, after Mussolini appointed the young, inexperienced, and uncultured fascist Grandi as under-secretary in the foreign ministry, as a sort of attached spy to the general secretary. Since that time, Contarini has been sick, and appears only sporadically in the ministry. The result is that total chaos rules there; no one is prepared to give out information, and it is impossible to have political conversations with anyone, except the busy Mussolini. It is hard to say how long this situation will last, and if it will lead to Contarini's removal from office, or whether this extremely versatile man will again succeed in regaining his old position of authority.[27]

Should the older diplomats disappear, Neurath feared an increase in a system of "alarms and threats, a policy of sabre-rattling and surly speeches [which] has come to set the tone of Italian pronouncements in foreign policy." But Neurath believed that Mussolini was becoming ever more aware of the limitations of Italian power, thus decreasing the chances that Italy would embark upon any reckless policy.[28]

Neurath left Italy unfavorably impressed by fascism, and only selectively enthusiastic about Mussolini. Still, he had seen a disruptive force civilized by the patient professionals, and had come to believe that both domestic and foreign advantages had been achieved under the dictatorship. With an inherent fatalism, coupled with the neutrality demanded of a diplomat, Neurath had apparently seen nothing during his Italian experience to make him unalterably opposed to a duplication in Germany of a similar governmental form. He himself doubted the successful transplanting of fascism, so largely theatrical and inherently Italian. He did nothing to help the German Nazis come to power, nor did he try to stop them. When the time came, Neurath would follow his own advice and the example of the Italian diplomats in the 1920s by staying in office and cooperating with the new government, hoping to curb dangerous excesses and smooth rough edges.[29]

Neurath's years in Rome also became a testing ground for his views on the complicated intricacies of postwar diplomacy and the role of power politics. He had come to Italy with strong convictions about Germany's immediate goals: the restoration of normal relations with former enemies, the removal of the humiliating restrictions of the peace treaties, and the rightful resumption of a place in the world community of nations. Yet he never believed that Italy would assist in this campaign. After Mussolini became minister-president, announcing that he would henceforth "follow an exclusively Italian policy," Neurath was even more reserved: "The Italians forget too easily that they are not alone in the world, and that England and France would see to it that the Italian tree would not grow very large. Moreover, these two states have the power to ensure that."[30]

In the following years, Neurath repeatedly cautioned Berlin against relying upon Italy. Mussolini, he was sure, was concerned "only with finding successes of the moment in order to strengthen his [domestic] position." To Berlin he was explicit:

> The Italian is and remains an opportunist in politics. This characteristic is deeply rooted in the popular folklore and runs like a red thread through the official Italian policy of the past decade.... In my opinion, our policy toward Italy can only be determined by the viewpoint that we should seek to obtain the greatest possible advantages from their undoubted need at present for allies, but otherwise we must remain perfectly clear that it is impossible to rely upon this country's attitude.[31]

Neurath's approach dominated the negotiation of a commercial treaty between Italy and Germany in 1925. Recognizing Mussolini's greater need, he did not regard the treaty as significant in drawing the two nations together. Should German interests appear threatened, Neurath was ready to scrap the talks. He remained convinced that relations between the two countries would continue uneasy, citing as his reasons the lack of control by fascist leaders within Italy, the threat of Italian activity in South Tyrol (the German-speaking area which Austria ceded to Italy in 1919), and Italian opposition to a union of Germany and Austria (*Anschluss*). Not friendship for Germany, but rather Italy's "attempt to free herself from the embrace of the allies, in particular the French neighbor," was the primary concern in Rome.[32]

Throughout the interwar years, Neurath was unusual among German ambassadors in that he did not encourage the Berlin government to strive for intimate relations with the nation to which he was accredited. Some officials interpreted this attitude as indifference; in fact it was the result of his inflexibly realistic understanding of the situation. He was not an enthusiast; he knew how many were the potential points for disagreement between Italy and Germany, and was satisfied that the proper slogan for most problems was "caution and prudence." "The observation of this principle," he wrote in 1927, "has never been more applicable than in relations with Italy."[33]

In addition, he showed his awareness that foreign policy rested not on ideas or will, but upon domestic situations. Repeatedly, he warned Berlin of Mussolini's "well-known aspiration to evaluate every foreign policy move by its domestic implication," and of Italy's weakness as a potential ally: "Italy is not consolidated enough either in its domestic political structure, its economic unity, or even in its military power so that it could be seriously considered as a rallying point for some European power grouping."[34]

Finally, Neurath's experiences in Rome showed him how German foreign policy should operate. No dogmatist who advocated systems, nor intellectual who explored new theories, he was interested only in the most precise evaluation of the existence and potential use of power. He analyzed Germany's postwar situation in terms of lost military, economic, and international power. Only a determined and realistic program could remove the limitations to Germany's role in the world. The argument then prevalent in Berlin was that demonstrations of good intentions would ultimately persuade the allies to revise the peace settlement. But Neurath maintained that only the restoration and manipulation of power (economic as well as military) would alter the treaties. Thus, he rejected the official policy of seeking redress through cooperation in the League of Nations, and he frequently complained that Germany had sold itself cheaply in joining in 1926.* He would have made final evacuation of the Rhineland the price of membership; that a nation could enter this body with a portion of its land under foreign occupation seemed to him ridiculous. Convinced that the League was only a disguised extension of the wartime alliance, Neurath was clearly not "one of the unqualified admirers of that institution."[35]

In the early 1920s, with Germany still weak, Neurath believed that the most diplomats could do was to keep open the lines of communication and to reassert the right to be treated as a sovereign nation. Thus, he refused the supplicant's role in bargaining with nations like Italy. Serious negotiations now, he advised, would only reveal German weakness; it would be better to await the restoration of power, when Italy would once more fear the neighbor to the North. Similarly, he was suspicious of attempts to extend border guarantees by treaties with Italy, Austria, Poland, and Czechoslovakia, in pacts similar to Locarno, opposing all attempts to reach agreement before German power ensured a proper hearing for German demands.[36]

This attitude emerges in his contemplation of closer ties with Austria. From

*Writing in prison after the war, Neurath recalled: "In order to set aside the discriminations of the Versailles Treaty, I along with Counsel Müller [Geneva] advised Stresemann at our meeting in Lugano to make the German entry into the League of Nations, which was strongly desired by England, dependent upon the revision of that Treaty. Stresemann, however, was strongly under the influence of the English Ambassador D'Abernon and Foreign Secretary Austen Chamberlain and rejected this advice, declaring that we could accomplish that goal easier from within the League." Neurath, "Skizze."

Rome, where he judged the related issues of Austria and the South Tyrol as "obstacles to German-Italian relations which were carefully and deliberately created by the authors of the Versailles-dictated peace," Neurath warned against prematurely raising these questions, expressing for the first time a fundamental conviction:

> As long as the Rhineland is not evacuated and the [Locarno Pact] not yet signed, it would be absurd to open discussion on the *Anschluss*. That issue has already once . . . been thwarted by premature and careless discussions at Weimar right after the revolution. A renewed alliance of all our neighbors, including those deep in the Balkans, now threatens to complicate the question if we continue to negotiate and discuss it as an acute issue. More than in any other political question which awaits a solution, our policy regarding *Anschluss* must always be: "Always think about it, never speak about it." Never, that is, until the moment arrives when we can not only speak, but also act.[37]

By the end of his Italian stay, however, Neurath believed the time was approaching for a more active policy. If political and economic conditions improved, Germany could raise the question of the Corridor, Upper Silesia, and union with Austria. In foreign office speculations, Bernhard Wilhelm von Bülow, director of the League of Nations desk, and soon to become state secretary, agreed with Neurath's consistently expressed view that Italy would be of little assistance in this struggle, while the friendship of Great Britain would be crucial. Obviously, Germany ought to have an ambassador in London who would contribute to the friendly atmosphere needed to carry out a more dynamic foreign policy. From 1928 on, advocates of such a line within the foreign office pressured to post Neurath to London, as part of the new era in German policy. As Köpke noted to Neurath:

> In my opinion, someone must be in London who will not drown in the ocean of legal formulas, and will not be satisfied merely to pray constantly his rosary of logic. You know England, know the English, speak completely effortless English, and would not let yourself be overly impressed in London. Moreover, you would carry out in excellent fashion the business at hand.[38]

At first Neurath was unwilling to accept the transfer, stressing that his health had not been good since his mild heart attack of 1925, which was followed by complications diagnosed as angina pectoris. The London climate might intensify his troubles and further worsen a chronic throat condition. President Hindenburg brushed aside these objections, reminding Neurath of his duty and ordering him on his honor as an officer and nobleman to accept the new assignment. Reluctantly, Neurath agreed. To his family, he commented that Germany needed someone in London who would not be browbeaten by the British, and who would be able to hold his own in the delicate conversations now underway.[39]

In London

Political pressures from Hindenburg were not alone responsible for Neurath's appointment. The foreign office saw 1930 as a crucial year for the arrangement of international conferences and the creation of a suitable atmosphere for them. Although Neurath did not seem to the liberal press a good representative of the "new Germany" and the appointment was strongly criticized, Berlin needed a man with diplomatic and technical accomplishments. Neurath was so judged by one of his contemporaries: "Here he was completely in his own element. He revealed all those Swabian gifts which enabled him tenaciously and adroitly to exploit the weakness of the enemy even in the most difficult moment of the negotiations, thus winning an acceptable compromise."[40] Moreover, Neurath and his wife were charming hosts, who knew English society and were personal friends of Queen Mary. In the task of winning British support for Germany's intensifying drive in foreign policy, Neurath's appointment was eminently logical.

The Neuraths arrived in London in early November 1930, and were immediately welcomed. Within a very short time, he had renewed old acquaintances and through the good graces of the Queen entered London's most exclusive circles. In later years, Neurath liked to recall his official reception at the court: the Queen broke the dignity of the occasion to exclaim, "Surely it is not my little Constantine!" recalling in friendly fashion her days at the Württemberg court. Soon Neurath and his wife transformed the embassy into a center of society. The success of their endeavors can be measured by the massive reception of January 18, 1931 in honor of the sixtieth anniversary of the founding of modern Germany. Despite his original hesitations, and the rash of illnesses which England's climate did intensify, Neurath soon came to enjoy his new position and served Germany well during his brief term.[41]

Unlike his experiences in Rome, however, which shaped his personal approaches to contemporary political phenomena, Neurath apparently learned only a diplomatic lesson during his years in London: the lack of British support for German recovery. During his years there, the smoldering issue of reparations and war debts was fanned by the financial crisis following the New York stock crash. The German government, weakened by the spectacular growth in numbers of both Left and Right radicals (especially after the elections of September 1930), decided to stabilize domestic affairs with foreign victories, by raising such territorial issues as the Polish Corridor, *Anschluss,* and the Saar. The army, in particular, urged renewed efforts to achieve arms equality and rearmament. The chancellor hoped for a cancellation of reparations or at least a moratorium on payments, and the new foreign minister, anxious to initiate some bold move which might bolster his own ministerial seat, proposed a customs union with Austria. All required assistance and support from Great Britain, and Neurath discovered that such aid was not available.[42]

In the disastrous summer of 1931, all of these plans swiftly collapsed. The preconference disarmament talks in Geneva produced a draft unacceptable to

Germany, and Berlin regarded with pessimism the general conference scheduled for February 1932. Even the startling invitation to have the German chancellor visit England (the first such visit in history) produced discouraging results. Despite friendly discussions and President Hoover's proposed moratorium on all intergovernmental debts and reparations, the chancellor returned to Germany with his revisionist program stalled and the financial crisis verging on catastrophe. Neurath summarized the results succinctly: "The English do not want to contribute to the restoration of Germany." It was an insight he would not forget.[43]

At home, the German government realized that solutions to domestic chaos could not be obtained in London, Vienna, or Geneva. The chancellor found he had no choice but to "pile decree on decree, shut his eyes, and hope for the best." But as domestic failures accumulated, Berlin once again turned to seek foreign success. Chancellor Brüning, succumbing to the urgings of his foreign minister, sponsored the idea of a customs union with Austria. Although Neurath and many diplomats were skeptical about the timing of this "bone of contention thrown before Europe," the plan proceeded, only to result in total defeat. One observer criticized the effects: "Under the impetus of the call for activity, German foreign policy is pursuing too many aims at one and the same time . . . thus running the risk of blocking one road, while pursuing another." It was the exact sentiment Neurath always voiced.[44]

The unexpectedly severe economic crisis had destroyed the forward impetus of German policy, and increasingly domestic exigencies became prominent. Neurath, who thought himself above such political developments, was caught up in the turmoil that would eventually destroy the Weimar Republic, even as it elevated him to the foreign ministry. He brought to the new position, however, not the insights of a politician, but the experiences and lessons of a successful ambassador. This was to be both his strength and his weakness in the days ahead.

CHAPTER

4

NEURATH BECOMES FOREIGN MINISTER

Everywhere the ravages of the world economic crisis of 1929 pushed foreign policy out of the limelight, sharpening the focus on domestic politics. This trend was especially evident in Germany. By 1930, an increasingly polarized political life preoccupied most citizens, and even professional diplomats could not remain neutral and unaffected. The key issue was the need to restore political and economic stability, without which, Neurath and his colleagues knew, a successful foreign policy was impossible. During his years as ambassador, Neurath had personal knowledge of the bad effects of mixing domestic and foreign affairs. In late 1925, a series of incidents had shown him the serious disadvantages.

Foreign Minister Gustav Stresemann, long a champion of German minorities abroad, reacted adversely to reports that Mussolini was terrorizing the South Tyrol in an attempt to destroy that area's German culture and language. Neurath viewed developments more calmly. While he sympathized with the wish to preserve linguistic and cultural heritages, as in the situation of the Germans in North Schleswig, he believed that Berlin could undertake nothing. He was therefore upset when the German press, with the support of the middle class and conservative parties, launched an intensive campaign against alleged anti-German measures in South Tyrol, charging that Rome had forbidden Christmas trees, destroyed German monuments, outlawed sermons in German, and forbidden the teaching of the German language.[1] Neurath cautioned:

> I have nothing at all against some precise listing of fascist excesses against the German minority and an objective criticism of the existing conditions, but I must warn strongly against immoderate polemic; that would serve neither our political relations with Italy, nor the interests of the South Tyroleans.

Until the German press stopped making wild charges, nothing could be done: "Riding about on our principles will not bring us out of the dead-end street, into which mutual polemics have brought us." In particular, he asked that the *Tägliche Rundschau,* because of its well-known close relations to Stresemann and his party, be asked to cease its anti-Italian campaign, or at least not print patently absurd stories.[2]

Stresemann's response was patronizing. Germany, he told Neurath, was not a fascist state which could silence the press. Since the crisis originated with Italy's blatant provocations, no improvement could be expected until the fascists ceased their attacks. In concluding, Stresemann rebuked Neurath: "Do not shut your eyes to the violence being done to Germans and do not grow accustomed to thinking that German press criticism of the violence to German culture and language poisons the atmosphere."[3]

Neurath would not let this scolding go unanswered. In a lengthy dispatch he acknowledged Italian responsibility, which he had ever emphasized to Rome authorities:

> But it is also my duty to call to the attention of my superiors those developments in Germany which seem likely further to poison the atmosphere, placing us in the wrong and annulling or at least weakening the effect of our diplomatic protests. Among such developments must be counted the various false reports recently appearing in the German press ... and the exaggerated accounts of acts of terror in the South Tyrol.

Taking up Stresemann's implied accusation of his pro-Italian position, Neurath concluded:

> I have expressed my views of the value of Italian friendship so often that I thought I would certainly be free of a charge of Italophilia. But in view of the main differences which we have with England and France ... I can scarcely appeal for support from Italy with any chance of success if the German press continues, either consciously or not, to exceed the justifiable degree of criticism of the Italian situation. I refer only to the excesses, for in the easing of the atmosphere, even the German side must try to cooperate.
>
> The accusation that I am blind to the violence being done to Germans is completely unsupported, and I reject it with the greatest firmness.[4]

From the beginning, Köpke, the minister-director of the concerned department, had tried to stop the "idiotic" press campaign, protesting "propagandistic babble such as that about the Christmas trees," but to no avail. His analysis for this failure is instructive:

> The explanation for this is surely Stresemann's emotional involvement in the whole question of the South Tyrol. In the past, he has expressed himself most temperamentally over this question, mostly when these issues were raised by the Right. You know that the whole idea behind the German National's parliamentary question on what the foreign minister planned to do in regard to the question of minorities before the League of Nations

sprang primarily from their attempts to ridicule earlier statements by the minister on this issue and force him to acknowledge that in such issues, particularly regarding the South Tyrol, Germany has undertaken no direct measures, and in the future will not be able to undertake any successful steps, even in the League. From this political party environment, perhaps we can understand why the minister, in spite of our constant pressure, could not decide in time to destroy by his initiative the ever-growing outcry over Mussolini's policy in Italy.[5]

To Neurath, such preoccupations did not excuse Stresemann's activities, but rather confirmed his conviction that political considerations made a rational foreign policy all but impossible.*

A year later, Neurath and Stresemann chanced to meet in San Remo while on vacations; over a number of days, they held "open political discussions" concerning foreign policy. Neurath came away convinced that Stresemann judged everything from the perspective of party politics. Köpke too frequently complained of "Stresemann's tendency to handle all foreign policy questions more or less chiefly from the party tactical point of view." Neurath subsequently told friends and family that Stresemann, trapped by politics, had failed to take advantage of favorable foreign opportunities.[6]

Neurath was saddened yet not surprised to find himself suddenly unpopular with Stresemann, who now worked to get Neurath retired from Rome or dispatched to some less important position. In 1927, he offered Neurath the vacant post of ambassador to the United States. Unlikely to fit enthusiastically into the American democratic society, Neurath feared he would be ineffective. Rejecting the offer, he recommended his own embassy secretary, Friedrich von Prittwitz und Gaffron, and was relieved when the latter was appointed. A year later, Stresemann offered an appointment to Moscow. Neurath rejected this offer too, suspicious that it had been made in the hope that he would soon discredit himself and retire from the service. Neurath knew no Russian, had never been involved with East European affairs, and his aversion to Bolshevism was well known. A personnel policy blatantly springing from political considerations, this offer offended Neurath's sense of expertise. Professionalism and politics, in his view, made very poor traveling companions. Many years later, after examining some documents from the "Stresemann era," Neurath commented: "Whoever wants to

---

*In his postwar "Skizze," Neurath admitted that he was often an "uncomfortable subordinate for the various foreign ministers. Stresemann, for example, often complained about me." To Köpke, he expressed his anger that the German press and political leadership judged everything by domestic politics. Neurath to Köpke, January 2, 1926, AA K428/K123485. Subsequently, independent investigation by the foreign office completely supported Neurath's conclusions that the burden of guilt for creating the aggravation over the Tyrol issue rested with "the larger German journals which have indiscriminately and uncritically reprinted and commented upon all manner of tendentious reports originating from known examples of yellow journalism." These investigations found that Italian reprisals had *followed* the initiation of the German press attacks. Fritz von Twardowski to AA, January 28 and February 3, 1926, AA 2784H/D538150–53 and ADAP B/III, 94–96.

learn can clearly see there how foreign service personnel questions should never be handled."[7]

In 1929, Neurath's convictions were confirmed when the press and Stresemann's office charged that he had not observed the proper embassy celebrations of Constitution Day (August 11) and that in Rome he had deliberately shunned prominent German writers (Emil Ludwig and Gerhard Hauptmann were mentioned) because of their political convictions. Subsequently, an official parliamentary committee looked into the high expenses incurred by Neurath's embassy and alleged financial deals with the fascist movement. Liberal journalists, especially Professor Bernhard, were irate, claiming the incidents demonstrated Neurath's opposition to the republic. While ostensibly defending his ambassador, Stresemann seemed to side with the critics, concluding that Neurath had "not played a very happy role" in the controversies and lacked both tact and a proper sense of etiquette. The charges were unproven, however, and testimonials introduced into the formal hearings by the foreign office claimed that Neurath was "the right man for the post," praising his "meritorious activity." Despite his vindication, Neurath was deeply hurt by the attendant publicity, exaggerated by an unsympathetic and politicized press.[8]

Well aware of Stresemann's antipathy, Neurath recalled many years later (in 1944):

> This feeling was entirely mutual. I never hid that fact, and [Köpke] had frequently to exhort me, when finally I did not even want to visit Berlin again. But I was decided that should the Stresemann era continue, I would let it develop into a complete break, and then resign.
>
> Incidentally, Stresemann's antipathy might have been influenced by the fact that the old gentleman [i.e., Hindenburg] had a well-known intention of making me Stresemann's successor, despite the fact that I rejected this unreasonable demand—as Stresemann must also have known—on more than one occasion, and only after Stresemann's death, and as a result of general pressure, did I make the sacrifice in 1932.[9]

This account of the quarrel seems plausible, for by 1928 Neurath and Hindenburg had become quite friendly, while the president's relations with Stresemann remained correctly cool. Neurath had always admired Hindenburg, enthusiastically welcoming his presidential candidacy in 1925. The wedding of Winifred von Neurath to Hans-Georg von Mackensen, oldest son of Hindenburg's friend and comrade, Field Marshal von Mackensen, however, was the first occasion upon which Neurath became personally acquainted with the president. During his visit to the Mackensen estate in 1927, he spoke at length with Hindenburg; their close personal ties seem to date from then.[10]

The two men took an instant liking to each other. Both enjoyed quiet walks and hunting, and they represented an older era and a tradition vanishing in the world around them. In the view of a critical observer, they were similar in another respect: Hindenburg was even less an intellectual than Neurath, "far more interested in the chamois-buck than in politics." Within a short time, Hindenburg developed a deep confidence in Neurath, and welcomed his presence and advice. By the end of 1928, it was no secret that of all his ambassadors, he liked Neurath best. Knowledgeable sources claimed that only the president's intervention prevented Stresemann from retiring Neurath from Rome. Thus it was expected that if a cabinet of "experts" were appointed by the president—and such speculation increased after 1928—Neurath would have a prominent place in it.[11]

Within the foreign office, Köpke's latest witticism made the rounds: time would bring not wisdom, but Neurath *("Kommt Zeit, kommt [Neu]rath")*. Everyone was sure that if the rightist parties were ever able to assemble a cabinet, Neurath would be included. Already in the summer of 1925, Neurath's life had touched the boundaries he had always drawn between politics and his own professional career. That August, Köpke wrote of Neurath's future involvement:

> I am inclined to believe that you do not want to remain in the service for longer than two or three more years. Moreover, I think it very likely that during the next spring, the whole political picture will make necessary a change in personnel in the office, and I believe . . . you will be forced, under these altered political circumstances, to accept either the post of foreign minister, or state secretary. The rightist parties have considered you for a long time now as the coming man [for these posts], even though you have always refused them, in my opinion correctly, after full consideration.[12]

Indeed, the British ambassador recorded in his diary in July 1925: "The German Nationals are said to have a new cabinet ready, with Gessler as chancellor, Neurath (the present ambassador in Rome) as foreign minister." But Neurath was opposed to becoming involved with cabinet politics, and replied to Köpke's letter:

> I won't speak about your additional speculations concerning my person. You know that I have an absolute abhorrence for coming to Berlin, regardless in whatever capacity. Only the fatherland's most extreme need, and the proof—which is still not forthcoming—that *I* particularly can be of help, would persuade me to give up this point of view. But for the present, the question is not acute.

Even had the friendship with Hindenburg not developed, Neurath's fate seemed linked with the future of conservatism in Germany.[13]

But more immediately important was Hindenburg's decision—sometime in 1927—that Neurath was the logical man for London. Stresemann, in the words of a contemporary, "strove with tooth and nail against posting Neurath to London." When the president announced that he would appoint no other candidate, Stresemann decided to maintain the aging and ineffective incumbent, rather than send Neurath. In the summer of 1929, Stresemann openly feared Hindenburg would select Neurath as the next foreign minister, and would do anything to block this eventuality.[14]

Hindenburg's Choice

Stresemann's fears were fully justified. As early as March 1929, Hindenburg had invited Neurath to take a day off from his annual cure at Bad Wildungen and join the president's hunting expedition. On that occasion, Hindenburg expressed his desire that Neurath succeed Stresemann, who was then seriously ill. Shortly thereafter Stresemann died, and the president officially asked Neurath to assume the post.

On both occasions, Neurath declined, citing lack of political party support. In his postwar testimony, he described his reactions: "In view of the party conditions in the Reichstag in those days, I saw no possibility for a stable foreign policy. I was not a member of any of the thirty or so parties, so that I would not have been able to [find] ... support in the Reichstag." Reluctantly, Hindenburg agreed, but elicited Neurath's promise that in time of emergency, he would stand ready to serve. With his family, Neurath discussed Hindenburg's flattering insistence, but always added: "Hopefully nothing will come out of this. I lack any domestic support."[15]

Neurath's analysis was acute; the shaky coalition cabinet could only appoint as minister someone who could control Reichstag votes. Thus, the position went to Julius Curtius, a former minister of economics, who knew little of foreign affairs but whose appointment guaranteed continued support from the DVP, Stresemann's party of moderate conservatives and businessmen. The deepening world depression, however, made the newly organized cabinet short-lived. On May 27, 1930, it lost a vote of confidence, and on the following day Heinrich Brüning of the Center (Catholic) Party was entrusted with the formation of a new cabinet calculated to win support from the moderate parties.[16]

In the ensuing discussions, Neurath's name again figured prominently, but the popular *B. Z. am Mittag* commented: "It must be immediately added that very strong political opposition to this candidacy must first be overcome. For there is opposition from the camps of the Left as well as from the circles of the middle parties." Most observers believed that the foreign office would go to the newly formed People's Conservative Party (*Volkskonservativen,* or VK). Brüning and Curtius, however, reached a political agreement and the latter remained in office. As part of this deal, Brüning suggested that the London post should be filled by a member of the VK or another conservative politician, thus repaying the concession concerning Curtius. The foreign minister claims he refused such arrangements. Nevertheless, two months later, Neurath was appointed to the Court of St. James's, and many believed it was a political maneuver.[17]

The *Vossische Zeitung* was especially indignant. Writing as the rumors were beginning, Georg Bernhard suggested the time had come for Neurath's "well-deserved retirement."

> **Herr von Neurath is no representative of the new Germany.** In Rome, he evaluated every writer who came by the standard whether or not he was accepted to him, while at the same time he received indiscriminately every-

one who was distinguished or had an official position in the former German Empire. This should not be taken as a reproach to his character. On the contrary, it is a sign of the honorable and upright nature of a gentleman, who undoubtedly displayed such an independent nature before his royal master at the Swabian Court as he now does in making no secret of his opinions. We are inclined to evaluate this attitude much higher than the fawning servility of many officials.

But while such a constituted person might gain many advantages for German policies at the Italian court and among the associates of the Duce, some real representative of the new Germany must be sent to England. . . . We must send abroad men who can serve as propagandists for the young German Republic.[18]

Despite his years opposing political involvement, Neurath's career was being influenced by political machinations.

Still head of a minority cabinet, Brüning moved to a dictatorship under presidential emergency powers. When the foreign policy mistakes of 1931 threatened a cabinet collapse, he agreed to sacrifice Curtius. Dependent upon the president and aware of Hindenburg's desire for a professional diplomat in this position, the chancellor and officials of the foreign office agreed on the qualifications of the replacement:

The successor should not be a parliamentarian; he must come either from the active diplomats or from officials within the Berlin office. He must have a lengthy foreign experience and his name must be well known abroad. He must be able to demonstrate successes in his foreign career in order to be acceptable domestically, and he must be acceptable to the Right.

In conversations following the cabinet resignation, Hindenburg expressed his well-known preference for Neurath and ordered him to Berlin. Observers were certain that any other candidate would "run into the opposition of Hindenburg." Indeed, the president rejected all other names suggested, particularly stressing their poor relations with conservative groups. Hindenburg "wanted precisely a candidate who would ease Brüning's position with the Right and not make it harder." But he could not persuade either Brüning or Neurath.[19]

Uppermost in Neurath's mind were both personal and political considerations. He was satisfied with his position in London. Popular with the people and the government, he had won the confidence of the British foreign office and achieved excellent relations with the royal family. He had little reason to desire a change, and he did not look forward to accepting the more arduous job of minister. Aware of his own limitations as a public speaker, he felt ill at ease with politicians for whom spoken improvisations were an everyday affair. Moreover, he told friends, he was not given to the quick decisions demanded by such a post: "The readiness of the Swabian always to see the other side of an argument and to recognize the justice of another's position robbed him of the possibility of making quick retorts and could even expose him occasionally to the suspicion of concealing something."[20]

His other objection was more significant. Neurath despised the Reichstag and believed that President Hindenburg should suspend its legislative powers. News reports circulated that Neurath had refused the job "because he is of the opinion that foreign policy must remain free from parliamentary influence." Regretting the antics of the politicians, disapproving of party influence, and despairing of meaningful initiative under parliamentary control, Neurath agreed with his friend Magnus Freiherr von Braun who asked:

> How can foreign policy follow any long-range goals, if the leading statesmen must always cast one eye on the outcome of the next election, never knowing if they will even *be* in office in the near future. Such a foreign policy will always be a patched-up affair at best. Foreign policy is seldom compatible with popularity.[21]

Neurath's reluctance to become foreign minister proceeded from his conviction that the political nature of the cabinet itself must be altered.

Neurath advocated a presidential cabinet of experts as the best means for restoring stability. The revisionist foreign policy which he desired could not function in the chaos of coalition governments, but required stable leadership which could mold public opinion. He opposed the view that foreign policy could produce domestic stability. As an experienced diplomat, he recognized the folly of negotiating from weakness. Thus, he made his acceptance of a cabinet seat conditional upon a strong government, with presidential support. Finding no such plan in Berlin, he announced his intention to "stay in London."[22]

Hindenburg was similarly unsuccessful with Brüning, who claimed that while Neurath might provide a certain "shield against the wind from the Right," he would cause as much trouble as had Curtius "only with the omens reversed." Attacks would now come from the Socialist Party, whose votes and benevolent tolerance the government required. Unable to convince Hindenburg to consider other candidates, Brüning himself assumed the office. Neurath and his family were relieved. "Thank God," Baroness von Neurath wrote in her diary, "Brüning takes over the foreign office." A few months later, Neurath pleaded with an embassy visitor: "Just leave me alone here. Tell Berlin to let me stay in London."[23] But Neurath's own desires soon became irrelevant.

Enter the Nazis

Increasing political disturbance in Germany, the growth of right-wing parties, and Brüning's inability to stabilize the situation brought Neurath closer to domestic involvement. Initially, Neurath viewed the growth of National Socialism as a seriously disruptive threat to German foreign policy. In the early 1920s, he had frequently referred to Hitler's party as a "reactionary-nationalistic German movement," whose triumph would bring "a return to the political methods which had made the world war possible." Despite the substantial Nazi victories in the national elections of September 1930, and in local elections in 1931, Neurath paid little more attention to the movement, relying for his information upon foreign office circulars, which stressed that "in concrete specific problems of foreign policy [Hitler's aims] do not essentially differ from those of the present government and its predecessors."* Neurath was reassured by dispatches which argued that should the National Socialists come to power, "the larger economic viewpoints, as well as the basic principles of our foreign policy will remain the same."[24]

Although Neurath never trusted National Socialism and its promises, which too closely resembled the opportunistic policies of Italian fascism, he was attracted by one feature of its program: "The precondition for a fruitful foreign policy [the foreign office circular quoted Hitler as saying] must be the inner health of the German people, and that can only be achieved through the resurrection of the national drive for self-preservation and a restoration of its military spirit." From his embassy in London, Neurath had diagnosed the failure of German foreign policy in 1931 as springing from such inner disunity and weakness.[25] Although he made no effort to learn more about the Nazis, he must have been reassured by this note.

Meanwhile, the domestic scene worsened. Entirely dependent upon Hindenburg's support, Brüning's cabinet faced with alarm the expiration of the president's term in the spring of 1932; no alternative to the eighty-four-year-old president had yet been found, and a concerned Brüning was forced to suggest extending the president's term by a constitutional amendment. Startled by Hindenburg's opposition to the idea, the chancellor called upon the president's conservative friends, including Neurath. At Brüning's request, Neurath visited the president in early December 1931 and talked with him at length about the term extension.[26] Eventually, Hindenburg told Brüning to proceed with plans for the constitutional amendment.

Celebration of the Christmas holidays in London was overshadowed by rumors of an impending Nazi coup; on January 6, 1932, Neurath was again called to Berlin for consultation, where he was again sent to the president. Brüning's talks with representatives of the rightist parties had broken down so that the term extension legislation was now impossible. Hindenburg was not likely to allow himself to be a candidate for reelection against the united opposition of his former supporters. Neurath was again asked to convince Hindenburg to run. In lengthy discussions, they reviewed the condition of Germany and the Reichstag chaos. When Neurath urged that the president must accept the responsibility for another campaign, Hindenburg raised the possibility of a shift to the Right, with a presidential cabinet that would include men like Neurath, but he admitted that such seemed unlikely at present.[27]

Undoubtedly at this time, Neurath mentioned a meeting that had occurred a few days earlier, arranged by a retired diplomat, the Prince zu Wied.[28] Through

---

*Pointedly, Neurath told English diplomats that even if the NSDAP "became so strong that they succeed in taking over the government, they will have to add much water to their wine after they assume responsibility." Neurath to AA, December 3, 1930, AA K1976/K512835.

this aristocratic member of the NSDAP, Adolf Hitler had invited Neurath for a private conversation. No record was kept of the meeting, but shortly afterwards Neurath gave an account of the occasion to friends:

> Neurath said he found a medium-sized, ill-dressed rather common looking man, who seemed also to be shy. The remarkable thing about [Hitler] was the eyes, which burned with unquenchable fire, and the voice, which had an extraordinary quality of persuasion. Hitler spoke for almost two hours, more a monologue than a conversation. He described the situation as very dangerous, said revolution might break out any day, sweeping away all barriers, and he insisted that if such were the case, he could do nothing [to stop it]. He spoke about his idea of what a government should be: reliable men, not extremists from any party; a government capable of upholding Germany's sacred right to freedom and dignity. Neurath's impression was not wholly negative. He was struck by the will power and the sincerity of some of the opinions expressed.[29]

The conversation confirmed Neurath's belief that Hitler lacked fixed foreign policy goals, and did much to banish from Neurath's mind the idea that Hitler was the fanatic depicted by the press.* Later the same evening, Neurath received another visit from the Prince zu Wied, who bore a message from Hitler: would Neurath take the foreign ministry, if Hitler should become chancellor in a National Socialist government? Not surprised, Neurath responded with characteristic diplomacy: "Ready in principle, [he] withheld his definite decision until all the conditions for such an offer were present."[30]

Obviously, Hitler was trying through Neurath to influence the one man who could block his rise to power: Paul von Hindenburg. Aware of the president's preferences, Hitler was prepared to work with Neurath and the ploy succeeded. Neurath's account of his meeting with Hitler certainly helped persuade Hindenburg to offer himself for another election campaign, and may have contributed to the destruction of the Brüning cabinet. Previously the president had no alternative to Brüning, because of foreign policy considerations, even though his heart had long been set upon a cabinet of experts ruling with the support of the Right. That Hitler would choose as foreign minister the man whom Hindenburg had himself selected more than three years earlier made the break with Brüning neither so terrible nor difficult. Following his own reelection in April, the president indicated that the time for such changes would probably come shortly after the Prussian elections, perhaps as early as May 1932.[31]

Events in early 1932 deepened the crisis and Neurath reluctantly sensed an inevitable fate. Two weeks after his return to London, he fell seriously ill. After

---

*Neurath's impressions were similar to those of Wilhelm Groener, who told a staff meeting on January 11, 1932 that Hitler made a "sympathetic impression as a decent, modest chap with good intentions. His air is that of a diligent, self-made man ... determined to wipe out revolutionary ideas.... Hitler's purposes and goals are good; but since he is a fanatic, so full of enthusiasm and volcanic forces, he undoubtedly continues to use the wrong means now and then." Printed in Otto-Ernst Schüddekopf, *Das Heer und die Republik: Quellen zur Politik der Reichswehrführung 1918 bis 1933*, 32.

two months in Bad Wildungen, he returned to Great Britain in late March, believing that rest, more than medicine, had wrought his recovery. During the opening of London's social season in late May, he received with surprise the news of Brüning's fall and his own selection as foreign minister.[32]

Although Neurath had hoped to avoid a cabinet appointment, the machinery which eventually ensured his nomination had been in operation for months. On February 13, 1932, leaders of the German Nationals and veterans' organization had met with Hermann Göring, Hitler's deputy, to agree upon an opposition cabinet. In the discussion, Göring rejected all nominees for foreign minister until Neurath was proposed. Here at least there was rare unanimity. General Kurt von Schleicher, the wily director of the political division of the Army command, however, was the prime mover behind the plots which toppled Brüning, and he had plans to form the new government by himself. For foreign minister, he had selected Rudolf Nadolny, a professional diplomat, ambassador in Ankara and chairman of the German delegation at the disarmament conference. If the new cabinet had been formed solely through political manipulations, Nadolny—who had already been approached and agreed "it would be best if I took over the ministry myself for then the fewest blunders would occur"—would have been appointed. But Schleicher, like Brüning before him, encountered Hindenburg's implacable insistence upon Neurath. On May 24, six days before Brüning's resignation, Neurath's name appeared on Schleicher's list, thus confirming the importance of presidential initiative in all these steps.[33]

On the afternoon of May 30, the Brüning cabinet resigned. Apparently Hindenburg had already accepted Franz von Papen as chancellor-designate, but no agreement had been reached as to the other ministers, except for the understanding that Schleicher would become minister of defense. On the same afternoon that he had curtly dismissed Brüning, Hindenburg sent for State Secretary von Bülow, the highest permanent official of the foreign office. From Köpke's letter of the same day, it is clear that Neurath was now the favorite: "I found that Bülow was by now completely in favor of Neurath's candidacy, surely influenced in part by the news which had reached him that Nadolny and Hassell had at least similar chances. He opposed these last two candidates as did I."[34]

After leaving the president, Bülow told Köpke that the meeting had proceeded perfectly. Hindenburg had been delighted at Bülow's mention of Neurath. Without waiting for the state secretary's complete presentation, the president proclaimed Neurath his choice, and instructed Bülow to wire him at once. On the morning of May 31, the future minister received the following telegram:

The president requests you, in view of your former promise, to assume the foreign ministry in the presidential cabinet now being formed, which will be made up of right-wing personalities free from political party allegiance and will be supported not so much by the Reichstag as by the authority of the president. The president addresses an urgent appeal to you not to refuse your services to the fatherland in this difficult hour. Should you not be able to give an affirmative answer immediately, I ask you to return [to Berlin] at once.[35]

Through his son who was coincidentally in Berlin, Neurath replied that he would await reports of the cabinet's composition, thus ascertaining its political goals before making a final decision. On the next day he left London to report to Hindenburg. As the ship crossed the channel, Neurath wrote a letter revealing the considerations uppermost in his mind:

> I answered [the president] that I must make my decision depend upon some previous insight into the contemporary relations in B[erlin], and upon the composition of the cabinet, but would come to B. at once. It seems to me no longer possible to escape. You know how difficult this decision is for me. The situation is as bungled and unclear as it could ever be, and only 13 days before the Lausanne [Reparations Conference].*

On May 31, Hindenburg gave Papen his charge, suggesting the name of Neurath (and perhaps some other names for various positions), which surprised Papen who apparently had expected to assume the foreign ministry himself. On the same evening, Papen instructed Bülow to offer Neurath the foreign ministry. Bülow replied that the president had already made the offer, thus distinguishing Neurath from the other cabinet members, and making him independent of Papen and Schleicher in the fate of the cabinet. While the other members were told that Hindenburg had selected them to be in a cabinet of "his friends," such a description fits accurately only Neurath's appointment.[36]

Arriving in Berlin in the early hours of June 2, Neurath learned from the papers that the cabinet was substantially complete. For the first time, he heard the identity of the new chancellor and the other cabinet nominees. Many of the men were known to him from their years of government service (for example, Magnus Freiherr von Braun and Lutz Graf Schwerin von Krosigk), but he was disturbed by newspaper reports that this "cabinet of authority" was designed to be only a caretaker until Hitler was given power, as well as by rumors that the rapidity with which the cabinet had been formed bespoke a careful plot headed by Schleicher and Junker elements. Neurath was reluctant to enter this potentially seething cauldron. Telegraphing his wife shortly before his meeting with the president, he expressed distaste for participation in such a government. His wife's written reply—which of course reached Neurath after the decision had been made—can suggest the troubled spirit with which Neurath approached his new duties:

> My thoughts are with you, and I would like to be by your side in the difficult hours which you are perhaps at this very moment enduring (it is 10:00 now), and which still stretch before you in the days ahead. I can however do nothing more than constantly send a burning request to Providence that He lead you on the right road, and make your decision and responsibility not too

---

*Neurath to Theda Freifrau von Ritter, June 1, 1932, Ritter Papers. Baroness von Neurath, in "*Lebenslauf,*" noted that the main reason for the journey was that Neurath did not know who was going to be chancellor, and he would not make his decision until after he had learned this fact. Rereading the letter in prison after the war, Neurath wrote: "I remember very well how I wrote it in my cabin on the ship and in what a mood I was in . . . and how unwilling I was to go to Berlin." Neurath to Baroness von Ritter, March 13, 1946, Ritter Papers.

difficult. I understand perfectly that this is not a question of what is more agreeable to us, but rather that you are the man who can help and must help, if your sacrifice is not already condemned to futility. Under the present constellations—which do not please me at all—I am, I confess, perplexed as to how that would be possible, and I shudder to think that your sacrifice might be in vain. But the older one grows, the more one realizes that one knows nothing, and perhaps even if we don't understand it, still everything works out for the best. I am convinced that after difficult conflict you will make the right choice.[37]

Although her letter also reported favorable reaction to the rumors that Neurath would become the new minister, her own hope was that he avoid the ordeal ahead: "I wish only that you do not undertake anything too arduous for your person. May God grant that you be spared that." Queen Mary, she added, shared her opinion and said "You must not leave here."

Even as his wife trembled before the prospects, Neurath's fate was being decided in a meeting with Hindenburg, in which Neurath "stated [his] own aims and ideas regarding foreign policy." Like all their talks, it was a rambling encounter in which the serious business of government policy and personnel was masked by frequent references to the clichéd vocabulary of duty, military camaraderie, and service to the fatherland. Neurath expressed his distaste for the position, and Hindenburg, measuring his arguments to the man, replied that he also disliked the many responsibilities of his office. He expected from Neurath a similarly selfless dedication. So great was Neurath's antipathy to the job that he made his acceptance depend upon two conditions. He demanded presidential support leaving him free to implement foreign policy without cabinet interference. Second, the cabinet must receive full presidential support in any struggle with the Reichstag, thus essentially ending parliamentary government. Hindenburg promised both. Neurath's fear of serving in a cabinet along with untried political figures like Papen, and loathsome (in his view) intriguers like Schleicher, was calmed when Hindenburg assured him that the government was not an expedient, but a genuine attempt to restore order by a cabinet of experts. The president said that Hitler himself had expressed pleasure at Neurath's appointment, wished him a long tenure at the foreign office, and promised a written guarantee not to oppose the new cabinet.[38]

Like the other new ministers, Neurath trusted Hindenburg to honor these promises and accepted the appointment. Hindenburg had assembled a cabinet of nonparty conservatives to provide a political program for his own "authority without a program." The attempt must be made, not because the omens for success were good, or because Neurath took any personal pleasure in the challenge. Rather his participation was a direct response to Hindenburg, a personal dedication to the worthy president, who symbolized both the honor and duty of the German nation.

As he left the president's office, Neurath met Schwerin von Krosigk who asked if he were to be congratulated. Neurath's reply indicates his own deepest feelings: "No," he said, "you are to extend your sympathies; I have been forced to accept the post."[39]

CHAPTER

5

THE PROFESSIONAL DIPLOMAT AS MINISTER

Neurath's First Six Months in Office

In German diplomatic circles, the appointment of Neurath was welcomed. They approved of him personally as a man who in years of diligent work had established cordial and cooperative relations with ministry officials and diplomats abroad, and it was assumed that under a professional the service would function more harmoniously than it had for years. After several politicians as minister, Neurath was expected to restore foreign office initiative, thus preventing precipitous action and advancing the programs the diplomats deemed necessary.[1]

But paradoxically, the appointment of a professional diplomat eventually weakened foreign office influence. In the republican system, the foreign minister's ability to defend his experts' program before the cabinet and Reichstag depended upon his party's strength in the coalition and how effectively he used "party tactics in order to implement his foreign policy aims."[2] No civil service minister, regardless of whatever virtues he possessed or the cooperation he received from subordinates, would have this kind of strength; nor would the policy he advocated necessarily influence the cabinet. Neurath was well aware of this weakness. "I will be the first minister to be fired," he told his son, "as soon as there is a return to a regular party cabinet. I have no party behind me."[3] His policies were only as strong as the help he could solicit from the president. As this assistance weakened (long before the death of Hindenburg in 1934), the influence of the foreign office program declined.

Next, the foreign minister needed the support of his fellow cabinet officials in order to implement his own policy. But Neurath was ineffective as a speaker, inarticulate in public discussions, and preferred to rely upon position papers previously prepared and distributed. He did not make friends or confidants easily, and never achieved a closeness with any of his cabinet colleagues. Many came to believe that no matter how strongly Neurath personally supported a program, he lacked the eloquence and friendships necessary to spur its implementation by the cabinet.[4]

Another element in the gradual deterioration of foreign office influence was Neurath's adherence to a civil service code that implied unquestioning submission to the authority of the state. Conscientious experts would hesitate to fight for a political program if their actions might in any way embarrass the government. As one member of the foreign office told Hermann Rauschning in the earlier 1930s:

> It is not our business to determine the course of policy. It is our duty to be loyal officials.... We are habituated to representing policies against our own better judgments. We are not even privileged to prevent a collision between our convictions and the policy we are to represent by voluntarily resigning. There are situations in which our resignation might inflict the most serious injury on the Reich. It is our duty to practice self-suppression to the very utmost.

Commendable as such sentiments might be in the civil service, a cabinet minister with a program to advance needed a more independent and political approach. Yet Neurath himself told Rauschning: "There are situations in which the patriot no longer has any right to insist on his own better knowledge and judgment." The civil service limitation has seldom been better expressed. "One must never allow personal feelings to intrude," he frequently told his daughter. "Duty comes first." In Neurath's subsequent career, these views became dominant. First displayed in the conflicts in the Papen and Schleicher cabinets, Neurath's tendency to view his role as one of self-sacrifice and obedience greatly contributed to his eventual tragedy under Hitler.[5]

Another danger to German foreign policy was inherent in Neurath's appointment: official policy became isolated from domestic developments. Deprived of the insights of politicians like Stresemann and Brüning, who for all their faults as foreign minister at least knew the domestic political situation, the foreign office increasingly pursued its policy as a self-contained entity, having no relationship to either domestic or broader developments. Neurath and his staff grew isolated, viewing German policy as a legal-juridical expression, acting, as one observer noted, as if abstractions (equality of status, sovereignty, international rights) were realities. In such issues as disarmament, reparations, and treaties, the Wilhelmstrasse seemed unaware that legal subtleties were only reflections of political conditions, useless when foreign governments saw conflicting evidence on the domestic German scene. Neurath's appointment intensified the one-sided outlook of the professional staff of the foreign office.[6]

Finally, since he was so well trained in the foreign office approach, Neurath was probably unqualified to conduct that thorough reevaluation of policy which Germany, after 1932, required. Writing after the war, he recalled his decision

> to continue Germany's foreign policy in the same direction followed by previous cabinets, that is, characterized by negotiations, especially with the victorious Versailles powers, in order to dismantle further the burdens of this treaty.... In this way, the poisonous international atmosphere created by the untenable demands of the treaty would be removed through a process of negotiations.[7]

As early as 1930, Neurath and most German diplomats considered Stresemann's policy of "finesse" to have failed, for Germany was still denied the basic rights of national security and sovereignty. It was expected that the new foreign minister would establish a harder line, to end a period of political inactivity and bring initiative at an opportune moment. Indeed, Neurath seemed willing to do just that, for he had long regarded "the egoism and pursuit of power of each individual Great State as the only true basis of policy," and one of his first acts upon entering office indicated his rejection of Stresemann's belief that full restoration of Germany's status would automatically follow from cooperation with other nations. Stresemann had framed and displayed in the foreign minister's office the telegram from Geneva confirming Germany's seat in the League of Nations. Neurath ordered the memento removed and the telegram restored to its proper entombment in the files. A picture of Bismarck was chosen to fill the empty spot.[8]

Neurath emphasized that while "politics of gradual and partial revision" remained the official program, an era of cooperation through a broad political-security system established to achieve good will as the prerequisite for treaty revision had come to an end. In its place, Germany seemed to embark upon a collision course with the rest of the world. Yet given his own personality and diplomatic background, Neurath was not likely to be innovative in guiding a new program. Determined to free Germany from the international system created at Versailles, Geneva, and Locarno, he was prepared to destroy that system while giving little thought to the more dangerous situation arising from a rearmed and restored Germany in the heart of a hostile Europe. Moreover, he seemed surprisingly incapable of adjusting his program to altered political situations. Thus, in the question of reparations and disarmament, he pursued Brüning's tactics, apparently unaware that the new government lacked the necessary foreign prestige. Oblivious to the suspicions aroused by Papen's cabinet, he failed to prevent his own government from committing a number of egregious errors. This weakness first became apparent in the delayed Lausanne Conference on reparations which opened in June 1932.[9]

Reparations

Official German policy on reparations had been established in December 1931 when Brüning announced that Germany could no longer fulfill its obligations and requested a meeting to revise the Young Plan, even as he sent a private communication that Germany did not expect outright cancellation but would settle for a moratorium or a final reparations payment. Convinced by Brüning's boast that Germany stood only a "hundred yards" from its goal, the new government looked to inherit his arrangements at the conference. Although Neurath insisted that Germany could pay nothing and needed a suspension period, he too thought privately that the best solution would be a final sum payment. He believed that things would work themselves out, and he promised British acquaintances that Berlin would be reasonable. State Secretary Bülow, however, knew that France would not allow Germany to secure a revision of reparations in an isolated settlement, but would demand political concessions. He proposed that Germany could "divert the French demands onto a less dangerous track" by suggesting a consultative pact among the major powers:

> It is quite likely that England in particular could be won over to such a pact. Without any extensive or specific stipulations, and without limiting in any undesirable way our freedom of action, the pact could be so worded that it would be regarded by the public as a document to ease tensions and restore mutual trust.

Neurath agreed with Bülow's plan, and had even proposed a similar idea to the British ambassador on his own.[10]

The foreign office, however, was not the sole determiner of German policy. Despite Neurath's statement to the British ambassador that he had received from Papen "full responsiblity in this department," the new chancellor immediately announced that he would personally lead the delegation to Lausanne. Long an advocate of French-German cooperation, Papen was convinced that before revision of the Versailles Treaty could succeed, France and Germany would have to settle their outstanding differences. He thought to make use of what seemed to him the perfunctory termination of reparations to achieve some great détente with France and raise the issues of equality, armaments, and economic recovery. He did not inform the foreign office of his plans, and he admitted in his memoirs that he had not bothered to study the documents which the diplomats had prepared for him. He and Schleicher needed a victory at Lausanne to ensure their domestic success, and they naively assumed they would win one.[11]

The Lausanne Conference opened inauspiciously. Neurath's suspicions proved well founded; the French were adamant. While Germany and Great Britain agreed on full cancellation, Minister-President Edouard Herriot demanded a final sum payment of seven billion gold Reichsmarks. The Germans flatly refused, relying upon the British to mediate. When the French replied with the notion of political concessions, the German delegation countered with Bülow's Four Power consultative pact, but Herriot then suggested an alternative guarantee of the domestic and foreign status quo, and Papen rejected this proposal out of hand. Neurath wired Berlin that the conference seemed about to collapse:

> On Monday we will again hold detailed discussions with the French, and express our rejection now and in the future of any further reparations payments. We will attempt, however, to prevent the occurrence of an absolute rupture, as well as the presentation of specific French demands. I hope we will succeed. When the German-French conversations end, I assume the English will come forward with a compromise solution. Whether or not this would be acceptable to us cannot be decided until the proposal is presented.[12]

But Papen was impatient. Without consulting the foreign minister, whom he suspected would have objections, he proposed to Herriot a French-German political, financial, and military alliance (aimed against Communism), as part of a more "meaningful" approach to diplomatic relations between the two countries. Neurath was subsequently so shocked by this irresponsible amateurism that his son spent most of the night searching for tranquilizers to prevent his father from having a heart attack.[13] Afterwards, Neurath did not hide his opposition. He did not return to Berlin with the chancellor to consult with the cabinet and even left Lausanne for a day in order to avoid the crucial meeting with the French and British in which Papen introduced the political issues of equality and disarmament into the reparations talks. "In spite of all official denials," one newspaper correspondent wrote, "Neurath could not have more clearly distanced himself from Papen's accomplishment." In fact, by failing to block the chancellor's moves, Neurath permitted Papen to stumble into an impossible position. The chancellor completely misunderstood the realities of the conference, acting as though all the world wanted the end of reparations, and Germany could expect to derive political advantages by agreeing to cancel its own obligations! The British and French predictably reacted sharply against what seemed a German trick; they agreed that only the payment of a final sum could end reparations. German hopes for cancellation were destroyed, along with its reputation for honesty in negotiations.[14]

Still unwilling to let the conference consider only the "minor" question of reparations, Papen plowed ahead. Without consulting Neurath and in flat contradiction to the cabinet's orders, Papen now told the British that Germany would consider a final sum payment, if Great Britain and France would repeal the war guilt clause and recognize German equality at the disarmament conference. British Prime Minister J. Ramsey MacDonald and Herriot were furious about the new demands. Dismayed over Papen's clumsy approach, Neurath hastily arranged a tactical meeting of the German delegation, which suggested a final sum payment, accompanied by a political memorandum to be issued after the meeting either by the major powers or by Germany alone. Ignoring telegraphed instructions from Berlin, Neurath proposed this solution to MacDonald, placating his wrath, and simultaneously persuading the cabinet to face realities and accept the final sum without a political declaration, leaving the negotiations up to the delegation in Lausanne. Reluctantly, the cabinet (and Papen) agreed. The policy which the foreign office had originally proposed had now, after the chancellor's dangerous improvisations, become official.[15]

Even after this decision, General Schleicher continued to complain of the violation of German honor inherent in the payment of a final reparations sum, but his protests had little effect. Neurath's negotiations concluded swiftly; he skillfully exchanged the meaningless and unattainable political statement on war guilt and equality for a final sum of three billion Reichsmarks. Here he clearly revealed his famous talent, handling both foreign statesmen and Papen with tactful determination, and salvaging the best settlement Germany could have obtained. With bad grace, Papen accepted Neurath's solution. Under protest, the cabinet approved, thus solving finally the perplexing problem of reparations.[16]

Unfortunately, Neurath could not offset all Papen's actions. Insulted by the chancellor's inept attempts to exert pressure and alarmed by Herriot's revelation of

Papen's desire for a military pact against the Soviet Union, the British were convinced of German treachery. They left Lausanne firmly committed to friendship with Paris. In his desire to achieve French-German cooperation (and a victory for the home front), Papen had recreated the Entente Cordiale, set back chances for an early agreement at the disarmament conference, and delayed the advancement of treaty revision.[17]

Subsequently, Neurath deliberately absented himself from the cabinet meeting in which Papen reported his "triumph" over reparations. In his opinion, the chancellor had raised awkward political questions, revealing an alarming propensity for "flamboyant gestures and unstudied reversals of position." Instead of solving the question of reparations in an atmosphere of trust, the conference operated amid tensions and adjourned in mutual suspicion. In settling reparations, the diplomats failed to facilitate the forthcoming disarmament talks. Papen was the chief cause of this failure, but Neurath could have taken charge earlier and perhaps prevented much of it. Although in a particularly strong position in the cabinet, he registered his disapproval of unwise policies by the relatively empty gestures of withdrawing from the conference city and refusing to attend cabinet meetings. Such protests needed the reinforcement of more dramatic confrontations or even threats of resignation, and in this first crisis of his ministerial career, Neurath showed clearly that the phlegmatic, easy-going nature which had been one of his assets as an ambassador might make him an ineffective minister. Under a strong and intelligent chancellor, conscientious obedience and loyalty might have been desirable in a foreign minister. But Neurath served under Papen, Schleicher, and Hitler, and as the Lausanne Conference revealed, he would have to exercise a less congenial, and more determined, aggressiveness, in order to prevail.[18]

Disarmament

Events surrounding the disarmament conference a few weeks later demonstrated a similar confrontation, this time with the strong-willed minister of defense, General Kurt von Schleicher. Although he eventually was able to reassert his authority, here too Neurath at first failed to prevent independent actions which jeopardized his policy and needlessly complicated the international situation. For years, in cooperation with the military, the foreign office had simultaneously pursued two broad approaches for restoring military power. The first called for general disarmament, in which all nations would disarm down to the level imposed on Germany by the postwar treaty. By 1927, however, most officials in Berlin concluded that the major powers would not cooperate, and recommended its termination, despite the strength of German arguments based on the disarmament portions of the Versailles Treaty, on the League of Nations Covenant, and on the obvious dangers of under-defended frontiers. At the same time, the Berlin diplomats were not prepared to adopt openly the second approach and admit the secret rearmament in which they had collaborated for years by approving violations of the treaty limitations as long as they were carried out cautiously and with foreign office knowledge. Aware of eventual discovery, the diplomats had believed foreign nations would tolerate these illegal measures, as long as Germany did nothing rashly overt.[19]

By 1930, these two approaches fused into a campaign for equality of status (*Gleichberechtigung*). Germany refused to sign the draft agreement for the forthcoming disarmament conference which left intact the military clauses of the Versailles Treaty, and informed the other powers that if armaments could not be leveled down, they would have to be leveled up, in order to guarantee equality. Although German diplomats continued to use the language of general disarmament, the policy was that only a reorganization increasing military strength (*Umrüstung*) could satisfy requirements for security. Thus, in his opening speech to the disarmament conference, Chancellor Brüning stressed Germany's "legal and moral right" to equal treatment and equal security, and State Secretary Bülow instructed the German delegation to leave no doubt that "equality of status should be the *prerequisite* for our participation in the conference." The Wilhelmstrasse was certain that once the principle of equality was recognized, the unilateral limitations of the Versailles Treaty must disappear and Germany could legally build the army it was already assembling illegally. Thus the fight for equality at the disarmament conference was not merely theoretical, but part of a determined drive to rebuild military strength.[20]

The foreign office had urged Brüning to ensure the principle of equality a prominent place on the agenda. In informal talks at Bessinge in April 1932, the chancellor had promised that Germany would not increase its armaments for five years or mass-produce the newly permitted weapons, but would undertake only certain specific reorganizational measures, if a general disarmament agreement applicable to all states would replace the Versailles clauses, and all states would have a right to the same kind of weapons. Although Germany promised to remain at its present military level, Bülow explained to Neurath on May 4, 1932, "we naturally do not mean literally the status quo, a fact which the chancellor explained very clearly and openly." Although the French were not present at Bessinge and further meetings were not held, the German foreign office believed that Great Britain, the United States, and Italy had unequivocally approved the Bessinge proposals. When Neurath became minister in June, he was told that German foreign policy rested explicitly on this "agreement." As Bülow informed him: "We must try to get the stalled disarmament conference going again. We must try to force even the French to recognize the German standpoint [on equality of status], now that the English, Americans, and Italians have, in private conversations with Chancellor Brüning, already expressed their approval."[21]

While Neurath and Bülow assured Europe that German policy would seek only an adjustment of military strength within a system of general disarmament, the picture had changed drastically: the Brüning cabinet which had won credence abroad had been replaced by one whose conservative and nationalist tone was alarming to many observers. Thus, even though the policy remained unaltered, the trust in German good faith which Brüning had worked so hard to create had evaporated. In addition, although Neurath had secured the chancellor's approval that "our old basic idea" would remain the same, Schleicher, the real power in the cabinet, found the inherited policy weak. He was ready to demand immediate military equality. Vigorously opposed, Neurath ordered officials not to deviate from his instructions. The issue abruptly became more tangible when the disarmament conference adjourned for the summer, after compiling a fall agenda with no mention of German demands for equality. Schleicher insisted that the government leave the conference, immediately renouncing the binding power of the Versailles military clauses.[22]

Believing such a policy dangerous and impossible of fulfillment, Neurath suggested instead rejection of the Geneva resolution, but limiting further reaction to an announcement that Germany would refrain from active participation until equality was placed on the agenda. Since Neurath knew that Germany was already proceeding to rearm on the assumption of equality, rejection of the resolution and a call for negotiations were tactical expedients to place the issue of equality on the top of the priority lists of European diplomatic problems.* Any public discussion of this issue would aid Germany; agreement on the principle would automatically increase its military strength, replace the Versailles Treaty, and prevent a return to unilateral disarmament. Even should France refuse to recognize any form of equality, world opinion would probably then support some degree of rearmament. Neurath envisioned his task as twofold: gaining recognition of increased military strength while securing an atmosphere favorable to the peaceful settlement of outstanding territorial and political issues. Far from being a break with peaceful negotiations, Neurath's proposal was a crucial stage in his campaign.[23]

Schleicher, after the disappointing election returns of July 31, strongly disagreed, complaining that the government needed some spectacular triumph abroad in order to consolidate at home. In a series of radio speeches, public appearances, and articles, he called for immediate restoration of military power. Neurath, who was not consulted, feared that foreign statesmen might conclude that a more aggressive policy was now in ascendancy. Schleicher sought to give such an impression, and on August 2, 1932, angrily demanded a thorough cabinet discussion of foreign policy. Neurath seemed too moderate, and Schleicher resented the minister's statement that "my announcements about Germany's future freedom of armaments are only for domestic consumption and not to be taken seriously abroad."[24]

Although Neurath believed he had prevented any change in the program, in the German note delivered to the French on August 29, 1932, the absence of familiar conciliatory phrasing allowed the French and British to conclude that Germany now demanded the right to rearm, threatening to "take the law into

---

*Even after the war, Neurath insisted this was a correct decision: "The strongest incentive to war is always a state without arms, therefore it seemed to me that the first and most accessible step on the way to the establishment of peace was equalization of armaments." "Notizen."

their own hands," should the conference not agree. In fact, the only threat contained in the note was more in the nature of a time bomb: after five years all discrimination against Germany must end either in general disarmament or German rearmament. Such had been Brüning's program which had been "approved" at Bessinge, yet now a British note rejected all German claims to equality which might in any way be construed as rearmament.[25]

The forward course of German policy seemed stalled. Oblivious to the changes in foreign relations attendant upon the formation of the new cabinet and Schleicher's aggressive speeches, Neurath continued to blame other states "who refuse to disarm and to undertake the same obligation which Germany now has." With apparent official approval, other officials were also saying that in the face of this refusal to disarm, open rearmament by Germany was necessary and justified. This schizophrenic approach produced confusion and hesitancy, sometimes masquerading as patience and tenacity. Neurath himself claimed to be hopeful: "We will clear this obstacle," he told the French ambassador. "I am not a nervous man; I am patient. We will arrive at [an agreement]." With studied nonchalance, he left Berlin to shoot game at his lodge. In truth, the situation threatened the future development of German policy.[26]

In this deadlock, the British government proposed a Big Five conference, and Neurath agreed. For the time being, Schleicher could not interfere since he was immersed in the campaign for Reichstag elections scheduled for early November. In preparing for the talks, Neurath's office returned to its original program: equality of status, with military reorganization symbolizing that equality. Neurath drew up eight propositions stressing that equality had to find some expression in Germany's altered military strength. The tone was strikingly conciliatory and, as one observer noted, did not exceed those demands "put forward by Dr. Brüning in April." But the message was clear. "Armaments permitted to one nation as defensive . . . must be permitted to all." Bülow added to the French ambassador, "One cannot treat us like savages, to whom one permits only bows and arrows." Foreign nations were informed that none of the plans then under consideration was satisfactory enough to persuade Germany to return to the conference. "They will try to offer us the principle of equality," Neurath had warned the office in Berlin, "but in practice they will wish to continue the existing obligations." He was determined to prevent declarations which might preclude future increases in arms and material. Although the Papen cabinet resigned prior to the opening of these talks, the President personally entrusted Neurath with full authority to negotiate Germany back into the Geneva conference.[27]

Neurath's subsequent success revealed the extent to which German policy might have worked had internal rivalries and unwarranted interference from other ministers not paralyzed the government. Meeting Sir John Simon, the British foreign secretary, at Geneva, Neurath easily produced an acceptable formula: a new disarmament agreement would replace all previous treaties, the duration of this new convention would apply to all nations, and equality in *kinds* of weapons would be recognized for all nations while practical applications of this principle would be negotiated. Optimistically, Neurath wired Berlin:

> I believe that we have now achieved what we intended, namely to erect a front of the three chief powers against France. However, we should not surrender ourselves to any illusions, since there are still a series of difficulties to be overcome in negotiations over the writing of a declaration allowing our return to the disarmament conference.[28]

Forced to interrupt these promising talks by a call from Berlin where the Papen cabinet was being replaced by Schleicher's, Neurath again secured Hindenburg's approval for his course of action.

Upon his return, he found little unity among the four powers, and when MacDonald began discussing a new United States plan calling for a 25 percent reduction of all weapons over a period of three years, Neurath felt strong enough to interrupt. He brought the conversation back to the original formula and submitted his own rough version of an agreement. The French replied with a brief two-sentence draft stating that equality of status would be *one* aim of the conference. Pleased, Neurath introduced two questions, making German acceptance of the French formula and return to the conference dependent upon assurances that equality would find "practical effect in every respect, and become the starting point, not the goal of the conference." As anticipated, the French rejected such a commitment, and the tables had been turned. Now it was France who seemed isolated and stubborn, bearing sole responsibility for future talks.[29]

French resistance had some basis in fact. German intentions were clearly set, as expressed in a letter from Bülow to the chancellor's office, December 10, 1932:

> For obvious reasons, it has not been possible to explain to the French that they would be no worse off by recognizing our demands (even in the distorted French version) than by rejecting them. For it was inexpedient for us to announce that, should the conference fail, we would in any case take the freedom which the formula of equality would give us.

In other words, Germany would proceed on the assumption of equality of rights, no matter what the conference decided. Neurath's job was to *prevent* declarations which might preclude German rearmament and to use a negotiated rearmament agreement as impetus to other issues. He half expected that the talks might end in a deadlock, but trusted the guilt would be "ascribed to France."[30]

In lengthy day and night negotiations on December 10, however, an agreement acceptable to everyone appeared. Despite last minute attempts by the British to include a section strongly condemning any increase in armaments, Neurath was able to maintain his position, and the final formula stipulated equality as the principle of the disarmament conference and of all subsequent agreements. "Now there is no reason for us to abstain further from the conference," Neurath wired Berlin, and the cabinet gave permission to sign the agreement.[31]

Thus, Neurath achieved a major victory. The recognition of the principle of equality meant the end of the unilateral Versailles obligations and gave Germany grounds for demanding legal rearmament, either in a disarmament treaty which would raise German military levels, or in default of such an agreement.* There was full justification for Schleicher's position when he told a group of army officers: "Now we have a completely free hand for anything which we wish to demand as equality of status. Our theoretical thesis, 'equal security for everyone' is now valid. The danger remains that this matter might be postponed or obstructed. This would force us to undertake the 'freedom to rearm.' "[32]

Another aspect of Neurath's December victory was that Germany had not given away anything. "We are in no way tied down or limited," Bülow told reporters. Neurath himself boasted of "completely excluding English stipulations that the implementation of the equality principle should in no case lead to a strengthening of our armaments." To the cabinet, he insisted that the military clauses of the Versailles Treaty were no longer in operation. By asserting his own leadership over foreign policy, the foreign minister reversed the dangerous drift toward unilateral abrogation, and preserved or restored the good relations with the other European nations, so necessary for handling future talks. This triumph rightfully belonged to Neurath, who had handled the lengthy sessions with skill and finesse. He excelled in this type of negotiations: quiet, behind closed doors, without parliaments or the press to disturb proceedings.[33]

Pleased with the results, he was not entirely optimistic. "The battle is not yet won," he told his delegation shortly after the talks ended. "There will be many difficulties to overcome." To Bülow he was more specific: "We should probably expect that in the future the French will raise difficulties about this declaration in the disarmament conference. If the other side then does not stand by its promises in regard to equality of status, we will be forced once more to leave the conference." Nevertheless, the agreement highlighted Neurath's hopes for the future: "Finally, the others see that we must be handled differently," he told his friends the Ritters. "For the first time I can see some light breaking through the clouds."[34]

In his cabinet report, Neurath suggested that should "the agreement over our basic equality of status not be adhered to," the government should leave the conference once again. Aware that Europe remained united on the question of German rearmament, however, he warned his colleagues that difficult negotiations were the only path and he opposed any attempts to force the pace except by careful discussions. There must not be, he warned, any flagrant violation of treaty obligations, a pointed reminder to those who might be tempted to use the new situation to increase unilateral rearmament at too rapid a pace. Aware that plans

---

*As early as June 18, 1932, the United States and British delegation to the conference had agreed that should no disarmament convention come into force, it would be impossible to force Germany to abide by the terms of the Versailles Treaty. Thus Bülow was justified in telling a press conference on December 12: "There can never be a return to the military clauses of the Versailles Treaty, for our equality of status has been explicitly and unconditionally recognized by the leading powers on last Sunday." See DBFP 2/III, 527, and AA, RM 18 1-adh, Bd. 3.

for the reorganization of the army had been moving forward, and that the acquisition of "samples" of the outlawed weapons had already begun, Neurath believed these measures did not exceed any standard which was likely to be adopted at the disarmament conference. He feared only the development of a more aggressive pattern; his warning to the cabinet was intended to avert such an eventuality.[35]

During the following weeks, Neurath anxiously insisted that the chancellor grant priority to the foreign office even in military aspects of foreign affairs. When General von Blomberg, the chief military member of the disarmament delegation, insisted that Germany reopen negotiations over the demilitarized Rhineland and submit to the conference specific demands for the reorganization of military strength, he justified his proposals by noting "that the realization of the crash program to guarantee Germany's security can only be achieved outside the restrictions of any agreement." Neurath flatly rejected this position, and on January 14, 1933, he informed Blomberg: "We should always maintain that the amount of military armaments required for our security would depend upon the successful disarmament on the part of the highly armed states." Utilizing reports that certain army officers objected to his policy regarding disarmament, Neurath demanded and received Schleicher's support. The revised instructions to the disarmament delegation accurately summarized Neurath's own program: "The delegates must focus their tactics on the goal of achieving a positive resolution of the conference, i.e., an agreement which would rest upon equality of status and which would offer a stipulated basis for considerable military reorganizational measures during its lifetime."[36]

Neurath was convinced that only within the relative security of negotiated agreements among all European powers could Germany safely restore its armed strength.* As desirous as Schleicher for this rearmament, Neurath feared a unilateral approach. Germany's territorial problems—the demilitarized Rhineland, the Saar, the Polish Corridor, and Austria—could only be solved by a degree of cooperation with foreign nations. Years of development were needed before Germany could even dream of imposing a solution by force; moreover the danger and insanity of a military move of this kind made Neurath categorically reject the use of force. Rearmament must proceed, but slowly, so as not to antagonize foreign neighbors and, even worse, international relations. The December agreement was for Neurath only a part, however integral, of his general campaign for treaty revision.[37]

Thus, within six months, Neurath had successfully tackled two of the most difficult issues in postwar German foreign policy: reparations and armaments. In both he had championed a moderate position, which eventually prevailed. Yet in the events surrounding these victories, a disturbing tendency was present. Skilled

---

*In his postwar "Notizen," Neurath repeated his conviction that "a weak Germany in the heart of Europe was always a danger to peace." His perception of the line of German policy since 1921 was its determination to "remove the discrimination of the postwar treaties, thereby restoring German equality with all other nations. . . . In this way, through negotiations, the poisoning of the international atmosphere created by infeasible treaties would be removed."

in negotiating intricate details, and keenly aware of the broader picture, Neurath lacked the tenacity to uphold his own opinions in disputes with fellow cabinet members and the army. His success occurred when he did not have to cope with a vigorous opposing policy. He had outlasted Papen and patiently outwaited Schleicher. Thus, despite Neurath's forceful warning to the cabinet, there was no guarantee that he himself could or would dissuade a German government from undertaking policies against a united Europe. Temperament, civil service training, and his own nationalistic conservative outlook could probably persuade him to accept even ill-timed programs of unilateral action, just as he had—from time to time in the summer of 1932—tolerated Papen's excursions and Schleicher's dangerous ideas. This unfortunate weakness did not augur well for a man who enjoyed the president's unlimited confidence and who, one month later, would accept the assignment of preventing unprofessional and intemperate foreign policy excesses in the Hitler cabinet.

CHAPTER

6

THE NONPOLITICAL MINISTER

In the Papen and Schleicher Cabinets

The Papen cabinet, personally selected by President von Hindenburg, seemed outwardly unified. Seven of the ten ministers were aristocrats, including one count and four barons. In family and education all the members were conservative, but not active in the DNVP or other rightist organizations. None had close party ties and for the first time in the Weimar Republic not one was a member of the Reichstag or of a previous cabinet.[1] The most important unifying factor in the new cabinet was the civil service background of the majority. Five members were experienced professionals from the federal administration, two had served under individual states, and one was an international railroad administrator. "We were all civil servants of the old school," one minister later wrote, "accustomed to thoroughness, caution, and openness with each other. This fact facilitated our teamwork." These men believed themselves experts, assembled under the president and commander-in-chief to master the political and economic chaos:

> Papen and all of us wanted to replace the parliamentary system, which had become completely unbearable, crushed by the economics of selfish interest and party fights, and thus condemned to sterility. We wanted to replace it by means of respectable work, order, and legality, such as we had known in earlier times. Papen really wanted a cabinet of gentlemen in the English sense. . . . [Men] who would take their responsibilities seriously and without fear.[2]

They felt superior to the republic's political organizations, able to provide the sense of direction and leadership necessary for German renewal.

But in reality, while sharing a vague conservative and authoritarian ideology, the Papen cabinet was deeply divided. Attempts to set goals and fashion programs were unsuccessful, for they lacked a realistic political philosophy. Instead of becoming an effective center of conservative forces, the cabinet remained only a collection of conservatives lacking structural solidarity. From the beginning, conflict, both personal and ideological, plagued the government. Because he had been instrumental in its formation, General Kurt von Schleicher expected to control the new cabinet, but his domineering manner was disruptive. His meddling and sarcastic witticisms alienated professional administrators, who rejected his claims to superior knowledge in their fields. Similarly, Papen did not win the support of his own ministers, who grew suspicious of his leadership ability. "Papen has a certain charm," Frau von Neurath reportedly remarked, "but nobody takes him seriously." Shortly after the cabinet's formation, a foreign office employee congratulated the new chancellor on his appointment. Aglow with success, Papen concluded the brief conversation with a remark, the careless dash of which expressed his approach to the arduous tasks which lay ahead: "Let's go a'ruling!" His tastes were not for the solid, mundane duties of government, and from the start Neurath believed he would eventually have to be replaced.[3]

More important than clashes of personality, however, was the tripartite split over the correct approach to Germany's political problems. Schleicher planned for a rightist coalition to rearm Germany and restore its international position. He wanted to utilize the army's latent political power to form a cohesive political block absorbing even radical Nazi elements. Papen, on the other hand, wanted to initiate constitutional reforms (creation of an upper house, increased cabinet and presidential powers, revision of Reichstag prerogatives, even monarchical restoration) as a prelude to restoring a prewar system under an all-powerful presidential cabinet. The eight civil service ministers believed that the purpose of the experimental presidential cabinet was to allow professional administrators the chance to correct the chaos of depression Germany. Officials like Neurath believed the present cabinet was an excellent form to provide authoritarian centralism, military recovery, and administrative reform and saw no reason for either Schleicher's political maneuvers or Papen's constitutional amendments.[4]

The civil service ministers, a cabinet majority, set the tone. They discouraged interference within their own areas of competence, and abstained from discussions outside their particular specializations. Consequently, it was impossible to conduct meaningful discussions of the domestic political situation. Neurath, for example, flatly refused to discuss domestic issues, telling friends that he served as foreign minister, not minister of the interior. This self-defeating attitude prevented the Papen government from even defining its own purpose, and hampered its effectiveness as an administrative and legislative body. Faced with Papen's dilettantism, the machinations of Schleicher, and the absence of any political program, Neurath and the other ministers were undecided and hesitant, thus materially contributing to the crisis which eventually ended the republic. In the long run, with the appointment of Hitler, these "neutral" and "disinterested" ministers helped create the tragic dictatorship which destroyed them all.[5]

In the cabinet's first major political actions (lifting the ban on the *Sturmabteilung*, or SA, and the Lausanne Conference program), the Schleicher-Papen influence dominated, supported by the hesitant civil service ministers. But in the decision to have the federal government assume control of the State of Prussia, the attitude of these ministers was decisive. Perceiving advantages for his rightist coalition, Schleicher had hoped the move would appease the Nazis and the DNVP who had long clamored for the removal of the Socialist-Center coalition which governed Prussia. Papen had hoped that a domestic triumph might rally support for the constitutional changes he contemplated. The civil service ministers, however, actively pushed through the takeover because they saw in it a removal of the administrative dualism which had hitherto prevented full implementation of financial, economic, and commercial stability.[6]

After the July election (in which the Nazis doubled their mandates while the DNVP—the cabinet's only official support—lost seats and the middle-class parties disintegrated), internal differences became marked. Schleicher feared that the rise of National Socialism would inundate the rightist movements, and he now advocated Nazi participation in the government, even suggesting Hitler as chancellor. Papen agreed that the Hitler movement "must be brought into responsible leadership in the state," but his principal objective was to prevent a Nazi-Center majority coalition which might replace him. For the political security of the cabinet, he told the ministers: "... the Führer must be tied down; the [Nazi] movement cannot be left in our rear. Otherwise it will be a permanent impediment to the Reich government." After the war Papen maintained that "I and the entire cabinet considered the participation of the NSDAP in my government as imperative and desirable." Documents do not support this conclusion; the civil service ministers, a numerical majority, did not agree.[7]

To the minister of the interior, Wilhelm Freiherr von Gayl, taking in even a few Nazis would be dangerous, since they sought full power and would not permit the cabinet or the army to remain neutral. He urged that the cabinet issue strong measures to master the economic and political situation, suspend the Reichstag, and demand additional powers from the president, beyond those granted by the constitution. The other civil service ministers agreed. Neurath argued that Nazi membership in the government would ruin Germany's credit and foreign policy. Others suggested that the return to law, order, and economic development would be disastrously impeded by Nazi participation. Only Lutz Graf Schwerin von Krosigk, the minister of finance, broke the ranks to suggest that civil war might be avoided "by making the poacher the game warden." In the end, although Schleicher and Papen were permitted to continue their negotiations, the ministers believed Hindenburg's presidential cabinet would continue unchanged in power.[8]

In a special meeting with Hindenburg at Neudeck on August 29, 1932, Papen, Schleicher, and Gayl requested powers to dissolve the new Reichstag which had not yet met, and received permission to delay elections beyond the constitutional limit. Papen claimed that the cabinet would utilize the interim period for "constitutional and administrative reforms." Surprised by a vote of no-confidence during the Reichstag plenary meeting of September 12, Papen used the dissolution order, forcing the cabinet to decide whether or not to use the other presidential decrees as well. This crisis again revealed the tripartite division. Papen wanted to use the president's power to dissolve the Reichstag, refuse new elections and proclaim emergency constitutional amendments. Schleicher lamely suggested new elections to discredit the party system.[9]

The civil service ministers were genuinely concerned about constitutional violation and abuse of presidential powers for the purpose of amending the constitution. They now supported Schleicher, who cleverly exploited their faith by arguing that the purpose of elections was to establish the validity of the present cabinet. With ill-concealed regret, Papen agreed. Actually, the cabinet had reached an impasse. They could not benefit from new elections without some party, but no cabinet minister ever tried to form one. Obviously Papen and Schleicher had not scheduled new elections to produce political support. Rather, since the majority of the cabinet was not yet ready to approve flagrant violations of the constitution, the elections were a useless last resort. Gayl argued in vain that the president, if faced with a cabinet ultimatum, would abandon his insistence upon constitutional methods. The crucial opposition of the civil service ministers to such a course of action, however, always prevented Papen or Schleicher from taking such an ultimatum to Hindenburg.[10]

In the two months preceding the November elections, the cabinet was very busy with financial and economic subjects, but no preparations were made for the impending elections. Only once, during the transportation strike, when Nazis and Communists appeared to cooperate against the government, did the cabinet show any concern about politics. Then General von Bredow, speaking for the defense ministry, assured the ministers that the army was prepared for all emergencies. From the point of view of those who believed in the existing presidential cabinet, the elections of November 6 were a victory. The Nazis lost two million votes and thirty-four seats; Schleicher's and Papen's plans for a wide rightist coalition did not materialize. No basic alteration in Germany's political alignments had taken place, even as the civil service ministers had predicted. Yet in the ensuing discussion, their front in the cabinet now crumbled, as four ministers conceded that only Nazi participation could consolidate the strength of the presidential cabinet. Faced with Papen's old solutions, Schleicher exploited the civil service dilemma to urge negotiations with the parties. After these failed, the cabinet could approach the president, informing him that the Reichstag should be indefinitely suspended, and the government run directly under the president. To Papen's dismay, Schleicher persuaded the ministers to accept this devious plan.[11]

Important in this new turn of affairs was the ministers' dissatisfaction with Papen's leadership. But Papen retained the president's trust, and he planned to drop obstructionists like Neurath who had failed to support his constitutional reforms. When it seemed that Papen would actually survive, the civil service ministers rebelled. In the November 25 cabinet meeting, some ministers inquired whether the army could contain the increasing civil disturbances. While Schleicher assured them the army was ready, many ministers, including Neurath, seemed disturbed by the prospect of Papen's reappointment. Nevertheless, on the next day, Hindenburg officially empowered Papen to form a new government, promising full presidential backing.[12]

Before accepting the president's commission, Papen consulted with those cabinet ministers he wanted to retain, and learned of opposition within the civil service bloc. In a meeting the next morning, Papen saw the extent of his isolation. Beginning with Neurath, who spoke of domestic and foreign dangers, the ministers refused to participate in any new Papen cabinet. Only after these opinions had been presented did Lieutenant Colonel Ott offer his hastily assembled report (based upon recently concluded war games), claiming that the army was unable to guarantee law and order should the unrest continue. Although Ott's presentation flatly contradicted both Schleicher's solemn assurances and the opinion of most high army officers, its conclusions were accepted. Even in the absence of supporting evidence, the cabinet would have abandoned Papen.[13]

The explanation for this turn of events is not Schleicher's plots, as many have insisted, but the altered attitude of the civil service ministers. They had never seriously considered Papen's program of constitutional reform; now that he had received presidential backing, his plans could no longer be ignored. Schleicher had little to do with the timing or scope of the cabinet's actions; later he truthfully told army officials: "... the cabinet itself had requested Papen not to assume the position again. Some did not want to share this ride with him." Without the ministers, Schleicher could not have brought down Papen. Only the advice of these trusted confidants persuaded Hindenburg to part from the man he had grown to trust.[14]

However dissatisfied Neurath might have been with Papen's inept management, he did not want to replace him with the domineering Schleicher. Concerned about foreign policy, he warned Hindenburg that should he appoint the general, "we'll have the whole world against us." Neurath believed a Schleicher cabinet should be a last desperate measure. "Politics and generals who dabble in politics," he was fond of saying, "are a dangerous mix." As the crisis continued, some cabinet members suggested that Neurath or Franz Gürtner, the minister of justice, should temporarily assume the chancellorship, but Neurath absolutely rejected these ideas.[15]

By December 1, it appeared that Papen would again be confirmed in office. Schwerin von Krosigk asked Neurath to see Hindenburg to prevent the appointment. Neurath, who had already spoken with the president, now saw Schleicher as the only alternative. Reluctantly, the president and his most trusted minister accepted Schleicher hoping that he might stabilize domestic politics. The new cabinet (announced on December 6) possessed little unity. From the first day, Schleicher faced presidential distrust. Cabinet meetings were seldom harmonious. Schleicher's insolence and inappropriately jesting manner impeded serious discussion. Moreover, the new chancellor's low opinion of most of his colleagues (including Neurath, whom he "frequently described to others as a totally incompetent diplomat") was well known. Most observers did not expect the cabinet to last thirty days. Yet in the first month, while political tensions remained high, most Germans seemed willing to give Schleicher a chance. Neurath received full authorization to continue his moderate policy at the disarmament conference, and indeed Schleicher followed Neurath's draft on every point in delineating the government's program in his maiden speech. As chancellor, he seemed more tractable than he had as the power behind the throne.[16]

Since his foreign policy required domestic tranquility, Neurath could support Schleicher as long as he provided stability at home. Still, he never overcame a natural dislike of the general and grew increasingly critical as Schleicher embarked upon a program designed to win broad rightist representation, from the Nazis to the Center Party. Neurath failed to see how the cabinet would be strengthened by such moves. To include prominent politicians would alter the whole concept of a presidential cabinet. Although the chancellor claimed that Hindenburg knew and approved of his plan, the cabinet rejected it out of hand.[17]

Schleicher's weakness now stood as clearly revealed as had Papen's two months before. He too had failed to achieve the political stability which would facilitate a government-led recovery. Neurath's uneasiness grew when the general suggested adopting military measures to impose order upon the country. Neurath wanted domestic calm, not incipient civil war. Although the chancellor spoke bravely of the reserves he could muster, and indicated that Hindenburg was anxious to dissolve the Reichstag for another test of strength at the polls, Neurath and his fellow ministers were beginning to suspect that the general's feet were made of clay. But Neurath was even more dismayed to learn that Papen and members of the president's camarilla were pushing Hindenburg toward a restored presidential cabinet under the former chancellor. The latter had already sounded out some ministers about serving in a cabinet enlarged to include representatives from Alfred Hugenberg's conservative party, the DNVP. Because everyone knew Hindenburg's unalterable opposition, no one suspected that Papen might also include some Nazi participation. The only alternative seemed to be a new Papen government, but Neurath and many believed that such an appointment would precipitate civil war. A new crisis seemed imminent.[18]

The Appointment of Hitler

In the late evening of January 27, rumors spread that Hindenburg had rejected an offer to dissolve the Reichstag. Neurath expressed a willingness to speak with the president in order to block Papen's appointment. In the cabinet meeting the next day, after Schleicher officially confirmed Hindenburg's intention to reappoint Papen, Neurath, as closest to the president, was asked to explain to him the grave domestic, economic, and foreign dangers involved. But Schleicher, returning from an interview with the president, reported Hindenburg's intransigence. Indeed, the president seemed to be "moving through the motions of an accustomed waltz." Without elaborating on the membership of the new cabinet, Hindenburg had characterized his decision as unalterable; further discussions would make his already burdensome task more difficult. He awaited the present cabinet's immediate resignation.[19]

Shortly thereafter, when Papen outlined the idea of Nazi participation to Krosigk, the latter was pleased and thought that Neurath and Gürtner, at the very least, would participate in such an enlarged cabinet. Later that evening, however, Neurath made it clear that he was unwilling to talk with Papen about cooperating in any government under his leadership. Opposition to Papen and disenchantment with Schleicher now convinced Neurath (and other ministers) that only a government with mass support (such as Hitler could provide) would improve the domestic situation. Neurath knew of no discussions of such a possible cabinet, but independent of their outcome, he had already altered his previously expressed fears of a cabinet with Hitler, and now welcomed the formation of a rightist coalition which would include the Nazis.[20]

As early as 1930, Neurath had regarded Hitler's rise to power as inevitable, in the light of intolerable domestic conditions. The force of such events, he said, was stronger than individuals; sooner or later Hitler would have his day. In January 1932, private conversations with Hitler had dispelled some of his doubts about the man's capabilities, but then during his six months as foreign minister, Neurath was unimpressed by Hitler's truthfulness or reliability. In a lengthy discussion with Hindenburg during this week in January 1933, Neurath mentioned his mixed feelings about possible Nazi participation, particularly as it might arouse foreign hostility, thus damaging the new impetus of his foreign policy. On the other hand, while Hitler was still occupied with those internal party problems necessarily following the successful "revolution," the dynamic appeal of National Socialism might be harnessed to advance foreign goals. "In the view of Neurath and his friends," Hermann Rauschning was later to write, "the revolutionary élan of the Nazis must be made use of in foreign policy as long as it continued undiminished, that is to say, until it had been worn down by the natural obstacles it faced."[21]

Neurath viewed National Socialism in the light of the lessons he had learned in Italy. No more positive about it than he had been about fascism, he believed that the movement could be used to gain certain advantages. In time, its radical wing and divisions would be reduced in importance, as the idea of the state became dominant among the party leadership. The critical period for Germany would be, as in Italy, the years immediately following the seizure of power, when radical forces possessed the maximum power and the "idea of the state" was weakest. If, however, members of the civil and military establishments stayed at their posts and worked with the newer men, the transition could be accomplished with a minimum of damage. Thus, in the face of personal antipathy for Hitler and the principles of party rule, Neurath answered the president's request and agreed to remain in office to guide foreign affairs.[22]

Neurath also believed that a Hitler-conservative coalition could overcome the parliamentary obstacles, political divisions, and lack of popular support which had plagued the former presidential cabinets, thus allowing the nation to unite behind a dynamic foreign policy. While responsible elements were in control, Hitler's discipline would be a healthy antidote to the prevailing democratic confusion. "Successful foreign policy," Neurath once wrote, "is not possible if there is no correctly led and determined will of the people behind it. Foreign policy and internal disunity are irreconcilable opposites." A new government, while providing internal unity, might even educate the Nazis. Perceptively, Rauschning noted this motivation:

> I am perfectly sure that [Neurath] acted from the highest of motives: he was trying to train the Nazis and turn them into really serviceable partners in a moderate nationalist regime. . . . He felt that it was his duty to make the best of the Nazis, and this could not mean getting rid of them as quickly as possible.
> He regarded himself as the protector of a young and undisciplined element out of which he flattered himself that he could form a politically serviceable one.[23]

Neurath's naive optimism about handling Hitler reflected a general lack of political realism among German conservatives. Bülow, one of the best-informed men in the government, assured friends that the presidential form of the cabinet was absolutely secure; the Nazis would never win an absolute victory at the polls, and therefore the presence of men like Neurath would guarantee a balance of power within the cabinet. Later Neurath explained that once Hindenburg's dream of a cabinet of experts was destroyed, a combination of politicians and "experts to temper the revolutionary party" became the only logical expedient. "Hindenburg obligated us to hold on as long as possible." Recalling his experiences in Italy, he predicted that for the Nazis too, "much water will have to be added to their wine after their acceptance of the responsibilities of government." Neurath never wavered from this conviction; even after the war, he claimed never to have seen "a party or a party leader, who has not essentially altered that program which he proclaimed during the campaign for power in the state."[24] In 1933, Neurath saw no reason why Hitler would prove an exception to this rule.

But as late as January 29, Papen was still enlisting cabinet members for a "fighting cabinet" of Papen and Hugenberg. Such a possibility seemed to Neurath the real threat; rumors abounded that Hitler's inclusion in the government (the "great solution") had been dropped. Neurath learned that Hindenburg expected him to remain, no matter what the nature of the cabinet's composition. He agreed with Krosigk, however, that should the "small Papen" solution prevail, neither of them would accept a post in the cabinet.[25]

Circumstances in Berlin remained confused; Neurath remained a passive observer. Only when the ministers arrived at the president's palace at 9:00 on the morning of January 30, in response to a hurried call, did they learn that a Hitler-Papen-Hugenberg cabinet had been formed, and that the swearing-in ceremony would take place within two hours. Neurath was dumbfounded; up to that moment, as Krosigk noted in his diary, both he and Neurath believed that Hindenburg would never appoint Hitler.[26] After receiving the news, however, Neurath made no objection, feeling bound by his promise to remain in office.

Confident that with the president's support, he could continue to control foreign policy, Neurath had agreed to make himself available. His administrative approach to politics, his semi-feudal conception of duty to Hindenburg, and his belief in the necessity for domestic order, encouraged him to enter his third cabinet within seven months. Papen and Schleicher had failed to provide internal stability, and Neurath did not lament their fall. Determined as always to view things optimistically, he remarked to the British ambassador "that the Hitler experiment had to be tried some time or other."[27] The present seemed as good a time as any.

CHAPTER

7

NEURATH AND DOMESTIC ISSUES IN THE HITLER CABINET

The Conservative Coalition

As Neurath entered the Hitler cabinet, the essential power structure appeared unchanged; the presidential appointees, all of them nonparty experts, retained key positions, in charge of foreign policy, the army, justice, and finance. With the support of the president, they would surely make both Nazis and German Nationals conform to earlier policies.[1] Few observers noted the fundamental conflict between nonparty authoritarianism and single-party dictatorship. Neurath and the other presidential appointees believed themselves responsible only to Hindenburg, welcoming Reichstag support but rejecting parliamentary domination. As leader of the largest party, however, Hitler aimed to create a National Socialist majority in the country and in the Reichstag. Because the advocates of the nonparty presidential system held a substantial cabinet majority, Hitler was cautious in approaching the political power of the state. Yet in eighteen months he transformed Germany into a Nazi dictatorship, aided as much by the political attitudes of his cabinet colleagues and their lack of unity as by the more well-known aggressiveness of the Nazi party.[2]

Even under Papen, the ministers had functioned primarily as individual experts. Under Hitler this tendency intensified. Ignoring constitutional provisions which made the chancellor only *primus inter pares,* the civil service ministers accepted Hitler's position that the cabinet merely advised the chancellor, who alone made government decisions.* On this point, Neurath's approach was more compatible with a dictatorship than a republic; he distrusted an all-powerful

---

*"Hitler took the position," Neurath wrote in "Notizen," "that individual ministers needed to know about general policy and his plans and intentions only as much as was necessary to carry out the business of the individual ministries." Schwerin von Krosigk reached a similar conclusion (*Es geschah,* 202): "The cabinet was forbidden to observe a divergence of opinion. Lammers conveyed the desire of Hitler that the ministers were to bring matters to the cabinet only after all points of conflict had been removed. If this was not possible, a conference of the involved ministers would be called with Lammers as chairman, and in extreme cases under Hitler. Hitler reserved the right to

cabinet in which majority rules would bind every minister, just as he disliked the majority rules of a parliament. He preferred a system in which the cabinet existed in order to ratify decisions already made by the responsible ministry. Thus he did not object to the idea that only he and the chancellor should conduct foreign affairs. After all, the new chancellor was unfamiliar with foreign nations and unskilled in diplomatic practices; he would necessarily rely upon his foreign minister who enjoyed the president's full support. The danger lay with interventions from other members of the cabinet. Thus, Neurath refused to utilize his own position to discuss domestic financial, economic, or political developments. This compartmentalized attitude was unwise, but with an untried chancellor and a divided cabinet, it was understandable for Neurath to attempt to preserve the unity of foreign policy by removing it from the domain of the cabinet. Such procedures, however, eliminated any possibility for the cabinet to contain Hitler's domestic rule, and Neurath was apparently willing to pay this price. In this gap, Hitler erected his personal dictatorship.

In tacit approval, Neurath watched Hitler evade cabinet discussions by ordering proposals back to special committees, stressing the responsibility of ministers to resolve differences of opinion in advance. When Hitler told the ministers that the cabinet should avoid all controversies, Neurath accepted this new arrangement with only a minor protest. The turning point was the Enabling Law of March 24, 1933. Neurath and his colleagues accepted the draft, believing it would greatly simplify the administration of government and facilitate the legislation necessary for Germany's economic and financial recovery without consulting a divided and deadlocked Reichstag. Although Hitler promised to make only occasional use of the bill's powers, in 1933 alone the government promulgated more than 210 decrees and more than 550 before 1936.[3]

This flurry of legislative activity obscured the undermining of the cabinet's power as a political institution. The increasing number of proposals on the agenda and participating members—including now many subordinate experts—swelled cabinet meetings to unmanageable proportions. Thus, the presentation and debate of an agenda of thirty-five items by forty men would have been impossible, even had Hitler encouraged free discussion. This multiplication of detail—an inevitable result of the enlarged powers now vested in the cabinet—made the form of a general meeting impractical. Hence, Neurath and others welcomed Hitler's inclination to make the important decisions in smaller groups outside these meetings. Thus the cabinet itself was bypassed: had a measure already won the approval of the responsible ministers, Hitler dismissed cabinet discussion as superfluous. Increasingly, he requested cabinet approval for vague and unformulated ideas, such as the necessity for reform of labor organizations; specific measures were then drawn up and proclaimed as cabinet-approved bills. As a result, cabinet

---

decide when a difference of opinion could be mentioned in the cabinet. . . . Each minister presented his draft, on which everyone had already agreed, and Lammers recorded that all were agreed. From time to time, Hitler delivered a monologue on some question which interested him at the moment."

meetings became conferences during which measures were accepted largely without debate. "In the cabinet, the Führer's authority carries all before it," Goebbels exulted in his diary. "There is no more voting. The Führer decides. Everything moves much faster than we hoped."[4]

With regularity, Hitler transferred decision making to interdepartmental conferences, and large cabinet sessions became less frequent. During the first 18 months of Hitler's chancellorship, the cabinet met 74 times. Thereafter, in the next 54 months, only 27 meetings were called, and the cabinet was totally eliminated in 1938. Invariably these meetings contained only superficial discussion of the proposed laws; most bills were recorded with the laconic remark, "the cabinet has taken notice." By January 1937, Hitler alone was responsible for passing laws, and was merely advised beforehand by the involved government bureaus.[5]

Divisions among the non-Nazi members also solidified Hitler's arbitrary power. As the center of the moderate conservatives in the cabinet, Neurath saw no reason to seek support from the three rightist politicians (Papen, Seldte, and Hugenberg) or even to form a bloc with the other civil service holdovers from the Papen cabinet. The government's strength, he believed, was not conservative unity, but individual reliance upon the president.[6]

Personal animosities also prevented the establishment of a workable majority in the cabinet. Neurath regarded Papen as a liability; their mutual antipathy was intensified by frequent rumors that Papen would shortly replace Neurath as foreign minister, and by Papen's excursions into the field of foreign policy. In meetings, they seldom agreed or cooperated on anything. Neurath's relations with the other non-Nazi members were similarly unsatisfactory. He and General von Blomberg disagreed over an armaments policy and the role of the army minister in foreign affairs. Toward Franz Seldte and Alfred Hugenberg (the Stahlhelm and DNVP leaders), Neurath was aloof and shared the president's active dislike of Hugenberg. Underlying these personal antagonisms was the old civil service distrust of politicians. From the start of this coalition government, Neurath and the other civil service ministers distanced themselves from the rightist politicians.[7]

It was thus misleading in January 1933 to emphasize, as did many contemporaries, conservative control of the power centers of the nation. Conservatives had not the ability, the program, or the will to unite, and the new cabinet of "National Concentration" contained a triple division. On one side stood the Nazi members, opposing them were the nationalist politicians, and in between (and often in opposition to both) were the presidential appointees, the conservative civil servants. When Neurath referred to himself as a dam to hold back the Nazi stream, he described his unique position as presidential confidant, and not his membership in any conservative coalition in the cabinet; no such unit existed.[8]

In the summer of 1933, the conservative civil service ministers, led by Neurath, actually helped destroy the last chances for conservative unity by forcing the resignation of Alfred Hugenberg, chairman of the DNVP and holder of four important government posts: two ministerships each in the Reich and Prussian cabinets. Never sympathetic either toward Hugenberg's economic theories for

German autarky or his brand of radical conservatism, the civil service ministers clashed with him from the first. At the London Economic Conference in June, with his economic program repudiated by his own colleagues, a disgruntled Hugenberg decided, over the objections of other delegation members, to publicize his views on national economy, German colonies, and the necessity for living space in the East. Neurath disavowed the Hugenberg memorandum, and Hitler approved the foreign minister's prompt action. Subsequently, Hugenberg sought a cabinet reversal of Neurath's arbitrary decision to exclude him from participation in future delegations. Failing to win cabinet support, he resigned.[9]

These events laid bare the strained relationship among the non-Nazi members of the cabinet. Unaware that only organized cabinet opposition with popular backing might contain Hitler, Neurath and the other civil service ministers edged out the only non-Nazi member with a political organization at his disposal. The unfortunate coincidence of Hugenberg's absurd indiscretion in London and the political naivete of the ministers guaranteed the capitulation of the cabinet before the militant Nazi minority. Subsequently, two new Nazi ministers replaced Hugenberg, and since Joseph Goebbels and Rudolf Hess had also received cabinet rank, Nazi membership swelled to seven. When Franz Seldte joined the Nazi party, Hitler possessed an absolute majority in the cabinet.[10]

The non-Nazi ministers sank into hopeless isolation. Blomberg, entirely dependent upon his pro-Nazi advisor, General Walter von Reichenau, seemed more concerned with preserving army leadership than with questioning the direction of domestic politics. Papen, thwarted in his ambitious dream of a conservative union, became a political Catholic, fighting for the Church, the Concordat, and cooperation of the Nazis in an anti-Bolshevik crusade; he too lost interest in safeguarding domestic liberties.[11] Not surprisingly, the four civil service ministers—Neurath, Schwerin von Krosigk, Gürtner, and Eltz-Rübenach—retired to the relative security of their own departments; by spring 1934, the base for any organized opposition had collapsed. In failing health and isolated at Neudeck, President von Hindenburg was ineffective. Neither cooperation among the cabinet ministers nor presidential powers had proven strong enough to curb the Nazi dictatorship.

As the institutional checks to Hitler's power were weakened, whatever chance remained for influencing events rested with individual ministers. Neurath held a uniquely strong position as President von Hindenburg's favorite and the senior cabinet minister. Had he openly opposed domestic changes, Hitler would certainly have been forced to slacken his drive toward absolute power, for he knew that his fate rested upon those ministers who had the ear of the president. It was frequently rumored that Hindenberg would resign should Neurath be forced out of the government. Certainly during the first eighteen months, Neurath's resignation would have triggered a presidential crisis which Hitler might not have survived. Even after the president's death, Neurath's public resignation would have seriously damaged the government both at home and abroad. "A change in the foreign office," one Nazi official wrote in May 1933, "would only disturb our political relations, and considering the tense situation is not desirable."[12]

Neurath and the Chancellor

Aware of his potential power, Neurath told friends on more than one occasion that he considered himself a rock in the middle of a brook, slowing down the course of the water. His failure to take advantage of this personal influence is typical of his personality. Thousands of other Germans during these months were motivated by attitudes similar to those prompting Neurath to support the Nazi cabinet. First, he believed that the Hitler coalition represented a "national resurrection," a return to decency and normalcy after the aberrations of Weimar. As early as 1925, Neurath had written that the "great majority of the German people were tired of socialism, democracy, profiteering, and humiliation."[13] Suspicious of democratic institutions, inspired primarily by a civil service dream of order, Neurath and his colleagues believed the time had come for regeneration, the reintroduction of discipline, and the repression of that licentiousness and debauchery which they instinctively associated with the republic*. Thus, as Hitler gradually dismantled the Weimar constitution, replaced the parties and parliaments, and ignored guarantees of civil rights, Neurath was not unduly alarmed. He welcomed the repressive legislation against Communists and disruptive elements and accepted the destruction of local administrative autonomy, of which as a Swabian he had been proud. "It was nothing more than the logical continuation of the century old search for German unity," he later wrote—an inevitable historical development, not a Nazi innovation.[14]

Second, Neurath was fascinated by authority. The role of the civil servant, and the professional diplomat, was to administer and guide, not master. Customarily gentle, he treated Hitler with the elaborate courtesy extended to foreign rulers and representatives; in the presence of the emotional chancellor, he never lost his calm dignity. Yet as Hitler and his closest advisors settled into power, Neurath showed no eagerness to become involved with them, or to share in this power. Later he would complain that Hitler had been a difficult man to locate, seldom in Berlin, traveling around the countryside or spending long weekends at Berchtesgaden. Moreover, Hitler's antipathy to written communications paralyzed the lifeline between the chancellor and the foreign minister. While all this is certainly true, Neurath accepted the new situation with somewhat passive resignation. Influenced by years of ambassadorial training, he resolved not to bother Hitler except in grave matters. "I follow the old maxim: don't go to your prince unless you are summoned," he told his friends the Ritters.[15]

Although present during most important meetings concerning domestic developments, Neurath was generally silent. Easily embarrassed by rude manners, he hated scenes and was unable to summon up the kind of response necessary to impress Hitler. It is impossible to imagine Neurath raising his voice, pounding on the table, or demanding even for a moment the immediate and absolute attention

---

*Thus Neurath's cabled assurances to foreign observers: "Recent national revolution in Germany, which aims at stamping out Communist danger and cleaning public life from Marxist elements, proceeded with exemplary order; cases of disorderly conduct being remarkably few and trifling." Neurath to Cardinal O'Connell, March 25, 1933, Archives of the Archdiocese of Boston.

of his superior. Neurath was clearly at a loss in verbal confrontations. Foreign office wags wondered whether the slow-speaking minister ever managed a single reply during conversations with Hitler. Ignoring formal reports and refusing to employ written communications, the chancellor used meetings to formulate his own thoughts, not to discuss the suggestions of his advisors. In such situations, he solicited emotional responses. Neurath found this behavior unsettling, and the lengthy monologues frankly boring. Irritated by Hitler's failure to listen, he often complained: "I am called upon to give advice, and then not given a chance to say a word!" Gradually, Neurath learned to tolerate the required conferences impassively, seldom venturing an opinion. When he suspected in advance that Hitler planned one of his extensive talks, Neurath tried to absent himself.[16]

Neurath never sought to build a more personal relationship with his chancellor. The polished diplomat was not at ease with the Austrian fanatic, and made no secret of his feelings. Several times officials suggested that in the interest of getting closer to Hitler, the minister ought to have the chancellor down to his estate for a visit. Invariably, Neurath declined: "Whatever would we be able to say to each other?" he indignantly asked his daughter. Throughout his ministry, Neurath seldom met Hitler except at official functions. An independent spirit, he was scornful of the Byzantine adulation demanded by Hitler and scoffed at the growing legions of the chancellor's "myrmidons." Neurath was never invited to Hitler's intimate sessions, often held late at night and composed of party leaders and unofficial advisors. Despising the whole atmosphere, Neurath underestimated the importance of these meetings and Hitler's fantasizing monologues. Hitler, in turn, came to view Neurath as a useful foreign minister, who was, however, politically unimaginative. As both the cabinet and the president progressively lost the ability to influence Hitler, Neurath failed to assert himself with the Führer.[17]

Neurath was similarly uncomfortable with other members of the Nazi hierarchy. He regarded Goebbels' private and political morals as despicable, and forbade his daughter to attend parties sponsored by Frau Goebbels. Not even for Göring's assistance, the value of which Neurath appreciated, was the foreign minister willing to disturb his regularized life. Rising early to walk in the Tiergarten before work, Neurath retired punctually at ten every evening. He did not entertain in a fashion to impress the new men of power. An incident early in 1933 is representative. Neurath arranged a dinner party at which Göring was guest of honor. Invited for seven, Göring did not appear until nine. Dinner was served immediately, and arising from the table an hour later, Neurath nodded to his guest and said a polite but firm good night, clear signal that the party was over.[18]

Increasingly, Hitler relied upon old cronies for advice. Considering the civil service a "refuge of mediocre talents," he bypassed the formal apparatus of government without producing a replacement organization. Instead the Führerstate became "a confusion of privileges and political contacts, competences and plenipotentiaries which became finally a fight of everyone against everyone."[19] Neurath remained aloof, and his power base suffered.

A third reason prompted Neurath's acquiescence. Aware that he was "much distrusted" within the Nazi party and perhaps destined to be replaced soon, Neurath felt obligated by the president's command to guide German foreign policy. Therefore, he centered his relations with the Nazi rulers on his primary function: foreign affairs. Despite the serious undermining of the cabinet as an institutional check, Neurath believed that individual ministers would ultimately prevail. Frequently questioned by friends as to why he remained in office, Neurath inevitably had recourse to military metaphors: "I cannot simply run away from my flag," he told the Ritters, "leaving my post unguarded, just because I am not particularly pleased with the general course of the battle." By staying, he could still have influence, as long as he limited his activities to foreign policy matters. After the war, he readily admitted that "domestic developments concerned me only insofar as they might influence foreign policy."[20]

A fourth reason for Neurath's support of the government was his conviction that the chancellor, despite an emotional approach to political matters, would in important decisions follow the dispassionate advice of his ministers. The trained civil service must be silent and survive, in order to channel revolutionary zeal into more legal operations. If events transpired as they had in Italy, Neurath believed responsible government would triumph. He suppressed a personal antipathy toward many domestic developments, even reconciling himself to a dictatorship, on the assumption that the advice of men like himself would ultimately prevail. Neurath never entirely rid himself of this delusion.[21]

A fifth and final factor must be mentioned. Neither ambitious nor power hungry, desirous of no personal gain, and motivated by an overwhelming love of his country, Neurath took no public stand on ethical or moral issues. Writing home in the summer of 1933, the French ambassador concluded that Hitler's triumph had resulted in large measure from the absence of strong and courageous personalities who could oppose the new trends. Neurath certainly must stand in this indictment. Like the protagonist in Bertold Brecht's parable "Measure against Violence," Neurath had no desire to make a show of backbone and invite disaster. No physical coward, he expected to outlive the current violence. Germany, he believed, was in the hands of an agent of authority who had asked: "Will you serve me?" Neurath, like Brecht's hero, chose to serve the agent of violence until the intruder grew fat and died. After the funeral, he hoped to clean house, breathe a sigh of relief, and answer "No." To remain in office and outlast the disturbances would be better than glorious and useless defeat.[22] Such reasoning, crucial for the obedient civil servant, reveals a flawed personality, unable to cope with the pressures of opposing a fanatical and unreasonable, but nevertheless legal, authority.*
The domestic crises set off by Hitler's reign proved overwhelming for the loyal Neurath, who lacked the internal weapons, and the professional training, to oppose with greater vigor the actions of the authority he served.

---

*On July 25, 1943, when he was clearly aware that the war was lost, Neurath expressed similar opinions to Köpke: "How are we to emerge from this war with even a modicum of decency? I have no idea at all. All I do know is that in the end, the old, decent men will have to occupy and pick up the pieces of political and military positions in order to save whatever can be saved." Köpke Nachlass.

In the early years of the Nazi government, at least three important domestic developments, blending foreign policy implications and personal involvement, should have moved Neurath to action. These were the party's rowdy behavior toward its opponents (including Christian and conservative elements), the massacre of June 30, 1934 (the so-called Röhm purge), and the growth of anti-Semitism as official government policy. Neurath's ineffectiveness within the cabinet and his attitude toward the National Socialist state can be measured only after a closer look at his reactions to these events.

Neurath and the Nazi Revolution

By the end of 1933, many conservatives were becoming alienated from the Hitler regime, especially as a result of SA actions, which culminated in a vulgar disruption of the aristocrats' ball in honor of the Kaiser's birthday on January 27, 1934. Field Marshal von Mackensen, related to Neurath by the marriage of his son to the minister's only daughter, wrote to President von Hindenburg, seeking an end to the Nazi harassment, but Neurath remained strangely silent. Conservative organizations were either "coordinated" under the Nazi party, or as in the case of some monarchical groups, simply outlawed. When friends with close connections to the former royal families queried Neurath on his inaction, he responded characteristically that he was the foreign minister, not the minister of the interior.[23]

Simultaneously, a small but militant group of "German Christians," encouraged by the appointment of a Nazi, Ludwig Müller, as Hitler's plenipotentiary to form a united German Evangelical Church, gained the official support of the party. By the end of 1933, Müller had secured the external unification of the various Länder churches and the formal proclamation of the Aryan paragraphs within the church's new constitution. But the scandalous means by which the union had been created and the force exerted to bring about compliance with the new regulations evoked widespread opposition. The open rebellion by thousands of pastors in the early months of 1934 persisted despite strong countermeasures.[24]

Amid this unrest, Neurath received dozens of appeals from churchmen and prominent lay leaders protesting the arrest of pastors and the general intimidations. Especially frequent were petitions from his friend Bishop Theophil Wurm of Stuttgart, who was convinced that Hitler's real intention was the eventual eradication of Christianity in Germany. Neurath arranged talks between the Lutheran bishops and Hitler, but he undertook no personal intervention, even refusing to support Mackensen's attempt to have Hindenburg issue some public statement. Sidestepping Wurm's appeal with the laconic remark "I will not meddle in this affair," he limited his action to forwarding all letters to the minister of the interior (Dr. Frick, one of the three original Nazi cabinet members) with the request for "friendly consideration." Eventually, he also sent a memorandum to Hitler mentioning possible damage to foreign policy resulting from the church conflict.[25]

Soon the situation worsened. In August 1934 Bishop Müller announced a united Protestant German church: "Anyone who cannot join in with us," he declared, "should keep quiet or stand aside. If he does not, I will force him to do so." In a carefully controlled national synod, Müller won approval for his plans, and a bizarre ceremony, featuring an SS guard of honor, formally installed Müller as Reichs Bishop. Dissenting church leaders, including Bishop Wurm, denied the competence of the synod, but were placed under house arrest. The hasty assembling of regional synods to confirm the new constitution sparked widespread protests which received much foreign publicity. Only then did Neurath bestir himself to convince Hitler how seriously this dispute damaged German prestige. Hitler agreed to Neurath's demand that Müller cease his bombastic campaign of church unification.[26]

The peaceful atmosphere was short-lived. On October 6, Bishop Wurm was again arrested; on October 10, a new Württemberg synod called for his immediate replacement, and the next day Gestapo officials proceeded against the Bishop of the Bavarian Evangelical church. Appalled, Neurath flew to Berlin for closed meetings with Hitler and Frick. During lengthy sessions, Neurath repeatedly referred to adverse foreign reaction, "particularly in the circles which hitherto have not been hostile to developments in Germany," and "argued for hours with Hitler about this conflict." On October 16, Neurath handed Hitler a strong memorandum contending that world opinion saw the German state as instigator of this persecution of the church, and that the resulting criticism was "a further complication in our foreign political situation and a threat to the execution of our rearmament policy."[27]

Largely because of Neurath's intervention, the two bishops were released, and Müller's chief lieutenant was forced to resign. To seal the peace, Neurath arranged a private interview between Hitler and the two bishops, but did not support their plea that Reichs Bishop Müller be removed. Eventually, Hitler refused to dismiss Müller, and the Evangelical church remained in turmoil. In these events Neurath's actions fall into an easily perceived pattern. First, he avoided open disputes, except in matters directly concerned with foreign affairs. Even then, he would wait until damage was imminent; then he preferred to employ personal talks with Hitler, rather than a cabinet discussion.* His intervention in the church conflict was successful, he believed, because he had not raised moral questions, but had demonstrated that Müller's actions were disruptive in foreign affairs. Neurath was authorized to inform Müller that it was intolerable "that measures taken by any kind of Church institution should jeopardize the whole of Reich policy and upset the work of reconstruction."[28] But once the dangers to foreign policy disappeared, Neurath ceased to press for a just and equitable solution of this domestic issue.

These examples of Neurath's inaction might have plausible excuses. Neurath had never been an active monarchist, never participated in political organizations which advocated a restoration. Similarly, although he professed his Christian faith, Neurath had never been particularly active in the Evangelical Church. His decision to remain silent in the face of threats might have reflected a personal

---

*When the prosecutor in the postwar trial pressed Neurath as to why he had not brought these matters before the cabinet, Neurath replied: "For the simple reason that it seemed to be more effective to tell Hitler directly." IMT, XVII, 23.

noninvolvement with these institutions. Such reasoning, however, cannot apply to another event which occurred simultaneously, namely, the suppression of the university student corps. All agree that the Corps Suevia of the University of Tübingen was very close to Neurath's heart. Yet when that group was threatened by the Nazis, Neurath maintained his characteristically detached stance.

Shortly after Hitler's appointment as chancellor, several Nazi organizations began to harass the student corps, which they claimed were led by "liberals and Freemasons." In the ensuing uproar, Rudolf Hess appointed a special commission charged with coordinating the student organizations. On May 20, 1933, at a convention in Goslar, the *Allgemeine Deutschen Waffenring* (ADW), the central organization of 20 corporation-unions and more than 860 corps, under pressure from the Hess commission, introduced a series of decrees implementing the Führer principle and the exclusion of all non-Aryans. At its annual meeting a month later, the Koesener-SC, the association of 124 corps to which Neurath's fraternity belonged, disagreed with the ADW rulings, and adjourned without implementing the new decrees. Although most associations soon complied, the Corps Suevia at Tübingen remained aloof.[29]

In the spring of 1934, the ADW reminded its member corps that non-Aryans must be expelled: refusal to comply with this instruction would bring expulsion from the national organization and even liquidation. Neurath's own corps could no longer procrastinate. The Corps Suevia had two Jewish members, and numerous friends wrote Neurath for advice. On April 12, Neurath replied to one:

I have recently been thoroughly briefed by [Hans] Lammers [state secretary in the chancellor's office], over the evolution of this directive and have established that it already represents a compromise, and that at present there is no longer a possibility of changing anything in it. There is no need to mention that the situation created by this directive is singularly regrettable. The only question is whether or not we are justified, for the well-being of the corps, in requesting this sacrifice from two corps brothers, in order to save the existence of the corps which is in any case severely threatened. In carrying out the recent law concerning civil servants, I must daily face decisions which pose frightful hardships upon the officials involved. But as things stand, in most cases nothing can be done. I am therefore of the opinion that also in the case of our two corps brothers, we must ask them to make the sacrifice and return the corps insignia. It goes without saying that nothing will change in our personal relations with them.[30]

But the officers of the corps refused to accept the resignations of the two Jewish members. As a result, on May 16, 1934, Neurath felt compelled to write directly to the officers in Tübingen, repeating once more his conviction that while a formal expulsion of the two men would truthfully "contradict the feelings of loyalty which all of us have sworn to our corps brothers," the real question was whether or not the "continuation of the corps could be justifiably jeopardized because of two of its members." In his own mind, there was no doubt at all about the hierarchy of values involved:

Should I be confronted with the decision whether or not the interest of the whole corps is more important than the interest of individual members of the corps, I would, without any hesitation, have to decide for the first. Membership in a corps grants not only rights, but also demands, to a higher degree, certain obligations toward the entire corps.[31]

The Union of Old Tübingen Schwaben, the governing body of the Corps Suevia, ignored the advice of its distinguished colleague, and suspended itself at once. The gesture was in vain, however, for in late May, along with four other corps, it was expelled from the Koesener-SC union, because of its refusal to break a fraternal oath with Jewish brothers.

Shortly thereafter, some corps members tried to solicit Neurath's support for a move to oust those leaders who had failed to cooperate. Neurath refused, claiming it would damage the reputation of the corps to reverse itself now, or to repudiate its leaders at this critical stage.[32] Subsequently, Neurath remained loyal, undertaking discussions with prominent leaders in the government throughout 1934 in a vain attempt to work out some possible solution permitting the continuation of the corps. As in the case of the churches and the conservative organizations, Neurath believed it was imperative for these institutions to work within the new system, for only thus could they preserve some degree of effectiveness. He was disappointed that all of his efforts failed. In 1942, when his corps faced confiscation of its property and holdings, Neurath, his son, and three others assumed responsibility as trustees, and sold the property, holding the money until such time as the corps might be reconstituted.[33]

Thus, even in areas impinging upon personal feelings and foreign policy, Neurath carefully avoided moral stands, but advocated moderation. He tried to do his best with words of encouragement, acts of personal loyalty, and even some initiative with leading government members. He had lived through the destruction of the monarchy and its way of life; he assumed that he and Germany would also be able to survive the destruction of the republic and the rest of the institutions which even the revolution of 1918–19 had left intact.

The foreign minister did not regard the various domestic developments too tragically, believing that natural factors would eventually topple Hitler's government. In the turbulent spring of 1934, he surprised many with his optimism. "Let it run its course," he remarked about the Nazi party. "In five years, no one will remember it." Concerning the restless SA, "those brown characters" as he called them, Neurath believed Hitler faced serious "growing pains."* Conservative faith in the powers of the president, in the unity of the cabinet, and in the ability of the moderate ministers, was now reduced to the pious hope that the Nazi party would eventually disintegrate from within, possibly as early as the summer of 1934. A

---

*Quoted in Rauschning, *Voice,* 150. General Kurt Freiherr von Hammerstein-Equord, the former commander-in-chief of the army, expressed similar views to Rauschning (*Men,* 9–10): "Don't interfere. Let it run its course! Any sort of interference is only one more short-circuiting. This sort of thing must be left to run itself out.... Cures cannot be forced. I regard all this as a fever which must run its course."

social reporter for a Berlin newspaper referred to the prevalent attitude in the foreign office: "Bredow told me today that at the Wilhelmstrasse they are hopeful for the speedy finish of the National Socialist government. The bosses of the party are continually knifing each other. When that has gone far enough, they think, the whole structure will topple. Even . . . Bülow is optimistic."[34]

Neurath believed that rifts within the party would eventually eliminate Hitler's dictatorial rule. As early as 1933, he told the French ambassador: "I saw the same conflict develop in Italy, and for some time I have predicted it here to Field Marshal von Hindenburg." In the tense summer of 1934, Berlin seethed with rumors of interparty difficulties. Military leaders put their troops on alert, and Neurath heard rumors of threatened demonstrations by the SA-Röhm wing of the party. Although present historical opinion doubts that either Röhm or the SA planned a putsch in June 1934, Neurath and many of his contemporaries had quite another impression. Circumstances and a bizarre set of events involving his son combined to convince him that Hitler had indeed suppressed a dangerous SA insurrection and was justified in the executions of Röhm and the principal conspirators.[35]

Neurath and the Rule of Law

In 1934, Ernst Röhm, with some of his closest friends, spent Easter vacation on a short, unofficial visit to Yugoslavia and Italy. Constantin von Neurath, son of the foreign minister, then attached to the Rome embassy, served for a few days as guide and protocol leader for the visiting delegation. Neurath's son inadvertently overheard a frank and lengthy discussion between Röhm and his friends concerning future SA "demonstrations" in Berlin. Although not certain of all the details, Neurath was sufficiently alarmed to report the conversation and its contents to his superior, Ambassador Ulrich von Hassell, who suggested that he file a report.[36]

On July 14, two weeks after Röhm's murder, the younger Neurath was summoned to Berlin where he was arrested at the airport. For three days in prison, no one told him what charges had been filed against him nor, even more surprising, did anyone inform the minister that his son was in custody. Hassell's July 18 telephone call asking when Neurath would return gave the office its first inkling of the situation. Notifying officials that something seemed amiss, the foreign minister informed Hitler's office. Late that same afternoon, young Neurath was brought before the chancellor who was nervously pacing up and down with the report in hand. Abusing the young diplomat, Hitler accused him of not directly forwarding his knowledge about a planned putsch. Neurath replied that it was inappropriate for a minor official to send a personal report to the head of state. He had followed correct procedures and his actions were beyond reproach. Accepting this explanation, Hitler embarked upon a lengthy monologue, citing the threatening situation, reading from a source he identified as "Schleicher's Diary," and elaborating on the theme of betrayal. As abruptly as he had begun, Hitler told Neurath he was free to return to his post, and left the room.[37]

The significance of this incident lies in its impact upon the elder Neurath. Informed on the evening of June 30 that "apparently there was a rising of the SA," Neurath was not surprised by the party's rapid mobilization, but he was shocked by the brutal murders. He could make no logical pattern of a conspiracy which would include such diverse figures as Ernst Röhm, General Schleicher, Erich Klausner, General Bredow, French ambassador François-Poncet, and his own protocol chief, Vico von Bülow-Schwante. Doubtful about the putsch, Neurath decided to submit his resignation to President von Hindenburg. He arranged an interview, but before it occurred, the arrest of his son and the reports of Röhm's conversations in Italy, convinced him that Hitler had prevented a large SA uprising at the last moment. Given this new information, Neurath abruptly changed his mind. Subsequently, he dismissed the violence as "growing pains" and shared the relief of many that the radical wing of the party had been eliminated. Although he was now prepared to stay in office, he decided, nevertheless, to see the president.[38]

In Neudeck on July 19, 1934, Neurath made what was to be his final report to the president; Hindenburg was so ill he could no longer follow the presentation. He seemed obsessed with the future of Germany, repeatedly requesting that Neurath stay on to guide foreign policy. Once again Neurath gave his promise, convinced when he left Neudeck that the president was near death. This meeting was influential in resolving whatever hesitation Neurath might still have had about remaining in office. "If all the good men desert the flag now," he told his friends, "what will be the result? Sheer chaos." After the war, Neurath admitted having many times clasped hands with brutal and murderous revolutionaries in the course of his long diplomatic career. In 1934, believing it necessary for his country's sake, he was ready to do so again: "Not vanity, nor hunger for power moved me to stay at my post, but simply and solely the hope that I might be able in this position to contribute to the well-being of my Fatherland and the general public."[39]

Although historians have correctly seen the massacre of June 30 as the final consolidation of Hitler's dictatorial power, Neurath was unaware of such significance. He certainly did not perceive that the Rechtsstaat had fallen before the whims of men without respect for old laws or desire to create new ones. Instead, Neurath conceded that the time had come to embody the altered political realities in new laws, which could be impartially administered. Hence, he did not oppose Hitler's unconstitutional move to unite the offices of president and chancellor immediately prior to Hindenburg's death in August 1934, nor the requirement that each cabinet minister take a personal oath of allegiance to Hitler. The subtle process of rationalization had already begun: with a censored press, the absence of public discussion or political forums, one's only chance to influence affairs was to cling to established positions.[40] To maintain a modicum of influence remained his goal, even when Hitler embarked on a course of anti-Semitic legislation, which should have prompted the foreign minister to question his continued presence in the government.

Since anti-Semitism was an integral philosophical part of the Nazi program, it is not surprising that Neurath faced its practical manifestations shortly after

Hitler was installed in office. In late March 1933, Hitler notified the cabinet of a party decision to boycott all Jewish stores and products. Neurath later told the British ambassador that "he himself had been taken by surprise and . . . deplored the [Nazi] action." Hitler, however, interpreted the stunned surprise of the non-Nazi ministers as tacit consent. After the cabinet meeting, when the civil service ministers, led by Neurath, tried to block the boycott by appealing directly to Hindenburg, Neurath pleaded with "the greatest insistence" that the president stop Hitler's plans.[41]

The president promptly summoned Hitler and spent an hour trying to persuade him to cancel the boycott. The interview "developed into a serious struggle, amounting almost to a presidential crisis." Despite Hindenburg's plea, and Neurath's threat to resign should such boycotts become official government policy, Hitler did not disavow his party's plans, but offered to limit the boycott to one day. Unhappy with this token compromise, Neurath continued to press. On March 31, he brought the issue before the cabinet, with disappointing results. Despite protests from Krosigk and Paul von Eltz-Rübenach (minister of transportation), and a face-saving plan proposed by Neurath and supported by Schacht, the chancellor would postpone the boycott only if the foreign minister could produce declarations from Great Britain, France, and the United States denying intentions on their part to boycott German goods. Neurath was given less than twelve hours to produce the statements, an impossible task which he tried desperately to perform. His eventual failure deeply disturbed him. The French ambassador found him "preoccupied and discouraged" and undeceived about the disastrous effect of the boycott on German prestige abroad. "Until midnight last Friday [March 31]," he told François-Poncet, "I believed that I had prevailed and that the boycott would not take place." The minister achieved for his efforts only the "suspicion and hostility" of the party, and one diplomat noted that his position within the cabinet became "more difficult every day." For Neurath it was a major reversal showing the ineffectiveness of Hindenburg, the presidential appointees, and even the cabinet in restraining Hitler. It was the last time Neurath attempted to mobilize a cabinet majority to block a move by the chancellor.[42]

On April 5, Neurath entertained Hitler at the first dinner party given by the foreign minister for the new chancellor. Although Baroness von Neurath recalled the evening as "stimulating," Neurath himself must have felt uneasy about the man who was now in power. For the first time, he was overwhelmed by an awareness that he had failed to prevent his own government from embarking upon a disastrous program. To this man of realistic views, an official policy of anti-Semitism was simply irresponsible. Unmoved by ideological considerations, he was baffled by Hitler's recalcitrance on this ill-advised policy. In a number of private conversations he attempted to illustrate the potential dangers, but he found Hitler "intransigent." To friends he sadly reported that "it was useless to talk [about the Jewish question] for Hitler has a passion here upon which no reason will prevail."[43]

Neurath's approach to this problem was complicated by his own divided mind on the issue of anti-Semitism. Like most Germans, he shrank from the violence with which the Nazis mishandled individual Jews, but he also shared with many in the middle and upper classes the idea that in recent years Jewish intellectuals and publicists had gained a disproportionately great control over public affairs in Germany. Thus, while he deplored the effects of repressive measures on foreign policy, he welcomed regulations to "clean up" German public morals. As he claimed in a September speech, the anti-Semitic decrees were an "absolutely necessary cleansing of our public life."[44]

In this dilemma, Neurath evolved a second approach to Germany's domestic problems. While continuing his earlier stance of noninvolvement, except in individual instances, he concluded that in view of the Nazis' arbitrary harassment of Jews, there must be some "regulation by statute" of the legal condition of Jews in Germany. Unable to dissuade Hitler on the issue of anti-Semitism, Neurath hoped that at least public outrages could be avoided through legal procedures which would peacefully and legally exclude Jews from some of the professions. Thus in April 1933, even as he appealed to Hindenburg to help restrain party excesses against individual Jews, he and his colleagues sponsored a series of decrees limiting the number of Jews in the universities and various professions, especially those concerned with medicine, communication, and the civil service. The ministers hoped that these laws would stop the "radical agitation" of the Nazis and facilitate a return to the rule of law.[45]

In approaching the flagrantly illegal actions of the Nazis, and especially the SA, Neurath was always handicapped by his belief that normalcy lay just around the corner. This attitude was described by one of his aides:

> Neurath never really understood what was happening domestically in Germany. He always believed that if he would only stay in office, do his duty, and preserve foreign contacts, one fine day he would wake up and find the Nazis gone. That was about as close as he ever got to a formal program. Hold on to your post; the Nazis, just a temporary appearance, would soon disappear.[46]

Thereafter, although Neurath tried his best to ameliorate the condition of individuals, he—and most German conservatives—must be indicted for their apparent disregard for that principle of equal human and civil rights, the violation of which lies at the heart of these discriminatory decrees. Closing his eyes, Neurath rationalized that in time, given proper administration, brutal treatment of Jewish people and property by irregular Nazi units would end, and even second-class citizens (such as the Jews had now become) would find protection. The rule of law, rather than of justice, became his model. This conviction was shared by many officials, especially in the ministry of the interior, who were working on methods to define the existing legal condition of Jews. In the late summer of 1935, Hitler convened the Reichstag for the annual party rally. At the last minute he decided that the proposed law to make the party banner the national flag was not sufficiently important and requested decrees defining Reich citizenship and the legal position of Jews. The cabinet was not consulted about these decrees—the infamous Nuremberg Laws of 1935—but at the last moment, Neurath became involved. Because of the hasty drafting, the experts asked that the proposed draft be postponed or altered. Justice Minister Gürtner agreed and asked Neurath to "hinder this nonsense with citation of possible foreign reactions"; Neurath agreed to see Hitler. But the chancellor dismissed all his arguments rather sharply: "Foreign reactions—of which he was by no means certain—were of no importance to him at all."[47]

This incident shows both the narrowing limits of Neurath's power and his characteristic reaction. He made no protest over the innocent victims who would now suffer, despite the fact that they included some of his closest advisors and friends. He indicated little concern over the implications of these laws, considering them merely a clearer definition of the existing legal situation, not initial steps in a more deadly kind of persecution. Although he realized that he could not protect the Jewish officials of his office, he did not attempt to resist, retaining until the end a conviction that Hitler's anti-Semitism was a fact of life to which German foreign policy makers would have to adjust.[48]

The Case of Eltz-Rübenach

Neurath's record in domestic policy making within the cabinet is lamentable. That of the other ministers, even of those directly concerned with internal matters, is little better. Only a single, isolated example exists of determined opposition to a government-sponsored decree after 1934; it also shows how far ministers were prepared to go in meeting Hitler's ideas and how reluctant they were to make an issue of opposition. In November 1936, as part of fourteen laws proposed for enactment, the cabinet received an advance copy of a decree concerning the Hitler Youth. It required for the first time the formal enrollment of all boys in this Nazi organization, one function of which was "to train the entire German youth physically, spiritually and morally in the spirit of National Socialism in order to serve the *Volk* and the national community." Despite a clause mentioning the role of the parental house and the school, the dominant influence was clearly to be the Hitler Youth organization. Paul Freiherr von und zu Eltz-Rübenach, minister of transportation and a devout Catholic, strongly objected. In a private conversation with Hitler he criticized the Hitler Youth's open warfare against Christianity. In a two-hour monologue, Hitler replied that he did not intend to destroy the churches. The decree was presented unaltered at the December 1, 1936 cabinet meeting, and Hitler delivered a three-and-a-half-hour oration, ending with the introduction of the bill. In the subsequent silence, only Eltz-Rübenach spoke out, criticizing the Hitler Youth's campaign against religion. "Nothing can end well," he insisted, "if the youth are taught to despise that which the parents revere." He would agree to the law only if Hitler promised to suppress these tendencies. In his own memorandum, Eltz-Rübenach recorded that "thereupon, the Führer nodded his head to me and said 'yes.'" The cabinet minutes only make mention of Eltz-Rübenach's agreement with the reservation that "nothing should be done to destroy the religious values which the parental home has planted in the hearts of the young."[49]

No other cabinet minister supported Eltz-Rübenach. Yet only a few months earlier, Neurath had departed from his usual silence to oppose implementation of National Socialism in the schools at the expense of the classical educational system. At a public gathering for the centennial of his Stuttgart Gymnasium, after a number of speakers called for a change in the "outdated and irrelevant" system, Neurath had startled the audience by rising to his feet and announcing with uncharacteristic emotion: "All that I am I owe to this Gymnasium system, and it is precisely more of this system that we need today."[50] But in the cabinet he avoided such provocative statements, and unlike Eltz-Rübenach never reached that point at which the government's domestic program so contradicted his personal standards that resignation was required.

Had he harbored such thoughts, the moment came a few months later in January 1937. On the occasion of the fourth anniversary of the cabinet, Hitler announced his decision to enroll all the ministers in the party. Neurath knew nothing of this plan; he had always prided himself as being above parties and had little reason to join one now. At the same time, he could not reject what was obviously offered as an honor. When Hitler approached him as the first to receive the "Golden Party Badge of Honor," Neurath accepted without comment. A few minutes later Eltz-Rübenach was next. Stopping the chancellor, he explained his inability, as a believing Catholic, to join a party which continued to persecute his church. Hitler was stunned, the cabinet aghast. As he left the room, Eltz-Rübenach was asked to resign. With his full cooperation, the whole affair was kept quiet. A loyal civil servant, Eltz-Rübenach did not wish to cause scandal or controversy; unable to move Hitler on the youth issue, he saw resignation as the end of the matter. His brave move, therefore, had absolutely no public effect.[51]

Neurath never considered himself a party member; he never paid dues and told friends, even in later years, that he had no reason to join the party. In September 1937, returning from a vacation for Mussolini's first official visit, he found his tailor waiting at his office with a complete SS uniform; thus he learned of Hitler's arbitrary enrollment of all cabinet members in the SS.* At first, Neurath indignantly refused to cooperate, but Hitler assured him that the costume was a formality, an honor something like the Order of the Garter! Neurath then offered to appear in the uniform of the Olga Grenadiers. Hitler replied that he wanted his cabinet to show their solidarity with National Socialism in order to impress Mussolini. Neurath acquiesced, after stipulating that he would under no condition renounce church membership nor consider himself in any way responsible to Heinrich Himmler. Hitler reasserted the purely honorific nature of the title, and

---

*According to his dossier in the party files, Neurath received party membership number 3,805,229 automatically with the "Golden Badge of Honor," but the files contain no correspondence or other evidence of active membership. His appointment as SS Gruppenführer (number 287,680) is dated September 18, while Neurath was still in the mountains. His formal "application" bears the date September 29, after the Mussolini visit had been completed. Information from Berlin Document Center.

Neurath accepted his explanation, wearing the uniform only rarely (and painfully) and without ever asserting any of the prerogatives of this elite group. Shortly thereafter he made a special request of his son. "In case of my death, I am completely opposed to having a so-called SS funeral, and I want you to refuse such a ceremony should I die, since I want in no way to be identified with the personalities and methods [of that organization, membership in] which has been forced on me as an intended honor."[52]

To the end, Neurath maintained an ineffective and undramatic independence. He thought he fulfilled his moral duties by half-steps undertaken to mitigate individual sufferings. He helped Jews leave the country, refused to cut off pensions, and used his influence to intervene for Bishop Wurm, former Reichstag President Paul Löbe, and other victims of the harsh laws which, ironically, he did not oppose in the cabinet.[53] Throughout these years he remained his own man, one of the few who still spoke openly to Hitler and preserved some independence of thought in Berlin. Such independence, however, does not mitigate his guilt, and indeed only compounds it; for six years, this German aristocrat and gentleman sat silently doing little to retard the implementation of the Nazi dictatorship. For all his rationalization about duty and hierarchy of goals, when confronted with a struggle for which he was untrained, Neurath simply lacked strength of character. Despite his emotional defense of a humanistic education, nothing indicates that he benefited significantly from the broader implications of such an education. Repeatedly, the natural impulses of the man were suppressed by the training of the civil servant. Even had Neurath succeeded in maintaining Germany's moderate foreign policy, his association with the domestic tyranny of Adolf Hitler was enough to tarnish him in the eyes of a civilized world.

CHAPTER

8

NEURATH'S INFLUENCE ON FOREIGN POLICY: 1933–1936

Encouraged by the successes of 1932—the end of reparations and the acknowledgment of German right to equal treatment in the disarmament talks—Neurath and the higher officials of the foreign office optimistically believed the time had come for a more dynamic policy, especially in the territorial issues, such as *Anschluss* with Austria, the recovery of the Polish Corridor, and the remilitarization of the Rhineland.

> I was firmly decided [Neurath wrote after the war] to continue Germany's foreign policy in the same direction followed by previous cabinets, that is, negotiations with the victorious Versailles Powers in order to dismantle further the burdens of this treaty. The line of German policy was clear and unequivocal. It ran like a red thread through the foreign programs of all German cabinets since 1921, namely removal of discriminations and restoration of . . . our sovereignty. In this way, the poisonous international atmosphere created by the untenable demands of the treaty would be removed by a process of negotiations.[1]

Long resentful of the impotence of the Republic, Neurath believed the government's new-found domestic strength could be used to eliminate the humiliations of unilateral disarmament, and restore to Germany "the ability to speak in Europe and in the world with the language of a major power."[2] Not surprised by the hostile foreign reaction to Hitler's inauguration, Neurath hoped to utilize even this to rebuild German power. Only when foreign nations learned to expect an independent policy from Berlin, he thought, could such become a reality.* The new

---

*Writing in prison after the war, Neurath noted: "Wars have their origins always in an unsatisfactory status quo or in a violated sense of honor. No strong people who love honor will permit themselves to be permanently discriminated against by other nations." "Notizen."

nationalist coalition might achieve the spectacular foreign successes denied other German governments. He anticipated no serious problems from Hitler.

Crucial to this biography is the precise delineation of Neurath's goals and the degree of influence he exerted. Succeeding chapters will investigate the conflicts which eventually erupted between Neurath and Hitler; although elements of disagreement were present from the beginning of their collaboration, concurrence between the two on the central and immediate goal—restoration of German military power—temporarily disguised more fundamental disagreements. While Neurath regarded war as disastrous for Germany, both in the immediate and distant future, he believed Germany must rearm in order to be able to threaten force should the lost territories not be recoverable by peaceful means. Neurath insisted that all military planning be subordinated to responsible aims enunciated by the foreign office. Even before 1933, he had dismissed Hitler's theories of *Lebensraum* as the fantastic ramblings of a man whose "short-sighted" and "amateurish" infatuation with demagogic phrases could play no role in German policy. Neurath hoped to correct Hitler's "erroneous views" and convert him to the equally ambitious goal of restoring German military, political, and economic sovereignty through elimination of the Versailles Treaty. Such a restoration, he believed, would inevitably enhance Germany's role in European and world affairs.[3]

Neurath's confidence is reflected in his reaction to Hitler's speech on February 3, 1933 at General von Hammerstein-Equord's dinner in honor of Neurath's 60th birthday. Hitler broadly sketched out his goals before the military commanders. Domestically, he would war against Marxism and the "cancerous sore of democracy." To create a powerful German state required a period of peace in foreign affairs, but sooner or later the government must solve what he considered the outstanding problems, primarily economic in nature. Many solutions were available, he told the generals, but he personally preferred the idea of the conquest of living space in the East, and its "ruthless Germanization." Without elaborating further on this or other goals, Hitler announced that most important would be to create a powerful military, rooted in the national "will to arms." "The most dangerous time will come," he concluded, "during the creation of the military forces. Then we will discover whether France has statesmen. If they do, they will not grant us the necessary time, but will fall upon us at once (probably with their Eastern satellites)."[4]

Despite such candid remarks, Hitler's audience that night treated the speech as propaganda: "Speaking is always more audacious than action," one general remarked. Most believed the new chancellor, just three days in office, was telling the military men what he thought they wanted to hear. Neurath found the speech immature in tone and content, the reflections of a man ignorant of foreign policy. He told his wife that the meeting was to encourage close cooperation between the government and the army, but privately he shared the sentiments of another participant that Hitler's "exorbitant designs would collide with harsh reality, and be rerouted in a more moderate direction." After the war, he recalled this conviction:

My lengthy experience in the foreign service would, however, compensate for Hitler's lack of knowledge about foreign countries, for he had never traveled beyond the German or Austrian frontiers. From the beginning, I had to contest Hitler's frequently naive views on foreign nations and on national mentalities and try to correct the misinformation he had gathered.[5]

Hitler's creation of a special foreign policy bureau within the party on April 1, 1933, was interpreted by many as a first step in closer supervision of the foreign office. This move, coupled with Hitler's earlier speech, prompted Neurath to clarify any potential confusion about future policy. Writing after the war, Neurath disputed that he or any leader ever pursued a rigid plan: "One can undertake to reach some goal; the methods, however, will come only out of the respective conditions.... I should like to meet just once any statesman who has not been forced in the course of time and developments to alter his political decisions and adjust them to circumstances."[6]

His own goal had been simple enough: "What we wanted," he wrote, "was a strong national state; the restoration of its authority and sovereignty over all German territory; the establishment of a Greater-German culture community; the restoration of German prestige in the world." Two months after Hitler assumed office, Neurath summarized this program in a lengthy report, which he read at a cabinet meeting on April 7, 1933. Given his dislike of lengthy public presentations, this exposition is of the utmost importance. It clearly illustrates Neurath's views and how he hoped to convert Hitler's vague schemes into a realizable program. Indeed, Hitler's influence upon the course of German policy after 1933 can be evaluated only after one understands Neurath's proposed program.[7]

After reviewing both Germany's problems and advantages, Neurath urged the cabinet to defer concrete initiatives concerning borders and lost territories "as long as Germany is not militarily, financially, and economically strong enough, and especially not before the disarmament question has been solved." Germany's weak military position—the German military was contained to a 10:110 ratio with the combined forces of France/Poland/Czechoslovakia—must be adjusted to an equal status. In reply to Hitler's recent statements about alternative goals, Neurath stressed:

> The other general foreign policy goals of Germany arise out of the revolutions in the political and economic constellations, especially in Europe. [The goals are determined] by our geographical situation, our economic principles (overpopulation, lack of natural resources), by the necessity for all industrial countries to open up new lands, to oppose the industrialization of agricultural lands, and so forth.

For Neurath, however, the "most important task was the strengthening of Germany in every respect, but avoiding at the same time all political and economic danger zones." This self-conscious pursuit of German interests spurred all Neurath's efforts.

Because a fully independent German program lay years away, all "foreign conflicts must be avoided as long as possible." He concluded this section with a characteristic note:

> Any untimely rush-forward in our foreign political demands would probably unite all the important powers against us and endanger the realization of these demands for many years to come. For us, a foreign political truce for several years would be the natural complement to a four-year program of domestic reconstruction. A period of relative foreign calm would allow us to strengthen ourselves in quite a different way than by unleashing constant foreign political disputes which can never lead to success.

While the reproach to Hitler was undisguised, Neurath was not advocating inaction. As he wrote in 1946:

> When I became foreign minister, I undertook an obligation on behalf of the German people to liquidate once and for all the impossible and absurd terms of the Versailles Treaty. Under the existing conditions that could only be accomplished by peaceful means, not by war, for a war would unnecessarily risk everything. . . . No methods were employed [by me] which were not generally and internationally recognized practices, and permitted by general standards. One such method was the military strengthening of Germany, after the highly armed states had refused to carry out their own obligations to disarm, as required by the Versailles Treaty, and after all attempts at limiting or equalizing arms had failed.
>
> Had Hitler not lost his patience in 1937 and replaced this peaceful policy which he had hitherto followed with one of power politics, I am convinced that all the remaining problems could have been solved.[8]

Neurath never believed that Hitler would use Germany's restored power to launch an aggressive war. The foreign minister assumed that rearmament would merely restore the traditional balance of power. Not surprisingly, over the next three years, Berlin's program more frequently bore Neurath's imprint than Hitler's. During these years the chancellor had to deal with an operating foreign office, an experienced and incumbent foreign minister, a competent staff, and a policy successfully restoring German prestige. Hitler's personal influence was limited by his own lack of experience, the absence of qualified advisors from within the party, and debilitating jurisdictional conflicts within Nazi organizations. From 1933 to 1936, the foreign office played the crucial role, while Hitler and his coterie of party men had an almost insignificant effect.

Because their own program carried the day, Neurath and his advisors were slow to perceive that Hitler's ideas of geopolitics, racism, and aggressive opportunism did not complement their approach. They did not so much underestimate Hitler as believe that responsible statesmanship and a rational program would prevail. Few commentators have taken such reasoning seriously, preferring to regard Neurath and his advisors as deluded by self-importance or as cowards conceding to Hitler's determined plans. But in reality, between 1933 and 1936, German foreign policy was formulated and implemented by the Wilhelmstrasse.

Rearmament

Neurath believed that by the December 11, 1932 declaration, Germany had won the legal basis for rearmament, and he awaited European recognition of some degree of actual arms build-up. After Hitler came to power, this policy remained unchanged. Hence, at the reconvened disarmament conference, Neurath urged passive expectation upon the German delegation and reminded the victor nations of their responsibilities:

> German demands upon the disarmament conference remain the same as before: disarmament of the highly armed states, adjustment of weapons to benefit those states already disarmed, equal weapons and equal freedom of arms for all.... For more than twelve years, we have waited in vain for the highly armed states to carry out their obligation to disarm.... Our patience is now exhausted.[9]

Hitler introduced no increased pressure and perceptive foreign diplomats properly attributed the hard line to Neurath. In early May, he warned: "If no agreement about general disarmament is reached and the full sovereignty of the states in armaments is thus declared as a principle, it will have to hold good in the same manner for Germany." Throughout these months, Neurath believed the other nations would come to their senses "once the exaggerated and foolish, partly downright malicious reports about the events in Germany and the alleged intentions of the new government have ceased." Thus, despite adverse foreign reactions, Neurath urged that Germany continue to issue both reassurances and threats to leave the disarmament conference. The chancellor's speech of May 17, and Neurath's address on September 15 stress the same theme: "There is only one choice: realization of our equality of status or the collapse of the whole idea of disarmament. For the incalculable consequences of the latter, Germany would not bear the responsibility."[10]

Under Neurath's handling, German diplomacy showed "an unusual and not customary adroitness" in the disarmament crisis. In the fall of 1933, when the British and French agreed on a plan involving a probationary period and a ban on all rearmament, Neurath urged that Berlin respond by leaving both the conference and the League of Nations. He, not Hitler, insisted upon the break, hoping to force a recognition of German rearmament. He urged the publication of a detailed yet moderate program of rearmament, which would convince hostile countries that an armaments agreement, including German increases, was preferable to the inevitable arms race. In proceeding, Neurath followed one of his favorite maxims: "One must not lose one's nerve, nor assume that we can accomplish anything by clamor or paper protest." With Neurath in attendance, the program was made public, and simultaneously, the minister approved the secret measures by which Germany would evade the remaining restrictions of the Versailles Treaty. The beginning of open rearmament was near.[11]

On February 10, 1934, Neurath briefed Hitler: while Germany should encourage discussion and prevent a united British-Italian-French front, the ultimate goal remained "the achievement of a satisfactory settlement by treaty, which we can in good faith sign and observe." The chancellor approved, indicating his desire at least for "tacit toleration of German rearmament." All of these ideas appeared in the declaration of April 16, which formed the basis of German military policy for the next years. But German sincerity went untested, because on the following day, France rejected all further disarmament talks, declaring a refusal to legalize illegal German rearmament. Neurath advised patience; by means of continued honesty in negotiations *and* cautious arms-building, the major powers would come around. But in the summer of 1934, such a course was perilous. At the foreign office, they spoke of "the beginning of the rearmament crisis."[12]

Bülow reflected this fear when he wrote Neurath: "No kind of rearmament in the next few years could give us military security.... Our only security lies in a skilled foreign policy and in avoiding all provocations." He urged Neurath to block further rearmament, especially in the air force. The foreign minister did not agree. After the war, he expressed the logic of his approach. "The strongest invitation to war is the existence of a disarmed state; hence equality of armaments appeared [to me] as the first and most feasible step on the road toward keeping the peace." As long as the pace of rearming remained moderate, Neurath wanted to continue applying pressure.[13] A cabinet report of January 1935 contained his traditional advice:

> I believe that our policy on all these matters must be determined by the question of armaments which should have first place in our deliberations. The most important thing for us is to obtain scope to complete our armaments, and we must subordinate all other problems in foreign policy to this end.

Always he resisted the impulse to negotiate prematurely:

> The other powers will certainly approach us of their own accord with their stipulations about the armaments question; we have no occasion to speed this up and place ourselves, instead of them, in the role of petitioners.... We are opposed by a united front insofar as the other powers are unanimously determined to restrict our freedom of action and bring us back into an international combination before we have sufficiently developed our armaments.[14]

In general, Neurath's tactic prevailed. The public announcement of the existence of a German air force was part of his plan, as well as the invitation to Sir John Simon to visit Berlin in March 1935. Indeed, the events of these years point to a skilled coordination between the foreign office and the military. The first minor interruption in this program was Hitler's sudden decision to cancel the Simon talks following the publication of a British White Paper criticizing German rearmament. Departing for Berchtesgaden with Joachim von Ribbentrop in tow, Hitler decided to respond dramatically by introducing conscription. Although at least one official guessed what was going on and warned Neurath, no communication passed between Hitler and the foreign minister until an emergency meeting of

March 15. General von Blomberg opposed the decision, rejecting Ribbentrop's arguments as "foolish rubbish," but Neurath did not agree. Even before Simon's visit had been canceled, he had worried that the British might be coming with false expectations of bargaining for "high stakes in particular fields of national defense." Neurath welcomed conscription as removing "the uncertainty regarding German armament measures for defensive purposes." "It was better," he told the Polish ambassador, "to play an open hand." To Ambassador von Hassell, he was even blunter:

> As our efforts to reach a direct understanding on [armaments] with France have been frustrated by the completely negative attitude of the French government, we have now had to take our fate into our own hands and forge the weapons which we consider necessary for our own defense.
>
> It was clear from the outset that the reintroduction of universal military service would at first cause a great stir abroad. That we nevertheless decided shortly before the Anglo-German conversations to lift the veil from our rearmament measures was because we could only hope to find a way out of the tangle of political intrigue by putting all our cards on the table . . . if we were to make clear once and for all that we had already assumed equality of rights in the field of rearmament.[15]

Neurath's sole hesitancy stemmed from the poor procedures by which Hitler had arrived at his decision. In private conversations with friends, he decried Hitler's "surprises": "There is simply no way of following Hitler, for he pursues no rigorous law of logic. He does not embark upon any systematic solution of problems, but leaps from one to another." Most alarming, Hitler did not seem interested in discussing any long-range plans. As far as Neurath could see, the chancellor preferred to withdraw from Berlin and "await inspiration." To the foreign minister, this was no way to run a government.[16]

Still, Germany was achieving restoration of its military position, and the tone of the other policies between 1933 and 1936 was determined not by Hitler, but by Neurath's report of April 7, 1933. There, the foreign minister had emphasized that after rearmament, revision of the Versailles Treaty must dominate all considerations. Despite present weakness, Germany was ready to assert its ambitions, and "all future goals . . . must take second place" to this immediate task. Neurath noted the positive factors which were present: favorable geographic location, a huge population with a high standard of living, world confidence in German expertise. Although the economic base had been weakened by the world depression, Germany was no worse off than its competitors and the domestic markets remained secure. With recovery, German products and industrial power would make a strong showing. The gradually dawning recognition of the injustice Germany had suffered in 1919 would also play a role. All of these factors encouraged Neurath's hopes for success in pushing treaty revision along many fronts. The key was economic. As long as Berlin committed no rash acts, returning prosperity would force many nations to consider the pragmatic advantages of "exchanging political concessions for tangible economic gains." Neurath believed that economic recovery would inevitably lead to expansion of Germany. Even had Hitler never come to power, the diplomats were prepared to engage in this more dynamic program.[17]

In his cabinet presentation, Neurath had insisted that a number of territorial questions be raised, yet he urged that "in order to bring about revision with the best possible results, and with the least sacrifice on our part, we must be able to choose the most advantageous time for each part of the revisionist program." Thus, he predicted one more partition of Poland, making it dangerous for Germany to raise prematurely such issues as Danzig, Memel, the Huttschiner territory, North Schleswig, Eupen-Malmedy, or the former colonies. Instead, he urged utilizing the Wilsonian principle of self-determination and building economic ties with the nations involved. In this slow campaign, however, a crisis might at any time enable Berlin to bring a specific territorial question up for solution. In preparation, the government must preserve close ties with German minorities abroad, and pursue "an elastic association with all the other states, determined in every instance by the character of the problem under consideration."[18]

This straightforward presentation aimed at total reversal of the military defeat of 1918 and the restoration of German power in central Europe. To Hermann Rauschning, Neurath depicted a reinvigorated Germany, bordered on the east and west by satellite countries; however, his program did not rest upon the foundations to which Hitler so often returned—race, war, destiny, or *Lebensraum*—but on Germany's industrial strength:

> With careful planning, the world depression gives us the great chance to overcome the general distress faster than all the other nations, thereby achieving an advantageous reorientation of the world's economic situation. Such a method of procedure would allow us to create a favorable economic position, at least in Europe. By excluding political conflicts and concentrating on economic questions, we will also be able to avoid those dangers of war, which at present we could not master.

He was sure Hitler would be convinced that economic power was the key to the future.[19]

Indeed, during these first three years, Hitler's dogmatic pronouncements about foreign policy found no implementation and little if any discussion by the diplomats. Yet it was not for want of trying. Frequently, Hitler (or his party comrades) did launch radical thrusts which supposedly reflected a National Socialist ideology. Austria is, of course, the foremost example, but there were others, including Rosenberg's fantasies in Romania, Ribbentrop's adventures in Great Britain, and Göring's romances in Italy. Neurath energetically opposed such programs, and he eventually prevailed. Thus, it was Neurath's approach of quiet diplomacy that prepared the ground for the triumphant restoration of German power, and shaped foreign policy in these years. To that program, we must now turn.

Western Policy

To most Western neighbors, Neurath and the foreign office paid little attention; Belgium, Holland, Switzerland, and the Scandinavian countries were deemed too insignificant to warrant detailed considerations, and Spain and Portugal were too removed from the mainstream of European politics. Postwar boundary adjustments had disrupted amicable relations with Belgium and Denmark, yet whenever Hitler implied that Eupen-Malmedy or North Schleswig were not important issues, Neurath always intervened to keep alive these territorial claims.[20] Toward other states, Neurath also suggested reserve. The 1933 Concordat, in his view, included too many German concessions. Good relations with the Holy See were more a matter of domestic than international politics, and Neurath always suspected that Vatican good will produced little real advantage. The United States, too, seemed indifferent to European affairs; serious efforts at friendship would be wasted. "For the future," he told the cabinet, "we will not be able to count on the basic sympathy nor the active support of Washington in European quarters."[21]

Hitler's chancellorship did not alter German policy toward any of these countries, even though some hostile foreign reactions did complicate relations. But Neurath trusted that economic and trade arrangements, not political assurances, would straighten things out. Of more primary importance was the friendship of France and Great Britain. During the Weimar Republic, France was considered essential to the redevelopment of German strength. Stresemann had tried friendly bilateral cooperation; Curtius and Brüning had pursued a European solidarity which would persuade Paris to abandon objections to treaty revisions. Neurath opposed both approaches:

> An understanding with France, in the sense of a permanent friendly formation of mutual relations, is for the foreseeable future as good as impossible. All that we can do for the time being is to regulate our relations with France so that she does not feel directly threatened, and hinder us.

In time, France would drop its stubborn insistence on perpetuating all the clauses of the postwar treaties, but for now, unpleasant tension was periodically unavoidable. "Our interest, however, demands that these moments of tension do not accumulate and do not follow too quickly upon each other. Experience shows that the French consistently resign themselves to any development that is not pursued too violently or too impetuously." In contrast to Hitler's view of France as an hereditary enemy, Neurath noted: "Any basic and demonstrative alienation of France by Germany would be misplaced, because no German goals can be achieved without French cooperation."[22]

Despite a strong military position, French hegemony in Europe was ending, Neurath believed, and Paris would not hinder Germany's peaceful growth, unless unduly provoked. He was careful to present dramatic events like the October departure from the League in such a way as not to threaten France. Yet when Papen persuaded Hitler to make some dramatic gesture to establish French-German understanding and thus avoid the Saar plebiscite (scheduled for 1935),

Neurath rejected the suggestion, and refused also to discuss a plan to guarantee the boundaries of Eastern Europe. He persuaded Hitler that France, if left alone, would accept German power. Ultimately his counsel prevailed; acute observers noted that the principal obstacle to an understanding between France and Germany was Neurath and his foreign office.[23]

Neurath's views on German-British relations were similar. Although Neurath believed that in London "a certain change in our favor is already noticeable," he had always doubted whether Great Britain wanted a strong Germany. To seek an alliance would be futile, he told the cabinet: "England will never place itself in opposition to America and France for our sake." Neurath knew the chancellor desired closer ties with Great Britain, and he later wrote:

> Hitler had the serious intention of coming to a peaceful understanding with England. He had naive ideas concerning the English mentality, and I had to point out repeatedly that the methods he had adopted during his domestic rise to power were entirely unsuited to win English sympathies.

Based on his experience, Neurath believed Great Britain would cooperate only as long as Germany sought treaty revision by peaceful and legal means, and did not try to rush events. Since such was his intention, he was hopeful of British tolerance and not discouraged by French opposition.[24]

In the summer of 1934, this cool but amicable period of relations with the Western powers abruptly ended with the Röhm purge and the assassination of Austrian Chancellor Engelbert Dollfuss. Thereafter, relations rapidly deteriorated. Shaken by foreign outrage, Hitler retreated from his search for greater friendship. Faced with a series of Western proposals for improving the uneasy situation in Eastern and Southern Europe, however, Neurath pursued a dilatory policy. To him, these proposals implied renewed recognition of the territorial or military clauses of the Versailles Treaty, for negotiations during a period of German weakness would only produce German concessions. Advocating no precipitous action which might unite Europe, Neurath kept avenues open, even while preserving the tensions necessary for the progress of his revisionist claims. This was the task he accomplished for Hitler in the years after 1933.[25]

Privately, Hitler fussed about his foreign minister's lack of imagination and initiative; Joachim von Ribbentrop, who had promised to provide Western allies for National Socialist Germany, swished from capital to capital, raising hornets' nests with such extravagant suggestions as the idea expressed to Lord Lothian that an agreement "between the two calm races in Europe" would stabilize the entire world situation. But after the summer crises of 1934, the international realities demanded the professional diplomat's cautious approach. Neurath's patience was almost immediately rewarded. In late 1934 the negotiations preliminary to the plebiscite in the Saarland proceeded smoothly; it seemed the French were beginning to accept German rearmament. Although in the cabinet Hitler claimed that this "clear success" resulted from Germany's "resurgence as a Great Power," and was a "vindication of Germany's internal reconstruction," the Saar negotiations and the easing of the Austria affair stemmed almost exclusively from the calm tone which Neurath had persuaded Hitler to adopt. Throughout this period, the chancellor depended heavily on his foreign minister, and on the day of the Saar plebiscite (January 13, 1935), he insisted that Neurath accompany him to Berchtesgaden—the first and last time the minister was so honored—to await the results of the voting.[26]

Thus, Neurath experienced what he called one of the greatest triumphs of German diplomacy: 90.5 percent of the Saar population voted to return to Germany. Fears and rumors that France would block the return of this rich area proved groundless. When Hitler expressed gratitude to his foreign minister, no one could question his sincerity. Two weeks later, Hitler's presence at an intimate family dinner celebrating Neurath's sixty-second birthday seemed to mark a period of even closer association.[27]

Neurath knew that the reinstatement of conscription in the spring of 1935 would not please the Western powers, but he thought it might speed negotiations. Thus, he was not surprised when a British note of protest came together with an inquiry as to whether or not Sir John Simon would still be welcomed in Berlin. As Neurath had always predicted, Great Britain would be the first to adjust to Germany's new power position in Europe. He was not discouraged when the meetings failed to produce anything more spectacular than an agreement for future talks on naval armaments. He was also unmoved by subsequent British actions condemning German rearmament. "The whole process leaves me cold," he told the Turkish ambassador. Convinced that his policy would continue to be successful, he anticipated no new approaches from Great Britain. He did not know that he had reached the high-water mark of his influence on Germany's Western policy.[28]

Eastern Policy

German policy in Eastern Europe centered on the related questions of Poland and the Soviet Union. Toward the smaller neighbors (Czechoslovakia, Hungary, Yugoslavia, Romania, and the Baltic states), Neurath adopted a simple policy: separate them from ties to France and encourage the dissolution of their mutual cooperation through German economic penetration. Of these countries, only Czechoslovakia, because of its geographic position and sizeable Sudeten-German minority, figured prominently in Berlin's deliberations during these early years. In 1928 and 1931, the German foreign office had proposed (and Neurath had encouraged) a Central European economic union, to include both Czechoslovakia and Austria, but Prague had rejected such ideas. Neurath suspected that Minister-President Eduard Beneš wanted to block a resurgent Germany by turning the Little Entente (Czechoslovakia, Romania, and Yugoslavia) into a permanent confederation of Central Europe. Determined to break French hegemony and expand German influence in this area, Neurath saw Beneš as an obstacle to the achievement of these goals.[29]

In the early months of 1933, relations with Prague worsened following arrests of German citizens and the banning of the National Socialist party. Neurath reacted by creating funds to aid Sudeten-German organizations, which were told to "make their own policy; the Reich could not help them for a long time." This subsidy program originated in the foreign office, without pressure from the chancellor or Nazi groups. On May 16, 1935, the signing of the Soviet-Czech pact made a policy reevaluation necessary. Konrad Henlein's Sudeten-German Party had won a resounding election triumph, consolidating two-thirds of all the Germans in Czechoslovakia into one block. The foreign office now hoped to use this group as a counterbalance to Soviet influence. "If the Henlein party pursues a clever and courageous policy and remains united," one official noted, "it could frequently become quite a source of embarrassment to the government and gain many advantages for the Germans." Out of such hopes was born a new program. Neurath aimed only at temporary advantages, for he was skeptical of over-reliance upon German minorities abroad. Moreover, he was convinced that until territorial disputes with Poland were settled, Germany should do nothing in Czechoslovakia.[30]

Dominating German policy in Eastern Europe were relations with Poland, which to Berlin included within its borders "clearly German territory." In 1925 Stresemann had expressed the official policy:

> Since a military intervention against Poland is out of the question, there remains only the possibility of winning over the world to the idea of returning the German territory in the East, by demonstrating that Poland—in its present form and especially in light of the unjust settlement of the boundary with Germany—poses a danger to European peace.

During Poland's financial troubles in 1925 and 1926, the foreign office urged: "Our goal must be to postpone any final and permanent economic and currency stabilization for Poland until that country is ready for a settlement of the boundary question in line with our wishes, and until our political power position is sufficiently strengthened." Although some diplomats argued that "the Corridor and Upper Silesia would return to the Reich only as a result of a war and the resulting destruction of Poland's power position," the foreign office thought it premature to resolve problems by military action. On one point, however, there was agreement: Berlin must reject any political pact which would recognize its borders with Poland.[31]

Neurath supported this program, rejecting all partial solutions to the territorial problems. Shortly after Hitler took office, the minister expressed his position:

> In Poland the conditions requisite for the initiation of any successful negotiations for revision have not yet come about. If, owing to some untoward circumstances, we had to negotiate at present about the Eastern problem, we would be bound to come off poorly. We must bear in mind that the revision of the eastern frontier is an indivisible problem and that there will be only one more partition of Poland. There would be no point in seeking a

solution of the Corridor question by itself. Demands for which we cannot gain satisfaction on that occasion will never be fulfilled later on. For there can be no doubt that the revision of the German-Polish boundary will end with some Eastern Locarno or some similar binding commitment.[32]

In the electoral campaign of February and March 1933, violent anti-Polish sentiments in the German press created widespread unrest in Warsaw; Marshal Pilsudski decided on a dramatic step to test "Germany's actual state of readiness." The resulting Polish occupation of the Westerplatte, a fortification in Danzig harbor, and rumors of Polish support for a preventive war against Germany forced Hitler to restrain his party's militancy and strengthened his dependence on Neurath. In his cabinet report of April 7, the foreign minister outlined the tactics which he believed should control future German policy:

> An understanding with Poland is neither possible nor desirable. We must maintain a certain amount of German-Polish tension in order to interest the rest of the world in our revisionist demands and in order to keep Poland economically and politically weak. The situation is in no way without danger, since the present Polish government is apparently playing with the idea of a preventive war, in the knowledge that the progressive strengthening of Germany will only impair her prospects and reduce France's allegiance to the alliance. Naturally our territorial demands are the cause of this situation. As a result, it is unavoidable that for a period of time, we must retire these demands from public discussions. The preservation of the financially dependent German community in Poland, especially in Upper Silesia as well as in Danzig, is of particular concern and costs us very considerable sums of money.[33]

Some restoration of peaceful relations was necessary and Neurath persuaded Hitler to begin preliminary talks. On May 2, the chancellor received Alfred Wysocki in Neurath's presence in an unspectacular meeting which ended with a mutual declaration to discuss existing problems bilaterally. Neurath was particularly careful to ensure that the public communique contained no mention of existing boundaries, and later told the newly elected Nazi president of the Danzig Senate: "Don't commit yourself too deeply [in discussions with the Poles]. We are still far from being able today to decide for or against Poland." Some normalization of relations might be in order, but Germany must be careful not to be "swindled by the Poles." After another meeting in November, Neurath told German diplomats not to expect "a special treaty," but only a press communique. A few hours later, however, Hitler informed him that he intended to sign a formal nonaggression pact. Neurath dissuaded him of this idea, which would "greatly restrict Germany's political freedom of action for many years." Although the Polish representative left thinking he had won such a pact, Neurath drafted a "somewhat unusual form of a detailed declaration" which deleted all references to existing boundaries and became a harmless text of friendly and mutual respect.[34]

Afterwards, Hitler lost interest in Poland and turned his attention toward Austria. For the next few years, Neurath pursued his "cool reserve" toward Poland. The Eastern Problem remained unsolved; the Danzig and Corridor "wounds" still bled, even though the public exchange of insults between the two countries decreased. The professional diplomats retained a hard line. German policy, Ulrich von Hassell advised Hitler, must aim always at terminating the "mutilations" in the East, and seek a way to keep the rest of Europe quiet while Berlin "takes on Warsaw one way or the other." The German ambassador to Warsaw agreed: "Poland will always remain our enemy." Neurath believed the Western nations would eventually force Poland to some compromise over German claims. The complex problems which "inevitably existed between [these] two states," he said, were insoluble, and the German-Polish détente had not altered the political situation in Europe. No one knew how to recover the area then controlled by Poland, but in the meantime, preventive war had been avoided without abandoning the revisionist program. The goals Neurath had sketched out for the cabinet in April 1933 had come surprisingly close to realization.[35] Until 1936, the official policy of the German government regarding Poland remained unaffected by innovation.

Similar developments appear in Germany's relations with the Soviet Union. Neurath had no intention of enlarging upon the republic's cordial but reserved relations. He believed in preserving a moderate German-Soviet friendship as a check to the hostility of France and Great Britain. The deteriorating relations in 1932 he attributed to Papen's maladroit "grand strategy" and the increasingly anti-Communist stance of the German government. Hence he welcomed Foreign Commissar Litvinov's assurance that the Soviet Union "considered it quite natural that Germany should treat communists in Germany exactly as enemies of the state are treated in Russia." On the eve of Hitler's chancellorship, Neurath was campaigning actively for ratification of the extension of the Berlin Treaty, renewed on June 24, 1931.[36]

Hitler's inauguration did not seriously upset this balance. Although Neurath rejected the idea that Germany should take the initiative, he believed that a gesture would be sufficient to restore the previous calm. In the first year of the new government, nothing indicated any altered attitude; even the dismantling of German military experimental stations in that country was carried out in a friendly atmosphere and according to a prearranged schedule. As early as February 15, after a discussion with Hitler, Neurath noted with obvious pleasure that "the chancellor is convinced about the importance of the Russian problem and about the necessity to maintain our previous political, economic-political, and military-political line; he will not allow any sort of changes to occur in German policy toward Russia." But Neurath did not rely solely on promises. In March he secured ratification of the long-postponed extension of the Berlin Treaty. "In the light of the present foreign policy situation," he had advised Hitler, "it appears to me advisable that our relations with the Soviet Union be placed once more on a firm legal basis." As outstanding economic and fiscal matters were amicably arranged, the future seemed promising.[37]

Nevertheless, relations between the two countries deteriorated, largely as a result of the anti-Communist election campaign in Germany and the attendant Soviet reaction. To counter Russian fears, Neurath suggested in his cabinet presentation of April 1933 that Germany concentrate on an economic program. Relations between the two countries would always remain cool, yet without giving the impression of "running after the Soviet Union," relations could be improved. In the last analysis, Neurath insisted, "we cannot do without the Russian rearguard cover against Poland." The limited goals behind Berlin's program were clear in foreign office instructions for the new ambassador, Rudolf Nadolny; these stressed the value of Soviet friendship primarily in a revisionist context as pressure upon Poland and to prevent "the incorporation of the Soviet Union in any political front directed against Germany." But Nadolny, an advocate of closer Soviet ties, was convinced that German salvation lay in some alliance with the Soviet Union. He was one of those anomalous diplomats who eventually function more as the representative of the country to which they are accredited than of their homeland. Moreover, Nadolny had for years criticized Neurath and wanted desperately to become foreign minister. He had already sounded out leading Nazis for support, and looked upon his mission to Russia as an opportunity to produce a détente so impressive as to make him Neurath's successor.[38]

Upon his arrival in November 1933, Nadolny at once began exceeding his instructions, bombarding Berlin with suggestions for winning Soviet friendship. Embassy officials were dubious about his chances for success. Aware of recent Russian overtures to the French, and Litvinov's strongly worded address to the Central Executive Committee, Neurath believed the Soviets were ready to sever relations with Germany and he instructed Nadolny to adopt "cool, self-assured reserve" and an attitude of "watchful waiting."

> The great importance of Russia for Germany in the political, economic, and military areas is in no way underestimated by us, and there is not the remotest intention of taking a stand against Moscow on our initiative. But there is no purpose in making attempts which are hopeless from the very start to change the attitude of the dominant statesmen of the Soviet Union.[39]

Unlike his ambassador, Neurath correctly saw that the new Soviet proposals (such as the March 1934 guarantee of territorial integrity for the Baltic countries) were motivated by hopes of neutralizing German influence and ensuring the expansion of Russian imperialism. Subsequently, Litvinov confessed that he had proposed the Baltic pact merely to see if German assurances "were honestly meant or not." The fact that Nadolny was taken in by the move further demonstrated to Neurath his incapacity (or unwillingness) to follow the official policy. He ordered the ambassador to reject any discussion "which might even indirectly imply a recognition of Germany's borders in the East" or in other ways limit German freedom of action in that area. Dissatisfied, Nadolny offered to come and present Hitler with his proposal of a treaty of friendship with the Soviet Union.[40]

Once in Berlin, Nadolny was assured by foreign office personnel that things could be worked out. Bülow and Richard Meyer, the experienced director of the East European desk, composed a supporting memorandum, which exceeded even the ambassador's requests. Stating that "the political importance of the Soviet Union is too great for us to be able simply to remain passive in relation to the present developments," it urged that Germany "use the next appropriate opportunity to enter once more into a serious political discussion with the Russians." The goal must be to lure the Soviet Union "away from the idea of seeking to bring about its security as a state by means of an anti-German policy, in particular in an alliance with France." But Neurath composed a report dismissing Nadolny's arguments and stressing instead his own conviction that nothing could be gained by a German initiative. Hitler agreed. After a noisy argument with Neurath, Nadolny angrily submitted his resignation. In these events, Neurath was dominant; nothing indicates any desire on Hitler's part to initiate a break with the Soviet Union. Although some have attributed Nadolny's removal to a clash of personalities, it really sprang from Neurath's conviction that revision of Germany's eastern borders should not be further complicated by pacts with the Bolsheviks, whose own expansionism in the East was at odds with German interests.[41]

Subsequently, Neurath rejected measures aimed at improving Soviet-German relations by replacing Nadolny in Russia with an old friend, Friedrich Count von der Schulenberg, the ideal person to maintain "with a great deal of patience" a policy of cool reserve. During the next six years, this "patient, impersonal and disengaged spectator of the passing show" followed Neurath's instructions to the letter, keeping all doors open without antagonizing anyone, and yet also without undertaking any initiative. Until 1936, Neurath maintained these "correct, if not friendly relations, while keeping foreign policy entirely separate from differences in domestic politics." All overtures were rejected, since to Neurath, the price of friendship with the Soviet Union was to abandon the full restoration of Germany's international influence, and he would not pay that fee. In all these decisions, Neurath recorded, the chancellor "was in complete agreement with our conception and tactics."[42]

When as a result of German intransigence the French-Soviet pact was announced on May 2, 1935, Neurath was not disturbed. Such an alliance, he had once observed, "is no threat to us, since we have no aggressive intentions." Shrewdly, he calculated the effects of the pact which, by reopening the balance-of-power question, made a reexamination of the Locarno Treaty necessary. Hence, he predicted, the pact "might possibly be far more embarrassing for other countries than for Germany." Assured almost immediately by the Soviets that Berlin could, if it chose, make the new agreement meaningless merely by engaging in talks with Moscow, Neurath preferred to use the opportunity to raise the subject of the demilitarization clauses of the Locarno Treaty. As always, his approach to the Soviet Union was solely tactical.[43]

Southern Europe

Despite the fundamental influence of the professionals on foreign policy making, Hitler and individual Nazi leaders did introduce some new elements, especially toward Italy and Austria. But these contradictory moves lacked coordination: experimentation and expediency—which were the hallmark of these events—cannot be made a coherent "system." Thus even in these areas of his own choosing, Hitler, albeit reluctantly and impatiently, eventually had to turn to Neurath for advice and to heed the program the foreign office suggested.[44]

Neurath had always thought Italian-German friendship was valuable only for keeping Italy out of an anti-German coalition. In the fight to restore German strength, Rome was an unreliable support. His April 7, 1933 cabinet presentation explained his position: "Our political relations with Italy rest upon one principle: closest cooperation on every front where common interests are present, but no firm binding of Germany to Italian policy." Indeed, Neurath believed the issue of the German-speaking Tyroleans and the Austrian question would always prevent close cooperation between Italy and the Reich. But Hitler disagreed, regarding Mussolini as the only continental leader with whom he could properly ally himself. For this alliance, which was the keystone of his foreign policy ideas, he was willing to sacrifice the insignificant 1,800,000 Tyroleans, and as for Austria, he was sure he could prevent Mussolini from interfering.[45]

A clash between the chancellor and the foreign minister erupted early. In March 1933, Mussolini initiated conversations in Rome on revision of the territorial clauses of the Versailles Treaty, especially with respect to the Polish Corridor and the Hungarian boundaries. He suggested that "an understanding of the four great European powers [France, Germany, Great Britain, and Italy]" could break the deadlock at the disarmament talks and introduce the subject of territorial revisions. Thus was born the Four Power Pact, which affirmed "the principle of revision." Neurath was immediately suspicious about Mussolini's motives for so gratuitously advancing German policy. He feared that Berlin might be drawn into a hostile environment which would reaffirm, rather than revise, the status quo. This suspicion was apparently confirmed when Mussolini accepted British and French amendments seriously weakening the already vague commitment to Four Power action independent of the League and the disarmament conference.[46]

Even before consulting Hitler, Neurath dispatched negative reactions to the proposals, yet suggested that if certain objectionable sections were removed, Germany could sign "because despite the small concrete content of its stipulations, the signing itself would ease the atmosphere." The Italian government tried to bypass the minister to deal directly with Hitler and Göring. When the latter returned from Rome with a compromise wording contradicting Neurath's instructions, the foreign minister announced the new proposals "had now not only become entirely worthless for us, but in addition contained commitments that could become very inconvenient for us at some later time." Summoning the Italian ambassador, Neurath insisted upon a return to the earlier forms. Hitler approved. Despite Göring's intervention, Neurath remained in control.[47]

Foreign observers viewed apprehensively an era of close Italian-German cooperation. Ironically, Neurath was also concerned, fearing the price Mussolini might one day extract. Telling foreign statesmen the treaty was as useful as "recognizing the neutrality of the moon," he made clear to Hitler that he would accept it only as "a sacrifice to improve the atmosphere," and not as signifying closer ties with Rome. When the negotiations ended uncertainly, Neurath was relieved. "If it has not done anything good," he remarked to the French ambassador, "at least it will not be able to do anything bad." The Mussolini pact—as Neurath always called it—had not altered the formal, cool ties with Italy. This principle dominated German policy in the following years.[48]

But Ulrich von Hassell, the German ambassador in Rome, rebelled, urging an alliance system of economic, military, and financial cooperation, even at the sacrifice of some German interests. Rebuffed, his dispatches criticized government policy ("a needless sermon," Neurath wrote on one). Hassell believed that Italian friendship was the most important goal of German policy, and he joined the irrepressible Papen in urging Hitler to visit Italy soon. Neurath feared a meeting with Mussolini might end discordantly or, more likely, with a German commitment to the status quo in Austria and the recognition of Italian influence in the Danube area. Better postpone such talks, he thought, than run risks, but Hitler, disturbed about the worsening Austrian situation, decided to approach Mussolini.[49]

The Venice visit in 1934 was not a success. Hitler and Mussolini seriously misunderstood each other, perhaps because the Italian insisted on conducting the conversation in German (of which he had only an imprecise command), and because Hitler refused to permit any foreign office representative to be present. The two men left convinced of full agreement, but in fact both adhered to previous positions and had only "roared at one another like bulls" (a phrase attributed to Neurath). Hitler thought he had secured approval to replace Austrian Chancellor Dollfuss and to include Nazis in the Vienna government, while Mussolini believed that agreement had been reached to handle all future problems concerning Austria in concert, even as Italy continued to support Dollfuss. Aware of these discrepancies, Neurath's office tried to resolve them, but to no avail. Despite ideological and rhetorical agreement, the Austrian situation remained unimproved. An aide who saw Neurath and Hitler together shortly after the state banquet recalled his impressions: Neurath seemed at home and at ease, even in the impressive Venetian palace. Hitler was nervous, talking rapidly, and looking every inch an insignificant man, out of place in elegant society. His first appearance on the broad stage of diplomacy had not been auspicious. Neurath believed Hitler had learned an important lesson: foreign affairs differed from domestic policy.[50]

Hitler became more dependent upon Neurath during the next month after the Röhm purge and the death of Hindenburg. When confronted by the Austrian Nazi uprising in July, the attendant murder of Dollfuss, and Italian mobilization on the Brenner Pass, Hitler welcomed Neurath's help and in general adopted a program shaped not by his own preference for an Italian alliance, but by Neurath's refusal to put Germany into Italian tutelage. Toward Austria, too, Neurath's policy eventually prevailed. As early as 1926, Stresemann had expressed the government's official policy supporting *Anschluss*, even if the international situation at that time meant that "we cannot loudly agitate for it." Neurath agreed; he had long warned that public acknowledgment of such aspirations must first await a more favorable foreign atmosphere and restoration of Germany's economy. A viable economic solution for Austria's troubles, he believed, would eventually overcome even the most hostile foreign opposition; until such time, Berlin could only hope to prevent Austria from further compromising future relations in its search for financial help from abroad.[51]

When he became foreign minister, Neurath ordered German missions to exclude Austria from conversations until the major problems had been settled. Premature discussions, he wrote, "might have the result of anticipating the subsequent development of our *special relations* with Austria." Hitler's appointment made this policy more difficult, but did not alter it. In time, Neurath argued, the synchronized strength of the National Socialists in Germany and in Austria would produce closer cooperation between the two countries, but for the present he petitioned the chancellor to "refrain from giving any encouragement to National Socialists in Austria." The immediate task was to prevent political disturbances in Vienna.[52]

Events beyond Neurath's control made this program impossible. In early March, after the Nazi successes in the German elections, the Austrian chancellor found himself unable to rule with the deadlocked parliament, yet afraid lest general elections produce National Socialist triumphs. He decided to form a presidential dictatorship, suppressing all opposition parties, including the Nazis and the Social Democrats, who had for the past fifteen years been the strongest advocates of *Anschluss* with Germany. After extended deliberations, the foreign office decided to assist the Austrian National Socialists, while not compromising Germany's official stance of noninvolvement: "The external picture must be and remain that the National Socialist movement in Austria came to power on its own strength and with no help from Germany beyond that of a compelling example." This decision—taken independently of the chancellor—originated in the long-range revisionist plans of the diplomats. Closer ties depended now upon the success of the Austrian Nazis; their triumph in Vienna would permit joint policies (*Gleichschaltung*) without a formal union. This idea, subsequently adopted by Hitler, but first proposed by Neurath and the foreign office, provided an ingenious means of avoiding those constitutional and international prohibitions which had doomed all previous attempts at an agreement.[53]

Hitler first revealed his own approach to Austria in discussions with the Italian ambassador in late March. Claiming no desire for *Anschluss*, he insisted on the primacy of party politics, even in foreign affairs. He demanded the ouster of Dollfuss, a scheduling of new elections, and the inclusion of Nazis in the new government. Obviously Hitler regarded himself as leader of the opposition party in Vienna, not just as a foreign head of state. Thinking official involvement unnecessary, he demanded only the nazification of Austria and was convinced that his party resources were sufficient to gain this victory. Thus, by a different route,

Hitler formulated a program similar to the one devised by the foreign office, namely, no overt campaign against Austria.[54]

The chancellor put Austrian matters entirely in the hands of Theodor Habicht, an Austrian citizen and inspector of the Austrian Nazi party. Neurath acquiesced, hoping to minimize the illegal radical policies. Almost immediately, he was disappointed. Repeatedly, Hitler refused to treat Austrian representatives as ministers of a sovereign state; once Neurath abruptly terminated an interview when Hitler angrily threatened Austria with economic reprisals if the government did not stop persecuting "his party." Increasingly, Hitler listened to the staff of Austrian experts from the party. In May 1933, he accepted their plan for a thousand-Mark visa for all Germans planning Austrian travel. With this serious disruption of the lucrative German tourist trade, the Dollfuss regime would surely topple, and a Nazi government be installed. Not consulted until Habicht had already spread the news that "Hitler and Neurath" had decided on the measure, the foreign office reiterated its warnings against overt German involvement:

> Any attempt to bring the Austrian problem to a head at this time through official German policy entails very considerable risks for us. There does not seem to be adequate justification for accepting such risks at a time when we are so dependent, as we are today, on an atmosphere as favorable as possible for the solution of other questions of vital importance to the German people, and which have still greater priority.[55]

Although the foreign office argued against intervention "since the party's own momentum will undoubtedly carry the National Socialist movement in Austria to its goal sooner or later, even without such artificial support," in the decisive cabinet meeting of May 26, the foreign minister was no match for the chancellor's forceful rhetoric. "The contest will be decided before the end of the summer," Hitler confidently told the ministers, sweeping aside Neurath's prediction that the measure would only create "general resentment against Germany." Thus the undeclared war between the Nazis and the Dollfuss government moved closer to open conflagration with the support of official Berlin authorities.[56]

Policy toward Austria seemed hesitant, however, even confused. While Hitler believed that public pressures and a cessation of the tourist trade would destroy Dollfuss, Neurath and the foreign office hoped for the introduction of Nazi elements in the Dollfuss government and the restoration of "friendly relations with Germany." Meanwhile, the Austrian Nazis pursued policies aiming at a forced *Anschluss*. This triple split made Neurath's job difficult. Although Hitler was intransigent,* throughout the summer, the foreign minister diligently set out to destroy Habicht's optimistic picture of the chances for speedy success and to warn of possible intervention by Great Britain, France, and Italy. Surprisingly, a round

---

*On June 15, 1933, Hitler told Hans Steinacher: "I will hold out against Austria, five, ten, fifteen years. It doesn't matter how long, if we remain resolute! I will hold out ... strong as steel. For the past fifteen years I have been engaged in battle—if one counts the world war, then twenty years. I have good nerves." Hans Steinacher's diary, kindly provided to the author by Hans-Adolf Jacobsen.

of conversations (at Stuttgart, Munich, Berchtesgaden, and Neuschwanstein) was successful. Although Hitler remained hostile toward Dollfuss and would not curtail the Nazi drive for power in Vienna, he accepted Neurath's demands and ordered that the public campaign against the Dollfuss government be terminated. This experience convinced the foreign minister that while the Austrian situation would remain a sore point for some time, Hitler would eventually adhere to a program of moderation.[57]

Meanwhile, the foreign office was aware that the Austrian Nazis were not completely under control. When Habicht failed to secure direct negotiations with Dollfuss and recommended intensification of Nazi agitation, Hitler ignored his advice, making all future requests subject to Neurath's prior approval. Next, as retaliation for various arrests in Vienna, Habicht persuaded Hitler to order an official tabulation of all Austrians living in Germany in order to determine some appropriate response, but Neurath's protest removed the order. Other dramatic events showed Habicht that Hitler was listening to the professional diplomats, not to the party organization in Munich. Warned of a Nazi uprising coordinated with an invasion by the Austrian Legion (of Nazi refugees), Neurath informed Hitler, who called in the responsible officials and ordered an end to all plans for a coup. In early February 1934, Hitler summoned the German envoy in Vienna and listened patiently to his lengthy exposition. Five days later, he received the military attaché and General von Blomberg. In both these meetings, held in the absence of party representatives, Hitler approved an approach contradicting his 1933 crusade. Once again, the diplomats seemed to have prevailed.[58]

Yet even as Hitler began to soften, Dollfuss, bowing to pressures from Rome, inaugurated a fascist-type dictatorship in Vienna. After a complicated series of discussions, on February 17, 1934, Great Britain, France, and Italy issued a joint declaration announcing their determination to preserve the integrity and independence of Austria. Neurath's campaign to win over Hitler had taken a little too long. When Dollfuss ruthlessly suppressed the Socialists in Vienna and grew increasingly dependent upon Mussolini, it seemed that a fascist block would soon extend from Italy through Vienna, Budapest, and Sofia. On the day before the joint declaration Mussolini warned Berlin that he would never permit *Anschluss*. More important, "for him, the *Gleichschaltung* of the Austrian government with the National Socialist regime in Germany was synonymous with formal *Anschluss*." In one sentence, Neurath's foreign office program, followed since March 1933, evaporated. The value of supporting the National Socialists in Austria was now doubtful; unexpected Italian intervention might jeopardize future developments. Neurath decided he would have to act fast to prevent Italy from posing as the protector of Austria.[59]

Using alarming reports of a proposed meeting in Rome of Hungarian, Austrian, and Italian representatives, and information that the French government would coordinate moves by the Little Entente and this new Danubian bloc, Neurath went to Hitler with a clear and present danger. Deeply concerned, Hitler agreed with Neurath's proposed new course toward Austria: attacks on the

Vienna government would cease and the Nazi party would concentrate on long-term consolidation in order to "make it impossible for any Austrian government to rule in the long run without this, the most effective and strongest party in the country." Although Habicht remained in charge of the Austrian Nazi organization (based in Munich), relations with Vienna would henceforth be handled with other foreign policy. Pleased, Neurath looked forward to an early opportunity to break off the struggle with honor.[60]

But Hitler was not totally satisfied. Seizing upon earlier suggestions by Papen and Hassell, he decided to settle the Austrian question through talks with Mussolini. Neurath objected to reaching any settlement under "Italy's patronage" and proposed a six-point program which included removing visa restrictions, lifting bans on newspapers, proclaiming a mutual amnesty for prisoners, and opening talks about including some Nazi representatives in the government. Surprisingly, Hitler agreed. Reversing his earlier position, he declared himself "entirely disinterested in Austria, politically and economically" and prepared "to write Austria off for years to come and hand her over to economic fertilization by Italy." Thus, Neurath withdrew his opposition to the meeting in Italy, and Berlin reverberated with the disappointment of the Austrian Nazis who considered Hitler's new course a desertion. Neurath even succeeded in having the Austrian Legion demobilized.[61]

As noted above, the Venice meetings proved useless, but Neurath returned with some optimism. Except for the unpredictable Austrian Nazis, he believed affairs were generally under control. Confident enough to leave for a vacation on his estate, Neurath was surprised by the "absolutely unexpected" putsch by the Austrian National Socialists (led by elements from Habicht's Munich office) and the Dollfuss murder. Recent studies have established that Habicht's organization planned and executed the revolt in a last desperate gamble to confront Hitler with a *fait accompli*. Not directly involved with the putsch, the chancellor had previously approved Nazi participation if the Austrian army were to lead an uprising. When he learned that only Austrian Nazis had been involved, he was furious.[62] Although both Göring and Papen subsequently claimed to have influenced Hitler's reaction, the chancellor was again guided by the foreign minister. He dismissed Habicht, closed the anti-Austrian propaganda centers, and moved the last of the refugee camps away from the borders. Once again, Neurath served as Hitler's *rocher de bronze,* securing broad authority to ensure a uniform policy in the future. The resulting ban on public discussion of the German-Austrian policy by party members, issued August 8, 1934, represented both Hitler's admission of the existence of parallel programs and foreign office determination to avoid further duplication.[63]

Despite the events of July 1934, the foreign office policy remained unaltered. When the new German ambassador to Vienna, Franz von Papen, pressed for dramatic German gestures to restore friendly relations, and when Hassell insisted that improvement could come only from Rome, Neurath rejected both. "We must now quietly wait for matters to develop, and watch for any opportunity for positive action.... At present I cannot see such an opportunity." Neurath reported that the "chancellor is in agreement with our position." During the next few years, this harmony continued. Köpke summarized official policy when he wrote: "Time is definitely on our side where the Austrian question is concerned." Neurath convinced Hitler to veto Papen's proposals. "He has agreed with my view," Neurath wrote on one dispatch, "that no commitment whatever concerning Austria should be entered into in any way beyond the assurance of nonintervention in Austria's internal affairs."[64]

Neurath's most immediate problem was Hassell, who constantly insisted that "we ought to come to an agreement in principle with the Italians on policy in the southeast [of Europe] beginning with Austria." But Neurath opposed mediation through Rome and cited such unfriendly acts as Italian sponsorship of the Stresa Conference in April 1935 in reaction to the introduction of conscription in Germany:

> The extremely hysterical Italian outbursts and measures... would perhaps have surprised me, but for the fact that during my eight and a half years' service in Rome, I frequently witnessed similar demonstrations.... What Italy's underlying reasons are for the military measures she had taken are not clear to me to this day. Every now and then I have the impression that Signor Mussolini does not know them himself.[65]

Two months later, Neurath concluded that the Italian initiative had stemmed from Mussolini's plans for Abyssinia. Desiring a quick settlement of the Austrian question in order to turn to Africa, Mussolini might desire German friendship, but Neurath was more reluctant than ever to heed Hassell's appeals to "foster our ties with Rome to prevent the Franco-Italian front from becoming firmly established." As Italy enmeshed itself in Africa, the foreign office prescribed Berlin's response: "We do not wish to have anything whatsoever to do with the Italian-Abyssinian conflict." As Mussolini became more involved, the price for Italian cooperation in Europe would fall. Then Neurath would talk and not before. He wrote bluntly to Hassell:

> The desire suddenly shown by the Italian government to be on good terms with us once more can, of course, be explained by the difficult position in which they find themselves as a result of the Abyssinian adventure, and in which they will probably become still more deeply involved.
> We have no occasion to hasten to extricate the Italians from this predicament. Perhaps one day a situation will arise therefrom which will enable us to discuss and settle the Austrian problem with Italy.... I am the last man to underestimate the advantages of maintaining good relations with Italy; on the other hand, I have had enough experience of Italian politics not to overrate these advantages.

When the Abyssinian conflict erupted into war, Neurath convinced a wavering chancellor to declare and enforce strict neutrality.[66]

Although both Hassell and Hitler wanted closer ties with Italy, Neurath was adamant: "This does not tempt us," he wrote on one dispatch, labeling recent overtures "very clumsy," making "no impression on those of us who know the fickleness of the Italians." Neurath advised Mussolini to end the conflict swiftly "by means of a suitable compromise," and throughout the difficult period of the League debates on sanctions and the Hoare-Laval proposals for a division of Abyssinia, he steered Germany in a neutral course. In January 1936 his patience seemed rewarded. Deeply involved in the war, Mussolini informed Hassell that he was willing for Austria, "as a formally quite independent state ... to become a German satellite." Had Hitler still sought a German-Italian détente he would have jumped at this opportunity. Instead, Neurath ordered Hassell to reject it "in the politest possible manner ... for it will tie our hands to get a change in the present form of government in Austria, for the foreseeable future." Two weeks later, Neurath cautioned Papen too against taking any initiative: "Now, as previously, we do not consider it advisable for any understanding with Austria to be achieved under Italy's aegis." German strength was beginning to reassert itself in many ways; the foreign office believed it had successfully directed policy in southeastern Europe along lines of slow but fruitful growth, and the harvest time was nearing.[67]

Weltpolitik

Throughout the preceding sections surveying the continuity and success of Neurath's policy, one theme predominates: he feared that European states might prematurely trap the German government into some alliance perpetuating the status quo. He aimed at avoiding such commitments while rebuilding strength. As he wrote after the war: "The endeavors of German foreign policy in the years 1933 through 1936 were directed towards winning a political base of preeminence." In his fear of premature concessions Neurath stood alone, and he attempted to guide the nation's policy with a sense of moral decency and historical self-respect. As events would soon make obvious, no treaty or alliance was so sacred to Hitler that it could not be signed with dispatch and quickly broken, should circumstances warrant. German policy in these years, on the other hand, was predicated on the belief that pacts and international agreements would be honored. Thus Neurath was most careful in guiding Germany's grand strategy regarding the spate of pact proposals which emerged after 1934.[68]

All his life, Neurath objected to broad pacts. In 1934, when France and the Soviet Union proposed an Eastern Locarno to include Germany, Poland, Czechoslovakia, the Soviet Union, and the Baltic states, guaranteed by France in return for a Soviet guarantee of France's western boundaries, he was uninterested. The pact seemed a thinly-veiled disguise for Soviet-French containment policies, and he preferred to have the two states openly sign an alliance, not escape responsibility through the myth of "collective security." Similarly, when France and Italy proposed in January 1935 a Danubian pact, embracing Germany, Austria, Italy, Hungary, Czechoslovakia, and Yugoslavia, with the possible future inclusion of

France, Poland, and Romania, Neurath reacted negatively. Should Berlin ever accept this plan, he warned, it would encounter constant diplomatic protests over real or pretended acts of union between Germany and Austria. He advised Hitler to "procrastinate and to prevent the pact from being concluded, by making demands which would be unacceptable to our opponents." His principal objection to both pact proposals was clear: "The other powers are unanimously determined to restrict our freedom of action and bring us back into an international combination before we have sufficiently developed our armaments." Neurath remained calm, unmoved by the hostile world reaction to the reintroduction of conscription. Were Germany to be stampeded into discussions because of such reaction, he told Hitler, "the distrust in which we are held would be in no wise reduced, but on the other hand, every critical or negative statement of ours would be used to demonstrate yet again our malice and to brand us once more as the disturbers of European peace." Hitler accepted Neurath's advice, and discussions of the pacts never really got started.[69]

By early 1936, Neurath's patience was rewarded. After the fiascos surrounding the League's involvement in the Abyssinian conflict and the Japanese invasion of China, he advised Europe to seek a new order, one based not upon the old realities of 1918 but upon the new situation of 1936. Europe must cooperate "in a spirit of mutual trust between the Great Powers concerned":

> As soon as [the Abyssinian conflict] has been settled, the time will come jointly to examine the question of what *new basis* can be devised for cooperation among the Great Powers, either by adapting the Locarno Treaty structure to present-day conditions, or by creating other structures which would accord with the political situation then prevailing. Whether this should be done in conjunction with a reform of the League of Nations, or outside the League, it is as yet impossible to foresee. That the old Geneva system, with its supplementary assistance pacts, is reducing itself to absurdity, is a fact of which France is now, to her cost, becoming aware. It will therefore be a question of taking in hand, in the light of the experience newly gained from the present conflict and of the political situation then prevailing, a work of reform with the object of securing a peaceful future for Europe. In this task, our cooperation will most certainly not be lacking.[70]

This dispatch illuminates Neurath's overall policy. The new basis for European relations, the reform of Locarno and the League, had to conform with the emergence of German power. Ever since 1932, he had worked to create the proper atmosphere, and now it had arrived. To understand his favorable view of the situation in 1936, we must return briefly to May 2, 1935 and the announcement of the French-Soviet mutual assistance pact. The Locarno Treaty (1926) rested explicitly upon the principle of full reciprocity: France, Belgium, and Germany renounced use of force against each other, a promise guaranteed by Great Britain and Italy. The promise included never to use or plan to use military force against each other. When a French pact with the Soviet Union was first discussed, both French and British diplomatic authorities concluded that any French commitment to possible military intervention against Germany would violate the Locarno Treaty. Paris spent many months trying to avoid this problem by bringing the Soviet Union into the League and attempting to secure an Eastern Locarno. This grand design foundered on Neurath's implacable opposition, and the Abyssinian conflict presented additional complications. Reluctantly the French government agreed to the pact with the Soviet Union; fearful of Germany's growing air and naval power, Great Britain approved. Berlin protested that the pact destroyed the moral and legal foundations of the Locarno Treaty, and Neurath knew at once that he could thereby raise the issue of the demilitarized Rhineland. For many years, he had anticipated such a moment, and he yearned for a way to restore this last necessary ingredient for German security.[71]

In March 1935, at the time of the introduction of conscription, Neurath had warned against any open violations of the demilitarized zone, for they might lead not only to sanctions but military invasion as well. By the summer, however, he moved to eliminate this last military discrimination through a negotiated settlement which would adjust the Locarno Treaty to the new situation. While insisting on quiet in the zone, "in keeping with the restraint and reserve demanded for reasons of state," Neurath ordered thorough legal evaluations of the Soviet-French pact. Writing in prison after the war, he recalled: "Upon completion of the French-Soviet Treaty on May 2, 1935, we immediately informed the French government of the incompatibility of this action with the Locarno Treaty ... and substantiated other contradictions at the end of July 1935. ... We left no doubt at all that we considered this step to be a violation of the Locarno Treaty."[72]

Indeed, as early as May 8, Neurath announced that "a new situation has been created with regard to the Locarno Treaty by the Franco-Russian alliance." To the French ambassador, he was more direct: "You have not yet learned," he said, "that one can no longer treat us as in the days of the Versailles *Diktat*." When the ambassador claimed that Germany was overreacting, Neurath exploded:

> For the past 15 years, people have preached at us that we should remain quiet, and everything would work itself out. Our experience, however, has shown that the *beati possidentes* have never made a serious effort to alter the situation which is so favorable to themselves, unless, from time to time, they have been energetically reminded that others do not find themselves in such a state of well-being as themselves.[73]

In his draft for Hitler's speech to the Reichstag on May 21, 1935, Neurath emphasized his point concerning German demands and inserted a counterattack to the League's condemnation of German rearmament:

> The German government [Hitler announced] would be specially grateful for an authentic interpretation of the retrospective and future effects of the Franco-Russian military alliance on the contractual obligations of the individual parties who signed the Locarno Pact. The German government also does not wish to allow any doubts to arise as to its own belief that these military alliances are contrary to the spirit and letter of the Covenant of the League of Nations.

Admitting that he had recently ordered the unilateral termination of the disarmament clauses of the treaty, Hitler followed Neurath's tactic:

> The German government hereby most solemnly declares that these measures of theirs relate exclusively to the points which involve moral and material discrimination against the German people and of which notice has been given. The German government will therefore unconditionally respect the articles of the Versailles Treaty concerning the coexistence of the nations in other respects, including the territorial provisions.

Significantly he added: "And those revisions which shall be rendered necessary in the course of time will be put into effect only by the method of peaceful understanding." To prevent any confusion, Hitler stressed that his government would not sign a treaty it could not uphold. He pledged "scrupulous" adherence to every treaty signed voluntarily, even before 1933. "In particular, they will uphold and fulfill all obligations arising out of the Locarno Treaty, so long as the other parties are on their side ready to stand by that pact." The grand lines of Neurath's policy were here clearly confirmed by Hitler himself.[74]

The official response from Great Britain, France, and Italy was not friendly. Meanwhile rumors abounded that remilitarization of the Rhineland was imminent, and Neurath seemed determined to compound them. Apparently ready for a war of nerves, he chose to start the renegotiations of the postwar security system with a discussion of the Rhineland. Hitler was not yet involved; the foreign office initiated both the evaluation of the French-Soviet pact's illegality and its violation of Locarno. Obviously Neurath wanted to create an atmosphere in which France and Britain would be forced to terminate the demilitarized zone. Thus when the British ambassador suggested London might conclude agreements to establish air bases in Belgium and France, Neurath countered with a proposal to set up antiaircraft positions, in violation of the demilitarized zone requirements. While present at this discussion, Hitler said nothing; later the same day, in a cabinet meeting, he summarized developments and supported Neurath's approach:

> Negotiations, which would deal with the determination of the limits of armaments according to the needs of the parties to the negotiations, could definitely take place. It would then probably emerge that it might be in the interests of Britain as well as of France to consent to the abrogation of the provisions concerning the demilitarized zone.[75]

When the foreign office learned that Italy considered denouncing the Locarno Treaty, Neurath was convinced a break would be forthcoming. Although officials in Berlin continued to insist that no German fait accompli would occur, as long as the other side remained true to the spirit of the Locarno pact, the French ambassador concluded that German diplomats were preparing the way for invalidation of the demilitarized zone clauses. That such was indeed the case has escaped the attention of most observers, because in the first weeks of January 1936, Hitler had not yet given serious thought to the problem. The foreign office proceeded without his orders; legal experts submitted position papers on demilitarized zones throughout the world. One of these concluded with a call that "this policy of interference in German affairs, which is a policy designed for disruption of peace, must end once and for all, in the interest of peace and the return to proper international law." In mid-January, leading generals strongly supported the foreign office plan to obtain "within the course of 1936 the abolition of the servitude which affects the demilitarized zone." Clearly the first steps had begun.[76]

During his London trip in late January (for the funeral of King George V), Neurath frankly discussed the issues with the new foreign secretary, Anthony Eden. Repeating his opposition to the French-Soviet pact, Neurath issued a transparent threat: "If, however, the other signatories or guarantors of the Locarno Pact should conclude bilateral agreements contrary to the spirit of the Locarno Pact, we should be compelled to reconsider our attitude." Bolstered, Neurath returned believing that Britain would restrain French impetuosity. François-Poncet believed the German foreign office was waiting for the right moment to renegotiate "a sensible modification of the clauses of the Locarno Treaty which concern the demilitarized zone." French diplomats in London were alarmed by indications of British willingness to negotiate; Neurath's calculations seemed accurate.[77]

Then on February 13, Prince Bismarck, embassy councillor in London, talked with the head of the Central Department of the British foreign office. In confidence, Ralph Wigram indicated that he had been ordered to prepare a "working agreement," covering many areas, between France, Great Britain, and Germany. Most important was Wigram's "obscure allusion to its being possible to render an air pact still more interesting by omitting from it things contained in the Locarno Treaty." From the context of previous discussions, these "things" could only be the demilitarization clauses. This top-secret report, reinforced by a second conversation a few days later, was given to Neurath on February 15; now the real breakthrough was becoming apparent. Unfortunately, the chancellor had already decided on another way of solving the problem.[78]

Throughout January and early February 1936, Hitler kept in the background, staying mostly in Berchtesgaden. He had participated in the opening of the Garmish Winter Olympics (February 6 through 15) and during those days received news about the general staff talks between France and Great Britain, and secret information that the French and Russian general staffs had agreed to link up in Southern Germany in the eventuality of a war against the Reich. Now Hitler feared that the British-French military talks, ostensibly directed at Italian aggression in Abyssinia, were really steps toward a military encirclement of Germany. Impulsively, he decided upon dramatic action. The French government's decision on February 11 to seek ratification in the parliament of the French-Soviet pact (initialed nearly nine months before) was part of the impetus. In Garmish, Hitler consulted military leaders who recommended stationing troops in the Rhineland. The chancellor delayed a final decision pending discussions with the foreign office. Flying into Berlin briefly on February 12 to meet Neurath, he learned for the first time of the minister's own interest in somehow raising the question of the demilitarized zone.[79]

The same day, Hitler met with Neurath, Dirk Forster (*chargé d'affaires* in

Paris), and Joachim von Ribbentrop. Hitler asked for likely foreign reaction to a unilateral move; Neurath believed such a step was unnecessary, while Forster predicted dire consequences. Only Ribbentrop encouraged sending in troops, claiming that the British government would welcome it. Hitler reserved a decision, setting aside his foreign minister's suggestions that a more measured approach would also produce results. After discussing the issue with Ambassador Hassell in Munich, who also supported a diplomatic, not military, solution, Hitler announced that troops would be dispatched into the Rhineland as soon as the French Senate ratified the pact. With reports from Great Britain so promising, Neurath was upset that Hitler was even contemplating unilateral action. Still, London's stance might be merely diversionary, aimed at *preventing* Germany from taking decisive steps in reaction to the ratification of the French-Soviet pact. Shortly *before* Hitler's final decision, Neurath told Hassell that he viewed Britain's overtures as deceptive, and had reluctantly decided to support unilateral action. He was convinced there would be no adverse moves by the other side.[80]

Although always counseling more deliberate action, the foreign minister never opposed the principle involved in reoccupying the Rhineland. Indeed, he was the first to link it as a response to the French-Soviet agreement and had himself initiated the issue of the demilitarized zone. Anticipating little British help, and having failed to persuade Hitler to move with greater diplomatic finesse, Neurath was a prisoner of actions he had himself advised. To resign because of the chancellor's arbitrary and independent moves seemed to him a personal reaction, which might imperil the chances of success. Moreover, Neurath was convinced that the great powers would react only with speeches and notes. Thus to resist Hitler's desires was both futile and unnecessary. General Fritsch later told Hassell that Neurath had done all that could reasonably be expected. If he ultimately accepted Hitler's decision, it was because he had come to accept the argument that the move would not cause serious damage or run tremendous risks.[81]

During these discussions, another factor became crucial. Ever since the British-German naval agreement which he had negotiated, Ribbentrop had clearly become Hitler's favorite. During the remilitarization plans, Ribbentrop slavishly parroted Hitler's opinions and opposed Neurath, who lamented that against the emotional and feverish activity of the "party people," his sole weapon was his "well-known sang-froid." He did not disguise the fact that serious disputes raged within the government, but should he force his opposition too far, Ribbentrop was waiting for his position. This, too, encouraged Neurath to stand at his post.[82]

When the day of action came, Neurath supported the move he deemed unavoidable. Acting, as one of his friends noted, "instinctively like a German foreign minister," he devoted his energy to making the occupation successful, and minimizing the risks by means of a carefully worded declaration which offered a justification and held out the hope of a return to the League of Nations. By keeping the number of troops small, he believed Europe would not consider it a "flagrant" violation. Word from France and Great Britain indicated there would be no mobilization. Although some of the highest officials (including Hitler) were less than certain of success, Neurath remained confident, and was generally the "man of nerves" during the crisis. On trial after the war, Neurath did not excuse his actions, insisting that he alone had been correct in assessing probable foreign reactions. On the eve of the move, when Blomberg and Göring were inclined to pull back, Neurath lectured them: "I do not think the moment is very well chosen, but now that you have gone so far, it is impossible for us to go back. You must under all conditions carry through the plan."[83]

Several days after the initial occupation, alarming reports of adverse foreign reactions were received. When Hitler himself began to waver, Neurath reportedly calmed him with the remark—pronounced in a distinctly thick Swabian dialect—that "now that we're in there, we'll stay there." A laconic note of the foreign office caught the same spirit: "Nervousness not shared here. The foreign minister is discussing the matter with Blomberg." Throughout these days, Neurath implacably opposed all gestures of compromise: Germany would refuse any "unilateral restrictions on our own security measures." In later years, Hitler several times recalled these tension-filled days, indicating that they were among the worst of his life. He referred to Neurath's iron nerves, which had greatly helped the situation.[84]

Although Hitler had made the final decision, the program had come from Neurath and the goal was his. Although some commentators have seen the reoccupation of the Rhineland as the first aggressive step toward world war, the evidence does not support that view, and Neurath's motives are clearly beyond reproach. For him, the termination of this last military restriction of the Versailles Treaty was the culmination of a program of revision which he had initiated years before. Significant light is shed on Neurath's attitude by an incident which occurred on the very day that German troops reentered the Rhineland. After addressing the Reichstag with his startling news, Hitler, accompanied by Neurath, boarded the train to await developments in Munich. That night, in the home of the Ritters, Neurath listened to a radio broadcast which gave details of the troop reception. Baroness von Ritter recalls that he was close to tears:

> He considered it to be the greatest triumph of German diplomacy in this century. He believed that at long last a major wrong done to Germany had been removed, and that now at last Germany could take its place with other nations as an equal partner in international affairs. He was very deeply moved by this event. In fact, I seldom saw him so moved.[85]

This heavily symbolic scene summarizes much in Neurath's attitude. During the many years of his diplomatic career, he felt humiliated by Germany's enforced disarmament and general weakness. As foreign minister, he hoped peacefully to remedy that wrong. One day, without paying any price to Italy, France, Great Britain, or the Soviet Union, Germany would regain its former power, thus abolishing the humiliation of 1919. Since 1932 this program had dominated German policy and in the spring of 1936 created the conditions for a reassertion of Germany's rightful position. One looks in vain for the initiation of any diplomatic revolution by Hitler. The conclusion is inescapable: had some other government controlled Germany during these years, the policy of the foreign office with Neurath in charge would have remained unchanged. While he might have been spared some embarrassments (such as the unnecessary crisis over Austria), the tone and outlook of foreign policy would have remained keyed to revisionism on all fronts.

Still, the Rhineland action of 1936 marks an important change. For the first time, Adolf Hitler showed a pronounced interest in arriving at decisions independent of his official advisors. Although Neurath still believed that German policy would continue along the lines he had drawn—and he too aimed at hegemony in Central Europe—a more independent Hitler, flanked by personal and nonprofessional advisors, now represented a threat more serious than any Neurath had faced before. Unless the foreign minister could prevent the gradual whittling away of the influence and power of his foreign office, unless he could find a suitable replacement for the large number of advisors who had previously assisted in guiding policy, he feared that more troubling times lay ahead. To these problems and the dangers they posed for Neurath and Germany, we must now turn.

CHAPTER

9

CHALLENGES TO NEURATH'S LEADERSHIP: 1933–1937

As early as July 1933, Mussolini complained:

> There seemed to be six if not seven members of the German government who acted from time to time as foreign minister. Hitler, . . . Neurath, Göring, . . . Papen, Goebbels and Rosenberg, not to mention General Blomberg who was brought into all discussions of foreign affairs. This rendered dealing with the German government a matter of considerable difficulty.

Four months later, François-Poncet observed that Neurath and his staff were fighting for the very existence of the foreign office:

> In the domain of foreign affairs, there no longer reigns any more than in other areas of government that order, unity, and discipline which the Third Reich brags to have brought with it. There is not merely one minister, nor is there only one foreign office. There are a half-dozen. When it is a question of Austria, Habicht is heard. When it is a question of Hungary or Romania, one perceives that Rosenberg and his office still retain a particle of authority. When it is necessary to take up the Saar, or the Vatican, or France, one addresses Papen. When there is reason to send a message to Mussolini, it is Göring who leaps into his airplane. Even the influence of the whimsical Dr. Hanfstaengl comes into play when America is under discussion.
> In the middle of all this competition, the indolent, timid, and irresolute Neurath is obligated to defend his position, his person, and even the officials of the Wilhelmstrasse, who are scorned by the Nazis, but who still form a compact group crowding around their minister. So much the worse if Germany's foreign relations suffer, and if those whom foreigners would consider the sole authorized interpreters of the thoughts of the government demolish, on the one hand, that which Neurath seeks to erect on the other.[1]

Neurath, who saw foreign policy as a matter of patient attention to detail, judicious evaluation of dispatches, and reasonable decisions, was horrified by this new brand of diplomacy, well described by a contemporary journalist:

> Never before had there been so much traveling here and there, one day in this place, the next in that, traveling in Pullmans, in automobiles, and in airplanes. Germany's foreign policy was characterized by a fantastic haste, a permanent state of excitement, and a fanatical zeal. There appeared a swarm of eager men who concocted different schemes every moment, but who never produced well-prepared ideas which had been thought through to their logical conclusions. Everything struggled along in a zig-zag line. . . . One is left with the impression that the apparatus of German foreign policy was an aggregation of more or less flimsy ice floes, occasionally forced together, but only to drift apart again and scatter on the open sea.[2]

Indeed, in foreign policy matters after 1933, Neurath faced that characteristic confusion of the Third Reich proper to the "conqueror state." This term describes not only the conquest of domestic power and its ultimate extension toward foreign territories, but also includes the principle that official power resides not in institutions, but in those individuals capable of wrestling out some satrapy of their own. The myth that Hitler was a Machiavellian genius cleverly introducing confusion and duplication of offices, paralyzing independent action and preparing the way for his own plans, dies hard. Yet the legend bears little relationship to reality. Hitler simply preferred to avoid administrative decisions. His aversion to bureaucratic procedures of decision making permitted individuals to fill the resulting vacuum with their own spheres of influence. The chancellor tolerated such conflicts largely out of indolence. Despite numerous appeals that he delineate divisions of authority, Hitler refused: "Führer decisions" came only *after* the struggle had already been resolved. The man who emerged master of a given situation, able to carry out actions independent of other governmental and party agencies, received Hitler's approval to continue doing that which he had already achieved. Hitler seldom prevented or alleviated conflicts, and he never altered administrative organizations, either to create order out of chaos, or complexity where clarity had previously prevailed. Rather, he was content to approve any individual or group which had consolidated power, regarding with cynicism and indifference the sacrifice either of colleagues or ideology. Such was the ordering principle of the Third Reich, the conqueror state.[3]

When one observes the many challengers who appeared in the field of foreign policy in the years following Hitler's inauguration, this process clearly emerges. Although some interpreters have regarded these rivals as Hitler's veiled means of controlling the traditional instruments of policy, that view does not withstand careful scrutiny. As the preceding chapter showed, Neurath was the decisive voice in Hitler's councils throughout the early years. Other advisors gained influence, not because the chancellor wanted to remove or replace Neurath, but out of a jumble of conflicts and internecine struggles. The foreign minister's failures to master the methods of the conqueror state impaired his ability to influence Hitler, thus contributing to the radicalization of German foreign policy.

Personal Rivalries

Between 1933 and 1936, however, Neurath upheld his authority despite numerous challenges. When Alfred Hugenberg, the powerful chairman of the German Nationals and minister of both economics and agriculture, intruded ineptly into international politics by a public call for German colonies and land for expansion, Neurath forced his cabinet resignation. He curtailed the interventions of other ministers, especially Franz von Papen, the vice-chancellor. Neurath despised Papen's tendency "to engage in all sorts of activity," not merely because these moves were never cleared with his office, but because they were erratic and irresponsible. Neurath's opposition was not based upon a fear that Papen would replace him, as some have suggested, but arose out of his skepticism about Papen's abilities. Neurath considered the Concordat (which Papen had negotiated) over-generous; it confirmed his belief that ambitious amateurs menaced foreign affairs. When the irrepressible Papen launched his own plan for a French-German cooperation committee to negotiate the future of the Saar, Neurath requested a presidential inquiry, and officially disowned that action. After the murder of Dollfuss, Neurath approved Hitler's suggestion that Papen ought to become the new minister to Vienna, but vetoed Papen's request to be directly responsible to the chancellor. Neurath found Papen's suggestions as ambassador usually premature and singularly unhelpful, and often arbitrarily independent. While this poor relationship had little influence on German policy, it was symptomatic of the complicated atmosphere within which Neurath had to function.[4]

Prominent Nazis, like Göring and Goebbels, were a more serious matter. From the start, Hermann Göring set about creating a special role for himself. In late June he decided to form a centralized intelligence and telegraph service, with its own special coding and decoding departments. All police, military, and diplomatic telegrams were to be routed through this new organization, thus making available to Göring all diplomatic correspondence. Neurath flatly refused to consider this arrangement, ending the matter abruptly. But Göring remained convinced that he had a future in foreign affairs. Contemptuously he dismissed the professional diplomats as bureaucrats who "spend the morning sharpening pencils and the afternoon at tea parties." To compensate for their inactivity, he traveled abroad (seldom briefing Neurath), seeking to advance the cause of close German-Italian relations. Neurath found such interference intolerable, and in a cabinet meeting on May 12, 1933, personally rebuked Göring, calling his "inordinate trust in the fascist government of Italy" entirely misplaced. Although the foreign minister reaffirmed his sole right to direct policy, Göring continued to claim (as in October 1933) that he had been assigned German-Italian relations "as his own special area." Still, despite Mussolini's preference for dealing with Göring, and the latter's frequent trips to Rome, no important changes in policy ensued.[5]

Undeterred by his failure in Italy, Göring turned to Central Europe, where he blithely assured the Romanian minister that Germany did not aim at territorial revision of the postwar treaties! When foreign governments made inquiries, a furious Neurath went to Hitler, subsequently recording the chancellor's comment that "he had never renounced revision of the Versailles Treaty, not even to the Poles." The sobering effect of these events upon Göring was always short-lived. In March 1935, he told Ambassador Lipski that Hitler had asked him to take "the relations between the two countries under his special protection." Thereafter, at the first appearance of trouble, such as negotiations over railroad traffic across the Corridor, Göring stepped into the breach, claiming that "the chancellor had entrusted him with the settlement of the Corridor question." The foreign office was unable to dispel the impression that "Göring is the only person who can help in such difficulties." These interventions did not change German policy, but unduly complicated its leadership. In Polish spheres, Göring achieved that independence which Papen had failed to establish in Austria, and eventually Neurath had to concede the point. In the summer of 1937 he told one visitor: "Don't take Göring seriously. In Germany, everyone concerns himself with foreign policy."[6]

Neurath's intense personal dislike for Joseph Goebbels prevented any such painless resolution to the rivalry which developed when the latter tried to take over the press department of the foreign office. The outcome of Neurath's resistance was that Goebbels controlled only the dissemination of German propaganda abroad, while the other functions of the press bureau remained intact (until 1943). Goebbels soon relinquished his ambition of gaining influence over foreign policy. Although subsequent clashes, like the one over propaganda in Danzig, continued to plague their relations, Neurath kept Goebbels from upsetting the workings of his policy. At times, the foreign minister probably suspected the chancellor of deliberately encouraging these rivals, but generally he was correct in regarding these unfortunate activities as independently initiated.[7]

This explanation illuminates Neurath's relations with Rudolf Hess, Hitler's deputy and party secretary, who attempted to monopolize that aspect of foreign policy which dealt with German-speaking communities living abroad—the so-called *völkisch* question. For years, numerous institutions and individuals had been active in programs securing and protecting the culture of German groups throughout the world. After the Versailles Treaty, this activity increased, especially toward the 1.3 million "border" Germans (those living in areas removed from German control by the treaty), and toward the nearly 12 million *Volksdeutsch* (people of German descent and language) living in successor states to the Austro-Hungarian Empire. Supported by the German foreign office, various organizations flourished under the republic, without any political goal more specific than the encouragement of German culture abroad. Hitler's promise to unify all Germans naturally excited and revitalized these organizations. As a result, the foreign office suggested that "all subordinate organizations be given orders to adhere strictly to the instructions from Berlin." In June 1933, Rudolf Hess circulated plans for a new organization to coordinate all *völkisch* activities abroad. Without specific directions from Hitler, he set up the Volksdeutsch Council (the

VDR), but from the beginning it lacked a clear idea of its competence, and Neurath specifically challenged its claim for autonomous responsibility. In addition, a debilitating disagreement within its own ranks paralyzed activity, and Hess seemed unable to make decisions or exert effective control over the far-flung operations. Thus, Neurath succeeded in limiting its role to an advisory one under foreign office supervision.[8]

But in 1934, Hess named the VDR as sole supervisor of ties with the Sudeten Germans, and early in February 1935, under the adventurous Ernst Bohle, the VDR pushed for a more dynamic relationship between Berlin and the German groups in Poland. On April 17, 1935, Neurath protested "the increasing tendency among certain offices within the Reich to intervene in the affairs of minorities." His first real challenge to the VDR was successful. Abruptly altering course, Hess limited Bohle's authority to German citizens living abroad; theoretically, the VDR continued to be concerned with the minorities in Europe, but never effectively functioned again. Subsequently Heinrich Himmler founded his own *Volksdeutsch Mittelstelle* (VDM) and launched a campaign to consolidate and nazify all *völkisch* organizations throughout Europe, by threatening to end financial aid from Germany. While Neurath was foreign minister, however, the foreign office blocked the intimidating orders. *Völkisch* affairs were not centralized until July 1938, and not until then did the VDM gain any real influence on foreign affairs. No evidence substantiates the oft-repeated charge that German foreign policy revolutionized *völkisch* elements in order to use them as "instruments of National Socialist expansion." Hess's VDR and its own rivals were manifestations of the anarchy within the Third Reich, and as long as Neurath was minister, their existence was not influential.[9]

In all these cases, Neurath competed with individuals who indulged in foreign affairs either out of a propensity to meddle or a desire to consolidate political power. His counterattacks were firm, but not spectacular, and he was sometimes willing to stop short of total victory, rationalizing these men's rights, as cabinet ministers, to be informed about foreign affairs. Moreover, as Rauschning noted, although Neurath and the professional diplomats were sometimes worried by the reckless irresponsibility of many of these men:

> the officials of the foreign ministry did not take these activities seriously. They felt satisfied that they would put the fellows in their place. They had done so with the wild men of the Weimar regime, of whom there had been plenty at first. If this had been possible with intelligent men, some of them with experience of the world, it should be easy with the uncouth and uneducated Nazis. They were a perfectly illiterate lot. Their *faux pas* were a source of continual amusement.[10]

Institutional Rivalries

In general, Neurath's optimism was correct. Concessions to individuals like Papen, Göring, and Hess were minimal and did not threaten the unity of policy. But simultaneously, the office itself was seriously challenged by rival Nazi institutions.

The challenges presented by the organizations of Rosenberg, Bohle, and Ribbentrop were thus more dangerous than any individual incursion into the field of foreign affairs. The first major organization to appear was the *Aussenpolitisches Amt der NSDAP* (APA), created on April 1, 1933. Its head, Alfred Rosenberg, made no secret of his ambition, announcing that now "the particular desires and the unique aspirations of National Socialism will find expression within the area of foreign policy." Rosenberg had long been the party's expert on foreign affairs. In 1927, he had published a book entitled *The Future of a German Foreign Policy*, and after the electoral successes of 1930 was a member of the Reichstag foreign policy committee. Subsequently he traveled to Great Britain and Italy where he was generally regarded as a "future German foreign minister." As late as 1931, Hitler promised to make Rosenberg head of the foreign office, but President Hindenburg had specified that Neurath must stay in that position. On the evening of his inauguration, Hitler reportedly opined that "the best thing to do with Party Comrade Rosenberg is to put him as state secretary in the foreign office." This remark was immediately reported to Neurath, who blocked the appointment. As a result, Rosenberg alone among the old Nazis received no promotion.[11]

The creation of the APA was not a deliberate assault on the foreign office. Indeed, no evidence exists that Hitler and Rosenberg had agreed on a program or planned to substitute "new methods and new personnel for the outdated practices and old men of the Wilhelmstrasse." Rosenberg received no such instructions, at least, and not even a budget until 1937! In retrospect, his appointment was typical of Hitler's procedures. Rosenberg was given a title around which he might erect a power base, but nothing more. As events would show, he lacked the strength to carry out his dream. The APA remained merely an inexpensive plum for Rosenberg. As Hitler told Neurath, it was a "harmless compensation, in order to be rid of [Rosenberg]"; the chancellor "did not intend to separate himself" from Neurath, whose determination to prevail was thereby strengthened. "He will not let himself be eased out," one official noted, "but will remain, no matter what the cost."[12]

In May 1933, Rosenberg's visit to London provided Neurath with ammunition to demonstrate the incompetence of this "arrogant ignoramus," whose poor showing and stupid remarks to the press forced the German ambassador to conclude that the visit "had caused England's hostility toward the new Germany to break out with full force." The usually neutral *Times* concluded that "his visit will hardly be regarded as a success even by those who were responsible for it." Neurath informed Hitler that the head of the APA had damaged German policy and should not be permitted to make further trips; in his diary, Rosenberg bitterly blamed his troubles on the professional diplomats, while his field workers claimed that Neurath had carefully collected the most unfavorable newspaper articles "in order to speak with the Führer and ease out Rosenberg." In any case, Rosenberg never recovered his privileged position.[13]

The APA remained troublesome in bringing various foreign visitors directly to Hitler. Even Neurath's decree of May 1935 failed to stop these unauthorized interviews or continued bungling. Protected under the APA, for example, were Habicht's activities in Austria. Only after the Dollfuss murder did Neurath succeed in removing him. Similarly, when Rosenberg's agents pushed nonaggression pacts with Yugoslavia and Czechoslovakia, the foreign minister's personal protests were required to stop the talks. The feud between the APA and Neurath erupted most severely when officials whom Rosenberg had sent to Manchuria so threatened German policy in that area that the foreign minister wrote to "emphatically protest against this manner of conducting official business" and demand the cessation of all activities. Once again, the APA was ordered to stop and in time Rosenberg's office was reduced to clipping newspaper articles and arranging receptions for unimportant people. Eventually, Hitler forbade APA trips abroad so that the organization ceased to be a serious rival. Nevertheless, as was typical, it continued to exist, to prove occasionally embarrassing because it retained direct access to the chancellor.[14]

Although a recent study has argued that APA activities were important in foreshadowing the ideological content of a "Nazi foreign policy," little evidence supports this interpretation or suggests that Hitler ever discussed plans with Rosenberg or other APA members. The organization was only one of a number of auxiliary groups struggling for power within the Nazi hierarchy, and it never enjoyed Hitler's specific support. The one concrete proposal it developed and carried to fruition—the creation of a pro-Nazi dictatorship in Romania—failed miserably after only a month, revealing "how little political skill the leading heads of the APA possessed and how much they allowed their actions to be determined by their own wish-pictures and ideological cliches." The events also illustrate dramatically why Neurath energetically fought Rosenberg and the APA at every step.[15]

A more serious threat to the discipline and autonomy of the foreign service emerged in a Nazi party organization created in 1931 for the purpose of working among German citizens abroad. After Hitler's inauguration, Rosenberg made a futile attempt to gain control of this Hamburg-based group to consolidate the power of the APA. In the ensuing struggle, Ernst Bohle protected the autonomy of his group by placing it under Rudolf Hess. In the fall of 1933, Hess recognized the organization, which controlled more than 350 local groups in all major foreign countries, as the sole intermediary supervising all communication with party members abroad, promoting it to an independent bureau of the NSDAP (*Hauptleitung*) with a branch office in Berlin.[16]

Throughout 1933, most Nazis anticipated Hitler's immediate appointment of a Nazi as foreign minister, thus permanently coordinating the foreign office. In December, faced with Rosenberg's disgrace, Neurath's tenacious hold on his position, and the chancellor's apparent satisfaction with the professional diplomats, Bohle became more ambitious and suggested that his organization of subordinate groups abroad and party men within Germany was ready-made for initiating and implementing a Nazi foreign policy. Bohle's organization offered what had hitherto been lacking in party circles: a cadre of men familiar with foreign countries and already integrated within an orthodox Nazi organization. Inspired by the installation of two more Nazi cabinet ministers on December 1 (Hess and Röhm), Bohle proposed himself as head of a ministry to develop a policy to unite all Germans abroad and reform the foreign service. In a letter to Hess of December 4, 1933, Bohle stressed the necessity for purging the service:

> The foreign office in its present form offers by and large no guarantee that Germany will be represented abroad in a vigorous and positive National Socialist sense. On the other hand, since it does not appear likely that any basic alteration in this matter can be achieved for years to come, we could, in preparation, utilize the interim period (which should not be wasted) so that such a ministry could carry out the necessary steps.

Despite nearly a year in office, National Socialism had not won over many of the diplomats. As Bohle noted:

> Although I have learned that the ambassadors and consuls make at least some effort to understand us and to represent the National Socialist state abroad, I must however add that these gentlemen—mainly very charming and clever people—are certainly not the energetic type of foreign representative which Germany needs in its present difficult situation.

The creation of a ministry based upon party organizations abroad would, Bohle believed, "strengthen the party vis-à-vis the foreign office, and thereby greatly facilitate the nazification of the foreign service."[17]

In addition, Bohle suggested such a ministry might create a new instrument for German policy; previous governments had ignored the potential in the millions of Germans living abroad as citizens, emigrants, and friends of the homeland. Bohle proposed organizing them. Although a recent study has read into this memorandum a carefully formulated policy emanating from Hitler, Bohle had not as yet even spoken with the chancellor, who apparently never learned of this proposal. Bohle's ideas merely served to increase his own power position. Although Hess dismissed the proposal, on February 17, 1934 he named Bohle a *Gauleiter* of a new organization, the *Auslandsorganisation der NSDAP* (hereafter AO), which would be in charge of all party communications between Germany and groups abroad and responsible for party members who lived or traveled in other countries. In this last category fell, of course, all German diplomats who were party members.[18]

Immediately, AO organizers tangled with the resident German community leaders in many countries, and Neurath was deluged with reports of the damage caused by zealous Nazis who sought control of local groups. This activity, Neurath later recalled, "was very annoying to our representatives and ambassadors because the [AO] mixed in everything, and every head of that organization thought he would be a better ambassador than the official ambassador." Repeatedly, the diplomats recorded the suspicions and shattered unity following this nazification process, while Bohle's men inundated the AO office with accusations that the professional diplomats were harming the party.[19]

Conflict between the foreign office and the AO intensified in 1935 when Bohle began an active campaign to unite under his leadership all German groups in Poland. After ineffective protests from the Wilhelmstrasse, Neurath personally intervened. In response, Hess limited Bohle's control to German party members who lived abroad. Bohle had failed to dislodge Neurath's hold over minorities, but the minister's victory was transitory. On February 4, 1936, after the assassination of Wilhelm Gustloff, AO leader in Switzerland, Hitler considered closing that organization. In response, Bohle suggested a special federal bureau within the foreign office, with himself as state secretary, charged with initiating personnel changes and supervising German citizens abroad. On February 27, he discussed his ideas with Hitler. Although Hess submitted a strong supportive draft, the chancellor rejected the proposal, approving only a weak formula to create special "party attachés" in important embassies. Moreover, he asked that the proposed draft be sent to Neurath. With much of the world aroused over Germany's recent violation of the Locarno Treaty, Hitler had second thoughts about antagonizing his foreign minister. Furious at the proposal, Neurath moved with thoroughness. Requesting his staff to prepare a reply, he utilized previously composed indictments of AO activities to attack Bohle's group and he recommended its termination:

> The uncontrolled activity abroad of irresponsible party functionaries who frequently are totally inexperienced in the realm of foreign policy has already delivered many setbacks to our efforts among Germans abroad. These defeats can scarcely be reversed and further burden official German policy with the heaviest load.[20]

Neurath complemented these startling indictments with the suggestion that the proposed party attachés be subordinated to the foreign office, excluded from all political activities, and answerable to the local German diplomats. On the same day, he unleashed another attack. Recent AO activities in Romania had become so embarrassing that he now requested Hess to prevent "the willful activity of unauthorized and irresponsible groups and personalities within Germany." Specifically, he requested that all money and aid sent by the AO be terminated, since "in the last analysis, the money was being used to finance the civil war among Germans" in Romania.

Bohle and Hess recognized their miscalculations. In rejecting Neurath's plan, they jeopardized their entire program, but to accept would be to sign the death warrant of the AO power base. Their frustration surfaced in Hess's protest over "improper procedures." After a short delay, they tried to salvage some victory, nominating six party attachés. Neurath replied that until "the working methods of the AO are subjected to a thoroughgoing revision," he would approve no appointments.[21]

This state of affairs persisted, but in July 1936 the outbreak of the Spanish Civil War showed that AO representatives could meddle, even without official status. Although evidence does not support the claim that the AO "influenced an important decision in National Socialist foreign policy," its members did transmit messages from Franco, thus enabling Hitler to consider aid, against the advice and indeed in the absence of his professional advisors. But this involvement was an isolated and uncharacteristic AO activity. The AO individuals who were involved were not the harbingers of a new foreign policy; they had merely permitted Hitler to bypass the foreign office.[22]

More typical was Bohle's futile attempt (in late 1936) to gain control of the organizations in Poland. Neurath's staff warned Germans living in that country that "as long as German foreign policy is not in a position to help them, the Volks groups must orient themselves more in the direction of Warsaw than in the direction of Berlin." To this official repudiation of the AO program, Neurath appended a brief note: "This position is shared by the Führer." Thus, during Neurath's ministry, the AO added nothing new to German policy. Bohle's appointment in early 1937 to a special position within the foreign office at first seemed an unexpected victory for the organization which Neurath had so long opposed. This interpretation overlooks an important distinction. Neurath had successfully prevented the AO from introducing a revolutionary policy, and the appointment was a tactical move to protect his staff's independence. By the end of 1936, Neurath ruefully noted the appearance of a more dangerous threat—Joachim von Ribbentrop. Driven toward some modus vivendi with the party hierarchy in order to withstand this new power, Neurath had decided to gamble on Bohle's malleability. And indeed, once installed in the Wilhelmstrasse, Bohle was as cooperative as he had earlier been obstructionist. Despite some grumblings and occasional forays, Neurath had won. Other Nazi adventurers began to fear that Bohle's assimilation might creat a block so firm as to destroy other Nazi groups interested in foreign policy.[23]

The Rise of Ribbentrop

Bolstered by foreign success, and personal influence with Hitler, Ribbentrop now became the focus of Neurath's concern. A relatively new party member, fluent in foreign languages, and rich in worldly experience and acquaintances (gathered as a distributor of fine champagne and liquors), and slavishly reverent of Hitler, Ribbentrop inched his way into favor, volunteering his services in relations with France and Great Britain, two countries of which he claimed intimate knowledge. From this slender base, he aimed to become Hitler's advisor in foreign affairs.[24]

As early as 1933, Neurath took an instant and permanent dislike to Ribbentrop upon the latter's submission of an essay in application for the post of state secretary in the foreign office. Neurath found the memorandum amateurish and ignorant both of history and policy. Appalled by the arrogance of this "awful fellow," Neurath did not disguise his contempt. Even publicly, he ridiculed Ribbentrop's social pretensions. Among officials, his hostility soon became well known; his remarks when Ribbentrop was named ambassador were widely quoted: "Ribbentrop will soon discover that . . . it is easier to have compliments paid to one as a representative of a brand of champagne than as representative of the government of the Reich." The usually reserved Neurath could not hide his hatred for this man "who did not have even the most primitive notions about foreign and political affairs." The jovial minister burned with fury in Ribbentrop's presence. At first, he thought Ribbentrop a fool, a stock character, the rank opportunist, frequently the butt of jokes.* Gradually, Neurath reevaluated these conclusions, seeing in Ribbentrop an evil man who exercised a dangerous influence over Hitler. Ribbentrop was a *"Treiber,"* always accelerating the pace Neurath worked so hard to regularize. As Neurath worked to smooth out difficulties, Ribbentrop thrived on crises. Always either up or down in mood, he was the very opposite of the even-tempered Neurath. After 1936, Neurath took increasingly less pleasure from his position, but he clung all the more tenaciously to his post, in fear of Ribbentrop's malevolent influence.[25]

Some commentators have suggested that a more energetic Neurath might have blocked Ribbentrop's rise. But Neurath's antagonism was quite clear, and his failure lay in method, not intention or action. He opposed Ribbentrop at every turn with rational and methodical arguments, but not in the truculent and emotional style which would have been the only effective way to destroy this man who had mastered the techniques of intimidation, pounding on desks, kicking open doors, and yelling to make a point. Yet ultimately it was Hitler's inability to judge the worth of people around him which preserved Ribbentrop; indeed, Neurath's open antagonism may ironically have contributed to the chancellor's decision, for he was notoriously willing to believe good of anyone denounced by bureaucrats. Neurath tried hard enough to neutralize Ribbentrop, but the ways of an honest civil servant were no longer effective.[26]

Ribbentrop's rise began inauspiciously; in February 1933, after hearing Hitler describe his personal foreign policy, he offered his service. He traveled to London and then in December visited Paris, extending a private invitation to Minister-President Edouard Daladier to visit Germany for conversations with Hitler. No records authorizing these trips have been found; probably, Ribbentrop acted independently. As late as December, he is still not included in the large list of "experts" then active in foreign affairs, but on February 5, 1934 (after Rosenberg's disgrace), Neurath informed his ambassadors that Ribbentrop, "who enjoys the confidence of the chancellor," was destined for various private missions in France and Great Britain. The minister ordered that Ribbentrop remain in contact with the embassies and asked the ambassadors to deliver their "observations and impressions" directly to the minister. It soon seemed that Ribbentrop would suffer Rosenberg's fate. He and his wife made a poor impression and were generally dismissed as "intriguing busy-bodies." Annoyed by his pretensions, foreign diplo-

---

*On the day following the Röhm massacre and the arrests of hundreds, Neurath's secretary Kotze greeted Ribbentrop with the remark that he was glad to see he had not yet been arrested! Observers were delighted as Ribbentrop paled and fled. Neurath told the story on various occasions, obviously enjoying the joke. Information from author's interviews with Frau von Kotze, Frau von Mackensen, and Hosso von Etzdorf, May 7, July 3, July 8, and August 19, 1968.

mats called his visits "inconvenient," and Neurath remarked that Ribbentrop, although friendly with the chancellor, was "insufficiently acquainted with details of a complex problem to be able to speak with authority." Utilizing a complaint from the German ambassador in Paris, Neurath arranged for an official presidential inquiry into Ribbentrop's activities. His own contribution was a highly critical memorandum to Hindenburg which concluded: "Such agents have often been active in the past and especially since the war. Their success and hence their usefulness are generally slight." As expected, Hindenburg agreed on the inadvisability of employing "such middlemen" in the future. Neurath believed that he had now disposed of Ribbentrop for good.[27]

Hitler, however, critical of the timidity, leniency, and reticence of his professional diplomats, welcomed Ribbentrop's zeal. Yet nothing suggests any determination on his part to replace Neurath. Indeed, the next step in Ribbentrop's rise occurred accidentally. Shortly after returning from his unsuccessful trips, Ribbentrop attended a dinner hosted by Vico von Bülow-Schwante, protocol chief in the foreign office. Observing the numerous accredited diplomats at the dinner, Ribbentrop, who held no official position or title, felt mortified by his lowly place at table. Subsequently he complained to Hitler that the foreign office had deliberately slighted the chancellor's special envoy. Revealing a characteristic sensitivity to imagined slights, Ribbentrop asked Hitler to end this ignominious treatment. Subsequently, Hitler had a long conversation with Neurath, during which much of the chancellor's distrust and dislike for the foreign service rose to the surface. Neurath defended his officials, but the chancellor demanded some sign of good faith. Eventually, Neurath bowed to Hitler's desire that Ribbentrop receive a title, Commissioner for Disarmament Questions, with rank equal to that of an ambassador. The foreign minister agreed on condition that Ribbentrop be responsible to Neurath and inform the foreign office of all negotiations.[28]

As long as Ribbentrop limited himself to the complexities and nuances of that almost dead issue, he could do little damage. Neurath was sure he would soon tire of the tedious work; to make sure, the minister assigned the reliable Erich Kordt to Ribbentrop's staff to prevent the new commissioner from pursuing an independent policy. The foreign office expected that Ribbentrop would quickly demonstrate his incompetence. Bülow cautioned diplomats not to improve any of his reports, for "the total foolishness of the man must clearly be manifested." But in spite of these "traps," and Ribbentrop's obvious incapacity for diplomatic service, he was not dismissed but was invited increasingly to conversations with Hitler who warned him not "to tell a soul in the foreign office."[29]

Although the official announcement of Ribbentrop's position emphasized the limited nature of his work, he proclaimed that he would function as a "traveling ambassador," offsetting the staid officials of the foreign service. Thus, he demanded to see all telegrams and dispatches. Bülow arranged that he receive disarmament documents, but specifically instructed officials not to include "secret matters, nor those items normally discussed at the meetings of departmental heads." In one communication, Ribbentrop was described as a sort of liaison between the chancellery and the foreign office; he should be received with courtesy, but given only limited information. But Ribbentrop insisted that he was not "just another official, but the Führer's representative in the foreign office," and continued to pester Neurath for permission to view all documents. The minister steadfastly refused. This firm but unspectacular opposition did not deter Ribbentrop, who found new sources for complaint, such as his demand to rank above all ambassadors and be equal to the state secretary. On all these matters, Neurath procrastinated, convinced that within a short time, "the complete stupidity of this new man in the field of foreign policy would be demonstrated clear as day."[30]

Impatient, Ribbentrop tried another approach. In the late summer of 1934, he set up his own office in the former palace of the Prussian Crown Prince (Wilhelmstrasse 64), directly across from the foreign office. Originally, this private organization numbered thirteen workers; by the end of 1935, more than thirty. Many commentators have erroneously regarded the Ribbentrop Bureau as Hitler's special foreign office, created to implement a policy at odds with that of the old diplomats. But consistent with the conqueror state, Hitler had neither ordered the creation of such an office nor designated any special tasks for it to accomplish. Only in 1936, after Ribbentrop had already won a position of importance as Hitler's confidant, did the bureau itself become important, and even then it served only as its chief's vehicle for personal advancement, providing him with a place of power within the Nazi structure. When Ribbentrop finally became foreign minister in 1938, he promoted only a few of his personnel to the office across the street. Then his famous bureau faded into oblivion.[31]

In the meantime, the bureau pursued no organized policy. In late 1935, when Hermann von Raumer became affiliated with it, he found the place in total confusion. His account bears repeating:

> October 15, 1935: I feel myself fatally unhappy. No one in the "Department" has his own room, or even his own secretary. Everyone just sits around, smoking, gossiping, and waiting for the boss. I was clearly informed that there was no "bureaucracy" here, and therefore no office file, since according to Ribbentrop that has been the start of every bureaucracy. If we need a particular document, two large Renaissance trunks full of papers are emptied out on the floor, and all the secretaries and adjutants look through the pile until they find the letter.[32]

Clearly such an office could assume no permanent role in the determination of German foreign policy.

Another incident is illustrative. Raumer was once awakened by a 2:00 A.M. telephone call from Ribbentrop, who asked for the length of time it would take the German ambassador in China to reach Berlin. Without knowing the reasons behind this request, Raumer and the Ribbentrop Bureau hastily assembled the information, which Ribbentrop delivered to Hitler at noon of the same day. Shortly thereafter, Neurath was called to the chancellery, where Hitler informed him: "Look, Herr von Neurath, this is how the Ribbentrop Bureau operates. You told me that Ambassador Trautmann would need six weeks for a trip to Berlin. Ribbentrop has just told me: 'I have carefully examined the facts; he can be here in ten days.' "[33] This insignificant incident reveals Ribbentrop's role; unlike the naysayers of the foreign office, he and his staff encouraged Hitler to regard any hesitation as timid and disloyal traits of the professional diplomats; Ribbentrop's staff would carry out immediately Hitler's slightest whim.

The failure of Ribbentrop's first official trip as Commissioner for Disarmament Questions, in November 1934, bolstered Neurath's confidence. The responsible British officials treated Ribbentrop coolly and requested the German ambassador to terminate such visits. "Apparently Ribbentrop himself was totally perplexed by the failure of his mission," Ambassador Hoesch wrote, in accounting for the reasons:

> As you know, the English become ever more intractable when someone tries to force something upon them, when they don't want [to discuss] it. This special visit of Herr von Ribbentrop fell in ever-increasing fashion into that category. I think it is impossible for any such attempts at direct conversation through the person of Herr von Ribbentrop to be useful.[34]

On the basis of Hoesch's complaint, Neurath angrily wrote Hitler:

> You asked me last night whether I had received reports from Ribbentrop and news of his visit to England. I had to deny both. I have just received this enclosed letter from Ambassador Hoesch, and I feel obligated to forward it to you at once. From reports in the English press and from private correspondence which has reached me from England, I already had received the impression that Ribbentrop's trip had been a complete disaster. This impression is confirmed by the enclosed letter of Herr von Hoesch. I believe that there should be no repetition of this visit, at least not in the near future.

Despite this strong letter, Ribbentrop's reputation with Hitler remained high. His own account of his visit was characteristically boastful.[35]

Neurath sought still other opportunities to confront Ribbentrop. Three months later, when the commissioner informed him that with Hitler's approval, he would hereafter send a representative to all foreign office briefing sessions, Neurath reacted forcefully:

> I must categorically refuse to keep you regularly informed of informational instructions which I or the state secretary give to the press, excepting, of course, on all questions of disarmament and related items, all material of which comes to you regularly.
>
> At this time, I would like to mention that recently you have no longer found it necessary to keep me informed, as the chancellor specifically ordered, of the activities you undertake at his instruction in the area of foreign policy. As yet I have not brought this to the attention of the chancellor, since generally he had informed me himself of his instructions to you. Nevertheless, I must remark in this matter that it is not the desire of the chancellor to separate individual areas of foreign policy from the responsible body of the

foreign office which I head. Even the disarmament question cannot be handled isolated from general policy.

It is therefore vitally necessary that you keep me regularly oriented; this condition was explicit at the time you were made responsible to my office. May I request that you return from time to time to that usual practice?[36]

Once again, this strong letter was to no avail. Although Ribbentrop had as yet achieved nothing tangible in foreign policy, and his predictions of Western reactions to German activities had been uniformly wrong, Hitler was pleased by his optimistic reports stressing European desires for friendship with the new Germany. Because these reports differed from Neurath's somber evaluations, Hitler jubilantly remarked that Ribbentrop was the only man who told him the truth. On February 25, 1935, not four weeks after Neurath's critical letter, Hitler named Ribbentrop Commissioner for Foreign Policy Questions, attached to the staff of the Führer's deputy. With this appointment, Ribbentrop emerged as the leading Nazi in foreign policy. Apparently, there was little that Neurath could do to stop him.[37]

Bolstered by this new sign of the Führer's confidence, Ribbentrop resolved to clarify his position within the state and the party. In March 1935, he asked Hitler to appoint him state secretary in the foreign office. Bernhard von Bülow, who had held that position since early 1930, was considered by most Nazis the most determined opponent to Hitler's government. Openly distrustful of the party leaders, Bülow had long recognized his exposed and dangerous position; moreover, he was not in good health. Ribbentrop, believing Neurath's position somewhat beyond his reach, was apparently willing to settle for second in command. At first, Hitler seemed favorably inclined. Later that month, when Sir John Simon and Anthony Eden visited Berlin, the chancellor refused to permit Bülow to participate in the talks, but included Ribbentrop. Shortly after the conference, Ribbentrop began to describe himself as the Führer's Commissioner for Foreign Policy. This produced several reactions. Alfred Rosenberg strongly protested to Hitler, citing Ribbentrop's limited field of authority, and Neurath rejected Ribbentrop's desire to be state secretary. The foreign minister described to Hitler how the appointment would disrupt the internal workings of the foreign office:

> If I have to take charge of all the petty details, from personnel to daily routine matters which are the special charge of the state secretary then I shall have no time to be foreign minister. If you appoint this total amateur, who has no ideas at all on how the office is run, it would mean that in effect I would have to serve as state secretary, while Ribbentrop would become foreign minister. I could not tolerate such a condition.

In essence, Neurath demanded that Hitler choose between himself and Ribbentrop.[38]

In this case, as in so many others, the chancellor refused to make a choice or clarify the situation. Without naming Ribbentrop either state secretary or *Reichsleiter* (the highest category of party official), Hitler gave him another new title and task. On June 1, 1935 he became Extraordinary Plenipotentiary and Ambassador of the German Reich on Special Mission, and was ordered to head the German delegation for the forthcoming naval talks with Great Britain. The details surrounding this appointment are not entirely clear. Although the initiative came from Hitler, Neurath accepted it because he and the diplomats had already predicted the uselessness of such talks. In particular, Hoesch in London believed the British would not negotiate seriously so soon after Germany had, through the restoration of conscription, flagrantly violated the Versailles Treaty. Neurath thought Britain would never settle the naval question without German concessions in such areas as an air pact. Hitler disagreed. "If you and Herr von Hoesch," he once yelled at Neurath, "do not believe that such an agreement can be reached, then I know someone who does believe it—Ribbentrop." Within a day, Ribbentrop was named to head the delegation.[39]

At first stunned by the nomination, Neurath eventually saw it as almost desirable. The German program of demands had already been drawn up; the technical aspects could not be influenced by "a champagne salesman who knows nothing of naval armaments." To keep the foreign office free from accusations of noncooperation, Neurath personally persuaded Erich Kordt to remain liaison officer on Ribbentrop's staff. "Even though no great success is expected," he told Kordt, "we must avoid the danger of being suspected of sabotage." Still Neurath was not going to permit Ribbentrop to enlarge his privileges. He once again refused Ribbentrop's familiar demand to see all the documents, and to the latter's angry reply that such refusal violated Hitler's wishes, Neurath reiterated his previous stand on pertinent access. He concluded abruptly:

> I take advantage of this opportunity to call your attention to two points: (1) In your letter of appointment of last year, it is clearly stated that you are responsible to me as foreign minister. I know of no alteration in that decree. (2) For months now, I have heard nothing about your foreign policy activities, either orally or in written reports.[40]

But all Neurath's attempts to bring Ribbentrop into line were upset when, to the surprise and chagrin of the foreign office, the British greeted Ribbentrop's arrogant manner with conciliatory speeches and, after a short period of negotiations, met all the German demands. A triumphant Ribbentrop returned with British permission to tear up the naval sections of the Versailles Treaty; Germany could build a modern fleet, as long as it did not exceed 35 percent of Great Britain's. Hitler was jubilant; his instinct that Britain sought German friendship had proven more correct than the expert evaluation of his foreign office. Ribbentrop, the despised outsider, had brought home the first real destruction of the circle of hostile forces surrounding Germany. No wonder Hitler lorded it over the diplomats, and many years later still recalled the consternation which reigned in the Wilhelmstrasse when Ribbentrop won this important prize.[41]

This success marked the turning point in Ribbentrop's career. Among his party comrades, he was hailed as "the greatest diplomatic genius we have in the foreign

CHALLENGES TO NEURATH'S LEADERSHIP: 1933–1937 133

service." In the following year, his every move won approbation and the size and importance of his organization soared. Convinced that Ribbentrop would certainly become foreign minister now, many party members flocked to his standard. By 1936, the Ribbentrop Bureau employed more than 150 workers. Public and foreign recognition followed. For the first time, Neurath had to admit failure in controlling a man who now posed a serious threat to the unified conduct of policy. Within a short time, all Berlin spoke of the antagonism, and even outsiders alluded to the fact that "Ribbentrop's genius found little appreciation in the eyes of Neurath and Bülow." The diplomats redoubled their efforts to discredit the upstart, pointing out that his success in London had been an isolated phenomenon; his activities in Paris and elsewhere were spectacular failures. But with unlimited funds at his disposal, and the apparent confidence of the chancellor, Ribbentrop seemed immune to their criticism. Some diplomats privately advised that the foreign office come to terms with the new man, but Neurath chose to preserve his relationship with the party through Bohle. He would have nothing to do with Ribbentrop.[42]

Long convinced that Hitler would eventually recognize Ribbentrop's incompetence, Neurath believed stronger resistance would only jeopardize the foreign office program. Had the minister been any more antagonistic towards Hitler's friend and new advisor, most contemporary observers believed it would have been the professional diplomats and not Ribbentrop who would have suffered. As it was, nearly four years after the triumph of National Socialism in Germany, the foreign office remained uncoordinated with the system, and unenthusiastic about new directions. Despite intense pressure from party sources, its personnel was still a loyal and compact force. All of the rival organizations had failed to destroy this unity, but now Neurath and the foreign office faced its most severe test, as a combination of Ribbentrop's successes, and a series of unexpected deaths, began to take their toll.[43]

CHAPTER

10

NEURATH AND THE PERSONNEL CRISIS: 1936–1937

From the beginning of 1933, the foreign office had been handicapped by the new chancellor's general dislike of diplomats and specifically of certain men in leading positions both abroad and in the central Berlin office. Before the new government was two months old, the party began regularly gathering personnel information on this "society of conspirators." These reports ranged from accounts of "Jewish influence upon the local consulates," to individual denunciations, including even evaluations of the foreign minister:

> Very well qualified diplomat of the old school. Monarchist, Protestant, but not energetic enough to rule with a strong hand in the foreign office (especially in the light of the many Jews who swarm around the office), or to carry out the remedies we require there.[1]

Nevertheless, no purge of foreign office personnel, like those of other ministries and organizations, occurred. As late as 1938, the homogeneous group of trained experts who ran the foreign service in 1933 remained in control. Of the nearly ninety ranking diplomats stationed abroad, only two resigned or were removed for political reasons. Fewer than a half-dozen "outsiders" were appointed to posts abroad, and of these, Ribbentrop was the only high party official who succeeded in holding or advancing his position. More significantly, only a few of the nearly 100 higher officials in the central office were replaced; in only one case during the five years of Neurath's administration did political or party pressures force such a removal. Prompted by party criticism, three others left voluntarily, but in general Hitler left the personnel politics of the Wilhelmstrasse in Neurath's hands. General sentiment among diplomats, still widespread today, attributed this remarkable record to the minister's stubborn persistence; even unfriendly critics have conceded Neurath this success in the face of persistent tension and an atmosphere of suspicion and criticism.[2]

The first serious threat to the integrity of the office came with the passing of the April 1933 anti-Semitic legislation, under the guise of "restoring the civil service." Providing for the immediate retirement of all Jewish and politically undesirable individuals, this measure aimed primarily at the higher officials. Neurath ignored the new law, claiming that foreign service appointments were the sole prerogative of the president, and not subject to civil service rules, but he was powerless to protect his officials from SA terror. Shortly after the appearance of the anti-Semitic law, Brown Shirts forced entrance into the home of Consul General Moritz Schlesinger. Called home from his office, Schlesinger was brutally beaten, his apartment ransacked, and his wife hospitalized in nervous shock. Although Neurath demanded punishment for the guilty parties and indicated no intention of removing Schlesinger, a sixteen-year veteran in the foreign office, the victimized official eventually resigned.[3]

A more organized threat was Hitler's decision to assign to the foreign office Josias Erbprinz of Waldeck and Pyrmont, SS Gruppenführer and special friend of Göring. Reluctantly Neurath gave Waldeck a minor position in the personnel bureau, while privately assuring officials that it was a meaningless gesture. Still, Waldeck's mere presence was threatening. Not all were as openly courageous as Bülow who refused to receive Waldeck in his SS uniform. When the prince ingenuously replied that his civilian clothes were unavailable until after Easter, Bülow reportedly replied: "So be it. I will receive him only after Easter." But Waldeck's presence terrified many, and in two cases, he was responsible for the resignation of officials of Jewish descent. Neurath's protests over flagrant intervention in the personnel policies of his office were unsuccessful.[4]

Still, the minister seemed relieved to have weathered the storm with only three sacrifices. But when Waldeck next demanded the right to participate in the selection of future officials, citing recent orders from the ministry of the interior concerning the removal of undesirable elements, Neurath reacted forcefully:

> Thank you for relaying to me a copy of Minister Frick's letter of July 14. In regard to the execution of the law for the restoration of the professional civil service, I must question the right of the minister of the interior to prescribe for my ministry. As you know, I specifically discuss all personnel questions with the chancellor, and during my last visit to Munich, I received full support for all the measures I had undertaken.

But Waldeck was undeterred, causing Neurath to return sarcastically to the same subject in November:

> Now that the Erbprinz of Waldeck has brought forward his objections to the planned personnel changes, he has fully executed his duty. I alone, as the responsible minister, must make the decision whether or not there are objective and legal reasons in individual cases to warrant the personnel changes, in spite of his objections. In all these instances, I have had discussions with the chancellor, before forwarding the nominations to the president.

Frustrated in these attempts, Prince Waldeck bribed a secretary to obtain incriminating information on certain officials. Angrily, Neurath demanded from Himmler some explanation for Waldeck's disgraceful conduct. Within a few weeks, the prince ceased to appear in the foreign office. Such attempts to break down the service from within failed as long as Neurath was present.[5]

Indeed, the foreign office congratulated itself on the relatively quiet way it had survived the rise of the Nazis. Amid rumors that the party planned to purge the service, Neurath and his advisors believed they could save the official structure: with the cooperation of some friendly party men, sufficient numbers of the professional diplomats would join the party "en bloc." In June 1933, Neurath informed all members of the service that they were free to apply for party membership if their consciences permitted such action. Significantly, neither Neurath, State Secretary Bülow, nor any of the minister-directors or higher officials in the Berlin office became members. Neurath was not actively proselytizing; he made no effort to compile information on which diplomats had joined the party, and as late as 1938 such lists were not available.[6]

The strategy was successful. In August 1933, Bülow noted to a foreign diplomat that although there had been numerous routine changes recently, "not one single party functionary or member has been named German representative abroad or even to a significant post in the foreign office." He was confident that the chancellor had decided to see policy "exclusively carried out by members of the German foreign service. If the situation were different, he would also not find [Bülow] in this room." To those seeking to use party affiliations in order to gain appointments, Bülow was blunt:

> We ignore party suggestions to enroll individual persons in the foreign service. The foreign office personnel questions, when they arise, are personally discussed between the minister and the chancellor. The chancellor has, moreover, determined that in principle the foreign service will carry on with its existing personnel without additions.[7]

The independence of the foreign service continued under strong attack; in September 1933, Neurath's office obtained a copy of a confidential proposal from Rudolf Hess's staff, calling for the creation of a special state secretary (Bohle) to supervise the nazification (*Gleichschaltung*) of the office. Rejecting the idea that the diplomatic corps could be captured either by installing a few party members or by winning converts, this report urged a broad effort "to anchor the spirit and *Weltanschauung* of the party deep in the foreign policy and bureaucracy of the foreign office," so that mutual ties would unite diplomats and politicians. Aware of these pressures, and desiring to accommodate the party without surrendering the independence of his ministry, Neurath instructed the personnel division to form liaisons with Ernst Bohle, whom he regarded as a "safe" Nazi who would influence Hess and keep extremists like Waldeck out of the office. Bohle's attitude pleased Neurath when they met in Hamburg on December 26, and the foreign office clearly got the better of their subsequent relationship. Although Bohle boasted that "our influence on the foreign office grows from week to week," personnel officials found him uninterested in interfering with the staff or its procedures, and willing to content himself with recruiting diplomats for the party. Through Bohle the ban on admittance to the party was lifted, and Neurath believed that by means of token converts, the service could avoid future attacks.* The foreign office seemed securely off-limits for purges, and in January 1934, one chancellery official complained that in spite of strong efforts, only a small number of undesirable diplomats had been removed.[8]

Then in mid-June 1934, Alfred Rosenberg charged that foreign office personnel were "sabotaging" the chancellor's orders. Hitler refused to take action, telling Rosenberg: "I do not want just now a fight with the old man [President Hindenburg, who was seriously ill], for I do not want to embitter his last days. Later, however, the whole camarilla over there [in the foreign office] must be driven out with one blow." Rosenberg had to content himself with anticipating the "very sudden and bitter awakening" which Hitler planned for the diplomats. But even after the president's death on August 1, 1934, Hitler refrained from a foreign service purge. He was well informed that within the foreign office the prevalent view, fostered even by Neurath, regarded National Socialism as a temporary aberration which would destroy itself; yet Hitler also knew that the proliferation of unofficial persons and groups in foreign affairs, while giving an appearance of dynamism, had actually paralyzed policy making. The chancellor needed Neurath, and thus he honored the foreign minister's insistence on protection for his staff, even as Hitler continued to express his dislike of them. He singled out the leading diplomats abroad (especially the ambassadors in London and Paris) and the principal officers in Berlin (especially Bülow, Köpke, and Meyer) for particular abuse, but made no move to touch their positions. No serious disruption occurred in the staff or the recruitment of career diplomats in these early years.[9]

Then at the end of 1935, Neurath faced a serious personnel crisis. Suddenly, the foreign office found it increasingly difficult to gain Hitler's approval for even routine appointments and changes. The chief of personnel complained of the "growing mistrust of the foreign office," and a resultant decline in morale. He suggested making minor concessions, but Bülow was convinced that concessions were not the answer and was reluctant to sacrifice any official. In the summer, lists prepared for Bohle's routine examination were returned with the comment that the party believed "many of the gentlemen were unsuited for the anticipated positions." No specifics were forthcoming. In July and again in August, Neurath

---

*This protection did not, of course, always work. A most instructive case is that of Walter Poensgen. Having written a casual statement early in February 1933 unflattering to the Nazi party, he was denounced by Goebbels nearly a year later. Poensgen made the mistake of denying having written the letter, and when Goebbels produced a photocopy, Neurath could do nothing but accept Poensgen's resignation. In an interview with the author on July 4, 1968, Poensgen insisted that Neurath had acted correctly and had extended his protection over him even afterwards. "I am terribly sorry," Poensgen quoted Neurath as telling him, "but what on earth could have prompted you to write such a letter?" Then correcting himself at once, Neurath added: "But never mind, be happy! Now you can enjoy life as a private citizen and be out of this rat's nest."

requested additional opinions from the party; when these failed to arrive, he proceeded to make appointments on his own. By September, the personnel office was in an "intolerable condition," and its head complained of potentially dangerous delays in some important appointments. Matters were further complicated by Hitler's decree of September 24, 1935, making all appointments subject to approval by Rudolf Hess before submission to the chancellor. Distressed by the backlog, Neurath asked the personnel bureau to draw up an exhaustive exposition, and he requested a personal appointment with Hitler to discuss the issue. Also, in late 1935, the office was engaged in a long-planned reorganization of its central bureau, entailing numerous personnel changes, especially within the highest ranks. To protect his officials, Neurath would have to secure some clarification of his powers.[10]

Ribbentrop's Ambitions

During these same crucial months, Ribbentrop once again became an active factor. Despite his triumph in the English-German naval accord, Ribbentrop was dissatisfied because the victory had brought no concrete benefits. He remained a sort of hybrid, the chancellor's personal advisor, who enjoyed neither official nor party rank equal to his ambition. In the fall of 1935, he resurrected the idea of his appointment as state secretary. His new proposal was nothing short of a complete reform of the foreign office, with the state secretary becoming the single source of authority. He would head the personnel office, chair a central operating committee (composed of representatives from other state and party organizations, including the APA and AO) and supervise the daily running of the office. Responsible to this state secretary, an undersecretary would handle the remaining political, economic, legal, and press divisions. The foreign minister would become a figurehead, a member of a foreign policy council, along with Hess, Goebbels, Göring, Blomberg, Schacht, and, of course, Ribbentrop.[11]

Rumors abounded that Ribbentrop would soon become the real authority in the foreign office. When State Secretary Lammers relayed Hitler's "urgent wish" that Ribbentrop be rewarded with an appointment as state secretary, Neurath replied with a formal letter of resignation, dated October 25, 1935. This letter must be quoted at length, since its absence from the official publications of documents provides a distorted picture of Neurath's relationship to Ribbentrop:

> I have had abundant time to consider the appropriateness and practicality of this appointment [Neurath wrote to Hitler]. To my deep regret, I have come to the conclusion that for technical and personal reasons, it is impossible for me to agree to this plan. For one thing, I do not believe that Herr von Ribbentrop, even with the help of trained officials, is able to fill (in a manner required by the country's interest) this position, which demands an accurate knowledge of international relations, of the administrative machinery, and of the available personnel.
>
> Then too, I fear that Herr von Ribbentrop will not be able essentially to

alter . . . the personnel policy which I have followed in the interest of both party and state. Finally, however, for personal reasons, it is impossible for me to cooperate with Herr von Ribbentrop in any fruitful work, such as is necessary and mandatory for official business between the state secretary and the minister. Since my person ought never, under any circumstances, to be a hindrance in the implementation of your views, I hereby resign the position first given to me by the late President von Hindenburg and renewed by yourself, and I request that you release me from my official duties as soon as possible.[12]

Years of frustration exploded in this renunciation of his life's work, demonstrating Neurath's determination to oppose Ribbentrop's rise. Surprisingly, the move worked. On November 4, 1935, Neurath met with Hitler, who rejected his resignation, agreeing on Ribbentrop's unsuitability for the foreign office. There, however, the conciliatory friendliness stopped, as Hitler vigorously attacked the foreign service. "The office has refused to cooperate," he claimed. "It stands outside the party, refuses to understand the policies of the Führer, and continues to make difficulties everywhere." Warming to his theme, Hitler accused Neurath of protecting scoundrels and traitors, claiming to have been told by "an old party member and active diplomat," that along with many other officials, Gerhard Köpke, the prestigious minister-director of the West European desk, had expressed strong reservations about German policy and "uttered disparaging remarks concerning his special commissioner and ambassador, Joachim von Ribbentrop." While Neurath stoutly defended his friend of more than thirty years, the meeting ended without reconciliation. Hitler demanded a complete overhaul of the service, beginning with the state secretary. Refusing that, Neurath did promise to investigate its "loyalty."[13]

Neurath's alarm was the greater because of recently increased pressures to remove those Jewish officials whom he had succeeded in protecting. Ever since the Nuremberg Laws (September 15, 1935) had deprived Jews of citizenship, Neurath knew that he could no longer retain them. Under the guise of reorganizing the central offices, he planned to retire the exposed officials, with arrangements by which they would receive full pensions in foreign currency, thus enabling them to emigrate if they chose. The highest official concerned was Minister-Director Meyer, of the Russian and East European division. Now that Hitler had attacked Köpke, no matter how harmless his actual remarks had been, Neurath knew that sooner or later, some zealous Nazi would uncover the Jewish grandmother in the minister-director's family tree. So Köpke too would have to go. Early in 1936, both Meyer and Köpke, Neurath's closest advisors on European affairs, and the principal designers of the policy to which he had hitherto adhered, left the foreign service. Successfully camouflaging their departure so that neither suffered public exposure or financial inconvenience, Neurath could not so easily replace their firm loyalty and expert advice.[14]

The minister's obviously isolated and weakened position remained the talk of the capital, frequently centering on the "opposition between Neurath and Ribbentrop." Hitler spent more and more time with Ribbentrop, and during the discussion preceding the remilitarization of the Rhineland, the latter was always present, much to the chagrin of Neurath and Hassell who considered his behavior shameless. In all these talks, the slavish Ribbentrop merely echoed Hitler. In a particularly aggravating meeting, when the chancellor described three alternatives in such a biased way that a child could see his preference for the third, Ribbentrop startled the diplomats with a well-timed outburst of emotion: "The third, mein Führer," he gushed, "the third."[15]

When the League of Nations Council of Thirteen, meeting in London, invited Germany to send a delegation to discuss possible condemnation for the Rhineland remilitarization, Neurath was forced to accept Ribbentrop as the head of that group. Foreign office personnel were openly critical. "Herr von Ribbentrop," Bülow told the French ambassador, "has only an extremely superficial knowledge of France." Frustrated by being reduced to "simple organs of execution," the professional diplomats feared that Ribbentrop would destroy all their recent accomplishments. Hitler had his own reasons for the appointment. As he told the mayor of Hamburg, while Ribbentrop might someday become foreign minister, "first he would have to earn his spurs, like all his other collaborators." Ribbentrop was going to London, Hitler said, not primarily for the League meeting, but for personal talks with leading British statesmen. Relying upon Ribbentrop's conviction that London secretly welcomed the move into the Rhineland, Hitler aimed at winning the British away from their dependence upon a moribund French policy. "Ribbentrop is supposed to give some backbone to the English statesmen," Hitler said. "England has no idea how strong she might be, if only she would will it."[16]

But Ribbentrop's mission was as disastrous as his predictions of British motives had been erroneous. In the arrogant style which always so infuriated foreigners, Ribbentrop failed to convince anyone of German sincerity; a scant few hours after his presentation, the council found Germany guilty of violating the Locarno Treaty. On the next day, the other Locarno powers (including Italy and Britain) drew up a detailed and (for Germany) totally unacceptable set of proposals, calling for, among other things, immediate troop withdrawals from the Rhineland. Within three days of his arrival in London, Ribbentrop flew back to Berlin for consultations. Angrily, Neurath rejected the new proposals, sharing the view of many in Berlin that a more moderate approach to the British might have gained real dividends. He made no secret of his opinion that Ribbentrop was to blame.[17]

Nevertheless, Hitler again delegated Ribbentrop to deliver the formal German reply. In these matters, Ribbentrop communicated directly with the chancellor, consulting the foreign office only incidentally. His sparse London reports concluded with reference to "exhaustive telephone conversations" with the chancellor. Neurath finally requested Ambassador Hoesch to spy on Ribbentrop if necessary in order to get the information which was being transmitted over a special scrambler link between London and the chancellery. But despite Ribbentrop's bravado, he had not impressed the British, and no breakthrough in

German policy occurred. Neurath could still hope that Ribbentrop would reveal his incompetence by failing to deliver the British friendship he had promised.[18]

In the midst of these negotiations, on April 10, 1936, Ambassador Leopold von Hoesch suddenly died. Hitler had long considered him an obstructionist, once even calling him "Germany's greatest enemy." In an unusual gesture of support for this official whom Ribbentrop and the chancellor despised, Neurath personally attended the funeral and delivered a brief graveside eulogy. Hoesch's death closely followed that of the German ambassador to France, Roland Köster, and was accompanied in the same month by the retirement of the seriously ill personnel chief, Werner Freiherr von Grünau. Thus within four months, Neurath had lost his top two advisors within the office (Meyer and Köpke), his personnel director, and the two most important ambassadors of the foreign service. The most serious breach in the monolith of the diplomats had been opened not by the Nazis, but by death.[19]

With an uneasy eye on recent events, the foreign minister feared that Hitler would propose Ribbentrop for one of the available vacancies. But during the early months of 1936, conscious of his failures, Ribbentrop brooded over his apparent fall from favor with the chancellor, even as Neurath concerned himself with the closeness of the two. In an attention-getting maneuver, Ribbentrop began pushing for closer ties with Japan, as the first step in a grand alliance of all anti-Communist states, the future Anti-Comintern Pact. In the spring of 1936, Ribbentrop preached a Japanese alliance at every opportunity. Once, after Neurath had finished briefing Hitler on general foreign problems, Ribbentrop interrupted to point out that the minister had failed to mention prospects of a Japanese alliance. Shortly afterwards, when recalling the discussion, Neurath ruefully admitted that he had lost his temper at that point. "Enough of that," he had exploded at Ribbentrop. "Such planning is not at all in our self-interest. Please spare us your opinions on that boring subject."[20]

Within a short time, however, Neurath learned that talks were underway and that the Japanese believed Ribbentrop had authorization for the discussions. Against this background of events, Neurath apparently concluded that to designate Ribbentrop Ambassador to the Court of St. James's would remove the interloper from the scene. Thus he told the chancellor that with Ribbentrop's special knowledge of the British, he would make a splendid choice. To others he was blunt: "After three months in London," he told Papen, "Ribbentrop will be done for. They can't stand him there and we shall be rid of him for good and all." Ribbentrop saw the inherent dangers and as rumors about such an appointment intensified, he strove to consolidate his relations with Hitler. Under no circumstances would he leave Berlin without being absolutely sure of his power.[21]

This intention explains his decision to clarify his own position vis-à-vis Rosenberg, the APA, and the other Nazi leaders. Writing to Hitler on May 11, 1936, Ribbentrop indicated his final conviction: "In view of the nature of my talents, I can undertake useful work in the future for the Führer in the area of foreign policy, the reorganization of the foreign service, and the diplomatic training program of the party, only if I become a *Reichsleiter*." Ribbentrop told Hitler that such an appointment would free him from Rosenberg's constant complaint that he was exceeding his responsibilities; he could no longer afford to initiate "illegal foreign policy" which other Nazi leaders could challenge at every opportunity. "Such controversies in the last years have certainly absorbed more than a half of all my efforts," he wrote. "While professional disputes can strengthen one's efforts, in the long run a person of my temperament undertakes these personal struggles within our own ranks only at a serious damage to his own health."

Ribbentrop now insisted that his value as a special advisor could be maintained "only through legitimization of his position within the party." Should Hitler not make this appointment, Ribbentrop requested release from all his functions and permission to enter the SS and work with Heinrich Himmler.[22] For reasons still unclear, Hitler refused to elevate Ribbentrop to *Reichsleiter*, but assured him that no other advisor would replace him if he took the London position. During the second week of June, Hitler and Neurath had several conversations, following which the chancellor indicated that Ribbentrop would succeed Hoesch. Ribbentrop was despondent.

Then on June 21, Bernhard von Bülow, the astute and experienced state secretary, unexpectedly died. Nazi leaders did not hide their jubilation "since Bülow was an absolute enemy of the Führer's policies." Ribbentrop himself said that death had claimed, in the persons of Bülow and the German ambassadors in London and Paris, "the three greatest enemies of Germany."[23] In part, Ribbentrop's glee arose from his awareness that exile in London could now be avoided. Immediately, he resurrected the idea of becoming state secretary and reforming the foreign service. Many thought he would now receive this appointment, and no doubt Ribbentrop importuned Hitler, but here as before, his ambitions foundered on Neurath's opposition. Under no conditions would the foreign minister accept him in his office, suggesting that Ribbentrop's proper place was London, working for the British-German friendship he had so long advocated. Characteristically, Hitler procrastinated. On July 21, after tracking him down at the Bayreuth festival, Neurath raised the issue. Hitler agreed that Ribbentrop should be named ambassador. After Neurath left, Kordt found Ribbentrop locked in his room, sulking over his coming disgrace. Such behavior soon earned an unhoped-for success. On July 24, Hitler signed a special letter of appointment, naming Ribbentrop ambassador, while ordering him to continue all his other functions. He was to engage actively in creating a German-Japanese treaty, without involving the foreign office, and he could preserve the Ribbentrop Bureau. In addition, Hitler stipulated that "in *all* these positions, he would be directly subordinate and responsible to me."[24]

Two days later, a triumphant Ribbentrop relayed the Führer's instructions to Neurath, informing him that as ambassador he would pursue a totally independent program under Hitler's direction, aimed at improving German-British relations. Neurath was stunned. In the presence of his son, also a member of the foreign service home on a visit, the foreign minister flew into an uncharacteristic rage: "See how much influence I have! None at all." Despairingly, he described his declining power with Hitler; his advice and opinions went unsought, and when given were ignored. In party circles, he was regarded as a clown (a *Hans Wurst*).[25]

Attempted Resignation

Clearly Neurath would not tolerate the appointment under the stipulated conditions. From his estate the next day, Neurath wrote the chancellor that such regulations would "deprive me of any influence on one of the most important aspects of German foreign policy" and destroy forever the unity required for the successful implementation of foreign policy. Neurath asked for permission to resign:

> I can no longer bear the responsibility for such conditions. I know of no other way to restore this unity of leadership, except that you yourself take over nominally the foreign ministry, and simultaneously entrust to a state secretary acceptable to you the technical running of its administration.
>
> In any case, I myself can no longer remain at the head of the foreign office, and therefore repeat my request of last fall, to relieve me of my post as foreign minister of the Reich, no later than at the time Herr von Ribbentrop assumes his position as ambassador in London. It will not be difficult to find some plausible explanation for this move.

Neurath concluded with sincere assurances that his resignation stemmed from his conviction that "any division of responsibility in the leadership of foreign policy must damage the Reich." He felt compelled to add: "Even if I am no longer a cabinet minister, should you desire, I am always at your disposal with my advice and my lengthy experience in the field of foreign policy." On the basis of recent experiences, however, Neurath was sure this gesture would remain only a polite closing formula in a letter.[26]

Neurath expected that his resignation would be accepted; Hitler, however, found the move both surprising and unacceptable. With his characteristic distaste for deciding personnel matters, he ordered the matter shelved. "He always hoped," one party official noted, "that personnel questions would work themselves out." Some of Hitler's friends guessed that the chancellor's appointment of Ribbentrop to London was in anticipation that "Neurath would reach retirement age in 1937 [*sic*], and one could then expect Ribbentrop to become foreign minister in the coming year." Thus, the decision could be safely delayed.[27]

In a long talk with Hitler on August 10, during the Olympic games, Neurath repeated his strong desire to retire. According to Baroness von Neurath's memoir of her husband, "Hitler rejected this appeal with the remark that he could not dispense with Neurath, and had full confidence in him and would carry out his wishes." The resulting decision seemed a triumph for the minister. Ribbentrop was named ambassador and ordered to take up the post in the immediate future;

previous conditions mentioning direct responsibility to Hitler and independence from foreign office control were removed. Only Ribbentrop's special title, as plenipotentiary, distinguished him from other German colleagues. Still, the chancellor preserved Ribbentrop's role as "special advisor" and permitted the continued existence of his Bureau. Neurath's victory, though limited, satisfied him. With his rival gone from Berlin, he hoped the Nazi organization would return to insignificance. Foreign diplomats awaited the outcome of this long-smoldering battle:

> The duel between [Neurath] and Ribbentrop is common knowledge, and in Germany everyone is waiting to see the outcome, now that Neurath has succeeded in sending his opponent to work in a field which he himself described as the best for the development of German policy. Any success for Ribbentrop in London—which by the way is most improbable—would be a failure for Neurath. The latter knows it and is ready to use any weapon to prevent it.[28]

Among Ribbentrop's followers, there was general consternation, and all spoke about the fact that Ribbentrop "went reluctantly to London."

Further, the installation of Bohle to a position within the foreign office probably represents in some fashion another victory for the bureaucrats, that is, the old school diplomats, Welczek-Neurath. It appears that the psychological moment for the appointment of Ribbentrop as foreign minister has passed.[29]

But unfortunately, Neurath had not destroyed either Ribbentrop or the Bureau. Even before leaving Berlin, circumstances beyond the minister's control prepared for Ribbentrop a victory greater than any he had before enjoyed: successful negotiation and conclusion of the Anti-Comintern Pact between Japan and Germany. Thus, although he subsequently failed as a diplomat in London, Ribbentrop was above the criticism of the foreign office. His reputation with the chancellor remained undisturbed, even by his notorious *faux pas* of 1937, when he greeted the new King of England with a "Hitler salute." No matter how ignominiously (in the eyes of the foreign office) Ribbentrop might fail, his sycophantic readiness to serve continued to buy Hitler's favor.[30]

Neurath had offered his resignation in the summer and again in the fall of 1936 with relief. The difficulty of finding men who could provide the support he had previously taken for granted troubled him. Aggravated by the discouraging rise of men like Ribbentrop, he would now have to install a whole new generation of diplomats to replace his closest collaborators. Subsequent appointments were uneven. Hans Dieckhoff, originally scheduled to replace Köpke, served as acting state secretary. Accepting the position against his own better judgment, Dieckhoff was a good man who lacked energy. Quickly, he requested and received appointment as ambassador to the United States. Joachim von Ribbentrop, of course, was ensconced in London; Paris received Count Johannes von Welczek, an unimaginative but experienced diplomat. From then on, Berlin no longer received the crisp and insightful coverage of events in Western capitals which had long characterized the reports of Hoesch and Köster. The new personnel director was a friend of Ernst Bohle, and while this promised good relations with that segment of the party, for the first time control over personnel had passed to a man who was not a product of homogeneous diplomatic training. Within the reorganized Berlin office, the new Political Department was headed by Ernst Freiherr von Weizsäcker, the future state secretary. A Swabian like Neurath, he was a hard worker and a conscientious diplomat, but he lacked Bülow's energies and failed to develop his new office to its fullest potential. The director of the new European division was Ernst Woermann, an uninspiring civil servant mildly fascinated by the Nazis. Distrusting the recalcitrant attitude of the foreign office toward the chancellor and his followers, Woermann did not hide his dislike for Neurath. The director of the extra-European division was Otto von Erdmannsdorf, a party member who unlike his colleagues in the office "had always supported the party's position and sought to have close cooperation with it."[31]

Neurath could no longer count on a tightly-knit organization which instinctively shared his own philosophy of foreign policy and distrusted the dangerous tendencies in Hitler's ambitions. In the remaining years of his ministership, he had to confront the chancellor's independence with an instrument not adapted to concerted action. To many in the Wilhelmstrasse, it was time to come to terms with the National Socialist era. Tragically, in all these appointments, Neurath had not bowed to the will of the chancellor or the party. All were initiated from within the office and their unsatisfactory performance clearly reflects both Nazi inroads upon the ranks of the professional diplomats and the paucity of first-rate people within the service. Indeed, Hitler became increasingly correct in labeling the diplomats second-rate. With the exception of Weizsäcker, who was later to demonstrate his integrity, none of the new appointments was of help to Neurath or a credit to the foreign office.

The events surrounding the filling of the post of state secretary illustrate these trends. After months of procrastination, Dieckhoff finally accepted the title of acting state secretary, pending a suitable replacement. After a fruitless search, and always fearful lest he be forced to accept Ribbentrop or some other party leader, Neurath despairingly decided to appoint his own son-in-law, Hans-Georg von Mackensen. Even members of his family were surprised by the choice, for Mackensen was more soldier than diplomat. Reared as a companion to Prince August-Wilhelm, whom he served as adjutant in World War I, Mackensen joined the foreign service as secretary in Neurath's legation in Copenhagen in 1919. After unspectacular service in Rome, Brussels, Tirana, and Madrid, in 1923 he was named German representative in Budapest, where he stayed until Neurath called him to Berlin in 1937. The minister's decision stemmed from two considerations: first, and most important, he needed someone in this vital position upon whom he could rely absolutely. An energetic and ambitious man would have been preferable in the face of Nazi encroachments, but in Neurath's view all the dynamic men belonged to the other side; after an exhaustive review of all his officials, he decided to settle for mediocrity if he could at least be sure of loyalty. The second consideration was political. Mackensen was the son of the popular field marshal of the war, and was one of the few German diplomats abroad who had joined the party and the SS (1934). By bringing such a man to Berlin, Neurath could undermine the rumor that the office was hostile to the party and its policies. In this appointment, family advancement was not an important consideration.[32]

On the contrary, Neurath at first hesitated even to consider his son-in-law, and when first approached, Mackensen refused. He reconsidered his decision reluctantly and as a family favor. Eventually Gerhard Köpke had to intervene to urge Mackensen to accept. The new state secretary later admitted that "it took an appeal to the old soldier in me in order to change my position from my original and well-grounded refusal." He recalled that one of Köpke's phrases had supplied him with a decisive motive:

> ... namely the thought that I might thereby be of some help to that much esteemed man who has, for nearly five years, borne the full load of responsibility, and that he might gain some person next to him with whom he could freely and confidentially speak, if only to clear his own thoughts, such as he used to do with you, his friend of many years. This sentence helped me greatly in my soul's dilemma.

Neurath's daughter echoed a similar reaction. While fearing "a mountain of difficulties," she admitted in a letter to Köpke that after much hesitation, they had agreed to "swallow the pill" if for no other reason than "to help out the parents." She recalled that her father, "who hates to put things into words, was positively blissful" when her husband accepted the appointment.[33]

Mackensen's appointment clearly demonstrates Neurath's dilemma. After years of defending the integrity of the foreign office and resisting Nazi advances and those agents who were "frivolously and recklessly destroying all the laboriously acquired opportunities for solidly constructive political work," Neurath was forced to employ men who were not equal to the task. Still, he hoped that through his own strenuous effort he could prevent greater disasters. His son, who visited Leinfelderhof immediately after these major decisions had been made, described his father's improved outlook in a letter to Köpke:

> I am very happy that father has now been able to restore some order in his office, and I hope that the new collaboration [with Mackensen] will go well. Above all, hopefully from time to time, some lighthearted moments might soften the particularly difficult situations, for I believe he has recently suffered very much in this regard. Since your departure, things have generally been painted in bleak colors and accompanied with much grumbling. No humor ever seems to be present.[34]

Throughout these later years, Neurath expended much energy upon the fight against party intruders. In general he had won the battle, and as late as March 1937, Bohle complained to Hess of the "relative lack of National Socialist officials in the foreign service." But while winning, Neurath assumed perhaps too readily that he could thereby maintain his own style of foreign policy, believing as he did that Hitler's sometimes aggressive and dynamic turns originated with the unofficial advisors. After 1936, it was clear that men like Ribbentrop were only reflectors of Hitler's own attitudes; thus, Neurath's success in blocking these men did not thereby eliminate undesirable policies. Indeed, in order to defeat these men, Neurath sometimes was forced to take conciliatory positions. As a contemporary wrote, "fellow travelers, in order to maintain their positions and accomplish their goals, must proceed with greater caution and reserve in their criticism than older members of the ruling movement."[35]

Beginning in 1936, and stretching over the next years, Neurath repeatedly fell victim to this approach. Unable to maintain independent control of German policy, he considered it his duty to ride out the storm. "Better give way betimes," one official had reportedly told Rauschning, "than have the whole conduct of affairs turned over to those wild men, Rosenberg and Ribbentrop." While this had not been Neurath's philosophy in the early years of the Hitler government, it became so after 1936. Papen correctly noted that Neurath was "so severely taxed by the daily difficulties with the party that he could not propose a long-range policy." More accurately, by this time, Neurath was so fearful of what would befall German policy should his restraining hand be lifted that he was determined to hold on for as long as he could. In this process, he compromised some of the integrity he had once enjoyed.[36]

The ever-perceptive reports of the French ambassador in Berlin note changes in Neurath's evaluation of his own position. In the months following the Olympic games, he wrote, Neurath grew increasingly fearful of Nazi leaders. Personally moderate and conciliatory, he failed to take the more aggressive line, and Hitler had little time for him. In turn, Neurath developed a tendency to avoid the ordeal of meeting the chancellor, since he found that such discussions often deteriorated into near-monologues. By early 1937, the foreign office was isolated; Hitler no longer kept his foreign minister informed of his orders and never asked for real advice.[37]

Thus, by the middle of 1936, the process by which German foreign policy was determined was beginning to change in two new and important ways. The traditional instrument, the foreign office, was clearly on the defensive, having lost some of its best men. And Neurath, who in the past had established the tone and direction of German policy, had lost much prestige with Hitler. In this important year in which the restoration of German independence in international affairs was sealed, these changes were to play a crucial part.

CHAPTER

11

NEURATH AND GERMAN FOREIGN POLICY: 1936–1938

In August 1936 representatives from every nation gathered in Berlin for the Olympic Games. Coming as they did so shortly after the German remilitarization of the Rhineland, and the solemn condemnation of that action by both the Locarno powers and the Council of the League of Nations, the festive celebrations in the capital city of the Third Reich represented a major triumph for the government. "The whole world," Neurath remarked to friends, "has come to pay respects to the new power of Germany." A glittering array of princes, statesmen, and important people visited Germany, met its leaders, and left praising its accomplishments. The games were priceless propaganda, formally announcing renewed German prestige.[1]

By August 1936, the German government had realized nearly all the goals which Neurath had set in 1932. Moreover, those goals were achieved primarily through his own proposed methods of quiet and peaceful rearmament, without premature political commitments to foreign nations. With the remilitarization of the Rhineland, the final step in consolidation of military power had been taken, and Germany was now ready to pursue that independent foreign policy which had ever been Neurath's goal. For the immediate future, the foreign minister planned a cautious approach until the Rhineland "had been digested": "As soon as our fortifications are constructed and the countries of central Europe realize that France cannot enter German territory at will," he told William Bullitt, American ambassador to the Soviet Union, "all these countries will begin to feel very differently about their foreign policies, and a new constellation will develop." Revealing his own intention to build a new block of states in central Europe aligned with Germany (Austria, Yugoslavia, Czechoslovakia, and Romania), Neurath insisted that while he would welcome friendly relations with Britain, France, and Italy, henceforth all should know that "our policy will be a German policy and nothing else."[2]

Hoping that Germany would remain "quiet and inoffensive" for the near future, avoiding "any commitments which might restrict its future activities," Neurath now feared that he might be unable to keep Hitler within the parameters of this policy, for the chancellor seemed to be moving away from his foreign minister and ever closer to the adventurers and extremists within the party. "The Nazis are like children," Neurath told friends. "They want something, and cannot believe that anything should stand in the way of attaining it." After nursing German policy through the crises surrounding rearmament and the first steps freeing the country from Versailles, Neurath now worried about the chancellor's "impulsive nature and personal temperament [which] had always inclined toward violence." The foreign office shared these fears. "They despair," one observer noted, "but they always hope."[3]

After 1936, Neurath grudgingly had to admit that Hitler's command of foreign policy, while certainly unorthodox and irregular, was successful and thus could be opposed only with difficulty. He found himself forced to give way on small points, in order to maintain his position. As the chancellor began to bypass him in the determination of policy, the minister strove harder to preserve his influence. The challenges after 1936, accumulating only gradually but to an overwhelming level, seemed to make him cling ever more tenaciously to his post. Not until late 1937 was Neurath abruptly challenged, and he responded with decision and firmness, yet by that time he no longer influenced German policy.

Neurath in Control

This process was demonstrated in three different ways. The first occurred in those areas in which, by determined opposition, Neurath was still able to influence developments, yet at a price. The most important encounter of this kind was the Spanish Civil War. For Neurath, the unexpected outbreak of the war offered little concrete advantage for Germany. Unsympathetic with the rebels, he regarded as fraudulent the widely publicized threat of a "Communist" danger, and opposed German intervention. He recommended a negative reply to appeals for military assistance. His advice was simply ignored and in his absence, motivated by a vague desire to see the rebels prevail, Hitler dispatched airplanes and some troops on July 28 and 31, 1936, thus sustaining Franco and initiating civil war which was to lacerate Spain for the next three years.[4]

Subsequently, Neurath had difficulty persuading Hitler to agree to an arms embargo and a declaration of neutrality. For the first time in his career as minister—excepting of course the issue of Austria—he found that Hitler apparently wanted to involve Germany in a foreign adventure, with little regard for the traditional and limited program offered by the foreign office. Neurath was unable to stop the escalating involvement, and in November, Hitler formally recognized

Franco as Spain's legitimate ruler. He refused to accept the foreign office nominee as ambassador, appointing instead General Wilhelm Faupel, who immediately requested greater military assistance from Berlin. Neurath now stood firm: "Under no circumstances," he wrote to General Blomberg, "do I consider it feasible to send a complete division as General Faupel desires, especially at the present time." Surprisingly, in an important meeting on December 21, 1936, Neurath's arguments carried the day; Germany would supply arms and instructors to Franco, but no troops. Neurath was visibly relieved. On the following day he wrote to Hassell that while Berlin would plan for emergencies, "I still hope we will not have to carry out any such measures, but rather that we will be able to emerge with blue eyes from this Spanish witch's cauldron."[5]

Hitler had shrewdly seized the opportunity presented by Franco's uprising to maximize foreign advantages for himself, while minimizing the likelihood that others would interfere. This had been accomplished with only a limited German presence. For the first time, the chancellor's personal ruthlessness was complemented by astute diplomatic skill. Previous German successes, like the Rhineland occupation, for all Hitler's initiative in forcing decisions, had still been accomplished largely with the able advice of the foreign office. In Spain, such advice was not a factor.[6]

The anomaly of Neurath's position emerges in an incident of early January 1937. Alarmed over reports that German military volunteers were in Morocco, Neurath futilely urged that Hitler issue a denial, and he even threatened to raise the issue himself in public conversations at the forthcoming New Year's reception. Reluctantly, the chancellor agreed, and a conciliatory exchange took place. A few days later, Neurath confessed relief at conclusive British reports that no German troops were in Morocco. As he told a friend, although he had been assured that no troops were there, he still had "some uncomfortable feelings about the whole matter." Obviously, he no longer believed even Hitler's solemn assurances. Still, he hoped he had blocked further involvement. "The Führer," he told the mayor of Hamburg, "wants to get out of the Spanish affair and has ordered that not one single German more will be sent to Spain." Göring was instructed to tell this to Mussolini, and Neurath informed foreign diplomats that the moment for a broad solution of the Spanish question was approaching. Stubbornly, he defended his policy throughout the critical months of April and May 1937 when Italian defeats raised grave questions about Franco's eventual triumph. In particular, Neurath angrily rejected Faupel's argument that troops must now be sent to preserve Germany's "military reputation."* In May, he repeated that his policy was to "get out of that hornet's nest as soon as possible." The question was whether or not Neurath's advice would prevail.[7]

On May 29, 1937, unidentified airplanes bombed the German battleship

---

*Only the sending of troops, Neurath commented in a memorandum, "would place our military reputation really at stake."

Deutschland, participating in the Non-Intervention Committee's patrol off the coast of Spain; 23 sailors were killed, with nearly 85 wounded in the attack. A furious Hitler wanted to declare war on the Republican government; Göring and Goebbels pressed for military action and massive bombing raids. Neurath alone held out for some moderate response. After nearly six hours of discussions, Neurath's viewpoint prevailed; Germany left the committee, reinforcing its own naval forces in the Mediterranean. In addition, Hitler ordered a punitive strike against the fortress of Almería. Opposing even that action, Neurath was relieved that a potentially dangerous situation had been met with minimal response.[8]

The *Deutschland* incident shows clearly that Neurath was not averse to taking on Hitler and Göring when the risk of war was involved, and he was still successful as a moderating force. But the long-range determination of policy had now escaped him and he did little more than react to crises. His opposition to aiding Franco had blocked direct intervention, but he had failed to persuade Hitler to accept the alternative program of the foreign office, namely, "the prevention of a general conflict rather than the unconditional and complete victory of the Franco party in the Spanish Civil War." Although he no longer determined overall strategy, Neurath was going to influence at least the tactics and prevent worse counsels from prevailing. In this he was generally successful.[9]

Neurath Is Ignored

A second pattern occurred in which Hitler ignored Neurath, even on issues where the foreign office, without urging undue risks, believed that the time had come for a more active pursuit of hegemony over Austria, Czechoslovakia, and particularly Poland and the Free City of Danzig. In the days immediately following the remilitarization of the Rhineland, Berlin had been conciliatory toward Warsaw, but less than two months later, Göring argued that "it is no longer so necessary... to meet Polish desires to so great an extent," and in June Hitler decided to complete the nazification of Danzig. In these events, the foreign office was consulted only after decisions had been taken by party leaders. Since Neurath had encouraged Berlin's control of Danzig, Hitler's use of party members and other advisors stemmed not from expected foreign office opposition, but from his growing preference for working with party cronies who were now forcing the pace. Although the Poles believed that Neurath would have adopted a policy "more reserved and cautious than his colleagues'," the party and Göring henceforth directed policy toward Poland; Neurath was simply excluded.[10]

A similar picture emerges for Czechoslovakia. Neurath had long insisted that Berlin could not afford to become involved in "warlike complications in the foreseeable future on account of the Sudeten Germans." He and the foreign office funded the Sudeten German movement and actively sought to bring about a unification of all German elements in Czechoslovakia, but on January 18, 1937, Neurath specifically warned of the danger of divisions "through aggressive National Socialist propaganda," and reminded Konrad Henlein that the Sudeten problem "could not at present be solved, but must remain for some later altercation."[11]

Although all evidence shows that Hitler shared this view, he had, without informing Neurath, approved Ribbentrop's secret negotiations with Beneš, which stretched on for nearly six months. This suggests a conscious exclusion of the foreign office from deliberations, even though Neurath's policy also insisted that only the timing was premature for incorporating the Sudeten area with Germany. In January 1938, Neurath emphasized that "if the Czechs [had] kept to the original Masaryk concept [of a federal state with autonomy for all minorities], they could exist at least for some time longer. But as matters stand today, 'this stump will have to be severed sooner or later.'" When that would come, however, Neurath would have no voice in deciding.[12]

Similarly, the "Gentlemen's Agreement" signed between Vienna and Berlin on July 11, 1936 was achieved without foreign office involvement, although Neurath welcomed the détente, believing as he did that thereby the Austrian question had been "reserved for subsequent solution by us." With no immediate danger of countermeasures by other countries, the fruit was ripening on schedule. Although he strongly criticized Göring's attempt to blackmail Mussolini into approving German action, on his trip to the Balkans in June, Neurath kept the pressure on. He reprimanded Vienna for failing to integrate Nazi elements into the government, and told foreign minister Guido Schmidt: "My total impression is that the will to carry out the Agreement of July 11, 1936 is not present on the part of the Austrian government, and that we shall hardly succeed in regulating German-Austrian relations by this method."

The French envoy in Belgrade and his Austrian counterpart found Neurath's "bad humor" understandable, since the minister "had been clearly outflanked in Germany by Nazi elements, and finding himself in a difficult situation with no way out sought to create [in the Balkans] the support for his projects." But while Neurath had lost ground, he was not deliberately adjusting himself to Hitler's outlook. His stubborn stand regarding Austria was neither new nor inconsistent.[13]

Then, early in July 1937, Hitler appointed a new advisor with full authority to "handle questions connected with Austria in relation to the Party." Although directed to confer with Neurath on all aspects of his task, Wilhelm Keppler soon went his own way, and by October, Neurath believed that his program was in jeopardy. Desiring that Germany should "cause no explosion of the Austrian problem in the foreseeable future," he suspected that other elements—over which he had no control—were not averse to a threat of force. Nevertheless, Neurath refused to read into these events a drastic change and believed that if success were obtained peacefully, Hitler would be satisfied. Early in January 1937, after a speech on the occasion of the anniversary of German unification, the mayor of Hamburg asked Neurath if Hitler was forcing events toward a war. The mayor recorded in his diary the minister's reply: "He could assure me that the Führer was not thinking at all of a war, and believes that any war is absolutely ruled out before

1941. But it would be wrong to overemphasize this point, for then other countries would be able to do with us whatever they wanted."[14]

Neurath's acceptance of the realities of power politics, coupled with a thinning hope that Hitler shared his basic approach to international relations, explains why the minister remained unalarmed by the evolution of policy in Central Europe, even though he had little to do with its direction and execution.

Neurath Is Overruled

Finally, a third pattern of decision making in the years between 1936 and 1938 clearly emerges. Besides those areas in which Neurath's determined efforts could change the tactics of a program and those in which he was kept ignorant of specifics but generally approved the direction of the policy, there were decisions which he strongly opposed and failed completely to influence, notably the Anti-Comintern Pact, with its attendant German-Japanese and German-Italian alliances.

In the first three years of his government, Hitler seldom mentioned aggressive expansion in the East, but in the late summer of 1936, he prepared a Four Year Plan concretizing his earlier vision and linking the theme of expansion and living area in the East with that of a European front against Bolshevism. Only Japan and Italy possessed the authoritarian strength to join Germany in this historic mission against Moscow. A call to defend Europe against Eastern barbarism would fortuitously provide Germany with its missing living space (*Lebensraum*) and raw materials; to implement this policy, Hitler demanded the creation of sufficient military and economic power to wage a war of conquest. More precisely, he set two tasks: within four years make the German army operational and the German economy fit for war.[15]

Hitler's new interest in the grandiose idea of an international coalition which might facilitate German military and economic expansion parallels the Four Year Plan. Aware of Neurath's distaste for such schemes, Hitler shared his ideas with Ribbentrop. In the summer of 1936, on the same day he was appointed ambassador to Great Britain, Ribbentrop received Hitler's commission to work out some formal pact with Japan. Simultaneously, Göring was ordered to establish closer understanding with Rome. Neurath and the foreign office followed both trends with misgivings, seeking to avoid improvised agreements. During his own talks with Italian foreign minister Galeazzo Ciano, Neurath avoided definite commitments, but the visit nevertheless created the Italian-German ties which he had so long feared. Although the understanding offered Germany advantageous freedom for expansion, Neurath believed such actions would antagonize Britain and terminate his own hopes for the peaceful and gradual restoration of German hegemony in Central Europe.[16]

On the same day that Neurath and Ciano initialed their protocols, Ribbentrop signed the Anti-Comintern Pact with Mushakajo Kntomo. In December 1935, Neurath had blocked negotiations with Japan by strongly protesting to Hitler that any agreement—even ostensibly against the Soviet Union—would greatly damage relations with Britain. But in the summer of 1936, Ribbentrop and the Japanese military attaché in Berlin reopened talks. No documentary evidence suggests the motivation, but Ribbentrop's desire to compensate for failing to explain German policy to the League Council in London probably contributed. Also Hitler had become increasingly preoccupied with the Soviet menace. On June 6 and again on June 26, to visiting Japanese he compared Europe to a peaceful valley, unaware of dangerous rock outcroppings which at any moment threatened its existence: "I am of the opinion that this danger can be met in no other way than to break this gigantic block [the Soviet Union] into its historical parts. I am resolved to do everything necessary to facilitate and hasten this development, and it makes no difference on which side of the Soviet Union it occurs."

Thinking along the lines of his Four Year Plan, Hitler had ordered Ribbentrop to negotiate a treaty with Japan; the foreign office was kept ignorant until after Hitler had accepted the pact in late October. Deeply displeased, Neurath refused to participate in the drafting or signing, and relayed this reaction to the foreign office.[17]

The Anti-Comintern Pact was only the first step in a new world policy. Ribbentrop promised Hitler that other nations would join, and spoke glowingly of the recruitment of Italy, Poland, Bulgaria, Latvia, Romania, Brazil, and other South American countries. The chancellor was equally enthusiastic: "Bring England into the Anti-Comintern Pact; that would fulfill my dearest wish," he told Ribbentrop. "I have sent you to England as the best horse in my stable. See what you can do." Setting to work, Ribbentrop still faced the determined opposition of Neurath, who finally succeeded in having Hitler prohibit the Ribbentrop Bureau from all activity concerning the Pact. With undisguised glee, Neurath told Ribbentrop of the Führer's orders that Raumer abstain from all questions of the extension of the Anti-Comintern Pact. Round one seems to have gone to Neurath, and the grand alliance of Italy, Japan, and Germany appeared doomed.[18]

Then on July 7, 1937, the Marco Polo bridge incident opened the war between Japan and China. The foreign office urged neutrality, and during the Nuremberg rally of 1937, Neurath won Hitler's agreement to remain neutral, cooperating with Japan in principle while continuing trade and military support to China. From his embassy in London, Ribbentrop stressed Japanese strength, and challenged all doubts of Japanese success. Then Neurath learned from the Japanese ambassador that a tripartite pact (Japan-Germany-Italy) was under consideration. Although Neurath replied that "we did not desire such an agreement," his efforts were immediately undermined when Hitler and Göring expressed their desires for closer ties with Japan. As complications continued, Neurath worried even more about the growing friendship with Italy and its possible impact. During Mussolini's visit to Germany in September, the two dictators excluded the professional diplomats from their meetings, to Neurath's intense displeasure. Ciano, however, gloated: "The Rome-Berlin Axis is today a formidable and extremely useful reality. . . . I shall try to draw a line from Rome to Tokyo, and the system will be complete." Neurath was excluded when discussions started about Italy's adhering to the Anti-Comintern Pact. On October 18, Ribbentrop reappeared in Berlin and instructed his assistant Raumer to fly to Rome to negotiate the tripartite pact.[19]

Apparently, Ribbentrop was himself unsure of the extent of his authority, for he had not obtained Hitler's approval for this move, only his general agreement as long as Neurath had no objections. Aware of the foreign minister's opposition, Ribbentrop decided to bring Italy into the Pact singlehandedly, hoping thereby to recover his diminished reputation with Hitler. Yet Neurath's opposition was well known, and Ciano noted in his diary: "You can't change the way these old men's minds work. You must change *them*. It is deplorable to see how in Germany the foreign minister fails to act on the Führer's instructions." Unsympathetic to Neurath's views, Ciano was shrewd enough to realize that Ribbentrop might have exceeded his responsibility, and sent the Prince of Hesse to learn the chancellor's personal attitude toward the extension of the Anti-Comintern Pact. The answer was curious: "The truth is that Hitler was very angry with Ribbentrop, not because of what has happened—Hitler approves of the Tripartite Pact and claims to have originated it himself—but because, contrary to his instructions, Ribbentrop had kept the whole thing a secret from Neurath."[20]

Meanwhile, Ribbentrop tried to sell Rome on the idea of a military alliance "in anticipation of the inevitable conflict with the Western powers." On October 25, Hitler gave permission for Ribbentrop to sign a nonmilitary protocol, and shortly thereafter, for the first time, some official informed the foreign office; the helpless Neurath could only warn the German representative in China that a pact would be forthcoming. It was a humiliating blow.[21] When the ambitious Ribbentrop arrived in Berlin on November 6, expecting a hero's welcome, he found Hitler furious and upset at his deception and concerned about possible damage to the chances for German-British cooperation. Listening to Neurath, Hitler had belatedly realized the implications of this pact: "Anti-Communist in theory, but in fact, unmistakably anti-British." Hitler stormed out, leaving Ribbentrop to return to his London embassy—which he had not visited during the past six months—and find some new plan to regain the chancellor's confidence.[22]

But in the meantime, German policy had now clearly entered a new stage in which Neurath and the foreign office were both isolated and in opposition. A deep gloom settled over the Wilhelmstrasse; Ernst von Weizsäcker spoke for many when he said he found this *Weltpolitik* unintelligible. Neurath unleashed his frustrations by going on a hunting trip. He could only hope that Hitler himself was not yet resolved on the precise direction of future policy.[23]

1937 was a tense year within the halls of the German government. Hitler had clearly established his authority and all officials, no matter how high, awaited his orders. Still, he had not yet visibly charted a new course, and François-Poncet caught this state of suspended animation in a perceptive dispatch of mid-July:

> Hitler devotes less and less time to public affairs. He spends more of his time at his house at Obersalzburg and much less in the capital city. He leaves his collaborators free to carry on in their own manner in those areas

which they have seized for themselves. He concerns himself, insofar as he does, with foreign policy. Primarily, he occupies himself in new and grandiose construction projects, especially for the beautification of Berlin, which haunts his imagination. It is this which makes an observer remember Ludwig II of Bavaria. He designs, he corrects architectural drawings, he retouches models, he consults picture albums. All the same, nothing of importance is accomplished without his agreement.

The radical wing of his party reproaches him for his hesitations, his temporizing; they find him lulled into security, that he has become middle class, that he lacks authority. The moderate wing of his followers hold against him, on the contrary, that he acquiesces too much to the influence of extremists, that he tolerates the excesses of the anti-religious and anti-Semitic campaigns, that he has not rid himself of a clique of compromised people. But throughout all this, Hitler's authority remains intact. Everyone fears him, knowing his fits of temper and his brutal decisions. Neurath, among others, is visibly terrified of him.

Hitler's prestige among the masses is undiminished. He is *the* support of the Third Reich. He sustains it like the ash or fir tree of German mythology that holds up the world; if he collapsed, the world which he has built would collapse. His lieutenants know they would be swept away in his fall; but they, at least, believe in him, and their awareness of this solidarity with him sustains them even in disputes. Those who serve him without being his friends believe that after him would come chaos. And they prefer Hitler to chaos.[24]

With the ever-elusive Hitler, discussions seldom clarified matters, and frequently were downright painful. Neurath was never sure whether the Anti-Comintern Pact, with its worldwide implications, was a determined policy or merely a tactical maneuver. Worse, he could not know whether it arose from Ribbentrop's interference or the chancellor's conscious planning. The Führer's peripatetic and bohemian lifestyle prevented regular communications, and Neurath was increasingly unclear about the drift of the new policy. After World War II, a skeptical world heard the German foreign minister confess to knowing little of many aspects of German policy after 1936. When asked to explain, Neurath could only reply that perhaps Hitler talked about these things after he had gone to bed.*

New Impetus to Resign

Hitler's decision to embark confidently upon a program of aggressive expansionism cannot be precisely dated. Although apparent in some of the diplomatic moves

---

*Albert Speer confirms this state of affairs. Once, he recalled, Hitler ordered his adjutant to call Neurath late at night. When his aide replied that "the foreign minister has already gone to bed," Hitler ordered: "Tell him he's to be waked when I want to talk to him." After another telephone call, Hitler was told: "The foreign minister says he will be available in the morning; he's tired now and wants to sleep." Speer adds: "Faced with such resolution, Hitler could only give up, but he was in a bad humor for the rest of the evening." Albert Speer, *Inside the Third Reich: Memoirs*, 98.

of 1936, Neurath himself believed the change came during 1937. Recalling these events after the war, Neurath wrote: "I frequently urged him not to draw the bow too tight. He did not listen to me and told me lies. He made his decision eventually to carry out his wishes by force, I am convinced, first in the fall of 1937, shortly after the major German [military] maneuvers [on the occasion of] Mussolini's visit." Aware that his own influence had dwindled to nothing and that this new approach invalidated his whole program, Neurath presented his resignation, rather than follow Hitler in what would inevitably produce a European war. The exact events surrounding this move document the changed nature of German foreign policy.[25]

Neurath's last year as foreign minister was unusually active. During his previous five years in office, he had left Germany only four times: twice to Geneva ("involuntarily" as he described it)[26] for a League of Nations meeting, to London for the World Economic Conference in 1933, and in early 1936, as head of the German delegation at the funeral of King George V. In 1937, in rapid succession, Neurath visited Vienna (February), Rome (May), Belgrade and Budapest (June), and invitations were received from Warsaw and other capitals. Although these trips were purely formal, Neurath everywhere left a good impression as the herald for the respectability of Germany's new dynamism in foreign policy.

To Neurath, the London visit would be the most crucial. For years, he had held that Germany's return to the status of a major power could come only with British cooperation. Recent events—the Spanish Civil War and the Anti-Comintern Pact—had alarmed him because they placed Germany in opposition to London. Seeking an opportunity for personal discussions of the issues, he accepted the British invitation in June 1937, requesting only an agenda sufficiently broad to prevent speculation that Germany was coming to plead for special problems. He expressed a hope for "gradual *rapprochement* through practical cooperation." News of the visit was enthusiastically greeted in the Wilhelmstrasse, where it was predicted Neurath would remove Ribbentrop and lay the foundations for pacific cooperation between Germany and the Western nations.* Abroad, reactions were more guarded, but almost everyone welcomed the opportunity for some German representative besides Ribbentrop to meet with British diplomats. Regardless of the outcome, the visit seemed to bespeak a renewed influence for the foreign office.[27]

From the start, Ribbentrop opposed the visit. His ambassadorship had not been triumphant; indeed most diplomats attributed the lack of closer relations to his personality. It seemed likely that the energetic upstart would soon be finished. On June 15, this most irascible and independent free agent complained that he was not being kept informed and lectured Neurath that "double-track operations should by all means be avoided." No doubt he telephoned his protest to Hitler. On June 18, when an unidentified submarine fired a topedo at the *Leipzig,* on patrol

---

*Speaking to a German journalist during this time, Neurath indicated that he would certainly do something about Ribbentrop. "It is almost impossible for me to mend all the porcelain which my ambassador in London is breaking each day." Cited in *Deutscher Kurier,* September 20, 1952.

off the coast of Spain, Hitler demanded that Neurath postpone his visit. In Berlin, diplomats shared Göring's opinion that Ribbentrop had engineered this delay. As usual, the French ambassador recorded the rumors:

> The postponement of Neurath's trip to London has spread reports in Berlin that Ribbentrop, by adopting an intransigent attitude, seeks to render impossible a policy which would overshadow him. This is the rumor received and propagated here by the various missions. . . . It is certain that relations between the German ambassador in London and the head of the Wilhelmstrasse are not of the best. In the *Leipzig* affair, it seems there is friction between Ribbentrop and Neurath, and the latter believes the ambassador has not maneuvered very well. Certainly, the Führer himself is the one who judged it necessary to defer the foreign minister's trip. . . . One must remember, however, that Ribbentrop communicates directly with the chancellor over the head of the minister, who is never informed of the content of these conversations between the Führer and his special advisor.[28]

In any case, an obviously disappointed Neurath did not go to London, and despite repeated renewals of the invitation, the trip remained in abeyance. Still, in the fall of 1937, rumors abounded that Neurath had finally regained a position of importance, although the canceling of the London trip prevented any removal of Ribbentrop. This situation helps explain the curious reconciliation, in August 1937, between Rosenberg and Ribbentrop. Although both men subsequently insisted that their lieutenants had acted without authorization in drawing up an agreement delineating two spheres of foreign influence, the "peace treaty" between them was signed in early September. This circumstantial evidence supports the conclusion that Ribbentrop felt his position so weakened that he had to settle his difficulties with other party leaders. A document from these discussions indicates that a major motive was fear that the Neurath-Mackensen-Bohle clique would succeed in consolidating their hold on foreign affairs and eliminating all rivals in the process.[29]

During the Nuremberg party rally (September 8–13, 1937), the rumors continued to spread of Ribbentrop's recall from London, his replacement by Hassell, and, significantly, his future employment as state secretary in the chancellery office. Most observers also expected some drastic personnel changes in October, especially surrounding Hjalmar Schacht and the economics ministry. Even Ribbentrop's successful Anti-Comintern Pact extension did not restore his prestige. On the day of Ribbentrop's return to Germany, Vernon Bartlett criticized him in the London *News Chronicle,* for signing a pact directed against the country to which he was accredited. The writer succinctly summarized charges: he met only reactionaries; he never visited really important people; he consistently misinformed Berlin "because he believes only what he wants to believe"; he never understood that Great Britain would not participate in a crusade against Communism; and finally, he still headed the Ribbentrop Bureau which continued to pursue policies antithetical to the official one, thus demonstrating to all that one could not trust a German. Had Neurath himself dictated the article, it could not have better expressed his own grievances against Ribbentrop. Doubtless the minister welcomed this public discussion as strengthening his case with Hitler.[30]

The Hossbach Meeting

Thus, in the first week of November 1937, Neurath was in a better personal position than he had been for years. True, Hitler continued to employ Ribbentrop and other agents, keeping the foreign office ignorant of many details. But Hitler still desired Neurath's counsel. So it must have seemed, as the foreign minister received an invitation to attend a conference in the Reichs Chancellery on November 5, 1937, a meeting known after the war as the Hossbach discussion, after Hitler's military adjutant, Colonel Friedrich Hossbach, who was present and subsequently wrote an account of the crucial discussion. For the first time in nearly five years, Hitler assembled the military commanders-in-chief and the foreign minister to express his views on the nation's military and foreign policy. In clear and precise language, Hitler spelled out his program: at the first opportunity, he would pursue otherwise unobtainable political and economic goals with military action.[31]

In rambling fashion, Hitler reiterated his opinion that living space for the German race was the one viable solution to Germany's economic and demographic problems. Autarchy, participation in world trade, and the regaining of distant colonies would bring no permanent improvement in Germany's economic situation. At the risk of war with Great Britain and France, Hitler proposed to conquer a solid block of land in Eastern Europe. Claiming the Western nations would be caught off guard if Germany moved quickly, the chancellor desired "the resort to force with its attendant risks. . . . Germany's problems could only be solved by means of force." Hitler designated three contingencies under which he would use force to achieve the acquisition of territory. The first would occur by 1943, should the present status quo in Europe last that long. With the world rearming to fend off a German move, further delay would decrease chances of success. If he were still alive, "it was his unalterable resolve to solve Germany's problem of space at the latest by 1943–1945." Two circumstances, however, would provoke him to take action before 1943; both involved sudden reversals of France's continental power, either through domestic strife or foreign war. A civil war in France, Hitler predicted, was possible at any time, and French involvement in a foreign war was even more likely. "It might emerge from the present tension in the Mediterranean [arising out of the Spanish Civil War], and he was resolved to take advantage of it whenever it happened, even as early as 1938." The chancellor believed any French-Italian conflict would soon include Great Britain as well, and "the time for our attack on the Czechs and Austria must be made dependent on the course of this Anglo-French-Italian war." But whether domestic or foreign, French involvement would distract Europe long enough for Germany to make a "lightning" descent upon Czechoslovakia and Austria "simultaneously in order to remove the threat to our flank in any possible operation against the West." Confidently he assured the commanders-in-chief that should such expansion be executed quickly and efficiently, the major European powers would not lift a gun to stop it.

The inclusion of Czechoslovakia and Austria within the German empire would still not provide the necessary living space, but the compulsory expulsion of 3 million people would produce sufficient food for nearly 6 million Germans, and twelve new divisions could be raised from the added populations. Most important, these two states would complete the middle-European amalgamation from which even more decisive conquests of territory could proceed by 1943.

Hitler's audience was stunned. Colonel Hossbach, who had attended the meeting anticipating a technical discussion of armaments and raw materials, realized that the chancellor had seized the occasion to reveal very far-reaching intentions. Lacking stenographic skills, he nevertheless took careful notes. However, he was less concerned about giving a complete account of the ensuing discussion, and this part of his record is thus incomplete. Hossbach later recalled the "sharpness of the opposition," the content and form of which "did not fail to make its impression on Hitler, as I could see from his changing expressions." Hitler spoke for about two hours, and the subsequent discussion took up equal, if not more, time, yet Hossbach devoted only one-tenth of his account to the discussion and later admitted that he had committed a "sin of omission before history" in not having recorded "in greater detail and in the actual sharpness the arguments" that followed Hitler's presentation.[32]

Even in the truncated version, however, Neurath's opposition to Hitler's statements is clear. Challenging the chancellor's predictions of a French war with Italy, Neurath supported General von Blomberg and General Werner von Fritsch in opposing any action which might force Germany into military confrontation with France and Great Britain. All three speakers were certain that Germany would not be equal to such a challenge, and Neurath feared that accelerating the tempo would precipitate just such a military confrontation. Despite this opposition, Hitler repeated that "he was convinced of Britain's nonparticipation, and therefore he did not believe in the probability of belligerent action by France against Germany." The meeting ended with a brief discussion of some concrete questions of armaments.[33]

Any evaluation of the November 5 meeting must take into account Hitler's intention. Certainly many of his statements were of questionable lineage. His August 1936 memorandum on a Four Year Plan, for example, had urged war in the East as part of a crusade against Moscow, a disguise revealed as fraudulent not two months later when he told Ciano that Germany used the "mantle of anti-Bolshevism" in order to oppose a French-British alliance. Moreover the real motivation for that 1936 memorandum may well have been a desire to overcome military support for Schacht's economic policies.[34] A similar case can be made for the Hossbach meeting. It would have been uncharacteristic for Hitler to assemble the commanders-in-chief and the foreign minister to discuss his thoughts on the future. Although the postwar Nuremberg trials so interpreted the meeting, even a superficial understanding of the nature of German government in 1937 invalidates that conclusion. Hitler no more sought to plot an aggressive campaign with his military and diplomatic advisors than he chose to consult Neurath over the Anti-Comintern Pact or the Japanese-Italian-German alliance. These considerations suggest more devious and hidden motivations.

Neurath was surprised by Hitler's presentation. Nothing seemed to warrant a discussion at this time of the possible dangers of warlike involvements. Only a few months earlier, Blomberg had concluded that Germany faced no danger of attack nor was it prepared to unleash one. General von Beck, chief of the general staff, agreed that "Germany is in no position to run the risk of war in Central Europe." The generals were not, however, averse to using Hitler's ideas of "conquest in the East" to gain a greater share of the resources and supplies of the Four Year Plan. Thus, in an August 1937 memorandum, General von Fritsch urged Blomberg to secure preference for the army, "because no Eastern nation can be annihilated in the air or on the water."[35]

This last phrase provides a key to the Hossbach meeting. Hjalmar Schacht, the economics minister, had been for years locked in battle with Göring concerning the Four Year Plan, with its emphasis upon military requirements, which he charged was creating a shortage of consumer goods and encouraging inflation. In the summer of 1937, Schacht gained army support for his position and brought the matter to Hitler. Characteristically, the chancellor took no sides and failed to respond to Schacht's suggested pause in rearmament for a reappraisal of the economic and fiscal situation. In the early fall of 1937, Schacht and Hitler heatedly argued at Berchtesgaden, and Hitler later told Speer that Schacht was sabotaging the rearmament program. Thereafter, Schacht refused to appear at his office, and let it be known that he no longer considered himself minister of economics.[36]

When Hitler refused to announce a replacement, economic planning was paralyzed. On November 1, 1937, Hans Lammers complained of the stalemate:

> It is always difficult for the Führer to arrive at decisions in personnel matters. He always hoped that the problems would solve themselves. A settlement [regarding Schacht] has therefore not yet occurred, because the Führer will not agree to the appointment of only a state secretary, but would, rather, like to name a minister. He always hopes that personnel questions will just solve themselves.

At the advice of his staff, Blomberg prevailed upon Hitler to call a meeting of the three commanders-in-chief to discuss the rearmament crisis. The initiative for the discussion, therefore, was not Hitler's, which explains why Neurath, who was unaware of the difficulties regarding raw materials and financing, was totally unprepared for the invitation and the course of the meeting.[37]

Apparently, Hitler decided to turn the issue around, by discussing entirely different and unrelated matters. It was a favorite device. The armaments experts called for the occasion waited in vain. After the war, Göring testified that shortly before the meeting began, Hitler complained that Fritsch was making trouble about the speed of rearmament, and that the chancellor would utilize the occasion to pressure him. To Göring's curiosity as to the last-minute inclusion of Neurath, Hitler replied: "Well, he did not want to handle this purely from the military point of view, and so he wanted to make it very clear to the commanders-in-chief, especially Fritsch . . . that the foreign political situation required this forced tempo of armaments. For this reason, he had included the foreign minister, who knew nothing at all about the scheme."[38]

Even should some new document throw additional light on Hitler's motivations in calling the meeting, its crucial importance for Neurath would be the same. With the other participants, he dismissed Hitler's exposition of the three cases as naive and implausible. Still the minister could not so easily forget the discussion, as apparently others were able to do. To the prison psychologist after the war, he insisted that he had received an "entirely different interpretation of that Hossbach speech. It was not so 'academic' as Raeder [now] pretends." Neurath realized that Hitler was not giving a considered evaluation of his foreign policy, or even a rational exposition of solutions to some outstanding problems, for he was well aware of Hitler's obsession with building a "political triangle" of Japan-Germany-Italy, which was not even mentioned. Neurath would have been able to dismiss the meeting from his mind had it been only Hitler's attempt to avoid an embarrassing discussion of emerging economic issues.[39] But for the first time, Neurath saw unmistakably that the chancellor would not hesitate to unleash Germany's military force in a series of small wars when he could do so with impunity. At the very least he sought a major international confrontation by 1943, and minor disturbances whenever he could get away with them. For Neurath such military adventures were irresponsible and unnecessary; Germany needed diplomacy and economic growth to regain its territory and rightful place. Now, Hitler had determined on the quick military blow. Clearly, the man who had uttered "irresponsible remarks" in 1933 about living space and ruthless Germanization of Eastern lands had not been softened by the possession of power. On the contrary, five years had only strengthened his resolve to demonstrate Germany's recovered military strength.

Neurath was aghast. All his foreign policy had been predicated on the belief that Germany's restoration would come through peaceful means; he feared even minor tactical confrontations would escalate into a military crisis ending European civilization. Recalling these events during his trial, Neurath made his position clear:

> Although the plans set forth by Hitler in that long speech had no concrete form, and various possibilities were envisaged, it was quite obvious to me that the whole tendency of his plans was of an aggressive nature. I was extremely upset at Hitler's speech, because it knocked the bottom out of the whole foreign policy which I had consistently pursued—the policy of employing only peaceful means. It was evident that I could not assume responsibility for such a [new] policy.

In his more spontaneous notes written prior to this testimony, Neurath was even firmer:

> As long as Hitler pursued the one great line of foreign policy, namely the restoration of authority and sovereignty within the German Reich and the peaceful growth of German prestige in the world, he and I were in agreement. But in the fall of 1937, he suddenly adopted a warlike tone.... Had Hitler in 1937 not lost his patience and replaced his previous peaceful policy with one of force, I am convinced that all the remaining questions could have been solved. But since any policy of force, in my opinion, infallibly must have led to war, and indeed to a second world war, I could only view my task as destroyed.[40]

Decision to Confront Hitler

Neurath departed deeply shaken and the next day sought out Fritsch and Beck, hoping to "stop this nonsense which Hitler has now concocted." During his daily morning walk, his daughter noticed his troubled preoccupation. When questioned, he replied: "I fear that now there will be a war." With his colleague Vico von Bülow-Schwante, whom he saw shortly before meeting with the army leaders, he was even more dramatic: "Now Hitler's gone completely berserk." To another friend, he indicated his conviction that he would have to resign.[41]

Anguished, he discussed with the commander-in-chief and chief of the general staff a plan of action. Fritsch, who was scheduled to pay a courtesy call upon Hitler at Berchtesgaden before leaving on an extended Egyptian vacation, agreed to repeat the military considerations against any scheme to use force against Czechoslovakia or Austria. For his part, Neurath would assemble a full diplomatic brief for the chancellor, stressing that developments in Central Europe were proceeding well enough without force. Finally, Neurath and Fritsch persuaded Beck, with whom the foreign office had a record of close cooperation, to try winning over Blomberg. Beck's subsequent memorandum has survived and clearly reflects Neurath's ideas. Challenging Hitler's pessimistic outlook that only force could solve Germany's problems, he argued against an aggressive policy. European cultural lines, as Neurath often mentioned, had been stabilized for more than a thousand years and could not easily be altered. Instead of military expansion, Beck proposed Neurath's scheme of greater participation in world economy and trade. His argument reflected Neurath's successful policy:

> The enormity of French and British opposition to any extension of German living space or German power is beyond question. But it is out of place to label this opposition as irrevocable or insurmountable, especially in the light of the totally insufficient attempts in the past to overcome it. Politics is the art of the possible. All three nations coexist in this world, and all three are in Europe. It would therefore be far better first to exhaust all possibilities in trying to arrange some settlement, especially in view of the mutual power relationships. Moreover, such a policy would be more intelligent, even should it come to some future confrontation.

Beck's memorandum echoed Neurath's arguments during the Hossbach meeting: Hitler's historical parallels were inexact; the chronological predictions for the three cases were faulty; and the ability to reap benefits from an occupied Czechoslovakia or Austria was questionable.[42]

Despite a sound position, Fritsch's conversation with Hitler proved fruitless, Beck's attempt to convert Blomberg was equally unsuccessful, and Neurath was unable even to reach Hitler. Apparently alerted by his talks with Fritsch, the chancellor avoided seeing his foreign minister. Tenaciously, Neurath sought a hearing, for bolstered by recent Austrian and British developments, he was certain of eventual German success if the peaceful program continued. Hitler's rebuffs on this occasion humiliated him. As he told friends: "Twice I went over to the chancellery and asked to see Hitler. Once they told me outright that it was impossible to see him today. He was too busy. And the second time, they made me wait a full hour or more in the waiting room before an aide returned to say that he was terribly sorry, but the chancellor could not receive me today." The strain took its toll. Worry and anxiety brought on at least two severe attacks of his angina pectoris, and for several days in late November, Neurath was confined to bed. He remained in the blackest of moods, so unlike his usual self that many of his acquaintances noticed the change.[43]

Determined that Hitler hear the other side, Neurath suggested that the chancellor talk with Lord Halifax, then visiting Germany. Ribbentrop's staff reported on the background of this visit:

> Neurath hurriedly prepared the ground for this political visit, no doubt thinking of his own aborted trip to London, in order once more to bring the English government into closer ties with Germany. . . . In certain circles within the foreign office (especially the political division), they speculate that Neurath's pressure to receive Halifax encountered a certain resistance from Hitler. . . . Hence certain men of the foreign office doubt whether, in the light of these developments, the visit will be a success. And any debacle will automatically be Neurath's.

Indeed, the visit was a hastily planned gamble, and was unsuccessful. Hitler was morose and moody, stressing the failure of other countries to honor his proposals. While assuring Halifax of his desire for a peaceful solution of the Austrian and Czech questions, Hitler's outlook was not improved when Halifax repeated the invitation for Neurath to visit London. Weakly apologetic for the disastrous meeting, Neurath knew he could do no more. How ironic it must have been to him to hear the chancellor, a few days later, urge civil service reform so that the best men of the nation would again recognize "the honor there was in being an official." What function could an official serve, if he were not allowed even a hearing?[44]

Nevertheless, Neurath continued to take an active role in the foreign office during these trying days. He fought hard to keep Germany out of involvement in the China-Japan war, and was the principal force behind the offer of mediation between the two warring nations. Similarly, in the issue of Austria, he told visiting

French politicians that Germany could handle (without French tutelage) the Austrian and Czech problems. In a memorandum, Neurath claimed that he was "protesting against the attempt of the French to prevent any evolution at all." Thus, in both Asia and Europe, Neurath tried to demonstrate to Hitler an effective program that could make progress without resorting to military aggression.[45]

A secret memorandum of late December 1937 soberly evaluated the European political situation. Although the background and subsequent use of this particular document is unknown, it appears to be Neurath's reply to Hitler's recent statements, for a trained diplomat would certainly have wanted in his files a precise account of his own program. The document noted that in recent conversations both the French and British were distinctly more friendly, recognizing the legitimacy of Germany's boundary revisions, and decreasing their own demands for concessions. The time had obviously come to reopen serious negotiations, because in the past such accomplishments as rearmament and the abolition of the demilitarized zone had occurred only after Berlin had demonstrated its sincerity. In a covering letter, the head of the political division, Ernst von Weizsäcker, strongly supported this approach: "We ourselves are not yet strong enough to engage in European conflicts and shall therefore not seek any." He urged the improvement of Germany's political position through negotiations with France and Great Britain. With this argument, Neurath hoped to head off Hitler's proposed alternative series of small *Blitzkriegs*.[46]

But Neurath's inability even to present his viewpoint to Hitler was beginning to wear on him. Should the situation continue, he told his family, he would simply resign. Aware of his isolation and powerlessness, he had several times spoken of leaving. "There is no pleasure in the job anymore," he told Krosigk only a few weeks before the Hossbach meeting. To his son he confessed that if some suitable replacement were in sight, "I would gladly hang my cloak up on the nail," and go off to Württemberg. But in recent months, only Ribbentrop had stood in line as a possible successor. Neurath's new readiness to resign may have been partially related to Ribbentrop's disgrace with Hitler.[47]

In any case, when all his efforts to see Hitler failed, Neurath wrote early in December requesting an interview and indicating his desire to resign. The chancellor did not even acknowledge receipt of the letter. Still smarting from the unexpected opposition from Neurath, Fritsch, and Blomberg, Hitler had carefully isolated himself in Berchtesgaden to brood on his suspicions. Over the Christmas vacation, Neurath consulted several close friends. For the first time, he explained his situation to the Ritters, who advised him not to resign without once more trying to dissuade Hitler from his fantastic schemes. Reluctantly, Neurath agreed. Baroness von Ritter saw how his helplessness tormented him, when he said: "It is horrible to play the role of Cassandra." In any case, he would no longer cooperate in despised policies, no matter what the personal consequences. These concerns overshadowed the family festivities in Leinfelderhof. Following a New Year's dinner, Neurath, his son-in-law State Secretary Mackensen, and Karl Strölin, Lord Mayor of Stuttgart, conferred on the subject of Neurath's resignation.

Although not privy to the talks, his daughter remembers even after many years the unusual gloom surrounding the vacation. Neurath returned to Berlin uneasy about the future and determined to meet Hitler at the earliest opportunity.[48]

On January 14, 1938, Neurath was present when Hitler spoke with Polish leaders Josef Beck and Josef Lipski. The moods and themes of the Hossbach meeting prevailed, and in the presence of foreign statesmen Hitler revealed his preoccupation with Austria and Czechoslovakia. Although citing no timetable, he left no doubt in the minds of the Polish statesmen that he had closed the door on peaceful solutions. Using words resembling those of the November meeting, Hitler "declared with absolute firmness" that he would not hesitate to march "as quickly as lightning."[49]

This conversation gave Neurath additional courage and an opportunity. After the diplomats left, he insisted on an immediate interview with Hitler. The foreign minister began by expressing his doubts over the direction of the chancellor's policy, noting that even the generals were wary of the dangers of war. He reminded Hitler of his own words in 1933 that a new war would be "sheer madness." To force the issues of Czechoslovakia and Austria would bring war, and Neurath would "have no part" in such a policy, the more undesirable because it was so unnecessary. "Many of [Hitler's] plans could be realized by peaceful means, even if the process were slower." As Neurath was about to elaborate, probably by citing the recent favorable developments in Austria, Hitler burst into a torrent of words. "I can't wait any longer," he shouted, launching into a lengthy monologue. Then abruptly he dismissed Neurath without answering any of his points.[50]

Drawing himself to his full height, Neurath asked the chancellor to consider his request for immediate retirement. In words both blunt and courageous, he told Hitler: "I cannot be associated with an aggressive policy, which must inevitably lead to a new world war." A stunned Hitler, without replying, walked away. Furious, Neurath returned to his office and apparently wrote a letter repeating his request and asking for Hitler's immediate consideration. Despite his best efforts, Neurath had been unable to dissuade Hitler; it was time, he believed, that he should go.[51]

Neurath as a member of Corps Suevia, Tübingen, 1896.

Wedding picture of Marie (Mannie) von Felseck and Constantin Freiherr von Neurath, 1901.

Neurath as Consul in Copenhagen, 1919.

Ambassador Constantin Freiherr von Neurath with Benito Mussolini, Rome, December 29, 1926.

Ambassador von Neurath presents his credentials as the new representative of Germany at the Court of St. James's, November 18, 1930. (*United Press International Photo*)

The Hitler-Papen Cabinet, January 30, 1933: (from l. to r.) Chancellor Adolph Hitler, Vice-Chancellor Franz von Papen, Minister of Interior Wilhelm Frick, Foreign Minister Constantin von Neurath, Minister of Economy and Food Alfred Hugenberg, Minister of Finance Count Schwerin von Krosigk, Minister of Labor Franz Seldte, Minister of Defence General Werner von Blomberg, Minister of Transportation Paul von Eltz-Rübenach, Minister without portfolio Hermann Goering, Employment Commissioner Guenther Gereke, and Walter Funk, thought to be Hitler's liaison with industry when this picture was published in February 1933. (*United Press International Photo*)

THE STAFF OF THE GERMAN FOREIGN OFFICE

Foreign Minister Neurath and State Secretary Bernhard Wilhelm von Bülow

Minister Director Gerhard Köpke, Head of the West European Department (*United Press International Photo*)

Minister Director Richard Meyer, Head of the East European Department (*United Press International Photo*)

Hitler with Foreign Minister Neurath and State Secretary Meissner, on the balcony of the Old Chancellery, Wilhelmstrasse, Berlin, 1934. First reception after Hitler assumed the office and powers of the Presidency. (*United Press International Photo*)

Ambassador Ulrich von Hassell, Foreign Minister Neurath, Hitler, and Mussolini in Venice, February 26, 1934. (*United Press International Photo*)

Adolf Hitler and Foreign Minister Constantin von Neurath in formal attire, 1935. *(Photo Süddeutscher Verlag)*

Sir John Simon, British Foreign Minister, Neurath, and Hitler, Berlin, 1935. (*United Press International Photo*)

Hitler congratulated Neurath on his 65th birthday, February 2, 1938. (*United Press International Photo*)

THREE FACES OF CONSTANTIN FREIHERR VON NEURATH

An official picture of the German Foreign Minister in his office.

A typical picture of the passionate hunter.

The Honorary SS Obergruppenführer, on the occasion of Mussolini's state visit, 1937.

Neurath arrives at Leinfelderhof after being released from Spandau Prison, having served more than nine years of his 15 year sentence. He is welcomed by his brother, his wife, and daughter. November, 1954. (*Photo Süddeutscher Verlag*)

Neurath's last picture, Leinfelderhof, 1955.

CHAPTER

12

THE YEAR OF DECISION: 1938

On November 6, 1937, the day after Hitler's dramatic Hossbach conference, Joachim von Ribbentrop in Rome brought Italy into the Anti-Comintern Pact, thus establishing the Japanese-Italian-German "political triangle." Taken together these two events challenged both the democratic West and communist Russia. As Hassell wrote Neurath: "Here we are dealing with a new orientation of German foreign policy, which, upon the promptings of no less a person than the ambassador to London, consciously pits Germany against Great Britain, and openly reckons with a world war."[1]

Clearly, Hitler was searching for new directions, and Ribbentrop proposed a solution that complemented the chancellor's own prejudices: only force can change the status quo in Eastern Europe; a strong military alliance among Japan, Italy, and Germany would deter British intervention if German use of arms against central European nations were limited to quick and decisive takeovers. Before Hitler could implement this new approach, he would have to do something about the cautious Neurath, who, he told an acquaintance, loomed as a conscience. Neurath's reputation with the Nazi leadership sank to a new low point in these months. Rudolf Hess, near the end of the year, "went off into a tirade against Neurath and German diplomats in general and their links with International Diplomacy," while German and Italian party leaders agreed that Neurath was an uncooperative "anglophile," whom Ribbentrop would shortly replace. As Hitler himself gained self-confidence in foreign affairs, he had little use for a minister who saw "military as well as political difficulties, and thus betrayed the head of state." As he later explained: "When I formed the party, I demanded absolute courage, and people said to me: 'Look, if you demand that, no reasonable man will join you.' The so-called reasonable men then were always weaklings. I did not want them! I wanted fanatics, and I obtained them."[2]

Accustomed to independence and too proud to support a policy he despised,

Neurath was far from fanatical, and his offer to resign still stood. Yet despite Neurath's hostility to his program, Hitler was not prepared for an open break; once again chance permitted him to solve the problem by linking it up with another issue.

The Blomberg–Fritsch Crisis

On January 12, 1938, Field Marshal Werner von Blomberg, the minister of war, married Eva Gruhn, a "child of the people," in his own words, and as it soon developed, a woman with a police record for prostitution. The discovery of Frau von Blomberg's past and the Field Marshal's refusal to have the marriage annulled, coupled with charges of homosexuality brought against General Werner Freiherr von Fritsch, the army's commander-in-chief, created a scandal in the high command. Wide-ranging personnel changes were predicted and at least one observer sensed an uneasiness equivalent to that preceding the Röhm massacre of June 1934. Hitler decided to disguise the crisis in the military leadership by initiating personnel changes on many levels. He discussed the idea of removing Neurath with Göring, who strongly disapproved of replacing the minister with Ribbentrop. When Hitler explained that he would retain Neurath for future consultations, Göring suggested the formation of a privy council for foreign affairs. Characteristically, Hitler chose this means to avoid a difficult decision. Setting aside the man who still tried to "put the brakes" on numerous plans, he could camouflage the dismissal as a promotion and still have Neurath's expert advice whenever he wanted.[3]

Thus in late January, following Neurath's renewed request to resign, Hans Lammers recorded that Hitler "considered it advisable at this time to carry out a change in leadership. Baron von Neurath and his foreign office 'are not cooperating' and he had for some time now decided to replace Neurath with Ribbentrop. The latter would be commissioned with reforming the foreign office." But until the military personnel crisis had been resolved, Hitler kept this decision secret. On January 31, he promised leading generals to "divert the spotlight from the army, force Europe to hold its breath, and by new appointments to a number of positions, avoid the impression of weakness and rather suggest a concentration of forces."[4]

On February 2, 1938, Constantin Freiherr von Neurath celebrated his sixty-fifth birthday and fortieth anniversary in the foreign service. By official order, the press ran lengthy articles praising this devoted civil servant and patriot; Hitler announced that he would personally attend ceremonies in his honor. Neurath protested this "circus," but his wishes were disregarded. The foreign office scheduled gala receptions, one for the diplomatic corps, and another for the entire office staff. Adolf Hitler appeared at noon in the Wilhelmstrasse and presented his foreign minister with a large oil painting—Constantine's tomb! During the formal dinner, an adjutant detected a "sunset spirit." "All of the men in the room were either open enemies or were profoundly skeptical of the 'new Germany.' After six years of power, Hitler still had not cracked the foreign office, but the men in charge were growing old."[5]

Neurath was unimpressed by the festivities, and as the chancellor offered birthday congratulations, the foreign minister, in an uncharacteristic departure from diplomatic courtesy, reminded Hitler of his resignation requests, and asked once again to be released from his post. A stunned Hitler "looked as if he had swallowed the wrong way." Quickly recovering, he grasped the hand of his minister: "Herr von Neurath, I could never let you leave my side. You must make this sacrifice for me." Still holding Neurath's hand, Hitler turned to Frau von Mackensen who stood beside her father: "You know," he said, "this man is like a father to me. I can't let him go. I need him for foreign affairs." This pretty speech was familiar to Neurath who had heard it all before, but Hans Lammers was amazed. While Hitler was assuring Neurath of his full support, the papers dismissing the minister and appointing Ribbentrop rested, already signed by the chancellor, on Lammers's desk. Not 48 hours later, they would be released.[6]

Neurath contemplated joylessly the continuation of his unhappy situation. Nevertheless, he was pleased to receive an invitation early on February 4 to see the chancellor later that afternoon. The meeting was both long and friendly; Neurath told his friend Bülow-Schwante, immediately afterwards, that he had found Hitler amicable and calm. They had discussed and solved a number of problems. That evening, when Neurath had just finished dinner, Hitler's private adjutant, Julius Schaub, telephoned that he was to come to the chancellery at once. Neurath replied that there was obviously some mistake, since he had seen Hitler only a few hours before. Schaub left the phone to confirm his instructions and then replied: "No, it is no mistake, you should come right over." Neurath promised to return as soon as he had finished his excellent cigar.[7]

Arriving at the rather crowded chancellery sometime after 10:30 P.M., Neurath met Hitler who left the group to which he was talking and led his foreign minister into the Wintergarden. His opening words were blunt: "Look, I have appointed Ribbentrop as my new foreign minister." Neurath was stunned, and saw in a flash how he had been duped in the last few days. He immediately rose to leave, saying: "You may do whatever you want. There is no need to ask me." Hitler hurriedly waved him to a chair, and started to explain: "On all really important problems, I want to talk with you, therefore I have created a special institution, a secret cabinet council, and I want you to head it, for then you will still be at my side. I have great need of you in the days ahead. I cannot bear to have you leave my side." Neurath heard the chancellor out in silence; a few minutes later, he left the chancellery and made his way through the garden to his villa.[8]

His mood was reflected in the ironic greeting he gave his son as he entered his home: "You can congratulate me," he called out. "I have been sacked!" To surprised questions from his family, he only replied with bitterness: "Well, I have long ago learned you can't do anything with Herr Hitler. What else could I have expected from a man like that?" His greater concern was with the news that Ribbentrop had been designated as his successor. Only two weeks before, Hitler had solemnly assured Neurath that he would never appoint Ribbentrop foreign minister. Neurath telephoned the Ritters with the news. "Well, I have taken my exit," he began. His conversation was grave and his mood depressed. Although somewhat reticent about the event, he used an expression which Baroness von Ritter recalled with clarity: "If someone is building a house, Neurath said, and the house is practically finished, and then the master sends in inexperienced workers, the result is certain beyond any doubt. The house will fall in." This metaphor illuminates Neurath's reactions to his dismissal. Though he was obviously relieved to shed increasingly onerous responsibilities, his worst fears were being realized. Hitler was moving Germany ever faster toward military confrontations, and the structure which he had so carefully erected to avoid war would now surely collapse. Only a few days later, to his aide Herbert Siegfried, Neurath announced with abrupt finality: "Well, my dear Siegfried, I fear that now war can no longer be avoided."[9] This bitter realization continued to darken his normally jovial disposition.

Even though Neurath's departure was announced simultaneously with the changes in the military, civil service, and diplomatic corps, the impact was profound. Few believed Neurath would retain his influence in Berlin; most saw the minister's removal as the beginning of radical changes in foreign affairs. Although some diplomats had regretted Neurath's lack of dynamism, all acknowledged that he had at least tried to contain Hitler and had on some occasions prevailed. Foreign diplomats and moderate Germans alike lamented Neurath's retirement; one called it a "major disaster."[10]

Neurath sought to leave Berlin immediately, but Hitler ordered that he continue to occupy the foreign minister's villa. Ribbentrop chose to be housed in the more ostentatious presidential palace. All who knew Neurath testified to his humiliation when introducing his successor to the staff in the Wilhelmstrasse. To wish Ribbentrop well in the years that lay ahead took remarkable loyalty; thereafter Neurath hurried off to Leinfelderhof, to join his wife who had left Berlin immediately after her husband's ouster. Although his wife told friends that Neurath was through with public life and would never again return to Berlin, within a week he was back in the capital, upon the chancellor's request. "It took a true greatness of soul," Baroness von Neurath commented in her diary, "for Neurath to accept the invitation for Hitler's diplomatic dinner."[11]

Anschluss with Austria

Shortly after his return, Neurath found himself drawn back to foreign affairs. In late January 1938, when Hitler had been most preoccupied with the personnel crisis, Ambassador Papen achieved the breakthrough which Neurath had always expected. Austrian Chancellor Schuschnigg had agreed to meet Hitler, and Neurath was convinced that Austria would quietly pass into Germany's orbit.* But the

---

*In late February, Neurath pointedly told the French ambassador that "all controversies between ourselves and Austria were a matter for those two countries alone," and that Paris would have to reconcile herself to "the possible affiliation of Austria and Germany." He strongly advised Hitler to hold an early meeting with Schuschnigg. See Lipski, *Papers,* 328; Neurath's memoranda, February 19 and 23, 1938, in AA 1798/490297 and DGFP D/I, 212-14; and Eichstädt, *Von Dollfuss zu Hitler,* 267-78.

chancellor was too involved to even discuss the issue. After the personnel changes in Berlin, Hitler retreated to Berchtesgaden, where he seized upon Papen's mention of a meeting with Schuschnigg in order to camouflage even further the serious weaknesses within his government. The resulting agreement called for Nazi participation in the Austrian government and a general amnesty for all political prisoners. Neurath observed "with a note of melancholy," that Hitler and Ribbentrop were now "reaping the fruits of his work, for the initiative and the elaborate plan for Schuschnigg's meeting with Hitler were his." Still, he was encouraged that his evolutionary policy was still operating, and he talked to the British and French ambassadors to ensure this "normalization of relations with Austria," thus removing "a potential danger to peace." From these conversations, Neurath believed that no country "would start a war over the *Anschluss*," which he thought was near; his fears of irresponsible foreign policy under Ribbentrop had not as yet materialized.[12]

Ribbentrop too expected no problems in the days ahead, and on March 8 went to London to take official leave of his former post. But aware that Berlin's evolutionary methods would pull the reins of power gradually from his hands, Schuschnigg decided to provoke either the Austrian Nazis or the German government into some overt action. Hoping to exploit resulting world sympathy for Austria, he announced a plebiscite on Austrian independence, which he knew would increase the chances of German armed intervention. By using a rigged plebiscite, Schuschnigg sought to forestall the triumph of Neurath's program.[13]

Completely surprised by the announcement of the plebiscite, on the evening of March 9, 1938, Hitler met with Edmund von Glaise-Horstenau, a Nazi sympathizer and minister without portfolio in the Vienna government, who had coincidentally been visiting in South Germany when Schuschnigg made his announcement. Glaise-Horstenau found the chancellor overwrought and indecisive; after an unproductive two-and-a-half hour talk, Hitler suddenly announced his intention of seeking advice from professional experts. "Unfortunately, Ribbentrop is far away in London," he told his visitor, but then added: "You know what? There is someone very close by—the prudent and discreet Neurath. I will call him to me." On the morning of March 10, Hitler spoke with Neurath who urged him to oppose the plebiscite, which might conceivably produce an international guarantee of Austrian independence. Convinced that Schuschnigg had acted rashly and prematurely, Neurath told the chancellor this opportunity for Germany should not be allowed to slip away.[14]

Following this conversation, Hitler conferred with Wilhelm Keppler, his special advisor on Austrian affairs who had just returned from Vienna, and then with military representatives who opposed an attack, but suggested a "symbolic" occupation with a token number of troops. These meetings terminated at noon; General Keitel left with orders to plan for the invasion and occupation of Austria. The chancellor again spoke with Neurath, indicating the gravity of the situation, and his own decision to block the plebiscite, if necessary with an invasion. Neurath objected, suggesting that a partial mobilization of troops or general troop movement near the frontiers would serve the same purpose without risking war. Agreeing, Hitler asked Neurath to handle any resulting foreign complications. Although Neurath suggested calling Ribbentrop home, Göring objected, and Neurath ultimately agreed to serve in a special advisory capacity.[15]

Neurath regarded the foreign situation as favorable. France was paralyzed by another cabinet crisis and Great Britain would never object to peaceful handling of the Austrian question. Should violence be avoided, even Mussolini would agree to a change of government in Vienna. But Neurath strongly urged that no troops cross the border, unless they were invited by the legitimate Austrian government. Only if Vienna requested help for the maintenance of law and order should German troops move. Hitler listened in silence and later told close friends that in such situations, Neurath was always his best advisor. As Goebbels retold the story, "in decisive moments, such advice was better than gold."[16]

Expecting no further immediate developments, Neurath left the chancellery. In his absence, Hitler ordered the Eighth Army mobilized. Two hours later, Glaise-Horstenau left for Vienna bearing the party's ultimatum: cancel the plebiscite before noon, or the German government would regard the Berchtesgaden agreement as voided and undertake the necessary countermeasures. Accompanying the ultimatum were vague hints that Arthur Seyss-Inquart, a leading Austrian Nazi, would be welcomed as the new chancellor and that he might appeal for German troops. Simultaneously, another leading Austrian National Socialist was dispatched to Vienna to orchestrate party agitation for cancellation of the plebiscite and Schuschnigg's resignation, or civil war. Believing that official protests and veiled threats of military action would be sufficient, Neurath did not learn until much later of these orders to the Nazi party in Austria. Nor did he ever suspect how determined Hitler had now become to achieve a spectacular foreign success in order to divert attention from the domestic troubles, especially the unrest in the high command.[17]

Early on March 11, Neurath returned to the Reichs Chancellery, having learned in the meantime of the mobilization orders. He greeted Hitler with the pointed inquiry: were troops really necessary? Wouldn't diplomatic pressure upon Schuschnigg force withdrawal of the plebiscite? The chancellor was adamant, however, and indicated that troops would enter Vienna that night. Neurath repeated his previous arguments, but when the chancellor remained committed to invasion plans, Neurath introduced two prepared statements. One assured Italy that "the sole purpose of the [Austrian action] is to prevent the spilling of blood of the German race in Austria and to ensure that the Austrian nation, in conformity with its right of self-determination, [is] to decide its own fate." To this, Neurath added assurances of German recognition of the "Brenner frontier." His second concern was for Prague, which would feel threatened by any German military action. Hitler agreed that he "had no intention of proceeding against the Czechs," for he thought that relations between the two countries had improved of late. Pleased at this disavowal of the scheme mentioned at the Hossbach conference to settle the issues of Austria and Czechoslovakia simultaneously, Neurath's statement committed Germany "to the methods of procedure of the arbitration treaty of 1925. Breach of the arbitration treaty [would be recognized] as a *causus foederis*." Hitler approved both statements, but suggested that the second be held for future use. He immediately left to write a personal letter to Mussolini which, while incorporating Neurath's suggestions, was composed in a more flamboyant style. As usual, the Prince of Hesse was ordered to hand-deliver the message to Mussolini as soon as possible.[18]

In the meantime, Berlin remained uneasy. Papen, recalled from Vienna, found the chancellery tense, crowded with ministers, state secretaries, and adjutants. Hitler and his minions believed that either the plebiscite would be called off or Germany would overthrow the Austrian government. But the chancellor's approval of invasion plan "Otto"—which was nonexistent and was being hastily improvised by a reluctant general staff—carefully stipulated its implementation for March 12 only "if other measures prove unsuccessful." Hitler still could not make up his mind, and had not yet resolved to attack Austria. Believing Vienna would still retract the plebiscite plans, Neurath left the chancellery in the early afternoon to supervise developments in the foreign office. He was, therefore, not present when the appearance of Hermann Göring completely changed the picture.[19]

Hastily called out of the Court of Honor demanded by General Fritsch, over which he was presiding, Göring "grasped with both hands the lead vacated by the vacillating Hitler." Aware of how disastrously the revelations of the trumped-up case against Fritsch would rebound against the government, and knowing that already the ends had begun to unravel, Göring was determined to produce a foreign victory to prevent internal disgrace. In the next few hours, he turned the situation completely around. Shortly before 3:00, he placed the first of his telephone calls to Vienna. Upon learning that Schuschnigg had canceled the plebiscite, he decided to escalate Berlin's demands, insisting upon Schuschnigg's resignation and the formation of a new Austrian government under Seyss-Inquart. He also suggested that Seyss-Inquart now forward the request for German intervention. Unless these conditions were met by 7:30 P.M., German troops would invade Austria.[20]

At 5:00, tension visibly relaxed when word reached Berlin that Seyss-Inquart had been appointed chancellor. The army was instructed to cancel orders for invasion, but a few minutes later Göring discovered that the Austrian president had unexpectedly refused to appoint Seyss-Inquart. Convinced that Vienna sought to make Germany look ridiculous, Göring ordered draconian measures, telling those in the chancellery: "The existence of Austria is past history." General Muff, Germany's military attaché in Vienna, was to tell the Austrian president that "if by 7:30 P.M., Field Marshal Göring had not received the report that Seyss-Inquart had become chancellor, 200,000 men standing in readiness at the border would march in. The president would bear full responsibility for the consequences of his refusal."[21]

Following this powerful threat, the Austrian affair moved out of the domestic realm. No longer was it possible to claim that Austrians were giving ultimatums to Austrians. Without consulting the foreign office or Neurath, Göring stripped away the mask which even Hitler would have preferred to leave in place, and events gathered speed. Radio Vienna announced the resignation of the entire government, but no new cabinet was mentioned, and at 7:50 P.M., twenty minutes after Göring's ultimatum had expired, Schuschnigg went on the radio to denounce (erroneously as it turned out) the action of German troops crossing the frontiers, and to announce that the Austrian government, brutally threatened, was bowing to force. After a hurried conversation with Hitler, Göring again called Vienna. To the startled German military attaché, he announced his version of events: the Austrian cabinet had resigned except for Seyss-Inquart, who, as minister of the interior, had formed a caretaker government and invited German troops into the country. Without awaiting such an invitation, Hitler now signed the invasion orders, stipulating merely that the telegram from Seyss-Inquart must be forthcoming. Three minutes later, Göring called Vienna again, and dictated a draft invitation.[22]

During these hours, Neurath was in the foreign office, handling inquiries about German intentions. Apparently he learned of Berlin's ultimatum only after the war, when transcriptions of Göring's conversations became key documents in the prosecution's case. At 9:40 P.M., Seyss-Inquart's telegram arrived and Neurath immediately brought it to the chancellery, apparently unaware that troops had already been ordered to cross the frontier. Having read the telegram, Papen suggested heightening Germany's international stature by declining to make use of this invitation and refusing to implement military occupation. Reports from Vienna confirmed a generally quiet situation. To persuade Hitler to accept a moderate response, Papen spoke first to Fritz Wiedemann, Hitler's adjutant, and then tried to enlist Neurath's help in reversing the decision to dispatch troops. To their surprise, they found him calm and confident. Austria would offer no resistance; war was impossible. Moreover, he suspected that Hitler was immovable on this symbolic point: "He has dreamed for so many years of marching into Austria at the head of his divisions," Neurath told Papen and Wiedemann. "Let us give him that pleasure." Once again, Neurath fell victim to his fatal preconception: as long as war was avoided, Hitler's humors were relatively harmless and could be permitted.[23]

The next day was difficult. Substituting for Ribbentrop who was furious at being prohibited by a special order of the Führer from returning to Berlin, Neurath had to face diplomatic representatives, and tell some flat lies. His story did not vary: Schuschnigg's provocations had forced Austrian nationalists to demand his replacement by a new government, which in turn freely requested the presence of German troops. Berlin had not overtly exercised pressure nor issued ultimatums. Germany's hands were morally clean. For the respectable bureaucrat and diplomat of the old order, it was a sorry performance.[24]

Supernumerary in Berlin

Immediately following Ribbentrop's return, Neurath left for a month's stay at his Württemberg estate. Thus he had no part in the decision to carry out full *An-*

schluss, but when Hitler met him in late March in Stuttgart, and asked him to return to Berlin, he agreed. His partial success with Hitler over Austria led Neurath to hope for some degree of continued influence. Returning to Berlin in April, he found that the chancellor's zeal for the mammoth scale in architecture had finally extended to the graceful old villa in the garden of the foreign office. In 1937, Hitler had asked Albert Speer to redecorate the minister's home more in keeping with the importance of the office. The Neuraths politely but firmly rejected this offer. Now, in order to give proper setting to Speer's new Reichs Chancellery, the entire villa would be torn down. Reluctantly, the Neuraths moved into a newly purchased official residence in Dahlem, where Neurath kept his office until February 1939, after which he moved into a suite of rooms in the chancellery. From this vantage point, he still hoped to affect the counsels of government.[25]

Of course, Neurath did still have a title and staff. On paper, the Secret Cabinet Council, composed of eight prominent officials (five cabinet ministers and the three commanders-in-chief) made eminent sense. Since regular cabinet meetings had finally ceased, a small council to discuss the outstanding issues in foreign affairs would be an effective power. Hans Lammers's drafts for the new body provided that the council would meet regularly, prepare position papers, and provide Neurath, as president, with direct access to all materials touching foreign policy.* It was designed, apparently, as a new power center, fitting perfectly into the conqueror state. Neurath, however, was hardly the man to seize the advantages in such an opportunity.[26]

Moreover, still smarting over Neurath's activities preceding the *Anschluss* and jealous at anyone who might limit his own sphere of influence, Ribbentrop demanded that the proposed draft be withdrawn or drastically altered:

> As you know, the Führer and Reichs Chancellor has designated a secret cabinet council and its president, Reichs Minister von Neurath, in order to provide him with personal advice in matters of foreign policy on specific occasions. The secret cabinet council is not concerned with the conduct of foreign policy, for according to the decision of the Führer, this right rests *exclusively* with the minister of foreign affairs. Should foreign policy questions come before other ministries, they must necessarily turn them over to my office, since foreign policy decisions should and can be executed only through the foreign office.
>
> Information for the president of the secret cabinet council, therefore, can and may appropriately be provided only by the foreign office. Following the wishes of the Führer, therefore, I have reserved for myself, and so decree, the right to provide to the president of the secret cabinet council all information concerning the broad lines of our foreign policy.

---

*In his earlier versions, obviously influenced by Hitler's original ideas, Lammers described a council which would have direct access to all matters of foreign policy, and provide Neurath with broad powers. His final version, drafted after the *Anschluss*, reduced the council to the vague task of "advising the Führer in questions of foreign policy," but still required that Neurath be kept informed of "all developments in the Reich ministries, insofar as they concern foreign policy."

Simultaneously, Ribbentrop directed his staff to cease distributing foreign office material to Neurath. Since many of his most trusted former colleagues had been transferred, Neurath received no copies of official correspondence or memoranda, but only newspapers, which he avidly read. Forced to rely upon private conversations with friends in the Berlin diplomatic corps, and a few leaks from Ernst von Weizsäcker, the new state secretary who was well disposed toward him, Neurath was apprised of some important developments. Subsequently, Weizsäcker dispatched one of his own protegés to serve as adjutant and preserve the link between Neurath and the foreign office.[27]

Despite such handicapping arrangements, Neurath accepted this anomalous position, settling for whatever influence he could exert by his presence, in the hope thereby to gain access to Hitler and perhaps some modicum of control to restrain any dangerous drift in German policy. After forty years in international diplomacy, it was also difficult for Neurath to completely cut himself off from his past. Had 1938 been a year of peaceful unimportance, perhaps he might have become, as he had often expressly desired, just a gentleman farmer in Leinfelderhof. But a sense of responsibility drew him back from that comfortable fate. Because he considered his title as president of the secret cabinet council only a "device to soften the bad impression created by my departure," and suspected that Hitler did not really want to discuss matters with such a potentially important group, Neurath made no attempt to assemble the council or bring it into activity. In fact, the council never met, not even to organize itself. He would use its imposing facade to play a moderating role, and in his first effort (the Sudeten crisis of August and September 1938), he was spectacularly successful.[28]

Immediately following the Anschluss, Hitler had informed his generals that "the solution of the Czechoslovak question was not pressing. We must first digest Austria." Nevertheless, by the end of March 1938, the chancellor ordered new tactics: the Sudeten Germans must initiate a series of unacceptable demands. But Neurath, emphasizing the progress that had already been made, urged patience. He utilized a birthday call on Hitler to raise the issue. To his surprise, the chancellor agreed. "He stood," he told Neurath, "at the pinnacle of his foreign policy successes, and one should not go too far." To General Keitel he announced the same theme: "It is not my intention to smash Czechoslovakia by military action in the immediate future, unless an unavoidable development of the political conditions *within* Czechoslovakia forces the issues, or political events in Europe create a particularly favorable opportunity which may perhaps never recur." Consistent with his Hossbach comments, while not seeking to use force, Hitler would not, given the suitable moment, hesitate to order "a decisive and ruthless attack."[29]

Although Hitler was not yet committed to military action, Neurath learned of increased tensions among Western nations, who feared the Czech question would precipitate a European war. When Prague ordered full mobilization of its army on May 20, citing alleged (but erroneous reports of) German troop concentrations on the frontier, Hitler was outraged, and immediately decided to revise previous orders. From Berchtesgaden he told Berlin officials to expect a conference when he returned on May 28. By this time, Western diplomats were convinced that both appeals and threats went unheeded when presented to Foreign Minister Ribbentrop, who, they complained, "is so intent on what he is going to say himself that he will not listen; he is too stupid to understand what the other is saying or even appreciate its importance." Thus both the French and British ambassadors made special efforts to warn Neurath, in the hope that he would fairly present their messages. For his part, Neurath confessed uneasiness over dangers inherent in "Hitler's periodic explosions of furious rage," and admitted these explosions "would be fanned rather than damped down by Herr von Ribbentrop." Aware of the crisis "which might be produced in the event of a sudden incident," Neurath resolved to approach Hitler upon the chancellor's return and deliver the British and French warnings, thus blocking any rash action.[30]

During the afternoon of May 28, he participated in what seems to have been a large, somewhat impromptu conference in the chancellery's Wintergarden.* Before speaking with the commanders-in-chief, Hitler addressed a widely disparate group who were in the chancellery, including cabinet ministers, state secretaries, generals, military aides, and even adjutants. He devoted the bulk of his lengthy talk to the usual historical survey of how he had gained political power and restored Germany's military strength. After these preliminaries, he revealed his new decision. The unprovoked mobilization of the Czech army showed the danger to Germany's southeast flank. Supported by France and Great Britain, Czechoslovakia was a military threat which must be removed, if necessary, by obliterating the country from the maps of the world! According to General Beck's notes, Hitler then added:

> At the present moment, such a move is not possible since we have not yet developed our ability to achieve quick penetration of the Czech border fortifications, and the German fortifications in the West are insufficient. Moreover, some temporary delay offers certain advantages, namely to learn about Czech plans, and to prepare the German people psychologically.[31]

Thus, Hitler announced to a large audience that while perhaps not ready to act until the spring of 1939, he was firmly resolved to "first settle affairs in the East... then I'll give [the generals] three or four more years, and we will then settle the situation in the West." Once again, Hitler confirmed his Hossbach approach: military preparations should anticipate short, lightning campaigns, which would

---

*In the postwar trial, the prosecution admitted they did not have an exact list of participants and both Neurath and Raeder strongly contested that they were there. The evidence, however, indicates the contrary. In "Lebenslauf," Baroness von Neurath wrote that her husband attended a meeting of the "cabinet council" on May 28, and the subject of the meeting was "the Czech question which is becoming ever more serious." Knowing that Henderson and others "counted on him more than anyone else to use all his influence with Hitler to save Europe from... disaster," Neurath doubtless took it upon himself to try to raise the issue with Hitler. There was no meeting of the cabinet on May 28, but in his two postwar affidavits (November 21, 1945 and June 2, 1947), Fritz Wiedemann insisted that Neurath was present—along with twenty or thirty others—at this Wintergarden talk. See IMT, VI, 112; XIV, 141; and XVI, 646; and NA, Nuremberg Documents (hereafter cited as ND), PS 3037 and NG 1659.

not result in a general war, since Eastern and Western powers would remain disengaged. General Beck's reactions to this meeting parallel Neurath's after Hossbach six months before. In a memorandum for military leadership, Beck rejected the idea that Germany could use military force and avoid confrontation with France and Great Britain. If such a military confrontation came, "even should the campaign against Czechoslovakia end victoriously, Germany will lose the war." He was determined to force a reconsideration of this decision.[32]

Neurath had gone to the meeting fearful that Hitler and Ribbentrop had returned from Berchtesgaden with dramatic marching plans. He left more optimistic. The crisis precipitated by Czech mobilization had not resulted in war, and Hitler planned no immediate action. Since the chancellor had for the time being conceded the dangers of military confrontation with the Western powers, Neurath now saw no need to relay the British and French warnings. Wiedemann, however, hearing these plans for the first time, believed Hitler meant war. As he left the conference he sought out Neurath, indicating his concern that someone must go to Hitler and stop him. Having lived through a similar scene at the Hossbach meeting, Neurath was calm. Since the timetable Hitler mentioned was the spring of 1939, he told Wiedemann, "we have at least a whole year. Much water will flow through the Spree by that time. Many things can happen by then."[33]

Though Neurath's optimism is understandable, his lighthearted tone is less so. Apparently he was sure that the Czechs, like the Austrians, would eventually come to terms; thus as long as any premature confrontation was avoided, war would not become a reality. Others shared this viewpoint. As Weizsäcker wrote to a colleague on May 30: "If the other side does not force us, we shall prefer the chemical process to the mechanical process in [the Czech] theater." Nevertheless, that same day, Hitler signed a revised order for the military: "It is my unalterable decision," it begins, "to smash Czechoslovakia by military action in the near future."

> It is the business of the political leadership to await or bring about the suitable moment from a political and military point of view. An unavoidable development of events with Czechoslovakia or other political events in Europe, providing a suddenly favorable opportunity which may never recur, may cause me to take early action.[34]

The Sudetenland Crisis

Sometime during this period, Neurath learned about the failure of the moderates to win over Hitler, and heard from Weizsäcker of Ribbentrop's declaration that "the Führer was firmly resolved to settle the Czech affair by force of arms," and before winter. Despite warnings, Hitler had finally rejected the idea of a negotiated settlement; while he did not believe the Western nations would interfere, he would not be deterred from his plans even if they did. At summer's end, a concerned Neurath returned to Berlin to see Hitler who, pleading the press of business, promised a conversation "in the course of the week." On August 26, Neurath talked at length with Neville Henderson, the British ambassador, and blamed the tense situation on both the Czechs and on German extremists like Goebbels and Ribbentrop. The army, he said, was 100 percent against a war, and while impatient, Hitler had not yet made up his mind. Neurath denied Germany would attack while the British mission was still in Prague attempting to work out a diplomatic solution. Unconvinced, Henderson begged Neurath to inform Hitler that the British and French were prepared at all cost to resist armed aggression against Czechoslovakia. Agreeing to try, he attempted to soothe the upset ambassador, who reported: "[Neurath] knew Hitler pretty well and unless he had greatly changed, he did not believe that [Hitler] would burn his boats at [the Nuremberg party rally]. Herr Hitler preferred to do things in his own way and not as he was expected to do." Neurath did promise to attend the rally and try to moderate the chancellor's approach.[35]

Neurath decided to renew pressure on Hitler through the one remaining cabinet minister with whom he remained on excellent terms: Finance Minister Schwerin von Krosigk. During the last week of August, Neurath urged Krosigk to warn Hitler about the poor situation. Himself long concerned about the deterioration of Germany's financial condition, and prompted by Neurath and General Beck, Krosigk now wrote Hitler a serious warning. He urged immediate limitation of expenditures and a clarification of foreign policy which currently produced "deep anxiety for the future of Germany." Reviewing the current atmosphere, the finance minister urged that Hitler defer any military involvement, especially since "time works in our favor." Krosigk concluded his letter in words that reflected accurately Neurath's approach:

> I am firmly convinced that [the proper tactic would be] for Germany to await its hour with the calmness of the strong against all provocation, to complete its armaments in the meantime, to create especially that balance between military and economic preparations which does not now exist, and to create and publicize a demand [against Czechoslovakia] which in its righteousness is convincing to the German people and the outside world. The demand, for instance, for the right of self-determination for Sudeten Germans would weaken any slogan coined by Great Britain to bring its people into war against Germany, and would also put Czechoslovakia in the wrong before the world. [If such tactics are employed], the day will not be far off when the final *coup de grace* can be dealt to the Czechs.[36]

On his part, Neurath followed Hitler to Stuttgart in the hope of speaking with the chancellor, but saw only Weizsäcker, who had already sent a strong appeal to Ribbentrop to "change our warlike tactics," since Germany would necessarily lose the resulting war. As September began, the moderate's position was clearly stated in Beck's memorandum for the generals, Krosigk's for Hitler, and Weizsäcker's for Ribbentrop. While Neurath had supported all these moves, his failure to obtain a personal interview with the chancellor was frustrating, and he even contemplated "calling together the secret cabinet council for this occasion." But avoiding so dramatic and uncharacteristic a step, he continued to hang about on the peripheries of power, keeping informed and talking to many people. At the Nuremberg rally, where the deteriorating Czech crisis dominated his conversation, he was again unable to see Hitler, but met with numerous foreign diplomats. On September 11, in a long conversation with Ambassador Henderson, he stated again that he opposed the policy of confrontation, but could hold out little hope.[37]

The next day, Hitler's insulting and aggressive speech aimed at the Czechs intensified the crisis, since the Sudeten Germans had been simultaneously directed to create "incidents." On September 13, they erupted in insurrection and the Czechs again mobilized. Rapidly, Berlin escalated its demands from Sudeten autonomy to outright annexation, as Neville Chamberlain learned on his visit to Berchtesgaden. When war seemed inevitable, the situation suddenly eased. On September 19, Neurath told Henderson that the relaxation stemmed from the clarification of German demands, in which he may have had a hand. He argued that the future rested on the reactions of London and Paris; should they refuse to support Prague, the Beneš government must resign, making possible a peaceful transfer of the Sudetenland to Germany. Henderson agreed with Neurath that strong language by the West would force the Czechs to accept "a truly peaceful solution."[38]

Most German diplomats in Berlin also believed war had been avoided. Weizsäcker told Hassell that all signs pointed to peace. Shortly thereafter, Neurath left for his customary hunting trip in the Austrian Alps, convinced that a diplomatic solution was in sight. Since the British and French were properly applying pressure, he reasoned that a peaceful unification of the Sudetenland and Germany could not now be upset. He had obviously forgotten his own warning to Henderson concerning Hitler's unpredictability. As soon as Prague had accepted the general terms of the London conference, Neville Chamberlain flew to Bad Godesberg to settle remaining questions. There he learned Hitler had changed his mind, and was now demanding immediate military occupation of all areas with German majorities! Chamberlain returned to London on September 23, and on the same day approved Czech requests for permission to mobilize. Only a miracle could avoid catastrophe, Weizsäcker wrote to a friend. The foreign office believed that Hitler unquestionably desired a war against Czechoslovakia. "His resentment from May 22, when the English reproached him for yielding, carried him on his warlike course."[39]

While Neurath was still away hunting, Krosigk learned that mobilization was due at the expiration of the German ultimatum on September 28 at 12:00 noon. On his own initiative, he telephoned Neurath, reaching him on the evening of September 26. Briefly he sketched the recent developments and asked Neurath to return to Berlin to prevent a war. Stating his readiness, Neurath added that "in such cases, one must not arrive too early." As always, timing was most of the game. "Of course, Herr von Neurath," Krosigk replied, but since mobilization was at any moment possible, "one must also not arrive too late." After a pause, Neurath unenthusiastically answered, "Na ja, then I will come," and rang off. Relieved, Krosigk remarked to one of his colleagues: "Now it will go better. I have roused the old stag from his lair." It was not a moment too soon. Hitler's Sports

THE YEAR OF DECISION: 1938

Palace speech against Beneš on the evening of September 26 made war seem inevitable.[40]

Arriving in Berlin during the late afternoon of September 27, Neurath immediately learned from Bülow-Schwante (who was temporarily attached to Weizsäcker's staff), that invasion of Czechoslovakia was imminent. After a few questions, Neurath telephoned Göring, who confirmed that "war seems inevitable if this keeps up, since mobilization is already underway." Then Neurath asked: "Can't we go to the chancellor and stop this nonsense?" Göring agreed and arranged to meet him the next morning at the chancellor's office. Bülow-Schwante recalls that he left Neurath a few hours later, "looking very pleased with himself that he had been able to get Göring's support."[41]

September 28, 1938, the day of decision, found Hitler, contrary to his usual custom, up early in the morning. The chancellery hummed with the confused activity of generals, adjutants, and many others, but the Western diplomats had been at work too. Late on the evening of September 27, the British ambassador had received a new plan which he was ordered to deliver to Hitler, and François-Poncet also asked to be received. The tension seemed about to break. At 10:30 A.M., Henderson asked Göring to help, telling him of new arrangements under which some German occupation of the Sudetenland would be permissible, and assuring him that peace was possible. Returning to his embassy at 11:30, Henderson received Chamberlain's important telegram: "I am ready to come to Berlin myself," he wired, suggesting a conference with France, Italy and Czechoslovakia, and ending: "I feel certain that you can get all essentials without war and without delay."[42]

Unaware of these last developments, Neurath had left for the chancellery. On the way, by chance, he met Henderson, who had not yet received Chamberlain's suggestion for a conference, but did know of recent French and British moves toward meeting Hitler's demands. He asked Neurath to use his influence to delay invasion. Minor details, he implied, could always be worked out. Armed with this information, Neurath determined to get into Hitler's presence. On the way into the chancellery, he met Fritz Wiedemann, who was bringing the chancellor a telegram from President Franklin D. Roosevelt, calling for "a conference of all the nations directly interested in the present controversy . . . to be held immediately in some neutral spot in Europe." Neurath read the telegram, and remarking "what business is this of Roosevelt's?" stuffed it into his pocket. He did not refer to it again, probably fearing that Hitler would shun suggestions that came from the United States.[43]

Told that Hitler would receive no one, Neurath walked right in. Surprised, the chancellor inquired unpleasantly "What do you want here?" Neurath was not to be put off:

> I answered that I wanted to point out to him the consequences of his intended step. I explained to him that he would bring on a European war, and probably a world war, if he were to march into Czechoslovakia while negotiations were still in progress on the Sudeten problem. . . . I told him it

would be a crime he could never answer for if he shed so much blood unless all possibilities of peaceful settlement had been exhausted.

Neurath elaborated on the most recent developments, volunteering his knowledge that both Daladier and Chamberlain were ready to agree; to prevent war, they would themselves induce the Czechs to cede the Sudetenland to Germany.[44]

At this point Göring arrived and supported Neurath. Almost immediately, François-Poncet's scheduled interview (11:15 A.M.) was announced. Since Neurath already knew the content of the French message, he greeted the ambassador graciously and with encouragement. But Neurath and Göring had not yet persuaded Hitler. François-Poncet's reception was unfriendly, though Hitler was impressed by the ambassador's detailed map delineating the stages of German occupation. Suddenly, Hitler was summoned to another room, leaving François-Poncet with Ribbentrop. Hitler's new visitor was the Italian ambassador Bernardo Attolico, who brought a special message. Mussolini had received and would comply with a British request to mediate if Hitler were to postpone mobilization. The combination of Neurath's and Göring's visit with the French plan prompted Hitler to agree to a twenty-four hour postponement. The gesture was not really significant, since even in the original plan the invasion was slated only for September 30. While Hitler returned to François-Poncet, Attolico paused briefly with Neurath and Göring. Later, Neurath recalled that he had seen at once that Mussolini's intervention had given him a trump card. Immediately following François-Poncet's departure, Neurath and Göring returned to Hitler. It was now about 12:10 P.M., and the crucial action was about to begin.[45]

Neurath began bluntly: "Mein Führer, have you really resolved upon having a war under all conditions?" Taken aback, Hitler paused before answering, "What do you mean, 'under all conditions'? Naturally not." "Then," answered Neurath, "everything can be put in order." He continued: "There is really no reason to begin a war. You have named October 1 as the date on which you will take over the Sudetenland. Naturally this date must be respected. But you cannot possibly take over the whole of the Sudetenland in one day. So, you do it in steps!" In this way, Neurath raised Mussolini's idea of some international discussion, concerning the progressive occupation of the Sudetenland. He was not suggesting a conference on Czechoslovakia, only on the technical aspects of the occupation.[46]

At this point, a few minutes after 12:15 P.M., Ambassador Attolico returned with a new message: while Mussolini would unconditionally support Hitler, he personally favored accepting Chamberlain's proposal of an international conference. Hitler was annoyed. "I've received no communication from Chamberlain," he raged. Aware of some mix-up of orders, Attolico left to obtain the original proposal. Neurath and Göring returned to the task of pushing for negotiations. Neurath employed the direct questioning which had worked before:

"Mein Führer, since Mussolini has now involved himself with this whole question, and since you and he understand each other so well, wouldn't you want a chance to talk personally with him about this?"

"Yes, yes, you are right. I would like to talk to Mussolini."

"Since Chamberlain has made proposals, would it not also be good to have him invited to the talks?"

"That's true. I want Chamberlain to be there also."

"Mein Führer, if both Mussolini and Chamberlain come, don't you also want to have Daladier? In the last resort, the French are also interested in a solution to this question."

"Yes, Daladier should also come."

"If you hold this conference in Berlin, it will give the impression that you are ordering the European statesmen to appear before you. That would not make a good impression in the world. Wouldn't you rather meet Mussolini halfway?"

"That is a good idea. We will meet in Munich."[47]

Thus, even before Henderson arrived at 12:30 P.M. with Chamberlain's official suggestion of a five-power conference on Czechoslovakia (Germany, Czechoslovakia, France, Great Britain, and Italy), Neurath had persuaded Hitler to accept an international conference on the proper methods of transferring the Sudetenland to Germany. Upon entering the chancellery Henderson immediately felt an easing of tension. General Bodenschatz whispered in his ear: "Things are a little easier, but speak your mind," and Göring and Neurath left Hitler satisfied. They had succeeded in obtaining all Berlin's goals, while still preserving the peace. An amazed world learned at about 3:00 P.M. that the diplomats were on the way to Munich; war had been averted. Neurath was pleased that he and Göring had converted the idea of a general conference to a more definite and limited one. Still he knew that "that criminal fool Ribbentrop" would be furious at having been bypassed, and before leaving the chancellery, Neurath remarked that if new demands suddenly emerged at the Munich conference, Ribbentrop might still get his way.[48]

Thus Neurath and Göring sat down, together with Weizsäcker, to draw up a formal statement of German demands, approved by Hitler and dispatched at once to Mussolini. At Neurath's suggestion, Attolico added a note that other forces were operating in Berlin "that might cause Hitler to stiffen these demands before the meeting." Neurath's suspicions were immediately confirmed. A foreign office friend telephoned Wiedemann that Ribbentrop was preparing a new set of demands which called for Germany to liquidate all of Czechoslovakia, even at the risk of war.[49]

Wiedemann suggested to Göring, therefore, that Neurath accompany them to Munich, for his presence might prove helpful in calming Hitler and neutralizing Ribbentrop. Göring agreed, on condition that the chancellor approved. Catching Hitler on the run, Wiedemann got the chancellor's reluctant permission, but he added that unfortunately there was no room in his train to accommodate Neurath. When Wiedemann replied that Göring could make room, the chancellor nodded his approval. Both Wiedemann and Schaub, Hitler's other adjutant, were pleased that Neurath was going, but the latter confessed surprise, since only a few minutes before, Hitler had explicitly told his staff that Neurath should not accompany the official delegation. Wiedemann perceptively analyzes this situation:

That morning Neurath had surprised Hitler with the question whether he wanted to have war under all circumstances, and thereby was able to bring about a change in what Hitler really wanted. As a result, Neurath was not to be allowed to go to Munich. But in turn, I surprised Hitler with my question, and so he withdrew that order he had given only a short time before.[50]

The Munich Conference

Thus, despite his influence in getting the conference assembled, Neurath attended the Munich meeting almost accidentally. He traveled with Göring, and accompanied him in meeting Daladier at the airport. He was housed at the Regina Hotel, where Neville Chamberlain also stayed, and accompanied Göring and Daladier to the *Führerbau*. Neurath did not participate in the afternoon session, but when the conference adjourned for lunch, he left for the hotel with Chamberlain and returned together with him. Whenever he appeared and was recognized, Neurath was loudly cheered; the German public considered him the voice of reason and observers were pleased to see him at the talks.[51]

Apparently Neurath participated in the second general session, and milled with the groups during the pause preceding the signing of the final document. He spoke at length with Daladier, reassuring him that the French people would appreciate his actions, and also held a long talk with Chamberlain. The latter asked Neurath to arrange a private meeting with Hitler, specifying that Ribbentrop be kept ignorant of it. Neurath agreed and although the chancellor was at first reluctant, in this way the final Chamberlain-Hitler talk was scheduled. On September 30, after securing Hitler's signature to the "peace in our times" declaration, Chamberlain had another frank discussion with Neurath. Hoping for a normalization of British-German relations, he invited Neurath to visit London in the near future. Neurath sadly replied that he did not believe Hitler would permit such a trip. Privately, he was very uneasy about the future. Even before leaving Berlin, he had confessed to friends his innermost conviction that things would end badly. When Göring congratulated him on the glittering success of the conference, Neurath soberly replied that it would probably be the last time he would be able to do anything at all with the chancellor.[52]

Several weeks after Munich, Neurath invited his good friends the Ritters to his lodge in the Austrian Alps. It was, Baroness von Ritter recalls, a glorious afternoon, and the three of them took a long walk. The scene stayed clearly in her memory years later:

> I was extremely happy, because I believed that for the first time in many years the war clouds that seemed to menace Europe had dissipated, so I was really enjoying our outing. Suddenly, out of the clear blue sky, Neurath made a statement which frightened me very much, and which returned me to the reality of German political life, from which I had sought to escape.
>
> "If only I could believe that Hitler would honor this treaty!" Neurath said. "If only I could believe that Hitler would feel bound by the obligations he has assumed, then I too could look forward to the future."

That was October 1938, and it frightened me very much, but you see, Neurath was right. He usually was.[53]

Still, Neurath returned to his routine, alternating between Berlin and his Württemberg farm. Writing about these months three years later, his wife noted that "in particular, Neurath missed the daily work, and found it difficult to reconcile himself to the smaller sphere of activity." During the winter of 1938–39, he saw Hitler only once, to make a brief report of his November trip to Turkey, where he had led the German delegation for the funeral of Kemal Ataturk. Cut off from his relationships in the foreign office by Ribbentrop's orders, and by the transfer of Bülow-Schwante in late 1938, Neurath's life became strangely idle. Hassell, who saw him in December, found him in a "resigned mood," relegated to a room at 74 Wilhelmstrasse, an undignified setting. In February, he and his staff (an aide, an office manager, and two secretaries) moved to a suite of rooms in the new chancellery, but his position remained unchanged.[54]

Had fate been kinder, Neurath might have drifted into insignificance, spending increasingly more time on his estate and gradually vacating his rooms in Berlin. In such a case, his life would have ended happier and better. Had anyone examined the record of Neurath's public or private career through January 1939, there would have been no way of guessing that he would eventually be tried as a major war criminal. But strange new paths and greater tragedies were still to come for this aging official, whose best days now lay all behind him.

CHAPTER

13

NEURATH IN PRAGUE: 1939–1941

On November 10, 1938, after attending Hitler's speech to representatives of German journalists, the usually well-informed Georg Dettinger summarized his impressions of the future course of German foreign policy. Hitler, he said, clearly aimed at controlling lands in the East which were part of the German living area:

> His speech, however, offered no information about the method by which he would carry out this goal. One can assume that no definite menu exists, whose first courses were Austria and Czechoslovakia, and that these are to be followed by a predetermined procession of other specific dishes. One should rather conclude that only the "living space" tendencies have been fixed, and the method will be adapted to whatever opportunities present themselves. Thus, in every instance of an international crisis, or the development of apparent weaknesses in the domains of other states, [Germany will adopt methods] to come nearer to that final goal in one way or the other.

Neurath, too, suspected that Hitler was ready to use his successes with the Sudetenland and the *Anschluss* toward a general expansion in the East. While no fixed plans had as yet been set, the overall outline was clear.[1]

Still, in the months following Munich, Hitler did seem to hesitate, retracting his earlier determination to "crush" Czechoslovakia and force the Czechs to "get out of Central Europe." He seemed satisfied to leave rump-Czechoslovakia relatively independent, and Sudeten German leaders who insisted on the incorporation of all Czech territory seemed to have been overruled. The foreign office composed plans to stabilize rather than jeopardize rump-Czechoslovakia's position, and Hitler agreed, although he ordered the army to be ready to "liquidate" the state at a moment's notice. In late November the foreign office drafted a treaty of friendship between the two countries, which would "ensure German domination without entailing German administration of Czechoslovakia." Neurath agreed that Prague now posed no threat. He did not regret the fate of this unhappy country; nature had brought it within the German sphere of influence, and in time the Czechs would accept this reality.[2]

But toward the end of December 1938, Hitler decided to destroy the rump state he had guaranteed at Munich, and began covert encouragement of the secession of Slovakia and outright German occupation of the remaining areas. On February 13, 1939, Weizsäcker noted that "the remainder of Czechoslovakia will receive its death blow in approximately 4 weeks." He was unhappy at the prospects; comparing Czechoslovakia to a louse which in 1938 had caused problems by being in one's clothes, he wondered what sort of infection it would produce, once under the skin. Throughout January and February Prague was uneasy; many Czechs expected German occupation. Aware of close ties between Germany and the Slovakian separatists, Prague sent a special emissary to Berlin, offering numerous concessions, including the appointment to a cabinet post for any German designate. Despite a sympathetic hearing in the foreign office, the Czech offer was never even formally acknowledged. "The Führer is not interested," Ribbentrop's assistant noted.[3]

Informed by his aide Kessel of Hitler's intentions, Neurath reacted with despair and paralysis. "He shook his head, as if to free himself from a nightmare," Kessel recalls, "and then muttered something unintelligible." Shortly afterwards, Weizsäcker probably showed Neurath the memorandum he had composed opposing any military occupation. In any case, Neurath decided to speak with Hitler, and on March 9, dined with the chancellor, discussing at length the Czechoslovakian question. Repeating that Germany's important territorial claims were not in the Prague area, but in Memel, Danzig, and the Corridor, he maintained that occupation of Bohemia and Moravia would undermine foreign confidence and could be justified only if the Czechs committed some egregious error, such as armed reprisals against the Slovakian separatists. Even should such a pretext for intervention be forthcoming, Neurath argued, Germany ought to be satisfied with control of the economy and foreign affairs, in return for guaranteeing a semi-autonomous Czech cultural nation. The interview ended with no resolution. The next day, Neurath left Berlin for his country estate; he had given his last warning, and had been ignored. In subsequent developments, Neurath was uninvolved.[4]

When President Emil Hácha repealed his previous dismissal of the Slovak government and dispatching of troops to restore order, Hitler was taken aback, and ordered Slovak leaders to initiate armed revolt. Hoping to preserve some independence for his endangered nation, Hácha traveled to Berlin to place Czechoslovakia under Hitler's personal protection. Following this unexpected cooperation, Hitler dropped his intention to annex the Czech lands outright, but he would not be denied their occupation. On March 15, the world awoke to the sound of German troops entering Prague. In an atmosphere of improvisation, Hitler had no plans yet for the lands now seized. He asked party and legal advisors to suggest future relationships, specifying that unlike the union with Austria twelve months earlier, he did *not* want annexation. To fulfill his promise to Hácha of guaranteeing "an autonomous development of [Czech] ethnic life as suited to their character," a new relationship would have to be devised.[5]

Impetuously accompanying the German armies occupying Bohemia and Moravia, Hitler spent the evening of March 15 in Prague Castle, where his experts proceeded, in noisy and somewhat confused fashion, to work out a constitutional form for the new administration. The principal influence appears to have been the legal advisor of the foreign office, Friedrich Gaus, who suggested that a protectorate status would preserve the fiction that President Hácha had voluntarily entrusted the country to Germany. In the decree, published March 16 in Prague, the Reich assumed control of all foreign policy, military defense, and international administration of transportation, postal, and telegraphic services. The remaining administration, however, would be provided by an autonomous Czech government, headed by a president. As "guardian of the interests of the Reich," a Protector responsible to the German chancellor would be appointed. Although the Protector was given broad powers,* the decree creating the Protectorate was vague. Desiring maximum advantage of Hácha's offer, Hitler's advisors suggested leaving open the crucial question of the degree of autonomy to be enjoyed by the Czech government.[6]

On the same day, Hitler received President Hácha in Prague, and told him that he would soon name as Protector a high official noted for objectivity, who would receive cabinet rank. Hácha begged him to refrain from appointing a Sudeten German. Apparently still undecided on the candidate, Hitler left Prague, arriving in Vienna late on the afternoon of March 17. During the trip he discussed with several advisors his concern about finding the right person. After the war, Lammers recalled these conversations:

> Since the angry storm of indignation in foreign lands over the creation of the Protectorate would not shortly come to an end, Hitler said, he needed for the post of Protector a personality who possessed an importance and reputation abroad, and who would be able to master cleverly, in diplomatic fashion and with a certain quiet hand, the task of bringing about the future peaceful cooperation of Czechs and Germans within the Greater German empire. This would not be an easy task, and since all the other candidates who had been discussed (old party members . . .) would not be equal to this responsibility, he concluded that only Herr von Neurath would be the proper man.

Neurath's name probably emerged first following his case against taking Czech lands. Despite the opposition of major party advisors, Hitler soon regarded him as an ideal person. To Goebbel's strong objection, the chancellor replied: "Neurath was the only man for the job. In the Anglo-Saxon world he is considered a man of distinction. The international effect of his appointment will be reassuring because people will see in it my decision not to deprive the Czechs of their racial and national life."

---

*The Protector's office was assigned six major responsibilities: to represent and protect the German interests; to ensure respect for the political leadership of the Führer; to confirm officials of the Czech Protectorate government; to advise the government on all measures, protesting against any detrimental to the Reich and, in emergencies, "order measures necessary in the common interests." Finally, he was empowered to rescind any laws, proclamations, or court decisions conflicting with Reich interests.

Meanwhile, Neurath had been alerted. To his son, he exclaimed: "When are they going to leave me in peace! Whenever some trouble breaks out, I am always the one they call upon to extinguish the blaze."[7] Called to Berlin for discussions, Neurath there learned of the creation of the Protectorate and the position of Protector. Late in the evening of March 17, Lammers summoned Neurath to Vienna for an interview with Hitler. En route, Neurath asked Kessel whether or not he should accept the post of Protector if it were offered. From the tone of the question, Kessel concluded that Neurath was tempted by the offer, which pleased the aide. Using a tactic he had worked out with Weizsäcker on the preceding night, he replied that an acceptance was possible only if Neurath demanded and received a written order from Hitler that the Gestapo, the SS, and the SD would have no authority in the Protectorate. "If you allow them to get a foothold," Kessel recalls saying to Neurath, "then the whole game is lost from the start. You must inform the chancellor that naturally it would take a few weeks for the German authorities to round up the more obdurate opponents, but after this brief period, the SS and SD must get out." All influence from central offices in Berlin must be forbidden. Neurath heard him out without comment.[8]

At the meeting in the Hotel Imperial on March 18, Hitler introduced the subject with a lengthy exposition of the history of the Czech problem and his decision to permit the continued existence of the Czech nation with cultural autonomy within the boundaries of Greater Germany. To ensure a peaceful evolution, he wanted Neurath to assume the office of Protector. He needed someone, he said, with foreign credibility, who could win and hold the confidence of the Czech people. At first Neurath refused, citing advanced age, his years of service to the Reich, his desire to retire to Leinfelderhof, as well as his lack of that administrative experience in domestic affairs which the job would primarily require. Hitler waved these objections aside, stressing the need to prevent violent unrest in that part of the world. Only Neurath's diplomatic skill could make the Czechs see the value of cooperation with Germany. Still Neurath wanted no part in the administration of conquered lands, and in particular the suppression of Czechs.[9]

Hitler now lost patience. He had been advised, he said, to dispatch some harsh administrator, one of the Sudeten Germans or perhaps an intimate of Ribbentrop, thus exploiting Neurath's known repugnance for his successor. "If you don't accept," he told Neurath, "then I will have to turn the matter over to Ribbentrop, and you know what that will mean. You will bear the full responsibility for whatever happens. I am offering the post to you, because you will create peace and order there. That and that alone is what I need." Neurath conceded. Remembering the advice of his aide, he stipulated that his position must be such as to guarantee the full autonomy of the Protectorate. He wanted no other agency active in the area, and he would tolerate no persecution of the Czechs. Hitler agreed, but when Neurath requested specific guarantees, the chancellor merely read aloud the final sentence of the decree which promised to serve "the real interests of the nationalities living in this area and to ensure an individual national life to the German and Czech peoples." Hitler added, however, that he would make the Protector responsible only to himself. With these assurances, Neurath reluctantly accepted the appointment. A few minutes later, he was presented to his new state secretary, Karl Hermann Frank, number two man in the Sudeten Nazi party and generally considered to be an exponent of radical anti-Czech sentiments. It was an ominous start.[10]

The Reichs Protector

Named Protector of Bohemia and Moravia on March 20, Neurath made his first official visit to Prague on April 5, while the country was still under martial law. In the city, he dedicated himself and his staff to the task of ensuring the "peaceful and firm development of Bohemia and Moravia within the area of Greater Germany." He left almost immediately to attend to final matters in Berlin and did not return until April 16, the day on which he officially assumed control. In explaining his decision to his family, Neurath was frank, especially when his incredulous daughter inquired how he could have accepted "after all Hitler has done to you and after he had lied to you." Neurath's reply was both typical and tragic:

> You are of course right. He has treated me shamefully! But we cannot turn down positions because of personal considerations. Duty comes first. I must do my duty. Ribbentrop is incompetent and no one knows where he is driving Germany. I must go to Prague in order to prevent at least that situation from erupting into war.

To Köpke he spoke of his role as "restraining both the German anti-Czech elements and the Czech Germanists, that is, the Sudeten Germans."[11]

Yet even as he announced that his intention was to treat the area as a Protectorate, "not a conquest," numerous German officials were already trying to limit the autonomy of Neurath's office and the Czech government. On March 16, Göring had notified all bureaus that he would control the economic life of the two provinces. Several days later, Himmler informed Neurath that all police and security measures would be carried out directly from Berlin. Other bureaus, especially Nazi party organizations, quickly demanded independence from Neurath's office. To counter these pressures, Hans Lammers's draft decree insisted that while Germany held final authority, it would make only limited use of this power, seeking rather to "bring the autonomous administration of the Protectorate into harmony with general interests of the Reich and to synchronize a few particularly important areas with the legal regulations of the Reich." His decree forbade any direct communications between German offices with Czech individuals and institutions. "The entire order of business will be carried out only through the office of the Protector," who was identified as the "single and sole representative of the Reich." Göring's office, the police, external and internal security organizations, as well as party bureaus, were pointedly informed of this restriction.[12]

Although Göring and others objected, on March 22, Hitler signed the decree recognizing the Protector as final authority. Three days later, Wilhelm Stuckardt, state secretary in the interior ministry, explained to a large meeting of higher officials the legal position of the Protectorate and discussed relationships among Neurath's office, the Protectorate (Czech) government, and Berlin. He stressed three themes: the Protector was in charge; German departments and officials were to stay out; the Czechs were to be treated firmly but fairly:

> It is the will of the Führer that the Czechs be handled conciliatorily in form, but with the greatest severity and relentless consequence in all matters. By his character, the Czech does not understand indulgence. The Czech is inclined to interpret all willingness to go halfway as weakness. But of course the treatment of the population according to strict principles must be fair.

It seems likely that Hitler—and the higher officials of the Reich—seriously intended to respect some Czech autonomy. Neurath, given the opportunity to comment on the proposed legislation, was pleased with the decrees and hoped that the chancellor would live up to his word. "If only I am left alone," he told one acquaintance, "we will succeed in working out some real cooperation between Germans and Czechs."[13]

On April 1, the decree formally establishing the Protector's authority appeared, along with a table of organization reflecting the hierarchical nature of Neurath's office. Both seemed to solidify his power. During the preceding week, State Secretary Frank had submitted a list of candidates for positions on Neurath's staff. All were party men from the Sudetenland who, he assured Neurath, knew the Czechs and the area. Neurath rejected them all. In discussions with the interior ministry, he emphasized the need to reconcile Czechs and Germans; the presence of prominent Sudeten Germans on his staff would only complicate this task. Agreement was reached on March 30 that "the skeleton crew for the Protector's office must definitely be assembled from civil servants within Germany." Naturally, Czechs would occupy all positions in the Protectorate government. The remaining questions concerning payment of civil servants, and police and SS supervision, seemed only minor irritants which would, Neurath was sure, vanish in time. Thus as he assumed his position in Prague, he had every reason to hope for success.[14]

Almost from the first, however, Neurath discovered the difference between Hitler's order for an autonomous Protectorate, and the practical realities in Bohemia and Moravia. Preceded into the country by a horde of German officials (many from the Sudetenland) who ensconced themselves in positions throughout municipal, county, and central governments, Neurath was at once locked in battle against men who enjoyed the support of the party and State Secretary Frank. In the initial skirmishes, Neurath had reasonable success. He flatly refused to countenance independent party activities and forced Hess, as party secretary, to forbid party leaders from bypassing the Protector's office. Simultaneously, he kept the justice ministry in Berlin from usurping full control of the courts in Bohemia and Moravia.[15] In two instances, he even forced changes in the original decree forming the Protectorate, twice postponing creation of the customs union (once after a formal public announcement had already appeared) and blocking German control of the postal service by arguing that it would be an "extensive limitation of the autonomy of the Protectorate." Although the conflicts dragged on until 1941, Neurath's arguments prevailed (to the surprise of many), and as late as 1942, Hitler instructed Lammers: "The Protectorate held a special position and was indeed an enclave within Greater Germany."[16]

Although there were obviously many difficulties, a strong Protector, with Hitler's support, might have mastered them and gradually created a truly autonomous position for himself and his protected Czech government. While recognizing the necessity of this undertaking, Neurath faced the task with insufficient abilities and ambitions, and he ultimately failed. As in so many other instances, Neurath discovered that Berlin did not want to pursue a uniform policy. While he tried to reconcile Czechs and Germans, other units pursued contradictory policies, and Neurath had long ago shown that he did not excel in the "conqueror-state" competition. Enjoying no party status, he was treated as an outsider by all. "This man has nothing in common with us," Goebbels wrote in his diary, "he belongs to an entirely different world." Goebbels was essentially correct, for Neurath was uninterested in creating an empire over which to preside. He approached his job in Prague as an administrator, carrying out his duties, and not attempting to enlarge his power base. As he had done in the Wilhelmstrasse, he would fight to maintain the integrity of his staff, but he was not industrious or interested enough to take on Behemoth. Moreover, more than he realized, Neurath was slowing down. Out of touch with his life's work in foreign policy, he became lazy and avoided systematic work, leaving affairs to his chief advisors and administrators. Thus as difficulties mounted, Neurath could not summon up the internal or institutional strengths to defuse the SS state and isolate the odious Sudeten German leader who held the number two spot in the Protectorate, Karl Hermann Frank.[17]

His failure began with the formation of his staff. From his own background, Neurath saw himself as a sort of ambassador, and he sought out other professional diplomats who shared this outlook. His first instinct had been to hire the head of the Czechoslovak and middle-European desk at the foreign office to lead his personal staff. When this idea fell through, and he was also unable to retain the services of his longtime aide, Kotze, Neurath selected Hans Völckers, who had briefly (1933–1934) served in his office in Berlin and subsequently been stationed in Havana and Madrid. Völcker's total lack of experience with Czech problems was matched by that of the other members of the staff. As his personal aide, Neurath brought Albrecht von Kessel, from the secret cabinet council. The remainder were also professional diplomats, without political ambitions, unprepared for the sort of challenges they were about to confront. To head the administrative group supervising the Czech government, Neurath hired Kurt von Burgsdorff, an experienced civil servant from Saxony. As under state secretary, he was a fine administrator who won the Protector's full confidence. Although he had joined the party in 1933, Burgsdorff was a decent, old-fashioned administrator, not unlike Neurath himself, and as a result, he did not enjoy high regard within Nazi circles. Consequently, he was no match for the power and influence which party officials soon exercised.[18]

Neurath and the staff he had gathered would have had difficulties enough in Prague had they faced only the motley crew of Nazi opportunists who were attracted to this new area. Their opponent, however, was the ruthless Karl Hermann Frank, "the perfect image of the German *halbgebildeter* whom National Socialism has raised to power." For Neurath, he was another Ribbentrop, only worse. As George Kennan, who was stationed at the American Legation, wrote in August 1939, it was difficult to know "whether Frank's ruthless zeal is the result of political ambition or of a self-righteous belief in the innate sinfulness of the Czechs." He was certainly the disruptive force in the Protectorate. The offspring of an old German family in the Sudetenland, he had spent his youth and mature life in the *völkisch* movement, eventually becoming a publisher and bookseller of German nationalist literature. His business failures, which he attributed to Czech hostility, prompted him to enlist in the Sudeten Nazi party, where he soon rose to national prominence. As leader of his party's delegation to the Czech parliament, and ranking SS officer in the Sudetenland, he became Konrad Henlein's chief lieutenant and head of the radical action wing. Disappointed after the Sudetenland was officially annexed that he had received only an appointment as deputy Gauleiter, he was infuriated when Hitler selected Neurath as Protector. He was even more annoyed when the Czechs let it be known that they welcomed Neurath for saving them from Frank. He began his term as state secretary determined to become the real ruler, and intimidated the staff with his arrogance and obvious hatred for the Czechs. "He was," one official recalled, "one of the most disagreeable men I have ever met, a low degenerate, and (unfortunately) clever criminal. A more hate-filled man would be hard to find." Völckers, who had ample opportunity to evaluate Frank, called him a "fanatic Sudeten German, who had a blind hatred for the Czechs, and was in addition a criminal without scruples."[19]

At first, Neurath thought to make quick work of Frank, who lacked government experience and administrative knowledge. It took time for him to realize that "Frank was deliberately sabotaging all of his plans for the pacification of the area." His aide later recalled that Baroness von Neurath had also viewed the situation with alarm. "My husband is far too trusting," she had exclaimed. "He believes what people tell him."[20]

Eventually, Frank thwarted Neurath, primarily because of his intimate relations with Himmler and ties with central SS headquarters. In the hours before Hitler arrived in Prague, the SS under Frank made systematic arrests. Although only a pale reflection of Himmler's incarcerations a year before in Austria (more than 70,000 had been involved), the detention of nearly 2,000 Czechs, without any legal pretext, foreshadowed the power which the head of the SS in the Protectorate would exercise. Warned by his advisors, Neurath had insisted upon controlling all police functions, but Himmler nevertheless entrusted the SS and other security organizations to Frank, in order to avoid placing them under Neurath. The Protector had accepted this compromise, believing the state secretary would be answerable to him.[21]

Arriving in Prague, Neurath realized his mistake. Using the threat of counterinsurgency as a ruse, the SS and security police had occupied most of the country. Their candidates were installed as provincial commissioners, each supervising two or three Czech municipalities. Appointed by Frank from among the Sudeten Germans, these men, with the support of the SS and without the knowledge of the Protector's office, began to exceed the "supervisory function" by simply taking over the administration of the local units. By the time Neurath sought to establish normal relations between the Czech government and his office, Frank's parallel corps of Sudeten administrators and SS groups had already established a third, and more important, locus of power. Independent of Neurath's staff and more powerful than the Czech officials, these men were soon joined by a motley crew of administrators representing various Berlin ministries. Between the Sudeten Germans, "many of them with various personal axes to grind," and these new arrivals whom Kennan correctly called the "carpetbaggers of occupation," any pretext of respecting an "autonomous Protectorate government" disappeared.[22]

Struggle for Autonomy

Neurath demanded information about these irregular groups and especially news of the SS arrests and confiscations; but his requests and investigations were either ignored or delayed by Frank, who sent alarmist reports to Berlin, justifying the illegal actions of the SS and provincial commissioners. Disguising the universal calm then prevailing in Bohemia and Moravia, he described "increased tensions," "passive resistance," and political rumors, against which he had been forced to apply the strictest measures, including extensive arrests. Frank insisted that the SS had been used because the German police units were "too weak to provide sufficient security." These reports were lies. More objectively, George Kennan described the quiet life of the Protectorate; the dominant tone and mentality recalled the "brave soldier Swejk": "a boggling willingness to comply with any and all demands and an equally baffling ability to execute them in such a way that the effect is quite different from that contemplated by those who did the commanding." Difficult as such a population might be to rule, it would be false to describe it as needing more police and a greater arbitrariness of rule.[23]

Aware that Neurath, possessed of suitable evidence, might yet prevail, Frank warned Himmler's office of Neurath's requested investigations. A tug of war began which an aide later recalled in describing the difficulties in gathering information on the true picture of events in Czechoslovakia:

> Frank found support with Heydrich and the Gestapo and these two petty conspirators agreed on a sophisticated plan of action with which to confront Neurath. While posing as the most devoted servants of the Protector, Frank and the head of the Gestapo in Prague .... SS *Obersturmbannführer*

Rasche, filled all the key posts, from the position of porter on up, with their trusted people, in order by this device to isolate Neurath completely from the outside world. Very quickly upon arriving in Prague, I discovered the growing isolation into which Neurath and the officials answerable to him were being maneuvered.... Through loyal German officials or through trusted Czechs, I learned that various arrests had been made in Prague, Brünn, and Pilsen. Informed by me, Neurath spoke with State Secretary Frank and the head of the Gestapo about these developments. Both men declared, with absolutely solemn faces, that nothing of the sort had happened at all. Neurath was not used to having his subordinates lie to him, and declared himself satisfied, but he nevertheless asked me to pursue any such rumors and keep him informed. I undertook this task, and was shortly able to provide him with the exact names of the arrested individuals.[24]

Unable to block these investigations and fearing that Hitler might listen to the Protector, Himmler dispatched Reinhold Heydrich, who visited Prague on May 9, 1939, for discussions with Frank and Neurath.

Alerted to his coming, Kessel, whose postwar affidavit has been quoted above, warned Neurath that Heydrich would demand further powers for the SS and security police, in order to unleash a reign of terror. He lectured both Neurath and the military commander, General Erich Frederici, on the realities of the SS terror in Germany, but no important discussion concerning the police occurred during the formal meeting with Heydrich and Frank. Afterwards, Neurath laughingly assured Kessel: "This time, you were wrong. Heydrich was quite reasonable. He demanded nothing of me. Nothing will be changed in the police powers in the Protectorate." Late that night, however, Heydrich returned to the palace, awakened Neurath and announced that a Czech plot had just been uncovered. Asking Neurath to sign a paper detailing special powers to the SS and SD (including the right of confiscation of property), Heydrich urged that given the "pressing importance for immediate action," the powers of the police and the SS in the Protectorate must now be administered directly by the Reich, independent of Neurath's office. Despite the warnings of his aide concerning this real purpose in Heydrich's trip, Neurath gave initial approval.[25]

Within a day or so, he recovered his senses and unearthed a whole series of SS deceptions. He wired Lammers requesting an immediate meeting with the chancellor. On June 1, Hitler received Neurath. Protesting the SS position in the Protectorate, Neurath demanded the removal of the Gestapo chief in Prague and strongly opposed all plans of consolidating the SS and police under direct Reich control. Apparently, Hitler agreed. The offending Gestapo chief was transferred on June 2, and a victorious Neurath returned to Prague. Since the new appointee proved a decent man, Neurath believed he had prevented the creation of an SS state in the provinces under his control.[26]

But Neurath's troubles were just beginning. In one of their earliest steps, the SS in Bohemia and Moravia seized the Land Office (created by the Czechs in 1919 to supervise land reform) whose thousands of acres were coveted by the SS's

Race and Settlement headquarters in Berlin. On April 18, Frank ousted or arrested all that bureau's Czech officials and named as its new head SS Oberführer Curt von Gottberg. Neurath protested to no avail. On June 2, after more arrests, Gottberg added the Czech ministry of forests to his empire. Again strong protests from Neurath's office went unanswered, and the Protector decided to take the matter directly to Hitler. On June 22, he demanded that Lammers silence Gottberg, who, with his SS colleagues, was announcing that "Hitler has declared that within ten years no Czech will be able to own land or property in Bohemia and Moravia." Neurath insisted that such statements "greatly prejudiced the policy which I am supposed to carry out in this country," and asked that the matter be brought to Hitler's attention. Several days later through Lammers, Hitler denied the statement, and disapproved of circulation of the story.[27]

The exchange left Gottberg unscathed. Arrogantly, he told officials that he was powerful enough to arrest not only Czech and German officials, "but also the state secretary and even the Protector himself." A few months later, on November 13, Gottberg was summoned to Berlin, informed that he had suffered a severe heart attack, was demoted, reprimanded in no uncertain terms, and ordered to disappear. Investigations had revealed that he and his immediate subordinates had misappropriated nearly a million Marks of Land Office money. Vindicated, Neurath demanded that the office revert to his control and nominated as its head one of his own trusted officials. Although Frank protested that "this measure delivers the Protectorate's land policy definitely into the hands of the bureaucracy and removes it from the control of the SS," Neurath prevailed. Through persistence and some good luck, he had ousted another opponent. He would not, however, have similar success with Frank or Heydrich.[28]

Although on May 9, Heydrich had won a major concession from Neurath concerning control of the police, no formal decree had yet appeared. On June 10, Lammers drew up drafts, sending copies to all departments except to Neurath, since according to Heydrich, the Protector's office had already approved. In early July, when the final drafts were circulated, Neurath received his first inkling of the proposals, and on July 14 wired a furious protest, demanding a conference. On July 21 in Berlin, Neurath's objections were strong and telling. The new regulations, he said, were "an attempt to separate the police from his administration and to set them up as an independent department." He particularly protested the provision that the Berlin office of the Gestapo and security police could "undertake direct actions in the Protectorate." Apparently, Neurath carried the day. The draft decree was withdrawn, and Lammers was instructed to rework it, while awaiting Neurath's counterproposal. Detailed negotiations dragged on through August, with Neurath demanding that police actions must have his "consent," while Heydrich would grant only that they be brought to the "knowledge" of the Protector. The outbreak of war on September 1 forced Berlin to decide promptly. Rejecting the Protector's arguments, the minister of the interior, with Hitler's approval, issued on the following day the new decree regulating the police, without Neurath's provisions or approval.[29]

Neurath had tried hard to curtail the powers of the Gestapo, SS, and security police, but failed. Thereafter his chance to influence decisively events in the Protectorate was severely limited. No longer consulted in advance, and often not even informed afterwards, the Protector's office could only protest and seek to mitigate some of the damage. Nevertheless, in June 1940 Neurath tried again to reassert his authority:

> Even in regard to the area of police powers, [he wrote Berlin], I am the representative of the German government, that is, in this case the competent representative of the minister of the interior. Therefore all measures for the preservation of security and order can, in principle, be decided upon only with my *previous* agreement and executed, normally, only through me and the departments subordinated to my office.

Such protests still produce some ripples. In July 1940, Lammers reminded officials that Neurath was the sole representative of the Reich, and in a private file note suggested there was no way to work out "a clear and general definition of the role of the Protector in relation to the Reich government." In other words, Neurath had not yet accepted Berlin's rule.[30]

While Neurath did defend to the best of his abilities the autonomous Protectorate, his efforts have not been properly appreciated. Indeed, when one reviews the many angry trips to Berlin to explain his views, and the wrestling over details of drafts assembled by unscrupulous men who sought only to deceive and unseat him, it is a wonder that the tired Neurath held on as long as he did. One of his aides in Prague, Werner von Holleben, concisely described Neurath's tactics:

> Neurath in general was not a fighter; he did not go after fights. He developed a more circumspect technique. Instead of flat and open opposition, he procrastinated. First he would give the appearance of being about to agree, then he would raise apparently minor points which would force a reexamination of the whole topic. In this fashion, he would succeed in getting his way, namely the postponement of adverse decisions. It was not a technique designed to win him medals or the title of hero, but it worked.[31]

Not until the fall of 1941, with Neurath's removal, did the full force of SS power reign in the Protectorate. As long as he was even nominally in charge, he prevented arbitrary terror. Among the Czechs, there was appreciation and gratitude for Neurath's role. In a dispatch of August 19, 1939, the astute George Kennan described the characters of the drama: "the dignified but inactive Baron von Neurath, the careerist intellectuals of the party, the underworld figures of the Gestapo, the correct and impassive officers of the Reichswehr," and above them all, the real leader, Frank. After five months of occupation, Kennan concluded: "[The Germans] have antagonized the Czechs without annihilating them, and they are now divided among themselves as to the best way of remedying the situation—some advocating more caresses and the others complete annihilation." At no time did anyone think Neurath belonged in the latter camp.[32]

In retrospect, these first months were crucial to Neurath's fight to preserve the autonomy of his Protectorate. By the end of that first summer, he was already aware of his failure to stop unauthorized excursions, and he complained to his family and friends of his isolation and powerlessness. Instead of creating responsible and honest supervision of established institutions, as he had anticipated, Neurath found himself involuntarily caught up in the power struggle for the future of Bohemia and Moravia. The decree creating the Protectorate had been deliberately vague about its future and, in the absence of strong leadership from the Protector, the rivalry of powerful men and organizations within Germany became Berlin's only definitive policy toward the area. Foremost was the party, which challenged the role of the bureaucracy and army upon which Neurath had relied to provide a moderating influence. Unfortunately, the party proved it could always prevail:

> In the permanent tension between the moderates and the radicals in the Protectorate, the latter held undeniable advantages. The vague delimitation of competencies favored ruthless individuals who could easily impose their will upon their obedient and conscientious colleagues of more moderate persuasion.

Sincerely desiring to reconcile Czechs and Germans, by September Neurath was defending a cause unpopular with prominent Nazis, with Berlin, and even with some of his own officials.[33]

In early 1939, various plans had called for the absorption of the Czech areas into Greater Germany, with a systematic suppression of all independent Czech life, making the territory and population German in character. Even after the creation of the Protectorate, many refused to consider it a permanent solution, and continued to call for a new approach to the Czechs. They were particularly critical of Neurath:

> Because of the great difficulties arising out of the question of competing jurisdictions between the individual state and party officials in the Protectorate of Bohemia and Moravia, important troubles are occurring which the politically astute Czechs know how to use for their advantage....
>
> There is no unified leadership in our policy toward the Czechs, since four Gauleiters are in charge of all party affairs and therefore of the leadership of the Germans in the Protectorate, while the Protector, as representative of the state administration, has nothing at all to do with matters concerning German citizens.
>
> Particular difficulties occur today as a result of the differing conceptions of affairs on the part of the Protector, on one hand, and that of his state secretary, Karl Hermann Frank, the Sudeten leadership in Reichenberg [i.e., Henlein], and the aims of old party comrades from the NSDAP on the other.[34]

On June 25, following reports that officials were being too easy on the Czechs, Hitler had directed that in the future the provincial commissioners should first consult with State Secretary Frank on political matters, "so that the proper decision could be taken." To counter this approach, Neurath and his office composed a concise and impersonal memorandum, "Viewpoints on the Task of the Protector in Bohemia and Moravia," which addressed the issues and provided an excellent picture of his hopes for the area and his approach. Unfortunately, it was not likely to gain support in Berlin. According to Neurath, German policy began with the principle that in an area of mixed nationalities, the well-being of *all* peoples living there must be guaranteed if peace were to be preserved. The Protectorate must not be considered "from the viewpoint of an imperialistic accretion of power by which means peace and stability would automatically follow," but must rather be viewed in terms of cooperation among the peoples not merely over years, but over centuries. His second principle was that all administration, including economic, political, and cultural policies, must be centralized under the Protector. Any deviation would confuse and muddy the chances for success.[35]

Three policy directions, Neurath insisted, had already been established: destruction of the Czech will for self-determination; preservation of a Czech national culture; and incorporation of Bohemia and Moravia into Greater Germany. The first could be attained only through a consistent policy that avoided duplicity and equivocation. "The German must above all act in worthy fashion and avoid any chicanery or petty annoyances, for these would only serve to encourage the Czechs to resist." While the "deep and natural desire for self-determination" was being curbed, Neurath insisted that greater care be taken to encourage the preservation of a Czech national culture:

> The Germans must never give the impression of interfering openly or with unilateral proclamations. In this way the whole problem of national culture will cease to be fertile ground for Czech irredentists, and gradually sink into insignificance. An interesting analogy for this procedure is Bismarck's handling of Bavarian particularism.

As he had shown in Denmark and Italy, Neurath was sympathetic to suffering minorities, but he believed that the issue of national cultural identifications must be overcome before Europe could enjoy real peace. While respecting the Czech right to a national culture, he believed it was in the best interest of all concerned, Germans as well as Czechs, to minimize cultural and national differences, in order to make the idea of a Czech nation academic. His vision of the future was concrete, and even, given other circumstances, realizable:

> If we permit the average man his individuality in [his private life, in speaking his native tongue, or worshiping God by local traditions] and at the same time show him the nearly unlimited advances open to him within the wide borders of Greater Germany, he will turn to these possibilities and forswear political games.
> Should this goal be accomplished in the great majority of the people, and accompanied by a constant emigration of portions of the upper classes into Germany proper, it is possible that within a relatively short time—perhaps in one or two generations—the Czech nation will sink into the insignificance

of an historical curiosity (such as the Bretons in France or the Wends in Lausitz), and the permanent incorporation of the lands of Bohemia and Moravia into the Reich will be complete.[36]

In regard to the integration of Bohemia and Moravia within Greater Germany, Neurath believed in granting provincial autonomy: "the Protectorate is by its nature only a control, not a German administration." In particular he warned against zealous German civil servants:

> German officials in Bohemia and Moravia must therefore always remember that they are called to work in a Protectorate, not in a German province or administrative unit. As a result, they must supervise here, but not administer. Every exercise of direct administration contradicts the spirit of the Protectorate.
>
> The Czech administration, based as it is on the tradition of the old [Dual] Monarchy, is not bad; it should be preserved in its now limited sphere, if for no other reason than as a harmless occupation for the upper classes.

At once conciliatory and firm, Neurath's policy, following his oft-expressed maxim that time and patience would solve most problems, urged the application of both: "The above exposition recommends a strict and conscientious action in the area of destruction of the will to self-determination, but in all areas, such as culture, national identification, social problems, and administration, it recommends a policy of the weak hand and the loose reins."[37]

Nothing indicates how Neurath's memorandum was received. On August 2 at the Bayreuth Festival, Neurath talked to Hitler, who was concentrating on the crisis with Poland. When Neurath requested a discussion of the Protectorate problems, the chancellor in turn asked advice on a possible treaty with the Soviet Union. Neurath welcomed the idea, believing it significantly advanced his evolutionary program and eliminated the threat of war. To Hitler's doubts about whether the Germans would accept such an abrupt ideological shift, Neurath replied that the chancellor "knew perfectly well that he could do what he pleased with the party." Despite a friendly atmosphere, Neurath was unable to bring the conversation back to the Protectorate, realizing that the threat of war overshadowed all concerns.[38]

Sufficiently alarmed by August 24 to interrupt his vacation, Neurath flew to Berlin for a private conversation with Hitler, which deepened his depression. "He had been unable to do anything against the pack of criminals surrounding the chancellor," friends observed. "Hitler had hardly listened to him, and had seemed very excited and far from reality." After waiting around for a few more days in hopes of somehow deterring a drift toward war, he decided to leave Berlin for Prague. There he found that Frank, on August 26, had drawn up a public warning against sabotage and dissemination of rumors. This document of "collective responsibility" made the whole Czech community responsible for any individual acts. Although his name appeared upon the decree, Neurath had not seen it before, nor was he aware that the Gestapo was planning, and eventually carried out, the arrests of nearly 2000 Czechs on the first day of the war. Pained by these events, Neurath intervened directly with Himmler for the release of nearly 1200, sharing the opinion that by such arrests Germany was ruining whatever chances existed for cooperation.[39]

War and Czech Unrest

Neurath had gone to see Hitler in August, prepared to resign. But the outbreak of the war he had long dreaded and predicted persuaded him to stay on. As he testified at his postwar trial:

> I told myself that during the war ... the Czechs would try, if not to throw off German rule, at least to disturb ... the military measures of the armed forces taken in the Protectorate and that ... due to this, the severest measures would be taken against the population on the part of Germany, which would cause the police, above all the Gestapo, to proceed with all kinds of terrorist acts. Through my remaining in office I wanted to prevent both of these things, and I also wanted to prevent a harsher treatment of the Czech population by the policy of conciliation and compromise which I followed.
>
> To lay down my office at a moment like that would have been desertion. But on the other hand, I believed that in a war in which the existence of the German people was at stake, I could not, as a German—which I am with full devotion—refuse my service and my knowledge. After all, it was not a question of Hitler or the Nazi regime, but rather of my people and their existence.[40]

The war brought into sharper focus the conflicting policies in the Protectorate. Under the pressures of mobilization, Frank issued new decrees concerning the prerogatives of the secret police and confiscation of property, and Berlin arranged a meeting on October 20 to reach a decision on the future of the Czechs:

> The regulation of these and nearly all other questions concerning the Protectorate [the meeting concluded] depends upon the previous decision in principle, whether the government wishes to pursue a policy of assimilating into the German stock the better racial elements of the Protectorate's population, or whether it is intended to separate the Czechs into their own restricted area. The representative of the ministry of the interior announced that his office had recently referred the whole question to the Führer for his decision.[41]

This crucial question would haunt Neurath for the rest of his life. Opinion on it within the Protectorate was divided, as Kennan's incisive report of October 1939 made clear:

> The moderates, still headed by Neurath, would like to give [the Czechs] something in the nature of real autonomy and make a serious attempt to reconcile them to German rule by concessions. The radicals, still headed by Frank, would like to smash them completely as a nation, destroy their intelligentsia, and make Bohemia and Moravia into German provinces.

Supremacy between these two groups can be decided only on the mat of Nazi party politics. Prague pundits say that the first round in the battle was won by Frank, that the second was a draw, and that the third is about to be fought out. They imply that the conservatives still have a chance to come out on top. That may be. But meanwhile the Czechs have been thrown at least 50 percent of the way back toward the status of a nation of peasants, servants, and laborers; and if the liberal views of Baron von Neurath finally carry the field, his conservative followers will have the dubious satisfaction of locking the stable door a good year after most of the horses have been stolen.[42]

Instead of this issue being decided by a discussion of the broader goals of the Protectorate—as Neurath had attempted by means of his memorandum—it was shrouded in the erupting controversy between Frank and Neurath following the first serious disorder in the Protectorate, the student demonstrations of October 28 and November 16, 1939. Although the prewar months had been calm, the outbreak of hostilities prompted underground organizations to demonstrate Czech hostility toward their German rulers. The security police had warned of trouble on October 28, the anniversary of the founding of the Czechoslovak Republic. Neurath, living like a prisoner "in a golden cage," as he wrote Köpke, believed that the police were exaggerating the dangers. Although the Italian consul thought Neurath's speech on October 24, which assured the world that all was well, contained an "excessive amount of optimism and not much truth," the Protector was sincere in these beliefs, On the same day, he left for his annual hunting vacation in Austria, leaving orders "to ignore demonstrations as far as possible and to interfere only if they assume the character of a serious danger to public peace and safety."[43]

As Neurath had predicted, the demonstrations were peaceful, silent, and in the words of one official, "spontaneous, unorganized expressions of national pride." Even security police reports show that the authorities always had control of the situation. Nevertheless, near the end of the day, through Frank's personal intervention, the SS and Czech police forcibly dispersed the last demonstrators and several people were injured. Briefed after his hurried return on October 31, Neurath reprimanded Frank: "Through his personal interference and the use of the SS," Neurath complained, "[Frank] had intensified the tumult."[44]

A recent study, confirming the harmlessness of the student demonstrations, has placed the incident in proper perspective:

> The conflict which opened in Prague on October 28 was more than a struggle between the subject people and the occupation regime. It was also a confrontation between the SS and the moderate Nazis to determine which was to play the decisive role in the country. Although the radicals apparently possessed no clear plan of action, they were determined to exploit any opportunities available while the moderates remained inactive.

Neurath's position was also clear: "I was never of the opinion," he testified after the war, "that this demonstration, which was carried on mostly by young people, should be considered especially important or that it should necessitate special police measures." But on November 11, Jan Opletal, a university student, died from wounds sustained during the demonstration. When student groups requested a public funeral, and the Czech government promised to assume responsibility for maintaining order during the ceremonies, Neurath permitted the funeral to be held. He warned that should there be further disturbances, however, he would intervene "with all the powers at my disposal." Privately, Neurath said he did not anticipate serious trouble.[45]

The funeral itself was peaceful, but was followed by another demonstration. The police acted firmly; three students were arrested, but promptly released. Clearly, the disorders were insignificant. Nevertheless, on November 16, Neurath, Frank, and General Frederici were summoned to Berlin where, in the presence of the Czech minister, František Chvalkovský, Hitler flew into a rage. Citing reports of sabotage and rioting in Bohemia and Moravia (all new to Neurath), Hitler screamed at Chvalkovský that his patience was at an end, that he had been good to the Czechs, but now "regretted having treated them with such forbearance." Unless Czech agitation immediately ceased, he would treat the inhabitants as he had the Poles, proceeding with undreamed-of severity, reducing Prague itself to ashes. Unless the students stopped their insane activities, he would not hesitate to line up every student and shoot them one by one! After the war, Neurath described his stunned reaction:

> I tried to calm [Hitler] but despite that, he made serious charges against the Czech minister and gave him instructions to tell the Czech government that if such events should recur, he would take the most severe measures against the people who were disturbing the peace, and furthermore that he would hold the entire Czech government liable. The language used by Hitler was quite uncontrolled and the proceeding was extremely distressing to us who were listening.[46]

Afterwards, Neurath and Völckers accompanied Chvalkovský out of the chancellery. Although Neurath had announced that he would remain in Berlin for several more days should the chancellor want to discuss any issues, Hitler asked only Frank to stay behind. Upset by the conference, Neurath did not expect any German move, nor did Chvalkovský mention reprisals in his telephone conversation with Prague. But shortly after Neurath had left, Hitler and Frank discussed plans for the prevention of future disturbances, and Frank flew to Prague, armed with Hitler's order to close the Czech universities and execute the student leaders responsible for recent disturbances. Between 3:30 and 7:45 A.M. on the morning of November 17, SS troops occupied the university buildings, arresting nearly 1900 students. By mid-morning nine randomly selected students were shot; throughout the city red placards announced the executions and the closing of all colleges and universities for three years.[47]

Although the public announcements bore his name, Neurath, still in Berlin, learned of the stupid and unnecessary brutality only on the afternoon of November 17. His horror turned to fury when he realized how Frank had tricked him and misused his name. One official described the situation in his diary after speaking with Neurath's assistant, Holleben: "He is as distraught and depressed as I am. He assures me that the entire affair is Frank's work. Neurath knew nothing about it until he read the full details in the newspapers! What should we wonder about more: the short-sightedness of our policies, or the shocking divisions within the office of the German Protector?"

Frank, supported by Himmler (who had mysteriously visited Prague only a few days before the demonstrations), seemed in control. When Neurath and President Hácha met on November 18, the Protector acknowledged his own frustration. He urged Hácha to reconsider his wish to resign over the incident, for that would only damage the Czech cause. He expressed the hope that the present excesses would cease, but freely admitted his own loss of effectiveness: "On October 28," he told the president, "Frank lost; now, on the contrary, after November 15, I am the loser."[48]

In Berlin, Lammers's staff noted the struggle between Neurath and Frank; the latter, with Himmler's support, "is striving for the total independence of the security and regular police": "Frank wants to use the events of October 28 (which in any case were limited to the city of Prague), in order to sharpen in general the course to be followed. The Protector and [Burgsdorff] seem to be of another opinion."

Behind the controversy, this report concluded, lay "essentially different approaches to the future of German policy in the Protectorate." Now that Frank had prevailed, Neurath apparently decided on a personal appeal to Hitler, but his request for an interview went unanswered. On December 2, Frank threatened the Protectorate population in a public decree: "From today on, we will employ the sharpest means without any warning. Whoever is not with us is against us, and whoever is against us will be ground to pieces." Clearly the situation was out of hand.[49]

When Neurath finally got his interview with Hitler, his hope that the chancellor would order the continuation of a moderate program was realized. Preoccupied with plans for extending the war in the West, Hitler insisted the Protectorate would remain intact and no large-scale resettlement of the country with Germans would take place, for "Germanization of [Poland] takes precedence, and there are hardly enough settlers available even for that program." Neurath protested his treatment by Frank and called the closing of the universities a foolish act. While Hitler reserved judgment on pleas that the students be released from the concentration camps and insisted that the universities remain closed, he ordered adherence to a moderate line: "The German authorities are to avoid anything that is likely to provoke Czech mass action, but any Czech defiance must be crushed with the harshest means from the outset." In answer to Neurath's request, the chancellor agreed to issue still another warning against Berlin's interference in Protectorate affairs.[50]

Although Neurath returned to Prague after Christmas in a somewhat strengthened position, he was discouraged by the general world picture. The war, he wrote friends, was far from over, and on the anniversary of the founding of the Protectorate, he wondered anxiously what other "surprises" were still to come. During these months, he tried to free the Czech students and curtail other elements of terrorist policy, but his arguments that the "liberation of the students would make a good impression on the Czechs," were rejected by the SS. Moreover, Frank retained his powerful position both in the Protectorate and in Berlin, while Neurath's became increasingly difficult.[51]

Despite Hitler's assurances to the contrary, rumors spread about some action against the Czechs. The surprising German victories in the summer of 1940 intensified fears that the Protectorate itself would be abandoned in favor of outright annexation and massive resettlement of Germans. Throughout 1939 the Sudeten Germans argued that the "Protectorate solution" had failed to "clarify relations between Czechs and Germans." Neurath had defended the Protectorate by arguing that his task was to "splinter the Czech population, not create specifically Czech reservations." With the outbreak of war, the Sudeten Germans again pressured for a permanent solution to the Czech problem. In reply, Neurath's office prepared a memorandum, "The Nationalities Policy of the Protectorate," suggesting that the issue of the future of Bohemia and Moravia "can only be solved later, after the war is over, as part of the greater problem of the minorities and internal colonization within Greater Germany." Arguing for time, he cautioned against any "discriminations against the Czechs, in order to facilitate the transition."[52]

He was surprised and disturbed by widespread reports in July 1940 of a possible partition of the Protectorate among the neighboring German administrative units, and the consequent total and rapid absorption of the Czechs into the German population. On August 6, he wired a strong protest to Lammers, labeling such talk "a threat to the unified direction of German policy" and requesting that all such plans and discussions be terminated. However, even Neurath's own officials were dissatisfied by the pace of events. "The question of assimilation" [of the Czechs], Burgsdorff told the provincial commissioners on August 15, "was particularly urgent.... The present proposed methods are not satisfactory." Only undesirable or antisocial types of Czechs were applying for reclassification as racial Germans, and due to the shortage of settlers, no more Germans were likely to be moving into the area.[53]

Policy Toward the Czechs

Meanwhile, new plans for reorganization circulated. Although differing in emphasis, all shared a common assumption and goal: Bohemia and Moravia must cease to be treated as a Protectorate and "Germanization of the area," either through extermination or absorption of the Czechs, must proceed at once. Before leaving on vacation, Neurath told his staff that he would work out a memorandum for Hitler which would oppose these new ideas and "defend the preservation of the Protectorate, by arguing its effectiveness in carrying out the nationalities struggle." Considering these wild plans foolish, Neurath believed he could dispose of them. Frank too was alarmed, since he had no desire to see his power base divided up among the neighboring Gauleiters. Privately he told officials that the Protectorate should be preserved for at least two or three more years. Then Hácha could be retired and a new Protector (clearly himself) could assume command. Despite differing motives, Neurath and Frank temporarily united to defend the Protectorate, and composed separate memoranda on the subject for dispatch to Hitler.[54]

In his memorandum of August 31, 1941, Neurath defended the continued existence of the Protectorate in order to prevent mass deportations and resettlements. He confided both motives and procedures to his friends the Ritters: "Quite aside from the sensible point of view, the people who are simply to be resettled arouse pity in one's soul. However, I believe I have discovered a way now to prevent the disaster. Time won is everything won, and frequently to postpone a thing is to do away with it."[55] Thus, Neurath adopted for the first time a strong line, guaranteeing permanent German control, and hoping that thereby all questions concerning Germanization would be postponed until after the war. In the meantime, the status quo should continue, ostensibly to prepare for these future developments. In reality, Neurath hoped that once the critical present situation was overcome, rational and humane considerations would prevail, and the gradual assimilation of the Czechs would continue. The first step must be the preservation of the Protectorate.

Neurath's memorandum parallels his earlier one on the goals in Bohemia and Moravia. The land had come peacefully to Germany, with little open area for new settlements. The Czechs did not love the Germans and accepted the situation out of fear and practicality. Hence, measures like forced emigration and importation of Germans would take many years, destroy the morale of a hard-working people who contributed significantly to the German war effort, and in general "create even greater difficulties for the clear and simple goal of a fusion of this land and its people with Greater Germany." Admitting that the "theoretically most perfect solution" might be the migration of all Czechs, Neurath rejected it on a number of grounds and concluded that it was not in the interest of Germany to eliminate the Czech people. From this conclusion, he criticized the various short-sighted and dangerous plans which were being proposed to divide the Protectorate. He issued a strong appeal for the concentration of leadership, not in Berlin or neighboring *Gaue* (districts), but in Prague, arguing that only the Protectorate form could emphasize the "Germanness" of many Czechs, and thus incorporate the area ever more firmly within the Reich. By separating the common people from troublemaking intellectuals, a peaceful assimilation and Germanization would occur. Above all, Neurath argued, the problem could not be solved piecemeal; only the present arrangements held any promise of success.[56]

Frank's memorandum was longer. It began with the conventional historical analysis of Germanic racial strains in the Czech people. Admitting that the Protectorate was a temporary instrument, he argued that competing plans of party leaders did not come to grips with the only feasible "permanent solution of the Czech problem," but benefited individual Gauleiters. Only full Germanization was the answer, and its process would come faster and more smoothly through the continued existence of the Protectorate. Imagining two possible solutions (emigration of the Czechs or their assimilation), Frank dismissed the first (as had Neurath) as impossible. The bulk of his memorandum, therefore, dealt with the question of a gradual absorption of the Czechs through the preservation of both the territorial unity and central authority of the Protectorate. Thus, although Frank gave greater emphasis to those measures best able to achieve Germanization, his essential message was the same as Neurath's: the status quo must be preserved. When Neurath looked over Frank's memorandum, he approved this conclusion and sent it to Berlin with his own, noting the complete agreement. Neurath knew he was engaged in a major battle in which he willingly accepted even Frank as an ally.[57]

Although the International Military Tribunal later called these memoranda plans for ruthless extermination of the Czechs and a calloused Germanization of their territory, Berlin officials correctly perceived the real issue. On September 11, 1940, Heydrich wrote a memorandum which must be quoted at length because it so clearly distinguished between the peripheral issue of Germanization and the real one—existence of the Protectorate:

> The memoranda of the Protector, Minister von Neurath, and that of the state secretary, SS Gruppenführer Frank, demand that some position be taken concerning the whole problem of the Protectorate, in particular the problems surrounding the possibilities of Germanizing certain portions [of the population], and the issue of the legal position of the Protectorate.
>
> By way of introduction, the surprising remark must be made that SS Gruppenführer Frank, who has always pushed a radical extermination policy against anything Czech, has suddenly—if in somewhat modified form—adopted Neurath's standpoint: namely a policy calling for the widest, if not total, assimilation of the Czechs![58]

Neurath's sole intention was to save the Protectorate and his evolutionary program. He appropriated a Nazi slogan—Germanization—in order to argue that its complexity would require the full attention of some centralized authority such as the Protectorate. Thus, he hoped to postpone the whole issue, perhaps forever. Subsequently, Lammers noted that such stalling had been Neurath's most successful tactic. "Hitler did not wish to disavow totally his Protector, especially not before giving him a chance to have a conference. Neurath's objections frequently succeeded in halting things, and thus defeating them." Later, Lammers specifically recalled Neurath's use of this device in regard to the proposals for restructuring the Protectorate in the summer of 1940. "It is inconceivable to me, even today," Lammers wote in an affidavit, "how the International Military Tribunal could construe anything damaging to Herr von Neurath out of these documents."[59]

In any case, Neurath's tactics worked. On September 23, Hitler received the

Protector and his state secretary. The chancellor had read the two memoranda and agreed in rejecting two solutions: the Czechs would never regain full independence from Germany, but similarly, the Czechs could not be disposed of through emigration. "No one would take the 7 million Czechs off our hands," Hitler said, "even if we wanted to do this." Accepting a program of assimilation, and echoing Neurath's remarks, Hitler predicted this policy might take 100 years in the fulfillment.[60]

At this point, the chancellor introduced a new thought; he approved the assimilation of "racially useful" elements, once "those portions of the Czechs who are enemies of the Reich are isolated or else subjected to special treatment [*Sonderbehandlung*]." Apparently Neurath here heard this concept for the first time, concluding that it meant isolating some people from the majority and subjecting them to special rules. He had no way of knowing, nor did he ever suspect, that in the Nazi rhetoric, *Sonderbehandlung* signified extermination. Frank, however, knew, and his subsequent version of Hitler's remarks clearly indicates such knowledge. He quotes the chancellor as saying: "Any Czechs with objectionable racial traits or who are known to be enemies of the Reich must be excluded from the assimilation process. These categories are simply to be eliminated." Had Neurath properly understood the phrase, he could not have commented in his own memorandum that Hitler expected the process to last at least a hundred years. Even for thousands of Czechs, extermination could be swiftly accomplished.[61]

Thus Neurath never knew he had been present at a meeting which considered extermination of Czech undesirables. His version of the meeting summarized what to him was the real decision: "No division of the Protectorate's territories. [Hitler] declared that only one central Reich office and not many various bureaus should handle questions involving Czechs." He believed that he had won a victory, and an official order resulting from the meeting confirmed his optimism:

> Following the preliminary discussions, the Führer has renewed the instructions that during the war, all discussions of changes in the existing borders of [German] Gaue and [Czech] Provinces must essentially terminate. This includes also questions concerning the relations with other Gaue and Provinces, and with the occupied territories. In order to avoid unrest, the Führer desires that no preparatory measures or discussions be undertaken concerning future changes in territory. This applies also to German relations to the Protectorate Bohemia and Moravia, and to [occupied Poland].

At the same time, Hitler ordered Lammers to enforce a plan of "gradually assimilating the Czechs." A satisfied Neurath believed that Hitler had abandoned schemes for emigration and deportations, and that all real changes had been postponed until after the war, a long way away. Writing to friends in November, he expressed his satisfaction that things were now working out very well, and that he could even find more time for hunting.[62]

Indeed, with Neurath in charge, the Protectorate remained off-limits, and even Göring's special interest remained unsatisfied. As one official noted, "the garden down there has been fenced in." In February 1941, Lammers reluctantly concluded that there was no point in trying to reorganize the Protectorate. "The more we try to clarify Neurath's position, the more we will get into trouble." With a tenacity not hitherto recognized, Neurath had fought for and won protection for the people and the area entrusted to him, preserving peaceful and stable conditions at least through the end of 1940. Unlike other occupied nations, the Czechs had not been subjected to rampant terror or abuse. Indeed, the exile government in London worried constantly about the absence of provocation. While Neurath was in charge, he administered a basically decent government which sought to protect, not destroy, the Czechs, and to ease them into a "realistic" relationship with Germany. He never sought to cause unrest, displacements of population, or bloodshed. As long as he was allowed to do his job, he kept this part of the Reich free from the general brutality and madness which seemed to reign both in Germany and in the world.[63]

Neurath's Ouster

But Frank's cooperation had hidden other motives. In January 1941, in Neurath's absence, he launched a bitter attack upon General Alois Eliáš, the head of the Protectorate government. In February he secretly urged Himmler to arrest Eliáš and sought to force the Czech government into dropping its neutral stance toward Germany's war. Frank's position was strengthened by the reverses of Italy in North Africa and the widespread rumors of a forthcoming German attack upon the Soviet Union. Neurath was alarmed by these developments; in February he wrote Köpke:

> Who knows what this new year will bring to us all! In any case, the political situation has grown considerably worse in the last weeks, and the military condition much more complicated through the turbulent "successes" of our allies. I do not as yet see an end to war, and when the peace bells are made ready to ring, these same allies will serve only as heavy weights on the clappers, if they have not already deserted us by then! In the meantime, our real bells are all being melted down.

He was particularly worried about how these events would alter the balance in the Protectorate:

> You will naturally understand the impact of the Italian "victories" and of the intensive interest by the United States in the prosecution of the war upon the flock entrusted to me. Now I can only ride here with spurs and a heavy bridle, but as long as I have ten divisions, things will work out. My occupation with these matters provides variety and prevents me from being lazy, but frankly, I would prefer a little less variety now and then.

Faced with these new trials, Neurath had difficulties freeing the students still in concentration camps. Only by taking advantage of Frank's temporary absence did he release 200 of them. Neurath's chief assistants confessed to the Czechs that in these months the Protector's influence was noticeably on the wane.[64]

Indeed, in early April 1941, in Neurath's absence, Frank utilized the German invasion of Yugoslavia to issue drastic warnings against public disturbances, denouncing the Protectorate's cabinet as "nay-sayers" and two-faced hypocrites. Hastily returning in a vain attempt to stabilize Frank's manufactured crisis, Neurath protested the "widespread interference in the autonomy of the Protectorate government." Nevertheless, he had to dismiss the cabinet minister whom Frank considered most obnoxious and suggest other changes to the president. As a departing German official noted in late May 1941:

> The conflict [between Neurath and Frank] has taken on such dimensions in the recent weeks, that within three or four months, one could expect some dramatic solution.... The loser would be Neurath since the Nazi party stood ruthlessly behind Frank, and accused Neurath of timidity and weakness.[65]

The outbreak of the war against the Soviet Union destroyed Neurath's remaining chances. Hitherto, the Czechs had been permitted to remain inactive under a benevolent rule. The Protector now realized that he would be unable to prevent the war from intruding upon his enclave. The Czechs gloated over this extension of the fighting and confidently predicted liberation by a victorious Russian army. On June 27, five days after the start of the invasion, trying to prevent unrest, Neurath forbade all discussions of the political future of the Protectorate.[66]

Throughout August 1941 the Protectorate was uneasy. For the first time, the Czechs followed the war with interest; many openly predicted that Germany had overreached itself. Allied propaganda efforts increased, and German officials feared sabotage. SD reports predicted chaos since the Czechs were ready to rebel. These accounts appear to have been greatly exaggerated; Neurath himself did not think the situation that serious, and made no special reports at all. Nevertheless, by September 10, he had to admit that affairs had taken a turn for the worse. His report of that date detailed 10 strikes and 25 incidents of suspected sabotage during the past week, as well as a rumor of a general strike set for the national holiday, October 28. Unconfirmed Czech sources mention a fiery meeting between Neurath and Frank on September 16 or 17, concerning these conditions and the necessary steps to restore order. Shortly thereafter, Frank decided the time was ripe to oust Neurath. As he candidly admitted in a 1944 speech, the war against the Soviet Union enabled him, by pleading the necessity of protecting front-line communications and national security, to pursue a harsh line against the Czechs. On September 21, Frank flew to Hitler's headquarters in East Prussia with SS and police reports accusing Neurath of allowing recalcitrant Czechs to pursue obstructionist tactics. On September 22, Himmler joined Frank in complaints of Neurath's prevention of sanguinary measures.[67]

As a result of these charges, Hitler ordered an unsuspecting Neurath to the Wolfschanze. There, in the presence of Frank, a furious Hitler informed Neurath that the Czechs had been deceiving him; the chancellor announced that he had appointed Heydrich to restore order in the Protectorate. Neurath was stunned, along with Frank, who had fully expected to become Protector. When Neurath objected, Hitler was adamant. He would smash Czech resistance, while Neurath could take a vacation, returning to Prague when the dust had settled. Then it was Hitler's turn to be surprised. Rejecting Heydrich's mission as unnecessary, Neurath refused to cooperate. If Heydrich were sent to Prague, Neurath would resign at once. "I will not return to Prague, ever," he added. As usual, Hitler solved such confrontations by doing nothing. Terminating the meeting, he told Lammers that Neurath should under no circumstances be consulted in the future, but he refused to approve or grant Neurath's request for resignation. Lammers was to announce that the Protector had requested sick leave. A furious Neurath left for Prague at once, packed his bags, informed his staff, and departed for Leinfelderhof within twenty-four hours, upset and angry.[68]

Although one recent study has suggested that the appointment of Heydrich represented only a superficial alteration in personnel, leaving essential policy unchanged, contemporary evidence and systematic analysis reveal a dramatic change. Heydrich recognized no Czech rights beyond subservience to Germany. On his first appearance in Prague, he attacked Neurath and his policies:

> The chief error was that the Czech government was treated as if it were an independent state, as if the office of the Protector were in some fashion an enlarged embassy, accredited to some foreign head of state. Because of this, the Czechs came to believe in the idea that they still had their own state, and that in this fashion the legal position and the international reality of March 16, 1939 had been overcome and forgotten. One cannot administer such an area, restructure it, and develop its sense of belonging to the German Reich if at the same time one approaches the inhabitants of this area with purely foreign policy ideas.[69]

Both Czechs and Germans recognized the "essential change in the nature of the Protectorate" from the moment of Heydrich's arrival. While Germans expressed the hope that "now sharp measures could be introduced against the Czechs," the Czech population generally regretted Neurath's dismissal. Most did not believe the story that he had suddenly become ill. One heard frequent expressions of regret for the "old man" who had been well-intentioned toward them. Another group soon felt the effects of Neurath's dismissal: within a few weeks, most of the higher officials of the Protector's office were fired, for following Neurath's "false policies."[70]

But while these officials merely went to other assignments, the heavy burden of change fell upon the Czech population. Almost at once Heydrich began a reign of terror. On September 27, he proclaimed martial law and began making arrests. On September 28, 6 people were executed; on September 29, 20; and on September 30, 58. Leading the list of those arrested was General Eliáš, head of the government. From September 28 through October 3, between 150 and 200 were condemned to death and executed. Records of the Prague courts alone show that between September 28 and October 9, 118 were condemned to death, 437 turned over to the Gestapo, and only 10 acquitted. In the words of one observer, "an era of blood-mad hatred has broken out."[71]

Within a short time, all Neurath's curbs upon Nazi policies were overturned. On October 9, Heydrich ordered the full imposition of anti-Jewish laws. By February 1942, all Jews were deported to Theresienstadt, which became the Protectorate's first concentration camp. By the end of October 1941, Germanization programs of Czech businesses had begun, led by Himmler's SS and the Land Office which Neurath had neutralized. More significantly, Hitler now abandoned whatever restraint he once employed in holding back German officials from dominating the country. In May 1942, he told Frank that in the future the Protector should be a purely nominal role. "Neurath was himself the perfect type of man for the job," Hitler added, "but he tried to influence policy as well as serve his representational role, and that was a mistake." In the future, German officials would dominate the entire area of government; the Protectorate ended abruptly.[72]

On the evening of January 23, 1942, in one of his table conversations, Hitler had the final word on Neurath's term of office in Prague:

> Every Czech is a born nationalist who naturally relates everything to his own point of view. One must make no mistake about him; the more he curbs himself, the more dangerous he is. The German of the old Reich let himself be duped by the apparent obligingness of the Czech and by his obsequiousness. Neurath let himself be completely diddled by the Czech nobility. Another six months of that regime and production would have fallen by 25 percent....
>
> Now they'll work, for they know we're pitiless and brutal. I don't despise them; I have no resentment against them. It is destiny that wishes us to be adversaries. To put it briefly, the Czechs are a foreign body in the midst of the German community. There is no room for them and for us. One of us must give way.[73]

For all his administrative weaknesses, Neurath had never harbored such thoughts. While he also believed that destiny had thrown the Czechs and Germans into competition for the same area, he preserved a conviction that with patience and time, the two sides could live in peace with each other. He was not given the opportunity to make his theory work, but he had certainly tried his best.

CHAPTER

14

LEINFELDERHOF, NUREMBERG, SPANDAU

From Leinfelderhof, Neurath requested official release from the title of Protector, arguing that "normal rule and administration of the Protectorate is now impossible." When Hitler refused to acknowledge his letter, he retreated to his mountain lodge. On October 10 he returned to Berlin, telling Lammers that after Heydrich's terror, he would never return to Prague. Removing his staff and office from the chancellery to the villa in Dahlem, he watched Germany draw ever closer to catastrophe. In April 1942 he visited Goebbels, hoping to bring from his disengaged situation a perspective which government officials might appreciate. But in typical fashion, Goebbels interpreted Neurath's concern as desire for another job and noted in his diary that the former Protector "had never been guilty of any incorrectness or disloyalty toward the Führer" and he hoped Hitler would make further use of him. Shortly thereafter, Neurath left Berlin to return to his estate. From there he wrote Köpke that he was enjoying retirement:

> Here we are enjoying the quiet life of the country. Physically, I am kept pretty busy, but that is good for me. There is so much to be done, and I am noticing for the first time how much I have permitted my own affairs to suffer during the long years of my activities for others. If one is here on a visit of days or weeks, and simultaneously filled with demands from other matters, there is no time and quiet opportunity to really look around thoroughly at the estate. . . . I greatly hope that I can remain here for as long as possible.[1]

In late October 1942, Neurath was brought back to Berlin by news he received from his son Constantin, who (after service in Lausanne, Rome, Brussels, and Milan) had been named diplomatic advisor to General Rommel in Africa. In October, he returned to Germany on sick leave, with a special report for Hitler on the military and political situation. Both before and after his presentation to the chancellor, he spoke with his father about the deteriorating course of the war:

[Constantin] spoke with very great concern, [Neurath wrote Köpke], about the situation in Africa, where indeed it does not look very good at all. Reinforcements have for a long time been cut off, especially since the "annihilated" [British navy] were able to land a huge convoy in Malta. Truly the English are bragging just a bit too much right now, and I hope that Rommel will be able to trounce them thoroughly again. But they have a huge superiority in men and material, especially in airplanes, when we need [ours] elsewhere. And now naturally the morale of our Italian allies has grown bad again. The English speculation on the demoralizing effect of their air attacks on Italian cities is justified. I know those "heroes."

Alarmed, Neurath believed the war was lost, and he decided to move to Berlin for the winter, to make some prominent officials face the dangerous realities.[2]

The move brought only further embarrassment. On February 2, 1943 (his 70th birthday), the German press sang his praises, and in offering Hitler's congratulations, Meissner presented a painting and a check for 250,000 Reichsmarks in the form of a special endowment. Neurath was surprised and furious. According to his daughter, who was present, he turned red and then deathly white: "I won't accept this," he told Meissner. "I won't be paid off with money, like some high-priced lackey." Meissner said he could not return the check and left the money. Insulted, Neurath consulted Schwerin von Krosigk, the finance minister, who said that the check, drawn from Hitler's private funds, could not be returned without the chancellor's approval. The Führer subsequently rejected both its return and Neurath's suggestion that the money go to charity. Ultimately, insisting that he would never touch the money, Neurath followed Krosigk's advice and placed it in a special bank account which in 1945 was still intact.[3]

His winter in Berlin was unproductive. His arguments concerning office space for his drastically reduced staff became rancorous. Moreover, heavy bombing raids were becoming a daily occurrence. When asked why he had built no air raid shelter, Neurath is quoted as saying: "When my wife and I experience a bombing raid here in Berlin, we prefer to come up here [on the balcony]. Should a bomb destroy us, God would have been good to us. After what has happened, we and the German people can expect nothing good in the future."

Following the destructive raid of March 12, he removed to Leinfelderhof. His mission in Berlin was over. The government seemed a madhouse full of insane officials. "Life is not easy anywhere in the world right now," he wrote during these days, "and it will not get any better for quite some time to come." Distressed by his failure to gain any serious consideration, he was irritated at the misplaced optimism which rejected outright any suggestions for opening negotiations. Köpke also criticized those irresponsible foreign office spokesmen who dismissed "peace feelers, either in the East or in the West," as unnecessary, "since this will be the year in which Russia falls apart militarily!" Confronted with such insanity, Neurath aimed merely at survival "until better times come once again."[4]

After his defeat in Africa in the spring of 1943, and from his new post as commander of the Mediterranean theater, Rommel too had become convinced that Hitler and his political advisors "were not equal to the tasks which awaited them." He prepared a devastating picture of the military situation, again selecting young Neurath, as his best authority on African and Italian affairs, to carry the report to Hitler. Faithfully executing this unpleasant task, despite Ribbentrop's and Keitel's attempts to prevent oral elaboration, Neurath was stunned by Hitler's retort: "No one has ever told me of all this." Even Rommel could not save young Neurath from being immediately recalled and posted, on Ribbentrop's orders, to the consul-generalship at Lugano, one of the backwaters of the war. At Leinfelderhof, Neurath was shocked. "It can't go on like this," he wrote. "It can't continue in such bad fashion." He had frequently discussed the issues with his son and this news, coupled with his own failures in Berlin, produced a despairing sort of paralysis, which his letters reflect:

> We are having beautiful summer weather during the last days and have much work to do before the harvest comes. At present this is a fortunate situation, since it leaves me little time for thinking about other things. I have no immediate intention of returning to Berlin. I can do nothing there at all![5]

On the occasion of Köpke's 70th birthday, Neurath wrote a letter which, he admitted, emphasized the changes since those days long ago when the two friends had sat over cigars and drinks, exchanging wise thoughts and nonsense. "The present humorless and jokeless times do not understand such behavior, of course, but they will live to regret it." This observation loosed a stream of ideas and hopes:

> In any case, the present moment is truly not suitable for joking. The clouds which seem to be gathering over us are growing ever more dark. How are we to emerge from this war with even a modicum of decency? I have no idea at all. All I do know is that in the end, the old, decent men will have to step forward and pick up the pieces of political and military positions in order to save whatever can be saved.
>
> This is not the proper form for a birthday letter, but the devil insists on writing another one. Many times I am overcome with rage at the folly with which such a good beginning was simply thrown away. This should not mean that we will simply let ourselves be conquered or that we have lost courage. That won't happen, even at the very end.
>
> If I decide to visit Berlin again—and at present I have absolutely no desire to do so—I will get in touch with you.

Here were Neurath's most fundamental convictions—his deep belief that Germany could have regained its rightful place without the horrors of war; his shock at the abdication of responsibility by the men in authority; his trust that decency could return only when the old soldiers, diplomats, and civil servants resumed their rightful positions. Though he had failed to be effective in Berlin and Prague in just such positions, he still believed in the rightness of his intentions and tactics.[6]

Still another letter survives from this bleak period. In reply to a series of suggestions on ending the war from a corps-brother, Neurath answered in late August 1943, describing his helpless preoccupation with how to "get out of this present situation with some salvation." He conceded that all suggestions would only be greeted with jeers by the present rulers in Berlin. "Last year I proposed an alteration in our course, because I was convinced that we could not go forward by continually adhering to our 1941 policy," but had received no encouragement:

> In particular, I was aware through long years of experience of the weaknesses of our southern ally [Italy] and of the true state of things there. From the beginning I tried to make people aware of this situation. Unfortunately, I was unsuccessful. My proposals were in another direction [from yours], but at the moment, even this way seems impassable. At present, I simply cannot say when and if the military situation would permit us to undertake a change of course, and whether or not there is time left for such a change. In any case, there is a great deal which we must change, including above all else more understanding for the psychological feelings of foreign nationalities than we have shown in the past or even continue to show today. But in spite of repeated attempts in this direction, I have not succeeded. Thus my departure from Prague. . . .
>
> I do not need to tell you that the general morale here is the same as in Hanover. Only complete idiots and individuals, who out of desire to advance their own positions hide their heads in the sand in ostrich fashion, can deny the seriousness of the present situation. During the whole of last winter, I stayed in Berlin in order to be near the influential authorities. But I had no success at all, and I found I could not get a hearing with the highest authorities at all except through written communication.
>
> Thus, after I had experienced the second severe bombing of Berlin in the spring, I moved to [Leinfelderhof], but continued my attempts to be heard. All in vain![7]

Neurath's attempts to consult with Berlin officials produced one desired result; in August 1943, Lammers sent Neurath a letter from the chancellor officially dismissing him from the position of Reichs Protector. Neurath was pleased, and answered Lammers graciously but could not bring himself to write Hitler. To friends he described the tragic period in Prague as a travesty. When pressed as to his reasons for serving, he replied: "Because I was such a blockhead and still believed Hitler."[8]

Contacts with Resistance Leaders

During the fall and winter of 1943 he no longer was deluded and reluctantly concluded that Germany could emerge from the war with honor only by somehow removing Hitler. Neurath first discussed this with his good friend the mayor of Stuttgart, Karl Strölin, a member of one of Stuttgart's oldest and most respected families, who had worked closely with Neurath on many official occasions. In 1937, he had confided to Strölin his doubts about the Hossbach timetable, and in 1939, Strölin spent several hours trying to change Neurath's mind about going to Prague. Shortly after the outbreak of war, Strölin began talks with General Ludwig Beck and Lieutenant-Colonel Hans Speidel (a fellow Swabian whom he had known since 1916), and after the defeat of France, twice visited military friends in Paris, expressing strong opposition to Hitler. In particular, Strölin criticized the German domestic situation. He told Speidel however, that it was also necessary to reevaluate foreign policy, "if we can even dignify by that name the chaos which now rules in Berlin."[9]

By the winter of 1943, Strölin was seeking Neurath's advice on chances for peaceful negotiations to end the war; both men concluded that Hitler's removal was the first prerequisite. In October 1943, after learning of the military situation in the East, Strölin proposed to the generals a limitation of the powers of the SS and SD, and for the first time "discussed concrete circumstances in the alteration of the domestic relationships, that is, the destruction of the government of the National Socialist tyranny."[10]

In their own talks, Neurath and Strölin had discussed, among other things, the proper replacement for Hitler. Opposing any idea of assassinating the chancellor, Neurath urged military arrest of the Führer and leading Nazi figures, placing them on trial for crimes against the German people. As long as Germany was involved in a war for her very existence, Neurath wanted no part in a murder plot. He encouraged, however, the "decent" military leaders like Beck and especially Field Marshal Rommel, whom Speidel served as chief of staff, to assume control of the government. Neurath was willing, even eager, to cooperate with such a "conspiracy."

In February 1944, Strölin talked with Rommel and in March with Speidel. Reluctant to become involved, Rommel asked for Neurath's opinion on the foreign policy situation, and the chances for peace should a change in government occur. He had met Neurath several times, had worked long and well with his son, and regarded the former minister as a sound judge of foreign affairs and a firm critic of the Nazi government. Strölin promised to arrange a meeting, but when this proved impossible, Rommel sent Speidel, who met with Neurath and Strölin at Freudenstadt on May 27, 1944.[11]

Neurath began the meeting with a lengthy exposé of Germany's desperate foreign situation. He described his attempts to dissuade Hitler from engaging in war and his warnings and proposals thereafter. He had reluctantly concluded that peace overtures would go unheard by the allies, as long as "Hitler and his flunkeys stood at the head of the Reich." Without some changes in government and in policy, however, catastrophe was inevitable. In his turn, Strölin painted a bleak domestic picture and informed Speidel and Neurath of plans for a new government under Carl Goerdeler, the former mayor of Leipzig. Together, Strölin and Neurath appealed to Rommel to place himself at the disposal of such a government. Neurath strongly argued that only Rommel had the foreign reputation to lend respectability to a new government and the necessary domestic prestige to command the armed forces, as regent or president. Although not optimistic about chances to win a successful peace, Neurath believed the allies would modify their demands for unconditional surrender, if a man like Rommel were in charge. After several hours of conversation, Speidel promised to transmit the appeal to Rommel. Ten days later, Neurath apparently composed a memorandum on the critical foreign situation, promising his help in any future government. Following these appeals, Rommel informed Strölin and Neurath that he would remain ready for any such eventuality, and asked for their future cooperation.[12]

Neurath's offer to help Rommel came from an old and tired man who was nevertheless still willing to cooperate with other "decent" people to alter Germany's course. Even though he, with Speidel and Strölin, opposed assassination, by 1944, Neurath had become sufficiently desperate to overcome a lifetime of loyalty and obedience to talk of setting aside the head of the state. Although in June he wrote of hopes for improvement he admitted that "there is certainly no way of knowing how long this present situation will last." His son found him in good health, but obviously troubled.[13]

In July 1944, the assassination attempt on Hitler surprised Neurath. He was shocked to hear that it involved conservative army officers and aristocrats, and especially that the bomb had been set off by the son of his old friend and colleague from the royal Swabian Court, Count Claus von Stauffenberg. Another shock was the deep involvement of Goerdeler, whose name had prominently figured in conversations with Speidel and Strölin. Neurath feared the abortive attempt would trigger a witch hunt. Although he had not mentioned his conversations to members of his family, his daughter became worried when rumors circulated that all of Hitler's old opponents—Neurath, Schacht, and Seldte, to name only a few—were either under arrest or in danger of being so. She hurried to Leinfelderhof to be with her parents. There she raised the subject of a plot to remove Hitler. To her surprise, Neurath replied: "Yes, these people spoke to me about it, but I told them that I would have nothing at all to do with an assassination."[14]

In his birthday letter to Köpke, two days later, Neurath expressed concern for the worsening situation. This letter accurately reflected Neurath's dilemma: what role could patriotic Germans take in a war which was ruining Germany?

> I am sitting down to the typewriter during one of the rare pauses in the mammoth air raid which has been going on against Stuttgart and surrounding areas for the past two days.... Who would ever have thought that in our old age, we would be experiencing dangers more serious than we faced twenty-five years ago? And we have no defenses! [During the First World War] you and I could at least fire back with our weapons. Now not only the years make this impossible....
>
> Naturally the worry about our country and the recent developments weigh heavy on my soul day and night. But that is true of all patriots of the German Fatherland. As I've said, the worst thing is this enforced inactivity; I feel so superfluous. But in spite of all this, I do not abandon courage and hope. As you know, such is not my nature.
>
> The attempted crime of the 20th naturally has affected me deeply. I did indeed know that there were criminals and fools in the land, and that stupidity is widespread everywhere, but hitherto I would not have believed it possible that German officers, in high positions, could be so lacking in conscience and so blinded as to believe they could effect a change in the political order in the country (with which they do not agree) by means of

murder, without at once plunging the Fatherland into chaos. What would have happened had the attempt on the life of the Führer succeeded? It can't even be imagined. The morale in the country is not good. There should be no deceiving ourselves about this. It would be wrong to assume that draconian measures would improve it, for unless such moves be skillfully administered, it is my experience that in employing such means many errors occur.

This is not really a birthday letter, but when the heart is full. . . . Let us hear from you soon, and how you are standing up under the constant attacks on Berlin. I have no idea when you will receive this letter. At present, we are cut off from the world![15]

News of widespread arrests (including Speidel) must have shaken Neurath, but he maintained a calm exterior until he heard that the Gestapo had learned of Field Marshal Rommel's involvement and given him the choice of suicide or a public trial for high treason. At Rommel's funeral, Neurath seemed a broken man, and his son believed that his arrest was imminent. Whatever the reasons, however, no case against Neurath ever developed.[16]

He remained on his estate, trying to protect "house and farm" from the war whose devastation drew ever closer. Despite his daughter's pleas to leave Leinfelderhof, which lay directly in the path of the armies advancing on Stuttgart, and join herself and her husband in the hunting lodge in the Austrian Alps, Neurath refused. As Frau von Mackensen wrote on July 23, 1944: "They won't leave the farm and in addition [they say] they would be bored and lonely up here. That might sound funny, but even though they have many more years under their belts than I do, they both are much too active and young in spirit to simply retire here and twiddle their thumbs."[17]

At Christmas 1944, Neurath wrote Köpke, enlarging upon old themes: the war was hopelessly lost; millions of Germans were suffering displacement and forced migrations; even he and his wife could probably not stay much longer in their family home to guard its possessions. For all that, he warded off despair by discussing measures to be taken *after* the fighting, when reconstruction began:

> There will be much severity and unpleasantness, but we will still hope that it will be better than what we have recently experienced, and that we will be able to achieve in the end a bearable peace, which could bring about the reconstruction of Germany and the restoration of the existence of the many scattered elements of our people. I grant you, this will take much work; it will require huge amounts of just, farsighted, and charitable endeavors, in order to overcome in some manner the intolerable suffering which has fallen upon millions of Germans.

This process would require all the best elements of the population, and he criticized the harsh measures taken against many aristocrats and professional civil servants, ostensibly because they shared ideas which the government claimed produced the assassination attempt. "The official explanation for the spiritual origins of the 20th of July," he wrote, "is certainly wrong, and at least not true as a generalization. . . . One will perhaps still have need of these conspirators in the future."[18] Although he could no longer be involved, he considered it necessary for aristocrats and civil servants to step forward (as he had after World War I) to help salvage whatever could be saved.

But this time, there would be no armistice and no peace conference for Germany. As the allied armies pressed ever deeper into the country, on March 26, 1945 (Palm Sunday) Neurath decided to abandon Leinfelderhof, and take refuge in his Alpine hunting lodge. He had made no plans, almost as if he could not face this unthinkable decision. The family possessions and documents were left on the estate, and only a few important items were taken to Bludenz. As he took a last tour of the grounds, he later recalled, he was filled with the most frightening premonition that he would never return. Through his son, who was working in Switzerland, Neurath had learned that his name was on the allies' "wanted list," and that he should expect to be arrested when the war ended. His immediate concern was to bring his wife to some safe place. Only this consideration prompted him to leave Leinfelderhof.[19]

War Criminal

On May 4, 1945 in Austria, French troops arrested Neurath and his son-in-law, Hans-Georg Mackensen, who had served as ambassador in Rome after his resignation as state secretary. Mackensen had no illusions about the future. "Now everything's finished," he told his wife. "I will never return here again!" Neurath was not as discouraged: "Don't worry," he told his family. "Nothing will happen to me. I have a good conscience, and most assuredly, I will return to you."[20]

Taken first to a French prison in Lindau, Neurath developed a serious infection, and in July underwent a prostate gland operation, not an easy experience for a seventy-two-year-old man. His recovery was slow and complications, including some old eye trouble, developed. By the first week of August, he was permitted out of bed, and then abruptly transferred to the prison hospital at Kirchberg, where his son-in-law Hans-Georg von Mackensen was also interned. Still unaware of his future, Neurath petitioned the French authorities for his release. His letters show the impact of the confinement: "In spite of the careful attention, I have had enough of the hospital. The more my strength returns, the smaller my room seems, and my inactivity and solitary state become more oppressive."[21]

Neurath's fate was as yet uncertain. After months of negotiations, representatives of France, Great Britain, the United States, and the USSR had drawn up a charter creating the International Military Tribunal to try major German figures on charges of crimes against peace and humanity, and an agreement to return lesser ones "to the scene of their crimes," where they would receive justice. Although the agreement was signed in London on August 8, 1945, the list of the major defendants had not as yet been determined. The British and Americans had engaged in a number of preliminary discussions and in June agreed on sixteen names. With the exception of Hitler, all the men were in the custody of their armies. The British were particularly insistent on a quick trial and a short list of defendants. In none of their conversations did Neurath's name figure prominently, even though they knew he was in prison. Only after the charter had been completed and the rules adopted did the London conference turn back to the question of defendants. On August 21, the Russians asked for a meeting, insisting that five prisoners whom they had captured should also be included as major criminals (including Fritzsche, a minor official of the propaganda ministry). Not to be outdone, the French now insisted that some of their prisoners should also stand trial as major war criminals. They could come up with only two candidates— Papen and Neurath—but they were adamant, and in the interest of international cooperation, these two names (and those provided by the Russians) were added. In such a fashion, and for reasons largely concerning political prestige, Neurath was brought to formal trial by the Allies.[22]

The official list, published on September 1, contained twenty-four names, including Göring, Ribbentrop, Rosenberg, Hess, Keitel, Raeder, Schacht, and Papen. On September 13, Neurath was moved to the main prison at Überlingen and then to Baden-Baden, where he joined nearly fifty other former German diplomats. In October, French authorities brought them all to Nuremberg, where Neurath was turned over to American officials. The formal indictment was issued on October 20 in Berlin; the trial began in Nuremberg on November 20, 1945.[23]

Upon arriving in Nuremberg, Neurath was subjected to a battery of interrogations, without the presence of a defense counsel. Thus the defendants themselves provided evidence to redefine the broad 25,000-word indictment. This indictment contained four major parts:

1. Conspiracy. The accused had pursued a common plan to seize unlimited power and conspired for the committing of all further crimes.
2. Crimes against peace. The accused had broken twenty-six international treaties in sixty-four cases, had begun a war of aggression, and had caused a world war.
3. War crimes: The accused had instituted a horrible blood bath and had ordered or permitted mass murder, tortures, slave labor, and economic exploitation.
4. Crimes against humanity: The accused had persecuted political opponents, and racial and religious minorities, and made themselves responsible for the destruction of whole groups of the population.

Convinced that his own indictment was a mistake, Neurath cooperated with the American investigators, going so far as to conduct his interviews in English. "If everyone had as clear a conscience as I have," he told the prison psychiatrist during these preliminary inquiries, "then it would be all right." The officer conducting the interrogations agreed. On October 4, 1945, Major John J. Monigan wrote to the American prosecution team that he thought the evidence did not warrant charging Neurath and in view of his age and health he ought not to stand trial. His suggestion was ignored.[24]

Neurath faced severe obstacles in preparing his defense. His only son was incarcerated in Switzerland; his wife was in Austria unable to leave; his daughter was busy trying to provide soap and washed clothes to an imprisoned husband and father. His papers were lost, his villa in Berlin destroyed in 1943, and Leinfelderhof plundered for ten days in April 1945. His health was not good, and to some of his interrogators, he gave the impression of approaching senility, a man "at 73, physically aged even beyond his years." With no experience in legal and criminal procedures, he was cavalier toward the proceedings, for to him it seemed the victors were less interested in a trial than in punishment of all German leaders. Shocked and saddened by the indictment, he told the prison psychiatrist: "I was always against punishment without the possibility of a defense." While Dr. Gilbert interpreted this ambiguous remark as a criticism of Nazi lawlessness, it was aimed at the forthcoming trial. Neurath could not conceive of a defense against "victor's justice," and summarized his feelings in a letter on the eve of the trial:

> In spite of all my energy, from time to time a sombre wretchedness overcomes me at the thought of all that stands before me, how long I will have to sit in jail, and what the victors have in mind for me. In this even my clear conscience does not help me. It is the end of a life full of decent, and, I can truthfully say, selfless work for the fatherland and for peace and humanity, and I now stand accused of violence against these very principles.[25]

The interrogations over and his indictment concluded, Neurath was informed of his right to legal counsel. Although his closest friend in Berlin was a lawyer, he had to choose from a list of three names provided by the court. Convinced that the trial would be a "typical political show-trial," he indifferently selected the first name, an East Prussian baron, Otto von Lüdinghausen. This fateful decision he was soon to regret. His family inaccessible, friends like Baroness von Ritter and her daughter arrived to help assemble his defense. They were appalled by the choice of Lüdinghausen:

> Within five minutes of talking to him [Baroness von Ritter recalls] I *knew* he was the wrong man and I wrote as much to Neurath, but by then the damage had been done. I tried to figure out a way to extract some good out of it, and we decided to include my daughter as his secretary. She might be able to put some heart into the case. For Lüdinghausen was the very opposite of Neurath—a Baltic baron, aesthetic and withdrawn. He never really understood Neurath, and did not try very hard to do so. From the beginning we had trouble with him. He had no animation; he did not understand the court system and did not put any backbone into the case. I am sorry to say, but Neurath was not served well by Herr von Lüdinghausen.[26]

The Nuremburg Trial

The prosecution began its case with broad charges of conspiracy and common participation in atrocities. German commentators and neutral newspapers found the charge particularly incomprehensible: it was highly unlikely that the 21 men in in the docket, ranging from top-ranking generals and leading politicians to civil servants and minor officials, had even talked together before, much less conspired. The *Basler Nachrichten*'s comments reflected this attitude:

> The indictment certainly does not represent historical truth. The variegated team of defendants never conspired or operated together, but were only commonly dependent upon a central authority. The sentence in which it is charged that "all" the defendants "acted in common concert and were united in their plans for mass murder" is simply not true. There are men among these defendants who did not approve these murders from a moral point of view, and who did not believe them to be helpful in the politics of war, for example Baron von Neurath.[27]

This uniform approach particularly discouraged the defendants. After only five days, Neurath wrote: "The trial will last months, and nothing can as yet be even suspected about the outcome. But following the whole attitude of the victors, it looks very black." A month later, he believed that little had changed:

> It will still last months, and it requires considerable effort to keep up health and spirits under the present conditions. Up to now, I have been fine. The exertions of sitting six hours daily on a wooden bench are serious, and added to that are the glaring lights and the heat. By evening I am mostly worn out, and then often cannot sleep for a long time.
>
> There is still nothing to report on the outcome of this trial. If it lasts very long, perhaps some interest will lapse, but there will still remain those indescribable, incomprehensible atrocities, of which I had no knowledge and for which now all are held responsible. Everything depends upon whether or not the court will permit individual defenses.

In the light of the conspiracy charges, he feared it would not.[28]

After a month of general charges aimed at full conviction of all the defendants, the prosecution took up individual cases. To the stupefaction of the defense lawyers, the prosecution freely departed from the original indictments, adding new charges and sections, and dropping others. Yet even here, no attempt was made to specify which charges were directed at which individuals, and the rules of the court prohibited counter-remarks by the defense. Neurath justifiably complained of this process:

> Tomorrow, [he wrote on December 15, 1945,] the prosecution will again fall upon me, and I must remain quiet. Until I am given a chance to reply, weeks will pass. That is the disagreeable part of this trial, that at first only the prosecution representatives have their say. The court itself created this procedure and rejects all defense proposals for change. They absolutely want to reach a condemnation, indeed if possible of all the defendants.[29]

Broad charges were made throughout, many of which had little or nothing to do with the individuals on trial. The case against Neurath, for example, was preceded and followed by a moving and dramatic presentation of atrocities in Western

Europe, especially in the concentration camps.* Moved to tears by what he now saw and heard, Neurath could only complain at being associated with all this:

> They are trying to blame me for as much as possible, including things of which I knew nothing and in which I was never involved. I am overwhelmed increasingly by a sense of outrage, as I learn about the atrocities from the concentration camps, and I am amazed that all that could have remained hidden from everyone.[30]

In the eyes of the prosecution, and apparently of the court as well, such association of charges was permissible since the whole system, not each individual, was on trial. Confused and angered by these procedures, Neurath insisted that he knew nothing about conspiracies, adding rather pathetically that if there were any, "Hitler must have done his conspiring with his little group of henchmen late at night," when he [Neurath] was at home in bed! He knew that the conspiracy charge would be the decisive point against all the defendants:

> The outcome of the trial [he wrote] will essentially depend on whether we have been able to convince the court that *NO* conspiracy and *NO* general liability existed, and that therefore each defendant should be tried for what he himself did that was wrong.... The principal guilty parties, admittedly, no longer stand before an earthly court.[31]

Faced with such charges and what he called "a monstrous trial with no trace of justice or search after truth, built only on hatred and sensation," Neurath was profoundly shaken and bitter. After a gloomy birthday in 1946 he wrote:

> If someone had told me that I would spend my 73rd birthday in jail, accused of crimes for the preparation of an aggressive war, for breaking international treaties, for crimes against humanity, against the Christian Church, etc., I would have pronounced him a fool. Yet, that has now become reality, despite the fact that the prosecution knows that their own charges are untrue. But life usually follows the old saying: "slander with audacity, something will always stick." This is all the more the case in this trial, since we can defend ourselves only months later, and in addition our defense lawyers are handicapped in every way.[32]

The prosecution's case against Neurath was fivefold: he held high position in the government from 1933 through 1945, as foreign minister, president of the secret cabinet council, and member of the defense council, and thereby had participated

---

*Deeply shaken by the documents presented in these January days (the French case on atrocities started on January 23, 1946, IMT, VI, 158ff.), Neurath frequently returned to the same theme in his letters: "New horrors are constantly sweeping over me as I learn about the atrocities of the concentration camps, and I stand amazed that all that could remain hidden, even that which in your own neighborhood must have been going on for years [Dachau was only 9 miles from the Ritters' home] and yet you knew nothing of it!" Two weeks later, he commented: "I have been particularly affected by the atrocities of which I learn only for the first time. I still can't understand that such things—and indeed not as isolated cases—were possible and that they could be kept secret. Yet for all this, I am now held responsible." Neurath to Baroness von Ritter, January 14 and 26, 1946, Ritter Papers.

in and was responsible for all the criminal acts of the German government. Second, by his actions within the government, Neurath had committed the crime of promoting and assisting the rise to power of the Nazi party. Third, as foreign minister, he had deliberately engaged in a "Nazi conspiracy for the consolidation of control in preparation for war," by leaving the disarmament conference, helping rearmament, introducing universal military service, and facilitating the remilitarization of the Rhineland. Fourth, as Hitler's intimate advisor, Neurath was accused of planning and executing "acts of aggression against Austria, Czechoslovakia, and other nations." Citing as evidence the Hossbach meeting and an affidavit by the former American consul in Vienna, George S. Messersmith, the prosecution claimed that Neurath was involved in a clear conspiracy, and subsequently "by accepting and occupying the position of Protector of Bohemia and Moravia, [he] personally adhered to the aggression against Czechoslovakia and the world." Fifth, as Protector, Neurath was accused of crimes against humanity for policies in violation of international laws governing war and peace, a charge rising largely out of plans for the "Germanization" of the Czechs.[33]

The heart of the prosecution's case was Neurath's good reputation, which he had preserved even while serving Hitler. Arguing that he had served as a fifth-column among conservatives in Germany and a tool for Hitler in international diplomacy, the prosecution insisted that had he not fully adhered to the National Socialist program (which in their view included plans for aggressive war), and not agreed with all aspects of German policy, both domestic and foreign, he would have broken with Hitler and spread the news of this disassociation to the general public. To the prosecution, Neurath's guilt lay in his continued good relationship with the German government, which made him responsible for the actions of that government.[34]

Neurath knew that in this form, the charges against him would probably stand. As he wrote on March 2, 1946:

> The trial has now taken on a wholly different face with this developing thesis that every individual is responsible for everything that happened. It is still unclear whether or not the court will recognize the fact that I did not know anything about all the atrocities and could have known nothing. I also do not know if I can succeed in proving that I always endeavored not only to preserve the peace, but to hold back Hitler from his plans, insofar as I even knew of them. It is only now clear to me that Hitler must have lied to me so many times, keeping his ulterior motives hidden, and indeed often suddenly changing them. This is naturally difficult to prove.

Especially angry at prosecution charges that he had, through his membership in the cabinet, "sold my honor and my reputation," Neurath was overwhelmed with shame at the atrocities, and with shock at the revelations of the "idiotic policies pursued by Hitler and his lackeys," but had no regrets about his own actions. Preparing his case, he recalled vividly the painful decision in 1932 to become foreign minister:

That is now thirteen years ago, and what fights and efforts I have experienced since then, and without any success except to end [in this trial]. But even though I frequently ask myself: "What would you do different, or what could you have done better?" I still come to the conclusion: I would even today do the same thing. It would naturally have been easier and more comfortable for me to have retired to Leinfelden. But would that have been the correct thing in the face of the needs of the Fatherland?

It was my destiny that was stronger than I. And so I must permit even what lies ahead to flow over me.[35]

Armed with this confidence, Neurath should have been able to defend himself. Had he been given access to his documents, a defense lawyer who understood the court procedures, and a court seeking historical truth rather than legal technicalities, he would have been acquitted. These he lacked and in particular, his lawyer never gained control of his case. When confronted by the court's rules on admissibility of evidence, use of witnesses, availability of documents and so forth, Lüdinghausen usually retired in confusion. Given the severe restrictions upon consultations between lawyer and client, Neurath was forced to undertake the difficult organization of his own defense. In his painfully difficult scrawl, Neurath wrote out his recollections, always conscious that "long imprisonment makes my age apparent here and there." Reluctantly, he admitted that his lawyer was largely useless, permitting the court to rule out some of his most important witnesses, and abandoning without protest his request for certain documents.[36] In court Lüdinghausen was incompetent. He failed to cross-examine witnesses properly, and his handling of Karl Strölin was so inept that this valuable witness became a liability. Subsequent witnesses were questioned with such imprecision that the court repeatedly reprimanded Lüdinghausen. In general, he took no pains to master the procedure of cross-examination. He believed it was unfair for the prosecution to attack a witness's testimony, and he complained of this technique in a letter revealing his own bewildered helplessness:

> The incalculable factor in predicting the course of this trial is the so-called cross-examination of individual witnesses by the four prosecutors. It is simply impossible to predict how long these cross-examinations will take. Up to now, they have frequently occupied more time than the examination of the witness by his own lawyer. Really, this cross-examination! This institution which is generally as good as unknown to us German lawyers in trial procedures is for all of us a nightmare. The major point of this process is mainly to picture the concerned witness as untrustworthy, and in order to reach this goal, the prosecution does not hesitate to use not only suggestive questions but also to fall upon the witness with new charges and documents, none of which has made its appearance beforehand. Moreover, they frequently and deliberately distort the meaning of these new documents, and thereby artificially construct some contradiction within the testimony of the witness, thus seeking to entangle him into further contradictions. None of us can predict what the prosecution can or will bring forward at such times, since

none of us knows what documents from the foreign office they have in their possession.... Herr von Neurath claims that there are no documents in existence which they can use to contradict the line pursued by his defense ... namely the peaceful intentions of the government. But we have lived through many bitter surprises in this connection.

Unlike several of his colleagues who subsequently turned the cross-examination to their clients' advantage, Lüdinghausen resigned himself to failure.[37]

Meanwhile, a series of court rulings further diminished Neurath's chances for a successful defense. The first ruled as "inadmissible" any evidence concerning the injustice of the Versailles Treaty. Next, the defense was denied the right to introduce new documents (out of an exaggerated fear of Nazi "forgeries"). Finally, on March 29, the court ruled that since it had permitted Hermann Göring to recount the general history and background of the Third Reich, other defendants could not "go over the same ground." This ruling openly recognized the prosecution's "conspiracy" thesis; since Göring was the number two man in the Nazi state, his version of history was definitive. Now, Neurath stood trial for participation in that Nazi history, and his defense would not be separated from that of the other men in the docket.[38]

Adding to legal worries, Neurath was plagued by fears for his family. His estates had been confiscated and, he heard, were to be parceled out; his personal property had been plundered. Even more alarming, his son was interned in Switzerland and subject to arrest upon his return to Germany. His son-in-law was already in prison at Überlingen where he would soon die. His wife and beloved daughter were in Austria, unable to communicate with him. He feared for their safety, especially as wandering bands of brigands were terrifying the countryside. "The treatment here becomes even unpleasanter and harsher," he wrote on January 6, 1946, "but that is nothing compared to my apprehension about Manny and Wini. Do you think they may have been put in a concentration camp? There's no trace of justice. The question arises, whether it is really worthwhile to go on living." These thoughts recurred as the trial dragged on through the spring and summer of 1946. Still, he had not been given a chance to begin his defense.

> What keeps up my courage, [he wrote to Baroness von Ritter,] is only the thought that I can be of some help to a few of my close friends in these troubled times. Otherwise, it would have been better for me to have quietly and solitarily passed away last summer after the operation—when it required only that I abandon my will to live. My life's work is destroyed, and at my age it is not possible that I will ever see the work of reconstruction.[39]

Finally, on June 22, 1946, seven months after the start of the trial, the court called on Dr. Lüdinghausen to present his case. For a complicated indictment such as Neurath faced, covering all foreign and domestic policy between 1933 and 1938, and the difficult question of the Protectorate, Lüdinghausen's presentation was surprisingly short and thin. His document book contained only 117 pieces, 92 of which were from official government publications. He filed only 7 original documents of historical importance, submitted only 10 affidavits, and called a mere 3 witnesses.[40] Although he knew that the prosecution could freely develop other charges during cross-examination, Lüdinghausen limited his case to precise and specific points. He assembled no material that would present Neurath in a light different from that given by the prosecution. In fact, his client's personality was rather lost in Lüdinghausen's case.

Before the Court

Neurath's lawyer had done little to prepare him for the ordeal on the stand. Despite his experience in the court during the preceding nineteen cases, he had Neurath limit his testimony to formal answers prepared in advance and read from the stand. These gave a painful and misleading impression. Neurath's hesitant speech and diplomatic way of choosing words carefully seemed characteristic of a man with something to hide, one who could not trust himself to oral sparring, but took refuge in prepared texts. The resulting testimony lacked vitality, and other defense lawyers thought Lüdinghausen had shown very little skill in its preparation. On rare occasions, when Neurath spoke without notes, he made a better impression, yet his lawyer then always led him back to the script. As a result, Neurath's testimony was counterproductive, trying the patience of the court, which repeatedly interrupted the narrative to criticize Lüdinghausen for permitting irrelevant details of history. The Tribunal concluded the first morning's testimony with a pointed reminder:

> Dr. von Lüdinghausen, we have been the whole morning at this and we haven't yet really got up to 1933. The Tribunal thinks this is being done in far too great detail. As I have already pointed out, a great deal of it is an attempt to show that the Treaty of Versailles was unjust, which is irrelevant.[41]

The court was correct. Although Neurath and his lawyer had known since late March that all arguments concerning the historical backgrounds would be dismissed, Neurath's case rested heavily upon such details. The afternoon session was no better; the court correctly described that testimony as largely "political history." His second day on the stand started off poorly and rapidly deteriorated. From the moment Lüdinghausen began questions on foreign policy, the Tribunal repeatedly interrupted, characterizing the testimony as "argument" not evidence. Lüdinghausen apparently did not understand the difference, and continued to muddle the defense. Unable to organize his material, he failed to concentrate upon what he had admitted to Neurath's family and friends was the critical point of the accusation: the term as Protector in Prague.[42]

The lawyer introduced this difficult aspect of the defense late on the afternoon of June 24. Noticeably weary after two full days on the stand, Neurath gave lengthy and rambling accounts of his motives and actions. Because of the late hour, he was forced to interrupt his testimony and appear on the following morning for still another day of examination. Courtroom observers noted a marked deterioration in Neurath's bearing: he seemed exhausted by the ordeal, and his own lawyer had failed to emphasize the positive aspects of his position. Still ahead lay the cross-examination.[43]

In his testimony on Prague, Neurath stressed efforts to prevent the occurrence of worse abuses; when he found himself no longer effective, he resigned. But Lüdinghausen failed to delineate the precise motivations for Neurath's acceptance of and continuation in office. As a result, the court was unimpressed with Neurath's contention that he had believed in Hitler's desire to reconcile Czechs and Germans, and had stayed in Prague hoping to achieve peace. On this unconvincing note, Lüdinghausen inexplicably rested the case for the defense. He did not even refer to events after Neurath left Prague and omitted completely his involvement with Strölin, and introduced no evidence to contradict the charge that Neurath continued to serve the Nazis until the end of the war.

To this point, Neurath's defense was at best uninspired; his lawyer presented him as a well-meaning, but rather incompetent and naive man, who although he held high office knew little of what was going on, and successfully opposed nothing. Even before the prosecution's cross-examination, Neurath's case was weak. Had he freely admitted that as foreign minister, he openly sought to restore German power, a responsibility which he accepted and which was no crime, his situation would have improved. Actions which the prosecution criticized should have been characterized as integral and sovereign acts of a German foreign minister; Neurath could have challenged the prosecution to prove that such duties were criminal! Instead, Neurath's attempted justification of all actions was confusing and left a "painful and unworthy" impression. Similarly, his best defense as Protector was to demonstrate his attempts to preserve the mild status quo which he had inherited; "criminal acts" occurred only over his objections and really began after he had left. Finally, he should have introduced the Strölin-Rommel conversations to show his awareness of the moral evil of the Nazi regime and his advice to those retaining sufficient powers to remove Hitler.[44]

While Lüdinghausen's incompetence is primarily responsible for this feeble defense, another cause operated. In the midst of the Nuremberg trial, Karl Hermann Frank, Neurath's state secretary in the Protectorate, was tried in Prague, condemned, and executed. At the same time, nearly 800 German and Czech collaborators were either executed or sentenced to die for their parts in the occupation. Lüdinghausen believed that were Neurath acquitted he would be extradited to Prague and probably executed. Hence, he told at least one source, the best defense would be for Neurath to be found guilty on minor matters and given a small sentence, part of which could then be commuted to time served. It would be dangerous to make Neurath available for Czech justice.* Thus Lüdinghausen defended Neurath against the serious charges, but chose not to introduce evidence (such as Strölin and Speidel material) which would entirely clear him.[45]

*On March 2, 1946, Neurath wrote Baroness von Ritter: "By the present course of this trial, I can scarcely hope to emerge a free man. And in addition, I must expect that afterwards I will be turned over to the Czechs." Ritter Papers.

Whatever the reasons, the defense rested with few positive points. One observer noted that Neurath did not seem physically equal to the task of defending both German foreign policy and that of the Protectorate. His generally poor performance discouraged all the defendants, who felt that Neurath's strong case had been damaged by an ill-staged defense. As the cross-examination began, the poor impression deepened. Facing Neurath was Sir David Maxwell-Fyfe, deputy chief prosecutor of the United Kingdom who with "icy civility" launched a devastating attack, firing a barrage of "sharp, at times even hate-filled questions," which confused the old man. "If Sir David keeps asking me questions in such an impudent tone of voice," he rather pathetically confided to the prison psychiatrist during the lunch break, "I'll give him a sharp answer. Just wait and see!" But few sharp answers followed, leaving the exchange completely one-sided.[46]

The British prosecutor did not pursue the broad lines adopted by the defense, but concentrated on four major charges. First, he claimed that by staying in office, Neurath showed approval of the government's crimes. When Neurath replied that he was "foreign minister, not minister of the interior," and that he had never heard of a cabinet minister leaving "if he does not agree with one particular thing," Maxwell-Fyfe retorted: "Every cabinet minister for whom I have any respect left a cabinet if it did something of which he morally disapproved." This good point, unfortunately, disguised a difference between the British and German cabinet systems. In spite of his rhetorical skills, Maxwell-Fyfe had hardly proved criminal charges, yet in presenting the verdict, the court emphasized Neurath's cooperation with the domestic policy of the Third Reich.[47]

The second charge involved Neurath's participation in aggressive foreign policy against the Rhineland, Austria, and Czechoslovakia. Maxwell-Fyfe argued that since Neurath knew the policy in these areas, he was also responsible for Nazi subversion and activities abroad. To this, Neurath ironically replied: "If I were responsible for every single [German] murderer. . . . who was active abroad, then I would have [had] a lot of work to do, would I not?" But such answers were hardly likely to convince, and Neurath had difficulty persuading the court that his policy in the Rhineland and Austria was pacific and not part of an aggressive conspiracy. When a report from Ambassador William C. Bullitt was interpreted by the prosecution as showing Neurath wanted to remain quiet "until the Rhineland had been digested" before expanding to aggression in the East and South, he challenged this interpretation, but did not thereby shake the conspiracy thesis. The prosecution used every event to bolster their conspiracy claim, while the defense could not cite the *absence* of evidence in Neurath's behalf. Finally, Maxwell-Fyfe challenged Neurath to name even one important order of Hitler's that he had refused to implement. Neurath replied that while he had "opposed all sorts of things," he could not provide details. The prosecution scored a telling point and Neurath seemed an unquestioning supporter of Hitler's illegal and wild expansionism.[48]

The third charge was that Neurath had known of and supported plans for aggressive war, because after the Hossbach meeting revealed Hitler's intentions, he had continued to serve in the government. Moreover, the prosecution introduced documents claiming to show that Neurath willingly cooperated with these plans by deliberately lying on the eve of the *Anschluss,* when he reassured the Czechs that Germany would abide by the arbitration treaty. When Neurath replied that he had merely relayed Hitler's message "with an absolutely clear conscience," Maxwell-Fyfe asked incredulously: "Did you still believe a word that Hitler said on the 12th of March 1938?" The prosecution's case rested upon the plausible theory that Neurath could not have been so naive. Thus he must have supported Hitler's plans to carry out such steps by serving in the secret cabinet council. The court apparently did not believe that the council never functioned, for in its final judgment, it defined Neurath's "crimes against peace" as participating in "formal relationship with the Nazi regime after 1938." In fact, Maxwell-Fyfe failed to establish that Neurath had planned or executed any criminal acts against peace, and had the prosecution ended its cross-examination with the year 1938, Neurath might well have been acquitted.[49]

But his ordeal was just beginning. After a recess, Maxwell-Fyfe turned to the fourth and most crucial charge: "criminal acts" in Prague. Introducing a surprise document—an unsigned letter by Neurath with two enclosures—he accused the former Protector of deliberately encouraging forced "Germanization," directing a "dreadful, callous and unprincipled" warfare against the Czechs. At first Neurath denied the authenticity of the documents, but the prosecution, producing another one, alleged that the harsh program of Germanization was jointly sponsored by Neurath and Frank. In this cross-examination, Neurath became confused and unable to follow the prosecutor. He was forced to defend not only his own ideas, but the plans and proposals of Frank and other officials which Maxwell-Fyfe lumped together. Equally unprepared, Lüdinghausen sat silent. Only once did Neurath react with animation; confronted with a proposal for mass deportations, Neurath angrily replied: "If you were to look through suggestions made by all your subordinates, then you, too, might find some proposal which you afterward rejected. Suggestions made by an advisor do not mean anything at all."[50]

At this point, the British prosecutor rested the case. Neurath's reaction to this damaging set of documents had bespoken guilt. His hesitations, faulty memory, and trouble in following the prosecution's arguments, made a poor showing. "His inability to talk well," one observer concluded, "his seeking for words, confirmed the unfavorable impression." Hans Fritzsche, Neurath's neighbor in the defendants' dock, watched Neurath's deterioration under pressure with pain and anguish. His account is accurate and insightful:

> It was painfully clear to everybody that [Neurath] lacked the ability to disentangle all this contradictory evidence, and his lawyer intervened pleading that his client was too tired to follow the argument. The Bench tried to clarify matters by a number of calm questions, but the old man was exhausted and returned to the dock in utter confusion.

Seyss-Inquart's lawyer came to a similar conclusion:

> The long imprisonment and his advanced age told on [Neurath], especially in the cross-examination, where he was confronted by the Englishman Sir Maxwell-Fyfe. [Neurath] left the witness chair completely disconcerted and confused. How differently had others conducted themselves in that chair, for example Kaltenbrunner. Neurath's fate was the tragedy of an old man.[51]

On the next day, Counsellor M. Y. Raginsky, assistant prosecutor from the Soviet Union, continued the cross-examination, using material from a Czech government document based upon interrogations of leading Czech collaborationists and State Secretary Frank, who had been executed three months earlier. Despite Lüdinghausen's protests that this document should not stand in evidence, the court accepted it. These unsubstantiated charges most seriously damaged Neurath's case.[52]

In his reexamination, Lüdinghausen attempted to refute some of the more serious impressions. In particular he concentrated on the prosecution's surprise documents. Now, Neurath remembered that "this entire affair and the origin of these memoranda are extremely difficult to explain." Correctly linking them to his troubles with outside interference by Nazi and German authorities, Neurath insisted that he had made "impracticable" suggestions "so as to declare them absurd later on." They were "a purely tactical maneuver to get at Hitler, because I was afraid that he would follow the radical suggestions made by Himmler and his associates." Unfortunately, Neurath had not recalled this connection when the documents were first produced in evidence, and his new testimony—which was an accurate account of the origins of the documents in question—did not overcome the effect of the cross-examination. Moreover, Lüdinghausen's later attempt to prove the documents were forgeries probably strengthened the case against his client.[53]

Before he left the stand on June 26, Neurath asked permission to comment on the charge that he had served a government which committed reprehensible and immoral acts. He read a statement which, although unappreciated by the court, summarized the philosophy of service which had motivated his whole life:

> I have already mentioned in the beginning that I had given my promise to Hindenburg to enter the government and to remain there as long as it was at all possible for me to follow a course unfavorable to any use of violence and to protect Germany from warlike entanglements. That was my task, and nothing else. But it was not only this promise I had given to Hindenburg, but also my sense of duty and my feeling of responsibility toward the German people, to protect them from warlike entanglements as long as it was at all possible, which bound me to this office. Beside these considerations, all my personal wishes which were quite different had to take second place.
>
> Unfortunately, my power and influence as foreign minister did not reach far enough to enable me to prevent pernicious and immoral actions in other spheres, as for instance, in domestic policy, although I did try in many cases,

not least of all in the Jewish question itself. However, I considered that my highest duty was to carry out the work assigned to me and not try to escape it, even if in another sphere where I had no influence things occurred which hurt me and my opinions very much.... It is not easy to belong to a government whose tendencies you do not agree with, and for which one is to be made responsible later on.[54]

Following this statement, Neurath was questioned closely by the three judges, who sought to establish Neurath's motivations, almost as if the court itself was dissatisfied with the legal process before it. The impression upon observers was bad, for the judges seemed to demonstrate "very negative attitudes toward Neurath." This atmosphere was not improved by Lüdinghausen's interrogation of his three witnesses. From Köpke he evoked only generalizations and from Dieckhoff only assurances of Neurath's good intentions. Völckers made long speeches of little substance, which tried the patience of the court and were largely ignored. A trial lawyer summed up the effect in his diary:

All three witnesses were not "led" well enough. Their testimony consisted more or less only of characterizations, and thus remained rather useless for the case. The prosecution even refrained from cross-examining!

In general the whole [defense case] was unsatisfactory, and this is all the more regrettable since Neurath's case certainly needed an improvement in tone and morale.[55]

Lüdinghausen suspected that he had failed to develop the potential of the case, and a few weeks later confessed his pessimism about the outcome:

With a clean conscience, I can say that I have really done everything which was within my power and intellectual capabilities in order to help [Neurath] and to save him from that fate which, God knows, he does not deserve. Whether all my efforts, all my work has been in vain now rests in the hands of a Higher Authority, and we can only beseech Him in prayer: grant him Your assistance.

My final speech was completed only a few days ago. The whole complex issue of the Protectorate was much larger and more difficult to compose than I had originally thought. I literally worked day and night on this section until I had brought it to the same loftiness and forcefulness as the political section. But this unhappy Protectorate affair remains my cross, and if he is condemned, it will be solely on account of this office. It is truly a vulgar and Sophoclean tragedy that this basically decent and honorable man should be found guilty without being himself guilty. Only because he followed his conscience and wanted to block shameful acts. But who here in Nuremberg worries about morality or immorality.[56]

Compounding his mistakes, Lüdinghausen composed a rambling final plea which lacked focus. A few days before he delivered it, Lüdinghausen revealed in a letter his tragic misunderstanding of his role at the trial:

The course of this trial has clearly shown that the mentality of the judges is at odds with legal concepts embodied in German law. Moreover, as the court frequently brought to our attention, it wanted to hear nothing about historical things and developments before 1933, nor about the guilt of other [nations]; even criticism of the Versailles Treaty itself was explicitly forbidden, and one had to handle discussion of this question very carefully.

In spite of these prohibitions, I sought to show in my [final plea], by a short presentation of the policies of the Western powers since 1919, the reasons why and how historical necessity produced a Hitler and National Socialism. Although I will have to abstain from reading this portion, because of the shortness of time allotted to my presentation, the very fact that it has been presented to the judges in the full copy of my text means they must take cognizance of it, and I will make specific mention of this in my presentation.

Instead of providing for Neurath's defense in accordance with the rules of the court, Lüdinghausen inserted his own quasi-historical conviction that Hitler and Nazism were the inevitable results of Western mistakes. Understandable as such views might be for a German lawyer in 1946, it was tactless to employ this argument to defend Neurath. To a large extent, Lüdinghausen contributed to Neurath's condemnation by his adamant refusal to adapt to the rules of the court. His overall impression had not been good. As one of the British judges noted in his diary, Neurath's defense lawyer was "tall, aristocratic, aloof, insensible to affront, with an extraordinary droning voice, and bearded like the poet. He loses himself in a maze of events, and produces an effect of complete and utter stupefaction."[57]

On July 26, 1946, the prosecution began its summary. To the dismay of the defendants and their lawyers, and despite months of testimony and witnesses, the prosecution repeated its earlier case, linking all the defendants in responsibility for the horrors of National Socialism and World War II. Not even the most questionable charges had been dropped. All the defendants were in a gigantic conspiracy, planning war and the extermination of the Jews. Neurath was described as "the old-school diplomat who cast the pearls of his experience before Nazis, guided Nazi diplomacy in the early years, soothed the fears of prospective victims, and, as Protector of Bohemia and Moravia, strengthened the German position for the coming attack on Poland." Whatever the justice of the first two statements, the third was not a criminal charge, and the fourth was entirely new, for no evidence or charge had suggested that Neurath was involved in the war against Poland. Obviously, the prosecution needed to link Neurath with at least one war.[58]

Similar exaggerations prevailed throughout the summation. Neurath was called "a foreign minister who knew little of foreign affairs and nothing of foreign policy." Without further documentation, the prosecution related the discredited story of his house being acquired through "seizure," and described his speeches as a "prostitution of . . . great words," his policies as rearmament for war, and his actions as motivated by his desire to wage war. He was accused of not heeding the warnings of his professional staff, of putting his "not yet tarnished" reputation at the service of a chancellor planning aggressive war, of making "no attempt to dissuade Hitler," but serving as a "mainspring of the party and state machine," and thus being "closely connected with . . . the crimes of extermination of which he was fully aware and which he himself decreed." He was charged with knowing, "from the very beginning," about aggressive plans in Austria and of being implicated in the assassination of Chancellor Dollfuss. After resigning as foreign minister, he blatantly reentered Hitler's service, and the prosecution escalated his "grimly cynical" reassurance to the Czechs to a major part of the charge.[59]

Doubting whether "mercy can survive Neurath's record in Czechoslovakia," the prosecution held Neurath guilty of the most odious crimes against the Czechs. With scathing reference to Lüdinghausen's plea for respect for the "holiness of the individual," the prosecution linked Neurath's name with "the most terrible document" put into evidence, namely the plan for the Germanization of the Czechs. This plan, the prosecution insisted, could be summarized in one word: annihilation. Zealously, Neurath's memorandum was rebaptized as a "biological device" for the subordination of Czechoslovakia. The prosecution then linked him with the other defendants in a ghastly recital of exterminations and executions. As one who claimed to profess familial and professional integrity, Neurath was accused of being more guilty than others and deserving of full punishment for the misery he had caused.[60]

Neurath's trial concluded with this final call for condemnation on July 30, 1946. His chances were not considered particularly good. Many defense lawyers believed he would be found guilty and sentenced to death. A poll of American reporters covering the trial also produced a guilty verdict, although only a small minority believed he would receive the death sentence. Lüdinghausen too suggested that in view of his client's sickness and old age, the court might be lenient, but his handling of the case had been so poor that Neurath's wife and daughter believed the death sentence inevitable. They began a writing campaign to prominent officials among the Allies, hoping that this expected punishment could be commuted to life imprisonment.[61]

During August, the court heard evidence and witnesses in the cases of organizations accused of being criminal in nature. On August 31, 1946, the defendants were asked to make their final statements. Neurath, in characteristic fashion, delivered the briefest of the day. Ignoring the charges against him, he asserted his clean conscience in a statement that is redolent of rather absurd gallantry, yet bespeaks the code upon which his life had been based:

> Firm in the conviction that truth and justice will prevail before this High Tribunal over all hatred, slander, and misrepresentation, I believe that I should add only this to the words of my defense counsel: my life was consecrated to truth and honor, to humanity and justice. I stand with a clear conscience not only before myself, but before history, and the German people.
>
> If, in spite of this, the Tribunal should find me guilty, I shall be able to bear even this, and take it upon myself as a last sacrifice on behalf of my people, to serve whom was the substance and purpose of my life.[62]

The court adjourned for September deliberations on verdicts and sentences. During these days of waiting, the rules of the prison were relaxed to permit visitors. Although Neurath at first refused to permit his wife to see him in prison surroundings, he eventually relented and his first reunion with Baroness von Neurath occurred on September 20. His daughter, whose husband had died only a few weeks before in an American prison camp, also visited the defendant. It was a painful experience, for the future looked bleak indeed. As Neurath had clearly implied in his final statement, he no longer believed in the possibility of acquittal.[63]

The Verdict

On September 30, the court reconvened to read the final judgment. It found that the prosecution had proven the charge of conspiracy to plan war and violate treaties. It accepted as demonstrated charges of crimes against peace, and war crimes defined as the murder and ill-treatment of civilians and noncombatants during the prosecution of war. Finally, the court recognized the validity of the charges of "crimes against humanity," including murder, extermination, enslavement, deportations, and inhumane acts against civilians, independent of the war.[64]

Neurath had been indicted on all four counts. While the trial had not strengthened the charges against him, the judges apparently had found it difficult to disentangle his particular situation from the general conspiracy charges. In a draft for the verdict, much was made of the fact that after leaving office he temporarily worked with Hitler again during the *Anschluss* crisis, thus proving his part in the conspiracy to wage aggressive war. Although the forced *Anschluss* was in other instances not considered a war crime (because it had not resulted in war), in Neurath's case, his actions on two days preceding the *Anschluss* became a critical issue in finding him guilty of conspiracy and crimes against peace. In addition, the draft cited the shooting of the nine Czech students as sufficient cause to find Neurath guilty on counts of war crimes and crimes against humanity.[65]

When the judges voted, the Russians, as usual, pronounced him guilty on all four counts, and the British agreed; the Americans and French were unusually hesitant. At the most, they seemed willing to convict him of war crimes, because of the nine murders committed in the Protectorate. Deadlocked on this issue (since it took three votes to convict), the judges also were divided as to a proper punishment. The Soviets, in their normal procedure, voted for death. The British spoke in favor of a life sentence. The American and French judges wavered between a five- and fifteen-year prison sentence. It was obvious that some compromises were necessary. After a "short round of horse trading," the Americans and French agreed to convict on all four counts, if Lord Lawrence would accept a sentence of fifteen years. The British judge agreed. In this irregular way, a majority was reached. Perhaps the countless horrors and the sea of blood which had inundated the courtroom simply stunned the judges, who found it finally appalling that such a man, having once left office, could return in the service of such a regime. Although in the case of Papen, one American judge admitted that it was the "duty of a man to serve" his government, none mentioned this mitigating factor in reaching a verdict on Neurath. Even given the new documents which explain so much else about this complicated trial, Neurath's sentencing remains inexplicable.[66]

Neurath received the court's verdict on October 1. In two brief paragraphs the Tribunal found him guilty of participating in the conspiracy to plan wars, and through his participation in the government after 1938 as president of the secret cabinet council also guilty of waging wars of aggression against Austria and Czechoslovakia.[67] In more lengthy fashion, the court also found him guilty of war crimes and crimes against humanity, because of his "criminal activities in Czechoslovakia." While admitting that perhaps the police and Gestapo might have been controlled by Frank and not Neurath, the court still held him responsible, for he was the "chief German official" and knew that "war crimes and crimes against humanity were being committed under his authority." In mitigation, the court mentioned Neurath's release of the Czech students, attempts to dissuade Hitler from sending Heydrich, and his eventual resignation. But in the opinion of the judges, all these gestures came too late.[68]

Neurath had been found guilty on all four counts; of his fellow defendants, only Göring, Ribbentrop, Keitel, and Rosenberg were declared guilty in every category. Except for Neurath, all were sentenced to die by hanging. Only Schacht, Papen, and Fritzsche were acquitted. The latter, who had come to know Neurath well during the trial, found his verdict the hardest of all:

> Papen and Schacht had been used to move on a plane where failure was forever liable to be mistaken for guilt, but in Neurath's long and placid life, there had been nothing whatsoever to warn him of the fate that was lying in store for him. He was no revolutionary, no soldier, no reformer, but a civil servant who, though he rose high, never crossed the dividing line that separates the maker of history from the mere administrator. He had been renowned as the very personification of honesty; and it was that which led to his downfall; for what Constantin von Neurath was mainly accused of was that he had prostituted his good name and reputation to the benefit of Hitler and the Hitlerite conspiracy.
>
> It was indeed this man's tragedy that Hitler had first used his good name and then sent him packing when he no longer required anything but blind obedience to his orders. And it was his hard fortune that at this trial he was examined by the ablest member of the prosecuting team—a man with whom he was altogether unable to cope.[69]

General reaction to the sentencing was summed up by one newspaper with satisfaction that Neurath had emerged so well since "he was always a decent man." In agreeing, the *Süddeutsche Zeitung,* however, argued that Neurath deserved the verdict for "the greatest political mistake of his life," namely "after he had rejected further responsibility as foreign minister for Hitler's policies aiming at war, and resigned, he allowed himself as Protector to be used in Hitler's criminal power politics." There was no doubt at all that the Protectorate affair had condemned him, and the newspaper added: "A man like Neurath did not need to take that position; he should really have retired completely from the politics of the

Third Reich." Neurath accepted the sentence with an emotion akin to relief. He was resigned to a harsh punishment and shared Lüdinghausen's fear that he would be demanded by the Czechs for a new trial. A few days after the sentencing, there were, in fact, published reports that Prague was unhappy with Neurath's verdict and would request extradition. Only much later did the family learn that the Czechs had not so requested, nor even demanded a particularly harsh sentence for their former Protector.[70]

Lüdinghausen and the family believed that the fifteen-year sentence would be significantly shortened. After all, Neurath was 73, sick with angina pectoris, and suffering from serious eye trouble. Within two or at the most three years, they believed, he would surely be released, in accordance with the procedures of German and European courts in such cases. Frau von Mackensen recalls this hope, which was also shared by various lawyers, as the last one preserved by herself and her mother in facing the years ahead. Neurath was not so optimistic. In April 1947, when his lawyer inquired whether he wanted to send an appeal for pardon, Neurath replied characteristically: "Under the existing circumstances, I believe it would be premature to undertake some action. We must quietly wait for the time being, and see how things work out."[71]

In Prison

In the summer of 1947, the allied military authorities decided to move the prisoners to Berlin's Spandau prison, where they would be under the alternating guard of the Big Four powers. Neurath's wife and daughter were permitted a final visit in Nuremberg. With reserve and dignity, Neurath repeated his conviction that he would certainly be home with them again. No one suspected how many years would pass before that day of reunion arrived. On July 18, 1947, chained like common criminals, Neurath and the six other prisoners were transferred to Berlin. Relieved of all personal possessions, he received a uniform marked with a large "3" and was assigned a solitary cell bearing the same number, which henceforth would become his name. Confined to cells at all times except for work exercises in the yard and eating periods, the prisoners were forbidden to talk to any fellow prisoners or staff or communicate with the outside world. The verdict of the Nuremberg trial had ordered them removed from human memory, and the prison regime aimed at that goal.[72]

Neither court nor prison authorities had reckoned on the persistence of Neurath's daughter, Winifred von Mackensen, wife of the former state secretary and ambassador to Italy. Traveling alone to Berlin in the bleak winter of 1947, she tried in vain to see her father. After four attempts, she succeeded in obtaining permission for a fifteen-minute visit in December. Although she had given various excuses to gain this permission, when asked to enter these in the official guard book, Frau von Mackensen wrote "because he is my father and I want to see him!" Disconcerted, the officials let her in, but subjected the interview to strict controls, with official observers. But Frau von Mackensen had achieved a significant break in the walls of Spandau; thereafter, prisoners were allowed the visit of one adult family member for fifteen minutes every two months![73]

After her second visit, on the occasion of her father's 75th birthday, Frau von Mackensen wrote her impressions of Neurath's prison life. She was already preparing for further campaigns:

> Since my father has been imprisoned in Spandau, I have been permitted to see him on two occasions, each time for a quarter of an hour. The last time was on February 2, 1948, his 75th birthday. In these quarter-hours, every word is written down by four men representing the various powers and two others observe our facial expressions. I am not allowed to bring anything for him to eat, and only a little tobacco or other toilet articles. Since he has been in Spandau, he never gets enough to eat, and is losing weight every week; this has been confirmed by four different doctors (American, Russian, English, and French). His sleep is interrupted every five to ten minutes by the glare of an electric torch. The normal garden work—six to eight hours per day—has at present been replaced with stupid and deadening prison work. The light in his cell is so bad that reading is a difficult strain. They have partially shaved his head, and whenever he is transported and when he was called to testify in Nuremberg, he is put in chains. The whole treatment is that accorded a common criminal and not a political prisoner.
>
> Except for my mother, to whom he may write one page a month (which takes three to four weeks to reach us), he is allowed to write no one else, and may also not receive letters from anyone. He may not write to his children, nor can he receive letters from them. Every two months he may have a quarter-hour visit from one of his immediate family. He is forbidden to talk in the prison, as if it were the strictest solitary confinement.[74]

Largely as a result of information which Frau von Mackensen supplied to the press, many of these conditions were changed in a general reform of the rules in December 1948. The most important improvement was in communication among the prisoners. Henceforth, the men could live a full communal life, separated only at night. Within a short time, Neurath was recognized as the patriarch of the prison; despite the rules, he became known to guards and prisoners alike as "the Baron." With his robust disposition, impressive appearance, and good humor, he became a sort of father confessor to his colleagues. "If we didn't have von Neurath," Speer claimed, "we would all go crazy. He is so practical." The prison chaplain agreed: "Neurath was a person of such urbanity that he always obtained from his fellow-prisoners whatever he wanted," he told one reporter. "He was an authentic gentleman, a perfect embodiment of correctness and good will." Before the year was out, "he had won the esteem of his comrades, the respect of the prison authorities and the sympathy of the guards." Because of his lifelong love for farming, Neurath was particularly pleased at permission to start a prison garden. As the only one who had any knowledge of agriculture, he took the whole task in hand. Soon, he was being jokingly referred to as "Obergartenbaudirektor" or chief director of the garden, by both prisoners and prison authorities.[75]

But despite these amenities, Neurath suffered under the prison restrictions, and was deeply mortified by the stringent regulations. Although he seemed content, his advice to his colleagues ("Think much, but say little. Feel much, but show little.") betrayed his own emotional suffering. His poor health was deteriorating, and he feared more than anything else that he would die without seeing his family and Leinfelderhof again. One of his colleagues, Admiral Raeder, noted the gradual decline: "Although he was in poor health, he never for a moment lost his natural dignity and bearing, and his calm acceptance of his situation was an example to everyone. But it moved me deeply to observe how his years were bearing down more heavily and his strength visibly ebbing."[76]

In the meantime, Neurath's family experienced further difficulties. On October 1, 1948, the "Liberation Ministry" of the new state of Baden-Württemberg opened formal charges against Neurath in a denazification trial. The object was to win condemnation of Neurath as a "major guilty person," thus enabling the state to confiscate his property, estimated by the courts to be in excess of 400,000 Marks. The family retained a Stuttgart lawyer, Dr. Helmuth Fischinger, who persuaded them that a trial would provide a welcome opportunity to reopen Neurath's case. He immediately began compiling affidavits and witnesses. Although the liberation ministry eventually decided to charge Neurath not only with the crimes of which he had been found guilty at Nuremberg, but also political crimes "leading toward the destruction of democracy in Germany," Fischinger believed the trial would force a revision of the Nuremberg verdict.[77]

To ensure fairness, Dr. Fischinger insisted that the court secure Neurath's transfer from Spandau to some local jail. Unless the prisoner were present to defend himself and to provide the defense lawyer with information, he argued, the trial could not take place. He persuaded the court that, unlike the Nuremberg Military Tribunal, it should grant the defendant the right to a full defense. On July 19, 1949, the American advisor to the denazification process informed the ministry that the Soviet Union had refused permission. He suggested that Neurath might give his testimony from Spandau. Unable even to communicate with Neurath, Fischinger rejected indirect testimony and requested a delay which might pressure the allied powers to grant the transfer.[78]

But in February 1950, the public prosecutor of Baden-Württemberg decided, in view of the importance of the case and the dangers inherent in delay (Neurath might die and thus avoid the loss of his property), to make a public accusation. Fischinger's plea against trying a man *in absentia* was overruled on June 20, and on October 4, 1950, the first public hearings in Neurath's new trial began.[79]

In his opening speech, Fischinger outlined the reasons why this trial should be held, claiming that several authorities had independently concluded that an impartial trial would overturn the previous verdict:

> In this Nuremberg trial, Neurath was so reduced by ill health, in the aftermath of an operation, that he was not up to the trial; in addition, his lawyer had done nothing to familiarize him with the British-American legal system. As a result, Neurath was simply bowled over by the prosecutor who was a past-master in the art of cross-examination. Neurath's case represents

a breakdown of the judicial system, and this must give us the incentive to ensure that the full story is properly presented before a German forum.

Since a pre-trial required Neurath's presence, he requested an order that the Spandau prisoner be brought to the Western Zone. The court conceded the point, and postponed the trial until Neurath could appear, but directed the ministry to continue gathering information. When the Allies finally refused to permit Neurath to leave Spandau and blocked Fischinger's access to his client, the Württemberg court decided again to postpone the case.[80]

Meanwhile, Neurath's health had become the subject of grave concern to prison authorities. An American physician, who described Neurath's sunken cheeks, shaking hands, and declining eyesight, told reporters that he could only hope for a quick death for this "wreck of a man," who appeared a "horrifying caricature of despair." In mid-1950, Neurath suffered a series of bad heart attacks, and British officials recommended outside hospitalization; the Russians, however, refused. When his illness grew worse, the authorities summoned Frau von Neurath, who arrived with her daughter. Following delays encountered when two adults tried to enter the prison instead of the permitted one, they found Neurath too exhausted to converse. Only at the end of their fifteen-minute visit did he rouse himself long enough to whisper: "I would like so much to die at home."[81]

To the surprise of his doctors, he recovered, but in 1951 suffered another serious attack. This time, the prison authorities forbade him even to mention his illness in his letters, promising to warn the family in time should there be danger of death! Again he recovered, but in the following years the attacks continued. "I am suffering again from angina pectoris," he wrote his wife in June 1951, "and sometimes the pains are awful. I have a heavy burden to carry under the circumstances, but to complain is not to my liking." In 1954, another series of attacks threatened his life and once more his wife and daughter were summoned. Although Neurath seemed near death, officials refused to permit Baroness von Neurath more than fifteen minutes, and also rejected her request to return on the following day. Each time, out of his determination not to die in prison, Neurath rallied.[82]

Meanwhile, Winifred von Mackensen had mounted an active campaign. In successful legal actions, she saved the hunting lodge in Austria from confiscation, and forced Baden-Württemberg to return Leinfelderhof, which the state had seized in 1946. Her crusade to free her father began with a public declaration she issued to the press, shortly after visiting her sick father in Spandau:

> It would have been better for my father to have been hung at Nuremberg than to live as he does at Spandau. I am his daughter and I love him, but I can say this because I know that is true. I do not seek to defend him; he has committed an error. He has been judged and found guilty, and that matter is no longer open for discussion. But he is so old, so ill, that even if he had once been dangerous he is certainly no longer harmful today. If they only authorize a release from here, they can place him under any type of surveillance they might design. His only desire is to die among his own, to be with his

wife with whom he has shared more than fifty years. My father had never been a member of the Nazi party, and that was officially recognized. He is simply a German.[83]

Tirelessly she wrote to prominent world figures, begging their intercession. Bolstered by sentence revisions for officials found guilty in subsequent trials, she intensified her pleas that the High Commissioners take similar action for her father. The press took up her campaign, using papers smuggled out of Spandau to Frau von Mackensen to attack the medical measures and rigorous punishment accorded to the prisoners there. In January and February 1951 a number of newspapers described the "scandal in Spandau" and printed side by side the prison rules applying to convicted murderers and Constantin Freiherr von Neurath. But her efforts secured no official action. Entering his seventh year in prison, Neurath seemed doomed to serve his full term or certainly to die before winning release. Rumors continued that the Soviet Union blocked all moves to free him, and Western appeals on his behalf to the control commission in Berlin added to the growing list of subjects which the commission could not take up, since it had not met since 1948. Truly, Neurath's fate seemed sealed.[84]

The only immediate result of Frau von Mackensen's campaign was a further easing of prison conditions. In November 1952, visiting rules were extended to one half-hour each month, and greater freedom was granted for written communications between the prisoners and members of their immediate families. Neurath's own correspondence during these years is almost exclusively concerned with his longing for home. On Palm Sunday 1953, eight years to the day he had left Leinfelderhof at the end of the war, he described to his wife his sad memories of that leavetaking:

> Handwritten letters make one feel closer to home than do typed ones. Palm Sunday 1945—I believe it was March 27—when we left to go to the children will always remain in my memory. The farewell to Leinfelderhof, and all the things which I had built and planted there in more than forty years was particularly hard, maybe because of a premonition of a long parting.[85]

His monthly letters inquired about the farm, the pigs and other animals, and gave instructions for improving the estate. In March 1948 he wrote: "The fields beyond the creek must be drained again. I believe you can buy the bricks at the best price in Vaihingen." In September 1949: "If there is sufficient money, it is time to build a new roof for the pigs' stall." His thoughts of the farm were always a mixture of nostalgia and practical advice:

> I am afraid that the three large elms behind the farm manager's house must be felled. They throw too much shade over the herb garden. It is sad to think of it, but it must be done. I remember precisely how my grandfather and I planted them over seventy years ago. The wood can be used in the repair of the roof work.[86]

In almost all of his letters, he returned to the theme of his beloved farm. In June 1951, he wrote: "Today I am thinking of father's death. Were it not for you, I could not but wish that soon I should be with him in our little graveyard at Glattbach. But as it is I am trying hard to hold on." For Christmas 1951, he noted his absence from the usual celebrations at Leinfelderhof:

> This is the seventh occasion on which I am sending you Christmas wishes and New Year greetings in this way. Never in our fifty years of married life were we parted, and even during the First World War, not at Christmas time. My thoughts will be with you and the family even more than ever. We are not allowed to have a Christmas tree here.... The holidays are not easy to bear, in spite of my philosophy.

And his birthday letter of March 1952 continues the same theme:

> I thought of you all on February 2nd. How often we celebrated this day. I wonder whether I shall ever see Leinfelderhof again? I remember our departure from there on Palm Sunday seven years ago. How right I was to feel heavy and depressed when we left.
>
> It is now just twenty years ago since Hindenburg demanded that I take over the Berlin post [as foreign minister] and we said goodbye to London. Remembering all our years together, I realize what they meant to us and, too, what you meant to me. My only regret is that after everything we shared together I now have to bring you sorrow. But I could neither foresee nor prevent it.
>
> It seems an eternity since you were here. Time flies and yet crawls here. Unfortunately my eyes are growing weak, as you can see from my writing....
>
> My trouble can't be overcome, after all my days are numbered and I can't be sorry about it in my present situation, though I would have loved to have come home just once more. I suffer great annoyance and worry and it is difficult to carry on, but carry on I must.

As the years went by, his letters reflected growing despair. For Christmas 1952, he wrote only a brief note:

> We are entering 1953 and with it my eightieth year of life, and though I have really lived long enough, I want to die at home and not in prison.
>
> For the New Year, I am sending you and Wini all the best wishes, above all that your health may remain good. I, on my part, will try my utmost to remain well and hold on, difficult though it is.
>
> The Christmas days, always so hard for the soul to bear, are over. How difficult they must have been for you, I know also. I have been thinking of the Christmases that we had with our parents. Those days are gone, but I must be grateful for them.[87]

Throughout the letters there runs also his sorrow over his separation from his wife. Such feeling intensified as their fiftieth wedding anniversary approached. His letter for that occasion is characteristic:

> Dearest Manny:
> I don't need to tell you how your visit here, though short, has made me happy and refreshed me. The winter was bad and I did not think I would live through it.

> It is splendid that some friends are visiting you on our wedding anniversary. That I can't be with you is particularly painful, but circumstances forbid me to tell you of my feelings. I can only thank you for all the love which you have given me in good and bad times during the fifty years.
>
> On the 30th, my thoughts will be with you more than ever. That you know. I wonder whether it will be as hot on that day as it was fifty years ago.[88]

Only once, and in a brief way, did he refer to the events which had brought him to Spandau. In a letter of March 1953, he wrote of his feelings shortly before being arrested in 1945:

> But I had a clean conscience and never thought that I would be held responsible for the deeds of others—deeds of which I knew nothing and which I would never have approved.
>
> The truth about this, though too late, will yet have its day. Anyhow, I would not act differently today if faced with the same situation.

But the years were beginning to tell, and in a letter of early 1954 he admitted: "I don't think I can stand it much longer."[89]

Early in 1953, a new press campaign began, which demanded on both legal and humane grounds that Neurath be freed. Dr. Fischinger persuaded Chancellor Adenauer to guarantee Western approval should the Russians ever change their objections to releasing Neurath. At Adenauer's suggestion, the family tried to approach Molotov directly. In January 1954, Neurath's case was officially brought before the Berlin Conference, but no agreement was reached. A few months later, Frau von Mackensen, through the aid of Pope Pius XII, found an intermediary willing to carry a personal message to Molotov, and in October she dispatched a lengthy appeal. Meanwhile, in September, Neurath suffered still another serious heart attack. His eyesight was deteriorating rapidly, and his speech was slurred and broken. Early in the year, the British dentist, "in order to simplify things," had extracted all his upper teeth and replaced them with a plate which fit so poorly as to make speech nearly impossible.[90]

In November 1954, Baroness von Neurath and her daughter had just returned from their bimonthly trip to Spandau, unaware that on November 2, for reasons not yet fully clear, the Russian representative to the control commission had suddenly proposed the immediate liberation of Neurath, "in view of his age and his state of health, and with the full agreement of Czechoslovakia." François-Poncet, the French representative, promised the full support and prompt response of the Western powers. On November 5, Frau von Mackensen received a telegram to report to Spandau the next morning at 11:00 A.M. Dr. Fischinger too had heard rumors that the Russians were prepared to discuss releasing Neurath, and he telephoned Chancellor Adenauer, reminding him of his promise. Within hours, full agreement was reached. Without preparation, Neurath was called for his weekend bath and, instead of normal prison garb, was handed an old suit. A few minutes later, he received his gold watch, the only personal possession he had carried into Spandau in 1947. Still, he did not realize what was happening, and later lamented that he had had no time to say goodbye to his fellow prisoners.[91]

As Frau von Mackensen waited in the prison hall, unsure whether the rumors would prove true, she received the first real confirmation, when she overheard the German servants complaining that the number "3" would not come off the overcoat. She had hardly time to digest this fact, when her father was escorted into the room. No one said a word, and impulsively Frau von Mackensen initiated the exchange: "May I take my father with me now?" she inquired. When no one said anything, the two simply walked out of the building arm in arm. After nine years and six months in prison, Constantin Freiherr von Neurath was once again a free man.[92]

Home

Without any identification papers, the 81-year-old man spent his first night of freedom in a Berlin hotel, while his daughter arranged for air transportation to Frankfurt. Although the press wanted interviews, Neurath could not control his emotions, and his daughter briefly described the recent events. When asked for his future plans, Frau von Mackensen replied that he wanted to go home as quickly as possible, "and walk through his fields once more." On November 7, an airplane bore Neurath to Frankfurt and from there a rented car brought him to Leinfelderhof, where he was greeted by a bedecked village and ringing churchbells. Deeply moved, Neurath tearfully greeted his 79-year-old wife. The German press had divided reactions, but Chancellor Adenauer and Bundespräsident Heuss sent congratulatory telegrams.[93]

Thereafter, never in good health, Neurath remained quietly on his estate making only an occasional trip such as to a reunion of fellow hunters in nearby Ludwigsburg. He received a few visitors, but their conversations were about friends and contemporary events. A local newspaper described his retiring life: "Mostly he preferred walking on the lawns and strolling slowly over the fields, breathing the healthy air of his *Heimat*. It was as if contact with his own soil gave him renewed strength." He never talked about the past, and rejected Dr. Fischinger's suggestions that his denazification case be reopened to set straight the verdict of Nuremberg. Sometime in 1955, when Neurath's life settled into this peaceful routine, his daughter thought he might want to dictate to her some sketches from his life. After reflection, the old man replied: "No, for I am afraid that they would not be too helpful. All I could say was how sad it was that I fell for all of Hitler's lies."[94]

After much physical suffering Neurath died peacefully on August 14, 1956 at the age of 83, nearly sixteen months after being released from Spandau. The prison chaplain commented that during the long years in Spandau, Neurath had lived only in order to die at home. Once released, his reason for holding on disappeared. "If he were still in prison," Pastor Schantz told a reporter, "Neurath would have lived for many more years." Neurath was content that his end should come in the midst of his family. He was buried at his request in the family plot at Klein Glattbach.[95]

His life had been an extraordinarily full and varied one, with shares both of triumph and of tragedy. This study has tried to place his experiences and actions in their historical framework, while not overlooking the human dimensions. Although there is nothing in his long career to impugn his absolute sincerity and steadfast honesty, history's final judgment on the man will probably not differ greatly from that expressed in the perceptive obituary of the *Deutsche Zeitung:*

> There is no reason to doubt Neurath's human virtues and his personal abhorrence of Hitler's criminal policies. But this statesman's shield can never be washed entirely clean. In the Nuremberg Trial and during his years up to 1954 in Spandau, Neurath had paid for his actions and his omissions. The reserve he maintained after his release (to which the Czechs too had agreed), speaks well for him. But his career is a perfect example that in political life, good intentions, vague conceptions, and a willingness to compromise differences, sometimes do not suffice; in fact, they may be fatal.
>
> Sharper understanding and decisive action following such decisions are more important, and only within this context can the other imponderables and diplomatic intuition take their place. Even personal "decency" and a refusal to involve oneself in intrigues—the one weapon which was still available to the diplomats of the old Wilhelmstrasse—are not always virtues.[96]

Neurath, a virtuous and decent gentleman, had allowed his talents and capabilities to serve forces which he only imperfectly understood and frequently rejected personally. Perhaps in another time, good intentions and private virtues would have sufficed. In Hitler's Germany they proved disastrous to a Baron born for another century.

Notes

CHAPTER I. *Introduction*

1. For Hindenburg's attitude, see Hindenburg to Berg, February 25, 1932, in Herbert Michaelis, Ernst Schraepler and Günter Scheel (eds.), *Ursachen und Folgen: vom deutschen Zusammenbruch 1918 und 1945 bis zur staatlichen Neuordnung Deutschlands in der Gegenwart,* VIII, 401–402. For the conservative ideology, see Hans-Joachim von Merkatz, *Die konservative Funktion, ein Beitrag zur Geschichte des politischen Denkens,* 12ff.; and Walter Bussmann, "Politische Ideologien zwischen Monarchie und Weimarer Republik: ein Beitrag zur Ideengeschichte der Weimarer Republik," *Historisches Zeitschrift,* 190 (1960), 57ff.

2. For the civil service attitude, see Herbert von Borch, *Obrigkeit und Widerstand: zur politischen Soziologie des Beamtentums;* and Arnold Köttgen, *Das deutsche Berufsbeamtentum und die parlamentarische Demokratie.* The attitude of the three groups was succinctly expressed in Major General Helmut Stieff's letter of August 21, 1931, in which he predicted that a presidential cabinet would free the government "from the chains of parliamentarianism, so that it could work independently." See Hans Rothfels, "Ausgewählte Briefe von Generalmajor Helmut Stieff," *Vierteljahrshefte für Zeitgeschichte* (hereafter cited as VJHZG), II (1954), 297.

3. In the preparation of this study, the author has attempted to complement the major books in this field, in particular Gerald L. Weinberg, *The Foreign Policy of Hitler's Germany: Diplomatic Revolution in Europe, 1933–1936;* the analysis of the foreign office in Hans-Adolf Jacobsen, *Nationalsozialistische Aussenpolitik, 1933–1938;* and the studies of the domestic origins of Hitler's dictatorship in Karl Dietrich Bracher, *Deutschland zwischen Demokratie und Diktatur;* Karl Dietrich Bracher, *Die Auflösung der Weimarer Republik;* Karl Dietrich Bracher, Wolfgang Sauer, and Gerhard Schulz, *Die nationalsozialistische Machtergreifung;* and Karl Dietrich Bracher, *The German Dictatorship.*

4. Recently, there has appeared a psychological analysis of Neurath's character (Florence R. Miale and Michael Selzer, *The Nuremberg Mind: The Psychology of the Nazi Leaders*). Apparently based upon a questionable understanding of history and frequent misinformation about Neurath (e.g., that he was a Prussian aristocrat), this scurrilous account contributes no new information about Neurath, but succeeds only in raising serious questions about the methods employed by the practitioners of such psychohistory.

5. In prison awaiting trial, in 1945, Neurath wrote two brief autobiographical sketches. One is an overview of his diplomatic life. The other, from which the above information is taken, concerns his life as a hunter and is entitled "Gebirgsjaeger." It is currently in the possession of Baroness Theda von Ritter, whose daughter served as the

secretary to Neurath's defense lawyer and who typed these sketches from Neurath's handwritten notes. Ritter Papers.

6. For this distinction between private and public virtues, see discussion in Ralf Dahrendorf, *Society and Democracy in Germany*, 285-96. Information also from author's interview with Frau von Mackensen, May 2, 1968.

7. This poem was given to the author by Frau von Mackensen, May 3, 1968. It is printed in the local newspaper's description of Neurath's funeral; see *Enz-Bote*, August 18, 1956.

8. Neurath, "Gebirgsjaeger," Ritter Papers.

9. Quotations from Albert Speer, *Inside the Third Reich: Memoirs*, 120 and 176. Information also from author's interviews with Hasso von Etzdorf and Albrecht von Kessel, July 3 and 30, 1968.

10. Neurath to Baroness von Ritter, March 2, 1946, Ritter Papers.

CHAPTER II. *Early Life: 1873-1919*

1. Information from *Gotharisches Genealogisches Taschenbuch der Freiherrlichen Häuser*, Teil B, 83 Jhg. (1933), 382; and "Die Familie des Freiherrn von Neurath," *Der Oberhesse*, March 5, 1938. For Constantin Franz's activities in Württemberg, see Julie Rath, *Württemberg und die Schleswig-Holsteinische Frage in den Jahren 1863-1865*, 57ff.; and Walter Schübelin, *Das Zollparlament und die Politik von Baden, Bayern und Württemberg, 1866-1870*, 33ff., 114ff., and 121.

2. Information from author's interviews with Frau von Mackensen, March 13 and May 2, 1968. In 1875, Neurath was appointed *Kammerherr*, a nobleman attached to the court, and subsequently became *Oberkammerherr* and head of the *Kammerherr* staff. He served as the chief courtier at all public ceremonies and as principal advisor on matters of titles, prerogatives, and the aristocracy. He was also a member of the court council and served for several years as one of Württemberg's representatives to the *Bundesrat* in Berlin. Information from Hauptstaatsarchiv Stuttgart (hereafter HSAS), E 14, Kabinettsakten IV, Bü. 470 and Bü. 229.

3. Information from author's interview with Theda Freifrau von Ritter, July 16, 1968. Baron von Ritter, the Bavarian representative at the Holy See, and his wife were very close to Neurath, and the Baroness graciously provided the author with Neurath's autobiographical "Skizze," written in prison in 1945. Neurath's two brothers, Wilhelm Heinrich Julius (born 1874) and Ernst Josef Baptist (born 1877), became army officers.

4. Information on Neurath's court titles is from HSAS, E 14, Kabinettsakten IV, Bü. 229. The incident concerning Queen Mary is discussed in Una Pope-Hennessy, *Queen Mary*, 239-40; and Jack Fishman, *Seven Men of Spandau*, 146ff. Information about his early life comes principally from an unpublished manuscript, "Lebenslauf Reichsminister Freiherr von Neurath," composed about 1940 in Prague by his wife. An invaluable guide, this 70-page typewritten draft, containing corrections in Neurath's own hand, drew heavily from Baroness von Neurath's diaries and letters which were destroyed at the end of the war. Intended as an outline for a future biography, the manuscript is in the possession of Frau von Mackensen, who kindly permitted the author to use it. Cited hereafter as Neurath, "Lebenslauf."

5. Information from author's interview with Frau von Mackensen, May 2, 1968.

6. Neurath, "Lebenslauf," and interview with Frau von Mackensen, May 2, 1968.

7. *Dienstzeugnisse* by Major von Donop, July 20, 1898; and Major Glansbetter, May 14, 1901; and Major von Rom, May 10, 1906; in HSAS, Heeresarchiv, Personalakten Reserveoffizier, N 4/6. Neurath served from April 1893 to April 1894, and participated in summer maneuvers in 1895, 1896, 1898, 1899, 1901, 1902, 1906, 1910, and 1914. His active service was reckoned at two years, two months and fourteen days. On March 30, 1909, Neurath wrote to his friend Gerhard Köpke: "Any considerations of proposals for peace and disarmament are suicidal." Unfortunately Minister-Director

Köpke burnt a large part of his letters shortly after the war. The present collection, which I have used with the gracious permission of Frau Gerda Klee, represents only a small portion of the original. It is cited hereafter as Köpke Nachlass.

8. Author's interview with Frau von Mackensen, May 3, 1968. See below, page 80, for a full discussion of Neurath's attitudes toward resigning.

9. Information from Neurath, "Skizze"; Neurath, "Lebenslauf"; and author's interviews with Frau von Mackensen and Dr. Ernst Woermann, May 2 and April 30, 1968.

10. Neurath was troubled all his life by illness and always insisted on a German doctor. Frequently, he returned to Germany for treatment and diagnosis. He told friends that he would never become too attached to any foreign post. He was too German! Information from author's interview with Baroness von Ritter, July 16, 1968.

11. Neurath to Köpke, June 24, 1907, Köpke Nachlass. Information also from Neurath, "Lebenslauf," and author's interview with Frau von Mackensen, May 2, 1968.

12. Information from author's interviews with Frau von Mackensen, March 13 and May 2, 1968. Documentary confirmation is impossible because a policy decision in Bonn inexplicably closed all personnel files of the Political Archives of the Foreign Office to scholarly investigation. For the new foreign secretary, see Ernst Jäckh, *Kiderlen-Wächter, der Staatsmann und Mensch: Briefwechsel und Nachlass,* I, 6, 17, and 80ff. Even while in London, Neurath had written of his distaste for the social life: "At least I am no longer troubled by any sort of homesickness for Berlin. I shit on society." Neurath to Köpke, July 8, 1907, Köpke Nachlass.

13. Information from Neurath, "Lebenslauf," and author's interview with Frau von Mackensen, July 8, 1968. The estate remained divided. Leinfelderhof remains in the possession of his daughter, Winifred, the widow of Hans-Georg von Mackensen. Klein Glattbach was sold by Ernst Josef's widow after the Second World War.

14. HSAS, Heeresarchiv, Personalakten Reserveoffizier, N 4/6; and author's interview with Frau von Mackensen, May 2, 1968.

15. Interview with Frau von Mackensen, March 13, 1968; the earlier story of Neurath's suspicions is based on information from Andreas Busse, kindly provided to the author by Professor Donald Rohr of Brown University.

16. Information on Neurath's war experiences are from Neurath, "Skizze," and HSAS, Heeresarchiv, Personalakten Reserveoffizier, N 4/6. He was the first officer of his regiment to win the Iron Cross first class.

17. Information from Neurath, "Skizze," and author's interview with Frau von Mackensen, May 2, 1968.

18. For a description of the state of affairs in Constantinople, see Richard von Kühlmann, *Erinnerungen,* 464ff.; and Wangenheim to Foreign Office, May 12, 1914, Politische Archiv des Auswärtigen Amts (hereafter cited as AA), Turkei 139, Bd. 32.

19. See Neurath to Bethmann-Hollweg, November 3, 1915, AA, Turkei 134, Bd. 34. His opponents reluctantly admitted Neurath's efficiency, "for he cloaked himself with professional arguments which were unanswerable." Captain Humann to Jäckh, August 1915, AA, Deutschland 135, Nü. 1, Bd. 5. For Professor Jäckh's role, see discussion in Fritz Fischer, *Griff nach der Weltmacht,* 124ff.

20. Information from Neurath, "Lebenslauf," and author's interview with Frau von Mackensen, May 2, 1968. For the initial harmony, see Metternich's dispatches to Bethmann-Hollweg, December 4, 1915 and following, AA, Turkei 139, Bd. 38; and AA, Deutschland 135, Nü. 1, Bd. 8. Concerning the quarrel with Metternich, I have been unable to locate Neurath's original report of January or February 1916; it may be located in the personnel records which are closed to scholars. See Neurath to AA, January 26; Neurath to Bethmann-Hollweg, April 28; and Kühlmann to Paul Weitz, September 14, 1916; in AA, Turkei 134, Bd. 35; and AA, Weitz Nachlass, Bd. 6. See also Erzberger's report of his trip, February 25, 1916, AA, Turkei 134, Bd. 35. For the controversy itself, Solf to Jagow, February 22; Treutler to AA, March 15; and Metternich to AA, with

marginal comments by Jagow, February 24, 1916; in AA, Geheim, Deutschland 135, Nü. 1, Bd. 1. I have found no evidence to substantiate the rumor reported in Miale and Selzer (*Nuremberg Mind*, 141) that Neurath was "dismissed by the German Foreign Office for disloyally reporting his ambassador's love affairs to Berlin." Typically, the authors make this unsubstantiated account the basis for their "Rorschach" analysis of Neurath. See ibid., 152.

21. Neurath to Rosenberg, August 4, 1916, AA, Geheim, Deutschland 135, Nü. 1, Bd. 1. Neurath mentions that Rosenberg's recent letter contained "more or less clear accusations concerning my conduct during this matter." I have been unable to locate this letter. Within the foreign service, Metternich was not much admired. Ow-Wachendorf (Bucharest) wired to the foreign office on September 9, 1916: "In spite of all his brilliant qualities, he does not fit at Constantinople." AA, Geheim, Deutschland 135, Nü. 1, Bd. 1. For Neurath's success in the city, including the story of how he taught the Sultan to eat asparagus with his fingers, author's interview with Frau von Mackensen, May 2, 1968.

22. Stumm to Zimmermann, n.d., written on the margin of Neurath to Stumm, August 4, 1916, AA, Geheim, Deutschland 135, Nü. 1, Bd. 1.

23. Neurath later insisted that he feared the Turks might well have joined Germany's enemies, "thereby permitting them access to Russia through the Dardanelles." Neurath, "Skizze." See also Metternich to Jagow, August 22, 1916, AA, Deutschland 135, Nü. 1, Bd. 1.

24. Neurath's condemnation of the squabbles are found in Neurath to Köpke, June 19, 1918, Köpke Nachlass. Magnus Freiherr von Braun, who occupied a similar position in the ministry of the interior, told the author on July 16, 1968 that Neurath chafed at the inactivity and lack of responsibility in this new job. See also Neurath, "Lebenslauf."

25. The Köpke Nachlass contain a series of reports from the "Kriegsziel Referat." In his official capacity, Neurath was closely related to this bureau. Writing in 1945, he claimed that the main reason he resigned was the "unhealthy policy toward Poland pursued by Reichs Chancellor von Bethmann and some generals." Neurath, "Skizze." The quotation about the differences of opinion is contained in Neurath's discussion with the prison psychiatrist as to why he resigned. Original manuscript of Dr. Gustave M. Gilbert's diary entry for February 2, 1946. The published selections (*Nuremberg Diary*) omit this incident. The author is grateful to Dr. Gilbert for permission to use the original manuscript for this study. In addition, Neurath told relatives that he despaired of future reform in the foreign office, and without reform no improvement in foreign policy was possible. See Strantz to Neurath, May 7, 1917, HSAS, E 14/16, Bü. 2078. Although Neurath subsequently recalled that he had resigned in December, the Stuttgart papers announced his appointment as *Kabinettschef* on November 23, 1916.

26. Neurath to Köpke, April 30, 1917. On November 27, 1917, Neurath wrote Köpke that his "royal corps-brother" had shown great understanding and provided him with an excellent stock of wine. Köpke Nachlass. Information also from HSAS, E 46/48, Bü. 598; and *Stuttgarter Neues Tageblatt*, January 12, 1917.

27. Author's interview with Baroness von Ritter, July 16, 1968. From Neurath's briefings, the king was well informed on all important points. See Theodor von Pistorius, *Die letzten Tage des Königreichs Württemberg*, 171–72.

28. Neurath to Köpke, April 30, November 27, 1917, and June 19, 1918, Köpke Nachlass. Baroness von Neurath later described these months in a similar tone: "Getting accustomed to the narrower sphere of the new position was hard for Neurath, in spite of his great veneration for his king." "Lebenslauf."

29. Neurath to Köpke, July 30, 1918, Köpke Nachlass.

30. Neurath to Köpke, July 30, 1918, Köpke Nachlass.

31. According to his daughter, Neurath frequently remarked that Germans prefer to be ordered. Author's interview with Frau von Mackensen, May 2, 1968. In 1938, Neurath told Polish Foreign Minister Beck that "in the forum of a parliament, when deputies

addressed the electorate, demagogy flared up." Jósef Lipski, *Papers and Memoirs of Jósef Lipski, Ambassador of Poland: Diplomat in Berlin, 1933–1939* (ed. Waclaw Jedrzejewicz), hereafter cited as Lipski, *Papers,* 324.

32. For unknown reasons, the entire documentary evidence concerning the revolution in Stuttgart, compiled by various government agencies, including a lengthy account written by Neurath, which were deposited in the Staatsarchiv, have been "misplaced," and apparently destroyed. The best description of background and events seems to be in Eric Koehler, *Zur Geschichte der Revolution in Württemberg,* 138ff. See also Karl Weller, *Die Staatsumwälzung in Württemberg, 1918–1920,* 95ff. Subsequently, many Swabians blamed the revolution on "foreigners," that is, Germans not from Württemberg. See Pistorius, *Letzten Tage,* 175. For best accounts of the occupation of the palace, see Pistorius, *Letzten Tage,* 27ff.; and General Christof von Ebbinghaus, *Die Memoiren,* 74ff. The only "victim" of the revolution was the leader of the palace watch who was slightly manhandled when he drew his saber to block the crowd's entrance. See Weller, *Staatsumwälzung,* 108.

33. See Koehler, *Zur Geschichte der Revolution,* 152–55. Subsequently, the king frequently charged that the people (not his officials) had betrayed him. In his funeral instructions, he forbade the cortege to pass through Stuttgart. Pistorius, *Letzten Tage,* 139, and author's interview with Frau von Mackensen, May 2, 1968.

34. This decision eventually caused Neurath's rupture with the royal family. After 1929, the pretender, Prince Philip (from a younger, Catholic line), claimed that the family's money had been severely depleted because the able Neurath had refused to continue in office. Author's interview with Frau von Mackensen, May 2, 1968.

35. For Neurath's specific request that officials continue to serve the republic, see Koehler, *Zur Geschichte der Revolution,* 160.

CHAPTER III. *Neurath as Ambassador: 1919–1932*

1. Neurath to Köpke, June 19 and 30, 1918, Köpke Nachlass.

2. Neurath to Ulrich Count von Brockdorff-Rantzau, January 1, 1919, AA, Deutschland 122, Nü. 2. "You can kiss my ass" was a common gross expression from Goethe's play. Information also from author's interview with Frau von Mackensen, May 2, 1968.

3. On the foreign office, see Ludwig Zimmermann, *Deutsche Aussenpolitik in der Ära der Weimarer Republik,* 36 fn. 3. Other information from author's interview with Frau von Mackensen, May 2, 1968.

4. *Geheimrat*—privy counselor—was a title usually granted to a senior advisor. Neurath to Brockdorff-Rantzau, January 1, 1919, AA, Deutschland 122, Nü. 2. Moritz Bonn, a professor of economics, claims he was offered the Copenhagen position "in late November 1918," but I have been unable to verify this. See Moritz J. Bonn, *Wandering Scholar,* 208ff. In his postwar "Skizze," Neurath wrote that he received the telegram from Brockdorff-Rantzau "shortly after Christmas." I have been unable to find the correspondence, which is probably located in Neurath's personnel file, closed to scholars.

5. I have been unable to verify reports that President Ebert took a direct interest in asking Neurath to reenter the service, but see Heinz-Günther Sasse, *100 Jahre Botschaft in London: aus der Geschichte einer deutschen Botschaft,* 56ff. Dr. Sasse was director of the archives in Bonn and had access to the personnel files, although he cites no sources. According to Neurath's "Skizze," he talked with Ebert, Philip Scheidemann, and Brockdorff-Rantzau before giving his agreement. See Brockdorff-Rantzau to Seckendorff, January 9 and 20, 1919, AA, Deutschland 122, Nü. 2.

6. Information from author's interviews with Baroness von Ritter and Frau von Mackensen, August 20 and July 8, 1968. In an interview with the author on April 3, 1968, Günther Altenburg recalled that Neurath told him in the early 1920s that the individual monarchies and duchies had outlived their histories, but as late as February 1933, Neu-

rath believed that the national monarchy might still be restored. See Karl Schwend, *Bayern zwischen Monarchie und Diktatur,* 524. Although none of Neurath's letters which survive from this period contains specific remarks on parliamentary governments, his opinions paralleled those of Köpke, who wrote him on January 16, 1925, and June 1, 1929 in the tone discussed in the text. Köpke Nachlass. But dislike for parliaments is not the "displeasure with the republic," of which Hajo Holborn accuses Neurath, nor does he document his claim that Neurath "radiated considerable ill-will toward a republican foreign policy." See "Diplomats and Diplomacy in the Early Weimar Republic," in Gordon A. Craig and Felix Gilbert, (eds.), *The Diplomats, 1919–1939,* 151. Neurath was against the parliament because he believed that professional civil servants—loyal, honest, and selfless—were more capable of carrying out a suitable foreign policy than politicians. Author's interview with Frau von Mackensen, May 2, 1968.

7. Neurath to AA, October 21, 1919, Microfilm of the German Foreign Ministry Archives (available from the United States National Archives), Serial 3384, Frame E011890 (hereafter cited as AA and serial/frame). Information also from Neurath, "Lebenslauf."

8. Information and quotation from Neurath, "Lebenslauf," and author's interview with Frau von Mackensen, May 2 and 3, 1968.

9. See Neurath to AA, October 19, 1920, AA 4867/E283009–011.

10. Neurath to AA, n.d.; and Neurath to AA, October 14, 1930; in AA 4792/E235928–29 and 3124/D647344. Author's interview with Frau von Mackensen, May 2, 1968. Earlier quotation is Neurath to AA, June 19, 1919, AA 4999/E250534–35.

11. Neurath to AA, June 14, October 14, and December 1, 1920, AA 4792/E235880–81, 4792/E235999–6000, 3124/D647345, and 3124/D647401–02. Also see Neurath's draft for instructions, November 23; and protocol of a meeting in the foreign office, December 18, 1920; and Neurath to AA, December 23, 1920 and April 1, 1921; in AA, 4792/E235980, 4867/E250031–32, 4867/E249952–53, and 4715/E228058–60.

12. Neurath to AA, May 23, June 20, and November 22, 1921, in AA 4792/E236124–25, 4792/E236129, and 4715/E228278. Neurath signed the draft treaty, which was finally approved in July 1922, after he had left Copenhagen for Rome.

13. Baroness von Neurath summarized Neurath's accomplishments in Copenhagen with some editorial comment: "Neurath's calm and firm personality had thus achieved Germany's first social triumph. Unfortunately, in front of the consulate waved the black/red/gold flag [of the Republic]," Neurath, "Lebenslauf." His own feelings are contained in Neurath to AA, November 3, 1921, AA 4867/E250553–55. Fearing that the head of the delegation would be offended if he followed the Danish request that he alone sign the agreement, Neurath suggested two signatures. See Neurath to Graf Wedel, June 4, 1921, AA 4715/E228215–16.

14. See unsigned note, September 15, 1920, AA K652/K170407. "The complaint against Schüler is in part that he hauled every possible worn-out horse out of the consular stable and sent them into the diplomatic racetrack. On the other hand, many hold him responsible for the appointment of outsiders, especially those who have been forced on the office by parliamentary supporters, for example Landsberg, Müller, and above all Samuel Saenger in Prague." For typical comments on the outsiders, see Hans E. Riesser, *Von Versailles zur UNO; aus den Erinnerungen eines Diplomaten,* 73; and Walter Zechlin, *Pressechef bei Ebert, Hindenburg und Kopf: Erlebnisse eines Pressechefs und Diplomaten,* 27. Information on Neurath's views was obtained in interviews with Dr. Walter Poensgen, Vico von Bülow-Schwante, and Dr. Wolfgang Sasse, July 4, May 24, and August 3, 1968. In *100 Jahre Botschaft in London,* 56, Sasse mentions, without documentation, that Neurath spent two extended periods in Berlin—a month in 1920 and five months in 1921. Claiming that the political archives was planning a study of the reform of the foreign service, Dr. Sasse refused to allow the author to see any of the numerous

memoranda which Neurath submitted on the reform question, with the exception of the one cited in note 16 below.

15. See Dr. Simons to Chancellor, December 20; Simons to Haniel, December 30, 1920; and Simons to Gneist, January 1, 1921; in AA K652/K170449, /K170446-48, and /K170516-17. The job description is from Sasse, *100 Jahre Botschaft in London,* 56. Final statement is from Neurath, "Lebenslauf."

16. Material from Neurath's "Memorandum Concerning the Education and Examination of Candidates for the Foreign Service," February 12, 1921, AA, Rep. IV, Personalia Generalia, Nü. 4, Allgm., Bd. 7. Additional information from author's interview with Frau von Mackensen, May 2, 1968.

17. See Neurath's memorandum, March 16; and Neurath to Simons, March 17, 1921; in AA K652/K170574-79 and /K170541-42. For rumors, see Gneist to Simons, AA K652/K170452-67.

18. The former embassy had been confiscated in 1916; after resumption of diplomatic relations in 1918, the German staff was housed in a Lutheran church and the ambassador and family had to live in a hotel. Neurath, "Lebenslauf." The quotation is from Neurath to Mutius, December 21, 1921, AA L219/L066927. For the messy situation involving Ambassador Berenberg-Gossler's agents and unprofessional agreements, see documents filmed as AA K19, and especially K524/K150254ff., and 2784H/D537336-57.

19. Information from author's interviews with Dr. Werner von Schmieden and Frau von Mackensen (who in the absence of her mother performed the duties of hostess for the delegation), May 1 and 2, 1968. For the conference, see Max von Stockhausen, *Sechs Jahre Reichskanzlei, von Rapallo bis Locarno: Erinnerungen und Tagebuchnotizen, 1922-1927,* 34ff.; and Harry Graf Kessler, *Tagebücher, 1918-1937,* 287-97. In his postwar "Skizze," Neurath recalled that at the last moment, Rathenau "got cold feet just as he and I were traveling to sign the agreement," and it took Neurath nearly two hours to restore the foreign minister's confidence.

20. Story comes from author's interviews with Frau von Mackensen and Baroness von Ritter, May 2 and July 16, 1968. See also Neurath to AA, December 16, 1923, AA 2784H/D537559.

21. See Neurath to AA, August 21, November 3, December 27, 1922, and December 19, 1925, in AA, K528/K151544-46, K428/K123487-88, K529/K151938, and K31/K003413-18.

22. His strongest condemnation of terror is in a report entitled "Mussolini and His Policies," December 2, 1924, AA 2784/D537797, but this theme is found in most of his reports on the subject of domestic politics within Italy. See Neurath to AA, December 27, 1922, March 13, April 11, and May 28, 1923, June 17, 1924, and January 8, February 16, October 17, and November 1, 1925, in AA K529/K151938, K520/K151950, K529/K151959, K529/K151969-70, K528/K151654-55, K528/K151705; AA Abtl. II, Italien, PO 29, Bd. 2; AA K529/K152087-90, and K528/K151716-17.

23. Neurath to AA, December 30, 1926, AA K528/K151757. The second quotation is Neurath to AA, October 18, 1926, AA K529/K152131-35. For his perceptive analysis of the various movements within the fascist party, see reports of December 19, 1925 and April 6, 1926, AA K42/K003413-18 and K529/K152114-15. See also Neurath to Köpke, May 7, 1923 and May 18, 1927, Köpke Nachlass. For the earlier criticism, see Neurath to AA, December 2, 1922, AA K428/K123497.

24. See Neurath to AA, November 24, 1924 and March 28, 1929, AA K428/K123560 and K528/K151808-13. He had long feared lest the party gain influence over foreign policy. See Neurath to AA, December 16, 1925 and December 24, 1927, AA K525/K150490-92, and K528/K151773-80.

25. From a report entitled "Evolution of Fascism," Neurath to AA, November 12, 1929, AA K529/K152516. For earlier quotations, see Neurath to AA, November 7,

1929, May 19, 1928, and January 17, 1929, AA K529/K152510, K529/K152199-212, and 2784H/D539056-72.

26. Neurath's testimony before the International Military Tribunal, *Trial of the Major War Criminals before the International Military Tribunal: Nuremburg, 14 November 1945–1 October 1946* (hereafter cited as IMT), XVI, 601. The second quotation is from Hans Dieckhoff's testimony, IMT, XVII, 123.

27. Neurath to AA, July 30, 1925, AA K525/K150487.

28. Neurath to AA, June 7, 1928, AA K525/K150569. See also his reports of January 17, 1929, May 19, 1930, and a secret report on Italy's war potential, ca. April 1930, in AA 2784H/D539056-72; AA Abtl. II, Italien, PO 1, Bd. 3.; and AA K27/K003312-14.

29. Information from author's interview with Constantin Freiherr von Neurath (Neurath's only son), and Baroness von Ritter (who as wife of the Bavarian representative to the Holy See, was very close to Neurath during these years), July 3 and 16, 1968. Neurath's attitude toward fascism is seen in Neurath to AA, June 1, 1927, AA Abtl. II, Italien, PO 1, Bd. 2, and in the postwar "Skizze": "Personally, I could never develop any close inner attitude in favor of fascism, even after I became personally friendly with Mussolini. Thus, during my eight years as ambassador, I participated in no fascist celebration or parade."

30. Neurath's two dispatches to AA, November 3, 1922, AA K428/K123487-88, and AA Abtl. II, Italien, PO 29, Bd. 1. Although Holborn claims that Neurath "spread the idea that the fascist government of Mussolini would help Germany in a revision of the Versailles Treaty," no documentation is offered for this statement, which in fact applies not at all to Neurath, but rather to such German National types as Ulrich von Hassell. See Holborn, "Early Weimar Diplomacy," in Craig and Gilbert (eds.), *Diplomats,* 151. See also Axel Freiherr von Freytagh-Loringhoven, *Deutschnationale Volkspartei,* 88.

31. Neurath to AA, June 3, 1924, AA K525/K150449-50. Earlier quotation is Neurath to AA, December 2, 1922. See also Neurath to AA, July 30, 1925, AA K428/K123499 and K525/K150486; and Neurath to Köpke, May 7, 1923, Köpke Nachlass. Neurath denied that Mussolini was following any general policy, either a "private fascist one," or a program aimed at the Entente powers. See Neurath to AA, December 12, 1922, and January 10 and 25, 1923, in AA K526/K150723, 2784H/D537366, and 2784H/D537386-88.

32. Neurath to AA, January 27, 1927, AA 6001H/E442561-68. For the treaty negotiations of 1925, see Neurath to Köpke, September 2, 1925, Köpke Nachlass; and documents filmed as AA 2784H/D537806-8061. Neurath's description of the hectic talks, which reminded him of an insane asylum in which he had to personally intervene in order to achieve a successful completion, is from a letter to his old friend Köpke, who was now in charge of the West European desk and so Neurath's immediate superior. Neurath's evaluation of the treaty and its problems are found in Neurath to AA, October 22; Neurath to Stresemann, October 28; and Neurath to AA, November 1 and December 16, 1925; in AA 2784H/D538046, 2784H/D538052-53, K528/K151716-19, and K525/K150490-92. For his similar actions during the negotiations of 1927, including his advice to break off talks rather than give in to Mussolini's demands to recognize again the Versailles Treaty, see documents printed in *Akten zur deutschen auswärtigen Politik 1918-1925,* Series B, Bd. III (hereafter cited as ADAP B/III), 437-40, 462, 467-68.

33. As early as 1925, Neurath warned that the South Tyrol and *Anschluss* issues blocked any real friendship between Italy and Germany. He repeated this conclusion in 1927, claiming that the situation was "getting worse from month to month," and as late as 1929, he argued that these two stumbling blocks were as large as ever. See Neurath to AA, May 3 and 6, 1925, December 20, 1927, and April 18, 1929, in AA K428/K123566-69, 2784H/D537928, K428/K123649-50, and K528/K151820-26. He urged, therefore, that Germany should seek only some informal and temporary relaxation of tensions.

See Neurath to AA, December 9, 1926, November 3, 1927, and January 17, 1929, in ADAP B/III, 483–84, AA K525/K150531–34, and 2784H/D539071–72. The quotation is from Neurath to AA, January 27, 1927, AA 6001H/E442567–68. His embassy counselor Prittwitz subsequently praised Neurath for keeping Berlin away from close ties with Rome. See Prittwitz to Neurath, May 22, 1930, AA, Prittwitz Nachlass.

34. Neurath to AA, May 2, 1928, AA K22/K003113. Earlier quotation is from Neurath to AA, January 27, 1927, AA 6001H/E442567–68.

35. Neurath shared the belief that France would use the League of Nations to impose a "lex gallica" upon Europe, permitting her to serve as both judge and policeman of the continent. The exchange between Stresemann and Neurath, March 24 and 25, 1926, is AA K652/K170911–12. See also Köpke to Neurath, June 23, 1925, Köpke Nachlass. Information on Neurath's attitude from author's interviews with Constantin Freiherr von Neurath, and Dr. Werner von Schmieden, May 7 and May 1, 1968. Neurath was kept informed of developments in Berlin by his good friend Köpke, who once commented in a letter that he had no one else in whom he could so freely confide "delicate and personal matters." Köpke to Neurath, February 16, 1926, Köpke Nachlass.

36. Neurath to AA, December 20, 1927, AA K428/K123650. Although Neurath wrote nothing specifically on the Polish question during his years in Rome, he apparently shared State Secretary Schubert's conviction that "the regaining of the Corridor and Upper Silesia" was "the most sensitive point of German foreign policy." Schubert to Neurath, April 28, 1926, AA 2784H/D538363.

37. Neurath to AA, May 3, 1925, AA K428/K123569. For his concern over a premature raising of the *Anschluss* question, see Köpke to Neurath, June 23, 1925; Neurath to AA, August 22, 1922; and Neurath to AA, May 14, 1925; in Köpke Nachlass; Microfilm of the files of the Reichs Chancellery Office (available from the National Archives), hereafter cited as RK, L232/L067409; and AA 2784H/D537934.

38. Köpke to Neurath, August 13, 1925, Köpke Nachlass; and Bülow to Smend (attached to Neurath's embassy in Rome), June 5, 1929, AA 5270/E325717–18.

39. For Neurath's reluctance, see his initial refusal to accept the appointment, unsigned note to Schubert, May 5, 1930, AA K652/K171117; and author's interviews with Frau von Mackensen and Constantin von Neurath, May 2 and 7, 1968. Cf. Julius Curtius, *Sechs Jahre Minister der deutschen Republik,* 147. Neurath's poor health is discussed in Köpke to Neurath, March 3, 1925, Köpke Nachlass. As an indication of his good relations in Italy, Neurath had to delay his posting to London (announced in May) until October at the request of the king who asked to receive him personally for a farewell visit. Unsigned note, October 1; and Schubert to AA, October 14, 1930; in AA 4620/E198858 and 6001H/E442748–49.

40. Friedrich von Prittwitz und Gaffron, *Zwischen Petersburg und Washington: ein Diplomatenleben,* 154. Significantly, this praise comes from a man who politically disliked Neurath. For criticism of the changes, see Georg Bernhard, "Das Revirement," *Vossische Zeitung,* May 4, 1930. Longtime State Secretary Carl Schubert had bitterly wanted to get the London appointment and never got over his disappointment: "I openly admit that the wound I received two years ago has never healed," he wrote Köpke on June 30, 1932, "and now once more starts to bleed." Köpke Nachlass. The occasion was the announcement that Ambassador Hoesch would replace Neurath in London. For Schubert's removal as state secretary, see Gottfried Reinhold Treviranus, *Das Ende von Weimar: Heinrich Brüning und seine Zeit,* 131 and 147. He is wrong, however, in believing that Schubert willingly accepted the ambassadorship in Rome instead of London.

41. According to Fishman (*Seven Men,* 147), this was Neurath's postwar version. It is similar to, and may have come from, Neurath, "Lebenslauf." Even Vansittart, who took a critical tone toward Neurath in his memoirs, admitted that London society had

"swarmed" the new ambassador and his wife. Robert Gilbert Vansittart, *The Mist Procession*, 447.

42. See especially Edward W. Bennett, *Germany and the Diplomacy of the Financial Crisis, 1931*, passim; and Wolfgang J. Helbich, "Between Stresemann and Hitler: The Foreign Policy of the Brüning Government," *World Politics*, XII (1959), 24-44. See also Francis P. Walters, *A History of the League of Nations*, 436; and the perceptive reports by the British ambassador, Sir Horace Rumbold, to the foreign office, July 3, August 12 and 19, and October 27, 1930, in E. L. Woodward and Rohan Butler (eds.), *Documents on British Foreign Policy 1919-1939*, Second Series, Volume I (hereafter cited as DBFP 2/I), 490, 491-93, 499-501, and 525.

43. Quotation is from Neurath, "Lebenslauf." Baroness von Neurath summarized Neurath's reactions to the London talks: "Although they very much enjoyed the German wine served in the embassy, the [British] still remained uncooperative, and the conference ended without positive results." Except, she added, "an 'A' for Germany's reputation." For discussion, see Karl Schwendemann, "Germany's Course in the Disarmament Issue," in Richard Schmidt and Adolf Grabowsky (eds.), *Disarmament and Equal Rights: Facts and Problems Dealt with in the Negotiations on Disarmament and Equal Rights, 1933/1934*, 14ff. See also Bennett, *Germany and the Financial Crisis*, 292; and Neurath to AA, July 13, 1931, AA 5138/E300357-58.

44. The best discussion of the project is F. G. Stambrook, "The German-Austrian Customs Union Project of 1931: A Study of German Methods and Motives," *Journal of Central European Affairs*, XXI (1961), 15-44; additional new material, especially concerning Curtius' motives and foreign office opposition led by Köpke, is found in Köpke Nachlass. The first quotations are from Köpke's memoranda February 21 and June 22, 1931. The criticism comes from Theodor Wolff's editorial in *Berliner Tageblatt*, March 24, 1931. The initiator of the action was Bülow, Curtius's new state secretary. Neurath, and the other ambassadors, were given no opportunity to present opposition, and the rest of the foreign office staff fell into line out of a "sense of authority," which implied that "the order to attack has been given and now we must all march along the whole line." Köpke to Rümelin, April 4, 1931; Hoesch to AA, March 6, 1931; and Köpke's memorandum, February 24, 1932; in Köpke Nachlass, AA K936/K240607-26 and K1148/K294599-603. For the attacks upon Curtius, see DBFP 2/II, 78, 251, and 278-79; and Heinrich Brüning, "Ein Brief," *Deutsche Rundschau*, 70 (1947), 485-89.

CHAPTER IV. *Neurath Becomes Foreign Minister*

1. See Köpke to Rümelin, June 1, 1929, Köpke Nachlass. For Stresemann's involvement, see his notes of a conversation with the Italian ambassador, December 14, 1925, ADAP B/III, 15-17.

2. Neurath to AA, December 28; Stresemann to Neurath, December 30, 1925; and Neurath to Stresemann, January 1, 1926; in ADAP B/III, 26-27, 28-29, and 38-39. Köpke admitted to Neurath that there was an agreement between the *Tägliche Rundschau* and the minister, but in all instances the newspaper has "a completely free political hand." He added that the minister refused to apply pressure to the newspaper. Köpke to Neurath, February 16, 1926, Köpke Nachlass. As late as April 1926, Neurath was still urging the foreign office to dissociate itself from the newspaper campaign. Neurath to Schubert, April 15, 1926, ADAP B/III, 240-42.

3. Stresemann to Neurath, January 3, 1926, ADAP B/III, 45-47.

4. Neurath to Stresemann, January 5, 1926, ADAP B/III, 47-48. In a subsequent letter, Stresemann denied that he had accused Neurath of tolerating excesses against the Germans, but he was convinced the ambassador was not exercising the proper zeal in protesting the "unheard-of persecution of the German elements" in the South Tyrol. Stresemann to Neurath, January 8, 1926, ADAP B/III, 52-53.

5. Köpke to Neurath, February 16, 1926, Köpke Nachlass. Upon receipt of another

Stresemann letter, Neurath commented: "I will forgo further unprofitable discussion [on this subject.]" AA K653/K171340. Neurath's attempts to prevent further German reactions are in Neurath to AA, January 15, February 10, March 28, April 7, and July 15, 1926; in Reichs Chancellery Files, Bundesarchiv, Koblenz (hereafter cited as BA, RK), R43/I, 78; and ADAP B/III, 200–201 and 300. The subsequent guidelines for the press incorporated most of what Neurath had been urging for months. See ADAP B/III, 50–51, 63, 103–105, 112–13; AA 2784H/D538169–76; and Köpke to Neurath, February 16, 1926, Köpke Nachlass.

6. Neurath was fond of saying that Stresemann rode with "slack reins," failing to give proper leadership. Author's interviews with Frau von Mackensen and Baroness von Ritter, May 2 and August 20, 1968. Information about the meeting is from Neurath, "Lebenslauf"; and Prittwitz to AA, February 7, and Schubert to Rome, February 8, 1927, in AA 2784H/D538622–23.

7. Neurath to Köpke, December 27, 1944, Köpke Nachlass. On the two appointments, information from Neurath, "Lebenslauf," and author's interviews with Frau von Mackensen (May 2 and July 8, 1968), Baroness von Ritter (July 16, 1968), and Constantin von Neurath (May 7, 1968). In the end, the president forced Stresemann to give a written guarantee that Neurath would be posted to London in the near future. See Hindenburg to Stresemann, November 22; and Stresemann to Hindenburg, November 24, 1928; in AA K1013/K266458–59 and K1013/K266463. For Stresemann's opposition, see Stresemann to Hergt, March 16, 1928, AA K652/K171019; and Kurt Freiherr von Reibnitz, *Im Dreieck—Schleicher-Hitler-Hindenburg: Männer des deutschen Schicksals,* 138–39. Only Hindenburg's personal interference preserved Neurath as ambassador. See Friedrich Lucas, *Hindenburg als Reichspräsident,* 32.

8. For the charges that Neurath did not celebrate Constitution Day, see Stresemann to Neurath, April 15, 1929, AA 2784H/D539125; Herbertus Prinz zu Löwenstein, *Stresemann: das deutsche Schicksal im Spiegel seines Lebens,* 300; and Prittwitz, *Zwischen Petersburg und Washington,* 166. In 1921, Neurath rented a hunting preserve in the Austrian Alps, and spent every August there until 1928 when he purchased another property; he continued his hunting vacations there until 1943. Neurath, "Gebirgsjaeger," Ritter Papers. For the other controversy, see Oscar Meyer (Reichstag member) to Schubert, March 22, 1929, AA K1013/K266479. Apparently Theodor Wolff and Henry Bernhard also wrote letters, but these are not available. The story is reconstructed in letters from Schubert to Bernhard, April 10; Stresemann to Neurath, April 12; Neurath to Stresemann, April 14; and Stresemann to Neurath, April 15, 1929; in AA 2784H/ D539122, /D539123, and /D539124–25. See also Theodor Wolff's article in *Berliner Tageblatt,* April 7, 1929; and Hanz Zehrer's article, "Nadolny," in *Die Tat,* August 1933. Neurath's actions were defended by a letter from Dr. von Harnack of the Prussian State Library who happened to be in Rome at the time; see Harnack to Schubert, May 3, 1929, AA 2784H/D539157. The charges concerning Hauptmann are found in Meyer to Schubert, April 22; Stresemann to Neurath, April 27; and Neurath to AA, April 25, 29, and May 2, 1929; in AA 2784H/D539138–39, /D539148, /D539150–51, /D539153–54, and /D539168–72. Subsequently, Neurath proved that he had not even been in Rome at the time of the alleged slight to Hauptmann. See Neurath to AA, April 8, 1929, AA 2784H/D539151. Stresemann's statement is found in a note by the state secretary of the Reichs Chancellery, May 8, 1929, RK K1013/K266486. See Krestmann's memorandum, May 7, 1929, AA 2784H/D539174–75. For the testimonials and newspaper citations, I am grateful to an official of the Political Archives in Bonn, who retrieved some material on the controversy from the personnel files.

9. Neurath to Köpke, December 27, 1944, Köpke Nachlass. Apparently Köpke had removed some documents from the official files, and, unfortunately, they have not survived.

10. For Hindenburg's relations with Stresemann, see Henry Bernhard, *Finis Ger-*

maniae: Aufzeichnungen und Betrachtungen, 23–24; and Elard von Oldenburg-Januschau, *Erinnerungen,* 219. Neurath had supported Hindenburg's election, and told the Italian government that it would have beneficial results. Neurath to AA, April 12, 1925, AA 4913H/E255744. Information also from author's interviews with Baroness von Ritter and Frau von Mackensen, July 16 and May 2, 1968.

11. Vico von Bülow-Schwante told the author on May 24, 1968, that in 1931, President von Hindenburg had praised Neurath so extravagantly that the family concluded Neurath would soon become foreign minister. See also Lucas, *Hindenburg,* 32.

12. Köpke to Neurath, August 13, 1925, Köpke Nachlass. The Köpke anecdote was frequently told to the author as an indication of the general feeling within the foreign office that Neurath would one day be minister. It is printed in Zechlin, *Pressechef,* 148.

13. Neurath to Köpke, September 2, 1925, Köpke Nachlass; and Edgar Vincent Viscount D'Abernon, *The Diary of an Ambassador,* III, 176. See also Bernhard, *Finis Germaniae,* 68. Although he expressed his abhorrence to the whole idea, Neurath gave the impression to his son's tutor, Gustav Strohm, that sooner or later he would be compelled to assume the position. Strohm to Friedrich Gaus, March 21, 1947, copy of letter in Köpke Nachlass.

14. Stresemann's opposition to sending Neurath is from Reibnitz, *Im Dreieck,* 138–39. For the extended controversy over presidential prerogatives, see documents filmed on serials AA K1012 and K1013, especially K1013/K266428–31, for its resolution. Köpke wrote of the "strong opposition against any possible sending of Neurath to London," and suspected that Stresemann was using the Ludwig/Hauptmann affairs, "a rather insignificant excuse," to delay Neurath's transfer. Köpke to Rümelin, November 30, 1928 and June 1, 1929, Köpke Nachlass. Neurath's meeting with the president to express his strong personal reluctance to leave Italy, and his sensing of Stresemann's fears is from Neurath, "Lebenslauf," and author's interviews with Frau von Mackensen, Constantin von Neurath, and Baroness von Ritter, May 2, 7, and July 16, 1968.

15. Information from author's interviews with Constantin von Neurath and Frau von Mackensen, July 3 and May 2, 1968. The quotation is from Neurath's postwar testimony, IMT, XVI, 599. See also the affidavit of Curt Prüfer that "Neurath could not consider himself suited to take over a ministry in a state ruled according to parliamentary procedure." IMT, XVI, 600. The idea that a professional diplomat should become foreign minister had long appealed to Hindenburg. In March 1929, he himself mentioned Neurath's name as a possible member of a rightist cabinet during conversations with Cuno Graf Westarp, then head of the German Nationals. Westarp's memorandum, March 18, 1929, cited in Bracher, *Auflösung der Weimarer Republik,* 323.

16. See Werner Conze, "Die Krise des Parteienstaates in Deutschland 1929/1930," *Historische Zeitschrift,* 178 (1954), 47–83; Thilo Vogelsang, *Reichswehr, Staat und NSDAP: Beiträge zur deutschen Geschichte, 1930–1932,* 70ff.; and Bracher, *Auflösung der Weimarer Republik,* 322. Werner Freiherr von Rheinbaben, the DVP's principal expert on foreign affairs after Stresemann's death, told the author (June 16, 1962) that he had urged his party to support either Neurath or Ambassador Hoesch for the position of foreign minister. See also Magnus Freiherr von Braun, *Von Ostpreussen bis Texas: Erlebnisse und zeitgeschichtliche Betrachtungen eines Ostdeutschen,* 238. For the background of the appointment and foreign office satisfaction, see Cabinet Minutes (hereafter cited as Cab. Mins.), October 10, 1929, BA, RK R43/I, 902; and Hencke to Twardowski, November 1, 1929, and Bülow to Kardorff, January 7, 1930, in AA Handakten Hencke and AA M269/M011345. Also see Curtius, *Sechs Jahre,* 107.

17. *B. Z. am Mittag,* April 8, 1930. See also Hencke to Twardowski, March 28, 1930, AA Handakten Hencke. Brüning had first thought of retiring Curtius and keeping the foreign ministry for himself. See Treviranus, *Ende von Weimar,* 131; and speculations in Hencke to Dirksen, March 28, and Hoesch to AA, April 9, 1930, in AA 2082H/450834

and K652/K171099. As a result, Curtius knew that his position was vulnerable and energetically began to pursue his own policies. Thus, he had to remove State Secretary Schubert, who was so closely associated with the Stresemann era. See Treviranus, *Ende von Weimar*, 147. Köpke, who for many years had been deputy state secretary, refused to be considered for the position and detailed his reasons in a memorandum, "What I Told Curtius," May 3, 1930, Köpke Nachlass. Bernard Wilhelm von Bülow, Curtius's final choice, was a nephew of the former Reichs Chancellor, and his selection was generally approved.

18. Henry Bernard, "Das Revirement," *Vossische Zeitung,* May 4, 1930.

19. These officials recommended Dr. Wilhelm Solf, former foreign secretary and ambassador to Tokyo from 1921 to 1928. First quotation is from Köster to Solf, September 15, 1931, BA, Solf Nachlass, 185. On September 10, 1931, Ambassador Rumbold wired London that Neurath was the center of rumors, but he believed Brüning would take over the position himself. See DBFP 2/II, 258–59. See also Curtius, *Sechs Jahre,* 208. Hindenburg's preference for Neurath is mentioned in Metternich to Solf, September 24, 1931. Three days earlier, Solf had written that although there would be objections to Neurath's name, he believed the president's preference would keep it in discussions. Solf to Metternich, September 21, 1929. Ultimately, Hindenburg rejected Solf who suggested it was because the conservatives "have never forgotten that I transferred too quickly from the old regime to the new one." He added, however, that he personally doubted whether Neurath wanted to be a part of such a risky venture. Solf to Metternich, October 29, 1931, BA, Solf Nachlass, 185. See also Eberhard von Vietsch, *Wilhelm Solf,* 303ff.; and Reginald H. Phelps, "Aus den Groener Dokumenten. VI: Die Briefe an Alarich von Gleich 1930–1932," and "VII: Das SA-Verbot und der Sturz des Kabinetts Brüning," *Deutsche Rundschau,* 76 (1950), 1016, and 77 (1951), 19.

20. Lutz Graf Schwerin von Krosigk, *Es geschah in Deutschland: Menschenbilder unseres Jahrhunderts,* 312. For Neurath's position in London, see L. Freiherr Geyr von Schweppenburg, *Erinnerungen eines Militärattaches,* 30 and 109. As late as 1937, Lord Halifax's remarks showed that in British circles, confidence in Neurath was still high. *Documents and Materials Relating to the Eve of the Second World War* (hereafter cited as *Documents and Materials*), I, 42.

21. Braun, *Ostpreussen,* 277ff. For newspaper reports, see *8 Uhr Abendblatt,* Berlin, June 2, 1932. Neurath's reputation is discussed in Erich Kordt, *Nicht aus den Akten: die Wilhelmstrasse im Frieden und Krieg, Erlebnisse, Begegnungen und Eindrücke, 1928–1945,* 46; and Friedrich Rosen, *Aus einem diplomatischen Wanderleben,* III/IV, 350.

22. See Solf to Metternich, October 10, 1931, BA, Solf Nachlass, 185. Information also from letters to the author from Erich Kordt and Dr. Ernst Woermann, July 9 and 25, 1963. For the despair even of democrats, see Bülow to Prittwitz, October 31; and Prittwitz to Bülow, November 5, 1931; in AA 4620H/E200005 and /E200021. See also the discussion of Groener's plans for a supra-party authoritarian cabinet, in Helmut Krausnick, "Vorgeschichte und Beginn des militärischen Widerstandes gegen Hitler," *Die Vollmacht des Gewissens,* 190.

23. The diary entry is from Neurath, "Lebenslauf," and the quotation is from Werner von Rheinbaben to author, June 16, 1962. According to Neurath's letter to Köpke, August 12, 1931, he had been in very poor health, twice confined to bed for extended periods. Köpke Nachlass. The idea of Neurath as a shield is from Solf to Metternich, October 29, 1931, BA, Solf Nachlass, 185. Other quotation from Rumbold to Marquess of Reading, October 7, 1931, DBFP 2/II, 280ff. For the claim that the SPD blocked the appointment, see Vogelsang, *Reichswehr, Staat, und NSDAP,* 132.

24. See Bülow to Rieth, September 30; Bülow to all missions, December 8, 1931; and Bülow to Prittwitz, January 25, 1932; in AA 4620/E198838, 3617H/D800704–40, and 4620/E200027. Also see similar views expressed in Newton to Sir John Simon, Novem-

ber 20; and Rumbold to Simon, December 18, 1931; in DBFP 2/II, 334–36 and 374–78. See also Neurath to AA, November 3 and 5, 1930, AA K1976/K512835 and 2363/D493503–04.

25. Quotations are from Bülow to all missions, December 8, 1931, AA 3617H/D800705.

26. Neurath, "Lebenslauf." Although neither mention Neurath's activities, the best discussion of Brüning's effort to convince Hindenburg is in John W. Wheeler-Bennett, *Wooden Titan: Hindenburg in Twenty Years of German History, 1914–1934*, 353ff., and Bracher, *Auflösung der Weimarer Republik*, 445ff.

27. Information from Neurath, "Lebenslauf," and Westarp's notes of a conversation with the president, February 25, 1932, cited in Bracher, *Auflösung der Weimarer Republik*, 452. For a discussion of the excitement surrounding the discovery of the "Boxheimer Documents" revealing Nazi plans, see Erich Eyck, *A History of the Weimar Republic*, II, 337; and Vogelsang, *Reichswehr, Staat, und NSDAP*, 145–46. See also Max Domarus, *Hitler: Reden und Proklamationen, 1932–1945*, I, 63–64.

28. The prince, at best an incompetent dilettante as a diplomat, had become an early member of the NSDAP. Through his wife, Princess Pauline of Württemberg, the only child of the last king of Württemberg, he maintained a confidential relationship with Neurath.

29. Henriette de Gourko to the author, August 1969. Mrs. de Gourko's mother, Marie Trarieux, was an old friend of Neurath and had followed his career with close attention. Mrs. de Gourko's account is based upon a diary notation made shortly after the conversation with Neurath. On Madame Trarieux, see Wipert von Blücher, *Deutschlands Weg nach Rapallo*, 57ff.

30. Neurath, "Lebenslauf."

31. Neurath was pleased that he had persuaded the president to run again. See Simon to Rumbold, January 12, 1932, DBFP 2/III, 19. For Westarp's account, see Bracher, *Auflösung der Weimarer Republik*, 453.

32. Köpke to Rümelin, February 16; Baroness von Neurath to Köpke, March 9; and Neurath to Köpke, March 27, 1932; in Köpke Nachlass. Information also from Neurath, "Lebenslauf."

33. For the fatal breach between Brüning and Hindenburg, and the role of General Kurt von Schleicher, see Vogelsang, *Reichswehr, Staat, und NSDAP*, passim; and Theodor Eschenburg, "Die Rolle der Persönlichkeit in der Krise der Weimarer Republik: Hindenburg, Brüning, Groener, Schleicher," VJHZG, IX (1961), passim. For the background of the February meeting, see Volker R. Berghahn, *Der Stahlhelm: Bund der Frontsoldaten, 1918–1935*, 205–206, especially fn. 5 for the meeting with Göring. For various accounts of Schleicher's support for Rudolf Nadolny, Ulrich von Hassell, and Brüning himself, see Hanz Zehrer, "Der Entscheidung entgegen," *Die Tat*, June 1932, 199. Nadolny was also pushed by Otto Meissner, the president's state secretary. See AA, Nadolny Nachlass. The quotations are from the original manuscript of the autobiography of Rudolf Nadolny, used with the permission of his widow, Frau Anny Nadolny. Several important items were removed before publication (as *Mein Beitrag*). For Hassell's candidacy, see Hermann Pünder, *Politik in der Reichskanzlei*, 127. For Brüning's name, see Otto Ernst Schüddekopf, *Das Herr und die Republik: Quellen zur Politik der Reichswehrführung 1918 bis 1933*, 343, fn. 845; Werner Conze, "Zum Sturz Brünings," VJHZG, I (1953), 281–82; and Kunrat Freiherr von Hammerstein, "Schleicher, Hammerstein, und die Machtübernahme 1933," *Frankfurter Heft*, XI (1956), 18. In the light of Neurath's discussion with Hitler in the preceding year, Vogelsang's speculation (in *Reichswehr, Staat, und NSDAP*, 197) that Joseph Goebbel's list of May 24, 1932 was subsequently added seems unnecessary. See Joseph Goebbels, *My Part in Germany's Fight*, 95. The *Vossische Zeitung*, June 1, 1932, called the consultation with party

leaders a "pure formality" since Hindenburg "has already for a long time now settled upon his choices privately."

34. Köpke to Rümelin, June 2, 1932, IMT, XL, 461–65. As with many of the documents introduced into the postwar trials, the original of this letter has disappeared.

35. Bülow to Neurath, May 31, 1932, IMT, XVI, 599. Improved translation by author from German text in Ritter Papers.

36. Author's interview with Franz von Papen, July 24, 1968. For the other cabinet members, see Braun, *Ostpreussen*, 208; Krosigk, *Es geschah in Deutschland*, 142–43; and the unfinished draft of the memoirs of Wilhelm Freiherr von Gayl, BA, Gayl Nachlass, 53.

37. Baroness von Neurath to Neurath, June 2, 1932, Neurath Nachlass, used with the permission of Frau von Mackensen. For the rumors, see *Vossische Zeitung*, June 1, 1932, evening edition.

38. Neurath, "Lebenslauf," and Neurath's postwar testimony, IMT, XVI, 600. For Hindenburg's promise, see *Zeugenschrifttum* Nü. 145 (hereafter cited as ZS 145), III (Schwerin von Krosigk), Archives of the Institut für Zeitgeschichte, Munich (hereafter cited as IZ); Gayl's memoirs, BA, Gayl Nachlass, 53; and Neurath's discussion reported in Rumbold to Simon and Simon to Newton, June 3 and 6, 1932, DBFP 2/III, 149–50 and 152–53. For Hitler's promise, see Franz von Papen, *Memoirs*, 151; and Meissner's memorandum, May 30, 1932, printed in Vogelsang, *Reichswehr, Staat, und NSDAP*, 458–59. Neurath probably also knew that Brüning had decided to appoint him foreign minister in a reorganized cabinet. By the end of April, the foreign office was full of such rumors. See Rumbold to Simon, June 9, 1932, DBFP 2/III, 170; and Köpke to Schubert, April 30, 1932, Köpke Nachlass. Assured of presidential support, Neurath entered the cabinet with absolutely no commitment to the chancellor.

39. Krosigk, *Es geschah in Deutschland*, 143; and author's interview with Lutz Graf Schwerin von Krosigk, April 26, 1968.

CHAPTER V. *The Professional Diplomat as Minister*

1. Neurath was the third professional diplomat to become foreign minister, but the terms of the other two (Dr. Friedrich Rosen, May to October 1921, and Dr. Friedrich von Rosenberg, November 1922 to August 1923) had been extremely short. Neurath was to remain minister for sixty-seven months, only seven months less than Gustav Stresemann. For foreign office reaction, see Köpke to Schubert, April 30, 1932. In November 1931, Köpke had opposed the idea that Brüning should take over the office himself, and on June 11, 1932 he had officially informed Schubert that the office regarded Neurath as the best possible candidate. Köpke Nachlass. Information also from author's interviews with Werner von Schmieden, Werner von Bargan, Walter von Poensgen, and Albrecht von Kessel, May 1, May 21, July 4, and July 30, 1968. Poensgen especially stressed how widespread was Neurath's support among the professional diplomats.

2. Walter Görlitz, *Gustav Stresemann*, 237. See also Henry Ashby Turner, *Stresemann and the Politics of the Weimar Republic*, 174–75.

3. Information from author's interview with Constantin von Neurath, July 3, 1968.

4. Information on Neurath's relations with cabinet colleagues from author's interviews with Lutz Graf Schwerin von Krosigk and Magnus Freiherr von Braun, April 23 and July 16, 1968.

5. Hermann Rauschning, *Men of Chaos*, 158–59. Information also from author's interviews with Frau von Mackensen, July 8 and August 9, 1968. How different was Neurath's attitude from that of his grandfather, who had resigned from his position as Württemberg foreign minister, when the king refused to accept his advice and ordered a change in policy. On July 10, 1854, the earlier Neurath had written: "I am unable to acknowledge that implementation of the king's orders is a minister's unconditional obliga-

tion." See letter and discussion in Götz Krusemarck, "Württemberg und der Krimkrieg," Ph.D dissertation, Kiel, 1931.

6. The best study of this new policy is Gaines Post, Jr., *The Civil-Military Fabric of Weimar Foreign Policy,* especially in his analysis of the blend of military force and foreign policy. See also Max Beer, *Die auswärtige Politik des Dritten Reiches,* passim; and Curtius, *Sechs Jahre,* 259. For the revisionist program of the foreign office, see Bülow to Smend, June 5, 1929, AA 5270H/E325717–18.

7. Neurath, undated "Notizen zur Anklage," Neurath Nachlass, used with permission of Frau von Mackensen. Cited hereafter as "Notizen."

8. Information from author's interview with Frau von Mackensen, May 2, 1968. The leading foreign office opponent of the League was Bernhard von Bülow, the state secretary. In his 1922 book, *Der Versailler Völkerbund: eine vorläufiger Bilanz,* 290ff., he attacked the idea that diplomacy and foreign policy could be fit into a parliamentary system. Neurath shared this opinion. For other quotations, see Rauschning, *Men,* 170.

9. Although originally scheduled for January 1932, the conference had been repeatedly postponed, and Brüning hoped such delays would help Germany. See Pünder, *Reichskanzlei,* 111. For a conflicting view, see Curtius, *Sechs Jahre,* 229. Quotation is from Giselher Wirsing, *Deutschland in der Weltpolitik,* 239. Information also from Rauschning, *Men,* 168 and 170, and author's interview with Herbert Siegfried, May 6, 1968.

10. Bülow to Erwin Planck, June 8, 1932, AA, II F Abr., Abr. 30, Bd. 3. Neurath's approval is recorded in an attached note. For British and French proposals of a political truce or at least an "Eastern Locarno," see DBFP 2/III, 135–36 and 159–71. For Neurath's assurances, see Bülow's report, May 4; Neurath's aide-memoire, June 6; and his report to the cabinet, June 13, 1932; in AA 4260/E200786; DBFP 2/III, 154–57; and BA, RK R43/I, 1456. For Brüning's actions, see Simon to Rumbold, December 31, 1931; and January 6, 1932; and accounts of conversations in Geneva, April 23, 1932; in DBFP 2/III, 6, 9, and 123 fn. 2. There is very little evidence to support Brüning's contention that he had practically ended reparations. See Köpke to Schubert, April 23, 1932, Köpke Nachlass. Also see Wolfgang Malanowski, "Die deutsche Politik der militärische Gleichberechtigung von Brüning bis Hitler," *Wehrwissenschaftliche Rundschau,* V (1955), 356; and Wilhelm Deist, "Brüning, Herriot und die Abrüstungsgespräche von Bessinge 1932," VJHZG, V (1957), 265ff.

11. Cab. Mins., June 13, 1932, BA, RK R43/I, 1456. For Neurath's statement that he "did not expect much to come of Lausanne," see Rumbold to Simon, June 3, 1932, DBFP 2/III, 150. For Schleicher and Papen's expectations, see Wilhelm Deist, "Schleicher und die deutsche Abrüstungspolitik in Juni/Juli 1932," VJHZG, VII (1959), 169. First quotation is from Simon to Newton, June 6, 1932, DBFP 2/III, 153. Franz von Papen told the author that he deeply resented Neurath's attempt to put the chancellor on the sideline. Interview, July 24, 1968. For his thoughts on French-German détente, see Papen, *Memoirs,* 124–25; and Franz von Papen, *Vom Scheitern einer Demokratie,* 214ff. Papen's admission of his inattention is from Papen, *Der Wahrheit eine Gasse,*164. It is deleted from the English translation, which, however, adds that he thought "the settlement of the reparations problem was largely incidental." Papen, *Memoirs,* 172.

12. Neurath to Köpke, June 25, 1932, Köpke Nachlass. Shortly before his death, Köpke burned most of his papers, including all correspondence between Neurath and Köpke for the years 1932 through 1938. This letter is thus the last document in the Köpke Nachlass for the years when Neurath was minister. For details of the conference, see Köpke to Bülow, June 18; Cab. Mins., July 1; and Neurath to London Embassy, July 16, 1932; in AA 4260/E200552, RK 3598/D790319, and AA 7360/E535741. For general discussion, see John W. Wheeler-Bennett, *The Disarmament Deadlock,* 48ff.

13. There is confusion as to the extent of Papen's proposals. See his memorandum, June 29, 1932, in *Documents on German Foreign Policy, 1918–1945,* Series C, Volume

I, page 91, fn. 2 (cited hereafter as DGFP C/I, 91 fn. 2). Also see British notes of June 20, 1932, in DBFP 2/III, 231. Information on Neurath's reaction is from author's interview with Constantin von Neurath, May 7, 1968.

14. Ferdinand Fried, "Die Heilige Allianz von Lausanne," *Die Tat,* August 1932, 397. See also the criticisms by two observers at the conference: Werner von Rheinbaben, *Viermal Deutschland,* 246; and Rudolf Nadolny, original manuscript for autobiography. The confusion of political demands so clumsily interjected into the conference is seen in Schubert to Köpke, July 13, and Köpke to Schubert, July 22, 1932, Köpke Nachlass. One of the best accounts of Lausanne is Paul Schmidt, *Statist auf diplomatischer Bühne, 1923–1945: Erlebnisse des Chefdolmetschers im Auswärtigen Amts mit den Staatsmännern Europas,* 245ff.

15. For Papen's decision, see Papen, *Memoirs,* 181. The German version (*Wahrheit,* 207) is more accurate: "For me the importance of the conference shrunk to the tiresome question of regulating reparations." For development, see Köpke to Bülow, July 1 and 2, 1932; and Cab. Mins., July 5 and 7, 1932; in AA 4260/E200535–57 and /E200571; and RK 3598/D790334 and /D790349–50. For British documents, see DBFP 2/III, 271ff.; and Wheeler-Bennett, *Disarmament Deadlock,* 46–47.

16. For negotiations, see DBFP 2/III, 332ff., 410ff., and 595–99. For Schleicher's protests to the cabinet and fellow officers, see Cab. Mins., July 7, 1932, RK 3598/D790356; and Schüddekopf, *Heer,* 346. Also see François-Poncet to Herriot, July 12, 1932, in *Documents Diplomatiques Français, 1932–1939,* First Series, Volume I, p. 17–21 (cited hereafter as DDF 1/I, 17–21).

17. The dramatic product of the Lausanne conference was the French-British pact announced on July 13, 1932, but actually drafted and approved on the morning of July 8 in Lausanne, a few hours *before* the successful formula for ending reparations had been achieved; see DBFP 2/III, 417–18; and DDF 1/I, 30–32. For Papen's glowing report to the cabinet, see Cab. Mins., July 11, 1932, RK 3598/D790360–75.

18. This was the only time in his long career that Neurath missed a cabinet meeting. It was obvious to many that he was annoyed at the way he had been treated. See Georg Schreiber, *Regierung ohne Volk,* 180; and Fried, "Heilige Allianz," 397. For Neurath's weak position, see also Earl R. Beck, *The Death of the Prussian Republic: A Study of Reich-Prussian Relations, 1932–1934,* 89; and Rumbold to Simon, July 12, 1932, DBFP 2/III, 441.

19. See especially Post, *Civil-Military Fabric,* passim; and Köpke's memorandum, November 21, 1927; and Forster's minutes, May 12, 1928; in AA K6/K000309–15 and /K000388–89. Good discussions are found in Christian Höltje, *Die Weimarer Republik und das Ostlocarno Problem, 1919–1934: Revision oder Garantie der deutschen Ostgrenze von 1919,* 220ff.; and Rolf Richter, "Der Abrüstungsgedanke in Theorie und Praxis und die deutsche Politik (1920–1929)," *Wehrwissenschaftliche Rundschau,* XVIII (1968), passim.

20. On January 15, 1932, Köpke wrote Schubert that the recent conference attended by Brüning, Curtius, Groener, Schleicher, and Bülow had revealed complete unanimity among the planning officials: the disarmament conference would never meet Germany's military needs. Köpke Nachlass. See also perceptive comments in DBFP 2/I, 583–84, and 2/III, 459ff. and 507ff. Quotation is Bülow to Nadolny, February 29, 1932, italics mine, AA 7360/E534980–81. See also Bülow's memorandum, February 25; and Nadolny to Bülow, March 12, 1932; in AA 3642/D811623 and 7360/E535052.

21. Bülow's memorandum for Neurath, June 2, 1932, AA 7360/E535360. This report was excessively optimistic. See Simon to Rumbold, August 29; and Secretary Stimson's declaration, September 1932; in DBFP 2/IV, 108–109 and 219. Earlier quotation is Bülow to Neurath (London), May 4, 1932, AA 4260/E200781–82. For the Bessinge meeting, see Nadolny to AA, February 22; and Nadolny to Brüning, March 18, 1932; in AA 7360/E534960–63, and /E535079; and Bülow to AA, April 18 and 26, 1932, in AA

7360/E535146-47 and /E535192. The best discussion is Deist, "Brüning, Herriot und die Abrüstungsgespräche von Bessinge," 265-72.

22. See Bülow to Nadolny, June 28; Nadolny to Bülow, July 2; Bülow to Schleicher, July 6; Bülow to Neurath, July 12; and Nadolny to AA, July 10, 1932; in AA 7360/ E535914-15, /E535921-22, /E535925-28, /E535902-03, and /E535512-17. Also see discussions in Otto Göppert, *Der Völkerbund: Organisation und Tätigkeit,* 249ff.; and German attempts to inspire a paragraph recognizing German equality, DBFP 2/III, 578-79. For French conclusions, see François-Poncet to Herriot, July 28, 1932, DDF 1/I, 124ff. The best discussion of Schleicher's role is Deist, "Schleicher und die deutsche Abrüstungspolitik," 165ff.

23. See Bülow's circular, August 20, 1932, AA 7360/E535798-815. For different interpretations, see Zimmermann, *Deutsche Aussenpolitik,* 468; and Deist, "Schleicher," 175. For the controversy within the German government, see Neurath to Schleicher, July 13, 1932, AA 7360/E535934; and Cab. Mins., July 13, 1932, RK 3598/ D790385. Nadolny's declaration of July 22, 1932 is published in DBFP 2/III, 589. Neurath deliberately refused to soften the impact of this move, telling the British and French that he no longer had any confidence in their promises. Neurath's memorandum, July 22, 1932, AA Büro Staatssekretär, RM, Bd. 3; and François-Poncet to Herriot, July 13, 1932, DDF 1/I, 28-29.

24. Schleicher to Papen, August 2, 1932, AA 3617H/D800776-77. For Schleicher's speeches, see Schüddekopf, *Heer,* 346 and 368-73. In vain, Neurath tried to explain that "naturally the tone in which the soldier speaks is different from that of a diplomat," but even his assurances that he had "remonstrated" with Schleicher did not allay fears. See François-Poncet to Herriot, July 27 and August 25; Rumbold to Simon, September 6; and Simon's memorandum, September 23, 1932; in DDF 1/I, 102-103, and 223; and DBFP 2/IV, 132-34, and 196.

25. Rumbold to Simon, September 8, 1932; Neurath to Nadolny, August 30; and Neurath to all missions, September 7, 1932; in DBFP 2/IV,150, AA 7474/H184108-10, and /H184253-55. For French and British notes and the German reaction, see DDF 1/I, 268-79 and 305-310; DBFP 2/IV, 172-75; and Cab. Mins., September 12, 1932, RK 3598/D790672. There were many rumors in Berlin that Neurath was planning to retire, but these were false. See Rumbold to Simon, September 19 and 28; and François-Poncet to Herriot, September 8, 1932; in DBFP 2/IV, 178 and 201, and DDF 1/I, 284-87. See also Köpke to Schubert, June 11, 1932, Köpke Nachlass.

26. Neurath implied that Schleicher was not really in charge. As he later told the British: "It would be a mistake to attach too much importance to the views of these officers." See Simon's memorandum, September 23; and Rumbold to Simon, November 15, 1932; in DBFP 2/IV, 198 and 285. The quotation is recorded in Neurath to Bülow, September 25, 1932, AA, RM 18 1-adh, Bd. 2. Also see Pompeo barone Aloisi, *Journal 25 juillet 1932-14 juin 1936,* 9. For an excellent analysis of German insensitivity to the rest of the world, see François-Poncet to Herriot, September 22, 1932, DDF 1/I, 365-71.

27. For Neurath's campaign, see his speech, September 24, 1932, cited in Schreiber, *Regierung,* 28; and his list, printed and discussed in Wheeler-Bennett, *Disarmament Deadlock,* 79-80. Quotations from Neurath to Bülow, September 25, 1932; and François-Poncet to Herriot, October 31, 1932; in AA 7474/H184746 and DDF 1/I, 642. For a discussion of Schleicher's involvement, see Vogelsang, *Reichswehr, Staat, und NSDAP,* 299ff. The perceptive French ambassador predicted that the diplomats would regain control of the situation soon. See François-Poncet to Herriot, September 22, 1932, DDF 1/I, 368ff. For the strategy planning in the foreign office, see Frohwein's memorandum, November 12, 1932, AA RM 18 1-adh, Bd. 2. None of these documents were submitted to Schleicher for his approval.

28. Neurath to AA, November 22, 1932, AA, RM 18 1-adh, Bd. 3. For the wording of

the agreement and for French alarm, see DBFP 2/IV, 287-302; and DDF 1/II, 4-11 and 43-45. In previous conversations, Neurath had always spoken of "samples," and Simon's account of this conversation also contains that phrase. Neurath's memorandum, however, does not. Apparently in his plan to get the British on his side, Neurath misled them into thinking that the older conversations still applied. See DBFP 2/IV, 267 and 297-98; and DDF 1/II, 17. Noting that Schleicher was now so involved with domestic developments that he could no longer become involved in foreign policy, the French ambassador doubted if Germany could pursue any real policy in the forthcoming talks. As always, François-Poncet tended to underestimate Neurath. François-Poncet to Herriot, November 17, 1932, DDF 1/II, 16-17.

29. For the discussions in Geneva before Neurath returned, see DBFP 2/IV, 314-78; and DDF 1/II, 120-26 and 145-56. Neurath's relief that the powers had failed to unite is in Weizsäcker to AA, December 3, 1932, AA, RM 18 1-adh, Bd. 3. For the French and British records of the negotiations, see DDF 1/II, 160ff.; and DBFP 2/IV, 328ff. Neurath's proposal was addressed to all the powers, but his own copy bore the title: "Questions of the French." AA, RM 18 1-adh, Bd. 3. He himself used the word "alarmed" in describing MacDonald's reactions. Neurath to Bülow, December 6, 1932, AA, RM 18 1-adh, Bd. 3. See also Bülow's memoranda of telephone conversations with Neurath, December 6 and 8; and Neurath to AA, December 10, 1932; in AA 7474/H185912-13, /H185924, and /H185975-76; and Aloisi, *Journal,* 32-34.

30. See Bülow's notes of a telephone conversation with Neurath, December 10, and an undated and unsigned memorandum, in AA 7474/H186014 and 3154/D672430. Earlier quotation is Bülow to Planck, December 10, 1932, AA 7474/H185960.

31. Bülow's notes of a telephone conversation with Neurath, December 10, 1932, AA 7474/H186013.

32. Cited in Thilo Vogelsang, "Neue Dokumente zur Geschichte der Reichswehr 1930-1933," VJHZG, II (1954), 426-27. For Neurath's views, see his article in the magazine *Heimatdienst,*draft in AA 7474/H186063-139.

33. Cab. Mins., December 14, 1932, RK 3598/D791266-67. Neurath's quotation is from his dispatch to all missions, December 13, 1932, AA 7474/H186017-18. The evaluation comes from one of the German participants; see Paul Schmidt, *Statist,* 250.

34. Author's interview with Baroness von Ritter, August 20, 1968. Bülow's record of a telephone conversation with Neurath, December 11, 1932, AA 7474/H186014-15. The first quotation is from Schmidt, *Statist,* 250-51.

35. Quotation is from Cab. Mins., December 14, 1932, RK 3598/D791266. For the rearmament, see reports of British attachés, DBFP 2/II, 515-25, and 2/III, 602-603.

36. For Blomberg's demands, see Nadolny to Neurath, January 11 and 13, 1932; and the working copies of the office proposals; in AA 7616/H188329-37, /H188348-52, and /H188326-328/10; and Neurath's memorandum, January 14, 1933, AA, St. Sek., RM, Bd. 3. On one proposal by Blomberg, Neurath wrote: "I believe that such a move would be tactically false, and therefore I cannot consent." He eventually prevailed. Quotations in text are from Neurath's memorandum, January 16; and Neurath to Nadolny, January 19, 1933; in AA, St. Sek., RM, Bd. 3; and AA 7616/H188347. These instructions conclude: "The attitude of the delegation must always take into consideration that should [the conference fail], we must not be in a state of political isolation which might limit our freedom of action." The same attitude dominated the draft which the foreign office prepared for Schleicher's speech of December 15, 1932: "The fate of the disarmament question, as the whole world agrees, is of decisive importance for the fate of the League of Nations, and therefore for our future cooperation in that institution." See Nadolny to Neurath, January 11, 1933; and Bülow to Planck, December 10, 1932; in AA 7616/ H188337, and AA, RM 1 f, Bd. 7. Also see foreign office draft for Schleicher's speech, January 17, 1933; Bülow to Nadolny, and Bülow to Prittwitz, January 19, 1933; in AA,

RM 1 f, Bd. 7; AA, II F Abr. 4, Nü. 1, Bd. 3; and AA 4260/E200843. Clearly Neurath was calling the tune.

37. By early 1933, Neurath thought the military would come into line, and there is evidence that they did. See General Liebmann's notes of the Stuttgart Army Command conference, January 15, 1934: Hitler and Blomberg, the officers were told, believed that France would accept any German military increase, as long as it was not officially announced. This was exactly Neurath's program. IZ, 167/51.

CHAPTER VI. *The Nonpolitical Minister*

1. For the characteristics of the cabinet, see Braun, *Ostpreussen,* 228-29; and the discussion in Thomas Trumpp, "Franz von Papen, der preussisch-deutsch Dualismus und die NSDAP in Preussen: Ein Beitrag zur Vorgeschichte des 20. Juli 1932," Ph.D. dissertation, Tübingen, 1963; and Joachim C. Fest, *Das Gesicht des Dritten Reiches—Profile einer totalitären Herrschaft,* 209ff.

2. Braun, *Ostpreussen,* 231. The five federal civil servants were Neurath, Lutz Graf Schwerin von Krosigk (finance), Magnus Freiherr von Braun (agriculture), Hermann Warmbold (economics), and Hugo Schäffer (labor). Wilhelm Freiherr von Gayl (interior) and Franz Gürtner (justice) came from the state level, and Paul Freiherr von und zu Eltz-Rübenach (transportation) had also had extensive civil service experience.

3. The incident about Papen's careless remark was reported to the author in an interview with Dr. Walter Poensgen, July 4, 1968. Baroness von Neurath's comment comes from author's interview with Herbert Siegfried, May 6, 1968. Information on cabinet from author's interviews with Magnus Freiherr von Braun, Lutz Graf Schwerin von Krosigk, Baroness von Ritter, and Vico von Bülow-Schwante, July 16, April 26, July 16, and May 24, 1968. For Schleicher's activities, see especially Papen's letter, printed in Thilo Vogelsang, "Zur Politik Schleichers gegenüber der NSDAP," VJHZG, VI (1958), 111; and Hammerstein, "Schleicher," 117. Also see Cab. Mins., August 15, 1932, RK 3598/D790548. Noting the strong opinions against Papen by his own colleagues, especially Neurath and Gayl, the British ambassador commented on the strange lack of loyalty within the cabinet. See Rumbold to Simon, August 4 and September 28, 1932, DBFP 2/IV, 21 and 201. See also Gayl's complaints against Schleicher in BA, Gayl Nachlass, 53. And see contemporary accounts in Walter Schotte, *Das Kabinett Papen, Schleicher, Gayl,* 79-80; Georg Schreiber, *Brüning/Hitler/Schleicher: das Zentrum in der Opposition,* 34ff.; and Calvin B. Hoover, *Germany Enters the Third Reich,* 53-54.

4. Schleicher's hopes for Papen as his "opening to the Right" is documented in ZS 281, IZ, and his program is discussed in Vogelsang, *Reichswehr, Staat, und NSDAP,* 203ff. Despite this treatment, and that in Bracher, *Auflösung der Weimarer Republik,* 529ff., a thorough analysis of the Papen cabinet and its ideology awaits an historian. Any evaluation must include Walter Schotte, *Der neue Staat,* 45ff., for which Papen provided the introduction. The best study in English (Beck, *Prussian Republic*) is too limited in scope to be the definitive work.

5. Most of the civil servants, Neurath included, believed their jobs would not last long. ZS 145 I (Schwerin von Krosigk), IZ; author's interview with Magnus Freiherr von Braun, July 16, 1968. Eltz-Rübenach refused to leave his job with the Baden railroads, asking instead for only a year's leave of absence. See Jürgen Huck, "Reichsminister Paul Freiherr von Eltz-Rübenach: Sein Leben und Wirken, 1875-1943," *Unser Portz,* II (1961), 41. Information on Neurath's attitude toward the Papen cabinet comes primarily from author's interviews with Frau von Mackensen, Constantin von Neurath, and Vico von Bülow-Schwante, May 2, May 7, and May 24, 1968. In an interview with the author on July 24, 1968, Franz von Papen complained that Neurath was absolutely stubborn on maintaining his monopoly over foreign affairs. He habitually prepared two reports, one for the cabinet and one for the president. See AA 7474/H185574 and Lucas, *Hindenburg,* 132.

6. For the administrative duplication and conflicts, see Arnold Brecht, *Federalism and Regionalism in Germany: The Division of Prussia,* 52–70; and Waldemar Besson, *Württemberg und die deutsche Staatskrise, 1928–1933: eine Studie zur Auflösung der Weimarer Republik,* 291–301. Although Vogelsang (*Reichswehr, Staat, und NSDAP,* 248ff.) has correctly noted that the coup was primarily a *Verwaltungsreform,* he overlooks the fact that Hindenburg had been won over to the idea by the civil service ministers' arguments for a unified administration. See Otto Braun, *Von Weimar zu Hitler,* 417. The political need for Papen and Schleicher to achieve some triumph in order to strengthen their position in the forthcoming election was only secondary. See Otto Meissner, *Staatssekretär unter Ebert, Hindenburg, Hitler: der Schicksalsweg des deutschen Volkes von 1918 bis 1945 wie ich ihn erlebte,* 238.

7. Papen's letter, November 12, 1957, is printed in Vogelsang, "Zur Politik Schleichers," 108. For the discussions, see Cab. Mins., August 10, 1932, RK 3598/D790528–32; and Walter Görlitz, *Hindenburg: ein Lebensbild,* 381. For Schleicher's views, see Paul Herre, *Kronprinz Wilhelm: seine Rolle in der deutschen Politik,* 201; and Vogelsang, *Reichswehr, Staat, und NSDAP,* 257ff. One of the most accurate summaries of Schleicher's position is found in Bredow (?), *The Berlin Diaries* (ed. Helmut Klotz), June 4, 1932, 38: "The meaning in brief of Schleicher's long harangue was that he wishes to tie the Nazis' hands by means of a forced marriage between them and the Center and Hugenberg." Although the authenticity of this book is difficult to establish, it appears to be the diary of Captain Bredow, a close friend and co-worker of Schleicher, who was murdered on June 30, 1934. In a letter to Göring on November 23, 1934, Reinhold Heydrich considered Bredow's authorship clearly established. Letter is from the Gestapo file of the Central and Western European Collection at the Hoover Institution on War, Revolution and Peace. While there may indeed have been some additions, I accept the book as essentially the diary of Bredow.

8. Cab. Mins., August 10, 1932, RK 3598/D790533–41. For the paralyzed Reichstag, see Lindsay Rogers, Freda Foerster, Sanford Schwarz, "German Political Institutions, II, Article 48," *Political Science Quarterly,* 47 (1932), 594ff. To the end of his life, Papen was bitter because Neurath and the other ministers believed in 1932 that they could somehow muddle through without constitutional changes. Author's interview with Franz von Papen, July 14, 1968. See also Graf Kuno Westarp, *Am Grab der Parteiherrschaft,* 122; and Sperr to Bavarian foreign ministry, August 2, 1932, cited in Vogelsang, *Reichswehr, Staat, und NSDAP,* 256. For the controversies, see also Besson, *Württemberg,* 312ff.; and Cab. Mins., August 15 and 27, 1932, BA, RK R43/I, 1457. Also see Otto Schmidt-Hannover, *Umdenken oder Anarchie: Männer, Schicksale, Lehren,* 322–23.

9. Meeting is described in Bracher, *Auflösung der Weimarer Republik,* 624; and in Meissner's memorandum, printed in Walther Hubatsch, *Hindenburg und der Staat,* 339–43. The Reichstag vote surprised not only ministers like Neurath (see Rumbold to Simon, September 12, 1932, DBFP 2/IV, 48), but also Hitler and the army. See Kurt C. W. Lüdecke, *I Knew Hitler: The Story of a Nazi Who Escaped the Blood Purge,* 457ff., and Bredow (?), *Berlin Diaries,* 168. In the Cab. Mins., September 24 and 14, 1932 (RK 3598/D790676–78, and /D790746–58), Schleicher deliberately misled the ministers, for he had no intention of retaining the presidential form of the cabinet as desired by the civil service ministers. See Gayl's account in his personal papers, BA, Gayl Nachlass, 53.

10. Cab. Mins., September 14, 1932, RK 3598/D790748. A week later, the Swabian representative reported that the cabinet was completely divided over a new constitution. See Besson, *Württemberg,* 306. The cabinet also opposed Gayl's arguments that frequent elections would bankrupt the parties. In his unfinished memoirs, Gayl wrote that the president had told him that he did not want to see the face of an "oath breaker" every morning in his mirror. BA, Gayl Nachlass, 53. For most of the cabinet, Papen was now becoming a liability. In August 1932, the Swabian minister wrote: "Papen always gives

the impression of a dilettante who does not realize the seriousness of the situation and thinks he can improvise his politics off the cuff." Besson, *Württemberg,* 296 fn. 2. According to author's interview with Frau von Mackensen on May 3, 1968, her father expressed similar views. If proof were wanting, one has but to read Papen's plans to make Crown Prince Rupprecht of Bavaria regent of the German republic. See Papen, *Vom Scheitern einer Demokratie,* 266ff. and 272–75.

11. Preceding the elections, Gayl and Papen campaigned for constitutional changes, and Schleicher made some public attacks against the Nazis, but none of these activities affected the election, and the publicity given to Papen and Gayl may well have frightened Schleicher, who drew noticeably away from Papen during these weeks. See Vogelsang, "Zur Politik Schleichers," 104; and Beck, *Prussian Republic,* 148. Following the elections, the author of the *Berlin Diaries* wrote on November 6, 1932 (201): "The country must be governed without the Reichstag! Bravo! Herr Hitler has lost his battle of the Marne. If we don't make any too bad blunders now, his dream has been dreamed once and for all. Schleicher is very well pleased. He will break with Papen, whose number has long been up in any case." For Papen's case against Schleicher, see Papen, *Vom Scheitern einer Demokratie,* 279ff. Subsequent events are recorded in Cab. Mins., November 9, 1932, RK 3598/D791161–68; and Meissner's postwar affidavit, Office of the United States Chief of Counsel for Prosecution of Axis Criminality, *Nazi Conspiracy and Aggression* (hereafter cited as NCA), Suppl. A, 507. By obtaining the cabinet's approval for negotiating with the Nazis, Schleicher had protected himself. If he succeeded, he had precluded any opposition from Neurath and the other ministers. In his memoirs, Gayl was especially angry about Schleicher's maneuver which prevented the cabinet from offering Hindenburg the chance to save a conservative presidential government in Germany. BA, Gayl Nachlass, 53.

12. See Bredow (?), *Berlin Diaries,* 206–207: "Papen is getting one facer after another. . . . The members of the cabinet are beginning to desert him." In the reorganized cabinet which Papen planned, he intended to take over the foreign ministry himself and to give still another position to his good friend Magnus Freiherr von Braun. Information from author's interviews with Franz von Papen and Magnus Freiherr von Braun, July 24 and 16, 1968. Events are recorded in Cab. Mins., November 25, 1932, RK 3598/D791206–15; Schwerin von Krosigk's diary entry for December 4, 1932, printed in Vogelsang, *Reichswehr, Staat, und NSDAP,* 330–31; and Meissner's memorandum, December 2, 1932, printed in Vogelsang, "Zur Politik Schleichers," 105–107. See also remark of November 26, 1932 in the *Berlin Diaries,* 216: "The opposition to a new Papen cabinet grows day by day. Bracht, Schwerin-Krosigk, and Neurath are fanning the blaze."

13. I have closely followed the account as preserved in Schwerin von Krosigk's unpublished diary (IZ) in my description of this meeting. In his published account, Schwerin von Krosigk is strangely silent, while Meissner (*Staatssekretär,* 246) and Braun (*Ostpreussen,* 255) give conflicting reports. In his original memorandum, December 2, 1932 (printed in Vogelsang, "Zur Politik Schleichers," 105–107), Meissner did not even mention a military report. But after the war, he made it the crucial event which changed the mind of the cabinet. See NCA, Suppl. A, 510. Although this interpretation has been adopted by most historians, in discussing my conclusions with Schwerin von Krosigk and Freiherr von Braun, both agreed with my interpretation. Interviews on April 26 and July 16, 1968. No cabinet minutes were apparently taken, but see Vogelsang, *Reichswehr, Staat, und NSDAP,* 332. Papen's numerous postwar versions (e.g., NCA, Suppl. A, 1450–51, *Memoirs,* 216–24, and *Vom Scheitern einer Demokratie,* 310–11) do not stand up to close scrutiny. On the illegitimacy of the Ott report, see Hans Rothfels, "Ausgewählte Briefe von General-major Helmut Stieff," VJHZG, II (1954), 297; and Schleicher's own report to the cabinet November 3, 1932, RK 3598/D791124. Schmidt-Hannover (*Umdenken oder Anarchie,* 313) insists that the war games which Ott cited

did not include the leading generals. But in conversations after the war, Ott assured Schwerin von Krosigk that the games were genuine, and only his own report assembled somewhat hurriedly. Information from author's interview with Schwerin von Krosigk, April 26, 1968.

14. Quotation is from Schleicher's speech to ministry officials, December 13-15, 1932, printed in Thilo Vogelsang, "Neue Dokumente zur Geschichte der Reichswehr 1930-1933," VJHZG, II (1954), 426-27. Subsequent information from Adolf von Carlowitz, cited in Bracher, *Auflösung der Weimarer Republik,* 675 fn. 96; and Braun, *Ostpreussen,* 255. The conclusion that it was the civil service ministers who persuaded Hindenburg is all the more likely in view of their later willingness to go to the president in order to block Papen's reappointment. See Cab. Mins., January 28, 1933, RK 3598/D791597.

15. Schwerin von Krosigk's diary, December 4, 1932, IZ. The first quotation is from Bredow (?), *Berlin Diaries,* December 7, 1932. Information also from author's interviews with Frau von Mackensen and Lutz Graf Schwerin von Krosigk, May 2 and April 26, 1968, who confirm that Neurath did indeed send such a warning to Hindenburg. On July 24, 1968, Franz von Papen told the author that his opponents frequently used Neurath in order to approach Hindenburg without going through the chancellor.

16. Information from Schwerin von Krosigk's diary, IZ, and from author's interviews with Schwerin von Krosigk and Magnus Freiherr von Braun, April 26 and July 16, 1968. For hopes that Schleicher would stabilize domestic politics, see *Der Ring* (organ of the *Herrenklub*), December 9, 1932, 845. For the workings of the new cabinet, see Andreas Dorpalen, *Hindenburg and the Weimar Republic,* 385ff.; Keppler to Hitler, December 19, 1932, printed in Vogelsang, *Reichswehr, Staat, und NSDAP,* 485; Braun, *Ostpreussen,* 261; and Cab. Mins., December 3, 1932, RK 3598/D791245.

17. Cab. Mins., January 16, 1933, printed in Vogelsang, *Reichswehr, Staat, und NSDAP,* 486-88. As early as November 1932, Schwerin von Krosigk had discussed such a cabinet in which the Nazis and Center would share power with the remnants of the presidential appointees. Brüning, however, would replace Neurath at the foreign office. Schwerin von Krosigk's diary entry, November 5, 1932, IZ.

18. Schwerin von Krosigk's diary entry, January 15 and 29, 1933, IZ. For Papen's preliminary talks, see *Frankfurter Zeitung,* January 27, 1933; and Hammerstein, "Schleicher," 122.

19. Schwerin von Krosigk's diary entry, January 29, 1933, IZ, and unsigned memorandum from the president's office, printed in Vogelsang, *Reichswehr, Staat, und NSDAP,* 490-91. Later attempts by army officers to request Hindenburg to reconsider his decision met similar rebuffs. See Hammerstein, "Schleicher," 166; and Hans-Rudolf Berndorff, *General zwischen Ost und West: aus den Geheimnissen der deutschen Republik,* 261.

20. Schwerin von Krosigk's diary entry, January 29, 1933, IZ. On July 24, 1968, Franz von Papen insisted to the author that he did not talk to Neurath about coming into a Hitler cabinet. He had assumed that Hindenburg had worked out all these details. I have been unable to find any confirmation of talks between Hindenburg and Neurath during these days. But given the evidence, it seems Baroness von Neurath was in error in "Lebenslauf," when she wrote that on January 29, "Vice-Chancellor [sic] Papen came on orders from Hindenburg in order to negotiate Neurath's entrance into the new cabinet."

21. Rauschning, *Men,* 172.

22. For Neurath's evaluation of similar developments in Italian fascism, see above, page 26. Information also from author's interviews with Frau von Mackensen, May 2, 1968, and Baroness von Ritter, August 20, 1968, and Mrs. Henriette de Gourko to author, August 1969. For the previous conversation between Hitler and Neurath, see above, page 42.

23. Rauschning, *Men,* 164. Earlier quotation from undated draft for Neurath's

speech, August 1934, AA, RM 1 c, Bd. 18. Conservative sentiment is expressed in Kurt Sontheimer, *Antidemokratisches Denken in der Weimarer Republik,* 332–33.

24. See Bülow to Prittwitz, January 25; Bülow to Dirksen, February 6; and Bülow to Prittwitz, February 6, 1933; in AA 4260/E200027, DGFP C/I, 21, and 22–24. Also see *Der Ring,* February 3, 1933, 75–76. Neurath's two quotations are from "Notizen" and Neurath to AA, December 3, 1930, AA K1976/K512835.

25. Schwerin von Krosigk's diary entries, January 29 and February 5, 1933, IZ. Information also from author's interviews with Franz von Papen and Lutz Graf Schwerin von Krosigk, July 24 and April 26, 1968; and Vogelsang, *Reichswehr, Staat, und NSDAP,* 386. In his postwar trial, Neurath testified that he had informed the president of his reluctance to serve in a Hitler cabinet, but that Hindenburg had insisted that he remain at his post. This interview apparently occurred before Neurath learned that Hitler would be appointed chancellor, in a meeting which discussed various theoretical possibilities. Schwerin von Krosigk told the author, on April 26, 1968, that he always assumed Neurath would stay on as foreign minister, and Meissner told the British ambassador on January 28, 1933 that "Neurath ... would no doubt be included in any government to be formed." Rumbold to Simon, January 28, 1933, DBFP 2/IV, 392. Neurath's testimony is IMT, XVI, 608–609.

26. Schwerin von Krosigk's diary entry, February 5, 1933, IZ. According to another account by an eyewitness (Theodor Düsterberg, *Der Stahlhelm und Hitler,* 74), nearly two hours passed before the ministers finally appeared in Papen's office to go to the president for the 11:00 A.M. ceremony. Neurath might have had an opportunity during this time to speak with Hindenburg, but apparently he did not, preferring to base his willingness to serve on previous conversations with the president. Information from author's interviews with Franz von Papen and Lutz Graf Schwerin von Krosigk, July 24 and April 26, 1968.

27. Rumbold to Simon, February 4, 1933, DBFP 2/IV, 407.

CHAPTER VII. *Neurath and Domestic Issues in the Hitler Cabinet*

1. Although Ambassador Herbert von Dirksen questioned whether Neurath and Blomberg could seize the initiative, most contemporaries ignored this problem. See Dirksen to Bülow, February 12; Rumbold to Simon, February 15; and François-Poncet to Paul-Boncour, February 4, 1933; in AA 4260/E200270; DBFP 2/IV, 421; and DDF 1/II, 562.

2. Neurath, Schwerin von Krosigk (finance), Franz Gürtner (justice), Eltz von Rübenach (transportation), Papen (vice-chancellor), General Werner von Blomberg (defense), Franz Seldte (labor), and Alfred Hugenberg (economics and agriculture) can be considered advocates of a presidential-cabinet system. The Nazis were Chancellor Hitler, Wihelm Frick (interior), and Hermann Göring (without portfolio).

3. For Neurath's views, see Cab. Mins., March 2 and 15, 1933, RK 3598/D791960; and IMT, XXI, 407. For Hitler's orders, see Lammers to all ministers, March 25; and Cab. Mins., March 2 and April 22, 1933; in AA, RM 1 c, Bd. 1; and RK 3598/D791960, and /D792374. For background, see Hans Schneider, "Das Ermächtigungsgesetz vom 24.3.1933," VJHZG, I (1953) 197–221; and Hans Schneider, *Das Ermächtigungsgesetz vom 24. März, 1933,* passim. For Neurath's skeptical attitude toward the Reichstag, see Lipski, *Papers,* 324.

4. Joseph Goebbels, diary entry, April 22, 1933, in *My Part,* 282. For Hitler's refusal to allow debate and his independent action, see Cab. Mins., July 14, September 26, 1933, and January 12, 1934; in DGFP C/I, 652; RK 3598/D793865ff.; and BA, RK R 43/I, 1468. Also see Otto Dietrich, *12 Jahre mit Hitler,* 249; and the good discussion in Eliot B. Wheaton, *Prelude to Calamity: The Nazi Revolution, 1933–1935,* 280ff. Earlier meetings contained about 5 items and required about 8 pages of minutes. The first cabinet session of the new type (July 14, 1933, RK 3598/D793208–50) had an agenda of 40

items, 42 pages of minutes, and 450 pages of documents and drafts. The number of participants rose from an average of 15 in February to more than 30 in June, and after September, proposals for cabinet discussions were to be submitted with 35 copies. See BA, RK RM 3, Bd. 1, and RM 3a, Bd. 6-7.

5. For the extra-cabinet conferences, see DGFP C/I, 647 and 848. For Hitler's effectiveness in these meetings, see Meissner, *Staatssekretär*, 618-19; and Joachim von Ribbentrop, *Zwischen London und Moskau: Erinnerungen und letzte Aufzeichnungen*, 46. The popular press began referring to the cabinet as the "Führerrat," but when a law was introduced on January 2, 1937 to change the cabinet to such an advisory body, Hitler refused to accept it. See Cab. Mins., January 26, 1937, RK 3598/D798500.

6. Neurath made little use of his free access to the president. For his reputation, see Rumbold to Simon, February 15, 1933 (DBFP 2/IV, 421), praising his "sound judgment and the capacity to visualize the consequences at home and abroad of political economic decisions." For Neurath's access to the president, see William E. Dodd, *Ambassador Dodd's Diary, 1933-1938,* 137. For Neurath's attitude, see his memoranda of July and December 1933, AA 6058/E447337-38 and 4619/E197836.

7. Information from author's interview with Baroness von Ritter, July 16, 1968, and Henriette de Gourko to author, November 1970. See also, John L. Heineman, "Constantin von Neurath and German Policy at the London Economic Conference of 1933: Backgrounds to the Resignation of Alfred Hugenberg," *Journal of Modern History*, 41 (1969), 160-88. Papen's low opinion of Neurath is seen in Papen, *Memoirs,* 332 and 342; and in NCA, Suppl. A, 447; and was confirmed in author's interview with Papen, July 24, 1968. Neurath's disdain for Papen is seen in Neurath to Bülow, July 31, 1933 and August 24, 1935; in DGFP C/I, 708, and AA 4619/E198170. Papen's aide and friend Fritz Günther von Tschirschky insisted that the rivalry between Neurath and Papen and his own unbounding ambition drove Neurath closer to Hitler. See ZS 568 (Tschirschky), IZ; and Fritz Günther von Tschirschky, *Erinnerungen eines Hochverräters,* 231ff. I found no other evidence to support this contention.

8. In the first decisions, the civil service ministers supported Hitler against Hugenberg and Papen, the conservative politicians. Neurath's attitude is described in Baroness von Ritter's postwar affidavit, May 28, 1946, IMT, XL, 444-49, and in conversations with the author on July 16 and August 20, 1968. For the general picture of a conservative power bloc, see Herbertus Prince zu Löwenstein, *On Borrowed Peace,* 2. For a true picture of the divided conditions, see Dorpalen, *Hindenburg,* 448-49; and Kordt, *Nicht aus den Akten,* 110. For Hitler's appreciation of Neurath's cooperation, see *Das politische Tagebuch Alfred Rosenbergs aus den Jahren 1934/35 and 1939/40,* ed. Hans-Günther Seraphim (hereafter cited as Rosenberg, *Politische Tagebuch),* 18.

9. See Heineman, "Neurath and London Economic Conference," passim.

10. On June 30, 1933, Hugenberg was replaced by Kurt Schmitt as minister of economics and Walter Darré as minister of food and agriculture. Both were Nazis. In December, Ernst Röhm and Rudolf Hess were given cabinet rank, but Röhm never attended meetings.

11. For Papen's lonely battles against dismissal of Catholics, sterilization, castration and cremation, see Cab. Mins., April 7, July 14, November 14, 1933, and May 15, 1934; in BA, RK R43/I, 1461-1469. In an interview with the author on July 24, 1968, Papen complained that each minister pretty much stuck to his own business; only he was interested in raising the general and broad questions which, he said, might embarrass Hitler.

12. From the diary of Mayor Krogmann of Hamburg, May 4, 1933, recording talks with Walter Funk and Hans Pfundtner of the ministries of the interior and economics. Forschungsstelle für die Geschichte des Nationalsozialismus, Hamburg (hereafter cited as FGN), Aussenpolitik 21, K-5. On those occasions when the conservatives did unite, Hitler inevitably gave way. See, for example, his dropping of the idea of a government

subsidy for the Nazi campaign after Neurath, Gürtner, and Schwerin von Krosigk opposed it. Cab. Mins., February 2, 1933, DGFP C/I, 18. For a strong criticism of these ministers, see Tschirschky, *Erinnerungen,* 231ff.

13. The quotation is Neurath to AA, April 12, 1925, AA 4913H/E255744. Information from author's interviews with Frau von Mackensen, Constantin von Neurath, and Baroness von Ritter, May 2, May 7, and July 16, 1968. The metaphor is from Baroness von Ritter's postwar affidavit, May 28, 1946, IMT, XL, 446. For the pseudo-conservatism, see Sontheimer, *Antidemokratisches Denken,* passim; and Klemens von Klemperer, *Germany's New Conservatism: Its History and Dilemma in the Twentieth Century,* passim.

14. For the decrees which essentially destroyed the Weimar constitution, see discussion in Karl Dietrich Bracher, *Nationalsozialistische Machtergreifung und Reichskonkordat: ein Gutachten zur Frage des geschichtlichen Zusammenhangs und der politischen Verknüpfung von Reichskonkordat und nationalsozialistischer Revolution,* 84ff. Neurath opposed such widespread measures; see Cab. Mins., March 2, 1933, DGFP C/I, 95. The quotation is from "Notizen."

15. Information from author's interview with Baroness von Ritter, July 16, 1968. For Neurath's difficulty in reaching Hitler, see Neurath to Hitler, April 2, 1933; Neurath to Bülow, August 25, 1934; and Phipps to Simon, November 28, 1933; in IMT, XXXV, 524; AA 4619/E198171-72; and DBFP 2/VI, 140. Also see Friedrich Hossbach, *Zwischen Wehrmacht und Hitler, 1934-1938,* 20.

16. Once summoned to the chancellery, he overheard Hitler's voice increasing in intensity behind a closed door. With only a slight hesitation, Neurath turned around and went back to his office, explaining to his companion that he had heard his quota of such ramblings for the month. Information from author's interviews with Baroness von Ritter and Herbert Siegfried, July 16 and May 6, 1968. On Neurath's embarrassment over one outburst from Hitler and his remark to his guest, "It is all terrible," see Phipps to Simon, May 16, 1933, DGFP 2/V, 243.

17. On one occasion, Hitler referred to Neurath as one of those "sterile old men in their second childhood who bragged of their technical knowledge and had lost their sound common sense." He claimed, however, he told them that "what they were up to was good enough for quiet times, when they can all go their sleepy way; but [these men] were not good enough for creating a new Reich. They must take the trouble to learn more modern methods. Neurath is unimaginative. Shrewd as a peasant, but with no ideas." Hermann Rauschning, *Voice of Destruction,* 67 and 275. For Neurath's attitude toward that "fellow" in the chancellery and his flunkeys, information from author's interviews with Baroness von Ritter and Frau von Mackensen, July 16 and May 2, 1968. As a passionate hunter, Neurath was perhaps aware of Hitler's frequent denunciation of that sport. See Dietrich, *12 Jahre,* 25 and 220; and Adolf Hitler, *Hitler's Secret Conversations, 1941-1944* (Harry Picker and Gerhard Ritter, eds.), 77 and 82.

18. Information from Herbert Siegfried, who was present, and from Frau von Mackensen, in interviews with the author, May 6 and July 8, 1968.

19. Estelle Peterson, *Limits of Hitler's Power,* 14. This concept is also delineated in Hans Buchheim, *Anatomie des SS-Staates,* 15. Other information from Hitler, *Secret Conversations,* 85, 106, 306, and 516-17. The last item, dated August 16, 1942, specifically cited Neurath as one of the difficult ministers: "The best method is always to settle the thing directly with the minister concerned," Hitler said, "and thus avoid tedious discussion, in which one will argue from the legal point of view, while another quotes principles of financial orthodoxy. That sort of thing drives me to fury."

20. First quotation from author's interview with Baroness von Ritter, August 20, 1968; second from "Notizen." See also Neurath's protest that he was the foreign minister, not the minister of the interior, in IMT, XVII, 20-26.

21. Köpke's testimony, IMT, XVII, 109. His original draft for this testimony, as

contained in his private papers, is more succinct. He attributed to Neurath the belief that "one must allow such revolutionary elements to develop. The hotheads will themselves develop prudence and reason, if they are given the time and opportunity to gather for themselves experience in responsible positions." Köpke Nachlass.

22. Bertolt Brecht, "Massnahme gegen die Gewalt," *Versuche I*, 22–23.

23. For the attacks upon conservatives, see Bella Fromm, *Blood and Banquets: A Berlin Social Diary*, 152; Walter H. Kaufmann, *Monarchism in the Weimar Republic*, 255; Bracher, *Machtergreifung*, 910ff.; and Bodo Scheurig, *Ewald von Kleist-Schmenzin: ein Konservativer gegen Hitler*, 129–37. Mackensen's appeal is discussed in Görlitz, *Hindenburg*, 418; and Neurath's monarchical ties are mentioned in Dodd, *Diary*, 92; and Schwend, *Bayern*, 524.

24. For the measures against dissenters, see Franz Zipfel, *Kirchenkampf in Deutschland 1933–1945: Religionsverfolgung und Selbstbehauptung der Kirchen in der nationalsozialistischen Zeit*, 400ff., and the general discussion on 35–54. Good also are J. S. Conway, *The Nazi Persecution of the Churches, 1933–1945*, 34ff.; and Hans Buchheim, *Glaubenskrise im Dritten Reich: Drei Kapitel nationalsozialistischer Kirchenpolitik*, 124ff.

25. Wurm to Neurath, March 8, April 3, 11, and 20, 1934; in AA L435/125129, /125182–83, /125218, and /125250–53. Wurm thanked Neurath for arranging a visit with Hitler, which is discussed in Theophil Wurm, *Erinnerungen aus meinem Leben*, 93. For Neurath's memorandum, see Neurath to Frick, April 23, 1934; and Neurath to Lammers, June 18, 1934; and Neurath's memorandum, June 18, 1934; in AA L435/125220, L434/124636, and DGFP C/III, 39–42.

26. See Neurath's memorandum, September 20, 1934, DGFP C/III, 419. Also see Conway, *Nazi Persecution*, 98; Zipfel, *Kirchenkampf*, 51; and Bismarck to AA, September 17, 1934, DGFP C/III, 415–16.

27. Neurath's improved version of an official memorandum, October 16, 1934, DGFP C/III, 486, fn. 4. The quotation about the argument is from Dodd, *Diary*, 180.

28. Neurath's memorandum, September 20, 1934, DGFP C/III, 418.

29. See P. Dietrich, "Die deutsche Landmannschaft: ein Beitrag zur geschichtlichen Entwicklung der DL im Rahmen des deutschen Korporationswesens," *Historia Academica*, 3/4 (1958), 85ff. Nevertheless, in October 1933, the National Socialist Student Organization took over all the independent student groups. See Werner Klose, *Freiheit schreibt auf eure Fahnen: 800 Jahre deutsche Studenten*, 234ff.

30. Neurath to Fontaine, April 12, 1934, Fontaine Nachlass, used with the kind permission of Wolfgang Fontaine.

31. Neurath to the head of the Corps Suevia, May 16, 1934, Fontaine Nachlass. Neurath sent a copy to the head of the Koesener-SC who had been leading the negotiations. Later he asked that this letter be kept secret. Apparently, Neurath sympathized with attempts to preserve the Koesener-SC by having all corps implement the anti-Semitic rule, and had agreed to bring pressure upon his own corps.

32. Neurath to Felix Suren, June 20, 1934, Fontaine Nachlass. Dr. Werner Fontaine was the leader of the Union of Old Tübingen Schwaben, and all the documents are from his files. Only 8 of the more than 860 corps in the ADW refused to follow the new regulations. On April 7, 1934, the *Deutscheburschenschaft* expelled its three corps which had refused to eliminate "non-Aryans and Freemasons." In May 1934, the Koesener-SC expelled Suevia/Tübingen, Borussia/Halle, Vandalia/Heidelberg, Suevia/Munich, and Rhenania/Strassburg zu Marburg. See Horst Bernhardi, "Die Göttingen Burschenschaft 1933 bis 1945," in *Darstellungen und Quellen zur Geschichte der deutschen Einheitsbewegung im neunzehnten und zwanzigsten Jahrhundert*, I (1957), 216; and Hans Peter Bleuel and Ernst Klinnert, *Deutsche Studenten auf dem Weg ins Dritten Reich: Ideologien-Programme-Aktionen, 1918–1935*.

33. Neurath to Fontaine, September 11, and October 23, 1934; and Blunck to Fon-

taine and to Neurath, June 7 and 12, 1934; in Fontaine Nachlass. In September 1935, the Koesener-SC was forced to disband. By skillful maneuvering, the Union of Old Tübingen Schwaben, under Fontaine, preserved its property from being confiscated or transferred to the Nazi organizations. In 1942, the land was sold, and proceeds were distributed among five trustees. Neurath and his son were two of these, and returned the money after the war. Dr. Harald Pickernell to Lüdinghausen (Neurath's defense attorney), June 3, 1946, Neurath Nachlass. See also Bernhardi, "Burschenschaft," 228–41.

34. Fromm, *Blood and Banquets,* 160. Rosenberg's *Politische Tagebuch* is full of angry comments about diplomats who were predicting the imminent fall of the Nazi regime; see 20, 27–38. The remark about "growing pains" is in Papen, *Memoirs,* 331. For Neurath's attitude, see also above, notes 21 and 22.

35. The quotation is François-Poncet to Paul-Boncour, February 28, 1933, DDF 1/II, 710. See also Phipps to Vansittart, May 30; and Phipps to Simon, June 23 and July 4, 1934; in DBFP 2/VI, 715, 775, and 785. For the background of the Röhm massacre, see Bracher, *Machtergreifung,* 928ff.

36. Information from author's discussions with Constantin von Neurath, May 7 and August 20, 1968. I have been unable to locate a copy of his report, but all such documents were apparently destroyed after Ribbentrop took over the foreign office. I have also failed to gain access to the Hassell diaries, still in the possession of the family, which may have some discussion of this incident. Röhm's vacation began on March 29, 1934, according to the *New York Times,* March 30, 1934, 10.

37. Information from author's discussions with Constantin von Neurath, May 7 and August 20, 1968. For the background of SA unrest, see Heinrich Bennecke, *Hitler und die SA,* passim; and Bennecke, *Die Reichswehr und der "Röhm Putsch",* 43ff.; and Robert J. O'Neill, *The German Army and the Nazi Party, 1933–1939,* 35ff. Although none mentions the Neurath episode, his account seems compatible with their conclusions that Röhm was in serious trouble, looking for some way to reassert his authority, and probably did speak in terms of blood in the street. Bracher alone *(Machtergreifung,* 946) denies Röhm even contemplated civil disorders and argues that Hitler invented this theory in order to justify the murders.

38. Information from Vico von Bülow-Schwante, whom Neurath had sent out to determine why guests were delayed in arriving at a reception at the Japanese embassy. Later, he discussed with Neurath the possible causes of the presence of troops in the streets. Subsequently, Bülow-Schwante himself was arrested, and Neurath had to work hard to get him released. Immediately thereafter, before he had heard about his son, Neurath spoke with Bülow-Schwante about resigning. Author's interview with Vico von Bülow-Schwante, May 24, 1968; and Bülow-Schwante to author, September 5, 1963.

39. Neurath, "Notizen." Earlier quotation is from author's conversation with Baroness von Ritter, July 16, 1968. Information also from Neurath, "Lebenslauf"; and from Köpke's notes for postwar testimony, which are more detailed than IMT, XVII, 108, in Köpke Nachlass. Information also from author's interview with Bülow-Schwante, May 24, 1968, and Henriette de Gourko to author, November 1970. See also Rauschning, *Voice,* 167–72.

40. Believing that Hitler would easily win a presidential election, Neurath cooperated in the new law. Neurath, "Notizen." For the succession and the oath, see Cab. Mins., August 1 and October 16, 1934, BA, RK R43/I, 1469 and 1470. Best discussion is in Bracher, *Machtergreifung,* 899ff. and 962ff. Thereafter, Neurath gave a glowing speech supporting the elections of 1934 (see AA, RM 1 c, Bd. 18), but he still preserved his independence, seeking on several occasions to block domestic measures which would "provide propaganda against the German government." See Cab. Mins., December 13, 1934, and June 26, 1935, BA, RK R43/I, 1471 and 1473. He made enough objections that he developed a reputation with Hitler for meddling. Years later, Hitler recalled that his proposals were "systematically rejected" by three ministers, one of whom was Neu-

rath. "And the infuriating thing is," Hitler added, "that most of these laws are no concern of the Ministers mentioned." Hitler, *Secret Conversations,* 516.

41. For background on the anti-Semitic program, see Helmut Krausnick, "The Persecution of the Jews," in Krausnick (ed.), *Anatomy of the SS State,* 23ff.; and Bracher, *Machtergreifung,* 227ff. For the boycott, see Goebbels, *My Part,* 269–71. Although Goebbels had discussed the proposal with Hitler at Berchtesgaden on March 26, the announcement for the March 29 cabinet meeting did not contain it on the agenda. For Neurath's actions, see Rumbold to Simon, April 1; and François-Poncet to Paul-Boncour, April 7, 1933; in DBFP 2/V, 15; and DDF 1/III, 185.

42. François-Poncet to Paul-Boncour, April 1, 5, 7, and 24, 1933; Rumbold to Simon, March 30 and 31, 1933; and Neurath to Hitler, April 2, 1934; in DDF 1/III, 128, 155, 185, and 310ff.; DBFP 2/V, 8 and 14; and NCA, Suppl. A, 951. Neurath subsequently took credit for the compromise solution of a one-day boycott. See Rumbold to Simon, April 1 and 5, 1933, DBFP 2/V, 15 and 25. The rumor of Neurath's attempted resignation is in François-Poncet to Paul-Boncour, April 1, 1933, DDF 1/III, 128.

43. See Aloisi, *Journal,* July 26, 1933, 141. On June 19, Neurath urged Hindenburg to reexamine the racial issue which was damaging Germany's international standing, but in a letter to Hitler of the same date, he did not even mention the Jewish question. See Neurath to Hindenburg, and Neurath to Hitler, June 19, 1933, IMT, XL, 465–70. Ambassador Dodd found Neurath embarrassed, but powerless over this issue. Dodd, *Diary,* 37, 103, and 157. See also affidavit of Madame Marie Trarieux, February 21, 1949, Neurath Nachlass; and Neurath, "Lebenslauf."

44. Information from author's interviews with Albrecht von Kessel, and Hasso von Etzdorf, July 30 and July 3, 1968. Neurath's comments in his speech of September 15, 1933 before foreign press representatives in Berlin follow an attempt by the foreign office to prevent a possible declaration by the League of Nations that German Jews were a "suppressed minority," and hence entitled to League protection. In August 1933, Bülow wrote Neurath that "it would naturally be desirable if the chancellor could say a few soothing words about the Jewish question." When he failed to achieve this, Neurath tried to release an official statement that all Jews were free to return to Germany with guaranteed protection under the law. When this too was rejected by Hitler, Neurath sought and received permission to emphasize that the whole issue was a domestic matter. He then added the particular comment about "cleaning up" German public morals into the text of a speech written weeks before. Later, when he tried to issue an official statement on Jewish rights in Germany, Hitler again refused permission. See Bülow to Neurath, August 1933; Neurath's speech, September 15; Kamphausen's draft for a statement, September 9; Cab. Mins., September 12 and 26, 1933; in AA, RM 1 f, Bd. 8; Schmidt and Grabowsky, *Disarmament,* 212; AA 3147/D665446–52; and DGFP C/I, 796–97 and 839. Nevertheless, when the laws were promulgated, Neurath did little to soften their impact, and insisted that they be applied even to prominent Jews such as Albert Einstein. See Neurath to Bülow, August 18; and Bülow to Pfundtner, August 17, 1933; in AA RM 88, Bd. 2; and AA St. Sek., Pol. A, Bd. 8.

45. Papen correctly notes (*Memoirs,* 286–87) that it was the moderate members of the cabinet who introduced the exclusion decrees. For statistics on Jewish membership in certain professions, see NSDAP to Hencke, April 13, 1933, AA 8787/612178. The nearly 45 decrees adopted between April and December 1933 are discussed in Bruno Blau, *Das Ausnahmerecht für die Juden in Deutschland, 1933 bis 1945,* passim. Hindenburg's letter and Hitler's reply are in Hubatsch, *Hindenburg,* 375–78. Information on Neurath's motives to create a legal situation is from his aide, Herbert Siegfried, in an interview with author, May 6, 1968.

46. Quotation from Albrecht von Kessel in an interview with the author, July 30, 1968.

47. Köpke's affidavit, February 5, 1949, Köpke Nachlass; and Bernhard Lösener, "Als Rassenreferent im Reichsministerium des Innern," VJHZG, IX (1961), 272–76. Accord-

ing to Lösener, some easing of the wording in the decree followed the intervention of Gürtner and Neurath. For background, see Bracher, *Machtergreifung,* 286–87. Neurath's aid for numerous Jews is well documented: Bernhard, *Finis Germaniae,* 149; Köpke's affidavit, February 5, 1949, Köpke Nachlass; author's interviews with Baroness von Ritter, and Walter Poensgen, July 16 and July 4, 1968.

48. For Neurath's protection of his own officials, see page 135. For the general belief that the Nuremberg Laws did not represent a new persecution, see Lösener, "Rassenreferent," 277.

49. Cab. Mins., December 1, 1936, BA, RK R43/I, 1475. See also Huck, "Eltz-Rübenach," 32ff. Huck's account is based on Eltz-Rübenach's report of the session, from the Eltz-Rübenach Nachlass.

50. This story was related to the author in an interview of April 25, 1968 by General Hans Speidel, also a graduate of the Eberhard Gymnasium and present at the celebration.

51. From Eltz-Rübenach's papers printed in Huck, "Eltz-Rübenach," passim, it is clear that the minister wanted to take some stand against the party after the Hitler Youth bill had passed, and awaited a suitable opportunity.

52. Information is from author's interview with Constantin von Neurath [son], May 7, 1968, and his "Personal Reflections of My Father's Relations to the NSDAP and Adolf Hitler," written in July 1945. This document, and a large number of affidavits, belong to the Neurath family lawyer, Dr. Helmut Fischinger, who graciously permitted the author to use them. Hereafter they will be cited as Fischinger Files. All these confirm the brief account in Neurath, "Lebenslauf." In an affidavit of December 18, 1948, Alois Binder, Neurath's chef, noted: "To my knowledge, it was very painful for Baron von Neurath whenever he had to appear in the SS uniform, and he did it only in the rarest of instances, when it could not be avoided." Fischinger Files. His request that his son refuse cooperation with the Nazis after his death seems a little unfair, however, when he was unprepared to do that himself.

53. Neurath's aid to Jews in the foreign service is detailed in *Das Auswärtige Amt der Weimarer Republik,* a house publication of the foreign office. After the anti-Semitic pogrom of November 1938, when Neurath was no longer in the cabinet, Hassell considered him to be "simply lazy and indolent" because he was doing nothing about the disgraceful events. See Ulrich von Hassell, *Vom anderen Deutschland: aus den nachgelassenen Tagebüchern 1938–1944,* 38. For Neurath's efforts on behalf of Paul Löbe, the former Reichstag president, see Bülow to Neurath, August 9; and Neurath to Bülow, August 14, 1933; in AA RM 88, Bd. 2; and DGFP C/I, 742.

CHAPTER VIII. *Neurath's Influence on Foreign Policy: 1933–1936*

1. Neurath, "Notizen." See also Bülow to Smend, June 1, 1929, AA 5270/E325716–18; and Bülow to Koch, April 19, 1931, printed in Stambrook, "German-Austrian Customs Union," 43.

2. The quotation is from François-Poncet to Paul-Boncour, May 9, 1933, DDF 1/III, 460. On August 10, 1932, Neurath had warned the cabinet that "from the foreign policy viewpoint, National Socialist rule would mean the ruin of Germany, since its [political] credit would be entirely dissipated." Cab. Mins., published in Vogelsang, "Zur Politik Schleichers," 96. For the rearmament issue, see Wolfgang Sauer's section in Bracher, *Machtergreifung,* 768ff.; and Post, *Civil-Military Fabric,* 159ff.

3. For Hitler's ideas, see Post, *Civil-Military Fabric,* 341–47; and the excellent studies: E. M. Robertson, *Hitler's Pre-War Policy and Military Plans, 1933–1939,* passim; and Charles Bloch, *Hitler und die europäische Mächte 1933–1934: Kontinuität oder Bruch,* passim. Speaking to a colleague in May 1933, Neurath emphasized that he stayed in office primarily to prevent worse things, "yes even the evil of war." Werner Freiherr von Rheinbaben, *Viermal Deutschland: aus dem Erleben eines Seemanns, Diplomaten, Politikers 1895–1954,* 272–73.

4. Notes by Lieutenant-General Liebmann, printed in Vogelsang, "Neue Dokumente," 434–35. See also discussions in Bracher, *Machtergreifung,* 748ff.; Vogelsang, *Reichswehr, Staat, und NSDAP,* 432; and Karl Dietrich Bracher, "Das Anfangsstadium der Hitlerschen Aussenpolitik," VJHZG, V (1957), 67ff.

5. Quotation is from "Notizen." For Hitler's attitude, see Rauschning, *Voice,* 275–78. The reactions to the speech are from Neurath, "Lebenslauf"; Krausnick, in *Vollmacht,* 203; Sauer in Bracher, *Machtergreifung,* 749 fn. 13; Vogelsang, "Neue Dokumente," 456; and ZS of General Liebmann, IZ.

6. Quotations from "Notizen." For a discussion of the foreign policy bureau, see Gordon to Secretary Hull, April 1, 1933, *Foreign Relations of the United States,* 1933, volume II (hereafter cited as FRUS 1933/II), 217; and François-Poncet to Paul-Boncour, April 1, 1933, DDF 1/III, 127–28. Also see full discussion below, page 122.

7. The Cab. Mins., April 7, 1933 (DGFP C/I, 255–60), contain only a general outline of Neurath's presentation. All quotations are from Bülow's "top secret" draft, which summarized his and Neurath's discussions. March 13, 1933, Deutsche Zentral Archiv, Potsdam (hereafter cited as DZA) 60966.

8. "Notizen."

9. From Neurath's article in *Volk und Reich,* March 3, 1933. For Neurath's position that aggressive initiatives should be avoided "since our intention to rearm would thereby be manifested too soon," see his handwritten note, February 8; Neurath to Nadolny, February 15; Bülow's memorandum, March 4; Neurath's dispatch, March 6; and Rumbold to Simon, March 10, 1933; in AA St. Sek., RM, Bd. 3; DGFP C/I, 43; AA 7360/E536258; AA 7360/E536271–73; and DBFP 2/IV, 501–502. Also see Bülow to Prittwitz, January 19 and February 6; and Bülow's memorandum, February 8, 1933; in AA 4260/E200843–44; and DGFP C/I, 23–24 and 27–28. For the December 11th declaration, see above, page 55.

10. See Neurath's articles in *Deutsche Allgemeine Zeitung,* April 12; *News Chronicle,* May 6; and *Leipziger Illustrierte Zeitung,* May 11, 1933. In all these, he was accused of trying to "out-Hitler Hitler." See François-Poncet to Paul-Boncour, May 11; Vansittart's minute and Rumbold to Simon, May 11; Heywood to Tyrrell, May 16, 1933; in DDF 1/III, 467; DBFP 2/V, 226–27, 227–28, and 260–61; and Aloisi, *Journal,* 120. For foreign office influence on Hitler's speech, see François-Poncet to Paul-Boncour, March 30, and May 18 and 23, 1933, DDF 1/III, 118, 515, and 560–62. Also see Richard Breyer, *Das deutsche Reich und Polen, 1932–1937: Aussenpolitik und Volksgruppenfragen,* 86–88; and Rumbold to Simon, May 17, 1933, DBFP 2/V, 252. The final quotation is from Neurath's speech on September 15, 1933 before foreign press representatives. The foreign office had originally proposed the speech to be delivered by Hitler. See Neurath to Hitler, April 23, 1933 (with enclosed draft); and Völcker's memoranda, September 13 and 15, 1933; in AA RM 1 f, Bd. 8. Selections are printed in Schmidt and Grabowsky (eds.), *Disarmament and Equal Rights,* 211ff. When the chancellor claimed he was too busy, Neurath delivered it himself. The quotation about malicious reports is from Köpke's memorandum, March 23, 1933, AA 3170/675807. For Neurath's fear of being "outvoted in Geneva," see Cab. Mins., May 12, 1933, DGFP C/I, 410.

11. Last quotation is from Neurath to Bülow, July 29, 1933, DGFP C/I, 701. Throughout the critical period from September to October, the decisive influence came from Neurath who noted that Hitler "was entirely in agreement with the course adopted by me at the negotiations." See Neurath's two memoranda of September 27 and 30; and especially his instructions of September 30, 1933; in DGFP C/I, 836–38; AA 4619/E197772; and AA 7360/E537372. By not printing this latter document, the editors of the DGFP permit the erroneous conclusion that Blomberg and Hitler had initiated a new hard line. But see Aloisi, *Journal,* October 5, 1933 (150–51), which noted that the German reply "repeated with greater intransigence what Neurath had said and demanded previously." Also see Neurath to Nadolny, October 11; and Bülow's instructions;

in DGFP C/I, 906–907 (with important sections added in Neurath's hand); and AA 7360/E537622-23. Ambassador Nadolny strongly opposed Neurath's program, motivated, as he admitted in a letter of 1937, by his desire to become foreign minister himself and introduce a new dynamism and initiative in foreign affairs. See Nadolny's draft letter for Hitler, c. May 27, 1937, AA, Nadolny Nachlass, Bd. 17. In this instance he traveled to Berchtesgaden to speak with Hitler, and even appealed over Neurath's head to President Hindenburg. See Nadolny, *Mein Beitrag,* and especially Neurath's anger reported in the original version. Also see Neurath to Nadolny, May 13, 1933, AA 7360/E536741; and Nadolny to AA, October 8 and 10, 1933, AA 7360/E537671-74 and /E537723; and Eden to Simon, October 9, 1933, DBFP 2/V, 668. For a perceptive analysis of Neurath's influence in these events, summarized in the opening quotation of the paragraph, see Arnal to Paul-Boncour, October 12 and 13; and François-Poncet to Paul-Boncour, October 18, 20, November 7, 1933, and especially January 20, 1934; in DDF 1/IV, 560–564, 595–601, 605, 719, and DDF 1/V, 489–90. Neurath's optimism is seen in his penciled remark on a British statement that German military figures "would produce disastrous effects." "Not so far," the minister wrote. Phipps to Hitler, December 20, 1933, DGFP C/II, 261.

12. See Neurath's memorandum, February 10, and Hoesch to AA, March 27, 1934, DGFP C/II, 462 and 681; and Hitler's statement to Rauschning (*Voice,* 155) that he would conclude "any pact which would allow Germany an army of four hundred thousand men, or even three hundred and sixty thousand." For the April 16th program, see Neurath to Hoesch, March 24; Dieckhoff's memorandum, April 14; and Neurath's memorandum, April 16, 1934; in DGFP C/II, 674–75, 742–43, and 747–48. There is no contemporary evidence to support the conclusion (see Gerhard Meinck, *Hitler und die deutsche Aufrüstung, 1933–1937,* 81) that this was a mask for further rearmament. French note is printed in DBFP 2/VI, 630–33. For Neurath's position, see his speech before the foreign press corps, April 27, 1934, AA B154/D669730-42. Also see his memorandum, March 29; and Neurath to Blomberg, May 16, 1934; in DGFP C/II, 688–89 and 821–22. Beck's memorandum is discussed in Wolfgang Foerster, *Generaloberst Ludwig Beck: Sein Kampf gegen den Krieg, aus nachgelassenen Papieren des Generalstabschefs,* 32–33. Final quotation is from Renthe-Fink's memorandum, May 29, 1934, DGFP C/II, 852.

13. Bülow to Neurath, August 16, 1934, DGFP C/III, 329. See also Bülow to Hassell, July 23, 1934, AA 6695/H100726-27; Beck's memorandum of a conversation with Bülow, printed in Foerster, *Generaloberst Beck,* 54; and discussion in Walter Bernhardt, *Die deutsche Aufrüstung 1934–1939,* 34ff. Neurath's quotation is from "Notizen." See also his memoranda, November 16 and 27, 1934, DGFP C/III, 634 and 677–78.

14. See Neurath's memoranda, January 16 and 17; Bülow's draft for Neurath's speech, January 23; and Neurath to missions abroad, January 27, 1935; in DGFP C/III, 821–22, 822, 853–57, and 861–67.

15. Neurath to Hassell, April 4, and Lipski to Beck, February 25 and March 23, 1935, in DGFP C/IV, 9–10, and Lipski, *Papers,* 175 and 180. Claiming that "France had definitely missed the opportunity for a preventive war," Hitler told the cabinet his plan to announce a German Air Force to coincide with the British-French call for immediate limitations on air power. Cab. Mins., January 24, 1935, RK 3598/796752-60. For the Simon visit and subsequent cancellation, see DGFP C/III, 904–905 and 964–65; FRUS, 1935/II, 294–96; and Robertson, *Hitler's Pre-War Policy,* 54–56. Although conscription had been long planned, most military experts wanted it introduced only in October 1935. See General Liebmann's notes, October 9, 1934, IZ; and Krausnick, *Vollmacht,* 257ff. For background to Hitler's decision, see Kordt, *Nicht aus den Akten,* 93; and Hossbach, *Zwischen Wehrmacht und Hitler,* 95–96. Despite the opposition of General von Blomberg, who feared that rapid expansion of the army threatened the esprit of the small officer corps, the matter was apparently not brought up at a cabinet meeting. Although Robert-

son *(Hitler's Pre-War Policy,* 56) suggests the contrary, Neurath's "Lebenslauf" reports only informal discussions outside of the cabinet.

16. Quotations are from author's conversation with Baroness von Ritter, August 20, 1968. Neurath visited the Ritters immediately after the proclamation of conscription.

17. All quotations are from Bülow's draft (March 13, 1933, DZA 60966) which Neurath followed exactly in the cabinet meeting of April 7, 1933.

18. Bülow's draft for Neurath's speech, March 13, 1933, DZA 60966, and author's interview with Constantin von Neurath (July 3, 1968), who considered his father primarily a realist. According to Rauschning *(Men,* 168ff.), Neurath once insisted that "the sphere of international relations was not to be formed . . . by utopian ideas of right, but by the interests of the Great Powers." His idea was to "keep all avenues open."

19. Bülow's draft for Neurath's speech, March 13, 1933, DZA 60966, and information from author's interview with Frau von Mackensen, May 2, 1968.

20. "The Führer," Neurath wired all missions on December 20, 1935, "was of course not thinking of Eupen-Malmedy, for which there can be no question of such recognition of the territorial status quo," and a month later he added: "In my view we should make an attempt to reach a provisional settlement of the Eupen-Malmedy question by negotiations." DGFP C/IV, 931 and 988–94.

21. Bülow's draft for Neurath's speech, March 13, 1933, DZA 60966. See also Dodd, *Diary,* June 25, 1935, 254: "It is not a little curious, but no German official has even intimated to me a German desire for an understanding with the United States."

22. Bülow's draft for Neurath's speech, March 13, 1933, DZA 60966. See also Neurath to Papen, February 9; and Neurath's memorandum, April 27, 1933; in DGFP C/I, 38–41 and 349–50.

23. For the Saar questions, see DDF 1/V, 100–103, 124, 244–47; DBFP 2/V, 714–15, and 2/VI, 123–24 and 141; and Bülow's memoranda, December 5 and 7, 1933, and Hoesch to AA, January 22, 1934; in DGFP C/II, 176–77, 184–87, and 402–404. For subsequent policy, see Neurath to Hindenburg, March 10 and June 8; and Bülow to Paris embassy, June 13, 1934; in DGFP C/II, 584–85, 853 fn. 2, and 905. Also see Neurath, "Skizze," and DDF 1/IV, 340–41, 365–67, and DDF 1/V, 246ff.

24. Quotations from Neurath to Bülow, July 20; Cab. Mins., April 7, 1933; in DGFP C/I, 701, and RK 3598/D792287; and "Skizze." Both the British and French ambassadors believed that Neurath was the author of the hard line. Phipps said he would rather deal with Hitler than with the "more civilized and more calculating Neurath," and the French were openly worried about Neurath's policy to pressure Great Britain in order to get the French in line. See DBFP 2/V, 725ff., and 2/VI, 81, 365–66, and 668; and DDF 1/IV, 756–57, and 1/V, 490ff. For his part, Neurath was sure that "sensible people in England" would sooner or later come to accept the new state of affairs. Neurath's handwritten note on Hoesch to AA, July 20, 1934, DGFP C/III, 200–204; and "Notizen."

25. Neurath told the French that he knew that "through such treaties, they wanted to entangle us in a new net and thereby deprive us of all freedom of movement." He would have none of this. Neurath's memorandum, November 10, 1933, DGFP C/II, 98. See also DDF 1/IV, 733–34; and Köpke's memorandum, November 13, 1933, DGFP C/I, 114–21. In this report, Köpke succinctly restated Neurath's oft expressed conviction that "dilatory talks" were necessary "in order not to grant premature concessions."

26. Information from Neurath, "Lebenslauf," and author's interview with Baroness von Ritter, July 16, 1968. See also Cab. Mins., December 4, 1934, DGFP C/III, 705–706. For Ribbentrop's trips, see Köster to AA, December 1, 1934, DGFP C/III, 696; and Bülow's note that Ribbentrop considered "all diplomats . . . to be complete idiots" (DGFP C/III, 735).

27. Neurath, "Lebenslauf." Even Neurath's staff had predicted the French would not return the Saarland. See DGFP C/III, 450ff. and 567ff.

28. Quotation is from Neurath's memorandum, April 5, 1935, AA 1368/356705. Only an informal agreement to have discussions in London over "Germany's desiderata in the sphere of naval armaments" was produced by the meeting, and even this was omitted in the excerpts of the official memorandum circulated to officials in the foreign office. See DGFP C/III, 1064–65, and Köpke Nachlass.

29. See Neurath's memorandum, February 22, 1933; and Noël to Paul-Boncour, January 19, February 2 and 17, 1933; in DGFP C/I, 68, and DDF 1/II, 469, 554–55, and 647–48. According to Hermann Rauschning (*Hitler Speaks*, 46), the chancellor insisted "the Czechs must get out of central Europe." Best discussion of the background of Czech-German relations is J. W. Brügel, *Tschechen und Deutsche, 1918–1938*, 214ff.

30. Koch to AA, May 22, 1935; earlier quotation from Rödiger to Koch, February 2, 1935, DGFP C/IV, 186–89, and AA 6144/E459637–38. Information on Neurath's attitude from author's interviews with Andor Hencke and Fritz von Twardowski, May 9 and 22, 1968.

31. Stresemann to Deutschen Ostverbände, December 28, 1925; and Stresemann to Sthamer, April 19, 1926; in ADAP B/II/1, 64 and 365. For Berlin's proposals, see Dirksen's memoranda, December 29, 1925 and April 17, 1926, ADAP B/II/1, 73 and 359–61. Final quotation is Rauscher to Dirksen, June 11, 1926, ADAP B/II/2, 7. Another official wrote: "It is totally impossible to bring about an alteration in the Danzig and Corridor questions through peaceful methods." Bernstorf to Kardorff, May 4, 1926, BA, Kardorff Nachlass, Bd. 8. For Berlin's determination, see ADAP B/II/2, 353–55 and 412.

32. Neurath to Papen, February 9, 1933, AA 9214/E647956–57. Partial translation in DGFP C/I, 40. See also Hoesch to AA, November 24, 1932; Bülow's notes on this dispatch; and Neurath's position in Cab. Mins., July 21, 1932; in AA 7474/H185833, /H185835, and RK 3598/D790427.

33. Bülow's draft for Neurath's speech, March 13, 1933, DZA 60966, partially printed in Hans-Adolf Jacobsen, *Misstrauische Nachbarn: Deutsche Ostpolitik 1919–1970*, 91. For background, see Köpke to Schacht, April 26; Moltke to AA, March 11; and Neurath's memorandum, March 16, 1933; in AA 7360/E536521; DGFP C/I, 146–47 and 164; and Hans Roos (pseud. for Hans-Otto Meissner), "Die 'Präventivkriegspläne' Pilsudski von 1933," VJHZG, III (1955), 359–61.

34. First quotation is from Rauschning, *Men*, 170. See also similar comments by Bülow, in Rauschning, *Men*, 166, and Breyer, *Deutsche Reich und Polen*, 91ff. First meeting is described in Lipski, *Papers*, 74, 80–81; and DGFP C/I, 356–57 and 375–76. Subsequently Neurath met Foreign Minister Beck at Geneva; see DGFP C/I, 840, and DDF 1/III, 706, and IV, 623ff. For the November meeting and communique, see Lipski, *Papers*, 96–99; and Meyer to various missions, November 16, and Bülow's memorandum, November 17, 1933, in DGFP C/II, 130 and 135. The draft communique is AA 2945/D575857. Hitler left Berlin immediately, leaving the foreign office to work out details. See DDF 1/V, 42. Best contemporary discussion is François-Poncet to Paul-Boncour, November 16 and 22, 1933, DDF 1/V, 70 and 80–88. See also unsigned "Comments on a German-Polish declaration," November 23, 1933, AA 2945/D575921. Neurath wired the Warsaw Embassy after the signing: "The wording of the declaration in no way implies a recognition of the present German eastern border but, on the contrary, gives expression to the idea that the declaration is to provide a basis for the solution of all problems, including therefore the territorial ones." Neurath to Moltke, November 24, 1933, cited in Breyer, *Deutsche Reich und Polen*, 103. Its omission from the DGFP series leads to such faulty interpretation of Neurath's action as that given by Ludwig Denne, *Das Danzig-Problem in der deutschen Aussenpolitik, 1934–1939*, 98. Breyer, however, also errs in suggesting that Hitler "instinctively" chose the declaration form. Neurath, not Hitler, made this choice. Polish surprise is registered in Lipski to Beck, November 30, 1933, which is also the sole surviving account of the Neurath-Lipski talks. Lipski, *Papers*, 100–103. For the opposition of the German diplomats, see Meissner, *Staatssekretär*, 344–45;

and DeWitt C. Poole, "Light on Nazi Foreign Policy," *Foreign Affairs,* XXV (1946), 134.

35. See Neurath to Moltke, November 14, 1934, DGFP C/III, 625–28. Earlier quotations are Hassell to Neurath, October 6, 1933; and Moltke to AA, October 16, 1934; in DZA 90751 and AA 6177/E464987–95. See also Cab. Mins., April 18, 1934; and Neurath's minute, July 23, 1935; in DGFP C/II, 755, and DGFP C/IV, 458 fn. 6. For the Danzig problem, see documents in DGFP C/III, and Lipski, *Papers,* 208ff.

36. See Marck's memorandum, n.d.; Dirksen to Meyer, June 7; Meyer to Dirksen, June 15 and August 23, 1932; in AA 7474/H186247–48, 9187/H249250, and AA Handakten Meyer. See also Max Beloff, *The Foreign Policy of Soviet Russia, 1929–1941,* I, 58ff. For background, see Theodor Schieder, *Die Probleme des Rapallo-Vertrags: eine Studie über die deutsch-russischen Beziehungen, 1922–1926;* and Hans W. Gatzke, *Stresemann and the Rearmament of Germany.* For the best study of the post-1933 relations, see Karlheinz Niclauss, *Die Sowjetunion und Hitlers Machtergreifung: eine Studie über die deutsch-russischen Beziehungen der Jahre 1929 bis 1935,* especially 58ff.; and Philipp W. Fabry, *Die Sowjetunion und das Dritte Reich: eine dokumentierte Geschichte der deutsch-sowjetischen Beziehungen von 1933 bis 1941.* Neurath's goals are described in "Skizze."

37. Neurath's memorandum, February 15; and Neurath to Meissner, March 29, 1933; in DGFP C/I, 22 fn. 5; and AA, Büro RM, Russia, Bd. 28. See also François-Poncet to Paul-Boncour, May 3, 1933, DDF 1/III, 409–410; and Niclauss, *Sowjetunion,* 122–130. Information also from "Skizze"; and Herbert von Dirksen, *Moscow, Tokyo, London: Twenty Years of German Foreign Policy,* 109.

38. Information on Nadolny from letters in AA, Nadolny Nachlass. Within the service, he was not much liked because of his tactless and undiplomatic temperament. Information from author's interviews with numerous diplomats, especially Herbert Siegfried, May 6, 1968. See also instructions for Nadolny, November 11, 1933; and Bülow's notes, September 26, 1933; in DGFP C/II, 122–23, and C/I, 850–51. Earlier information from Bülow's draft for Neurath's cabinet speech, March 13, 1933, DZA 60966. For discussion of Soviet suspicions even before Hitler came to power, see Payart to Paul-Boncour, June 2, 1933, DDF 1/III, 630–33. Neurath reported in "Skizze" that when he tried to get Hitler to tone down the Nazi party's anti-Communism, the chancellor refused, claiming it was the "principal ingredient which held the party together."

39. Neurath to Nadolny, January 17, 1933, DGFP C/II, 375. Three weeks later, the foreign office had to repeat: "From the standpoint of our policy as a whole ... the time has not yet come for an active policy toward Russia in domestic or foreign policy. Therefore 'cool reserve' is advisable." Bülow to Nadolny, February 12, 1934, DGFP C/II, 476. Neurath was more accurate than Nadolny in his evaluation of the Soviet atmosphere; see Alphand to Paul-Boncour, January 4, 1934, DDF 1/V, 400–401. For Nadolny's unauthorized activities within two months, see DGFP C/II, 202–203, 210, 226, 301, 331, 333, 338, and 352. Information on his staff's suspicions of these activities comes from author's interview with Fritz von Twardowski, May 22, 1968.

40. Neurath's memorandum, June 13; Siegfried's undated record of a telephone conversation; and Nadolny to AA, March 28, 1934; in DGFP C/III, 903; AA Abtl. IV, Russia, PO 2, Geheimakten, Bd. 1; and DGFP C/III, 683–85. There is little evidence to support Niclauss's conclusion (*Sowjetunion,* 171) that Litvinov's proposals aimed at restoring Soviet-German relations. Only Nadolny interpreted the move in that spirit, and he was always looking for signs of reconciliation. For the Baltic pact, see DGFP C/II, 367–79 and 373–75; and DDF 1/V, 499–500, 516–17, and 834–35. For the controversy with Nadolny, see Bülow to Nadolny, February 12; and Neurath's memorandum, November 14, 1933; in DGFP C/II, 474–78, and DGFP C/III, 98; and Lipski to Beck, July 13, 1934, Lipski, *Papers,* 148–50.

41. The AA memorandum, May 31, 1934, is printed in DGFP C/II, 862. For

Nadolny's proposals, see DGFP C/II, 739-40, 763-64, 775-76, and 863-67; and Nadolny, *Mein Beitrag,* 167ff. For the meeting, see letters between Nadolny and Meissner, April through May, 1937, in AA, Nadolny Nachlass, Bd. 17. Neurath's second memorandum has not been found. For discussion, see Erich Kordt, *Wahn und Wirklichkeit: die Aussenpolitik des Dritten Reiche. Versuch einer Darstellung,* 63ff.; and Gustaf Hilger and Alfred Meyer, *The Incompatible Allies: A Memoir-History of German-Soviet Relations, 1918-1941,* 263ff. For Nadolny in Berlin, see DGFP C/III, 860-67 and 882-83.

42. Neurath's memorandum of a conversation with Hitler, July 17, 1934, DGFP C/IV, 183. For Neurath's position, see his memorandum, June 13; Bülow's memorandum, October 25; Bülow to Schulenburg, October 26; and Meyer's memorandum, November 27, 1934; in DGFP C/III, 903, and C/IV, 532, 532-33, and 682-85. See also Carl E. Schorske, "Two German Ambassadors: Dirksen and Schulenburg," in Craig and Gilbert, (eds.), *Diplomats,* 488ff.

43. First quotation is in Lipski to Beck, July 13, 1934, Lipski, *Papers,* 148-50. Second is from Neurath's circular, July 17, 1934, DGFP C/III, 182. For Soviet assurances, see Schulenberg to AA, May 8; and Tippelskirch's memorandum, June 27, 1935; in DGFP C/IV, 138 and 372-73. The French documents confirm the difficulties to be overcome in drawing a real alliance. See DDF 1/IV, 165-67, 234-36, 271-74, 402-405, 535-42, and 677-79. For foreign office nonchalance, see DGFP C/III, 852-58; C/IV, 128-30; and Lipski, *Papers,* 179-82. The best exposition of this policy is a lengthy survey written in October 1935 by the longtime head of the East European desk, Richard Meyer, AA 6609/E497544-60. Meyer, Neurath's principal advisor on Eastern relations, was forced to retire because he was Jewish. Although Weinberg (*Foreign Policy,* 74-75) stresses that Hitler had some strong ideas of his own concerning the Soviet Union, he too admits that during the years under consideration, Hitler left the foreign office alone to wrestle as best it could with the problems.

44. See Dieter Ross, *Hitler und Dollfuss,* passim; Hans-Adolf Jacobsen, *Nationalsozialistische Aussenpolitik, 1933-1938,* 391ff.; and Bracher, "Anfangsstadium," 67ff.

45. See Adolf Hitler, *Mein Kampf;* Hitler, *Hitler's Secret Book* (Gerhard L. Weinberg, ed.); and discussion in Walter Werner Pese, "Hitler und Italien," VJHZG, III (1955), 113-26. In November 1922, Italian diplomats informed Mussolini that Hitler had said "for us, the South Tyrol question does not exist and will not exist in the future." See *Documenti Diplomatici Italiani,* 7th Series, 1922-1925, vol. I, p. 80 (hereafter cited as DDI 7/I, 80). Neurath was also aware of Hitler's ideas regarding Italy, for Schleicher informed his cabinet that Hitler demanded "a complete change of course in foreign policy. He wants to come to an understanding with Italy and turn against France." Cab. Mins., November 25, 1932, RK 3598/D791212. For Neurath's policy, see Neurath to Hassell, November 5, 1932; January 5, and February 7, 1933; and Köpke to Hassell, February 20, 1933; in AA 7474/H185407, 7680/E547644-49, DGFP C/I, 29-34, and 57-60.

46. The best discussion of the negotiations is Konrad Jarausch, *The Four Power Pact, 1933;* and Lothar Krecker, "Die diplomatischen Verhandlung über den Viererpakt vom Juli 1933," *Die Welt als Geschichte,* XXI (1961), 227-37. For Neurath's position, see Hassell to AA, March 10; Neurath's memorandum, March 14; Neurath to Hassell, March 24, April 5 and 12, 1933; in DGFP C/I, 132-34, 160-63, 211-17, 248, and 284-86. See also documents in DDF 1/II, 729-32, 757-61, 775-76; 1/III, 15-25, 33-38, 196-203; and DBFP 2/V, 56-57, 67ff., 76-80, 100-104.

47. See Neurath's report, Cab. Mins., May 12, 1933, RK 3598/D792586-87; and Hassell to Neurath, February 7; Neurath to Hassell, May 4 and 5; Neurath's memoranda, May 20 and 22, 1933; in DZA 60942; DGFP C/I, 377; AA 3170D/676187; DGFP C/I, 471 and 478-79. See also DDF 1/III, 329-30, 367-78, and 511-15; and DBFP 2/V, 364-65. For Neurath's actions over Göring, see his memorandum and note to the Italian ambassador, May 20; and his memoranda, May 22 and 24, 1933; in DGFP C/

I, 471 fn. 5, 478–79, and 482. On Göring's activities in Rome, see DDF 1/III, 530–32 and 545–48.

48. Neurath's quotations are reported in François-Poncet to Paul-Boncour, May 20 and June 8, 1933, DDF 1/III, 586, and 650–51. See also Graham to Simon, June 19, 1933, DBFP 2/V, 370. The negative AA position is seen in DGFP C/I, 57–60, 524–26, and 690. For French fears and reactions, see DDF 1/III, 644, 650, and 658. When the pact was finally signed in July 1933, it was already outdated and useless. It was neither the diplomatic accomplishment which Jarausch implies (*Four Power Pact*, passim), nor the embryo of the later Axis, as suggested by Paul Reynaud, *In the Thick of the Fight, 1930–1945*, 30.

49. In 1935, Hassell claimed that he had sent "sixteen reports, telegrams reporting further discussions with Mussolini, and private letters," in eight months, but still "Berlin had failed to respond to the idea." Undated memorandum, DGFP C/IV, 104–105. See also his various reports in DGFP C/I and C/II, and the reactions, well summarized by Köpke's remark on one dispatch: "Hassell, ceterum censeo!" DGFP C/II, 626, fn. 15. For Neurath's strong pressure, see Neurath to Lammers, March 20, 1934, DGFP C/II, 648–49.

50. For the background of the visit, see documents in DGFP C/II, 690ff. Hassell was under a cloud because of poor reporting, and officials were not impressed with his arguments. See especially AA 4260/E200420–26; 3086/D617469–74; and DGFP C/II, 685–86 and 735–36. For Hitler's motivations, see Weinberg, *Foreign Policy*, 98. After the war, Neurath called the meeting "not at all satisfactory," but there is very little documentation on his attitude. See NCA, Suppl. B, 1492; Aloisi, *Journal*, 198; and DGFP C/III, 63 and 65–66. The phrase attributed to Neurath is from Elisabeth Wiskemann, *The Rome-Berlin Axis: A History of the Relations Between Hitler and Mussolini*, 36. Impressions of the meeting were given to the author by Herbert Siegfried on May 6, 1968. See also André François-Poncet, *Souvenirs d'une ambassade à Berlin, Septembre 1931–Octobre 1938*, 130–31 and 239; and Fritz Wiedemann, *Der Man der Feldherr werden wollte: Erlebnisse und Erfahrungen des Vorgesetzten Hitlers im 1. Weltkrieg und seines späteren persönlichen Adjutanten*, 64.

51. Quotation is from Köpke's minute of conversations, March 29, 1926, ADAP B/III, 213. See also Stresemann's memorandum, printed in Jürgen Gehl, *Austria, Germany and the Anschluss, 1931–1938*, 4. The other good discussion is Nicholas von Preradovich, *Die Wilhelmstrasse und die Anschluss Österreichs, 1918–1933*. For Neurath's attitude, see ADAP B/III, 353–54.

52. Quotation is from Neurath to Hassell, February 7, 1933, DGFP C/I, 30; words are emphasized in the original. For background, see Neurath's memoranda, September 6 and November 12, 1932; and Kordt's memorandum, January 11, 1933; in AA, St. Sek., RM, Bd. 3; and AA 3086/D616407. See also DBFP 2/V, 60; and IMT, XXI, 402–409. Good discussion in Ulrich Eichstädt, *Von Dollfuss zu Hitler: Geschichte des Anschlusses Österreichs, 1933–1938*, 23ff.

53. AA 6077/E450600–602. Full discussion in Bülow's draft for Neurath's cabinet speech, March 13, 1933, DZA 60966. See also Köpke to Rieth, March 22, 1933, DGFP C/I, 193–94; and Ross, *Dollfuss*, 19ff.

54. See Köpke's memorandum, March 23, 1933, DGFP C/I, 207. For the discussions within the foreign office, see Köpke to Schoen, April 10; and Lammers to Neurath, May 4, 1933; in AA 6077/E450613–14 and 3086/D616474. Also see Ross, *Dollfuss*, 163.

55. Heeren's memorandum, May 20, 1933, DGFP C/I, 475. For the background and deliberations, see Neurath's memorandum, May 10; Köpke's memorandum, March 23; and Köpke to Schoen, April 10, 1933; in DGFP C/I 397–98, 206–207; and AA 6077/E450613–14. For criticism that Neurath was simply bowing before Hitler, see François-Poncet to Paul-Boncour, July 13, 1933, DDF 1/III, 889. The evidence does not, in my opinion, support this or Ross's argument (*Dollfuss*, 36ff.). Neurath was not constantly

changing his mind, but pursuing a rather straightforward course, against heavy opposition from Hitler.

56. See Völcker's memorandum, May 10, 1933; and Cab. Mins., May 26, 1933; in AA 3086/D616495-97 and DGFP C/I, 487-90. In the meeting, Neurath's strong opposition was weakened by his opening declaration of "agreement in principle" with pressure upon Austria. Shortly before this meeting, Bülow and Neurath reportedly told the British ambassador that they were in danger of losing their positions because of opposition to Nazi activities in Austria. Other rumors circulated in the capital about Neurath's weakened power base. See Phipps to Simon, May 16; and François-Poncet to Paul-Boncour, May 24 and 27, 1933; in DGFP 2/V, 243; DDF 1/III, 567-69; and 581.

57. According to a note by Köpke, "the Führer discusses all Austrian questions only with Inspector Habicht." June 19, 1933, AA, Abtl. II, Austria, PO 20, Bd. 1. See also François-Poncet to Paul-Boncour, May 24, 1933, DDF 1/III, 567ff. Neurath was well aware of the inherent dangers of involvement in Austria, but suspected (correctly) that Great Britain and France were not entirely pleased by Dollfuss's growing dictatorship. See documents in DDF 1/III, especially 41, 290-91, 374-75, and 493. He could, however, intervene only after evidence arrived concerning the dangers of foreign actions. For Habicht's optimism, see Heeren and Bülow's memoranda, July 31, 1933, in AA 3086/D616627-32 and DGFP C/I, 708-712. For the office's fears that some "disaster could occur over the Austrian affair," see Ross, *Dollfuss,* 64ff. When he learned (perhaps through an intercept of DDF 1/IV, 73-75) that the major powers were planning a common protest, Neurath moved rapidly to avert it. See Neurath, "Lebenslauf," and documents in DGFP C/I, 707-708, 718-19, 732, 740-41, 763-66, 770-72, and AA 2784/540208-11. For Neurath's satisfaction with his success, see memorandum, December 13, 1933, DGFP C/II, 224-25. His whole program is documented in Köpke's postwar affidavit, February 5, 1949, Köpke Nachlass. The recently published French documents show that other diplomats correctly perceived Neurath's program and worried lest Dollfuss lose a majority in the country. If that happened, they concluded, "no foreign power will be able to save him." See DDF 1/IV, 177-78, 195, 439, and 1/V, 346-47, 471-72, and 577.

58. See Rieth to AA, February 10 and 15; and evaluation in François-Poncet to Barthou, February 26, 1934; in DGFP C/II, 464-67 and 482; and DDF 1/V, 823. Best discussion of Habicht's role is Ross, *Dollfuss,* 101-125. Concerning the deportation plans, the diplomats learned that "while there had been talks between the chancellor and [Habicht] the chancellor had not quite expressed himself so decisively as the publication issued by [Habicht's office] might indicate." See Renthe-Fink's memorandum, January 17; and Neurath's memorandum, January 17, 1934; in AA 8663/E606483-84, and 3086/D617141. For Neurath's protests, see DGFP C/II, 437-38 and 466. The best summary of the policy then in effect comes from the French ambassador. Hitler, he wrote, did not desire Anschluss but only a National Socialist Austria, "which would continue to have an independent international life and which would remain in that situation as long as he judges suitable or as long as it is indispensable for peace." François-Poncet to Paul-Boncour, December 6, 1933, DDF 1/V, 177-79.

59. See Neurath's memorandum and Neurath to Hassell, February 16; and Köpke's memorandum, February 23, 1934; in DGFP C/II, 492-93, 494-95; and AA, Abtl. II, Austria PO 20, Bd. 1. For Mussolini's threats to defend Austria, "even in the trenches of Vienna," see Chambrun to Paul-Boncour, November 7, 1933 and February 7, 1934; and Puaux to Paul-Boncour, January 20, 1934; in DDF 1/IV, 721; and 1/V, 650-51 and 492. Other information from François-Poncet's dispatches, DDF 1/III, 46-47, and 1/V, 703-705, and 779-82.

60. The secret source for Neurath's report seems to be Barthou to Chambrun, March 1 and 2, 1934, but it is unknown how the foreign office obtained copies. That Neurath had already talked to Hitler about them is clear, however, from the chancellor's rages on

March 9 about Italy's presumptuous behavior "to install its domination over the entire Danubian valley." See DDF 1/V 847–48, 860–61, 910–11; and Neurath's memorandum, March 9, 1934, DGFP C/II, 577: The quotation is from Köpke to Rieth, March 15, 1934, DGFP C/II, 614–15. For the rest, see DGFP C/II, 598–99, 616–17, and 728. I cannot accept Ross's conclusions (*Dollfuss,* 189ff.) that "there is no evidence that the foreign office was actively involved with the determination of the new program." True, Neurath did not pound on the table until Hitler adopted a new approach, but when events forced even Hitler to be aware of the intolerable situation, he picked the alternative closest to hand—that of Neurath and the foreign office. Unfortunately, no documents exist from these talks with the chancellor.

61. Quotation is from Bülow's memorandum, April 10, 1934, DGFP C/II, 735–36. For background see Bülow to Neurath, April 7; and Neurath's directive, May 20, 1934; in AA 3086/D617464–74, and B154/D669536. With typical lack of understanding, Papen (*Memoirs,* 331) attributed Neurath's opposition to the meeting as resentment of "my intervention in his affairs." For rumors of Nazi discontent, see Neurath to Frick, May 24; and Köpke's memorandum, May 31, 1934; in DGFP C/II, 839–41; and IMT, XXXV, 617ff. Although the latter document was successfully used at the postwar trial to prove that Neurath had approved a Nazi uprising in Austria, recent scholarship (e.g., Ross, *Dollfuss,* 214–18) has shown that these rumors had no substance and that Neurath was justified in dismissing such a possibility.

62. Best analysis of Hitler's involvement is in Ross, *Dollfuss,* 228ff.; and Helmut Auerbach, "Eine nationalsozialistische Stimme zum Wiener Putsch vom 25. Juli 1934," VJHZG, XII (1964), 208ff. For Neurath's attitude, see "Lebenslauf"; and his conversation about conflicts with the SA, reported in Drummond to Simon, June 20, 1934, DBFP 2/VI, 763. Concerning the Venice meeting, see Renthe-Fink's memorandum, June 7, 1934, AA 6114/E454267–72. Ross (*Dollfuss,* 221ff.) has misunderstood Neurath's goal; removing the talks from the party level had already been accomplished. The danger lay in action from Rome, not Munich.

63. See Bülow's memoranda, July 26 and 27, 1934, DGFP C/III, 235–41 and 251; and Neurath to Köpke, July 28–29, 1934, Köpke Nachlass, excerpts printed in IMT, XL, 500–501. Papen overestimated his own contributions to the solution, for Neurath had discussed ways of easing the crisis, even before Papen's name came up for debate. See Papen, *Memoirs,* 229; NCA, Suppl. A, 438–42; and Tschirschky, *Erinnerungen,* 215. See also documents in DGFP C/III, 271–72, 299, and 352–53.

64. See Neurath's note on Papen to AA, November 3, 1934; and Bülow's circular, February 6, 1936; in DGFP C/III, 566 fn. 7; and C/IV, 1099. Papen summarized his own program in a dispatch to Hitler, July 27, 1935, which Neurath contemptuously dismissed. See DGFP C/IV, 496–502. For earlier quotations and background, see Bülow to Lammers, August 22; and Köpke to Hassell, October 23, 1934; in DGFP C/III, 356 and 525–28. Franz von Papen told the author on July 24, 1968, that Neurath consistently undercut his efforts to achieve an international agreement over Austria in 1934–1935. This is perfectly correct, but out of reasons of policy, not—as Papen and more recently Tschirschky have maintained—because Neurath was jealous. See AA 4260/E200810, and DGFP C/III, 336–43 and 463–66. For involvement with Hassell over the same problem, see AA 6001/E443041–44, and DGFP C/III, 300–305, 321–25, 455–59, 472–73, and 523–24.

65. Neurath to Hassell, April 1, 1935, DGFP C/IV, 9. The clearest rejection of Hassell's position is Neurath to Hassell, October 13, 1934, AA 7824/E567407–409. See also DGFP C/III, 525–28, and C/IV, 347–48 and 429–433, with Köpke's sarcastic "How, pray?" beside one suggestion. Weinberg's conclusion (*Foreign Policy,* 50 fn. 97) that Neurath bore a grudge against Hassell and feared him as a possible rival is in error. The majority of German diplomats shared a dislike for Hassell's pressure politics. Like some other ambassadors, he was more the representative *for* Italy, than *of* Germany. See

Köpke's remarks on Hassell to AA, June 21, 1935, DGFP C/IV, 337–39. Information also from author's interviews with Frau von Mackensen, Baroness von Ritter, and Herbert Siegfried, May 2, July 16, and May 6, 1968.

66. Quotation is Neurath to Hassell, June 24, 1935. Paragraphs separated by author, DGFP C/IV, 348. Earlier quotations are Hassell to AA, July 5, 1935; and Neurath's memorandum May 2, 1935; in DGFP C/IV, 417–19, and 113–14. Hitler accepted the policy summarized in Bülow's memorandum with Neurath's comments, August 19, 1935, DGFP C/IV, 348 and 563–65. Hassell's recommendations are found in DGFP C/IV, 523–24, 661–62, 684–91, 732–33, and 417–19. Once aware of Neurath's objections, Hassell tried to use personal influence with Hitler; see Hassell to AA, October 3, 1935, DGFP C/IV, 693–94. Despite the good press Hassell has enjoyed with historians (as a result of his later resistance), Neurath's program was certainly more perceptive. As late as 1937, Neurath was using all his influence to prevent a permanent alliance between Italy and Germany. See Mackensen's memorandum, October 7, 1935, AA 8006/E576545–65; and a series of documents in DGFP C/IV, 693, 703, 709, 727–28, 777–78, 794–96, 797–99, and 803 shows his concern to gain a neutrality declaration during the Abyssinian war.

67. See in particular Bülow's circular, February 6, 1936; and various documents in DGFP C/IV, 1096–99, 1100–1101, 1130–33, and 1204–1207. For the different approaches to Italy, see Neurath's comments on Attolico to Neurath, October 21; and Neurath to Bergen, November 13, 1935; in DGFP C/IV, 764–65, and 814–15. For other items, see Hassell to AA, October 17; and Neurath's remarks to Lipski, November 30, 1935; in DGFP C/IV, 744–47, and Lipski, *Papers*, 233–36. Also see Hassell to AA, January 7; Altenberg's memorandum, January 9; and Neurath to Papen, January 24, 1936; in DGFP C/IV, 974–77, 978–80, and 1028–31.

68. Quotation is from "Notizen." For recognition of Neurath's decent intentions, see François-Poncet to Paul-Boncour, June 4, 1933, DDF 1/III, 646–51. Baroness von Ritter informed the author that a friend of hers once quoted Hitler as saying that Neurath always loomed before him as his conscience. Interview of August 20, 1968.

69. See Neurath to Bülow, and Neurath to Hitler, August 7; Neurath to Hitler, September 2; and Neurath to Bülow, September 2, 1935; in DGFP C/IV, 542–43, 543–45, 605, and 606. Throughout the discussions, Neurath reported that Hitler expressed "complete agreement with our conception on tactics." Neurath's circular and memorandum, July 1934, DGFP C/III, 164–69 and 183. For the background and Neurath's negative attitude toward the pact proposals, even before talking to the chancellor, see Neurath to missions, June 8, 1934, DGFP C/II, 885–87; Lipski, *Papers*, 148–50, 153–57, and ff.; and DGFP C/III, 325–30; Köpke's memorandum, December 31, 1934, AA 2406/E510904–905; Bülow's memorandum for Neurath, January 23, 1935, DGFP C/III, 852–57; Neurath to embassies in Italy and France, January 27, 1935, DGFP C/III, 866; and Neurath's handwritten comment on Hoesch to AA, July 24, 1935, DGFP C/IV, 471–74. Official policy was confirmed in Neurath's conversations with Hitler; see DGFP C/III, 822, 839, and 858. The foreign office rejected the pact believing that "in its present form the Eastern Pact is directed against us and aims at putting new shackles on us." See DGFP C/III, 325–30.

70. Neurath to Köster, December 3, 1935, DGFP C/IV, 873. My emphasis. See also the analysis in François-Poncet to Laval, January 2, 1936, DDF 2/I, 3–9.

71. For French and British concern that the French-Soviet pact violated Locarno, see DDF 1/V, 234–36, 535–42, and 677–79; and DBFP 2/VI, 803ff. Especially at the first session of these meetings, Barthou admitted that unless the Soviet Union entered the League of Nations, and was thus covered by the general terms of the Covenant, "France could not give any guarantee in respect to a Treaty of Mutual Assistance in the East." Neurath's arguments closely paralleled those of the French ministers themselves. For German protests, see DGFP C/IV, 130–31 and 202–206.

72. Earlier quotation is from Neurath's dispatch, March 5, 1936, DGFP C/V, 12. For the discussions within the foreign office, the principals included Neurath, Bülow, Köpke, and the enigmatic director of the legal division, Friedrich Gaus. Neurath first raised the issue in the Simon-Hitler talks on March 25, 1935. Bülow spoke of the "dangerous military connection," on April 16, and Köpke wired Hassell on May 7: "You might also hint that, to your knowledge, Berlin is very seriously studying the difficult question of whether the Franco-Russian Pact is compatible with Locarno." Bülow's circular of the same date indicated similar concerns. See DGFP C/III, 1055; and C/IV, 58–60, 130, and 131.

73. Neurath's memorandum, AA 1368/356722-24; and Neurath to Hoesch, May 8, 1935, DGFP C/IV, 138. Neurath expected little from the naval talks, but thought they would prolong discussions. He accepted Ribbentrop as head of the delegation precisely because he and the diplomats considered them "negotiations of a technical character." Hoesch to AA, May 7, 1935, DGFP C/IV, 132.

74. Hitler's speech, DGFP C/IV, 171–79. According to Dodd (*Diary,* May 15, 242) Neurath told him "he had sent Hitler a memorandum on what ought to be said." I have been unable to find such a draft, but assume there was one, for a close comparison of this speech with known foreign office positions reveals Neurath's hand.

75. Cab. Mins., December 13, 1935; and Neurath's memorandum, December 16, 1935; in DGFP C/IV, 914 and 919. As early as November 18, Laval had made overtures in Berlin. Although Neurath eventually concluded that the move was solely motivated by domestic conditions, he was optimistic that future developments would bring France to the negotiating table. See DGFP C/IV, 825–29, 859–62, 866–68, 915–17, and 925–26. See also his memorandum of November 19; and Neurath to Köster, December 3, 1935; in DGFP C/IV, 835–37 and 872–74. For foreign reactions, see Neurath to all missions, July 27, 1935, DGFP C/IV, 492. Rumors are found in diary entry of October 28, 1935, in Fromm, *Blood and Banquets,* 209. Although the French documents are not yet available, see André François-Poncet's account of his alarming reports of November 21 and 26, and December 31, 1935, in *The Fateful Years: Memoirs of a French Ambassador,* 188–90.

76. Foreign diplomatic reports are in DDF 2/I, 1, 40–42, 71–76; FRUS, 1936/I, 181; and DGFP 2/IV, 998–1000. The foreign office position papers are AA 7881/E570782-93, /E570806, and /E570751-66. Information is from François-Poncet to Laval, January 15; see also reports of January 17 and 22, 1936, DDF 2/I, 85–86, 108, and 141.

77. See DDF 2/I, 174, 213, 232–33, and 245–47. For Neurath's experiences in London, see his memorandum, January 27, 1936, DGFP C/IV, 1039–40. Despite this openness, Neurath's message apparently did not get across, or else Eden, in his memoirs (*Facing the Dictators,* 372–73) is not being perfectly honest: "Though the German foreign minister was not a man to be trusted nor one who necessarily knew Hitler's mind, there was nothing in this interview to arouse any undue alarm." For the British-French military talks which were to play such an important role in Neurath's and Hitler's subsequent actions, see Hoesch to AA, January 6; Bülow's memorandum, January 10; and Neurath's memorandum, January 14, 1936; in DGFP C/IV, 972–73; AA 7881/E570741; and DGFP C/IV, 1002–1004. Also see French war office warning, January 27, 1936, that Germany would probably reoccupy the Rhineland should the French-Soviet pact be signed, DDF 2/I, 152–54.

78. See Bismarck to Dieckhoff, February 13; Bismarck to AA, February 15, 1936; and Geyr's report, March 24, 1936; in DGFP C/IV, 1136–39, 1147–49; and C/V, 335.

79. The best discussions are Robertson, *Hitler's Pre-War Policy,* 66ff.; and Max Braubach, *Der Einmarsch deutsche Truppen in die entmilitarisierte Zone am Rhein im März 1936: ein Beitrag zur Vorgeschichte des zweiten Weltkrieges.* See also Manfred Funke, *Sanktionen und Kanonen: Hitler, Mussolini und der internationale Abessinienkonflikt 1934–36,* 82ff. No notes have survived from Neurath's conversations dur-

ing these days in Berlin. The Fritsch-Hitler discussion is mentioned in Hassell's private notes, printed by Esmonde Robertson, "Zur Wiederbesetzung des Rheinlandes 1936," VJHZG, X (1962), 178–205. For British-French staff talks, see DDF 2/I, 16–17 and 24–25. The deep German suspicions are shown in Neurath's sarcastic comments, DGFP C/IV, 1002–1004. The secret information, which Neurath mentions in his postwar "Notizen," probably was involved with the presence of Marshal Mikhail Nikolaevich Tuckhachevsky, the Vice-Commissar for Soviet Defense, in Paris during the first weeks of February 1936.

80. See Hassell's memoranda, February 14, 20, and 21; and his private papers and diary, February 23, 1936; in DGFP C/IV, 1142–44, 1159–63, 1163–66; and Robertson, "Zur Wiederbesetzung," 202–205. To confirm this interpretation, see Hoesch to AA, March 6, 1936, DGFP C/V, 24–26. For the most thorough investigation of these events, see Funke, *Sanktionen und Kanonen,* 82ff. Hitler made no attempt to bring Ambassador von Hoesch (London) back for conversations, and I believe that Forster was included because he was, by chance, in Berlin. The negative reactions from diplomats are in AA 7881/E750630 and /E750775–76. Hoesch claimed military action would lead "with absolute certainty to an armed conflict," and Forster said that a flagrant violation of the Locarno pact would have serious results. But Hitler had a low opinion of Hoesch (see Krogmann's diary, March 20, 1936, FGN, K-6 Aussenpolitik 21), and an equally poor view of Forster (see Hans E. Riesser, *Haben die deutschen Diplomaten versagt?* 35).

81. For Neurath's attempt to dissuade Hitler, see Fritsch's remarks to Hassell, in Robertson, "Zur Wiederbesetzung," 204–205. See also François-Poncet to Flandin, March 25; and Atherton to Hull, March 26, 1936; in DDF 2/I, 656; and FRUS 1936/I, 269. In complaining that Neurath objected in private while deferring in talks with Hitler, Hassell misunderstood Neurath's initiative and disdain for a possible British response. See his memorandum, March 11, 1936, AA 4619/E198277. For Neurath's withdrawal of objections, see DGFP C/IV, 1166. For the items passed to the AA from Göring's investigating bureau and which encouraged Neurath's determination to act, the author is grateful to Werner von Schmieden, who discussed this aspect with the author on May 1, 1968.

82. Neurath's comment is recorded in François-Poncet to Flandin, February 13, 1936, DDF 2/I, 254. From Göring's announcement to the Poles, it appears that the decision had already taken place prior to February 20. See Breyer, *Deutsche Reich und Polen,* 156. Two days later, however, Neurath and Bülow described the project as still under consideration; see AA 769/270856–58. Also see DGFP C/IV, 1186; Dodd, *Diary,* 314–15; and FRUS 1936/I, 249.

83. The evaluation of Neurath's actions is from Rheinbaben, *Viermal,* 345–46. See also Funke, *Sanktionen,* 135ff. Quotation is from Baroness von Ritter, who told the author on August 20, 1968 that she had received the story from Neurath himself, late on the evening of March 7, 1936.

84. Neurath's remarks are mentioned in Kordt, *Nicht aus den Akten,* 30; Sigismund-Sizzo Fitz-Randolph, *Der Frühstücks-Attaché aus London,* 21–22 and 31–34; Geyr, *Erinnerungen,* 88. For Göring's panic, see Lipski's undated note, in Lipski, *Papers,* 252. The warning telegrams are printed in DGFP C/V, 61, 67–69, 95–96, 100–102, and 119–21. The foreign office comment about nervousness is DGFP C/V, 134 fn. 3. For Neurath's instructions, see DGFP C/V, 110–11 and 114–15. See also Generalfeldmarschall Wilhelm Keitel, *Verbrecher oder Offizier? Erinnerungen, Briefe und Dokumente des Chefs OKW,* 25; and Hans Frank, *Im Angesicht des Galgens: Deutung Hitlers und seiner Zeit auf Grund eigener Erlebnisse und Erkenntnisse,* 211–12. The reference to Hitler's appreciation of Neurath's iron nerves is from Mrs. Henriette de Gourko to author, November 1970.

85. Baroness von Ritter to author, August 20, 1968; and Köpke's affidavit, February 5, 1949, Köpke Nachlass. Himself a private citizen at the time, Köpke's testimony on behalf of Neurath, much of it never introduced at the trial, does not carry the burden of

self-defense. See also Neurath's own testimony, IMT, XVI, 624ff. Confirmation of this attitude was provided in author's interviews with Constantin von Neurath, and Frau von Mackensen, July 3 and August 19, 1968.

CHAPTER IX. *Challenges to Neurath's Leadership: 1933–1937*

1. Quotations from Graham to Vansittart, July 26; and François-Poncet to Paul-Boncour, November 9, 1933; in DBFP 2/V, 448; and DDF 1/IV, 742–43.

2. Max Beer, *Die auswärtige Politik des Dritten Reiches,* 73. Since Beer knew Neurath, it is likely that this book, which appeared in 1934, followed some discussion with the minister and reflected his displeasure with the situation. See also Roger Manvell and Heinrich Fraenkel, *Goering,* 143; and Kordt, *Nicht aus den Akten,* 91–92.

3. See Walter Petwaidic, *Die autoritäre Anarchie,* 18ff.; and Reinhard Bollmuss, *Das Amt Rosenberg und seine Gegner: Zum Machtkampf im nationalsozialistischen Herrschaftssystem,* 244ff. Also see French ambassador's remarks about "rivalries, ambition, competition of clienteles, intrigues, machinations, scandals of all sorts," in François-Poncet to Paul-Boncour, December 27, 1933, DDF 1/V, 356–57. Discrediting the general opinion that Hitler deliberately set officials against each other is the fact that he never made any attempt to duplicate offices competing with Goebbels, Himmler, or Bormann. Once these had won their fields, Hitler was content to live with them, as he was willing to watch Rosenberg, Bohle, Funk, Frick, and Schwarz ruin their chances. See Bollmuss, *Machtkampf,* 100–102; and Peterson, *Limits of Hitler's Power,* passim.

4. For Hugenberg, see Heineman, "Neurath and Economic Conference," 180ff.; for Papen's hostility, see Krogmann's diary, January 18, 1934, FGN, K-5 Aussenpolitik 21. Neurath's disgust is found in Bülow's memoranda, April 5 and 7; and Hassell to Neurath, March 22; and Neurath to Bülow, July 31, 1933; in DGFP C/II, 709; AA 3086/D617469–74; AA 3170/D675782–83; and DGFP C/I, 708. For Papen's role in the Concordat, see Alfons Krupper, "Zur Geschichte des Reichskonkordats," *Stimmen der Zeit,* 163 (1958/59), 279ff. Within the foreign office, it was felt that Papen had given away too much. Author's interview with Herbert Siegfried, May 6, 1968. For rumors that Papen would become foreign minister, see DDF 1/III, 127–28, 272–73, 343, and 1/V, 17; and Engelberg to Thost, March 19, 1934, AA, Partei-Dienststelle APA, Allg. 2/4. According to Hans Völckers (author's interview of June 12, 1968), President Hindenburg had personally reassured Neurath about his own position. For Neurath's actions in disavowing Papen's emmissary, Kurt Freiherr von Lersner, "so that nothing occurs which might damage in any way German interests" in the Saar, see Bülow to Köster, March 6 and November 26, 1934, AA 4260/E200619 and /E200634. For Austria, see NCA, Suppl. A, 447; and Bülow's memorandum, July 28, 1934, AA 4260/E200810.

5. Göring's remarks are in Breyer, *Das deutsche Reich und Polen,* 199; and Manvell and Fraenkel, *Goering,* 143. For the meeting of May 13, see documents in DZA 60952. Göring had given information to the Italian ambassador who had dispatched it to Rome. The foreign office intercepted it, and Neurath read the dispatch in the cabinet. Story is also contained in Nadolny's original draft of *Mein Beitrag.* For Göring's activities in Italy, see Hassell to Neurath, October 4, 1933, DZA 60952, and AA 3170/D617301–32. *Vorwärts* on February 15, 1933 mockingly concluded that Göring had taken over the foreign office as well. For his interference in Rome later that year, see Hassell's memorandum, November 10; Neurath's memorandum, November 20; and Phipps to Simon, November 10, 1933; in DZA 60952; DGFP C/II, 142–43; and DBFP 2/VI, 28. For Göring's intelligence service, see Bülow's memorandum, June 30, 1933, DZA 60954.

6. Last quotation is cited in J. G. Leithäuser, *Diplomatie auf schiefer Bahn,* 19. Neurath's earlier comments are from Rumbold to Simon, March 1; and his remarks on Renthe-Fink's memorandum, November 2, 1934; in DBFP, 2/IV, 431; and DGFP C/III, 560, 548–49, and 559–60. For Neurath's anger over Göring's "constant interference in foreign political matters," see Fromm, *Blood and Banquets,* 193; Rosenberg, *Das pol-*

itische Tagebuch, 52; and Neurath to Göring, April 1, 1934, AA 2945/D576024-25. On Poland, see Lipski, *Papers,* passim; and Comte Jean Szembek, *Journal 1933-1939,* passim.

7. For Goebbels at Geneva, see DDF 1/IV, 433-46. Neurath disliked Goebbels so much he once forbade his daughter to have anything to do with the family. Author's interview with Frau von Mackensen, May 1, 1968. See also Fromm, *Blood and Banquets,* October 6, 1934, 183.

8. See Stieve's memorandum, November 17, 1933, AA 8772/E611284. On the VDR, see Jacobsen, *Aussenpolitik,* 178-220. I do not think the evidence, however, warrants his conclusion that Hitler had a fixed plan which Hess was ordered to carry out. Rather, individuals (such as Haushofer and Hess) set out to create their own empire, and Hitler allowed them free rein. The VDR was created by underlings and then protected by Hess. Hitler had little or nothing to do with it. See DGFP C/II, 49, 107, and 136. For earlier quotation, see Richthofen to AA, April 11, 1933, AA, Abtl. IV, Nd. Denmark, PO 2, Bd. 10. This warning paralleled Neurath's cabinet report that a premature initiative concerning rectification of the Danish border would only strengthen the ties between Poland and France.

9. Neurath's challenge is Neurath to Hess, April 17, DGFP C/IV, 63. See also Dodd, *Diary,* March 6, 1935, 215. Despite impressive documentation, I am not persuaded by Jacobsen's conclusions (see *Aussenpolitik,* 220ff.). The evidence seems to confirm Neurath's judgment that despite all the fuss which Haushofer, Steinacher, and Bohle made, their power and the issue of German communities abroad were of no influence at all in the determination of German foreign policy.

10. Rauschning, *Men,* 190.

11. For earlier career, best treatment is Günter Schubert, *Anfänge nationalsozialistischer Aussenpolitik,* 220ff.; and Bollmuss, *Machtkampf,* passim. Ambassador von Neurath was absent from London during Rosenberg's visit, but his embassy described the visitor as "Hitler's future foreign minister." London to AA, December 3, 1931, AA, Pol. III, England, PO 2, Bd. 7. Although Rosenberg later insisted that Hitler had offered him only the post of state secretary, Schubert (*Anfänge,* 223-25) has shown that the offer was for the ministership. See also Kurt C. W. Lüdecke, *I Knew Hitler: The Story of a Nazi Who Escaped the Blood Purge,* 441 and 462; and Putzi Hanfstaengel, *Hitler: The Missing Years,* 197.

12. See Vienne to Paul-Boncour, May 8, 1933, DDF 1/III, 449-50. Neurath's threats of resignation are discussed in Lüdecke, *I Knew Hitler,* 596; Weizsäcker, *Memoirs,* 88; and François-Poncet to Paul-Boncour, April 1, 1933, DDF 1/III, 127-28. For the thesis that Hitler deliberately appointed Rosenberg to be a competitor of the foreign office, see Paul Seabury, *The Wilhelmstrasse: A Study of German Diplomats under the Nazi Regime,* 35. For assurances that Neurath was secure in office, see François-Poncet to Paul-Boncour, April 5; and Neurath's memorandum, May 11, 1933; in DDF 1/III, 167-68; and DGFP C/I, 404ff. Also see Heinz Sasse, *Zur Geschichte,* 16.

13. For Rosenberg's disgrace, see Engelberg (APA agent in Rome) to Thost (APA man in London), January 30, May 25 and 27, 1934, AA, Partei Dienststelle, APA Allg. 2/4; Schubert, *Anfänge,* 325; DBFP 2/V, 204, 212, 228; Hoesch to Neurath, May 15, DGFP C/I, 433; and Göring's comment to the Italian ambassador, May 15, 1933, DZA 60952. Rosenberg's position had fallen so low that he was listed as number 299 on the election lists for November 1933. The party believed that Neurath had destroyed Rosenberg. As late as 1937, when Ernst Bohle planned a London trip, one official warned him that "behind the invitation to London, there stood the thought that perhaps Rosenberg's experience there might be repeated. This would certainly not be unwelcomed in some circles." Bohle replied: "I believe I know the lay of the land a little better than the gentleman they so beautifully destroyed at that time." Benes/Bohle correspondence, July 29 and August 9, 1937, in AA, Chef AO, 41 Beamte.

14. The rule about unauthorized interviews is in Völcker's memorandum, May 24, 1933, AA, St. Sek. RM, Bd. 3. For APA activities, see DDF 1/III, 761-65, and 1/IV, 132-34. After the war, Göring admitted that foreign office information on Austria was brushed aside. See NCA, Suppl. B, 1146. On Austria and other countries, see especially Neurath to Lammers, April 20; and Engelberg to Thost, March 19, 1934; in AA 9327/E661475-77; and AA, Partei Dienststelle, APA Allg. 2/4. The final quotation is from Neurath to Hess, June 21, 1934, DGFP C/III, 57. See also Engelberg to Thost, May 13, 1934, AA, Partei Dienststelle, APA Allg. 2/4. Background is seen in Rosenberg, *Das politische Tagebuch*, 26ff., 30-41, and 49-52. For subsequent embarrassments, see Thomsen's memorandum, April 17; and Neurath's comment ("I know nothing of this") on Bülow's memorandum, July 31, 1935; in DGFP C/IV, 70-71 and 516-17. The description of the APA in Louis de Jong, "The Organisation and Efficiency of the German Fifth Column," in Maurice Baumont et al. (eds.), *The Third Reich*, 884ff., is now superseded by Jacobsen, *Aussenpolitik*, 51ff. The latter, however, tends to overestimate the importance of the office; it never, for example, reached 50 percent of its published size.

15. See Neurath/Rosenberg letters of September 1935, in AA, Partei Dienststelle, APA Allg. 2/5; and discussion in Jacobsen, *Aussenpolitik*, 84ff.

16. Best discussion is Jacobsen, *Aussenpolitik*, 90-100. Earlier works, which rely upon wartime publications, contain misleading information. The files of Bohle's office have survived only in fragments and were not microfilmed. They are housed in the Political Archives of the foreign office in Bonn.

17. Bohle to Hess, December 4, 1933. See also Bohle to Bormann, November 27; and Bohle to Hess, December 20, 1933; in AA, Chef AO, 49.

18. See discussion in Jacobsen, *Aussenpolitik*, 105ff., which depends less upon documentary evidence, however, than upon the author's concept of a "Nazi style" in foreign policy and the appropriateness of Bohle's suggestions to that style.

19. See Neurath's postwar interrogations; and Bülow's warning against duplication, June 29, 1934; in NCA, Suppl. B, 1490; and AA, RM, Aufz. des St. Sek., Bd. 2. Denunciations are discussed in Jacobsen, *Aussenpolitik*, 148-55, and 495-97.

20. For the origins of the conflict, see Neurath to Hess, April 17, 1935, DGFP C/IV, 62-65; and documents in AA, Abtl. VI A, Deutschtum 1, Bd. 18. The new move originated with Bohle to Hess, February 26, 1936, AA 6805/E516404-405. Bohle proposed that all AO officials be taken into the German foreign service "in order to legalize in the eyes of foreign states their efforts among the Germans abroad." He argued that traditional diplomats had "neither the ability nor the desire to take care of so many local Germans ... and to bring them into closer relations with the Reich." He insisted that under AO leadership, "the Germans living in foreign countries have become an active force in our foreign policy and can be utilized 100 percent." Subsequently, Lammers drafted a series of proposals, AA 6805/E516438-59. Tentatively approved by Hitler on March 8, and then almost immediately withdrawn so that it could be sent to Neurath, one draft reached the foreign office on March 19, 1936. On the same day, Lammers reported that Neurath flatly refused to cooperate. AA 6805/E516460-65. The quotation is from Neurath to Lammers, with enclosures, March 30, 1936, AA 6085/E516483-503. Although Lammers had not sent Neurath a copy of Bohle's original plan, it appears that the foreign office knew all the details.

21. See Hess/Lammers/Neurath letters of April 1936, in AA 6805/E516504-529, and Neurath's memorandum, April 20, 1936, AA 4619/E198287-88. In his earlier attack, Neurath demanded the subordination of the AO in all "political influence in a National Socialist sense upon the local German element and all political organizing, even if limited to German citizens." Neurath to Lammers, March 30, 1936, AA 6805/E516476-82. For another Wilhelmstrasse attack, see Bülow-Schwante to Zeberer, March 27, 1936, AA 6805/E516471-72. For Romania, see Neurath to Hess, March 31, 1936, AA, Inland II g, 222 Deutschtum, Bd. 3. See also Jacobsen, *Aussenpolitik*, 578.

22. For full discussion, see Manfred Merkes, *Die deutsche Politik gegenüber dem spanischen Bürgerkrieg 1936–1939;* and Jacobsen, *Aussenpolitik,* 423–24, from which the quotation is taken.

23. A full study of Bohle is needed. Best discussion is Jacobsen, *Aussenpolitik,* 132ff. For his work in the Wilhelmstrasse, see Kordt, *Nicht aus den Akten,* 186; and Sasse, *Zur Geschichte,* 17. Earlier quotation is from Twardowski's memorandum, November 30, 1936, AA, Inland II g, 221 Deutschtum, Bd. 2. Other information from Rümelin/Bohle letters of December and January 1936–37, in AA, Chef AO, 47. The best discussion of the AO is Jacobsen, *Aussenpolitik,* 148–55. For me, however, Jacobsen attributes far too much importance to the *völkisch* aspects. Despite Bohle's ambition in this area, the AO failed to introduce a new approach to foreign policy. Rather, Bohle was primarily interested in building a position of power; after 1937, in fact, he concentrated entirely on the personnel area.

24. Although he is the subject of several biographies, Ribbentrop has never been studied with the newly discovered materials utilized by Jacobsen, *Aussenpolitik,* 252–318, and Weinberg, *Foreign Policy,* passim. My information also from interview with Vico von Bülow-Schwante, May 24, 1968.

25. For Neurath's attitude, see Gilbert, *Nuremberg Diary,* 201, and Sasse, *100 Jahre Botschaft,* 66. The story of the essay is from Franz von Papen's interview with the author, July 24, 1968; his postwar testimony, NCA, Suppl. A, 450; and *Wahrheit,* 421. See also Ribbentrop, *Zwischen London und Moskau,* 42ff. Earlier quotations are from Ciano's notes of a conversation, October 24, 1936, and author's interview with Constantin von Neurath, July 3, 1968. For the former, see Ciano, *Diplomatic Papers* (ed. Malcom Muggeridge), 60. Neurath's anger over Ribbentrop was relayed to the author by practically all the diplomats interviewed.

26. Author's interviews with Erich Kordt, and Walter Poensgen, April 25 and July 4, 1968.

27. For Ribbentrop's early career, see Neurath to Hoesch and Köster, February 5, 1934, DZA 60975. As late as November 1933, when the French ambassador discussed the influence of various men over foreign policy, he mentioned Putzi Hanfstaengel, but not Ribbentrop; see DDF 1/IV, 739–45. For Ribbentrop's poor reception in London and elsewhere, see DBFP 2/VI, 393 and 407; and DDF 1/V, 869–71. For Neurath's reactions, see Neurath to Hindenburg, March 10; and Bülow to Köster, March 15, 1934; in DGFP C/II, 584–85 and 648. Compare with Neurath's own experiences with such amateurs in Constantinople; see above, page 12.

28. Story from author's interview with Vico von Bülow-Schwante, May 24, 1968. This account helps explain Ribbentrop's leap from apparent defeats to the first stages of his success. At the time, Hitler's dissatisfaction with the foreign office was not yet strong enough that he would order sweeping changes. See François-Poncet to Paul-Boncour, June 18, 1933, DDF 1/IV, 734.

29. Information from author's interviews with Erich Kordt, and Werner von Bargan, April 25, and May 21, 1968; and Kordt, *Nicht aus den Akten,* 70. See also Dettinger reports, cited in Jacobsen, *Aussenpolitik,* 254–55; and the resentment mentioned in Riesser, *Diplomaten,* 34–35; and Phipps to Simon, April 25, 1934, DBFP 2/VI, 657. Information also from Ribbentrop's postwar interrogation, NCA, Suppl. B, 1212–13 and 1182. Neurath's wire to Hoesch to keep an eye on the new man, May 4, 1934; Neurath's comments on Hoesch's report, July 17, 1934; and reports from Bismarck, Köster, and Hassell, May and June 1934; in AA 7466/H178673; AA B154/D669528; and AA 7466/H178685, /H178717–20, and /H178737. The English translations of Ribbentrop's dispatches (as in DGFP C/II, 805–809 and 826–31) disguise the inferior quality of the German originals.

30. Information from interview on July 4, 1968 with Walter Poensgen, who personally received the order from Bülow. Both Poensgen and Frau von Kotze (interview May 7,

1968) described Ribbentrop's scenes and Neurath's support for his staff, even after Ribbentrop took the matter to Hitler personally. See also Ribbentrop to Neurath, July 2, 1934, DZA 60975; and Jacobsen, *Aussenpolitik,* 263.

31. Author's interview with Hasso von Etzdorf, July 3, 1968. Best discussion of the bureau is Jacobsen, *Aussenpolitik,* 267-89.

32. Hermann von Raumer, unpublished manuscript entitled "Der Antikominternpakt," used with permission of Dr. Jacobsen. Written in the form of a memoir in 1955, this manuscript was taken in large part from a diary. For the role of the Ribbentrop Bureau, I am particularly indebted to information from Erich Kordt, interview of April 25, 1968.

33. Incident is related in Jacobsen, *Aussenpolitik,* 291-92, from a conversation with Raumer.

34. Hoesch to Neurath, November 16, 1934, DZA 60975.

35. Neurath to Hitler, November 17, 1934, DZA 60975; Ribbentrop to Neurath and Hitler, November 16, 1934, DGFP C/III, 638-41.

36. Ribbentrop to Neurath, January 14; and Neurath to Ribbentrop, January 19, 1935; in DZA 60975.

37. See Gordon A. Craig, "The German Foreign Office from Neurath to Ribbentrop," in Craig and Felix Gilbert (eds.), *The Diplomats,* 423-24; and Kordt, *Nicht aus den Akten,* 88.

38. Information from author's interview with Günther Altenberg, (April 3, 1968), who had the story directly from Kotze shortly before the appointment of Ribbentrop. Neurath alluded to this discussion in his letter to Hitler, October 25, 1935, IMT, XL, 470-71. For Rosenberg's action, see his "Aktennotize für Führer," May 4, 1935, cited in Jacobsen, *Aussenpolitik,* 301. Earlier information from Rosenberg, *Das politische Tagebuch,* March 12, 1935, 60. Bülow's ill health is mentioned in *Trials of War Criminals,* XII, testimony of Weizsäcker, 918-19 (hereafter cited as TWC). For the talks with Simon and Eden, see Schmidt, *Statist,* 303; and author's interview with Schmidt, July 16, 1968. The talks themselves are recorded in DGFP C/III, 1043-80.

39. Information from Sasse, *100 Jahre Botschaft,* 67. Although Sasse cited no sources, Hoesch visited Berlin between April 8 and May 1, 1935, and conversations may have taken place at this time. For the general expectations, information from author's interviews with Werner von Schmieden and Erich Kordt, May 1 and April 25, 1968.

40. Ribbentrop to Neurath, May 27; and Neurath to Ribbentrop, May 29, 1935; in DZA 60975. Earlier quotations from author's interviews with Constantin von Neurath, and Erich Kordt, May 7 and April 25, 1968. For the naval talks, which Berlin considered purely technical in nature, see program approved in Munich, May 31, 1935, DGFP C/IV, 132-33, 189-92, and 240; and Grand-Admiral Erich Raeder, *Mein Leben,* I, 301.

41. See Hitler's speech before the German press, November 10, 1938, printed in VJHZG, VI (1958), 186-87. Hitler referred to a "Legationsrat" (minor official) who first said nothing could be gained by talks with the British, and when Ribbentrop returned successful, this same man inquired: "But what is 35 percent; if it had been 50 percent, well then we could boast of it, but what is 35 percent?" From author's interview with Erich Kordt, April 25, 1968, it seems certain that Hitler was referring to Kotze, whose actual rank was Counsellor. He was removed from the Wilhelmstrasse by Ribbentrop and posted off to Riga where he died during the war.

42. See Köpke's memorandum of a conversation with the Prinz zu Wied, November 4, 1935, Köpke Nachlass. Information also from author's interviews with Werner von Bargan and Hasso von Etzdorf, May 21 and July 3, 1968.

43. Many former diplomats who knew the situation very well expressed to the author their belief that Neurath could not have pushed any harder. Interviews with Herbert Siegfried, Werner von Bargan, Hasso von Etzdorf, and Walter Poensgen, on May 6, May 21, July 3, and July 4, 1968. See also Dirksen, *Moscow, Tokyo, London,* 108.

CHAPTER X. *Neurath and the Personnel Crisis: 1936–1937*

1. Undated memorandum, c. March 1933, AA, Partei Dienststelle, APA 2/1.
2. In his study, Jacobsen (*Aussenpolitik,* 25ff.) mentions an additional twelve men who left the foreign service for reasons not yet known. Some of these may have left for political reasons. Until the personnel files are open to scholarly use, his account must stand as definitive. The outsiders given ambassador positions were Hans Luther (USA), Franz von Papen (Austria), Joachim von Ribbentrop (Great Britain), Heinrich Sahm (Norway), General Wilhelm Faupel (Franco Spain), and Hermann Kriebel (Shanghai). During the same period, however, more than eight diplomats retired, so that Nazi influence did not even include all replacements. See Jacobsen, *Aussenpolitik,* 623–32; and charts in DGFP C/I through C/V, and DGFP D/I.
3. Schlesinger, whose wife was Russian, was the department's top expert on Soviet policies. When asked why the SA had singled this victim out, Röhm replied: "It is very simple. This Jew in 1918, after the revolution, was a member of the workers' and soldiers' soviet; that is one thing we will never forgive." For this and other details of the incident, see François-Poncet to Paul-Boncour, April 24; and Rumbold to Simon, April 13, 1933; in DDF 1/III, 311–12; and DBFP 2/V, 43. In an interview with the author on July 4, 1968, Walter Poensgen, who was in the personnel division at that time, said Neurath arranged payment of pensions abroad for all officials who were removed. On July 28, 1933, Bülow informed Neurath that 83 officials had recently retired. AA K652/K171249–52. From the context, however, it seems most were routine changes, and not the result of political action.
4. Earlier story from François-Poncet to Paul-Boncour, April 24, 1933, DDF 1/III, 311. Information on rest from Walter Poensgen, interview of July 4, 1968. One of the involved officials was Erich Michelsen, who had served in Tokyo for many years before being posted to the Far East desk in the Wilhelmstrasse in 1926. In 1933, he was deputy director and head of the Orient section of the office, and was scheduled to become ambassador in Peking.
5. Quotations are from Neurath to Waldeck, July 25, 1933; and Neurath's memorandum, November 4, 1934; in DZA 60974, and AA K652/K171263–65. Information on Neurath's attitude from interview on July 4, 1968 with Walter Poensgen, who also recalled the incident of the bribed secretary. The pertinent documents concerning the removal of material from the files are in DZA 60974. For Neurath's letter to Himmler, July 2, 1934, see AA, RM 2, Bd. 8.
6. See Neurath to all members of the diplomatic and consular service, June 28, 1933; and Prüfer to all members of the diplomatic and consular service, September 30, 1938; in AA, Ref. Deutschland, PO 5; and AA, Inland II a-b 32, 151. For foreign office opposition, see François-Poncet to Paul-Boncour, August 1, 1933, DDF 1/IV, 133–34.
7. Bülow's memorandum, August 30, 1933; Bülow to Neurath, August 9, 1933; and Bülow's memorandum, January 25, 1934; in AA K652/K171258–59, /K171276, and AA 3619/E197707. See also Krogmann's diary for August 4 and 5, 1933, FGN, K-4, Aussenpolitik, 21.
8. See Rüdiger's minute, January 12, 1934, BA R 55/45; and Neurath's memoranda, November 7 and December 7, 1933, and January 1, 1934, AA K652/K171268, /K171270–72, and /K171274. See also François-Poncet to Paul-Boncour, November 9, 1933, DDF 1/IV, 742–43. In 1934, another official, Rudolf von Holzhausen, who was stationed in the consulate in Prague, was denounced by party members for a number of offenses, including marriage to a Jew. He demanded a hearing, and although Neurath was forced to transfer him from Prague, he was not dismissed from the foreign service. Documents in Köpke Nachlass. The proposed Gleichschaltung is contained in an unsigned memorandum, September 14, 1933, DZA 60974. For Bohle's optimism, see Bohle to Hess, February 26, 1934, AA, Chef AO, 49. For Neurath's decision to work through Bohle, information from author's interviews with Vico von Bülow-Schwante, and Walter

Poensgen, May 24, and July 4, 1968. Many details of this history, however, are still vague. Best discussion is in Jacobsen, *Aussenpolitik,* 468–69.

9. Rosenberg, *Das politische Tagebuch,* May 15 and 17, and August 2, 1934, 20, 22, 41–42. For Hitler's criticism, see also Fitz-Randolph, *Frühstücks-Attaché,* 46–51; Jacobsen, *Aussenpolitik,* 465ff. Hitler's information on AA opposition came from Albrecht Haushofer's memorandum, microfilm available from the National Archives (hereafter NA), T-235, frame 46.

10. See Grünau to Neurath, March 19 and October 3, 1935, DZA 60974. The best discussion of Nazi pressures is Jacobsen, *Aussenpolitik,* 469–77. Earlier books, such as Seabury, *Wilhelmstrasse,* 61ff., and Walther Hofer, *Die Diktatur Hitlers bis zum Beginn des zweiten Weltkrieges,* 68ff., are erroneous or misleading. For the reorganization, see DGFP C/IV, 1238ff. Basically, the foreign office returned to its pre-1919 format, abolishing the last of the republican reforms. For Ribbentrop's plans, see below.

11. See discussion in Jacobsen, *Aussenpolitik,* 313ff. Raumer believes the first draft of this idea was worked out in the winter of 1935–36. I think it was probably in October 1935, when Ribbentrop reopened the question of an appointment as state secretary. With Bülow in improved health, there was no reason to take up this question at that time, except to speed up the *Gleichschaltung* of the foreign office, and raise Ribbentrop's importance.

12. Neurath to Hitler, October 25, 1935, IMT, XL, 470–71. My translation. See also Dodd, *Diary,* July 11, 1935; and Meissner, *Staatssekretär,* 406–407.

13. No official record has been found of this meeting. Details are taken from a memorandum which Köpke composed on November 4, 1935, immediately after discussing the conversation with Neurath. Köpke Nachlass. Information also from Neurath, "Lebenslauf," and author's interviews with Frau von Mackensen and Constantin von Neurath, May 2 and 7, 1968. This was not the first time that Köpke and Bülow had been singled out. See, for example, François-Poncet to Paul-Boncour, August 1, 1933, DDF 1/IV, 132. Ironically, the diplomat who denounced Köpke was the son-in-law of Neurath's Württemberg king, the Prinz zu Wied.

14. For dismissals, which were disguised as sick leaves, see Bülow to Köpke, February 25, 1936, AA 4620/E200579; DGFP C/IV, 941; and AA L538/L155227. Meyer emigrated to Sweden, where his furniture and possessions were sent at foreign office expense, and where his full pension was paid, even throughout the war years. After the war, he returned to Germany and visited Neurath. Köpke joined a wire service agency in Berlin, and lived to testify in Neurath's behalf at the Nuremberg trial.

15. Hassell's undated diary entry, cited in Robertson (ed.), "Wiederbesetzung," 203. For Neurath's isolation, see François-Poncet to Flandin, February 13, 1936, DDF 2/I, 254; and Fromm, *Blood and Banquets,* October 12, 1935, 306–307. Quotation is from Krogmann's diary, March 5, 1936, FGN, K-6, Aussenpolitik, 21.

16. For AA attitude toward Ribbentrop, see Krogmann's diary, March 20, 1936, FGN, K-6, Aussenpolitik, 21; DGFP C/V, 274–75; DDF 2/I, 622; FRUS 1936/I, 233; and Fitz-Randolph, *Frühstücks-Attaché,* 31ff. Information also from author's interviews with delegation members Werner von Schmieden and Ernst Woermann, May 1, and April 30, 1968.

17. Neurath's actions are seen in his memorandum, and Neurath to Hassell, both March 21, 1936; and Bülow to Dieckhoff, March 23, 1936; in DGFP C/V, 231–32, 232–33, and 256–60. See also DDF 2/I, 632–33, 656ff., and 675–80.

18. On Ribbentrop's failure, compare his written reports with other AA comments; see DGFP C/V, 283–87, 289–93, 315–18, 330, 364–65, and 377–82. See also DDF 2/I, 693–94, and 2/II, 87 and 92–97. For the general view of Ribbentrop's reputation, see Corbin to Flandin, June 15, 1936, DDF 2/II, 456–57. The issue of spying on Ribbentrop is from Neurath to Hoesch, March 23, 1936, DZA 60964.

19. Köster died on December 31, 1935; Hoesch on April 10, 1936; Grünau had been ill since December, but retired only in April. See AA 5620/E200400-401. The reform of

the office was officially announced on April 30, 1936, AA 1780/406789–97. Hitler's opinion of Hoesch is recorded in Krogmann's diary, January 18 and May 8, 1936, FGN, K-6, Aussenpolitik 21. Neurath's fears after Hoesch's death are from author's interview with Hasso von Etzdorf, July 3, 1968.

20. Information from author's interview with Baroness von Ritter, July 16, 1968. When Weizsäcker was told of the project, he dismissed it as a "stupid thing," adding: "I can't understand such pretensions to world politics." Author's interview with Erich Kordt, April 25, 1968. Among German diplomats, there was near-unanimity with Bülow's conclusion that any understanding with Japan "did not fit in with our political scheme." Bülow's memorandum, March 7, 1935, DGFP C/III, 988–90. Kordt alerted the foreign office to Ribbentrop's intentions, but his warnings were dismissed. In November 1935, Ribbentrop received permission from Hitler to negotiate with the Japanese military attaché. The foreign office was not to be informed. Kordt, *Nicht aus den Akten,* 123–24 and 155–56. For proposals to send "a confidant of Ribbentrop's as ambassador," see DGFP C/IV, 1061–72. As Hermann von Raumer recalled the situation in his unpublished manuscript "Der Antikominternpakt," Ribbentrop tried to use the idea of a pact with Japan in order to win attention for himself: "Hitler had not received Ribbentrop for quite some time and he was in a growing poor humor. Daily he sat in the adjutant's room in the chancellery without being called for. Repeatedly, Ribbentrop pressured me whether I was ready to give him some final scheme. My negative answers did not improve his humor." Raumer finally proposed the Anti-Comintern Pact. On German relations in the Far East, see Ernst L. Presseisen, *Germany and Japan: A Study in Totalitarian Diplomacy 1933–1941,* 1–23; and Karl Drechsler, *Deutschland-China-Japan 1933–1939: Das Dilemma der deutschen Fernostpolitik,* 9–19.

21. Papen, *Memoirs,* 375; and NCA, Suppl. A, 471–72. See also Fitz-Randolph, *Frühstücks-Attaché,* 40, 61, and 64–66; and Dirksen, *Moscow, Tokyo, London,* 174.

22. Ribbentrop, "Notiz für den Führer," May 11, 1936, Bundesarchiv Koblenz, Files of the National Socialist Party (hereafter cited as BA, NS), 10/91.

23. Krogmann's diary, June 30, 1936, FGN, K-6, Aussenpolitik 21; and Sasse, *100 Jahre Botschaft,* 70. There is a brief reference to Neurath's discussion with Hitler in June in "Lebenslauf." The return of the Japanese ambassador with the message that his government desired closer cooperation in containing Bolshevism may have prompted Neurath's action to push Ribbentrop to London. See Meissner's memorandum, June 9, 1936, DGFP C/V, 603–604.

24. See Sasse, *100 Jahre Botschaft,* 71; Neurath to Hitler, July 27, 1936, IMT, XL, 473; and Neurath to Dieckhoff, mentioning "three long conferences with the Führer during which I was able to discuss all current questions," July 22, 1936, DGFP D/I, 289. On the same day, Ribbentrop was authorized to carry on the talks with Japan. He obviously expected little opposition from Neurath. See DGFP C/V, 899–900 and 814. Information also from interview with Erich Kordt, April 25, 1968. For speculations, see Krogmann's diary, June 28 and 30, 1936, recording conversations with Wilhelm Keppler and General von Blomberg, who told him that Ribbentrop had been slated to go to London, but that all plans had been changed by Bülow's death. FGN, K-6, Aussenpolitik 21.

25. Author's interview with Constantin von Neurath, May 7, 1968. Story also from Sasse, *100 Jahre Botschaft,* 71–72, but no sources cited. An incident mentioned in Neurath, "Lebenslauf," fixes this conversation as the third week in July; of these talks with Hitler, Baroness von Neurath made an unusual mistake, saying they were concerned with "the Austrian question which threatens to become acute." For Neurath's copy of Ribbentrop's appointment, see IMT, XL, 472.

26. Neurath to Hitler, July 27, 1936. IMT, XL, 473. My translation.

27. Krogmann's diary, August 2, 1936, FGN, K-6, Aussenpolitik 21. The information was obviously wrong; Neurath would be only 64 in 1937. Earlier in the year, Hitler told

both Krogmann and his personal adjutant Fritz Wiedemann that Ribbentrop would become foreign minister one day, but not just at present. Krogmann's diary, March 20, 1936, and author's interview with Fritz Wiedemann, July 25, 1968. The quotation about Hitler's handling of personnel matters is from Lammer's remarks to Krogmann, November 1, 1937, FGN, K-6, Aussenpolitik 21.

28. Ciano's memorandum, October 24, 1936, *Diplomatic Papers,* 60. Quotation is from Neurath, "Lebenslauf." Neurath later quoted Hitler as saying: "We won't discuss the matter any further." See Wiehl to Dieckhoff, November 15, 1936, AA, St. Sek., Schriften an Beamten 1. For Ribbentrop's disappointment, author's interview with Werner von Schmieden, May 1, 1968, and Raumer's entry, August 11, 1936, "Der Antikominternpakt." Ribbentrop's account (*Zwischen London und Moskau,* 90–91) is wrong; his wife's (Annelies von Ribbentrop, *Verschwörung gegen den Frieden,* 127) is, if possible, worse.

29. Likus's minute, October 1936, AA, Dienstelle Ribbentrop, Ribbentrop persönlich.

30. One perceptive official told Rauschning: "Ribbentrop is a magnificent instrument. He simply confirms the thing that Hitler knows by intuition." Rauschning, *Men,* 200. Upon arriving in Great Britain, Ribbentrop started lecturing the British on the values of anti-Communism. In February 1937, after a long absence, he returned to London in order to present credentials to the new king, George VI. In the process, he snapped out a "Hitler salute." The British press and public were outraged. Despite his assurances to Neurath and Hitler that his gesture was a symbolic manifestation of independent Germany, it appears Ribbentrop had just forgotten where he was. This, at least, was the story he told Paul Schmidt. Author's interviews with Paul Schmidt and Erich Kordt, July 16 and April 25, 1968. See Corbin to Delbos, November 11, 18, and 26, 1936, in DDF 2/III, 747, 800, and 2/IV, 53. The Neurath/Ribbentrop correspondence in April 1937 about the salute is in DZA 60977. Public reaction is seen especially in DDF 2/IV, 747 and 756–57.

31. See Wiehl to Dieckhoff, September 2, 1936, AA, St. Sek., Schrift mit Beamten, I. Information also from various interviews, especially with Frau von Kotze, Vico von Bülow-Schwante, Constantin von Neurath, and Baroness von Ritter, May 7 and 24, July 3, and August 20, 1968.

32. Information on Mackensen from various sources, especially author's interviews with Frau von Mackensen, Constantin von Neurath, and Baroness von Ritter, May 2 and 7, and July 16, 1968.

33. Mackensen to Köpke, and Winifred von Mackensen to Köpke, March 29, 1937, Köpke Nachlass.

34. Constantin von Neurath to Köpke, April 11, 1937, Köpke Nachlass. Earlier quotation is from Rauschning, *Men,* 175–76.

35. Beer, *Auswärtige Politik,* 69. Earlier quotation from Bohle to Hess, March 22, 1937, AA, Chef AO 41, Beamte.

36. Rauschning, *Men,* 7; Papen, *Wahrheit,* 385. The English translation (*Memoirs,* 342), on this point, is a complete distortion: "I considered Neurath too open to party influence."

37. See François-Poncet to Delbos, August 5 and 13, 1936, and February 18 and 22, 1937; in DDF 2/III, 138, 202–208, 2/IV, 802–812, and 2/V, 235–38. The latter dispatch spoke of negotiations with the Czechs which were deliberately hidden from the Wilhelmstrasse. See also Krogmann's diary, August 12, 1935, for an earlier attempt to bypass the foreign office. FGN, K-6, Aussenpolitik 21.

CHAPTER XI. *Neurath and German Foreign Policy: 1936–1938*

1. Author's interview with Frau von Mackensen, May 2, 1968.
2. Bullitt's undated memorandum of a conversation with Neurath, May 18, 1936, FRUS 1936/I, 300–302. Neurath confirmed its accuracy in "Notizen."

3. First two quotations from Bullitt's memorandum, FRUS 1936/I, 303; and Corbin to Delbos, May 4, 1937, DDF 2/V, 672. See also excellent reports of François-Poncet to Delbos, April 22 and 26, 1937, DDF 2/V, 517–18 and 568–69. Next quotation is from author's interview with Baroness von Ritter, July 16, 1968. Description is from François-Poncet to Delbos, June 16, 1937, DDF 2/VI, 131. For Neurath's minimal influence and fears, see Ernst von Weizsäcker, *Memoirs,* 109; and Leonidas Hill, "Three Crises, 1938–1939," *Journal of Contemporary History,* III (1968), 115.

4. See documents in DGFP D/III, 3–15; and Weinberg, *Foreign Policy,* 286ff.

5. See Neurath's memorandum, November 12; Neurath to Hassell, December 5; and Neurath to Blomberg, December 15, 1936; in DZA 60974, DGFP D/III, 152–53, and 168. For correspondence over military aid, see Faupel to Dieckhoff, December 5 and 10; and Dieckhoff's memoranda, December 5 and 11, 1936; in DGFP D/III, 154–55, 159–62, 165, and 165–66. The December 21 meeting is undocumented, except for Warlimont's postwar testimony, DeWitt C. Poole File, NA, 59, entry 637; and Neurath to Hassell, December 22, 1936, DZA 60974. When Hitler proposed that Neurath fly to Rome to coordinate a German-Italian program in support of Franco, Neurath flatly refused. For the earlier foreign office proposals, see Dieckhoff's memorandum, August 22; Neurath to Dieckhoff, August 24; and Dieckhoff's memorandum, August 24, 1936; in DGFP D/III, 50–52, 56–57, and DZA 60964 (this is the original document, excerpts of which are printed in DGFP D/III, 56–57). For French rumors, see DDF 2/III, 124.

6. The best discussion of Hitler's policy towards the Spanish Civil War is Weinberg, *Foreign Policy,* 299ff. Although he does not sufficiently emphasize Neurath's role, his presentation is superior to the other good discussion, Merkes, *Die deutsche Politik gegenüber dem spanischen Bürgerkrieg.*

7. See Krogmann's diary, January 18, 1937, FGN, K-7, Aussenpolitik 21; and François-Poncet to Delbos, January 17 and 19, 1937, DDF 2/III, 553 and 539. See also Faupel/Neurath exchange, April 14, 21, and 23, 1937, DGFP D/III, 267–70, 274–76, and DZA 60964.

8. In a footnote to his wife's brief account, Neurath added that the initial consultation between Hitler and himself occurred in a cow-stall at an agricultural exhibition in Munich, which they were coincidentally attending. Neurath, "Lebenslauf." For other details, see DGFP D/III, 296–97; and DDF 2/V, 820–21, and 2/VI, 22–29.

9. See DGFP D/III, 355ff. and 391–92; and DDF 2/VI, 153–57, 176–77, 197–98, 316–17, 334, and 423–24. In late June, diplomatic circles in Berlin were optimistic, since the British government had invited Neurath to talks in London. Then on June 15 and 18, unidentified submarines attacked the German cruiser *Leipzig.* Hitler canceled Neurath's visit. Many members of the foreign office believed that Ribbentrop had sabotaged the trip. For an excellent analysis and account of the differences of opinion between Neurath and Ribbentrop, see François-Poncet to Delbos, June 24 and 26, 1937, DDF 2/VI, 193–197 and 206–207.

10. The Wilhelmstrasse believed that the Danzig question was not yet ripe for a solution, since only force would bring it about, and force was "out of the question at the moment"; see Weizsäcker's memorandum, October 15, 1936, DGFP C/V, 1092. For Neurath's opposition, see his memoranda, October 26 and 29, 1936, DGFP C/V, 1143 and 1159. For the French impression that the move was skillfully and carefully orchestrated, see DDF 2/II, 594–600. See also Lipski, *Papers,* passim; and Szembek, *Journal,* 188.

11. Krogmann's diary, January 18, 1937, FGN, K-7, Aussenpolitik 21. Earlier quotation is from Neurath's memorandum, August 14, 1936, DGFP C/V, 898–99. The contrary opinion is expressed in Weinberg, *Foreign Policy,* 312ff. For another viewpoint, see Helmuth K. G. Rönnefarth, *Die Sudetenkrise in der Internationalen Politik: Entstehung, Verlauf, Auswirkung,* I, 137ff.

12. Lipski, *Papers,* January 13, 1938, 328, and 333–39. Best discussion of the Rib-

bentrop negotiations is Gerhard Weinberg, "Secret Hitler-Beneš Negotiations," *Journal of Central European Affairs,* XIX (1960), 366–74. The failure of the talks persuaded Hitler to wait for a more suitable time, which was precisely the advice Neurath was giving to all who would listen. See DGFP C/V, 1114; and DDF 2/V, 30–31, 170 and 235ff. For German reactions to increased attempts by Czechs to nationalize the German minority, see DGFP D/II, 36–44 and 76. Information on Neurath's position comes from author's interview with Frau von Mackensen, May 2, 1968.

13. On Austria, see Neurath's memorandum, November 21, 1936; Papen to Hitler, January 12, 1937; and the Austria-German agreement; in DGFP D/I, 347–48, 372–73, and 278–81. For Göring's trip, see Hassell to Neurath, January 29; memoranda of January 16, 23, and 30; Hassell to Neurath, January 29, 1937; in DZA 60952; DGFP D/I, 363–78; DZA 60952 (a 23-page document); DGFP D/I, 384–85 and 386–87. Also see DDF 2/IV, 564–65 and 574–77 for the French reactions. Neurath's trips to Vienna and Rome are discussed in DGFP D/I, 396–403 and 419; and especially his account of talks in Rome, May 3, 1937, in DZA 60952. Last quotations are from Neurath to Hitler, August 10; and Dampierre to Delbos, June 24, 1937; in DGFP D/I, 451–52, and DDF 2/VI, 198. See also Papen to Neurath, August 21, 1937, DGFP D/I, 454–58.

14. Krogmann's diary, January 18, 1937, FGN, K-7, Aussenpolitik 21. For the Austrian developments, see DGFP D/I, 448, 463, 477–78, and 494–95. In October, Neurath demanded a special meeting with Hitler and Göring "in order to provide Göring with the necessary instructions for his conversations with Mussolini regarding Austria." Neurath believed Hitler did not support Göring's ideas, which were too severe. See Keppler's memorandum, October 1, 1937, DGFP D/I, 463–64.

15. Undated and unsigned memorandum by Hitler, August 1936, DGFP C/V, 853–62. For Hitler's obsession with anti-Communism, see Jacobsen, *Aussenpolitik,* 446ff. Neurath did not know of this memorandum or of Hitler's precise plans, but as his conversations in Hamburg show, he was generally aware of Hitler's emphasis upon the year 1941. Krogmann's diary, January 18, 1937, FGN, K-7, Aussenpolitik 21.

16. The German foreign office raised all sorts of problems in the preliminary discussions. Evidence of their objections to close alliance between Italy and Germany is found in DGFP C/V 1004ff. Best discussion is Weinberg, *Foreign Policy,* 336–37.

17. I have been unable to locate any documents concerning Neurath's discussion with Hitler in December 1935. The story can be reconstructed, however, from DGFP C/IV, 948–57, and C/V, 271–73. Hitler apparently ordered the idea shelved, for Bülow could record on May 4, 1936 that Ribbentrop's negotiations "had been broken off." DGFP C/V, 502–504. Quotation from Hitler's conversation with Ribbentrop, Raumer, and Oshima, in Raumer, "Der Antikominternpakt." See also Meissner's account of the Hitler-Moushakajo conversation, June 6, 1936, cited in Theo Sommer, *Deutschland und Japan zwischen den Mächten 1935–40,* 31. Remaining information from Raumer, "Der Antikominternpakt," entry for November 23, 1936. Raumer was forced to approach Neurath for help in signing the pact, and knowing that the minister would be very angry, he tried to head off an outburst by suggesting that Neurath should approach Hitler directly if he had any questions. Subsequently, Neurath refused to join the Commission Against Communism, which was a part of the pact yet met only once, on January 29, 1937. In general, the best treatment of this issue is Sommer, *Deutschland,* 50–57, and he makes great use of the Raumer manuscript.

18. First quotation from Raumer, "Der Antikominternpakt," entries for October 1 and November 27, 1936, and March 1, 1937. Rest from Neurath to Ribbentrop, April 23, 1937, DZA 60978; and Raumer, "Der Antikominternpakt," entries for January 29 and March 1, 1937. To initiate negotiations, Ribbentrop overrode Raumer's hesitations: "You think just like the men over there in the foreign office," he said. "You must not always look at the difficulties. If Herr von Hassell won't cooperate, then we will carry it out without him." When Raumer inquired what Ribbentrop would say if someone treated him that

way, he was brushed aside: "Nonsense! We are dealing here with facts, not personalities."

19. Best discussion of the incident and the ensuing war is F. C. Jones, *Japan's New Order in East Asia: Its Rise and Fall, 1937–1945,* passim. Neurath's account of conversations with Hitler is printed in DGFP D/I, 750. For the Ribbentrop/Neurath dispute, see DGFP D/I, 758–60, 768–69, and 772. Information also from author's interview with Werner von Schmieden, May 1, 1968, and private papers which Dr. von Schmieden permitted me to examine concerning German relations with China. The decision for closer relations with Japan is discussed in Sommer, *Deutschland,* 64–65. Final quotations from Bülow-Schwante's memorandum of an automobile ride with Mussolini, October 2, 1937, DGFP D/I, 3–4; and from Count Galeazzo Ciano, *Hidden Diary, 1937–1938* (ed. Malcom Muggeridge), October 2, 1937, 16. See also Hassell's memoranda, July 7 and 12; and Neurath to Hassell, July 15, 1937; in DZA 60974; and Dirksen to AA, September 8, 1937, DGFP D/I, 757–58.

20. Quotations from Ciano, *Hidden Diary,* October 21 and 30, 1937, 23 and 26. For foreign office attempts to cut off Ribbentrop from access to diplomatic information, see Mackensen's memoranda, October 5, 6, 13, and 16, 1937, DZA 60978. For background, see Raumer, "Der Antikominternpakt," and author's interview with Erich Kordt, April 25, 1968. Raumer suspected that all was not right about Ribbentrop's orders and flatly refused to undertake a trip to Italy unless authorized by the foreign office. On October 19, however, Raumer received Hitler's orders, apparently delivered by Ribbentrop. See DGFP D/I, 5 fn. 10, and 16–18; and Raumer, "Der Antikominternpakt."

21. For the signing, see Mackensen to Trautmann, October 27, 1937, DGFP D/I, 776; Ciano, *Hidden Diary,* October 25, 1937, 24 and 25; and Ciano, *Diplomatic Papers,* October 22–24, 1937, 139. For the anti-British aspects of the agreement, see Hassell to AA, November 11, 1937, cited in Drechsler, *Deutschland-China-Japan,* 63; and Ciano, *Hidden Diary,* November 1 and 2, 1937, 27.

22. For Ribbentrop's attempt to come up with some new device to win Hitler's attention, see his memorandum of January 2, 1938, DGFP D/I, 162–68. The story of Ribbentrop's disgrace is from Kordt, *Nicht aus den Akten,* 173; and Raumer, "Der Antikominternpakt."

23. Author's interview with Herbert Siegfried, May 6, 1968.

24. François-Poncet to Delbos, July 22, 1937, DDF 2/VI, 444.

25. Neurath's postwar autobiographical "Skizze."

26. Neurath to Müller, August 19, 1933, DZA 60964.

27. In 1936, Neurath had visited London for the King's funeral, and had subsequently claimed it was profitable to have renewed old contacts. Neurath to Papen, February 7, 1936, DZA 60964. The British requested that he lead the delegation for the coronation of George VI, but Ribbentrop blocked this. Information from author's interview with Paul Schmidt, July 16, 1968. See also Schmidt, *Statist,* 354. For the 1937 invitation, see DGFP D/III 307–308, 311–16, 322–24, 443–44, and especially 335–36. For enthusiasms over the visit, especially for Schacht's reaction, see DDF 2/VI, 268–75, and 130–33, 142–43, 148–51.

28. Evaluation of Ribbentrop's failures is Corbin to Delbos, June 22; quotation is from François-Poncet to Delbos, June 26; and Ribbentrop to Neurath, June 15, 1937; in DDF 2/VI, 176–77, 206–207; and DGFP D/III, 341–42. For evidence of Ribbentrop's responsibility in blocking the trip, see Likus's note, June 25, 1937, AA, Dienststelle Ribbentrop, AA Angelegenheiten Teil II; and Göring's perceptive comment cited in Wiedemann, *Feldherr,* 161.

29. Likus's account, August 8, 1937, AA 1562/378108–109. The Austrian foreign minister believed that Neurath's position had been strengthened, and the French ambassador in Vienna reported that even Göring treated Neurath deferentially. See DDF 2/VI, 754–66 and 768–69. Neurath's disappointment is recorded in Dodd, *Diary,* June 23,

1937, 420; and was recounted in the author's interview with Fritz Wiedemann, July 25, 1968.

30. For the rumors circulating in Nuremberg, see Krogmann's diary, September 14, 1937, FGN, K-7, Aussenpolitik 21. For the criticism of Ribbentrop, see DNB report, November 6, 1937, DZA 60964. Ribbentrop had traveled so much that in December 1936 a formal question had been raised in the House of Commons: "Is not the position of German Ambassador in England a full-time job?" London *Times*, December 10, 1936.

31. Hossbach's memorandum, November 10, 1937, DGFP D/I, 29ff. German text is printed in IMT, XXV, 402-413. All citations, unless noted, are from the English translation.

32. See Hossbach, *Zwischen Wehrmacht und Hitler*, 217-19. The armament experts were never called in. The most thorough study of the actual Hossbach document has been by Meinck, *Hitler und die deutsche Aufrüstung*, 236-37 fn. 4, with letters from a number of the individuals involved. According to his conclusions, the Nuremberg document was a copy of the original Hossbach memorandum, made by Captain Graf von Kirchbach sometime in 1943. The original memorandum has disappeared. Kirchbach insisted that his own copy, and Hossbach's original, were both substantially different from the document which appeared in Nuremberg, and contained many more comments from Neurath, Fritsch, and Blomberg. Kirchbach suspects—and Meinck agrees—that the allied prosecution at Nuremberg made a new copy, leaving out large portions of the "opposition comments," as incompatible with their theories of a conspiracy. Thus, Meinck concludes, Hossbach did not commit a "sin of omission," but the court at Nuremberg committed a far more serious one. Tempting as it is to accept this conclusion, there is no way of proving it. Indeed, a recent examination of the issue (Bradley F. Smith, *Reaching Judgment at Nuremberg*, 141ff.) has shown that the original captured document was microfilmed and sent to the State Department on May 25, 1945, and that the State Department, a month later, brought it to the attention of the Nuremberg prosecution team. It was not until September 1945 that the Prosecution Office requested Washington to send a copy of the full document to Nuremberg. The document submitted to the trial is identical to the one sent to Washington in May, and thus the possibilities of falsification for the purposes of the trial seem ruled out. Unfortunately, the original of the Kirchbach copy has now disappeared, and thus no scientific tests on it can be undertaken.

33. Hossbach memorandum, DGFP D/I, 38.

34. See discussion in Meinck, *Hitler und die deutsche Aufrüstung*, 164-67.

35. See Blomberg's directive, June 24, 1937, IMT, XXXIV, 733ff. The last quotation cited is from Fritsch to Blomberg, August 1937, from a secret source included in Robert John O'Neill, *The German Army and the Nazi Party 1933-1939*, 131.

36. See Edward Norman Peterson, *Hjalmar Schacht: For and Against Hitler*, 281-89. Also see Speer, *Memoirs*, 116; and Schacht's postwar testimony, IMT, XII, 522.

37. Quotation is from Krogmann's diary, November 1, 1937, FGN, K-7, Aussenpolitik 21. For rumors about Schacht, see Mackensen's memorandum, October 28, 1937, AA 6981M/E521597. For Neurath's lack of information about the subject of the forthcoming conference, see Mackensen's memorandum, November 3, 1937, DGFP D/I, 777.

38. My translation from Göring's testimony of March 14, 1936. The English version (IMT, IX, 307) is not quite accurate.

39. Gilbert, *Nuremberg Diary*, May 20, 1946, 310. Raeder claims that Göring had tipped him off that Hitler's aim was "to spur the army to greater speed in rearming," and that after the meeting Blomberg also assured him that "the whole thing was not meant seriously." See Raeder, *My Life*, 267. For a similar opinion, see Erich von Manstein, *Aus einem Soldatenleben, 1887-1939*, 321. Kordt *(Nicht aus den Akten,* 172-74) suggests that Hitler did not mention the German-Japanese-Italian alliance, which would be signed that very day, because of Neurath's presence. This is questionable, in view of Hitler's

enthusiasm for the new alliance two days later in the Bürgerbrau speech, discussed in Elizabeth Wiskemann, *The Rome-Berlin Axis: A History of the Relations between Hitler and Mussolini,* 86–89. Rather, its omission seems to have occurred because it was out of place in a meeting discussing the "crisis of rearmament" to talk about an ambitious project of world alliances. Information also from author's interview with Lutz Graf Schwerin von Krosigk, April 26, 1968.

40. First quotation is from Neurath's testimony, June 24, 1946, IMT, XVI, 640. The second is from Neurath's "Notizen." See also Neurath to Baroness von Ritter, February 1946, Ritter Papers.

41. Information from author's interviews with Lutz Graf Schwerin von Krosigk, Frau von Mackensen, and Vico von Bülow-Schwante, on April 26, May 2, and May 24, 1968. On November 6, 1937, Neurath also talked about the discussion with Manfred Zimmermann, his friend and lawyer. His plans then were to resign at once. See Zimmermann's affidavit, IMT, XL, 442.

42. It may be that Fritsch decided at this time to have Hossbach give some record of the meeting to Beck. Since the Neurath/Fritsch/Beck meeting occurred on either November 7 or 8, 1937, such a suggestion may have provided the impetus for Hossbach to compile his memorandum. This may also account for the nature of the document, for it was to inform Beck and serve as the basis of a rebuttal of Hitler's points, not as a record of the full discussion. See Hossbach to Meinck, September 9, 1956, cited in Meinck, *Hitler und die deutsche Aufrüstung,* 238 fn. 40. For dating of the meetings, see John Wheeler-Bennett, *The Nemesis of Power: The German Army in Politics, 1918–1945,* 362. Beck's subsequent memorandum is printed in Foerster, *Generaloberst Ludwig Beck,* 80–82. The similarity of these views with those held by Neurath was frequently demonstrated in interviews with Frau von Mackensen, May 2 and 3, 1968. Neurath in particular stressed the issue of the peoples of Central Europe and the necessity for Germany to avoid any involvement in their problems. "They can never be the reason for us to run the risk of another war," he frequently said to his daughter.

43. Story related to the author by Baroness von Ritter, who heard it from Neurath during his Christmas vacation, 1937. Information on Neurath's heart problems comes from Baroness von Ritter's affidavit, May 28, 1946, IMT, XL, 444–45; and author's conversations with Baroness von Ritter, July 16 and August 20, 1968. After the Hossbach meeting, Neurath had three occasions to talk with Hitler. On November 9, he was in Munich with the chancellor, but had no opportunity for a private conversation. He may, however, have attended this SS gathering—for the first and last time in his life—precisely in order to try to see Hitler. Neurath file, Berlin Document Center. Next, on November 19, Neurath escorted Lord Halifax in and out of Berchtesgaden, but without any opportunity for a private talk with Hitler. See Papen to Neurath, November 11; and Neurath's notes on the visit, November 20, 1937; in DGFP D/I, 41 and 55–67.

44. First quotation is Likus's memorandum, November 19, 1937, AA 43/28854/2–54/3. See also DGFP D/I, 39–45. Last quotation from Cab. Mins., December 9, 1937, RK 3598/D798271–72. For the Halifax talks, see DGFP D/I, 55–67. Hitler was convinced that he had "put down" Halifax, and told Admiral Raeder that he "had no intention to let it come to a war with England, but believed that at present England is not yet ripe for an understanding. In any case, he is not ready to let the English determine the timing of such negotiations." Krogmann's diary of a conversation with Raeder, January 11, 1938, FGN, K-7, Aussenpolitik 21. For Neurath's embarrassed role, see Ivone Kirkpatrick, *The Inner Circle: Memoirs,* 95ff.

45. See Neurath's memorandum, December 3; and comment on Papen to Neurath, December 16, 1937; in DGFP D/I, 94 and 130. Best discussion of this mediation effort is in Sommer, *Deutschland,* 68–81; and Werner von Schmieden's manuscript account, used with his permission. There is absolutely no evidence to support Drechsler's conclusion

(*Deutschland-China-Japan,* 37) that Neurath sought a China alliance in order to wage war against the Soviet Union.

46. See Rintelen's memorandum, and Weizsäcker's covering letter, December 20, 1937, DGFP D/I, 147–51. Although there can be no doubt at all that the ideas contained in this document are Neurath's, Rönnefarth (*Sudetenkrise,* II, 36–37) errs in attributing the covering letter to Neurath.

47. Information from author's interviews with Lutz Graf Schwerin von Krosigk, and Constantin von Neurath, April 26, and July 3, 1968. See also Kordt, *Nicht aus den Akten,* 173; and Raumer, "Der Antikominternpakt."

48. I have been unable to find Neurath's letter, but information about it is contained in author's interviews with Herbert Siegfried, Frau von Kotze, Vico von Bülow-Schwante, and Baroness von Ritter, May 6, 7, 24, and July 16, 1968. For Neurath's depression, see affidavit of Baroness von Ritter, May 28, 1946, IMT, XL, 473; and author's interview with Frau von Mackensen, May 2, 1968. On the meeting at Leinfelderhof, see Mackensen to Strölin, January 21, 1938, AA 2185/472183; and Strölin's postwar testimony, IMT, X, 62. In general, see Harold Deutsch, *Hitler and His Generals,* 74ff.

49. See Lipski's report, January 14, 1938, Lipski, *Papers,* 333–39. Also see Neurath's memorandum, January 14; and Weizsäcker to Moltke, January 19, 1938; in DGFP D/V, 38–40.

50. Neurath's testimony, June 24, 1946, IMT, XVI, 641. For evidence that Great Britain was moving toward recognition of German influence in Austria and that Vienna would come to terms with Berlin, see Eichstädt, *Von Dollfuss zu Hitler,* 245.

51. Neurath's "Notizen," and testimony, IMT, XVI, 641. I have been unable to find the letter, but several sources mention that he wrote one; author's interviews with Baroness von Ritter and Vico von Bülow-Schwante, July 16 and August 20, and May 24, 1968. According to Baroness von Ritter, Neurath told her that he would not make a fuss or create an incident, but merely take his leave. He told Hitler that it would not be difficult to come up with a believable pretext. His postwar testimony is not explicit as to whether or not he wrote a letter. His prison notes, however, imply that he did: "When I could not dissuade Hitler from a warlike stance, in January 1938 I requested my resignation." "Notizen."

CHAPTER XII. *The Year of Decision: 1938*

1. Quotation cited in Wolf-Ulrich von Hassell's introduction to Ulrich von Hassell, *Vom anderen Deutschland,* 13.

2. Hitler's speech, January 25, 1939, in Hans-Adolf Jacobsen and Werner Jochmann (eds.), *Ausgewählte Dokumente zur Geschichte des Nationalsozialismus 1933–1945.* Other quotation is cited in Johann Adolf Graf Kielmansegg, *Der Fritsch-Prozess 1938: Ablauf und Hintergrund,* 35. For Neurath's position, author's interview with Baroness von Ritter, July 16, 1968; Ciano, *Hidden Diary,* November 21, 1937, 25, 26, and 35; Hassell to Neurath, January 19, 1938, DZA 60694; and Fitz-Randolph, *Frühstücks-Attaché* 243. Raeder even suggests that Neurath was invited to the Hossbach talks in order to get him to resign, but I have found no evidence to corroborate this theory. See IMT, XIV, 36. For Ribbentrop's proposals, see DGFP D/I, 162–68; and Rönnefarth, *Sudetenkrise,* I, 49–58. Hitler's pro-Japan attitude is seen in his remarks to Raeder that he was "happy that for the first time we have an ally who is really powerful." Krogmann's diary, January 11, 1938, FGN, K-7, Aussenpolitik 21.

3. For the crisis, see Krogmann's diary, February 2, 1938, FGN, K-7, Aussenpolitik 21; Fromm, *Blood and Banquets,* January 12, 1938, 263–64; and Jodl's diary entries for January 28, February 2, and 3, 1938, IMT, XXVIII, 360, 363, and 365. Apparently, Hitler was truly surprised and shocked over the Blomberg case. His further decision, however, to block the logical promotion of General Werner Freiherr von Fritsch as Blom-

berg's replacement was influenced by Göring and Himmler and his own determination to set aside this stubborn opponent of his plans. See Kielmansegg, *Fritsch-Prozess,* passim; and the excellent treatment in Deutsch, *Hitler and His Generals,* passim. For Neurath's removal, see Göring's postwar testimony, IMT, IX, 290–91; and Bullitt to Hull, February 7, 1938, FRUS 1938/I, 16. Göring told the prison psychiatrist: "Von Neurath was a man of standing and insight. He would contradict Hitler on occasion and reason with him." Gilbert, *Nuremberg Diary,* November 11, 1945, 18. Albrecht Haushofer reported to his father, February 10, 1938: "It is important to take into account that the intention of the highest authorities here is not to bar Neurath from having influence. They want to lift him higher, not kick him out." NA, T-253, 46.

4. Jodl's diary, January 31, 1938, IMT, XXVIII, 362; and affidavit of Hans Lammers, May 6, 1953, from the files of Dr. Helmut Fischinger, the Stuttgart lawyer retained by Neurath's family for a postwar denazification trial. These records, henceforth cited as Fischinger Files, were made available to the author through the generous cooperation of Frau von Mackensen and Dr. Fischinger. For the decision to postpone Funk's installation as Schacht's successor see Krogmann's diary, February 3, 1938, FGN, K-7, Aussenpolitik 21. Within the foreign office, observers believed the crisis solely concerned Blomberg; see Albrecht Haushofer to his father, February 3, 1938, NA, T-253, 46.

5. See *Berliner Morgenpost,* February 2 and 3, 1938. Information also from author's interviews with Frau von Mackensen and Vico von Bülow-Schwante, May 2 and 24, 1968. Quotation is from author's interview with Herbert Siegfried, May 6, 1968.

6. The story was told by Neurath in a telephone conversation with the Ritters on the evening of February 2, and relayed to the author by Baroness von Ritter, August 20, 1968. The incident is also described in Meissner's postwar interview, August 31, 1945, Poole Interviews, NA 59, 637; and Lammers's affidavit, May 6, 1953, Fischinger Files. Hitler's words were also quoted to the author by Günther Altenberg, April 3, 1968. He had the story directly from Kotze, Neurath's aide who was present.

7. Information from author's interview with Vico von Bülow-Schwante. One issue Neurath wanted to discuss with Hitler was the question of Ulrich von Hassell who had asked to be removed from Rome. See Neurath/Hassell letters, December and January 1937–38, DZA 60964. It is unclear why Hitler did not speak frankly with Neurath. According to Jodl's diary, the military personnel issue had been resolved on February 4 in the morning. See IMT, XXVIII, 366. Ribbentrop also was kept in ignorance; Kordt met him on the late evening of February 3, and found him in one of his darkest and most pessimistic moods. Author's conversation with Erich Kordt, April 25, 1968.

8. Author's interview with Vico von Bülow-Schwante, May 24, 1968. Bülow-Schwante discussed the background and course of the events with Neurath on February 5. Since the departure of Köpke, Bülow-Schwante was Neurath's closest confidant in the foreign office. See Neurath's statement to the American ambassador, Hugh Wilson, on February 19, 1938, cited in Charles S. Tansill, *Back Door to War: The Roosevelt Foreign Policy, 1933–1941,* 375.

9. Author's interview with Herbert Siegfried, May 6, 1968. Baroness von Ritter's recollection of a telephone conversation, described to author on August 20, 1968, is also contained in a letter to the author, November 1, 1970. Information also from Constantin von Neurath, May 7, 1968. Frau von Mackensen was busy that night and was unable to see her parents until the next day. For the public announcement, see Jodl's diary, IMT, XXVIII, 367.

10. See Sir Neville Henderson, *Failure of a Mission,* 108; Gilbert to Hull, February 5, 1938, cited in Tansill, *Back Door to War,* 374; and Albrecht Haushofer to his father, February 10, 1938, NA, T-253, 48.

11. Neurath, "Lebenslauf." Information also from author's interviews with Baroness von Ritter, and Frau von Mackensen, July 16 and May 2, 1968. According to an affidavit

of architect Paul Schmitthenner, February 25, 1949 (in the Neurath Nachlass), Neurath told him immediately afterwards that he would permanently stay in Leinfelderhof and wanted the house there enlarged. Schwerin von Krosigk, in an interview with the author on April 26, 1968, recalled that shortly after returning to Berlin, Neurath attended the reception and inadvertently picked up the card identifying the seat and dining partner of the "foreign minister." Only Krosigk's prompt intervention avoided a scene with the touchy Ribbentrop.

12. For the clear link between the Berchtesgaden talks and the domestic troubles with the military, see Deutsch, *Hitler and His Generals*, 340–41. Schuschnigg had already told Austrian Nazis that he would concede all of Germany's demands. See Gehl, *Austria, Germany, and the Anschluss*, 166ff.; and DGFP D/I, 500–502. Most diplomats in 1938 saw the Anschluss as only a question of time. See Eichstädt, *Dollfuss*, 260; and Johnson to Hull, February 17, 1938, FRUS 1938/I, 399–400. Neurath's lament about Ribbentrop's reaping his victory is in Lipski to Beck, February 19, 1938, Lipski, *Papers*, 342. Neurath's attitude is well described also in "Notizen." Gehl (*Anschluss*, 174) appears to be correct in suggesting that General Keitel's presence at Berchtesgaden was to demonstrate that no split in leadetship had occurred in Germany.

13. Gehl, *Anschluss*, 182ff. For German arguments that the plebiscite was a fraud, see Muff to AA, March 8, 1938, DGFP D/I, 562.

14. For background, see Likus memorandum, April 22, 1938, AA 43/28926. Ordered by Ribbentrop to conduct an investigation of Neurath's activities during these days, Likus talked with Glaise-Horstenau for his information. See also Keppler's testimony, in TWC, XII, 768, and IMT, XVI, 117. Also Weizsäcker to London, March 9, 1938, DGFP D/I, 562. According to "Lebenslauf," Neurath had conferences with Hitler on both March 10 and 11, 1938. This concurs with the Likus memorandum. Neurath's prison "Notizen," however, recalls only a discussion on March 11.

15. According to Jodl's diary (IMT, XXVIII, 371–72), Keitel was summoned to the chancellery only at 9:45 A.M. It is possible that Neurath suggested that Hitler talk to the military. The information about Göring's objections to recalling Ribbentrop is from "Notizen."

16. Krogmann's diary, October 21, 1938, FGN, K-7, Aussenpolitik 21. This incident helps establish that Neurath spoke with Hitler before such orders were given to Glaise-Horstenau on March 10, 1938. Thus, Weizsäcker's rather sarcastic comments in his late evening diary entry of March 10, 1938 are wrong. See Ernst von Weizsäcker, *Die Weizsäcker Papière, 1933–1950* (ed. Leonidas E. Hill), 122–23 (hereafter cited as Weizsäcker, *Papiere*).

17. For events, see IMT, XVI, 117. Glaise-Horstenau testified that his message contained only vague and tentative ideas. Seyss-Inquart called them "hints." Both men said they did not take the suggestion seriously. See Seyss-Inquart's affidavit, NCA, V, 981. On the importance of the domestic crisis which arose in military circles over the firing of General Fritsch, see Deutsch, *Hitler and His Generals*, 341–42.

18. Handwritten statements by Neurath, with a covering file note by Weizsäcker, AA 1649/391803–806. Only the first statement is printed in DGFP D/I, 585. The letter to Mussolini is DGFP D/I, 573–74, and is discussed in Ciano, *Hidden Diary*, 87. For Neurath's subsequent use of the second statement, see below, note 24 and page 231.

19. For Papen's account, see NCA, Suppl. A, 496. Hitler's directive is IMT, XXXIV, 336. The chancellor may indeed have thought the Austrians had not responded to his ultimatum, but Seyss-Inquart and Glaise-Horstenau had granted Schuschnigg a two-hour extension. See IMT, XVI, 117–18; and Gehl, *Anschluss*, 188. On Keitel's trick keeping the army's objections from Hitler, see Field Marshal Wilhelm Keitel, *Memoirs* (ed. Walter Görlitz), 179.

20. Quotation is from Deutsch, *Hitler and His Generals*, 343. See also Göring's

telephone conversation, NCA, V, 629–30; and Seyss-Inquart's testimony, NCA, V, 983. Shortly thereafter, Keppler was dispatched to Vienna with new demands, including a list of cabinet ministers, and a rough draft of a telegram requesting German intervention. See also Gehl, *Anschluss,* 188.

21. Göring's telephone conversations, NCA, V, 634ff. Quotation is from Muff's memorandum; in a covering letter, Counsellor von Stein noted that had he known about this, he would "have attempted to prevent this step." DGFP D/I, 589–90. On cancellation of the marching orders, see Jodl's diary, NCA, IV, 362–63.

22. For Schuschnigg's declaration, see DBFP 3/I, 17–18. Invasion was ordered at 8:30; the decree signed at 8:45, nearly an hour after the radio broadcast. At 8:48, Göring telephoned Keppler in Vienna asking for a telegram requesting troops. See NCA, IV, 363; V, 638–40; and VI, 1017. According to information from Fritz Wiedemann in an interview with the author on July 25, 1968, Neurath was not in the chancellery when these decisions were taken.

23. Quotation from Wiedemann, *Der Mann der Feldherr,* 122. In his recollections, Keitel holds a similar opinion (*Memoirs,* 59), namely that Hitler "wanted to take part in the triumphal entry into his Fatherland and personally accompany the troops." There is evidence, however, that Neurath tried to dissuade Hitler from going to Vienna; see Likus's memorandum, March 12, 1938, AA 43/28910. The telegram asking intervention (DGFP D/I, 580) was dispatched at 9:10 P. M., and arrived in Berlin at 9:40. Neurath stayed in the foreign office to that time and brought it immediately to the chancellery. Papen, who told the author that he was concerned lest the telegram be a forgery and become "another Ems dispatch," saw Neurath bring it in, and this is confirmed by the affidavit of Wilhelm von Grolmann. Information from author's interview with Franz von Papen, July 24, 1968, and Gehl, *Anschluss,* 191. Apparently, Neurath made no effort to find out what pressures his government had applied to the Austrians. He was content that the problem had been resolved to Germany's advantage and in a peaceful fashion!

24. See Neurath to Henderson, and Neurath to François-Poncet, March 12, 1938, AA 1798/409367–71, and /409431–34; and IMT, XXXI, 137–38. According to "Notizen," Hitler had told Neurath that Seyss-Inquart would invite German troops to enter the country, even before Neurath suggested a telegram asking for intervention. Surprisingly, Neurath did not have to answer for any of these events. The main charge against him in the Nuremberg trial for these days was that he had lied to the Czechs! On March 12, the Czech consul in Berlin, Voljtech Mastný, aware of his country's exposed southwestern frontier, asked Neurath for assurances that Berlin did not intend to attack Czechoslovakia. Although Neurath mentioned to Mastný the continuing concern of his government about Czech mistreatment of the Sudeten German minority, he assured the minister that Germany had no intention of using military force against Czechoslovakia. The allied prosecution, utilizing the Hossbach discussion, claimed that Neurath knew Hitler intended to attack Czechoslovakia at the first suitable opportunity, and therefore he was guilty of lying consciously and diabolically to Mastný. Neurath could never understand this charge, but it was a major element in his conviction of "crimes against peace." See IMT, XVI, 643–44.

25. Information from Neurath, "Lebenslauf," and Speer, *Memoirs,* 129. After the war, the prosecution produced an affidavit from Raymond H. Geist, former United States consul in Berlin (IMT, XXVIII, 251) which charged that Neurath had "appropriated" his new house from a Jewish owner at a fraction of its worth. The prosecution used this evidence to accuse Neurath of subservience to the Nazi regime. Subsequently, Neurath proved that the house had been purchased from official government funds, for a fair and just price, and that he had arranged that the funds be paid in foreign currency, thus allowing the owner (who was not Jewish but was married to a Jew) to emigrate. "Notizen," and Neurath to Oda von Ritter, January 7, 1946, Ritter Papers.

26. The decree setting up the council is IMT, XXVII, 171–72. Lammers's four drafts of the proposal for the composition and workings of the council, of February 17, undated, March 9, and March 19, 1938, are filmed as RK 6806/E516557, /E516577–78, /E516582–83, and /E516586.

27. Since Albrecht von Kessel was deeply implicated in the abortive plot to remove Hitler at the time of the Munich crisis in 1938, Weizsäcker hoped that posting him to the relative obscurity of Neurath's office might afford some protection for the young diplomat. For this and information on the files, author's interview with Albrecht von Kessel, July 30, 1968. Information on the transfer of Neurath's friends and the official ban on communications to him from author's interviews with Frau von Kotze and Vico von Bülow-Schwante, May 7 and May 24, 1968. On Kessel's involvement in the resistance, see Harold Deutsch, *The Conspiracy Against Hitler,* passim. Earlier document is Ribbentrop to Lammers, April 4, 1938, RK 6806/E516584–85.

28. Neurath's quotation is from "Notizen"; other information from Lammers's affidavit, May 6, 1953, Fischinger Files. In the postwar trial, the prosecution insisted the council must have existed, for it had a budget, offices, and letterhead stationery. Although the court never proved the charge, it agreed that by maintaining this "formal relationship" with the Nazi government, Neurath was guilty of participation in crimes against humanity. See IMT, VI, 641–44, and XVII, 50–54, and discussion, below, page 235. Information about Neurath's attitude after his dismissal is from discussion with Herbert Siegfried, May 6, 1968; and with Frau von Mackensen, May 2 and July 8, 1968. Although the author frequently heard charges that Baroness von Neurath was ambitious and wished to stay in Berlin with the prestige of a high office for her husband, the documentary evidence and my research indicates that in these matters, Neurath made up his own mind.

29. See Jodl's diary, IMT, XXVIII, 372; DGFP D/I, 197ff., and 204–205. Hitler's statement to Neurath is from a note of April 24, 1938, in Weizsäcker, *Papiere,* 126. I have been unable to find additional information on this meeting. For Hitler's plans, see Schmundt's notes, April 22, 1938, IMT, XXV, 415–17. Hitler's change of tactics may have been forced by Sudeten Germans; having seen their Austrian brothers join the Reich, large numbers of Sudeten Nazis protested to Henlein about the lack of dynamism in their own movement. See various documents in Václav Král (ed.), *Die Deutschen in der Tschechoslowakei, 1933–1937,* 186–94 and 207–208. For Hitler's decision, see Keitel to Hitler, May 20, 1938, DGFP, D/II, 300, and Keitel, *Memoirs,* 62–63. Despite Ribbentrop's frivolous talk about making war "right and left," it appears as if Hitler's position had not changed. "Czechoslovakian question is not urgent," he told Mussolini. Within the foreign office, most believed that Germany could not use force without setting off a war which Germany would lose. See Ciano, *Hidden Diary,* 112–13; Král, *Deutschen in Tschechoslowakei,* 206–207; and notes of May 13, 1938, in Weizsäcker, *Papiere,* 128.

30. Schmundt to Keitel, May 25; and Neurath's memorandum, May 19, 1938; in IMT, XXV, 431–32; and DGFP D/II, 292–93. For Ribbentrop's reputation, see Hugh Wilson, *A Career Diplomat. The Third Chapter: The Third Reich,* 35–36; Henderson to Halifax, May 27, 1938, DBFP 3/I, 384–85; Henderson, *Failure of a Mission,* 138–39; and notes of May 22, 1938, in Weizsäcker, *Papiere,* 128. Neurath apparently still had sufficient access to confirm fears of Ribbentrop's role.

31. Quotation from Beck's notes, in Foerster, *Generaloberst Beck,* 107–108. According to Wiedemann (*Der Mann der Feldherr,* 128), Hitler's words were violent: "It is my unshakeable resolve that Czechoslovakia should disappear from the map." From an account of the meeting given him by Walter Hewel, Ribbentrop's aide, Erich Kordt concluded that Hitler wanted primarily the destruction of Czechoslovakia, not annexation. See Kordt, *Nicht aus den Akten,* 228. Only one document survives that describes the meeting, General Beck's handwritten notes, printed in Foerster, *Generaloberst Beck,* 107–108. These notes agree completely with the other principal source, Fritz

Wiedemann's memorandum, September 5, (1939?), printed in ADAP D/VII, 544–45; and Wiedemann, *Der Mann der Feldherr*, 127–28. Supplementary evidence is found in Beck's memoranda of May 29, June 3, and July 16, 1938, printed in Foerster, *Generaloberst Beck*, 109ff.; and Weizsäcker's notes, May 31, 1938, in Weizsäcker, *Papiere*, 129.

32. The similarity of language in Wiedemann's 1939 memorandum and Beck's 1938 notes confirms Wiedemann's memoirs, for he did not have access to Beck's papers. See ADAP D/VII, 545; Foerster, *Generaloberst Beck*, 108–114; Wiedemann, *Der Mann der Feldherr*, 128–29. For analysis, see Rönnefarth, *Sudetenkrise*, I, 307–312. Immediately afterwards, Ribbentrop repeated the decision to a newspaper correspondent: as soon as the Western fortifications were complete and Austria absorbed, Germany would have "complete security from any attacks in the West," and would then "take up the Czech question with all decisiveness and effectiveness." Cited in Jacobsen and Jochmann (eds.), *Dokumente*, 103.

33. Author's interview with Fritz Wiedemann, July 25, 1968. Wiedemann said he had included this metaphor in his original manuscript, but editors had taken it out of the published version.

34. Directive, May 30, 1938, DGFP D/II, 358. See also Keitel, *Memoirs*, 62ff.; and Jodl's diary, IMT, XXVIII, 373. Earlier quotation is Weizsäcker to Trautmann, May 30, 1938, DGFP D/I, 864. In his notes of August 19, 1938, Weizsäcker recorded that Hitler intended to solve the Czech crisis in 1938, with force if necessary; see Weizsäcker, *Papiere*, 136.

35. Henderson to Halifax, September 3, 1938, DBFP 3/II, 224–26. For Lord Runciman's mission, see Rönnefarth, *Sudetenkrise*, I, 407–96. For Goebbel's activities, see Fitz-Randolph, *Frühstücks-Attaché*, 203–208. For Hitler's difficulty in making up his mind, see Ciano, *Hidden Diary*, I, 149–50. See Weizsäcker's memoranda, July 12 and 21, and August 19, 1938, in Weizsäcker, *Papiere*, 131ff.; the quotation is from the latter memorandum, which also contains the interesting fact that Hitler wanted to go to Prague in the invasion and intended to have Neurath take over the foreign office in his absence. Likus also warned Ribbentrop that there was open speculation that in the near future Neurath would again become foreign minister, while Ribbentrop would retire or be sent as ambassador to Italy. Likus's memoranda, August 9 and October 5, 1938, AA, Dienststelle Ribbentrop, Ribbentrop persönlich. For Neurath's talks with the British, see Henderson to Halifax, September 3, 1938, DBFP 3/II, 224–26; and Henderson, *Failure of a Mission*, 146–47. Neurath may also have participated in the conversations with Beck and Wiedemann, discussed in Foerster, *Generaloberst Beck*, 125–32. See also Neurath, "Lebenslauf." Earlier, Neurath had attempted to inaugurate discussions with Great Britain, by bypassing Ribbentrop. Fritz Wiedemann went to London for this purpose, and Neurath offered to handle any negotiations which might follow. Information from author's interview with Fritz Wiedemann, July 25, 1968; and Wiedemann's notes of conversations in London; and Halifax's account of the talks, July 18, 1938; in ADAP D/VII, 539–44; and DBFP 3/I, 587.

36. Lutz Graf Schwerin von Krosigk to Hitler, September 1, 1938, TWC, XII, 509–14. Author's translation. In interviews with the author, Schwerin von Krosigk and Frau von Mackensen mentioned his frequent visits to Neurath's villa in 1938. Schwerin von Krosigk confirmed that he had discussed the issue thoroughly with Neurath. Interviews of April 26 and May 3, 1968. See also Krosigk's talk with Weizsäcker, July 20, 1938, in Weizsäcker, *Papiere*, 132–33.

37. For Neurath's activities, see DGFP D/II, 662–63; TWC, XII, 799; and Neurath, "Lebenslauf."

38. Henderson to Halifax, September 19, 1938, DBFP 3/II, 413. See also Bullitt to Hull, September 14, 1938, FRUS 1938/I, 596. For the new stage of the crisis, see DGFP

D/II, 751–54, 786–802, and 810–11, and Hitler's orders to the Sudeten Germans, in Král, *Deutschen in Tschechoslowakei,* 300–301.

39. Diary entry for October 9, 1938, in Weizsäcker, *Papiere,* 144–145. For earlier information, see Hassell, *Vom anderen Deutschland,* 18; and FRUS 1938/I, 608–609. In the light of these documents, it is hard to explain Weizsäcker's alleged fury over Neurath's irresponsible absence (cited in Hassell's diary, October 10, 1938): "At the critical time, the president of the secret cabinet council did not bother himself, but went chasing after deer." Hassell, *Vom anderen Deutschland,* 22. Hassell, who was fond of criticizing Neurath, may well have exaggerated the incident, for it is difficult to understand what Neurath could have done in Berlin! That Neurath's optimistic evaluation of the situation had some basis in fact, see Rönnefarth, *Sudetenkrise,* I, 545ff.; and DBFP 3/II, 413 and 425. It appeared quite likely that Prague would make concessions. See also Brügel, *Tschechen und Deutsche,* 481ff.

40. Author's interview with Lutz Graf Schwerin von Krosigk, April 26, 1968. He had forgotten the metaphor he had used on that day until reminded of it a few years ago by a colleague. For Hitler's speech, see Brügel, *Tschechen und Deutsche,* 496–97.

41. Although he had already been assigned to Brussels, Bülow-Schwante was detained in Berlin by Weizsäcker, who told him he might as well wait out the crisis in Germany. Information from author's interview with Vico von Bülow-Schwante, May 24, 1968. For details of the mobilization, see NCA, III, 352.

42. See DGFP D/II, 985ff., and DBFP 3/II, 584–93.

43. For the telegram and its fate, see FRUS 1938/I, 684–85 and 727–28. In explaining to the United States ambassador why he had never received a reply, Wiedemann was careful not to tell the whole truth. See Wiedemann, *Der Mann der Feldherr,* 180–81. For Neurath's actions, see IMT, XVI, 647. In the jumbled atmosphere of the Nuremberg courtroom after the war, the presiding judge misunderstood Neurath to say that he had learned from Henderson that Chamberlain would come to Germany for a conference. From the timing of this conversation, however, that is clearly impossible. Neurath's prison "Notizen" give the information as cited in the text.

44. Neurath's testimony, IMT, XVI, 646–47.

45. See DBFP 3/III, 620; FRUS 1938/I, 698–99; François-Poncet, *Souvenirs,* 620; Schmidt, *Statist,* 411–412; and Rönnefarth, *Sudetenkrise,* I, 641–42. Neurath used the metaphor of the trump card in discussing these events with his friend the Evangelical Bishop of Stuttgart; see Wurm, *Erinnerungen,* 144. For the French move, see DBFP 3/II, 607–608.

46. Wiedemann, *Der Mann der Feldherr,* 180. In an interview on May 24, 1968, Vico von Bülow-Schwante gave a similar account; he said he had received the information from Neurath on the afternoon of September 18, 1938.

47. Wiedemann, *Der Mann der Feldherr,* 180–81. Later in the same afternoon, Neurath visited his friend Madame Marie Trarieux and her daughter, Mrs. Henriette de Gourko. From notes which the latter wrote at the time, both of these women confirm that Wiedemann's account of Neurath's conversation with Hitler is accurate as Neurath relayed it to them. Affidavit of Madame Trarieux, February 21, 1949, in Neurath Nachlass, and Mrs. Henriette de Gourko to author, November 1970.

48. Henderson to Halifax, September 18, 1938, DBFP 3/II, 597; and author's interview with Fritz Wiedemann, July 25, 1968. In this conversation and in his memoirs, Wiedemann insisted that had Neurath not appeared in the chancellery, there would have been war. This opinion is shared by many of Neurath's friends who believe he was the person most responsible for arranging the Munich conference. Weizsäcker strongly contradicts this in his diary entry of October 9, 1938 (Weizsäcker, *Papiere,* 145), but the anger is spiteful and without substantiating evidence.

49. See Wiedemann, *Der Mann der Feldherr,* 182–83; Weizsäcker, *Memoirs,* 154;

Wilson to Hull, October 21, 1938, FRUS 1938/I, 729; and Schmidt, *Statist,* 412ff. Information also from author's interviews with Fritz Wiedemann and Paul Schmidt, July 25 and 16, 1968. For proof that Neurath's fears about Ribbentrop were correct, see Ciano, *Hidden Diary,* 166, September 29, 1938; and diary entry of October 9, 1938, in Weizsäcker, *Papiere,* 145–46.

50. Author's interview with Fritz Wiedemann, July 25, 1968; and Wiedemann, *Der Mann der Feldherr,* 182–83. When Wiedemann later was posted to San Francisco as consul and heard that Neurath had been sent to Prague, he concluded that Hitler wanted to get both of them out of the way, and thus prevent repetition of their actions.

51. See *Berliner Morgenpost,* September 30, 1938; Schmidt, *Statist,* 414ff.; and Keith Eubank, *Munich,* 209ff. The cheering for Neurath is recorded in an undated memorandum from the Ribbentrop Bureau, forwarded to the foreign office on October 5, 1938, AA, Dienststelle Ribbentrop, Ribbentrop persönlich.

52. Mrs. Henriette de Gourko has reconstructed this conversation between Neurath and Göring from notes made at the time and sent it to the author, November 1970. On Neurath's reputation, see Szembek, *Journal,* October 10, 1938, 349–50. Neurath's activities during the conference are recorded in G. Ward Price, *Year of Reckoning,* passim, and Gilbert, *Nuremberg Diary,* 168. For the arrangement of the private Chamberlain/ Hitler talks, see Neurath's testimony, IMT, XVI, 647. Although both Henderson and Schmidt are silent on this point in their memoirs, the latter told me it was possible that Neurath accompanied Chamberlain to the Führer's residence. Certainly, Neurath and Chamberlain had a conversation immediately thereafter.

53. Baroness von Ritter to author, November 1, 1970, confirming information discussed in our interview, August 20, 1968.

54. Quotation and mention of meeting of November 26, 1938 are from Neurath, "Lebenslauf." Descriptions of the room changes are to be found in BA, RK R43/II, 1401 B. The quotation from Hassell's diary, December 17, 1938 (*Vom anderen Deutschland,* 22–23), continues by adding that Neurath "covers it up with a lot of hollow phrases." As has been noted before, Hassell was never a generous person in judging other people.

CHAPTER XIII. *Neurath in Prague: 1939–1941*

1. Dettinger Report, November 10, 1938, cited in Martin Broszat, "Die Reaktion des Mächte auf den 15. März 1939," in *Bohemia: Jahrbuch des Collegium Carolinum,* VIII, 262. For Hitler's speech, see VJHZG, VI (1958), 181–91. Neurath believed Hitler would make a "generous offer" to the Poles, thereby peacefully resolving that last problem—Danzig and the Polish Corridor. See Lipski, *Papers,* 453–54. Information also from author's interview with Frau von Mackensen, May 3, 1968.

2. For the pre-Munich plans of the Sudeten German Nazi party, see Král, *Deutschen in Tsechoslowakei,* 221–27. For the post-Munich suggestions and the foreign office plans, see Václav Král, *Lessons from History: Documents concerning Nazi Policies for Germanization and Extermination in Czechoslovakia,* 35–38; Král, *Deutschen in Tsechoslowakei,* 349–53, 357ff.; Woermann's memorandum, October 5, 1938, NA, ND, NG 3056; and documents in DGFP D/IV, 46–49, 56ff., 99–100, and TWC, XII, 515–18. The peace plan is discussed in H. Bodensieck, "Der Plan," *Zeitschrift für Ostforschung,* X (1961), 464–73; and Vojtech Mastný, *The Czechs Under Nazi Rule: The Failure of National Resistance, 1939–1942,* 28. Neurath apparently shared Hitler's belief that the Czechs must "realize that [their nation] is in the German sphere and it is in her own interest to adapt herself to the conditions of that sphere." DGFP D/IV, 70. The Czechs seemed to have decided to become good German vassals. See perceptive reports of the American representative in Prague, in George Kennan, *From Prague After Munich: Diplomatic Papers,* 8–11.

3. For the diary, see Weizsäcker, *Papiere,* 150 and 152. For the general background of the decision to proceed against rump-Czechoslovakia, see Heinrich Bodensieck, "Zur

Vorgeschichte des Protectorats Böhmen und Mähren," *Geschichte in Wissenschaft und Unterricht,* XIX (1968), 713–32. For Hitler's response, see DGFP D/IV, 221 fn. 1. The Czech offer is found in Altenberg's memorandum, March 1; and Weizsäcker to missions, March 10, 1939; in DGFP D/IV, 221–24, and AA 1941/435184–86. For the Prague atmosphere, see Kennan, *From Prague,* 28–33; and DGFP D/IV, 188–89.

4. Information from Albrecht von Kessel, in an interview July 30, 1968, and Kessel to author, February 15, 1969. Neurath, "Lebenslauf," records that on March 9, Neurath had a "private supper with the Führer and discussed thoroughly the Czech question which had momentarily grown so acute." My speculation about Neurath's conversation with Weizsäcker is based on the unlikelihood that Neurath would have received Kessel's warnings and not discussed them with his old friend and fellow Swabian. For Weizsäcker's views, see Weizsäcker, *Papiere,* 150–51. In supporting my contention that Neurath raised the same arguments with Hitler, two subsequent events are important. It seems unlikely that Hitler would have called upon Neurath to guarantee cultural autonomy for the Czechs, had Neurath not argued for such an approach. Similarly, it seems unlikely that Neurath would have suspected Hitler would offer him the position of Protector unless he had discussed with Hitler some problems concerning autonomy for the Czechs.

5. Upon the resignation of Eduard Beneš, Dr. Emil Hácha, President of the Czechoslovak Supreme Court, assumed the presidency. The foreign office was independently preparing some excuse for German intervention; see Král, *Deutschen in Tsechoslowakei,* 279–80. Hitler expected that the crisis would come later, and his actions bore an air of improvisation. In his study, Mastný (*Czechs,* 41ff.) suggests that Hácha's appearance in Berlin influenced Hitler's decision not to simply eradicate Czechoslovakia. It is also possible that Neurath's discussion with Hitler only a few days before may have been helpful in shaping the chancellor's reactions. For the Hácha/Hitler conversations, see DGFP D/IV, 263–69. The joint declaration is printed in DGFP D/IV, 270.

6. Hitler's proclamation, March 16, 1939 is DGFP D/IV, 283–86. For background, see Gaus's memorandum, March 15, 1939; and Lammers's affidavit, May 6, 1953; in AA 427/218198–200, and Fischinger Files. See also Mastný, *Czechs,* 47–49.

7. Lammers's affidavit, May 6, 1953, Fischinger Files. Hácha's notes of conversation with Hitler on March 20, 1939 are printed in *Dokumenty z historie československe politiky, 1939–1943* (hereafter cited as DHCP), I, 460. Hácha's other remarks are recorded in Ladislav Feierabend, *Ve vládě Protektorátu,* 19. From a comment recorded in Elizabeth Wagner (ed.), *Der Generalquartiermeister: Briefe und Tagebuchaufzeichnungen des Generalquartiermeisters des Heeres General der Artillerie Eduard Wagner,* 82, it seems that at one point General Fritsch's name was also under consideration. The first rumors in German diplomatic circles insisted that Konrad Henlein had been appointed Statthalter of Bohemia. See Halifax to Henderson, March 15, 1939, DBFP 3/IV, 272.

8. First two quotations are from Speer, *Memoirs,* 176, and author's interview with Constantin von Neurath, May 7, 1968. Information from author's conversation with Albrecht von Kessel, July 30, 1968, and Kessel to author, February 15, 1969.

9. No sources have survived, but the story has been reconstructed from two subsequent accounts: Lammers's affidavit, May 6, 1953, Fischinger Files; and author's interview with Baroness von Ritter, whom Neurath telephoned the evening of March 18, 1939. Constantin von Neurath and Frau von Mackensen also discussed this issue with their father and related the story to the author in interviews of May 7 and July 8, 1968.

10. Lammers's affidavit, Fischinger Files; and author's interview with Baroness von Ritter, August 20, 1968. There is no precise evidence as to when the decision to appoint Frank was made. On March 16, Frank was received by Hitler in Prague. After a few remarks about the modern architecture of the city, Hitler said: "Today is one of the most decisive of my life. We will unite once more that which by nature belongs together. We will not conclude an international treaty between Germany and Bohemia-Moravia, but we

will erect a Protectorate, which will reflect the majesty of the Reich." After a pause, the chancellor added: "For the next few days, Frank, keep yourself in readiness. I will need you." Returning to his office in Reichenberg, Frank received a call from Vienna to report there, where Hitler told him Neurath was Protector and he would be state secretary. Information from Karl Hermann Frank's papers, printed in Ernst Frank, *Karl Hermann Frank: Staatsminister im Protektorat,* 76–77.

11. Gerhard Köpke's draft for testimony at Nuremberg, Köpke Nachlass; author's interview with Frau von Mackensen, July 8, 1968, confirmed in author's interview with Constantin von Neurath, July 3, 1968. According to the latter, his father had told him he had to accept, "or else all sorts of nonsense would be done by us in Czechoslovakia, which would help nobody." Neurath later discussed the appointment with Karl Strölin, the mayor of Stuttgart, who strongly urged that he turn down the position. Author's conversation with Frau Magirus (Strölin's private secretary), July 24, 1968. In talking with Neurath shortly after his conversation with Hitler, General Keitel thought Neurath found the prospects "unedifying." Keitel, *Memoirs,* 82. Earlier quotations are from DNB report, April 5, 1939, AA, Under St. Sek., Protektorat. For Czech reactions, see Hubert Ripka, *Munich: Before and After,* 109; Vojta Beneš and R. A. Ginsburg, *Ten Million Prisoners (Protectorate Bohemia and Moravia),* 36–37; Detlef Brandes, *Die Tschechen unter deutschem Protektorat,* I, 29; and Kennan, *From Prague,* 111–13.

12. See Göring to all ministries, March 16; Himmler to Neurath, March (date illegible); Lammers to highest administrative offices, March 20; and Hess's order on party boundaries, March 21, 1939, in BA, RK R43/II 1326a; RK 3113/D632532; RK 5233/E310933–37; and BA, RJ R22/29. The quotation about conquest is from Madame Marie Trarieux's affidavit, February 21, 1949, Neurath Nachlass.

13. Quotation is from Mrs. Henriette de Gourko to author, November 1970. Andor Hencke, who served as liaison with Neurath, described the Protector's mood to the author in an interview on May 9, 1968 and in a letter, February 15, 1969. On October 12, 1945, Hencke told a team of American investigators that he judged Neurath as an aging gentleman who was "no longer energetic or ambitious." Poole Interviews, NA 59, entry 637. For decrees, see protocol of a meeting in Berlin, March 25; Lammers's note, March 25; Göring to Stuckhardt and Göring to Lammers, March 26; in RK 313/195974–98, RK 3113/D632806–808, RK 5233/E310932, and /E310944. For Hitler's decision, see Lammers's note, and Lammers to Körner, March 25 and 29, 1939; and the decree, April 1, 1939, in RK 5233/E310945, /E310947–48, and TWC, XII, 893, and original in RK 5233/E310959–62.

14. Frank to Neurath, n.d.; Pfundtner to Lammers, March 30; and Stuckhardt to all higher administrative offices, April 1, 1939; in BA, RK R43/II, 1329; and 1329a. The question of whose budget would cover the civil servants employed in the Protector's office was finally resolved on April 21, 1939, with all officials remaining on the payroll of the individual ministries in Berlin. One of the officials involved described to the author the resulting confusion: "Once Neurath had accepted this arrangement, there was henceforth no way for him to work against the ministries in Berlin with any chance of success, because it has always been true that the person who controls the purse also controls the activities and the policies. Thus Neurath's influence on events in Prague was from the very beginning extremely limited." Dr. Wolfgang Wolfram von Wolmar to author, June 26, 1974. For the documents, see files in BA, RK R43/II, 1329.

15. See Neurath's protest of April 11, and the resulting ruling of Hess, May 4, 1939, BA, RJ R22/29 and RK 3113/D632615. For Neurath's fight over party rights, see BA, RK R43/II, 1324. The files on Neurath's dispute with Gürtner are in BA, Reichs Justice Ministry (hereafter RJ) R22/29 and summarized in Neurath's report on June 26, and Gürtner's capitulation, August 3, 1939, in RK 5233/E310967–68, and /E310965–66.

16. Lammers's note, December 12, 1942, RK 4808/E237994. For background, see Woermann/Weizsäcker correspondence, February 1940; Neurath/Lammers/Ohnesorge correspondence, September and November 1940, and February, April, and May, 1941; in

AA 331/195881-83, AA 2312/484590, and RK 4808/E237821-23, /E237825-36, and /E237841-58. These insignificant cases indicate that there was good reason for Neurath to hope that Berlin would honor the Protectorate's autonomy. He was not, therefore, necessarily a fool or dupe in believing Hitler's assurances, for even as late as 1942, the chancellor was insisting on a special role for the Protectorate.

17. Quotation is from Speer, *Memoirs,* 176. For the discussion of administrative anarchy, see Walter Petwaidic, *Die autoritäre Anarchie,* 18ff.; and Mastný, *Czechs,* 96. The latter, however, gives a different emphasis to these aspects.

18. Altenberg turned down Neurath's invitation because he believed that with Frank as state secretary, little positive work could be accomplished. Hans Ulrich von Kotze also believed the job would end badly. Information from author's interviews with Günther Altenberg, and Frau von Kotze, April 3, and May 7, 1968. From April through July 1939, Kessel headed Neurath's staff, and then returned to Berlin upon the arrival of Hans Völckers. In July came two new assistants, Werner von Holleben, a professional diplomat who had served in Paris from 1932 to 1937, and Dr. Richard Thilenius. In general, Völckers handled all questions of domestic affairs; Holleben was in charge of protocol and representational functions; Thilenius supervised legal relations. Information from author's interviews with Kessel, Holleben, and Dr. Wolfgang Wolfram von Wolmar, July 30, June 21, and July 30, 1968; and Thilenius's affidavit, April 3, 1946, Ritter Papers. For Burgsdorff, see Mastný, *Czechs,* 94.

19. First quotations from Kennan's reports, August 19 and October 1939, in Kennan, *From Prague,* 218-19 and 232. Information on Frank is from his notes written in prison, in E. Frank, *Frank,* passim. Information also from author's interview with Hans Völckers, June 12, 1968. Quotation from Völckers's affidavit, December 13, 1948, Fischinger Files, and Wilhelm Dennler, *Die böhmische Passion,* 8. In his conversations with the author on April 3, 1968, Altenberg called Frank "a hardened person—hardened by his experiences in Czechoslovakia, which included the loss of an eye." Writing in 1948, Kessel claimed: "Frank united in his person a perverse hatred of everything Czech with a degree of duplicity which I have never seen either before or since." Cited in Erich Kaufmann's Plaidoyer for Neurath's defense, June 8, 1953, Fischinger Files.

20. Author's interview with Albrecht von Kessel, July 30, 1968, and Hans Völckers's affidavit, December 13, 1948, Fischinger Files. Frau von Mackensen told the author on May 3, 1968 that her father believed he would be able to clip Frank's wings in a short time.

21. See Himmler to Lammers, April 4; and Lammers to all departments, April 6, 1939, in BA, RK R43/II, 1329a. Also see the excellent analysis of the relationship between Neurath and the SS, in Richard Thilenius's affidavit, April 3, 1946, Ritter Papers. In Berlin, immediately prior to departing for Prague, Neurath told his old friend Madame Trarieux: "I will try to free Prague from the SS rule which has been established there." Affidavit, February 21, 1949, Neurath Nachlass. For the terror during the occupation of Prague, see Mastny, *Czechs,* 56.

22. Description of Sudeten officials from author's interview with Albrecht von Kessel, July 30, 1968, and Kennan's reports, May 23 and July 3, 1939, and October 1939, in Kennan, *From Prague,* 172, 188-89, and 232-33. For the provincial commissioners, a form of German sheriff, see Brandes, *Tschechen unter Protektorat,* I, 30ff.

23. See Stuckhardt to Lammers, May 2, 1939, TWC, XII, 894-96; and Kennan's dispatch, April 14, 1939, Kennan, *From Prague,* 117-18. Also see Kennan's other reports, in *From Prague,* 131-44 and 157-59. The fullest description of Frank's duplicity is in Kessel's 1948 affidavit, Kaufmann's Plaidoyer, Fischinger Files. On April 27, 1939, General Alois Eliáš became Minister-President of the new Czech government. See Mastný, *Czechs,* 60-61.

24. Affidavit of Albrecht von Kessel, 1948, for Kaufmann's Plaidoyer, Fischinger Files.

25. Information from author's interview with Albrecht von Kessel, July 30, 1968; and Neurath to Lammers, May 19, 1939, BA, RK R43/II, 1329. In his 1948 affidavit,

Albrecht von Kessel explained that Neurath requested to come to Berlin, especially after Frank attempted to "explain away" their first lies. Fischinger Files.

26. For removal of Rasch, see Heydrich to Lammers, June 2, 1939, BA, RK R43/II, 1325. Although Mastný implies (*Czechs*, 89–90) that Neurath was embarrassed by SS reports of fascist riots in Moravia and was unable to win his point, Neurath did not return to Prague empty-handed, and Kennan's dispatch of June 6 shows that the Czechs were pleased that Neurath was successfully defending them. They were aware, however, that Frank might still prevail. See Kennan, *From Prague,* 179. No records of the meeting have been found.

27. Gottberg was appointed on May 21, 1939; see RK 3113/D632686–87. For Neurath's actions, see his letter to Lammers, June 22; Lammers to Neurath, July 7; Feierabend to Darré, June 14; and Kennan's dispatch, June 6, 1939; in RK 1774/406076–77; /406080; RK 3113/D632581–85; and Kennan, *From Prague,* 182. For general discussion, see Mastný, *Czechs,* 88–89; and Robert L. Koehl, *RKFDV: German Resettlement and Population Policy, 1939–1945: A History of the Reich Commission for the Strengthening of Germandom,* 42ff.

28. Neurath's nomination of Theodor Gross is Neurath to Lammers, December 17, 1939, BA, RK R43/II, 1325. Quotations by Gottberg and Frank are from Mastný, *Czechs,* 121.

29. See Lammers's note, June 10; Neurath's note, July 7; Neurath/Frick correspondence, July 14 and 20, 1939, in BA, RK R43/II, 1325; and Lammers to Neurath, July 1, 21, and August 2, 1939, in BA, RJ R22/29. Hitler supported the Protector's position. For subsequent drafts, see Frick's circulars of August 5, 8, and 12, and the decree, September 2, 1939, in BA, RK R43/II, 1325.

30. Neurath to Lammers, June 29, 1940, and Lammers's undated note written on the reverse; and Lammers to all departments, July 24, 1940; in BA, RK R43/II, 1325, and RK 3113/D632555. For Neurath's lack of control over the police, see affidavit of Richard Thilenius, April 3, 1946, Ritter Papers, and *Zpověd K. H. Franka: Podle vlastnich výpovědi v době vazby u krajského soudu trestního na Pankráci* (Frank's confession in prison), 74.

31. Information from author's interview with Werner von Holleben, June 21, 1968. In his affidavit, May 6, 1953, Hans Lammers described the exact process: Neurath would frequently appeal for a Führer decision, knowing full well how much Hitler avoided such decisions, and thus, in effect, stalling the whole procedure. Fischinger Files.

32. Kennan's dispatch, August 19, 1939, in Kennan, *From Prague,* 218–19. Nevertheless, in the postwar trial, this was the crucial charge against Neurath, see below, pages 231, 235.

33. Since this study is primarily an examination of Neurath's role in Prague, and not a history of the Protectorate, the domestic developments of German rule there will not be further investigated. This is all the more unnecessary because of the recent appearance of two excellent books on this subject, Mastný's *The Czechs under Nazi Rule,* and Brandes, *Die Tschechen unter deutschem Protektorat.* Quotation is from Mastný, *Czechs,* 98. See also Brandes, *Tschechen unter Protektorat,* 36–37.

34. Likus's report of conversations with Kundt, June 8, 1939, AA 43/29459–61. See also Kennan's report, August 19, 1939 (*From Prague,* 222–23): "There are now indications . . . that the Germans are starting out on a campaign of indiscriminate Germanization wherever they see possibilities of progress in this direction." For the various plans, see Král, *Deutschen in Tschechoslowakei,* 221–27. Neurath must have known of these proposals. See DGFP D/II, 57ff. In late 1938, Ernst Kundt proposed to the foreign office that since it was impossible to Germanize the Czechs, a special Czech reservation should be created. See Král, *Deutschen in Tschechoslowakei,* 349–53.

35. Undated and unsigned memorandum in the foreign office file, AA 436/220888–99. From a covering letter, Weizsäcker to Kessel, July 3, 1939, it is clear that this docu-

ment was composed in late June and was part of Kessel's attempt to help Neurath determine a firm policy. Apparently drafted by Kessel after talks with Neurath and other officials, it was then sent to Berlin. See Neurath to Weizsäcker, July 6, 1939, AA 2050 /447410. For the struggles within the Protectorate, see Bormann to Frick, June 25; Frick to Neurath, July 14; and Stuckardt's order, July 20, 1939; in Král, *Deutschen in Tschechoslowakei,* 391; RK 3113/D632516; and /D632619ff.

36. Undated memorandum, AA 436/220899. Far from suppressing the Czech language as Frank wanted to do, Neurath sought to encourage German officials to learn it: "An official who knows a few words of Czech," the memorandum argues, "and uses them from time to time, can overcome the sense of inferiority in the Czech people, out of which there might easily spring passive resistance which would be hard to fight." AA 436/220894.

37. Undated memorandum, AA 436/220897-98. In a postwar affidavit (December 24, 1948), Carl Preuss, a minor official on Neurath's personal staff in Prague, wrote that Neurath always used the expression "a policy of the weak hand and the loose reins" in describing his program in the Protectorate. Neurath Nachlass.

38. See Poole, "Nazi Foreign Policy," 142; and August Kubizek, *The Young Hitler I Knew,* 286. This event is also discussed by Neurath in his "Skizze," written while in prison. In a memorandum of September 1939, Herbert Dirksen mentioned that he discussed the general crisis with Neurath in late July. *Documents and Materials,* II, 157.

39. Neurath's meeting with Hitler is mentioned in Neurath, "Lebenslauf." Quotation is from Mrs. Henriette de Gourko to author, November 1970, citing notes she made at the time. Possibly Neurath discussed the dangers with Weizsäcker and learned of the latter's despair. He was in Berlin at least through August 27. See Neurath to Lammers of that date, BA, RK R43/II, 1401 b. For events in the Protectorate, see Brandes, *Tschechen unter Protektorat,* 48. The public warning is IMT, XXXIV, 535-36. Composed on August 26 and dispatched to Berlin on August 27, it appeared on the walls of Prague on August 28, 1939. See BA, RJ R22/30. Earlier in the summer, in Frank's absence, Neurath had tried to arrange the political rehabilitation of Ernst Kundt, the Sudeten German leader of Prague and Frank's chief rival, who had been banished from the Protectorate. See Kundt to Neurath, August 4; and Neurath to Lammers, and Neurath to Weizsäcker, August 8, 1939; in BA, RK R43/II, 1324, and AA 1774/4063039ff. According to a report circulating during this time, Frank would not return because of Neurath's opposition to "Henlein radicals" but would be replaced by Kundt. See Brandes, *Tschechen unter Protektorat,* 283 fn. 118.

40. Neurath's testimony, June 24, 1946, IMT, XVI, 661.

41. Lammers's office memorandum, October 29, 1939, BA, RK R43/II, 1324. For the harsh new decrees, see Frank to Weizsäcker, September 22; and Lammers's notes of conferences on September 23 and 29, 1939; in AA 436/220904, and BA, RK R43/II, 1325.

42. Kennan's dispatch, October 1939, in Kennan, *From Prague,* 237-38.

43. Security police reports for October 3, 13, 25, and 28, NA, T-175, 258/570071, /750145, and /750158-60. The Italian report is Caruso to Rome, October 24, 1939, DDI, 9/II, 11. Neurath's views are from Neurath to Köpke, October 14, 1939, Staatsarchiv Nuremberg. This attitude confirmed to author in conversations with Frau von Mackensen and Frau von Kotze, May 3 and 7, 1968. Both had visited Neurath in Prague at about this time. The final quotation is from Holleben's affidavit, cited in Kaufmann's Plaidoyer, June 8, 1953, Fischinger Files.

44. Neurath/Hácha conversation, October 31, 1939, cited in Mastný, *Czechs,* 115, and IMT, XVI, 663. Holleben's quotation is reported in Dennler, *Böhmische Passion,* 9. See also SD report, October 30, 1939; and Heyden-Tynsch's memorandum, October 29, 1939; in NA, T-175 258/750172-73, and RK 331/195884.

45. Neurath's decree, November 14, 1939; Neurath's testimony, cited in *Persekuce*

českého studenstva za okupace, 56ff.; and IMT, XVI, 663. Earlier quotation from Mastný, *Czechs*, 112–13. For funeral, see Feierabend, *Vládě Protektorátu*, 112, and Brandes, *Tschechen unter Protektorat*, 89.

46. Neurath's testimony, IMT, XVI, 665. Völckers accompanied Neurath to the meeting and described Hitler's rage for the author on June 12, 1968. For the generally peaceful nature of the demonstrations, see Heydrich to Lammers, and Neurath to Hitler, November 15, 1939, in RK 3113/D632599–600 and /D632595. Information also from author's interview with Werner von Holleben, June 21, 1968. Although Brandes (*Tschechen unter Protektorat*, 91–92) claims that our knowledge of this meeting is limited to the possibly self-serving testimony of Neurath and Frank, there is also Chvalkovský's dispatch to his government (in *Persekuce*, 66ff.), which is probably the source for the remarkably accurate description in Hubert Ripka, *Two Years of the Protectorate*, 110–11. Some of the quotations are from that source; others are from Hans Völcker's description to the author. Frank's postwar version is printed in E. Frank, *Frank*, 90.

47. Frank did not even inform Neurath that he was taking his airplane. Best presentation is in Brandes, *Tschechen unter Protektorat*, 92ff., and Mastný, *Czechs*, 117ff. Of the 1850 students arrested, 1200 were transported to the concentration camp at Oranienburg. The remainder, mainly Slovaks, Yugoslavs, Bulgarians, and youths under 20, were released. All the surviving sources, except E. Frank (*Frank*, 90), agree that Neurath was not present. Apparently Neurath and Völckers left the chancellery with Chvalkovský, in order to calm him down. They both then went to Neurath's villa, where they discussed the whole unhappy and amazing reaction by Hitler. Brandes (*Tschechen unter Protektorat*, 91–93) errs in blaming the Protectorate government for inexplicable inactivity. From Chvalkovský's report, they did not expect any further German moves.

48. Dennler's diary entry, November 1939, *Böhmische Passion*, 11–12. Information also from author's conversations with Hans Völckers and Werner von Holleben, June 12 and 21, 1968; and from the letter and affidavit of Irene Friedrich, Neurath's private secretary, June 6, 1946, recalling Neurath's horror and dismay over the actions. Lüdinghausen files, currently in possession of Dr. Wolfram von Wolmar. The account of Neurath's visit with Hácha is from Brandes, *Tschechen unter Protektorat*, 94.

49. Lammers's office memoranda, November 9 and 22, 1939, BA, RK R43/II, 1325. See also affidavit of Curt von Burgsdorff, April 4, 1952, Neurath Nachlass. The final quotation is from Brandes, *Tschechen unter Protektorat*, 98.

50. Documentation for this meeting is sparse. Neurath repeated the key points to the foreign office representative in Prague who forwarded them to his office in a dispatch in December; see DGFP D/VIII, 338–39. See also Neurath's testimony, IMT, XVI, 665. For warnings, see RK 3113/D632522–24 and /D632653–54.

51. Neurath to Madame Trarieux, January 6, April 7, and May 12, 1940, de Gourko Papers. Neurath's improved position is discussed in the report of the underground agent Psel to London, January 25, 1940, cited in Brandes, *Tschechen unter Protektorat*, 100. His attempts to free the students are SS Aktenvermerk for Heydrich, February 25; and Neurath's memorandum, March 26, 1940, T-175, 119/264753, and IMT, XXXIV, 353–54. In January 1940, when two cabinet ministers fled and emerged in Beneš's government-in-exile in London, Neurath successfully insisted upon a moderate response. See Ziemke to AA, January 29 and 31, 1940, AA 1779/460443–44, and DGFP D/VIII, 723–24. Finally, in January 1940, Neurath tried to block a special fund of 100,000 RM for Frank, citing the danger that "this money would be employed without my knowledge and against my will and thus threaten the unified leadership of the Protectorate." In February, however, Himmler intervened and Frank received the money. For the correspondence, see RK 3113/D632811–26.

52. For the rumors, see Vokmar Hopf to Neurath, January 2, 1940; and SD reports, December 6 and 11, 1939, and March 1 and April 5, 1940; in Král, *Deutschen in*

Tschechoslowakei, 398-99; and NA, T-175, 258/750400-404, /750433, /750958, and /751195. For the fears, see Ziemke to AA, June 17; and SD report, June 20, 1940; in AA 766/270694-95, and NA, T-175, 295/751754. For the Sudeten German plans, see Likus's report, June 8; and Neurath to Lammers, August 27, 1939; in AA 43/29459-61, and BA, RK R43/II, 1325. For the situation after the outbreak of the war, see monthly report for March 1940, and Lammers's memorandum, October 22, 1939, in Král, *Deutschen in Tschechoslowakei,* 403, and BA, RK R43/II, 1324. Neurath's memorandum, April 23, and Neurath to Lammers, May 16, 1940, are from Král, *Deutschen in Tschechoslowakei,* 404, and RK 3113/D632738-39.

53. Memorandum of a meeting of the provincial commissions, printed in Král, *Deutschen in Tschechoslowakei,* 416. Neurath's original letter has not been found, but see Lammers to departments, August 6, 1940, AA K773/K204739. For the most important plan calling for a division of the Protectorate, see that of Dr. Jury, the Gauleiter of Lower Austria, July 25, 1940, printed in Král, *Lessons,* 47-53.

54. On August 19, 1940, Ziemke, the representative of the foreign office in Prague, wrote to the AA: "The plans for reorganization of the Protectorate grow each day." See also his dispatches of August 26 and 30, 1940, AA 423/217380-82, /217384-88, and /217389-93.

55. After the war, Neurath's memorandum of August 31, 1940 formed the single most important document in the successful prosecution of him as a war criminal, and so must be discussed here briefly as a document. The sole source is an unsigned copy, which was introduced as a surprise document in cross-examination, IMT, XVII, 59ff. and 95ff., printed in IMT, XXXIII, 252-71, supplied by the Czech government from files captured in Prague. No preliminary drafts have been found. Subsequently, Neurath testified that he believed the document was a forgery. He recalled a "much shorter" memorandum, and challenged the SS certificate of his name. Numerous witnesses support his contention that no SS man ever worked in his office. From the evidence introduced by the prosecution (IMT, XVII, 377), and from evidence discussed below (page 207), however, I believe the document is authentic. It was written by Neurath, duplicated in Frank's office (thereby receiving the SS attestation of signature). Crucial for this confirmation is Ziemke to AA, August 30, 1940, AA 423/217391-92. The quotation is from affidavit of Baroness von Ritter, May 28, 1946, IMT, XVI, 673. Baroness von Ritter told the author she had constructed this affidavit from letters in her possession from Neurath, which were subsequently destroyed. Interview with Baroness von Ritter, July 16, 1968.

56. Neurath's memorandum, August 31, 1940, IMT, XXXIII, 252-59. For Neurath's earlier proposals, see above, page 199. At no time did Neurath ever refer to Hitler's comment during the Hossbach discussion that there would probably be a need to effect the "compulsory emigration of two million people from Czechoslovakia." See DGFP D/I, 36.

57. Shortly before the dispatch of these memoranda, Neurath discussed his ideas with Ziemke. Peace and quiet, he said, prevailed in the Protectorate. Bohemia and Moravia could be made a part of Greater Germany through purely political means and this gradual evolution was only conceivable under the Protectorate form. Thus, through numerous channels, he hoped the message would reach Hitler. Ziemke to AA, August 30 and September 17, 1940, AA 423/217389-93 and /217394-99; Ziemke reported that he had read and possessed a copy of Frank's memorandum, but did not mention Neurath's. Frank's memorandum, August 31, 1940 is in IMT, XXXIII, 260-71. The prosecution at Nuremberg admitted that Neurath's own proposal was not criminal, but he was guilty of supporting Frank's, which was. None of the background and explanation for Neurath's actions were introduced into the trial.

58. Heydrich's memorandum, September 11, 1940, printed in *Zločiny nacistů za okupace a osvobozenecký boj našeho lidu,* 156ff.

59. Affidavit of Hans Lammers, May 6, 1953, Fischinger Files. The Lammers papers, which probably contain many more letters from Neurath, were given to Dr. Herbert

Grabert, of the Institut für deutsche Nachkriegsgeschichte in Tübingen. In correspondence with the author, Dr. Grabert refused permission to examine these files. Neurath had achieved success in the question of Berlin's desire to ban marriages between Czechs and Germans by demanding that the discussion be brought to Hitler, where the issue died without being implemented. See minutes of the meeting at the ministry of the interior, July 5; minutes of the meeting in the chancellery, August 26; Lammers's note, September 5; and Lammers to Neurath, September 14, 1940; in RK 4714/E227982–86; BA, RK R43/II, 1325a; and BA, RK R43/II, 1325.

60. Neurath's memorandum, September 25, 1940, RK 3113/D632626–28. Lammers called the meeting, but there is no further record. See BA, RK R43/II, 1325a.

61. Ziemke to AA October 5, 1940, IMT, XXXV, 439–40.

62. Neurath to Madame Trarieux, November 25, 1940, de Gourko Papers. Neurath's quotation is from his memorandum, September 25, 1940, RK 3113/D632626–28. Ziemke's dispatch to AA is October 11, 1940, AA 423/217414. For Hitler's order, see Lammers's staff memorandum, October 4, 1940, RK 3113/D632684–85. At the trial after the war, Neurath was stunned when the prosecution presented Ziemke's telegram and sought to use it to make Neurath responsible for having suggested to Hitler the "elimination" of undesirable Czechs. The prosecution used the last line of this telegram, which said that Hitler's decision followed the suggestion of Neurath and Frank, to prove the point. A proper interpretation would be that Hitler had decided in that meeting to preserve the Protectorate, and in so doing had followed the suggestions of both Neurath and Frank. Neurath's lawyer, however, did not see the distinction and failed to make this rebuttal.

63. See especially Mastný, *Czechs,* 162. For Neurath's success, see Lammers to Frick, February 1, 1941; and Oberlandrat to Protektor, September 6, 1940; in BA, RK R43/II, 1325; and Král, *Lessons,* 72. Under these circumstances, it is wrong to suspect that Neurath supported, or even was aware of some of, Frank's plans to push Germanization. In fact, no one seems to have tried to implement Germanization as long as Neurath was in charge. In so doing, they were following Hitler's announcement in June 1939 that he had no intention of trying "to turn Czechs into Germans." See Lammers's minutes of a meeting at the Obersalzburg, June 20, 1939, BA, RK R43/II, 1327.

64. Neurath to Köpke, February 11, 1941, Köpke Nachlass. The victories refer to the disastrous Italian defeats in North Africa in December and January, during which they lost nearly 130,000 prisoners. For Neurath's waning power, see Hubert Masařik, "The Last Months of General Eliáš," *Reporter,* XXI (1968), II. For the release of the students, see Ziemke to AA, February 7, 1941, AA 1779/406480. The huge troop concentrations and rumors of an attack upon the Soviet Union are from Dennler, *Böhmische Passion,* 38–39, 43, and 48. For Frank's actions in the Protectorate, see Ziemke to AA, February 11, 1941, AA 2380/D498382–83; and Mastný, *Czechs,* 162–65. Returning from his vacation, Neurath told the Czechs they should not take Frank's threats seriously; see Masařik, "Last Months of Eliáš," III.

65. Masařik, "Last Months of Eliáš," IV. According to this account, the official was Andor Hencke. Information generally confirmed in author's interview with Hencke, May 9, 1968. For the warnings by Frank, see his speech of April 8, 1941, cited in Václav Král, *Otzáky hospodářského a sociálniho vývoje v českých zemich v letech, 1938–1945,* III, 221. For the April 20 speech by Frank and the subsequent cabinet crisis, see Janson to AA, April 23, 24, and 25; and Neurath to Lammers, April 24, 1941; in AA 4714/E228007, AA 1779/406482–83, AA 2380/D498442, and RK 4808/E237830.

66. Neurath's decree, June 27, 1941, IMT, XXXIII, 328. On the same day, Neurath wrote Bormann asking that the party issue a similar decree, and on August 16, 1941, Lammers confirmed, to Neurath's great satisfaction, that Hitler had agreed there would be no changes in the territorial boundaries during the war. See RK 3113/D632641–44 and RK 4808/E238102. Ironically, the prosecution at Nuremberg subsequently at-

tempted to show that Neurath's decree was a dastardly attempt to lull the Czechs into a false sense of security! In fact, the Germans constantly violated Neurath's decree, and reports continued to circulate that the Czechs would be deported to the other side of the Urals. See Král, *Deutschen in Tschechoslowakei,* 448.

67. For background, see Mastný, *Czechs,* 176ff.; and Brandes, *Tschechen unter Protektorat,* 204–205. Author's interviews with Hans Völckers and Werner von Holleben, on June 12 and 21, 1968, confirmed the impression that the situation was actually very quiet. In late August 1941, Neurath even became involved with the expansionist party men, Bormann and Himmler, in one of his numerous controversies with Berlin over jurisdiction. See correspondence of July and August in RK 4808/E238094–8106. For the alarmist reports, see Krebs to Himmler, August 19; and SD reports of August 27, 29, and September 12 and 17, 1941; in NA, T-175, 66/258215ff.; and T-175, 278/489107–108, /489124–25, /489175–76, and /489188–91. Neurath's report of September 10, 1941, is not available, but is cited in Král, *Otzáky,* III, 232; and in Václav Král, *Pravda o okupaci,* 229. Frank's speech is printed in Král, *Deutschen in Tschechoslowakei,* 519–24. Other information and rumors from Lammers's affidavit, May 6, 1953, Fischinger Files; Dennler, *Böhmische Passion,* 55; and Brandes, *Tschechen unter Protektorat,* 208–209.

68. Information from "Notizen"; IMT, XVII, 16–17; and author's interviews with Baroness von Ritter and Hans Völckers, July 16, and June 12, 1968. Confirming evidence can be found in Lammers's affidavit, May 6, 1953, Fischinger Files, and Dennler, *Böhmische Passion,* 53–57. See also report of one official, who recorded that Neurath had "asked to be relieved of duties because of the wartime conditions." Gastberger to AA, September 28, 1941, AA 2380/D498101. Neurath's anger was described in Frau von Mackensen's interview, May 3, 1968. According to Dennler (*Böhmische Passion,* 53–57), Frank had supplied forged documents to Hitler. In discussions with the author, Werner von Holleben and Hans Völckers both agreed that Frank expected to get the appointment and had staged the crisis in order to remove Neurath, who apparently suspected nothing. On October 7, 1941, Hitler told one visitor that the Czechs regarded Neurath "as an affable old gentleman and mistook his good heart and leniency for weakness and stupidity." Cited in Mastný, *Czechs,* 180. Frank later claimed he had not been involved, but confirms that Hitler told him he would not scold Neurath, merely tell him to take a vacation. E. Frank, *Frank,* 99–100.

69. Cited in Cestmír Amort and Otto Hornung (eds.), *Heydrichiáda,* 126–42. For the faulty interpretation, see Brandes, *Tschechen unter Protektorat,* 233.

70. See Dennler, *Böhmische Passion,* 57 and 61. See also Gastberger to AA, October 2 and 7; SD reports, October 2, 1941; and Kaltenbrunner to Himmler, July 1, 1943; in AA 2380/D498053–55, /D498086–89; NA, T-175, 261/754915–17; Král, *Deutschen in Tschechoslowakei,* 455–56; and NA, T-175, 458/3046ff.

71. Quotation is from Dennler's diary entry September 28, 1941, *Böhmische Passion,* 57. Statistics are from Luther to Weizsäcker, October 10; and Heydrich to Lammers, October 9, 1941; in AA 2330/D498075, and RK 1774/406029–34.

72. Frank's account of a conversation with Hitler, May 28, 1942, in Král, *Deutschen in Tschechoslowakei,* 478. For the new order, see Heydrich to Lammers, October 9; Heydrich to Bormann, October 30, 1941; and AA note, February 28, 1942; in RK 1774/406029–34; Král, *Deutschen in Tschechoslowakei,* 462; and AA, Inland II A/B, 83-26.

73. Harry Picker and Gerhard Ritter (eds.), *Hitler's Secret Conversations,* 192.

CHAPTER XIV. *Leinfelderhof, Nuremberg, Spandau*

1. Neurath to Köpke, May 27, 1942, Köpke Nachlass. The other material is from a diary entry of April 15, 1942 in Louis P. Lochner (ed.), *The Goebbels Diaries, 1942–1943,* 171. See also Schacht's attempts in Schacht to Lammers, August 2; and Lammers

to Bormann, August 19, 1943, but Hitler refused even to receive him. BA, RK R43/II, 140a. Earlier quotations are from Neurath, "Lebenslauf," in a section which Neurath himself added in 1943. Writing from his mountain retreat to Köpke on October 3, 1941, Neurath said that all he could think of was the refrain of a popular song: "What happens now?" Köpke Nachlass.

2. Neurath to Köpke, November 7, 1942, Köpke Nachlass. The career of the son is recorded in "Lebenslauf." He served in Lausanne in 1932; Berlin, 1932–33; Rome, 1933–1936; Brussels, 1936–40, from where he was returned in an exchange of diplomats after the outbreak of the war. Neurath's decision to go to Berlin is found in Neurath to Madame Trarieux, November 5, 1942, de Gourko Papers.

3. See *Deutsche Allgemeine Zeitung,* February 2, 1943, for official press reports. The source for the scene with Meissner is author's interview with Frau von Mackensen, May 3, 1968, and Neurath's affidavit, May 23, 1946. On the subsequent history of the endowment money, information from author's conversation with Lutz Graf Schwerin von Krosigk, April 26, 1968; and letter of Reichs-Kredit-Gesellschaft, Bamburg, to Lüdinghausen, June 21, 1946, in Lüdinghausen file, currently in the possession of Dr. Wolfgang Wolfram von Wolmar.

4. Neurath to Madame Trarieux, June 13, March 14, and April 7, 1943, de Gourko Papers; Neurath to Köpke, March 14, and Köpke to Neurath, March 17, 1943, Köpke Nachlass. See also Hassell's diary, April 20, 1943, *Vom anderen Deutschland,* 272–73. Earlier quotation from Dr. Wilhelm Henninger to Baroness von Neurath, September 9, 1952, Neurath Nachlass. For the arguments over his office space, see correspondence of February and March 1943, BA, RK R43/II, 1401 b; and author's interview with Lutz Graf Schwerin von Krosigk, April 26, 1968. Neurath eventually gave some space to Krosigk, on the explicit condition that the rooms never be turned over to his neighbor in Dahlem, Alfred Rosenberg, who had been trying to obtain them. At the postwar trial, the prosecution produced a number of documents from Neurath's secret cabinet office during 1943 concerning the payment of money. See IMT, XXXIII, 574–76. They do not indicate what the money was paid for and Neurath could not account for them on the stand. See IMT, XVII, 53–54. The mystery still remains, for I have been unable to uncover any information at all on this subject.

5. Neurath to Madame Trarieux, July 18, 1943, de Gourko Papers. Earlier quotation was given to the author by Constantin von Neurath, July 3, 1968. Information on Rommel from Lutz Koch, *Erwin Rommel: die Wandlung eines grossen Soldaten,* 136–37 and 148–49; and author's conversations with Constantin von Neurath, May 7 and July 3, 1968.

6. Neurath to Köpke, July 25, 1943, Köpke Nachlass.

7. Neurath to Fontaine, August 28, 1943, Fontaine Nachlass.

8. Quotation given to the author in an interview on April 25, 1968 by General Hans Speidel. A distant cousin of Neurath's, Speidel questioned him during their meeting in Freudenstadt; see below, page 217. For Lammers's drafts of a letter, Lammers to Neurath, August 23, and Neurath to Lammers, August 28, 1943, see RK 5734/E415833–37 and /E415841–47.

9. Information primarily from Speidel's testimony for Karl Strölin, n.d., IZ, ZS 579. In discussing this issue with Strölin's private secretary, Frau Magirus, on July 24, 1968, the author was informed that the Strölin Nachlass (which she controls) contains nothing of interest for this story, since Neurath and Strölin were too careful to put anything into writing.

10. Speidel's testimony, IZ, ZS 579. Some conversations were held in Leinfelderhof and others in Strölin's office in Stuttgart. Confirmation of the frequent meetings from author's interviews with Frau von Mackensen, Frau Magirus, and Constantin von Neurath, May 3, July 24, and July 7, 1968.

11. Speidel's affidavit, December 20, 1948, Neurath Nachlass. Information also from author's interview with General Hans Speidel, April 25, 1968.

12. Speidel's affidavit, December 20, 1948, Neurath Nachlass; author's interview with General Hans Speidel, April 25, 1968; and Hans Speidel, *Invasion 1944: Rommel and the Normandy Campaign,* 63; and Gert Buchheit, *Soldatentum und Rebellion: die Tragödie der deutschen Wehrmacht,* 369-70. See also Helmut Krausnick, "Erwin Rommel und der deutsche Widerstand gegen Hitler," VJHZG, I (1953), 68.

13. Neurath to Madame Trarieux, June 11, 1944, de Gourko Papers; Constantin von Neurath (son) to Köpke, May 15, 1944, Köpke Nachlass. Information also from author's interviews with Frau von Mackensen and Constantin von Neurath, May 3 and July 3, 1968. It is difficult to understand why Neurath chose to introduce none of this material into his postwar trial. Perhaps Neurath himself did not want to become involved in an unseemly attempt to justify himself by citing talks which, ultimately, produced nothing. See discussion below, page 229.

14. For background on Count von Stauffenberg, see Joachim Kramarz, *Stauffenberg,* 21-22. For Goerdeler, see Wilhelm von Schramm, *Der 20. Juli in Paris,* 32-33. For Neurath's relations with the Stauffenberg family at the royal Württemberg court, see above, page 17.

15. Neurath to Köpke, July 26, 1944, Köpke Nachlass. Ellipses in the original.

16. Constantin von Neurath related to the author on July 3, 1968 a strange story of his fears that his father would be arrested at the funeral and the sudden appearance of an SS man who tried to divert the car. Neurath's broken state was also described in an interview with Lutz Graf Schwerin von Krosigk, April 26, 1968, who related how Neurath was more upset and concerned than he had ever seen him before. From Neurath, Krosigk learned for the first time that Rommel's death had not been a natural one.

17. Frau von Mackensen to Köpke, July 23, 1944. In a subsequent letter, September 29, 1944, she still complained that her parents refused to take refuge in the hunting lodge at Brandt, near Blundenz. Köpke Nachlass.

18. Neurath to Köpke, December 27, 1944.

19. Author's interview with Frau von Mackensen, May 3, 1968. See also letters printed below, page 242.

20. Author's interview with Frau von Mackensen, May 3, 1968.

21. Neurath to Baroness von Ritter, August 6, 1945, immediately after transfer to Kirchberg. Ritter Papers. Information also from author's interview with Frau von Mackensen, May 3, 1968.

22. Information on the background to the trial is now superbly presented in Bradley F. Smith, *Reaching Judgment at Nuremberg.* Other information from Sidney S. Alderman, "Negotiating the Nuremberg Trial Agreements, 1945," in Raymond Dennett and Joseph E. Johnson (eds.), *Negotiation with the Russians,* 49-98.

23. See *Bayerische Tag* (official American newspaper for the occupation), August 18, September 1 and 22, October 8 and 22, 1945. For indictment, see IMT, I, 24ff.

24. Summary is from Joe J. Heydecker and Johannes Leeb, *The Nuremberg Trial,* 82. Quotation is from G. M. Gilbert's original diary, undated, used with the permission of Dr. Gilbert. Major John H. Monigan, Jr., who conducted most of Neurath's interrogations, concluded that it was a mistake to have held them in English. Many points remained unclarified, even after these interrogations. Monigan to author, January 23, 1968. According to the files in the National Archives, Neurath was interrogated on October 2, 3, 4, 8, 18, and November 12 and 14, 1945. Some excerpts are printed in NCA, Suppl. B, 1488-1509. For Monigan's letter urging that Neurath be released, see Smith, *Reaching Judgment,* 71.

25. Neurath to Baroness von Ritter, November 18, 1945, Ritter Papers. Earlier quotations from Douglas M. Kelley, *22 Cells in Nuremberg: A Psychiatrist Examines*

the *Nazi Criminals,* 115, and G. M. Gilbert, *Nuremberg Diary,* 12. See also Poole, "Light on Nazi Foreign Policy," 138-39.

26. Information and quotation from author's interview with Baroness von Ritter, July 16, 1968. Earlier quotation is Neurath to his brother Wilhelm, November 1945, Ritter Papers. Frau von Mackensen informed the author on May 3, 1968 that she had a similar impression of the lawyer, but did not meet him until May 1946 when the authorities finally permitted her and her mother to leave Austria. For the selection process for lawyers, see *Süddeutsche Zeitung,* November 12, 1945. The German evaluation of Lüdinghausen is confirmed in a report from a Dr. Braun to Sir David Maxwell-Fyfe, November 27, 1945, which gives a frank appraisal of all the defense lawyers. Lüdenhausen is lumped in with a group which includes "not one who is really first class." They were lacking in experience and "will not be any more than the assistants of the better informed and cleverer defendants." He assures the British prosecution that all are guaranteed to provide an "unprovocative treatment of the case." Braun to Maxwell-Fyfe, British Foreign Office, 371, U 9486/16/73, 50998/07825. From another document in the foreign office files (Major Neave to the General Secretary of the IMT, October 24, 1945), it appears that Neurath did try to secure his own lawyer, before accepting one from the list provided by the court. I have been unable to throw any light on this subject. British Foreign Office, LCO 2 2982/X/LO6693.

27. *Basler Nachrichten,* October 20, 1945, article entitled "Die Anklageschrift."

28. Neurath to Baroness von Ritter, November 25; see also December 5, 1945, Ritter Papers.

29. Neurath to Baroness von Ritter, December 15, 1945, Ritter Papers.

30. Neurath to Baroness von Ritter, December 15, 1945, and January 14, 1946, Ritter Papers. The tears are recorded in *Nürnberger Nachrichten,* January 25, 1946.

31. Neurath to Baroness von Ritter, February 16, 1946, Ritter Papers. Earlier quotation is Gilbert, unpublished diary, and *Nuremberg Diary,* 73.

32. Neurath to Baroness von Ritter, February 3, 1946, Ritter Papers.

33. IMT, VI, 98-105.

34. IMT, VI, 113-17.

35. Neurath to Baroness von Ritter, March 13, 1946. Earlier quotations from Neurath to Baroness von Ritter, February 17 and March 2, 1946. Ritter Papers.

36. In early January, sets of bars were erected separating the defendants from their lawyers, and thereafter communication between Neurath and Lüdinghausen became extremely difficult. Neurath had to write out all his notes in his hard-to-read hand, and a typist had to transcribe them for the lawyer. His letters to Baroness von Ritter of January and February 1946 (Ritter Papers) are full of his complaints about these difficulties. Moreover, he still had not heard from his wife and daughter. Lüdinghausen was of little help, and permitted the court to eliminate Manfred Zimmermann and Msgr. Orsenigo as witnesses. Zimmermann was Neurath's closest friend, and was frequently described to the author as his "father confessor." The affidavit he submitted (IMT, XL, 447-53) gives some idea of the excellent evidence he might have offered. Then in February, Lüdinghausen's assistant, Professor Metzger, was arrested, setting back even further the organization of Neurath's defense. The family reluctantly came to the conclusion that Lüdinghausen was of little help in all these matters. Quotation is from Neurath to his wife, January 1, 1946, Ritter Papers. For the Metzger case, see Viktor Freiherr von der Lippe, *Nürnberger Tagebuchnotizen, November 1945 bis Oktober 1946,* 94, 137, 143, 174, and 193.

37. Lüdinghausen to Köpke, April 8, 1946, Köpke Nachlass. Neurath was aware of the dangers; see Gilbert, *Nuremberg Diary,* 173. See also Lippe, *Nürnberger Tagebuchnotizen,* 195, 247, 251. For the various witnesses, see IMT, XII, 58-61, 561-62; XIV, 141, 287-290. Included in those not cross-examined at all by Lüdinghausen were Seyss-Inquart and Glaise-Horstenau.

38. See IMT, X, 90, 180–83, and 230.

39. Neurath to Baroness von Ritter, January 6 and March 22, 1946, Ritter Papers. He first heard from his wife in March; in April she and their daughter were expelled from Austria, with all their property confiscated. Neurath to Baroness von Ritter, November 15 and 25, 1945, and April 9 and 11, 1946. On April 13, 1946, Neurath told Baroness von Ritter that he rejoiced that his family were back in Leinfelderhof where at least they would have enough to eat. Ritter Papers.

40. Of the documents, two were from Köpke's files (from which many had been offered), one apparently came from foreign office materials, and four from the surviving Neurath papers. None of these original documents have been found. Both Köpke and Dieckhoff, Neurath's principal witnesses, came early to Nuremberg in order to prepare for their testimony, but to no apparent advantage on the stand. Similarly, the affidavit which Lüdinghausen submitted from André François-Poncet was ineffective. See Lippe, *Nürnberger Tagebuchnotizen,* 323 and 338.

41. IMT, XVI, 615 and 620. See also Hans Fritzsche, *The Sword in the Scales,* 288; and Lippe, *Nürnberger Tagebuchnotizen,* 337 and 339. The poor atmosphere surrounding Neurath's testimony is described in Lippe, 341 and 399.

42. See the Tribunal's warnings to Lüdinghausen, IMT, XVI, 621, 626, 627–28, 641, and 650. In general, the court believed that he was "allowing the defendant to make long, long speeches. This is not the object of evidence."

43. See Lippe, *Nürnberger Tagebuchnotizen,* 339.

44. See Lippe, *Nürnberger Tagebuchnotizen,* 341 and 344.

45. Neurath's fear was confirmed in author's interviews with Frau von Mackensen, May 3 and July 8, 1968. This fear is corroborated by an aunt of Dr. Lüdinghausen who told Michel C. Vercel (*Les Rescapés de Nuremberg: Les "Seigneurs de la guerre" après le Verdict,* 37): "My nephew told me throughout the trial, that he ardently prayed that Neurath would not be acquitted." For the Czech trials, especially that of Frank which lasted from March 22 through April 28, 1946, see E. Frank, *Frank,* 167ff. The condemned Frank was executed on May 22, 1946. Shown a newspaper account, Neurath was not upset. According to Dr. Gilbert's *Nuremberg Diary,* June 4, 1946, 333, "At lunch, Neurath commented that it served him right. He was the one who had lied to him and exercised the reign of terror in Czechoslovakia."

46. Neurath's comment is from Dr. Gilbert's original manuscript, June 25, 1946. For the comment on the unequal duel between Neurath and Maxwell-Fyfe, see Lippe, *Nürnberger Tagebuchnotizen,* 340 and 344, and Fritzsche, *Sword in the Scales,* 288. Lippe, who was assistant lawyer for Admiral Raeder, specifically noted that Neurath's "defense lawyer did not operate with sufficient skill in order to provide him with assistance. By arrangement, Neurath read his prepared answers from notes, and only seldom spoke freely. When he did this, the impression was much better." *Nürnberger Tagebuchnotizen,* 399. Lüdinghausen's text for Neurath's testimony, carefully typed by Oda von Ritter, is in the Ritter Papers.

47. In the exchange described, the issue was whether Neurath approved the dissolution of the trade unions. In his statement, Neurath added that he did not think the issue was a question of morality: "It was a political measure, but not an immoral one." IMT, XVII, 23–27. Although the court did not mention this aspect of the prosecution's case in the final judgment—thus apparently accepting Neurath's arguments—a better defense lawyer could probably have forced the retraction of most of the extreme charges which arose from this issue.

48. See IMT, XVII, 35 and 44–45. The Bullitt memorandum has been discussed above; see page 148. Neurath also had difficulty with an affidavit by the interpreter Paul Schmidt that charged Neurath had not protested strongly enough against illegal German actions abroad. With justice, Neurath asked how Schmidt, "who was only an insignificant civil servant at the time," could possibly have been privy to his thoughts and actions. But

Lüdinghausen raised no objections to such testimony being entered as evidence, and Schmidt, who was in Nuremberg, was never summoned before the court. Schmidt told the author on July 16, 1968, that he had no evidence to give on this subject, but had merely passed on an impression to the prosecution. He agreed that Neurath's challenge to his testimony was absolutely valid.

49. IMT, XVII, 51ff., and XXII, 580. The technical proof submitted and accepted by the court was records of expenses by Neurath in 1943. For discussion, see above, page 176. For the "lying" to the Czechs, see above, pages 172, 306.

50. IMT, XVII, 72. Throughout this cross-examination, IMT XVII, 59ff., Neurath's memory was not sharp enough to recall the background of the events which had produced the prosecution's documents. See discussion above, pages 205–209.

51. First quotation is from Lippe, *Nürnberger Tagebuchnotizen,* 340 and 344; second is from Fritzsche, *Sword in the Scales,* 297; third is from Gustav Steinbauer, *Ich war Verteidiger in Nürnberg: ein Dokumentenbeitrag zum Kampf um Österreich,* 59.

52. IMT, XXII, 582.

53. See IMT, XVII, 95ff., and 373–76. Apparently Lüdinghausen was at fault in permitting Neurath to resume the stand. With a total misunderstanding of the problems, he permitted the court to establish that the covering letter was signed by Neurath, which it was not. For discussion, see Lippe, *Nürnberger Tagebuchnotizen,* 355, and above, pages 205–209.

54. IMT, XVII, 97–98.

55. Lippe, *Nürnberger Tagebuchnotizen,* 344–45. He characterized the three witnesses as follows: Köpke was "almost too good a witness"; Dieckhoff "very sparse"; and Völckers "not precise enough." This is an excellent evaluation, yet from Köpke's resources alone, Lüdinghausen could have assembled a formidable defense. As Neurath's closest friend and head of a major desk at the foreign office, Köpke could have demolished the charge that Neurath had engaged in deliberate treaty violations and planned for aggressive wars. Moreover, Köpke had an extensive diary covering the years in question. At Lüdinghausen's request, he prepared lengthy testimony summarizing German foreign policy from 1932 through 1936, yet of the nearly 26 sections which he submitted, Lüdinghausen used only 13. In the oral testimony, moreover, the lawyer failed to extract any demonstration of the consistently peaceful aspects of Neurath's policy. So harmless did Köpke appear that the prosecution dismissed him without the traditional cross-examination. Full texts are preserved in Köpke Nachlass. After the war, Köpke tried to have his diary published, but when he failed to obtain suitable terms, he burned it. Information given to the author by Miss Gerda Klei, who currently owns the Köpke Nachlass.

56. Lüdinghausen to Köpke, July 20, 1946, Köpke Nachlass.

57. Diary of Norman Birkett for June 24, 1946, from H. Montgomery Hyde, *Norman Birkett: The Life of Lord Birkett of Ulverston,* 520. Information from Lüdinghausen to Werner von Schmieden, July 16, 1946, Neurath Nachlass. The final speech is printed in IMT, XIX, 216–312. The lawyer read it beforehand to Neurath's family who were appalled that it contained so little reference to the defendant, his personality, motives, fears, or disappointments. Author's interview with Frau von Mackensen, May 3, 1968. See also Lippe, *Nürnberger Tagebuchnotizen,* 400, for comment on lack of focus. It is improbable that the Tribunal took the time to read it closely. Information also from author's conversation with Franz von Papen, July 24, 1968.

58. Summation was by the chief prosecutor, Justice Robert H. Jackson. For his role in the trial, see Eugene C. Gerhart, *America's Advocate: Robert H. Jackson,* passim. For charges see IMT, XIX, 417, 426–27, 445, 450, 525, and 557–58. Apparently the reason for including the new charge about preparing for a war on Poland was fear that the only real crime against peace must have occurred when an actual war broke out.

59. IMT, XIX, 453, 525, 557–58, and 572–73.
60. IMT, XIX, 496, 498, 515, and 523.
61. Poll of reporters, in Ritter Papers. See also Lippe, *Nürnberger Tagebuchnotizen,* July 11, 1946, 373; Lüdinghausen's letters of the period, however, reveal an unrealistic optimism. Lüdinghausen to Baroness von Neurath, April 20, May 25, July 14, August 31, 1946, Neurath Nachlass. The family's concern is voiced in their own letters to prominent officials, August 1946; copies of letters from Baroness von Neurath and Frau von Mackensen in author's possession.
62. IMT, XXII, 408. See also Lippe, *Nürnberger Tagebuchnotizen,* 483.
63. Information primarily from Lippe, *Nürnberger Tagebuchnotizen,* 486–95. Frau von Mackensen visited her father on September 17. A few days later, Göring, Neurath, Papen, and Keitel had a small party to exchange hunting yarns. The final visit of the families was September 27, 1946.
64. The original indictment is printed in IMT, I, 29–68. The court's judgment is IMT, XXII, 411–98.
65. For the process by which the guilty verdicts on Neurath were reached, see Smith, *Reaching Judgment,* 223–25.
66. Smith, *Reaching Judgment,* 228–29. On Papen, see 288.
67. IMT, XXII, 580–82. In a slight contradiction, the court found that the secret cabinet council had never met and thus could not be a criminal organization (see IMT, XXII, 519), yet Neurath's participation in this nonfunctional body was included in the verdict against him.
68. There is evidence that most of the judges had long ago found Neurath guilty. As early as July 11, even before the final arguments were presented, the defense lawyer Lippe recorded information from a reliable source that the verdict had already been reached. He correctly identified the three men who alone were acquitted: Schacht, Papen, and Fritzsche. Lippe, *Nürnberger Tagebuchnotizen,* 373. Moreover, as Smith has shown (*Reaching Judgment,* 120 ff.), the court began discussing the verdicts in June (!), while Neurath was still on the stand, and weeks before the written arguments of the defense lawyers were submitted. An analysis of the drafts of the verdict on Neurath (August and September 2 and 11, 1946) from the Francis Biddel papers confirms the impression that it was predetermined, and based but little on the evidence introduced into the Nuremberg trial.
69. Fritzsche, *Sword in the Scales,* 298. Although he had expected a death sentence and was relieved that Neurath had gotten off so well, Lippe recorded the courtroom comment: "I would have thought one [year] would have been enough." *Nürnberger Tagebuchnotizen,* 521–22.
70. See *Nürnberger Nachtrichten,* October 3; and *Süddeutsche Zeitung,* October 4, 1946; Vercel, *Rescapés,* 37; report on Prague is in Lippe, *Nürnberger Tagebuchnotizen,* October 3, 1946, 530. Information also from author's interview with Frau von Mackensen, May 3, 1968.
71. Notes of a conversation with Neurath, April 17, 1947, by Richard Thilenius who had served as Lüdinghausen's assistant. Neurath Nachlass. Throughout the winter of 1946–1947, Neurath was held in Nuremberg and provided evidence for the forthcoming continuation of the trials. The Staatsarchiv Nuremberg contains interrogations of Neurath from September and November 1946, and February 1947.
72. Information from Vercel, *Rescapés,* 66 and 71ff.; Fishman, *Seven Men of Spandau,* passim; and author's conversation with Frau von Mackensen, May 3, 1968. Conditions at Spandau are now most clearly illuminated by Albert Speer, *Spandau: The Secret Diaries,* especially 65ff.
73. Vercel, *Rescapés,* 85; and author's conversation with Frau von Mackensen, May 3, 1968.

74. Frau von Mackensen's report, February 13, 1948, Neurath Nachlass.

75. *Allgemeine Zeitung,* April 1, 1948; Vercel, *Rescapés,* 72, 78, and 98; Fishman, *Seven Men of Spandau,* 141.

76. Raeder, *Mein Leben,* II, 405; Vercel, *Rescapés,* 76–77; Fishman, *Seven Men of Spandau,* 154–55. In particular, Neurath objected to the lights flashed into his cell at night. For general conditions of the prisoners, see Speer, *Spandau,* passim.

77. Liberation ministry to public prosecutor, October 1, 1948; Prosecutor Schöbel to liberation ministry, January 12, 1949; Fischinger to Spruchkammer, January 8 and February 26, 1949, Fischinger Files. In the latter, Fischinger mentioned 34 affidavits and 38 witnesses whom he wished to call. These affidavits form the bulk of the Fischinger Files, which Dr. Fischinger graciously placed at the disposal of the author.

78. Fischinger to Spruchkammer, January 8, 1949, citing a letter from Carroll to General Clay, January 12, 1948; Spruchkammerakten, July 28, 1949; and Leeds to Koransky, August 12, 1949; in Fischinger Files.

79. Bauer to liberation ministry, February 4, 1950; public indictment, May 9; Fischinger to Spruchkammer, June 7; Spruchkammerakten, June 20; Fischinger to Spruchkammer, August 5, 1950; in Fischinger Files.

80. Protocol of the public session of the Spruchkammer, October 4, 1950, ruling by Dr. Reinhard Winker, President, Fischinger Files.

81. Dr. Vancil's communication to *Stern,* February 5, 1950; *Die 7 Tage, Illustrierte Wochenschrift,* August 28, 1953. Quotations from Vercel, *Rescapés,* 102.

82. Information from Fishman, *Seven Men of Spandau,* 142, 161, 173, 244–45; and Vercel, *Rescapés,* 102.

83. Cited in Vercel, *Rescapés,* 101–102. See also Fishman, *Seven Men of Spandau,* 263–65. The estate had been confiscated and the main house turned into a convalescent home. Frau von Mackensen demonstrated to the courts that the estate had been improved and enlarged with money provided by Baroness von Neurath. Hence she had the legal right to the property; the state returned it, but the house was then considered uninhabitable and razed.

84. For press campaign, see *Die Zeit,* April 21, 1949; *Heute,* November 23, 1949; *Stern,* February 5, 1950; *Der Mittag,* November 14, 1950; *Merkur,* November 17, 1950; *Deutsche Zeitung,* February 17, 1951; and *Münchener Allgemein,* January 28, February 11 and 18, 1951. The information smuggled from Albert Speer is included in Frau von Mackensen's February 1, 1952 report, Neurath Nachlass. See also *Deutsche Kurier,* September 20, 1952. Prominent persons to whom she wrote included President Truman, Pope Pius XII, and numerous bishops. Sentences for a number of officials found guilty in 1949 (including many foreign office personnel) were reduced in 1950. See TWC, XIII, 865ff. And see, for all this, Vercel, *Rescapés,* 99, 101, 132–36.

85. Neurath to his wife, Palm Sunday 1953, from Fishman, *Seven Men of Spandau,* 248, and 132 for new prison regulations, also cited in Speer, *Spandau.*

86. All letters cited in Frank Lynder, "Frau von Neurath erzählt," *Das Neue Blatt,* November 23, 1954.

87. Neurath to his wife, June 3, 1951; Christmas 1951; March 9, 1952; Christmas 1952; printed in Fishman, *Seven Men of Spandau,* 244–47.

88. Neurath to his wife, May 1951, printed in Fishman, *Seven Men of Spandau,* 243–44.

89. Neurath to his wife, March 1953, and undated letter of 1954, printed in Fishman, *Seven Men of Spandau,* 248 and 143.

90. See *Deutsche Zukunft,* January 31, 1953; and *Die 7 Tage, Illustrierte Wochenschrift,* August 28, 1951, which ran a long article entitled "Must Neurath Die in Prison?" Information also from *Nordwest-Zeitung,* November 9, 1954; and *Frankfurter Allgemeine Zeitung,* August 16, 1956; and author's conversations with Frau von Mackensen, and Dr. Helmuth Fischinger, May 3, and July 24, 1968.

91. See Vercel, *Rescapés,* 175; and *Ludwigsburger Kreiszeitung,* November 8, 1954. For the impact upon the remaining inmates of the prison, see Speer, *Spandau.*

92. *Stuttgarter Nachrichten,* November 8, 1954, and author's interview with Frau von Mackensen, May 3, 1968.

93. Telegrams are printed in *Stuttgarter Nachrichten,* and *Ludwigsburger Kreiszeitung,* November 8 and 9, 1954.

94. Author's interview with Frau von Mackensen, July 8, 1968. Information also from *Der Enz-Bote,* August 16, 1956, and author's conversation with Dr. Helmuth Fischinger, July 24, 1968. The denazification process was never held; the state lost all interest when it established that Neurath did not have as much property and money as had been expected. Despite the court's prohibition of all future publications by the men sentenced at Nuremberg, Neurath was the only one who did not write his memoirs.

95. Vercel, *Rescapés,* 180. Details of the funeral from *Der Enz-Bote,* August 18, 1956. The eulogy was delivered by Franz von Papen.

96. *Deutsche Zeitung und Wirtschafts Zeitung,* August 18, 1956.

Bibliography

Unpublished Sources

1. Documents of the German Foreign Office (AA).
   All the files cited in this work were examined in the original at the Politisches Archiv of the German Foreign Office, Bonn. They are cited by serial and number as recorded on the microfilms on deposit at the National Archives, Washington, D.C. To establish the original province of the document cited, the scholar is referred to the cross index edited by George O. Kent for the United States Department of State and the Hoover Institution on War, Revolution and Peace: *A Catalog of Films and Microfilms of the German Foreign Ministry Archives, 1920–1945,* 4 vols., Stanford, 1962ff. The German department or category number is cited only when the microfilm serial is missing on the original.
2. Documents of the German Reich Chancellery (RK).
   These were examined in the original in the Bundesarchiv, Koblenz, but are cited by microfilm serial and number when available. Many of these files, however, have not been filmed, and so the original German department or category number is used.
3. Documents of the German Ministry of Justice (RJ).
   Examined in the original at the Bundesarchiv, Koblenz, these files have not been filmed extensively and are cited by category and file number.
4. Handakten from the Ministerbüro Reichsaussenminister (Neurath), 1928–1944.
   These documents from the Deutsches Zentralarchiv Potsdam (DZA), files 60951–60987, were examined on microfilm acquired from the archives.
5. Documents from the Hauptstaatsarchiv Stuttgart (HSAS).
6. Documents from the Institut für Zeitgeschichte, Munich (IZ).
   Primarily an important collection of written and oral testimony (*Zeugenschrifttum,* cited as ZS) by eye-witnesses and participants, these documents are cited by number, except where the identity of the witness is public knowledge.
7. SS Personnel File for Constantin Freiherr von Neurath, from the Berlin Document Center.

8. Documents from the National Archives, Washington, D.C. (NA).
   These include the originals of documents introduced at the Nuremberg War Trials, and the DeWitt C. Poole collection of postwar interrogations. In addition, the archives house the microfilms of surviving German documents, the originals of which have been returned to Germany.
9. Documents from the files of Dr. Helmuth Fischinger.
   These files contain numerous affidavits and letters gathered by Dr. Fischinger of Stuttgart for Neurath's postwar denazification trial, which was never held. The collection is in the possession of Dr. Fischinger.
10. Unpublished letters from private collections.
    Werner Fontaine Nachlass, in the possession of his heirs.
    Gerhard Köpke Nachlass, in the possession of Frau Gerda Klei.
    Constantin Freiherr von Neurath Nachlass, in the possession of Frau Winifred von Mackensen, neé Freiin von Neurath.
    Papers of Baroness von Ritter.
    Papers of Madame Trarieux and Henriette de Gourko.
11. Unpublished manuscripts.
    "Das Auswärtige Amt der Weimarer Republik," Politisches Archiv, Bonn.
    Wilhelm Freiherr von Gayl, unfinished memoirs, Bundesarchiv, Koblenz.
    Dr. Gustav M. Gilbert, original manuscript diary, in the possession of Dr. Gilbert.
    Gerhard Köpke, "Aus dem alten Auswärtigen Amt," Politisches Archiv, Bonn.
    Mayor Krogmann of Hamburg, manuscript diary, Archiv des Forschungsstelle für die Geschichte des Nationalsozialismus, Hamburg (FGN).
    General Curt Liebmann, Aufzeichnungen, Institut für Zeitgeschichte, Munich.
    Rudolf Nadolny, original manuscript of his memoirs, in the possession of Frau Änny Nadolny.
    Constantin Freiherr von Neurath, "Gebirgsjaeger," c. 1946, in the possession of Baroness von Ritter.
    ———, "Notizen zur Anklage," written in prison, 1945–46, in the Neurath Nachlass.
    ———, "Skizze," an autobiographical sketch, c. 1946, in the possession of Baroness von Ritter.
    Marie Freifrau von Neurath, "Lebenslauf Reichminister Freiherr von Neurath," biographical sketch written in Prague, c. 1940, in the Neurath Nachlass.
    Hermann von Raumer, "Der Antikominternpakt," a memoir-history reconstructed from diary entries, from Dr. Hans-Adolf Jacobsen's private collection.
    Werner von Schmieden, manuscript memoir of the foreign office and German policy towards the Far East, in the possession of Dr. von Schmieden.
    Lutz Graf Schwerin von Krosigk, diary, Institut für Zeitgeschichte, Munich.

Interviews and Correspondence

The following people graciously provided information in interviews during 1968 and in correspondence during the following years:

Gesandter a. D. Dr. Günther Altenburg
Botschafter a. D. Dr. Werner von Bargen
Reichsminister a. D. Magnus Freiherr von Braun
Botschafter a. D. Vico von Bülow-Schwante
Botschafter a. D. Hasso von Etzdorf
Rechtsanwalt Dr. Helmuth Fischinger
Staatssekretär a. D. Andor Hencke
Gesandter a. D. Werner von Holleben
Gesandter a. D. Albrecht von Kessel
Minister a. D. Professor Dr. Erich Kordt
Frau Magaret Kotze
Frau Winifred von Mackensen, geb. Freiin von Neurath
Frau Magaret Magirus
Frau Änny Nadolny
Dr. Constantin Freiherr von Neurath
Reichskanzler a. D. Franz von Papen
Dr. Walter Poensgen
Staatssekretär a. D. Werner Freiherr von Rheinbaben
Theda Freifrau von Ritter
Gesandter a. D. Dr. Paul Schmidt
Gesandter a. D. Dr. Werner von Schmieden
Reichsminister a. D. Lutz Graf Schwerin von Krosigk
Botschafter a. D. Dr. Herbert Siegfried
General a. D. Dr. Hans Speidel
Gesandter a. D. Dr. Hans Thomsen
Botschafter a. D. Dr. Fritz von Twardowski
Gesandter a. D. Dr. Hans H. Völckers
Gesandter a. D. Captain Fritz Wiedemann
Gesandter a. D. Dr. Ernst Woermann
Rechtsanwalt Dr. Wolfgang Wolfram von Wolmar

Published Sources

Akten zur deutschen auswärtigen Politik, 1918–1945: aus dem Archiv des Auswärtigen Amts, Series B (1925–1933), Göttingen, 1966ff.

Amort, Cestmír and Otto Hornung (eds.), *Heydrichiáda: Dokumenty,* Prague, 1965.

Conze, Werner, "Zum Sturz Brünings," *Vierteljahrshefte für Zeitgeschichte,* I (1953).

Documents and Materials Relating to the Eve of the Second World War, 2 vols., Moscow, 1948.

Documents Diplomatiques Français, 1932–1939, Series 1 (1932–1935) and Series 2 (1936–1939), Paris, 1964ff.

Documenti Diplomatici Italiani, 7th Series (1922–1925), Rome, 1952ff.

Documents on British Foreign Policy, 1919–1939, First and Second Series, eds. E. L. Woodward and Rohan Butler, London, 1946ff.

Documents on German Foreign Policy, 1918–1945, Series C (1933–1937) and Series D (1937–1945), Washington, 1949ff.

Dokumenty z historie československé politiky, 1939–1943, eds. Libuse Otáhalová and Milada Cervenokova, Prague, 1966.

Domarus, Max (ed.), *Hitler: Reden und Proklamationen, 1932–1945: kommentiert von einem deutschen Zeitgenossen,* 2 vols., Munich, 1965.

Foreign Relations of the United States: Diplomatic Papers, Washington, D.C., 1861ff.

Gotharisches Genealogisches Taschenbuch der Freiherrlichen Häuser, Teil B, 83 Jhg. (1933).

Hitler, Adolf, *Hitler's Secret Book,* ed. Gerhard L. Weinberg, trans. Salvator Attanasio, New York, 1961.

———, *Hitler's Secret Conversations, 1941–1944,* eds. Harry Picker and Gerhard Ritter, New York, 1953.

———, *Mein Kampf,* trans. Ralph Manheim, Cambridge, Mass., 1962.

International Military Tribunal, *Trial of the Major War Criminals before the International Military Tribunal: Nuremberg, 14 November 1945–1 October 1946,* 42 vols., Nuremberg, 1947ff.

Jacobsen, Hans-Adolf (ed.), *Misstrauische Nachbarn: deutsche Ostpolitik 1919–1970: Dokumentation und Analyse,* Düsseldorf, 1970.

Jacobsen, Hans-Adolf and Werner Jochmann (eds.), *Ausgewählte Dokumente zur Geschichte des Nationalsozialismus, 1933–1945,* Bielefeld, 1961ff.

Kennan, George F., *From Prague after Munich: Diplomatic Papers, 1938–1940,* Princeton, N.J., 1968.

Král, Václav (ed.), *Die deutschen in der Tschechoslowakei, 1933–1947: Dokumentensammlung,* Prague, 1964.

———, *Lesson from History: Documents concerning Nazi Policies for Germanisation and Extermination in Czechoslovakia,* Prague, 1961.

———, *Provada o okupaci,* Prague, 1962.

Lipski, Jósef, *Papers and Memoirs of Jósef Lipski, Ambassador of Poland: Diplomat in Berlin, 1933–1939,* ed. Waclaw Jedrzejewicz, New York, 1968.

Lösener, Bernhard, "Als Rassereferent im Reichsministerium des Innern," June 26, 1950, in Hans Rothfels, "Das Reichsministerium des Innern und die Judengesetzgebung," *Vierteljahrshefte für Zeitgeschichte,* IX (1961).

Nazi Conspiracy and Aggression, 8 vols. and 2 supplements, Washington, D.C., 1946ff.

Persekuce českého studenstva za okupace, Prague, 1945.

Phelps, Reginald H., "Aus den Groener Dokumenten," *Deutsche Rundschau,* LXXVI (1950) and LXXVII (1951).

Pünder, Hermann, *Politik in der Reichskanzlei: Aufzeichnungen aus den Jahren, 1929–1932,* ed. Thilo Vogelsang, Stuttgart, 1961.

Robertson, Esmonde (ed.), "Zur Wiederbesetzung des Rheinlandes 1936," *Vierteljahrshefte für Zeitgeschichte,* X (1962).

Rothfels, Hans (ed.), "Ausgewählte Briefe von Generalmajor Helmut Stieff," *Vierteljahrshefte für Zeitgeschichte,* II (1954).

Schüddekopf, Otto-Ernst, *Das Heer und die Republik: Quellen zur Politik der Reichswehrführung 1918 bis 1933,* Hanover and Frankfurt, 1955.

Trials of War Criminals Before the Nürnberg Military Tribunals Under Control Council Law No. 10, 15 vols., Washington, D.C., 1949ff.

Ursachen und Folgen: vom deutschen Zusammenbruck 1918 und 1945 bis zur staatlichen Neuordnung Deutschlands in der Gegenwart. Eine Urkunden- und Dokumentensammlung zur Zeitgeschichte, eds. Herbert Michaelis, Ernst Schräpler, and Günter Scheel, Berlin, 1958ff.

Vogelsang, Thilo, "Neue Dokumente zur Geschichte der Reichswehr 1930–1933," *Vierteljahrshefte für Zeitgeschichte,* II (1954).

Zločiny nacistů za okupace a osvobozenecký boj našeho lidu, ed. Josef Čejha et al., Prague, 1961.

Zpověď K. H. Franka: Podle vlastních výpovědi v době vazby u krajského soudu trestního na Pankráci (Karl Hermann Frank's confessions and testimony during imprisonment at Pankrac), Prague, 1946.

Memoirs and Diaries

Aloisi, Pompeo barone, *Journal 25 juillet 1932–14 juin 1936,* Paris, 1957.

Bernhard, Henry, *Finis Germaniae: Aufzeichnungen und Betrachtungen,* Stuttgart, 1947.

Blücher, Wipert von, *Deutschlands Weg nach Rapallo: Erinnerungen eines Mannes aus dem zweiten Gliede,* Wiesbaden, 1951.

———, *Gesandter zwischen Diktatur und Demokratie: Erinnerungen aus den Jahren 1935–1944,* Wiesbaden, 1951.

Bonn, Moritz Julius, *Wandering Scholar,* New York, 1948.

Braun, Magnus Freiherr von, *Von Ostpreussen bis Texas: Erlebnisse und zeitgeschichtliche Betrachtungen eines Ostdeutschen,* Stollhamm, Oldb., 1955.

Braun, Otto, *Von Weimar zu Hitler,* New York, 1940.

Brüning, Heinrich, "Ein Brief," *Deutsche Rundschau,* LXX (1947).

——, *Memoiren, 1918–1934*, Stuttgart, 1970.

Ciano, Count Galeazzo, *Ciano's Hidden Diary, 1937–1938*, ed. Malcolm Muggeridge, trans. Andreas Mayor, London, 1952.

——, *The Ciano Diaries, 1939–1943*, ed. Hugh Gibson, New York, 1946.

——, *Ciano's Diplomatic Papers, being a record of nearly 200 Conversations held during the years 1936–1942* ..., ed. Malcolm Muggeridge, London, 1948.

Curtius, Julius, *Sechs Jahre Minister der deutschen Republik*, Heidelberg, 1948.

D'Abernon, Edgar Vincent Viscount, *The Diary of an Ambassador*, 3 vols., Garden City, N.Y., 1929ff.

Dennler, Wilhelm, *Die Böhmische Passion: Prager Tagebuch, 1939–1947*, Freiburg, 1953.

Diels, Rudolf, *Lucifer ante portas: zwischen Severing und Heydrich*, Zürich, n.d.

Dietrich, Otto, *12 Jahre mit Hitler*, Munich, 1955.

Dirksen, Herbert von, *Moscow, Tokyo, London: Twenty Years of German Foreign Policy*, Norman, Okla., 1952.

Dodd, William Edward, *Ambassador Dodd's Diary, 1933–1938*, eds. William E. Dodd, Jr., and Martha Dodd, New York, 1941.

Düsterberg, Theodor, *Der Stahlhelm und Hitler*, Wolfenbüttel, 1949.

Ebbinghaus, Christof von, *Die Memoiren des Generals von Ebbinghaus*, Stuttgart, 1928.

Eden, Sir Anthony, *Facing the Dictators*, Boston, 1962.

Feierabend, Ladislav Karel, *Ve vládě Protektorátu*, New York, 1962.

Fitz-Randolph, Sigismud Sizzo, *Der Frühstücks-Attaché aus London*, Stuttgart, 1954.

François-Poncet, André, *The Fateful Years: Memoirs of a French Ambassador in Berlin, 1931–1938*, trans. Jacques LeClercq, London, 1949.

——, *Souvenirs d'une ambassade à Berlin Septembre 1931–Octobre 1938*, Paris, 1946.

Frank, Hans, *Im Angesicht des Galgens: Deutung Hitlers und seiner Zeit auf Grund eigener Erlebnisse und Erkenntnisse*, Neuhaus bei Schliersee, 1955.

Fritzsche, Hans, *The Sword in the Scales*, trans. Diana Pyke and Heinrich Fraenkel, London, 1953.

Fromm, Bella, *Blood and Banquets: A Berlin Social Diary*, New York, 1942.

Geyr von Schweppenburg, L. Freiherr, *Erinnerungen eines Militärattachés London, 1933–1937*, Stuttgart, 1949.

Gilbert, Gustave M., *Nuremberg Diary*, New York, 1947.

Goebbels, Joseph, *My Part in Germany's Fight*, trans. Kurt Fiedler, London, 1935.

——, *The Goebbels Diaries, 1942–1943*, ed. Louis P. Lochner, Garden City, N.Y., 1948.

Hanfstaengl, Ernst, *Unheard Witness*, London, 1957 (American edition is entitled *Hitler: The Missing Years*).

——, *Zwischen Weissem und Braunem Haus: Memoiren eines politischen Aussenseiters*, Munich, 1970.

Hassell, Ulrich von, *Vom anderen Deutschland, aus dem nachgelassenen Tagebüchern, 1938–1944*, Zürich, 1946.

Henderson, Neville, *Failure of a Mission, Berlin 1937–1939*, New York, 1940.

Hossbach, Friedrich, *Zwischen Wehrmacht und Hitler, 1934–1938*, Wolfenbüttel, 1949.

Jäckh, Ernst (ed.), *Kiderlen-Wächter: der Staatsmann und Mensch, Briefwechsel und Nachlass*, Stuttgart, 1924.

Keitel, Field Marshal Wilhelm, *Verbrecher oder Offizier? Erinnerungen, Briefe und Dokumente des Chefs OKW*, ed. Walter Görlitz, Göttingen, 1961. Translated by David Irving as *Memoirs of Field-Marshal Keitel*, New York, 1966.

Kessler, Harry Graf von, *Tagebücher, 1918–1937*, ed. Wolfgang Pfeiffer-Belli, Frankfurt, 1961.

Kirkpatrick, Ivone, *The Inner Circle: Memoirs*, London, 1959.

Klotz, Helmut (ed.), *The Berlin Diaries, May 30, 1932–January 30, 1933*, New York, 1934.

Köhler, Ludwig von, *Zur Geschichte der Revolution in Württemberg: ein Bericht*, Stuttgart, 1930.

Kordt, Erich, *Nicht aus den Akten: die Wilhelmstrasse in Frieden und Krieg. Erlebnisse, Begegnungen und Eindrücke, 1928–1945*, Stuttgart, 1950.

——, *Wahn und Wirklichkeit: die Aussenpolitik des Dritten Reiches. Versuch einer Darstellung*, Stuttgart, 1947.

Kubizek, August, *The Young Hitler I Knew*, trans. E. V. Anderson, Boston, 1955.

Kühlmann, Richard von, *Erinnerungen*, Heidelberg, 1948.

Lippe, Viktor Freiherr von der, *Nürnberger Tagebuchnotizen: November 1945 bis Oktober 1946*, Frankfurt, 1951.

Lüdecke, Kurt C. W., *I Knew Hitler: The Story of a Nazi Who Escaped the Blood Purge*, New York, 1937.

Manstein, Erich von, *Aus einem Soldatenleben, 1887–1939*, Bonn, 1958.

Meissner, Otto, *Staatssekretär unter Ebert, Hindenburg, Hitler: der Schicksalsweg des deutschen Volkes von 1918 bis 1945, wie ich ihn erlebte*, Hamburg, 1950.

Nadolny, Rudolf, *Mein Beitrag*, Wiesbaden, 1955.

Oldenburg-Januschau, Elard von, *Erinnerungen*, Leipzig, 1936.

Papen, Franz von, *Memoirs*, trans. B. Connell, New York, 1953.

——, *Der Wahrheit eine Gasse*, Munich, 1952.

———, *Vom Scheitern einer Demokratie, 1930–1933*, Mainz, 1968.

Pistorius, Theodor von, *Die letzten Tage des Königreichs Württemberg: mit Lebenserinnerungen und Lebensbekenntnissen von seinem letzten Finanzminister, dem nachherigen Hochschullehrer*, Stuttgart, 1936.

Prittwitz und Gaffron, Friedrich von, *Zwischen Petersburg und Washington: ein Diplomatenleben*, Munich, 1952.

Raeder, General-Admiral Erich, *Mein Leben*, Tübingen, 1956. Translated by Henry W. Drexel as *My Life*, Annapolis, 1960.

Rauschning, Hermann, *Men of Chaos*, New York, 1942.

———, *Voice of Destruction*, New York, 1940.

Reynaud, Paul, *In the Thick of the Fight, 1930–1945*, trans. James Lambert, New York, 1955.

Rheinbaben, Werner Freiherr von, *Viermal Deutschland: aus dem Erleben eines Seemanns, Diplomaten, Politikers, 1895–1954*, Berlin, 1954.

Ribbentrop, Annelies von, *Verschwörung gegen den Frieden: Studien zur Vorgeschichte des Zweiten Weltkrieges*, Leoni am Starnberger See, 1962.

Ribbentrop, Joachim von, *Zwischen London und Moskau: Erinnerungen und letzte Aufzeichnungen*, ed. Annelies von Ribbentrop, Leoni am Starnberger See, 1954.

Riesser, Hans Edward, *Haben die deutschen Diplomaten versagt?* Geneva, 1957.

———, *Von Versailles zur UNO: aus den Erinnerungen eines Diplomaten*, Bonn, 1962.

Rosen, Friedrich, *Aus einem diplomatischen Wanderleben*, Vols. 3 and 4, Wiesbaden, 1959.

Rosenberg, Alfred, *Das politische Tagebuch Alfred Rosenbergs aus den Jahren 1934–35 und 1939–40*, ed. Hans-Günther Seraphim, Göttingen, 1956.

Schmidt, Paul, *Statist auf Diplomatischer Bühne, 1923–1945: Erlebnisse des Chefdolmetschers im AA mit den Staatsmänner Europas*, Bonn, 1949.

Schmidt-Hannover, Otto, *Umdenken oder Anarchie: Männer-Schicksale-Lehren*, Göttingen, 1959.

Schwerin von Krosigk, Lutz Graf, *Es geschah in Deutschland: Menschenbilder unseres Jahrhunderts*, Stuttgart, 1951.

Speer, Albert, *Inside the Third Reich: Memoirs*, trans. Richard and Clara Winston, New York, 1970.

———, *Spandau: The Secret Diaries*, trans. Richard and Clara Winston, New York, 1976.

Spitzemberg, Hildegard Baroness von, *Das Tagebuch der Baronin Spitzemberg*, ed. Rudolf Vierhaus, Göttingen, 1960.

Steinbauer, Gustav, *Ich war Verteidiger in Nürnberg: ein Dokumentenbeitrag zum Kampf um Österreich*, Klagenfurt, 1950.

Stockhausen, Max von, *Sechs Jahre Reichskanzlei: von Rapallo bis Locarno*,

Erinnerungen und Tagebuchnotizen, 1922-1927, ed. Walter Görlitz, Bonn, 1954.

Stresemann, Gustav, *Stresemann: His Diaries, Letters and Papers,* 2 vols., trans. and ed. Eric Sutton, New York, 1935.

Szembek, Comte Jean, *Journal, 1933-1939,* Paris, 1952.

Treviranus, Gottfried Reinhold, *Das Ende von Weimar: Heinrich Brüning und seine Zeit,* Düsseldorf, 1968.

Tschirschky, Fritz Günther von, *Erinnerungen eines Hochverräters,* Stuttgart, 1972.

Vansittart, Lord Robert Gilbert, *The Mist Procession,* London, 1958.

Wagner, Elizabeth (ed.), *Der Generalquartiermeister: Briefe und Tagebuchaufzeichnungen des Generalquartiermeisters des Heeres General der Artillerie Eduard Wagner,* Munich, 1963.

Weizsäcker, Ernst von, *Memoirs,* trans. John Andrews, Chicago, 1951.

———, *Die Weizsäcker-Papiere, 1933-1950,* ed. Leonidas E. Hill, Frankfurt/Main, 1977.

Wiedemann, Fritz, *Der Mann der Feldherr werden wollte: Erlebnisse und Erfahrungen des Vorgesetzten Hitlers im 1. Weltkrieg und seines späteren persönliche Adjutanten,* Velbert, 1964.

Wilson, Hugh, *A Career Diplomat. The Third Chapter: The Third Reich,* New York, 1960.

Wurm, D. Theophil, *Erinnerungen aus meinem Leben,* Stuttgart, 1953.

Zechlin, Walter, *Pressechef bei Ebert, Hindenburg, und Kopf: Erlebnisse eines Pressechefs und Diplomaten,* Hanover, 1956.

Secondary Works

Auerbach, Helmuth, "Eine nationalsozialistische Stimme zum Wiener Putsch vom 25. Juli 1934," *Vierteljahrshefte für Zeitgeschichte,* XII (1964).

Baumont, Maurice, John H. E. Fried, and Edmond Vermeil (eds.), *The Third Reich: A Study Published under the Auspices of the International Council for Philosophy and Humanistic Studies and with the Assistance of UNESCO,* New York, 1955.

Beck, Earl R., *The Death of the Prussian Republic: A Study of Reich-Prussian Relations, 1932-1934,* Tallahassee, 1959.

Beer, Max, *Die auswärtige Politik des Dritten Reiches,* Zürich, 1934.

Beloff, Max, *The Foreign Policy of Soviet Russia,* 2 vols., London, 1947.

Beneš, Vojta, and R. A. Ginsburg, *Ten Million Prisoners: Protectorate Bohemia and Moravia,* Chicago, 1940.

Bennecke, Heinrich, "Alternative der Not: Schleicher, Bürgerkrieg, oder Hitler," *Politische Studien,* 14 (1963).

———, *Hitler und die SA,* Munich, 1962.

———, *Die Reichswehr und der "Röhm Putsch"*, Munich, 1964.

Bennett, Edward Wells, *Germany and the Diplomacy of the Financial Crisis, 1931*, Cambridge, Mass., 1962.

Berghahn, Volker, "Die Harzburger Front und die Kandidatur Hindenburgs für die Präsidentschaftswahlen 1932," *Vierteljahrshefte für Zeitgeschichte*, XIII (1965).

———, *Der Stahlhelm: Bund der Frontsoldaten, 1918–1935*, Düsseldorf, 1966.

Berndorff, Hans Rudolf, *General zwischen Ost und West: aus den Geheimnissen der Deutschen Republik*, Hamburg, 1951.

Bernhardi, Horst, "Die Göttigen Burschenschaft 1935 bis 1945," in *Darstellungen und Quellen zur Geschichte der deutsche Einheitsbewegung im neunzehnten und zwangzigsten Jahrhundert*, Heidelberg, 1957.

Bernhardt, Walter, *Die deutsche Aufrüstung, 1934–1939: militärische und politische Konzeptionen und ihre Einschätzung durch die Aliierten*, Frankfurt, 1969.

Besson, Waldemar, *Württemberg und die deutsche Staatskrise, 1928–1933: eine Studie zur Auflösung der Weimarer Republik*, Stuttgart, 1959.

Blau, Bruno, *Das Ausnahmerecht für die Juden in den europäischen Ländern, Teil I, Deutschland*, New York, 1952.

Bloch, Charles, *Hitler und die europäischen Mächte, 1933–1934: Kontinuität oder Bruch*, Frankfurt, 1966.

Bluel, Hans Peter, and Ernst Klinnert, *Deutsche Studenten auf dem Weg ins Dritten Reich: Ideologien—Programme—Aktionen, 1918–1935*, Gütersloh, 1967.

Bodensieck, Heinrich, "Der Plan," *Zeitschrift für Ostforschung*, X (1961).

———, "Zur Vorgeschichte des Protectorats Böhmen und Mähren," *Geschichte in Wissenschaft und Unterricht*, XIX (1968).

Bollmus, Reinhard, *Das Amt Rosenberg und seine Gegner: Zum Machtkampf im nationalsozialistischen Herrschaftssystem*, Stuttgart, 1970.

Booms, Hans, *Die deutschkonservative Partei: preussischer Charakter, Reichsauffassung, Nationalbegriff*, Düsseldorf, 1954.

Borch, Herbert von, *Obrigkeit und Widerstand: zur politischen Soziologie des Beamtentums*, Tübingen, 1954.

Bracher, Karl Dietrich, "Das Anfangsstadium der Hitlerschen Aussenpolitik," *Vierteljahrshefte für Zeitgeschichte*, V (1957).

———, *Die Auflösung der Weimarer Republik: eine Studie zum Problem des Machtverfalls in der Demokratie*, 3rd ed., Villingen/Schwarzwald, 1960.

———, *Deutschland zwischen Demokratie und Diktatur: Beiträge zur neueren Politik und Geschichte*, Bern, 1964.

———, *The German Dictatorship: The Origins, Structure, and Effects of National Socialism*, New York, 1972.

——, *Nationalsozialistische Machtergreifung und Reichskonkordat: ein Gutachten zur Frage des geschichtlichen Zusammenhangs und der politischen Verknüpfung von Reichskonkordat und nationalsozialistischer Revolution*, Wiesbaden, 1956.

Bracher, Karl Dietrich, Wolfgang Sauer, and G. Schulz, *Die nationalsozialistische Machtergreifung: Studien zur Errichtung des totalitären Herrschaftssystems in Deutschland 1933–34*, Cologne, 1960.

Brandes, Detler, *Die Tschechen unter deutschem Protektorat, Teil I, Besatzungspolitik, Kollaboration und Widerstand im Protektorat Böhmen und Mähren bis Heydrichs Tod (1939–1942)*, Munich, 1969.

Braubach, Max, *Der Einmarsch deutscher Truppen in die entmilitarisierte Zone am Rhein im März 1936: ein Beitrag zur Vorgeschichte des zweiten Weltkrieges*, Cologne, 1956.

Brecht, Arnold, *Federalism and Regionalism in Germany: The Division of Prussia*, New York, 1945.

Brecht, Bertolt, "Massnahme gegen die Gewalt," *Versuche I*, Berlin, 1930.

Breyer, Richard, *Das deutsche Reich und Polen, 1932–1937: Aussenpolitik und Volksgruppenfragen*, Würzburg, 1955.

Broszat, Martin, "Die Reaktion des Mächte auf den 15. März 1939," *Bohemia: Jahrbuch des Collegium Carolinum*, VIII (1967).

Brügel, Johann Wolfgang, *Tschechen und Deutsche, 1918–1938*, Munich, 1967.

Buchheim, Hans, *Glaubenskriese im Dritten Reich: drei Kapitel nationalsozialistischer Religionspolitik*, Stuttgart, 1953.

——, "Die SS—Das Herrschaftsinstrument," in *Anatomie des SS-Staates*, Olten, 1965.

——, *Totalitarian Rule: Its Nature and Characteristics*, trans. Kurt P. Tauber, Middletown, Conn., 1968.

Buchheit, Gert, *Ludwig Beck: ein preussischer General*, Munich, 1964.

——, *Soldatentum und Rebellion: die Tragödie der deutschen Wehrmacht*, Rastatt/Baden, 1961.

Bülow, Bernhard Wilhelm von, *Der Versailler Völkerbund: eine vorläufige Bilanz*, Berlin, 1923.

Bussmann, Walter, "Politische Ideologien zwischen Monarchie und Weimarer Republik: ein Beitrag zur Ideengeschichte der Weimarer Republik," *Historische Zeitschrift*, 190 (1960).

Čelovsky, Boris, *Das Münchener Abkommen, 1938*, Stuttgart, 1958.

Conway, John S., *The Nazi Persecution of the Churches, 1933–1945*, Toronto, 1968.

Conze, Werner, "Die Krise des Parteienstaates in Deutschland, 1929–1930," *Historische Zeitschrift*, 178 (1954).

Craig, Gordon A., and Felix Gilbert (eds.), *The Diplomats: 1919–1939*, Princeton, N.J., 1953.

Dahrendorf, Ralf, *Society and Democracy in Germany*, Garden City, N.Y., 1967.

Davidson, Eugene, *The Trial of the Germans: An Account of the Twenty-Two Defendants before the International Military Tribunal at Nuremburg*, New York, 1966.

Deist, Wilhelm, "Brüning, Herriot und die Abrüstungsgespräche von Bessinge," *Vierteljahrshefte für Zeitgeschichte*, V (1957).

———, "Schleicher und die deutsche Abrüstungspolitik im Juni/Juli 1932," *Vierteljahrshefte für Zeitgeschichte*, VII (1959).

Denne, Ludwig, *Das Danzig-Problem in der deutschen Aussenpolitik, 1934–1939*, Bonn, 1959.

Dennett, Raymond, and Joseph E. Johnson (eds.), *Negotiation with the Russians*, Boston, 1951.

Deutsch, Harold C., *The Conspiracy Against Hitler in the Twilight War*, Minneapolis, 1968.

———, *Hitler and His Generals, The Hidden Crisis January–June 1938*, Minneapolis, 1974.

Dietrich, P., "Die Deutsche Landmannschaft: ein Beitrag zur geschichtlichen Entwicklung der DL im Rahmen des deutschen Korporationswesens," *Historia Academica*, III/IV (1958).

Dorpalen, Andreas, *Hindenburg and the Weimar Republic*, Princeton, N.J., 1964.

Drechsler, Karl, *Deutschland-China-Japan, 1933–1939: das Dilemma der deutschen Fernostpolitik*, Berlin, 1964.

Dyck, Harvey Leonard, *Weimar Germany and Soviet Russia, 1926–1933: A Study in Diplomatic Instability*, London, 1966.

Eichstädt, Ulrich, *Von Dollfuss zu Hitler: Geschichte des Anschlusses Österreichs, 1933–1938*, Wiesbaden, 1955.

Eschenburg, Theodor, "Franz von Papen," *Vierteljahrshefte für Zeitgeschichte*, I (1953).

———, "Die Rolle der Persönlichkeit in der Krise der Weimarer Republik: Hindenburg, Brüning, Groener, Schleicher," *Vierteljahrshefte für Zeitgeschichte*, IX (1961).

Eubank, Keith, *Munich*, Norman, Okla., 1963.

Euler, Heinrich, *Die Aussenpolitik der Weimarer Republik 1918–1923: vom Waffenstillstand bis zum Ruhrkonflickt*, Aschaffenburg, 1952.

Eyck, Erich, *A History of the Weimar Republic*, 2 vols., trans. Harlan Hanson and Robert G. L. Waite, Cambridge, Mass., 1962.

Fabry, Philipp Walter, *Die Sowjetunion und das Dritte Reich: eine dokumentierte Geschichte der deutsch-sowjetischen Beziehungen von 1933 bis 1941*, Stuttgart, 1971.

Feiling, Keith, *The Life of Neville Chamberlain*, London, 1947.

Fest, Joachim, *Das Gesicht des Dritten Reiches: Profile einer totalitären Herrschaft,* Munich, 1963.

Fischer, Fritz, *Griff nach der Weltmacht: die Kriegszielpolitik des kaiserlichen Deutschland 1914–18,* Düsseldorf, 1962.

Fishman, Jack, *The Seven Men of Spandau,* New York, 1954.

Foerster, Wolfgang, *Generaloberst Ludwig Beck: sein Kampf gegen den Krieg, aus nachgelassenen Papieren des Generalstabschefs,* Munich, 1953.

Foertsch, Hermann, *Schuld und Verhängnis: die Fritsch-Krise im Frühjahr 1938 als Wendepunkt in der Geschichte der nationalsozialistischen Zeit,* Stuttgart, 1951.

Frank, Ernst, *Karl Hermann Frank: Staatsminister im Protektorat,* Heusenstamm, 1971.

Freytagh-Loringhoven, Axel Freiherr von, *Deutschnationale Volkspartei,* Berlin, 1931.

Funke, Manfred, *Sanktionen und Kanonen: Hitler, Mussolini und der internationale Abessinienkonflikt, 1934–1936,* Düsseldorf, 1970.

Gackenholz, Hermann, "Reichskanzlei 5. November 1937: Bemerkungen über 'Politik und Kriegsführung' im Dritten Reich," in *Forschungen zu Staat und Verfassung, Festgabe für Fritz Hartung,* eds. Richard Dietrich and Gerhard Oestreich, Berlin, 1958.

Gatzke, Hans Wilhelm, *Germany's Drive to the West: A Study of Germany's Western War Aims During the First World War,* Baltimore, 1950.

———, *Stresemann and the Rearmament of Germany,* Baltimore, 1954.

Gehl, Jürgen, *Austria, Germany, and the Anschluss, 1931–1938,* London, 1963.

Gerhart, Eugene C., *America's Advocate: Robert H. Jackson,* Indianapolis, 1958.

Gilbert, Gustav M., *The Psychology of Dictatorship: Based on an Examination of the Leaders of Nazi Germany,* New York, 1950.

Göppert, Otto, *Der Völkerbund: Organisation und Tätigkeit,* Stuttgart, 1938.

Görlitz, Walter, *Gustav Stresemann,* Heidelberg, 1947.

———, *Hindenburg: ein Lebensbild,* Bonn, 1953.

Grauer, Karl-Johannes, *Wilhelm I, König von Württemberg: ein Bild seines Lebens und seiner Zeit,* Stuttgart, 1960.

Gruchmann, Lothar, *Nationalsozialistische Grossraumordnung: die Konstruktion einer deutschen Monroe-Doktrin,* Munich, 1965.

Hammerstein, Kunrat Freiherr von, "Schleicher, Hammerstein und die Machtübernahme 1933," *Frankfurter Heft,* XI (1956).

Heineman, John L., "Constantin von Neurath and German Policy at the London Economic Conference of 1933: Backgrounds to the Resignation of Alfred Hugenberg," *Journal of Modern History,* 41 (1969).

Helbich, Wolfgang J., "Between Stresemann and Hitler: The Foreign Policy of the Brüning Government," *World Politics*, XII (1959).

Heneman, Harlow James, *The Growth of Executive Power in Germany: A Study of the German Presidency*, Minneapolis, 1934.

Herre, Paul, *Kronprinz Wilhelm: seine Rolle in der deutschen Politik*, Munich, 1954.

Heydecker, Joe J., and Johannes Leebe, *The Nuremberg Trial: A History of Nazi Germany as Revealed through the Testimony at Nuremberg*, Cleveland, 1962.

Hildebrand, Klaus, *Deutsche Aussenpolitik, 1933–1945: Kalkül oder Dogma?*, Stuttgart, 1971.

Hilger, Gustav, and Alfred G. Meyer, *The Incompatible Allies: A Memoir-History of German-Soviet Relations, 1918–1941*, New York, 1953.

Hill, Leonidas, "Three Crises, 1938–1939," *Journal of Contemporary History*, III (1968).

Hillgruber, Andreas, *Hitlers Strategie: Politik und Kriegsführung, 1940–1941*, Frankfurt, 1965.

——, *Staatsmänner und Diplomaten bei Hitler: vertrauliche Aufzeichnungen über Unterredungen mit Vertretern des Auslandes, 1939–1945*, 2 vols., Frankfurt, 1967.

Höltje, Christian, *Die Weimarer Republik und das Ostlocarno-Problem, 1919–1934: Revision oder Garantie der deutschen Ostgrenze von 1919*, Würzburg, 1958.

Hofer, Walther, *Die Diktatur Hitlers bis zum Beginn des zweiten Weltkrieges*, Konstanz, 1960.

Hoover, Calvin Bryce, *Germany Enters the Third Reich*, New York, 1933.

Hubatsch, Walther, *Hindenburg und der Staat: aus den Papieren des Generalfeldmarschalls und Reichspräsidenten von 1878 bis 1934*, Göttingen, 1966.

Huck, Jürgen, "Reichsminister Paul Freiherr von Eltz-Rübenach: sein Leben und Wirken, 1875–1943," *Unser Porz*, II (1961).

Hyde, H. Montgomery, *Norman Birkett: The Life of Lord Birkett of Ulverston*, London, 1964.

Irving, David, *Hitler's War*, New York, 1977.

Jacobsen, Hans-Adolf, *Nationalsozialistische Aussenpolitik, 1933–1938*, Frankfurt, 1968.

Jarausch, Konrad Hugo, *The Four Power Pact, 1933*, Madison, Wis., 1965.

Jones, Francis Clifford, *Japan's New Order in East Asia: Its Rise and Fall, 1937–1945*, London, 1954.

Kalow, Gert, *Hitler, das gesamtdeutsche Trauma: zur Kritik des politischen Bewusstseins*, Munich, 1967.

Kaufmann, Walter H., *Monarchism in the Weimar Republic*, New York, 1953.

Kelley, Douglas McGlashom, *22 Cells in Nuremberg: A Psychiatrist Examines the Nazi Criminals,* New York, 1947.

Kielsmansegg, Johann Adolf Graf, *Der Fritschprozess 1938: Ablauf und Hintergründe,* Hamburg, 1949.

Klein, Burton Harold, *Germany's Economic Preparation for War,* Cambridge, Mass., 1959.

Klemperer, Klemens Wilhelm von, *Germany's New Conservatism: Its History and Dilemma in the Twentieth Century,* Princeton, N.J., 1957.

Klose, Werner, *Freiheit schreibt auf eure Fahnen: 800 Jahre deutsche Studenten,* Oldenburg, 1967.

Koch, Lutz, *Erwin Rommel: die Wandlung eines grossen Soldaten,* Stuttgart, 1950.

Koehl, Robert Lewis, *RKFDV: German Resettlement and Population Policy 1939–1945. A History of the Reich Commission for the Strengthening of Germandom,* Cambridge, Mass., 1957.

Köttgen, Arnold, *Das deutsche Berufsbeamtentum und die parlamentarische Demokratie,* Berlin, 1928.

Král, Václav, *Otzáky hospodářského a sociálniho vývoje v českých zemich v letech,* 1938–1945, 3 vol., Prague, 1958.

Kramarz, Joachim, *Stauffenberg: The Architect of the Famous July 20th Conspiracy to Assassinate Hitler,* trans. P. H. Barry, New York, 1967.

Krausnick, Helmut, "Der 30 Juni 1934: Bedeutung, Hintergründe, Verlauf," *Das Parlament,* Beilage B, XXV (1954).

———, "Erwin Rommel und der deutsche Widerstand gegen Hitler," *Vierteljahrshefte für Zeitgeschichte,* I (1953).

———, "Legenden um Hitlers Aussenpolitik," *Vierteljahrshefte für Zeitgeschichte,* II (1954).

Krausnick, Helmut, et al. (eds.), *Anatomy of the SS State,* trans. Dorothy Long, New York, 1968.

Krecker, Lothar, "Die diplomatischen Verhandlungen über den Viererpakt vom 15. Juli 1933," *Die Welt als Geschichte,* XXI (1961).

Krupper, Alfons, "Zur Geschichte des Reichskonkordats," *Stimmen der Zeit,* 163 (1958/59).

Krusemarck, Götz, "Württemberg und der Krimkrieg," Ph.D. dissertation, Kiel, 1931.

Leithäuser, Joachim Gustav, *Diplomatie auf schiefer Bahn,* Berlin, 1953.

Löwenstein, Hubertus Prince zu, *On Borrowed Peace,* Garden City, N.Y., 1942.

———, *Stresemann: das deutsche Schicksal im Spiegel seines Lebens,* Frankfurt, 1952.

Lucas, Friedrich J., *Hindenburg als Reichspräsident,* Bonn, 1959.

Malanowski, Wolfgang, "Das deutsch-englische Flottenabkommen vom 18. Juni

1935 als Ausgangspunkt für Hitlers doktrinäre Bündnispolitik," *Wehrwissenschaftliche Rundschau,* V (1955).

———, "Die deutsche Politik der militärischen Gleichberechtigung von Brüning bis Hitler," *Wehrwissenchaftliche Rundschau,* V (1955).

Manvell, Roger, and Heinrich Fraenkel, *Goering,* New York, 1962.

Masarik, Hubert, "The Last Months of General Eliáš," ["Poslední měsíce generálem Eliášem"] *Reporter,* III (No. 21) (1968).

Mastný, Vojtech, *The Czechs under Nazi Rule: The Failure of National Resistance, 1939–1942,* New York, 1971.

Mau, Hermann, "Die zweite Revolution: der 30. Juni 1934," *Vierteljahrshefte für Zeitgeschichte,* I (1953).

Meinck, Gerhard, *Hitler und die deutsche Aufrüstung, 1933–1937,* Wiesbaden, 1959.

Merkatz, Hans-Joachim von, *Die konservative Funktion: ein Beitrag zur Geschichte des politischen Denkens,* Munich, 1957.

Merkes, Manfred, *Die deutsche Politik gegenüber dem spanischen Bürgerkrieg 1936–1939,* Bonn, 1961.

Meskill, Johanna Margarete Menzel, *Hitler and Japan: The Hollow Alliance,* New York, 1966.

Miale, Florence R., and Michael Selzer, *The Nuremberg Mind: The Psychology of the Nazi Leaders,* New York, 1975.

Neurath, Constantin von, "Deutschlands Kampf um Gleichberechtigung in der Wehrfrage," *Velhagen und Klasengs Monatshefte,* 47 (1933).

Niclauss, Karlheinz, *Die Sowjetunion und Hitlers Machtergreifung: eine Studie über die deutsch-russischen Beziehungen der Jahre 1929 bis 1935,* Bonn, 1966.

O'Neill, Robert John, *The German Army and the Nazi Party, 1933–1939,* London, 1966.

Pese, Werner, "Hitler und Italien, 1920–1926," *Vierteljahrshefte für Zeitgeschichte,* III (1955).

Peterson, Edward N., *Hjalmar Schacht: For and Against Hitler. A Political-Economic Study of Germany, 1923–1945,* Boston, 1954.

Peterson, Estelle, *The Limits of Hitler's Power,* Princeton, N.J., 1969.

Petwaidic, Walter, *Die autoritäre Anarchie: Streiflichter des deutschen Zusammenbruchs,* Hamburg, 1946.

Poole, DeWitt C., "Light on Nazi Foreign Policy," *Foreign Affairs,* 25 (1946).

Pope-Hennessy, James, *Queen Mary, 1867–1953,* London, 1959.

Post, Gaines, Jr., *The Civil-Military Fabric of Weimar Foreign Policy,* Princeton, N.J., 1973.

Preradovich, Nicholas von, *Die Wilhelmstrasse und der Anschluss Österreichs, 1918–1933,* Bern, 1971.

Presseisen, Ernst L., *Germany and Japan: A Study in Totalitarian Diplomacy, 1933-1941*, The Hague, 1958.

Price, George Ward, *Year of Reckoning*, London, 1939.

Rath, Julie, "Württemberg und die Schleswig-Holsteinische Frage in den Jahre 1863-1865," Ph.D. dissertation, Tübingen, 1935.

Reibnitz, Kurt Freiherr von, *Im Dreieck—Schleicher-Hitler-Hindenburg: Männer des deutschen Schicksals*, Dresden, 1933.

Richter, Rolf, "Der Abrüstungsgedanke in Theorie und Praxis und die deutsche Politik, 1920-1929," *Wehrwissenschaftliche Rundschau*, XVIII (1968).

Ripka, Hubert, *Munich Before and After: A Fully Documented Czechoslovak Account of the Crises of September 1938 and March 1939*, London, 1939.

———, *Two Years of the Protectorate*, London, 1941.

Robertson, Esmonde M., *Hitler's Pre-War Policy and Military Plans, 1933-1939*, London, 1963.

Rönnefarth, Helmuth K. G., *Die Sudetenkrise in der Internationalen Politik: Entstehung, Verlauf, Auswirkung*, 2 vols., Wiesbaden, 1961.

Rogers, Lindsay, Freda Foerster, and Sanford Schwarz, "German Political Institutions: II, Article 48," *Political Science Quarterly*, 47 (1932).

Roos, Hans, *Polen und Europa: Studien zur Polnischen Aussenpolitik, 1931-1939*, Tübingen, 1957.

———, "Die 'Präventivkriegspläne' Pilsudski von 1933," *Vierteljahrshefte für Zeitgeschichte*, III (1955).

Ross, Dieter, *Hitler und Dollfuss: die deutsche Österreich-Politik, 1933-1934*, Hamburg, 1966.

Sasse, Heinz Günther, *100 Jahre Auswärtiges Amt, 1870-1970*, Bonn, 1970.

———, *100 Jahre Botschaft in London: aus der Geschichte einer deutschen Botschaft*, Bonn, 1963.

———, *Zur Geschichte des Auswärtige Amts*. Bonn, 1959.

Scheurig, Bodo, *Ewald von Kleist-Schmenzin: ein Konservativer gegen Hitler*, Oldenburg, 1968.

Schieder, Theodor, *Die Probleme des Rapallo-Vertrags: eine Studie über die deutsch-russischen Beziehungen, 1922-1926*, Cologne, 1955.

Schmidt, Richard, and Adolf Grabowsky (eds.), *Disarmament and Equal Rights: Facts and Problems Dealt with in the Negotiations on Disarmament and Equal Rights, 1933-1934*, Berlin, 1934.

Schneider, Hans, "Das Ermächtigungsgesetz vom 24.3.1933," *Vierteljahrshefte für Zeitgeschichte*, I (1953).

———, *Das Ermächtigungsgesetz vom 24. März 1933*, Bonn, 1961.

Schotte, Walter, *Das Kabinett Papen, Schleicher, Gayl*, Leipzig, 1932.

———, *Der neue Staat*, Berlin, 1932.

Schramm, Wilhelm von, *Der 20. Juli in Paris*, Bad Wörishofen, 1953.

Schreiber, Georg, *Brüning/Hitler/Schleicher: das Zentrum in der Opposition,* Cologne, 1932.

——, *Regierung ohne Volk,* Cologne, 1932.

Schübelin, Walter, *Das Zollparlament und die Politik von Baden, Bayern und Württemberg, 1866–1870,* Berlin, 1935.

Schubert, Günter, *Anfänge nationalsozialistischer Aussenpolitik,* Cologne, 1963.

Schüddekopf, Otto Ernst, *Die deutsche Innenpolitik im letzten Jahrhundert und der konservative Gedanke,* Braunschweig, 1951.

Schwend, Karl, *Bayern zwischen Monarchie und Diktatur: Beiträge zur bayerischen Frage in der Zeit von 1918 bis 1933,* Munich, 1954.

Scott, William Evans, *Alliance Against Hitler: The Origins of the Franco-Soviet Pact,* Durham, N.C., 1962.

Seabury, Paul, *The Wilhelmstrasse: A Study of German Diplomats under the Nazi Regime,* Berkeley, 1954.

Smith, Bradley F., *Reaching Judgment at Nuremberg,* New York, 1977.

Sommer, Theo, *Deutschland und Japan zwischen den Mächten, 1935–1940: vom Antikominternpakt zum Dreimächtepakt. Eine Studie zur diplomatischen Vorgeschichte des Zweiten Weltkriegs,* Tübingen, 1962.

Sontheimer, Kurt, *Antidemokratisches Denken in der Weimarer Republik: die politischen Ideen des deutschen Nationalismus zwischen 1918 und 1933,* Munich, 1962.

Speidel, Hans, *Invasion 1944: Rommel and the Normandy Campaign,* Chicago, 1950.

Stambrook, F. G., "The German-Austrian Customs Union Project of 1931: A Study of German Methods and Motives," *Journal of Central European Affairs,* XXI (1961).

Tansill, Charles Callen, *Back Door to War: The Roosevelt Foreign Policy, 1933–1941,* Chicago, 1952.

Taylor, A. J. P., *The Origins of the Second World War,* London, 1961.

Toscano, Mario, *The Origins of the Pact of Steel,* Baltimore, 1967.

Turner, Henry Ashby, *Stresemann and the Politics of the Weimar Republic,* Princeton, N.J., 1963.

Vercel, Michel Cretin, *Les Rescapés de Nuremberg: Les "Seigneurs de la Guerre" après le Verdict,* Paris, 1966.

Vietsch, Eberhard von, *Wilhelm Solf: Botschafter zwischen den Zeiten,* Tübingen, 1961.

Vogelsang, Thilo, *Reichswehr, Staat, und NSDAP: Beiträge zur deutschen Geschichte, 1930–1932,* Stuttgart, 1962.

——, "Zur Politik Schleichers gegenüber der NSDAP," *Vierteljahrshefte für Zeitgeschichte,* VI (1958).

Die Vollmacht des Gewissens, Munich, 1956.

Walters, Francis P., *A History of the League of Nations*, London, 1952.

Weinberg, Gerhard L. *The Foreign Policy of Hitler's Germany: Diplomatic Revolution in Europe, 1933–1936*, Chicago, 1970.

———, "Secret Hitler-Benes Negotiations," *Journal of Central European Affairs*, XIX (1960).

Weller, Karl, *Die Staatumwälzung in Württemberg, 1918–1920*, Stuttgart, 1930.

Westarp, Kuno Graf, *Am Grab der Parteiherrschaft*, Berlin, n. d. (1932).

Wheaton, Eliot B., *Prelude to Calamity: The Nazi Revolution, 1933–1935*, New York, 1968.

Wheeler-Bennett, John W., *The Disarmament Deadlock*, London, 1934.

———, *The Nemesis of Power: The German Army in Politics, 1918–1945*, New York, 1954.

———, *Wooden Titan: Hindenburg in Twenty Years of German History, 1914–1934*, New York, 1936.

Wirsing, Giselher, *Deutschland in der Weltpolitik*, Jena, 1933.

Wiskemann, Elizabeth, *The Rome-Berlin Axis: A History of the Relations Between Hitler and Mussolini*, New York, 1949.

Zimmermann, Ludwig, *Deutsche Aussenpolitik in der Ära der Weimarer Republik*, Göttingen, 1958.

Zipfel, Friedrich, *Der Kirchenkampf in Deutschland, 1933–1945*, Berlin, 1965.

Index

AA (Auswärtiges Amt), the German Foreign Office. *See* Wilhelmstrasse
Abyssinian War, Neurath's evaluation of, 108–110
Adenauer, Chancellor Conrad, 244–245
Allgemeine Deutschen Waffenring (ADW), and Corps Suevia, 77
Almeria, Neurath and the attack on, 150
Anschluss (Union with Austria): Neurath's attitude toward, 28–30, 103–104, 171–172; Hitler's attitude toward, 104–105, 284; Neurath's activities during, 170–175, 186; IMT verdict on these activities, 236
Anti-Comintern Pact, origins of and Neurath's attitude toward, 141, 144, 153–154, 157–158, 161, 167, 296
Anti-Communism, Hitler's belief it was the heart of his party, 281
Anti-Semitic legislation: Neurath and, 77–78, 80, 82; introduced into the Protectorate by Heydrich, 212
Assassination attempt on Hitler, Neurath's reaction to, 218–220
Ataturk, Kemal, 185
Atrocities, the IMT case against Neurath on, 224–225
Attolico, Bernardo, 182–183
August-Wilhelm, Prince of Prussia, 145
Auslandsorganisation der NSDAP (AO): beginnings and operation, 124
Aussenpolitisches Amt der NSDAP (APA): beginnings and operation, 122–123
Austria, 93, 116, 117, 151, 164–166; Neurath's attitude toward, 104–109, 152, 284–285; Hitler's attitude toward, 159–60. *See also* Anschluss
Austrian Legion, Neurath's curbs on, 106, 107
Austrian National Socialists, 104, 107
Austrian Plebiscite; Schuschnigg announces, 171; Hitler and Neurath's reactions, 171 ff.

Bad Godesberg, visit of Neville Chamberlain, 180
Baldurschwang, Neurath's hunting lodge in Allgäu, 5, 220
Baltic states, Neurath's policy towards, 96, 109
Bartlett, Vernon, strong criticism of Ribbentrop, 158
Basler Nachrichten, evaluation of conspiracy charge at IMT, 222–223
Bayreuth Festival, Neurath meets Hitler at, 1939, 200
Beck, Josef, 166
Beck, Colonel General Ludwig: discusses Hossbach meeting with Neurath, 161, 163–164, 302; notes of conference of May 28, 1938, 177–178, 307–308; Czech crisis of 1938, 179; discussions with Strölin on removing Hitler, 216–217
Belgium, Neurath's attitude toward, 94, 110
Beneš, President Eduard, 96, 152, 180–181
Berchtesgaden, 91, 113, 154–155, 165, 171, 176, 178, 180, 278; Neurath complains of Hitler's frequent visits to, 72; Neurath invited to only once, 96
Berchtesgaden Agreement of 1938, 171–172
Berlichingen, Götz von, Neurath's maternal ancestor, 7, 251
Berlin Conference of 1954, Neurath's case discussed at, 244
Berlin Treaty, renewed June 24, 1931, 99
Bernhard, Professor Georg, 36, 38–39
Bessinge, meeting of April 1932, 52
Bethmann-Hollweg, Chancellor Theobald von, 10, 250
Big-Five Conference, December 1932, Neurath and, 54–56
Bismarck, Prince Otto von (German Embassy in London), 113
Blomberg, Field Marshal Werner von: attitude toward disarmament conference, 57; in the

Blomberg (cont'd)
  Hitler Cabinet, 70–71, 92, 106, 115, 117, 150, 270; and the Hossbach meeting, 160–161, 163–164, 165, 301; marriage and subsequent fall, 168
Bludenz. *See* Baldurschwang
Bodenschatz, General Karl, 183
Bohle, Ernst: Neurath's opposition to, 121, 122, 123–125; named to position in Wilhelmstrasse, 126; Neurath works with in order to bypass Ribbentrop, 133, 136; works for the Nazification of the foreign service, 136, 146, 290
Boycott of Jewish Businesses, April 1, 1933, Neurath and, 81 f., 275
Braun, Magnus Freiherr von, 40, 44, 266
Brecht, Bertold, 74
Bredow, Major General Kurt von, 62, 79–80, 267
British-German Naval Agreement. *See* Naval Agreement between Great Britain and Germany
British White Paper, 91
Brockdorff-Rantzau, Count Ulrich von, 18–20
Brüning, Chancellor Heinrich, 1, 32, 38, 48, 52, 94; creation of dictatorship in Germany, 32; and controversy over Neurath as Foreign Minister, 38–40, 261; use of Neurath to persuade Hindenburg to run for re-election in 1932, 41–42
Bülow, Bernhard Wilhelm von, 30, 48–49, 52–55, 91, 100; supports Neurath for Minister, 43; expectations for Nazis in cabinet, 66; attitude toward Nazis and they to him, 131, 133, 135, 136, 137, 140; sudden death, June 21, 1936, 142
Bülow-Schwante, Vico von, Neurath's closest confidant after 1936, 128, 163, 169, 181, 185, 304; involvement with the Röhm Purge, 80, 274
Bullitt, William C., 148, 230
Burgsdorff, Kurt von, in the Protectorate, 192–193, 204–205

Chamberlain, Austen, 29 n
Chamberlain, Neville, 180–181; and Neurath at Munich Conference, 184, 310
Chvalkovský, František, 203–204
Ciano, Count Galeazzo, 160; opposition to Neurath, 153–155
Civil servants, Neurath's evaluation of those Italians who stayed to control Mussolini's fascism, 27–29
Civil Service Ministers: attitude toward the Papen Cabinet, 47, 60–64; push the seizure of Prussia, 61, 267; oppose plans for a new Papen Cabinet, 62, 63, 268; role in the Hitler Cabinet, 70–72, 74, 83; support the anti-Semitic legislation, 81–83; contribute to the neutralization of the cabinet, 69
Colonies, Neurath's opposition to, 93
Commissioner for disarmament questions, Ribbentrop appointed as, 128, 130
Commissioner for foreign policy questions, Ribbentrop appointed as, 131
Concordat of 1933, Neurath's evaluation of, 94, 119
Conference in the Chancellery, November 5, 1937. *See* Hossbach meeting
Conference in the Chancellery, May 28, 1938, 177–178
Conqueror State: the concept of, 118–119, 289; Ribbentrop Bureau an example of, 128; applied to Protectorate, 192
Conscription, introduction of, 91–92
Conservatives, German, 51, 59, 61, 64, 70; support Presidential Cabinet, 1, 17, 20; ready with an opposition cabinet in 1925, 37; in the Papen Cabinet, 59; in coalition with Hitler, 65, 70
Conspiracy: prosecution's case on at IMT, 221–225, 227, 234; contemporary evaluation of, 222–223; Neurath's opinion of IMT charge of, 223–225; Neurath found guilty of at IMT, 236
Constitution Day, controversy of Neurath and celebration of, 36, 256
Contarini, Neurath's evaluation of, 27
Corps Suevia: Neurath joins, 8; Neurath and the threats of Nazi coordination, 77–78
Court of Honor, Colonel General Werner Freiherr von Fritsch, 173
Crimes against humanity, IMT found Neurath guilty of the deaths of nine Czech students as proof of, 236
Cross-examination at IMT: Neurath's poor performance during, Lüdinghausen's complaints over, 226
Curtius, Julius, 38, 39, 94
Czech Mobilization, May 20, 1938, Hitler's reaction to, 176, 178, 180
Czech student demonstrations, October and November 1939: Neurath's attitude toward, 202–203; Frank's intervention in, 202; nine students shot and 1900 arrested following, 203–204, 316; Neurath's attempts to free students, 205, 209–210; as a charge against Neurath at IMT, 236
Czech universitites, closed by Hitler and Frank, 203–204
Czechoslovakia, 96, 109, 123, 151, 164–166, 172–173, 176–185; Neurath's attitude toward, 97, 152; Hitler's attitude toward, 159–160, 281

INDEX

Czechs: Neurath's assurances to during the Anschluss crisis, 1938, 172–173, 231, 306; Neurath's attitude toward as Protector, 178–180, 186–191, 197–201, 204–210; reaction to war against Soviet Union, 210; attitude toward Neurath as Protector, 197, 211; Lüdinghausen and Neurath fear they would demand a new trial for Neurath, 229 and n, 238, 323

DNVP (German National Peoples Party). *See* Conservatives
D'Abernon, Edgar Vincent Viscount, 29 n
Daladier, Minister President Edouard, 127, 182–184
Danubian Pact, Neurath rejects proposals for, 109–110
Danzig, 93, 98, 99, 151, 187
Darré, Walter, 271
Decree establishing Protectorate of Bohemia and Moravia, 188, 191
Defendants at IMT, preparation of list, 220–221
Denazification trial, Neurath summoned before, 240, 327
Denmark, Neurath's activities in, 20–23
Dettinger, Georg, 186
Deutschland incident, 150–151
Dieckhoff, Hans, 144, 145; witness for Neurath at IMT, 233, 323, 324
Disarmament Conference, Neurath's attitude toward, 31, 48, 51–58; the December Agreement of the Big-Five at, 54–57
Dollfuss, Bundeschancellor Engelbert: discussion of at Venice meeting, 103; forms a presidential dictatorship, 104, 106; murder of and German reactions, 93, 103, 107, 119, 123; prosecution at IMT attempts to link Neurath with murder of, 235

Eastern Locarno, Neurath rejects proposals for, 29, 95, 98, 109, 111
Ebert, President Friedrich, 19–20, 251
Eden, Anthony, 113, 131
Elections of November 6, 1932, 62
Eliáš, General Alois, 209, 211
Eltz-Rübenach, Paul Freiherr von und zu: in Papen cabinet, 266; in Hitler cabinet, 69, 71, 81, 270; opposition to Hitler Youth Bill and refusal of Golden Party Badge of Honor, 83–85
Erdmannsdorf, Otto von, 145
Eupen-Malmedy, Neurath's attitude towards, 93–94, 279
Extraordinary Plenipotentiary and Ambassador of the German Reich on Special Mission, Ribbentrop named as, 132

Fascism, Neurath's attitude towards, 25–27, 254; Neurath's comparison with National Socialism, 26–27, 41, 65–67
Faupel, General William, 150, 294
Filseck, Marie Auguste Moser von (Manny), married Neurath, May 30, 1901, 9. *See also* Neurath, Marie Freifrau von
Final sum payment, discussion of at Lausanne Conference, 48–50
Fischinger, Dr. Helmuth, 240–241, 244–245
Foreign nationalities, Neurath's criticism of German attitude toward, 216
Foreign Office, German. *See* Wilhelmstrasse
Foreign Service, German, *See* Wilhelmstrasse
Forster, Dirk, 113–114
Four Power Pact, rejected by Neurath, 102–103
Four Year Plan, Hitler's, 153–154, 160–161
France, 117, 172, 178; Neurath's attitude toward, 94–95; reaction to the remilitarization of the Rhineland, 114–115; Hitler's attitude toward, 94, 159–160
Franco, Francisco, 149–151, 298
Francois-Poncet, Andre, 80–81, 113, 117, 155–156, 182–183, 244
Frank, Karl Hermann: appointment as State-Secretary in Protectorate, 190, 211, 311–312; evaluation of by German officials, 193, 313; attitude toward the Czechs, 193, 194, 197, 201–202; Neurath's struggles with, 191, 193, 197–198, 201–202, 210, 212, 316; urges Berlin to clamp down more in Protectorate, 194, 196, 209–211; decrees and warnings to the Czechs, 200–201, 204, 210; and the Czech student demonstrations, 203–204; and the shooting of Czech students, 203–204; his memorandum on the future of Czechoslovakia, 206–207; manipulates the fall of Neurath, 210–211, 319; tried and executed in Prague, 229; posthumous evidence of introduced against Neurath in IMT, 231–232; Neurath's reaction to his execution, 323
Frederici, General Erich, 195, 203–204
French-Soviet Pact, Neurath's reaction to, 101, 111–112, 286
Freudenstadt, May 27, 1944, meeting of Neurath Strölin, Speidel, 217
Frick, Dr. Wilhelm, 75–76, 135, 270
Fritsch, Colonel General Werner Freiherr von: evaluation of Neurath, 114; reaction to Hossbach meeting, 160–165, 302; accused of homosexuality, 168; court of honor for, 173; under discussion as possible Protector, 311
Fritzsche, Hans, 221, 231, 237

Gaus, Friedrich, 188, 287
Gayl, Wilhelm Freiherr von, 61, 62, 266
Gemmingen-Hornberg, Mathilde Freiin von, Neurath's mother, 7
Geneva Disarmament Conference. *See* Disarmament Conference
Genoa Conference of 1922, Neurath's attitude towards, 24
George V, King of Great Britain, 113
German Air Force, public announcement of, 91, 278
German alliance with Italy, Neurath's attitude toward, 153
German alliance with Japan, Neurath's attitude toward, 153-154, 296
German Christians, attempts to coordinate the Lutheran Church, 75-77
German domestic politics, Neurath's attitude towards, 31-33, 40
German Foreign Service. *See* Wilhelmstrasse
German hegemony in central Europe, Neurath's support of, 153
German minorities abroad, Neurath's attitude toward, 93, 97, 120-121, 199
German nationals. *See* Conservatives
German police in the Protectorate, 190, 194, 201, 202; Neurath's protests over control of, 195-197, 313; issue of used against Neurath at IMT, 237
Germanization: discussion of in Protectorate, 204-208, 314; Neurath's plan to avoid, 205-207, 232; IMT use of Neurath's report, 225, 231-232, 235; Kennan's report on, 314; Neurath's views on, 318
Germanization of businesses, introduced by Heydrich, 212
Gessler, Otto Karl, 37
Gestapo in the Protectorate, 189, 200-201. *See also* German Police
Gilbert, Dr. Gustav, 222
Glaise-Horstenau, Edmund von, 171-172
Gleichberechtigung (Equality of Status), 52 f.
Goebbels, Joseph, 70, 71, 117, 119, 120, 151; and Neurath, 5, 172, 188, 192; Neurath's attitude towards, 72, 178-179, 290
Göppert, Otto, 10
Goerdeler, Carl, 217
Göring, Hermann, 93, 107, 150, 190, 208-209; views on Neurath, 43, 304; Neurath's attitude toward, 74, 102, 117, 119-121, 151-154, 289; fears during Rhineland occupation, 115; opposition to Ribbentrop, 158, 168, 172, 298; on Hossbach Meeting, 161-162, 301; and the Austrian Crisis of 1938, 173-174; and the background to the Munich Conference, 181-184; as defendant at IMT, 221, 227, 237

Golden Party Badge of Honor, controversy over, 84-85
Gottberg, Curt von, 196
Great Britain, 93, 112, 115, 167, 172, 178-179; Neurath's attitude towards as ambassador, 10, 30-32; Neurath's attitude towards as foreign minister, 95-96, 153, 279; Hitler's views of, 95, 159-160; Ribbentrop's actions in, 132-133, 144, 157, 297; Naval Pact with, 132-133
Groener, Wilhelm, 42n
Grünau, Werner Freiherr von, 141, 295
Gruhn, Eva, 168
Gürtner, Franz: in the Papen and Schleicher cabinets, 63, 65, 266; in the Hitler cabinet, 71, 83, 270
Gustloff, Wilhelm, 125

Habicht, Theodor: in charge of Austrian affairs, 105-110, 117, 123; and the Putsch against Dollfuss, 107
Hácha, Emil, 311; entrusts rump-Czechoslovakia to Hitler, 187; and Neurath, 188, 204, 207
Halifax, Lord Edward, 164
Hammerstein-Equord, General Kurt Freiherr von, 79, 87
Hanfstaengl, Ernst Franz (Putzi), 117, 292
Hassell, Ulrich von, 79, 92, 99, 107-109, 150, 158, 180; candidate for foreign minister, 43; disagrees with Neurath on policy toward Italy, 103 ff., 107, 283; evaluation of Ribbentrop and Tripartite Pact, 140, 167; on the remilitarization of the Rhineland, 114; evaluation of Neurath by, 185
Hauptmann, Gerhard, controversy over, 36, 257
Haushofer, Albrecht, 304
Henderson, Neville, 177 n, 178-179, 180-183
Henlein, 97, 152, 193, 198; rumors that he would be named Protector, 311
Herriot, Minister-President Edouard, 49-51
Hess, Rudolf, 71, 77, 124, 136, 138, 146, 191, 271; involved with Neurath and foreign policy, 120, 121, 124-125, 167; defendant at IMT, 221
Hesse, Prince Philip of, 155, 173
Heuss, President Theodor, 245
Heydrich, Reinhold: and the German police in the Protectorate, 194-197; reacts to Neurath's plans for future of Czechoslovakia, 207; actions in Prague after Neurath resigned, 211-212, 237
Himmler, Heinrich, 121, 136, 209; Neurath's refusal to be subordinate to, 84-85; supports Frank in Protectorate, 190, 193-194, 201, 204, 210-211

INDEX

Hindenburg, President Paul von, 1, 41-42, 247; support for Neurath over many years, 30, 36-37, 38, 43-44, 45, 257-258, 259; and the Papen and Schleicher cabinets, 1, 44, 61, 63-65, 267; and the Hitler cabinet, 65, 71, 81, 128; Neurath's last visit to and death of, 80, 103, 137; Neurath's loyalty to, 232, 243

Hitler, Adolf: first meeting with Neurath, 42, 45; aims for cabinet, 68; on anti-Semitic legislation, 81-83; on Röhm Purge, 79-80; speeches of, 87, 90, 111-112; decision to reintroduce conscription, 91-92; undermining of cabinet's powers, 69-70, 73, 272; on Hitler Youth Bill, 83-84; Golden Party Badge controversy, 84-85; evaluation of Neurath, 95, 272, 274-275; bohemian lifestyle of, 156; Neurath evaluates his growing sureness in foreign policy, 87-89, 92-93, 99, 116, 149-153, 156-157, 167; reaction to murder of Dollfuss and attitude toward Austria, 104-109, 171-174; attitude toward Czechoslovakia, 176-178, 180, 186-187, 307; on Danzig, 151; attitude toward Italy, 102, 107-109, 282; attitude toward Japan, 154; views on Poland, 98-99, 166; actions during the Spanish civil war, 149-151, 298; attitude toward the Soviet Union, 99, 154, 200, 281; visits Mussolini, 103, 107; decides on the remilitarization of the Rhineland, 113-116; prepares Four Year Plan, 153; and personnel of the Wilhelmstrasse, 134, 137, 138, 139, 141; and Ribbentrop, 128, 130-133, 138-140, 142, 152, 154-155, 296-297; and APA, 88; and AO, 126; and Keppler, 152; and Rosenberg, 122, 131, 137; delivers Hossbach talk, 159-163; and reactions to Hossbach meeting, 163-165; handles Neurath after Hossbach meeting, 143, 158, 164, 166, 168-169, 298; and the Blomberg-Fritsch affair, 168-170; and the Anschluss, 170-174; and the Czech crisis 1938, 177-178, 180-184; at the Munich conference and afterwards, 184, 186; relations with Neurath after dismissal, 171, 175, 185, 200; occupies Prague, 186-188; appoints Neurath as Protector, 188-190; attitude toward the Protectorate, 191, 192, 203-204, 208; replaces Neurath, 211-212, 319; gift to Neurath, 214

Hitler Cabinet: appointment of, 64-67, 270; splits within, 68-71; role of the civil service ministers in, 68-71, 272; declining importance of, 69-71

Hoare-Laval proposals, 109

Hoesch, Leopold von, 130, 140, 141, 155, 295

Holleben, Werner von, 197, 204, 313, 319

Holzhausen, Rudolf von, incident of, 294

Hoover, President Herbert, 32

Hossbach, Colonel Friedrich, 159-160

Hossbach meeting, November 5, 1937, 159-163; themes of repeated, 167, 176, 177-178; Neurath's evaluation of, 162-163, 216; introduced into IMT against Neurath, 225, 231

Hossbach Memorandum, evaluation of as a document, 301

Hugenberg, Alfred, 64, 70-71, 119, 270

Hungary, 96, 102, 109, 117

Huttschiner Territory, 93

IMT (International Military Tribunal): agreement on and opening of, 220-221; Neurath's opinion of, 222-225; Prosecution's case against Neurath at, 224-225, 234-235; Neurath before the, 228-236; rulings of which hampered Neurath's defense, 226, 227; Lüdinghausen and the process of, 226-227, 228; uses issue of Hossbach, 160; uses issue of Neurath's new house, 306; uses issue of Neurath's assurances to Czechs, 306; uses issue of Neurath's memorandum on future of Czechoslovakia, 207, 318; Neurath as Protector as seen by, 231, 233; Neurath's cross-examination before, 229-231; deliberations of over sentencing of Neurath, 236-237, 325

Italy, 93, 109, 112, 115, 153-154, 172-173; Neurath's views of as Ambassador, 25-30; Neurath's view of as foreign minister, 33-35, 101-103, 108-109, 153-156; Neurath's evaluation as a wartime ally, 209

Japan, 153-154; and the Tripartite Pact, 155, 162; Neurath's rejection of all proposals, 153-154, 296

Judges at IMT, voting of on Neurath, 236-237

Kabinettschef, Neurath's role as, 15-16

Kaltenbrunner, Ernst, 232

Keitel, Colonel General Wilhelm, 171, 176, 215, 221, 237

Kennan, George, reports from the Protectorate, 193, 194, 197, 201, 310, 314

Keppler, Wilhelm, 152, 171

Kessel, Albrecht von, 187, 189, 192, 195, 307

Kiderlen-Wächter, Alfred von, 10-11

Kirchberg Prison, 220

Klausner, Erich, 80

Klein Glattbach, 7, 11, 249; Neurath buried at, 245

Kntomo, Mushakajo, 153-154

Köpke, Gerhard, 10, 14, 144, 146; Neurath's correspondence with, 15, 16, 17, 30, 36, 37,

74, 190, 202, 209, 213, 214, 215, 218, 219, 248–249, 262; diary of, 324; discusses Neurath's future role, 37, 43, 258; as head of the West European desk in the Wilhelmstrasse, 34–35, 108, 254; criticized by Hitler and forced to retire, 137, 139, 141, 295; witness at IMT for Neurath, 233, 323, 324
Koesner-SC, 77–78
Köster, Roland, 141, 145, 295
Kordt, Erich, 128, 132, 142, 307
Kotze, Hans Ulrich von, 127 n, 192, 293, 313
Kriebel, Hermann, 294
Krogmann, Mayor of Hamburg, 152, 296–297
Krosigk, Lutz Graf Schwerin von. *See* Schwerin von Krosigk, Lutz Graf

Lammers, Hans, 77, 138, 197, 291; evaluation of Hitler's attitude toward personnel questions, 161; involved in Hitler's removal of Neurath as minister, 168–169; drafts for Secret Cabinet Council, 175, 307; involved with Neurath over Protectorate, 188–190, 192, 195, 196, 204, 205, 207, 209; evaluation of Neurath's tactics as Protector, 314; ordered to remove Neurath, 211, 213, 216
Land Office, Czech bureau seized by SS, 195–196
Lateran, Treaty of, Neurath's attitude toward, 26, 253
Lausanne Conference, 48–51. *See also* Reparations
Law restoring the civil service, impact upon the Wilhelmstrasse, 135
Lawrence, Lord Justice, and the sentencing of Neurath, 236–237
League of Nations, 110, 111, 157, 278; Neurath's attitude towards, 29, 48, 90, 114; condemnation of Germany by, 140, 148, 154
Lebensraum, 87, 93, 153
Leinfelderhof, Neurath's estate, 5, 11, 146, 165–166, 170, 176, 211, 249, 304; Neurath moves to from Berlin, 214, 216; Neurath leaves on March 26, 1945, 220; Neurath returns to, November 7, 1954, 245; confiscated in denazification process, but recovered by Frau von Mackensen, 240, 326
Leipzig incident, 157–158, 298
Lindau Prison, 220
Lipski, Ambassador Joseph, 120, 166
Litvinov, Maxim, 99, 100
Locarno Treaty, Neurath's attitude towards, 29, 48, 101, 110–112, 113
Locarno-Type Treaties. *See* Eastern Locarno
Löbe, Paul, 85
London Agreement, on International Military Tribunal, 220

London Conference, during the Czech crisis, 180
London Economic Conference, 1933, 71
Lothian, Lord, 95
Ludwig II, King of Bavaria, 156
Ludwig, Emil, 36
Lüdinghausen, Otto Freiherr von: selected as defense lawyer, 222; weakness of, 226–228, 231, 232, 233; criticism of, 322, 324; prosecution's evaluation of, 322; IMT's evaluation of, 234; fears that Czechs would demand Neurath for new trial, 219 and n, 323; evaluation of his case and expectations for trial, 233–235; reaction to the sentencing, 238
Luther, Hans, 294

MacDonald, Prime Minister J. Ramsey, 50–51, 55
Mackensen, Hans-Georg von: married Neurath's daughter, 36; appointed State Secretary, 145–147; discusses Hossbach meeting with Neurath, 165–166; arrested in 1945, died in prison, 220, 227
Mackensen, Frau Winifred von, nee Freiin von Neurath: 2 n, 9–10, 36, 219, 221–222, 227; on her husband's appointment, 146; discusses Hossbach meeting with her father, 163; witnesses Hitler's refusal to accept her father's resignation, 169; attempts to help her father in prison, 238, 239, 241, 244, 245
Mackensen, Field Marshal August von, 74–75
Manchuria, APA activity in, 123
Marco-Polo Bridge, incident of, 154–155
Mary, Queen of Great Britain, 8, 31, 45
Mastný, Vojtech, 306
Maxwell-Fyfe, Sir David, 230–232
Meissner, Otto, 214
Memel, 93, 187
Messersmith, George S., 225
Metternich, Count Wolff, Neurath's troubles with, 13–14, 250
Meyer, Richard, 100, 137, 139, 141, 282, 295
Michelsen, Erich, incident of, 294
Molotov, V.M., 244
Monigan, Major John J., 221, 321
Müller, Reichsbischof Ludwig, 75–76
Muff, General, attache in Vienna, 173–174
Munich Conference, Neurath and, 181–185, 310
Mussolini, Benito: Neurath's relations with, 24–25, 26, 102, 119; meets Hitler in Venice, 103; evaluates duplication in German foreign policy, 117; Neurath's evaluation of his Abyssinian adventures, 108; and German relations with Austria, 106, 108, 109,

172, 173; visits Germany, 84, 154, 157; and Munich Conference, 182–183

Nadolny, Rudolf, 43, 100–101, 278, 281
National Socialism: Neurath's early views of, 40–41; Neurath's comparison with fascism, 26–27, 65–67, 74, 79
National Socialist Domestic Revolution, Neurath and, 75–79
Naval Agreement between Great Britain and Germany, 114: Neurath's pessimism about, 132, 287; Ribbentrop named to negotiate, 132, 138
Neurath, Constantin Alexander Freiherr von (son), 9, 78, 213–215, 221, 320
Neurath, Constantin Hermann Freiherr von: personality and characteristics, 2–6, 21, 72, 249; early life, education and consular service in England, 7–12, 248; military experience and in World War I, 9, 11–12; controversy with ambassador in Constantinople, 11–14; resigns from foreign service and is appointed Kabinettschef, 14–16, 250; in the Revolution of 1918/1919, 16–17; attitude toward the Weimar Republic and politics, 16, 18–21, 40, 72, 250, 251, 252, 258; as Consul in Denmark, attitude toward the Versailles Treaty, 20–22, 33; active in personnel reforms, 23, 252; as Ambassador in Rome, attitude toward Mussolini and fascism, 24–30, 34–35, 41, 65–67, 74, 79, 254, 258; controversies with Gustav Stresemann, 33–37, 256, 257, 258; as Ambassador in Great Britain, 30–32, 257; friendship with President Hindenburg who pressures new appointments, 36–40, 41, 43–45, 258, 259
_____, as minister in the Papen and Schleicher cabinets, 45–48, 58–64, 65–67, 266, 268; at the Lausanne Reparations Conference, 49–51; determines policy toward the Geneva Disarmament Conference, 52–58, 263, 264, 265; achieves big victory in the December Declaration of Equality of Status, 54–56
_____, as minister in the Hitler Cabinet: first impressions of Hitler and National Socialism, 40, 41–42, 65–67, 276; strengths and weaknesses of a civil service minister, 65, 66, 68–72, 81, 83–85, 270; and the National Socialist domestic revolution, 75–85; and the German Christians, 75–77; confronts Anti-Semitic Legislation, 80–83, 275; experiences the Röhm Purge, 78–80, 274; views the demise of Corps Suevia, 77–78, 273, 274; accepts the Hitler Youth Bill, 84–85; receives Golden Party Badge of Honor, 84; last visit with President Hindenburg, 80; enrolled by Hitler in the SS, 84–85, 276; personal relations with Hitler, 72–74, 81, 96, 151 n, 272, 274, 275
_____, views on foreign policy: accepts role of power politics, 10, 21–22, 28–30, 34–36, 47–48, 53, 86–87, 109, 248, 253, 319; fears premature negotiations, 91, 93, 97, 98, 109, 279; makes a programmatic report to the cabinet, 69, 74, 86–88, 92, 94, 97–98, 100, 102; toward rearmament, 90–93; toward Western Europe, 94–96; toward Eastern Europe, 96–101; toward Southern Europe, 101–109, 110–116, 276
_____, directs German policy: toward League of Nations, 90, 110–111; toward Austria and the Dollfuss government, 103–108, 152, 284, 285; toward Poland and the Friendship Pact, 97–99, 151, 280; toward the Soviet Union, 99–101, 200, 281; toward Italy, despite Hitler and Hassell's desires for closer ties, 102–103, 108–109, 282, 283, 289; toward the Saar Plebiscite, 94–96; toward the Sudeten-Germans and other German nationalities abroad, 151–152; toward Great Britain, 95, 113, 132, 147, 287; toward the Naval Agreement, 132–133; toward proposals for an Eastern Locarno, 109–110; toward the French-Soviet Pact, 101, 110–112; toward the remilitarization of the Rhineland, 112–116; despite Hitler's announced policies, 87–89
_____, challenges to his official leadership: from Hugenberg, 70–71, 119; from the APA (Rosenberg), 122–123, 139, 141–142; from the AO (Bohle), 121, 123–126, 136, 291; from Waldeck, 135–136; from Göring, 119–120, 152; are examples of the Conqueror State, 118–119, 289; and his fight to prevent Nazification of the Wilhelmstrasse (foreign service), 136–137; makes him see Hitler's opposition to many of his officials, 136–138, 139, 141–142, 294; forces him to respond with new appointments, 145–147
_____: struggles with Ribbentrop, 114, 126–133, 138–141, 143–145, 152–159; becomes aware of Hitler's growing independent policy, 92, 93, 148–149, 151–157, 163–166; opposes strongly the Anti-Comintern Pact, 141, 153–155, 296, 299; warns against alliance with Japan and the Tripartite Pact, 141, 153–155, 161–162, 167, 296; urges non-involvement with the Spanish Civil War, 125–126, 149–151, 298; employs traveling to make his point that all was in order, 152, 157, 300; is surprised and

Neurath (cont'd)
furious over the Hossbach meeting, 159–164, 165, 167, 302; requests his resignation, 131, 138–139, 143, 164–166, 169; remains involved in foreign policy, 164–166; celebrates his 65th birthday and is fired, 167–170

———, President of the Secret Cabinet Council, 174–175, 306; activities during the Austrian Crisis, 170–174; assurances to the Czechs during the Anschluss, 172–173, 306; continues to warn of foreign policy mistakes, 176–180, 308; gets involved in the Czech crisis leading to Munich Conference, 180–185; 310; attempts to influence policy after Munich Conference, 185, 187, 200–201

———, Protector of Bohemia and Moravia: appointed as, 2, 188–190, 191, 312, 313; attitude toward Czechs, 152, 178–80, 186, 187, 189–191, 197–201, 204–210; discovers Conqueror State in Protectorate too, 192; works out plans for future of Czechoslovakia in order to avoid violent Germanization, 200–202, 204–209, 314, 317; fails to control budget of his own officials, 191, 312; struggles with Karl Hermann Frank, 191, 192, 193–195, 210, 313, 316; fails to block Frank's independent actions in Protectorate, 194–195, 200–204, 210; and the Czech student demonstrations, 202–204, 316; tries but fails to gain control of German Police and SS, 189, 192, 193, 194–197, 201, 210–211, 313; Frank uses Czech unrest in 1941 to force his retirement as, 210–213, 216, 319; Heydrich's reign of terror in Protectorate after his ouster as, 211–212

———, in retirement at Leinfelderhof and Berlin: Hitler refuses to permit publication of his resignation, 212, 213; Hitler's gift of 250,000 RM for his 70th birthday, 213–215, 320; Rommel's warnings received through his son, 213–215; discussions with conspirators on removing Hitler, 215–220, 321; arrested at end of war and sent to Nuremberg for trial, 220–221

———, defendant before the IMT (International Military Tribunal) in Nuremberg: attitude toward the IMT, 222–224, 225, 226; prosecution's case against, 224–225, 234–235; Lüdinghausen's defense of, 226–228, 232, 233, 234, 322; performance on the stand, 228–236; cross-examined by Sir David Maxwell-Fyfe, 230–232; fears that Czechs would demand him for a new trial, 229 and n, 238, 323; final statements by, 232–233, 235; first reunion with his wife and daughter, September 20, 1946, 236; IMT deliberations over verdict, 236, 325; sentencing of and reactions by, 237–238; in Spandau prison, 239–245; writes letters from Spandau, 241–244; suffers ill-health in Spandau, 241–242; released from prison, 244–245; dies at Leinfelderhof, August 14, 1956, 245

Neurath, Constantin Karl Freiherr von (father), 7, 248
Neurath, Ernst Josef Baptist Freiherr von (brother), 11, 248, 249
Neurath, Marie Freifrau von (wife): MS biography of her husband, 248; attitude toward Neurath's appointment as minister, 44–45; evaluation of Papen, 60; reports Hitler's statements rejecting Neurath's resignation, 143; on her husband in Prague, 193; Neurath's letters to on their 50th wedding anniversary, 243–244
Neurath, Wilhelm Heinrich Julius Freiherr von (brother), 248
Newspaper criticism, of Neurath, 34, 36, 38–39
North Schleswig, Neurath's attitude toward, 22, 93–94
Nuremberg Laws of 1935, 82–84, 139
Nuremberg Rally of the NSDAP: in 1937, 154, 158; in 1938, 179–180
Nuremberg Trial. See IMT

Obersalzburg. See Berchtesgaden
Old Tübingen Schwagen, Union of, 78, 274
Olympic Games in Berlin, 143, 147, 148
Opletal, Jan, student demonstrator killed, 203
Orsenigo, Msgr. Cesare, 322
Ott, Lieutenant Colonel, 63
Otto, Operation for conquest of Austria, 173–174

Papen, Franz von: appointed chancellor, 1, 43, 60–64; thought he would also be foreign minister, 44; Neurath's low opinion of, 45, 60; bitterness toward Neurath and other civil service ministers, 267; policy toward Lausanne Conference, 49–51; blamed for deteriorating relations with the Soviet Union, 99; involved with the fall of Schleicher and appointment of Hitler, 65–66, 268; in the Hitler cabinet, 70–71, 270; interference in foreign policy, 70, 94, 103, 107, 117, 119, 121; as Ambassador to Austria, 107–109, 170–171, 173–174, 285, 294; evaluation of Neurath, 147; as defendant at IMT, 221; case is seen by IMT as quite different from Neurath, 236–237
Papen Cabinet: content and program, 59–63; attitude of the civil service ministers toward, 60–64; role of ministers in, 68
Parliamentary government, Neurath's opposition to, 40, 258

Pius XII, Pope, 244
Plans for future of Czechoslovakia: Neurath and, 204–207; rumors of differing, 201–202, 317; Sudeten-Germans and, 205; conference in Berlin over, 201. *See also* Germanization
Poensgen, Walter, the case of, 137 n
Poland, 93, 96, 109, 110, 151, 154; Neurath's attitude toward, 97–99, 151, 280
Polish Corridor, 86, 97–99, 102, 187; AO activities in and Neurath's protests, 120, 125–126; prosecution's attempts to link Neurath with war on, 234
Poll of reporters at IMT, 235
Power politics, Neurath's support of this concept: toward Denmark, 21–22; toward Italy, 28–29; as foreign minister, 86–87; fears of negotiations before restoration of power, 91, 93, 97–98, 109, 279; Neurath's belief time had come for new German program of, 110
Presidential Cabinet: concept of, 1, 45, 247; Neurath's support of, 40, 64
Prittwitz und Gaffron, Friedrich von, 35
Private virtues, as the motivating force behind Neurath, 4
Protector of Bohemia and Moravia: discussion of candidates for, 188, 311; appointment of Neurath and his reactions, 2, 188–191, 312–313; Neurath's staff as, 313; as chief reason Neurath was sentenced at IMT, 237–238
Protectorate Bohemia and Moravia, 188–212; budget for civil servants in, 191, 312; plans for future of, 198–201, 204–209, 317, *see also* Germanization; divisions of programs within, 198; Neurath's role in, *see* Protector of Bohemia and Moravia
Prussia, Seizure of, 61, 267

Raeder, Grand Admiral Erich: on Hossbach meeting, 162, 301; at conference on Czechoslovakia, 177 n; defendant at IMT, 221; on Neurath in Spandau, 240
Raginsky, M.Y., 232
Rapallo Treaty, Neurath's attitude towards, 24
Rasche, SS Obersturmbannführer, 194–195
Raumer, Hermann von, 129, 154, 296, 299
Rauschning, Hermann: on weakness of civil service ministers, 47; evaluation of Neurath's motives and accomplishments, 65–66, 78, 93, 98, 121, 147
Rearmament: German policy of, 51–56; Neurath's policy of, 90–93
Reform of the Foreign Office. *See* Wilhelmstrasse, reform of
Reichsprotector. *See* Protector of Bohemia and Moravia

Reichsprotektorat. *See* Protectorate Bohemia and Moravia
Remilitarization of the Rhineland, 86, 112, 115–116, 148, 151; Neurath's attitude towards, 29, 112–116, 148–149
Reparations, Neurath's policy towards, 48–51
Resistance, Neurath's involvement with, 216–219
Revolution of 1918–1919, Neurath's attitude toward, 16–17
Rhineland, Occupation of. *See* Remilitarization of the Rhineland
Ribbentrop, Joachim von, 93, 122, 299–300; Neurath's opinion of, 114, 126–140, 157 n; opinion of by Bülow and other diplomats, 142; rise of in foreign affairs, 91, 92, 95, 122, 126–133, 134, 138–143, 147, 152; visit to London, 130; special new titles for, 128, 130–131, 132; Neurath accepts Ribbentrop to lead naval talks with Great Britain, 114, 132, 287; and the Rhineland remilitarization, 114, 140; ambitions for a position in foreign office, 131, 138, 142; Neurath's opposition to, 138–139, 143; uses idea of Anti-Comintern Pact to get back in Hitler's good graces, 141, 153–154, 296; reconciles himself with Rosenberg, 141–142, 158; works on the Tripartite Pact despite Neurath's opposition, 154–155, 165, 167; posted to the Court of St. James's despite his objections, 141, 142, 144, 294; alienates British by his actions, 144, 157, 158, 297, 298, 301; is appointed as foreign minister, 168–170, 304; in London during the Austrian crisis, 171, 174; and the Munich Conference, 178–179, 182–183; opposes Secret Council and cuts Neurath off from sources, 175–176, 177, 185; is used by Hitler as a threat to force Neurath to become Protector, 189; removes Neurath's son, 215; as defendant at IMT, 221; IMT verdict on, 237
Ribbentrop Bureau, 129, 133, 142, 154, 158, 164
Ritter, Theda Freifrau von, and Neurath, 44, 56, 72, 74, 115, 165, 169–70, 184–185, 206; opinion of Lüdinghausen, 222
Röhm, Ernst, 75–80, 124, 271, 294
Röhm Purge, 75, 79–80, 95, 103, 168
Romania, 93, 96, 110, 117, 120, 154; Neurath protests party activities in, 123, 125
Rome-Berlin Axis, 154
Rommel, Field Marshal Erwin, 213–215, 217–219
Roosevelt, President Franklin Delano, 181
Rosenberg, Alfred, 93; billed as Hitler's future foreign minister, 290; interferes in foreign policy, 117, 122, 123, 127, 290; disgrace after London visit, 122–123, 290; reconciles himself with Ribbentrop, 131, 158; charges

sabotage by Neurath, 137; Neurath's attitude towards, 122–123, 290; as defendant at IMT, 221; IMT verdict on, 237
Rump-Czechoslovakia, Hitler's decision to eliminate, 186–188

SA Bann, discussions on lifting, 60–61
SD (Sicherheitsdienst), 189, 210
SS (Schutzstaffel): Hitler's decision to enroll all cabinet ministers in, 84–85; Neurath's attitude toward his enrollment in, 85, 276; Neurath's opinion of its activities in Protectorate, 189, 192, 193, 194, 195, 196, 313; closes Czech universities, shooting nine students, and arresting 1900 students, 203; denies Neurath's request to free students, 205; sends reports to support Frank's case against Neurath, 210, 319
Saarland Plebiscite, 94, 95, 96, 119
Sahm, Heinrich, 294
Sanders, General Otto Liman von, 12
Scandinavian countries, Neurath's attitude toward, 21–23, 94
Schacht, Hjalmar, 81, 158, 160–161, 218; before IMT, 221, 237
Schäffer, Hugo, 266
Schantz, Prison Chaplain, 245
Schaub, Julius, 169, 183
Schleicher, General Kurt von: helps form Papen cabinet, 43–44; supports Rudolf Nadolny for foreign minister, 43; attitude toward Papen cabinet, 60–62; Neurath's opinion of, 44, 45; interferes in foreign policy, 49–51, 53–58; forms his own cabinet, 1, 63; views of his own cabinet, 63–64; opinion of Neurath, 63; murdered during the Röhm Purge, 80; diary of alleged by Hitler as proof of Röhm conspiracy, 79
Schlesinger, Moritz, incident over, 135, 294; Röhm explains reasons for attack upon, 294
Schmidt, Guido, 152
Schmitt, Kurt, 271
Schüler, Edmund, 23, 252
Schulenberg, Friedrich Count von der, 101,
Schuschnigg, Bundeschancellor Kurt, 170–174
Schwerin von Krosigk, Lutz Graf: reports Neurath's attitude toward becoming foreign minister, 45; views of the Papen cabinet, 44, 61, 63, 266; opposes the restoration of the Papen cabinet, 63, 65, 66; in the Hitler cabinet, 71, 81, 270; discusses Hossbach meeting with Neurath, 165; warns Hitler over the Czech crisis, 179; summons Neurath for help in Czech crisis, 180; is consulted by Neurath on Hitler's gift of 250,000 Marks, 214
Secret Cabinet Council, 168–169, 175–176; Ribbentrop's opposition to, 175–176; IMT's opinion of, 307, 325
Seldte, Franz, 70–71, 218, 270
Seyss-Inquart, Arthur, 172–174
Siegfried, Herbert, 170
Simon, Sir John, 54–55, 91, 96, 131
Slovakia, 187
Soden, Julius Freiherr von, 15
Solf, Dr, Wilhelm, 259
South Tyrol, Neurath's views on, 28–30, 33–35, 102; Neurath's controversy with Stresemann over, 33–35, 256–257
Soviet Union, 96, 109, 115; Germany policy towards remains unaffected by Hitler's inauguration, 99; Neurath's attitude toward, 99–101, 110–111, 200; controversy between Nadolny and Neurath over policy toward, 100–101; Hitler's fears of, 154–155, 160–161; Hitler and Neurath discuss alliance with, 200; Protectorate influenced by outbreak of war with, 210; Neurath condemned at IMT by judges from, 236–237; refuses to release Neurath for denazification trial, 240; refuses to release Neurath from Spandau, 242; agrees to release Neurath, 244
Soviet-Czech Pact, May 16, 1935, 97
Spandau, Neurath in, 238–246; release of Neurath from, 244–246; Neurath's health in, 241–242
Spanish Civil War, 149–151, 157, 159; Hitler's attitude toward, 149–151; Neurath's attempts to minimize German involvement in, 149–151, 157, 298; AO activities in, 125–126
Special Treatment (*Sonderbehandlung*), Neurath's ignorance of meaning of word, 208
Speer, Albert, 5, 156 n, 161, 175; evaluation of Neurath in Spandau, 239
Speidel, Lieutenant Colonel Hans, 216–219
Stauffenberg, Count Claus von: Neurath and family, 17, 218
Steinacher, Hans, 105n
Stresa Conference, 108
Stresemann, Gustav, 94, 97, 103; controversy with Neurath over South Tyrol, 33–35; controversy with Neurath over politics, and desire to remove him as ambassador, 33–37, 256, 257, 258; Neurath and many in Wilhelmstrasse reject his policies, 29 n, 48
Strölin, Karl, 165–166, 216–218, 312; Lüdinghausen's failure to use as a good witness for Neurath at IMT, 226, 229
Stuckardt, Wilhelm, 191
Sudeten-Germans: Neurath's support for, 96–97, 121, 151; organized in Henlein's National Socialist party, 97; insurrection of as pretext for Hitler's claims, 176, 180; atti-

tudes toward the Protectorate, 194; Neurath's difficulties with as Protector, 190–191

Tägliche Rundschau, 34
Territorial Revisions, Neurath's advocacy of, 93–94, 120, 279
Theresienstadt, Heydrich sets up first concentration camp in Protectorate at, 212
Thilenius, Richard, 313
Thousand-Mark Visa, 105, 284
Tripartite Pact, Japan, Germany, Italy, 154, 155, 161, 162, 296

Überlingen Prison, 221
Umrüstung. *See* Rearmament
United States, Neurath's attitude toward, 94, 279
Upper Silesia, Neurath's demands for, 97
USSR. *See* Soviet Union

Vatican, 117
Venice, visit of Hitler and Mussolini at, 103
Versailles, Treaty of, Neurath's obsession with, 20, 22, 48, 49, 53, 86, 89, 90, 92, 95, 102, 111–112, 115, 120, 132; Lüdinghausen's use of at IMT, 234
Villa Volkonsky, 24
Völckers, Hans, 192, 313; discusses Frank's intrigues against Neurath, 203–204, 319; witness for Neurath at IMT, 233, 324
Volksdeutsch. *See* German minorities
Volksdeutsch Council (VDR), 120–121
Volksdeutsch Mittelstelle (VDM), founded by Heinrich Himmler, 121

Waldeck and Pyrmont, Josias Erbprinz of, 135, 136
War between Japan and China, 154–155
War crimes, shooting of nine Czech students held as proof of Neurath's guilt at IMT, 236
Warmbold, Hermann, 266
Weizsäcker, Ernst Freiherr von, 145, 180, 296, 307; disapproves of Hitler's Weltpolitik, 155, 296; on Neurath's memorandum of December 1937, 165–166; relations with Neurath, 176; alarmed by the Czech crisis, 178–179; works with Neurath to prepare Munich Conference, 183; learns of Hitler's decision to destroy rump-Czechoslovakia, 187; approves of Neurath as Protector, 189
Welczek, Count Johannes von, 144
Westerplatte, Polish occupation of, 98

Wied, the Prince zu: intermediary between Hitler and Neurath in 1932, 42–42, 260; denounced Köpke to Hitler, 295
Wiedemann, Fritz, 297, 308; during the Austrian crisis, 174; present at the conference of May 28, 1938, 177 n, 178; accounts Neurath's actions in preparing the Munich Conference, 181–184
Wigram, Ralph, 113
Wilhelmstrasse (German Foreign Office, and German Foreign Service): state of in 1919, 19; reform of service in 1920s, 18, 23, 252, 253; Neurath's participation in reform of service in 1920s, 23; Neurath's attitude towards "outsiders" in, 12–13, 12 n, 23; welcomes appointment of Neurath as minister, 39, 46, 261; attitude towards Germany's domestic politics in 1932, 33; remains prime determiner of Germany policy, 89; policy toward disarmament, 51–52; policy toward Poland, 97; policy toward Danzig, 298; policy toward the remilitarization of the Rhineland, 112–116; attitude toward early demise of Nazi amateurs in foreign policy, 79, 120; denunciations of by Göring and other Nazi officials, 117, 119, 134; challenges to its official leadership, 117–134; struggles with the AO, 124; conflicts with Ribbentrop, and his plans for reorganization, 127–129, 133; Neurath protects service from Nazification, 136; personnel crisis for, 135–147; many in the service think time has come for reconciliation with Nazis, 145, 147; others reject Hitler's "Weltpolitik," 155; hopes that Neurath can finally get rid of Ribbentrop, 157; celebrates Neurath's 65th birthday, 168; Neurath's criticism of for optimism during 1943, 214
William II, King of Württemberg, 7; Neurath's relations with, 15–16, 20–21; and the Revolution of 1917, 17; death of, 20
Winter Olympics, of 1936, 113
Woermann, Ernst, 145
World Economic Conference in London, 157
Wurm, Bishop Theophil, 75–77, 85
Wysocki, Alfred, 98

Yugoslavia, 96, 109, 123
Young Plan, 48

Zimmermann, Manfred, 302, 322

Compositor:	Computer Typesetting Services, Inc.
Printer:	Braun-Brumfield
Binder:	Braun-Brumfield
Text:	Autologic APS-5 Times Roman
Display:	Autologic APS-5 Times Roman
Paper:	50 lb. P&S Offset Vellum